D1203107

EX LIBRIS
JUN 4 1975
Presented by the
JEWISH CHAUTAUQUA SOCIETY
NEW YORK, N. Y.
Religious Freedom
is the Life-Blood
of Democracy
1499

# STUDIES IN PHARISAISM AND THE GOSPELS

*First and Second Series*

# LIBRARY OF BIBLICAL STUDIES

edited by

HARRY M. ORLINSKY

*Professor of Bible*

Hebrew Union College - Jewish Institute of Religion

New York City

# STUDIES IN PHARISAISM AND THE GOSPELS

BY

I. ABRAHAMS, M.A.

READER IN TALMUDIC, UNIVERSITY OF CAMBRIDGE,
FORMERLY SENIOR TUTOR, JEWS' COLLEGE, LONDON

Prolegomenon by
MORTON S. ENSLIN

*FIRST SERIES*

KTAV PUBLISHING HOUSE, INC.
NEW YORK

BS
2555
.A32
c.2

Reprinted by permission of Cambridge University Press.
First Published 1917 and 1924.

New Matter
Copyright 1967
Ktav Publishing House, Inc.

Library of Congress Catalog Card Number 67-11899
Manufactured in the United States of America

## PROLEGOMENON
## POST ANNOS QUINQUAGINTA

Some books are antedated before the ink on their pages is dry; others are as useful decades after their first appearance as they were when first they came from the press. The two volumes *Studies in Pharisaism and the Gospels,* combined in one set of covers in this current reissue, are definitely of the latter sort. Long out of print, their reappearance will enable many students—both professional and aspiring—long forced to consult them in libraries, to have them in more convenient reach. In addition, because of the nature of the essays and collected notes which comprise their content, as evidenced by the title their author gave them, they will most certainly prove attractive to many readers concerned in the continued task of breaking down walls—not of religious commitment and proper pride in ancestral heritage, but of suspicions and prejudices especially easy to retain and express even if awkward to justify, not to mention to prove.

Jesus was born, lived his life, and died a Jew—proud of his heritage and sure of the reality and validity of God's promises. His early followers, both during his brief ministry and in the years following, were also Jews. But gradually this situation changed, and the movement which came to be known as Christianity became not only a new religion but one recruited in large part from the gentile world. Although its Jewish heritage was not abandoned—a solid core of moral requirements, reflective of God's own character, essential to covenant with him; an appreciation of a Scripture, unlike all other books, which was God's richest gift to man—it tended to become forgotten in the hostility that developed and continued between the two groups, now far apart and increasingly forgetful of the common heritage, but both alike convinced that theirs was the only true religion to which eventually all others must turn.

Precisely because of this common heritage and the confidence shared alike by both in their unique status in the plan and purpose of God, it has not been surprising that the early hostility between the two "chosen people" continued and resulted in suspicions and hatred—each for the other—at times far more intense and tragic than toward the rest of mankind. Since much of this common heritage is persistent in both and with obvious similarities, it has not been surprising that each saw and appraised these common elements very differently when viewed as theirs or the other's. Qualities which are virtues when practiced by oneself and one's own are too often vices when discerned in one's rivals. Thus the epithet "hypocrite" is the unfortunate but not unnatural rejoinder in the twentieth century as well as in the first, despite the fact that the tale of the years has presented, to those who had eyes to see, attempts toward lessening suspicions and hatred of the other without any loss of personal conviction or devotion to the heritage that is one's own.

It is here that one of the values of Dr. Abrahams' work is most evident and the reissuing of these fruits of insight and understanding at the present time most happy. Quite apart from the scholarly worth of these reprinted essays and notes is their author's so evident wish to lessen the needless and too often perverse hostility between sons and daughters of a common Father. Israel Abrahams has properly been styled "an unhyphenated Jew." He detested controversy, and cleavage, and the use of party labels. None of his severest critics ever charged him with having renounced in any degree his loyalty to the Synagogue. Of him one of his fellows wrote in appreciation:

> *His earnest hope was to make the Jew of today both know and love the faith, history, literature and ritual of his forefathers, neither sinking this heritage in oblivion nor permitting the particular and the ephemeral to crush the universal and the eternal, or suffering a dead past to strangle a vigorous present. Between the extremes of formalism and iconoclasm he walked in balanced equipoise, a steadfast Jew, true to his God, a lover of his brethren.*[1]

I am not aware in any of his many writings, and few men have written more, of any indication of the slightest interest in turning a Christian into a Jew. I am sure that the verb he would have employed to characterize such an attempt would have been *pervert,* not *convert.* Rather his concern was to make good Jews better and to lessen their prejudices against their fellow Christians; he was perfectly content to permit his Christian colleagues to attempt the same wholesome task with those to them akin: Walls of prejudice were to him anathema. In the words of the psalmist: "And by the word of my God do I leap over a wall."[2]

At the time that Abrahams wrote, almost exactly a half century ago, much was being written by Christian scholars, especially in Germany, about the nature of Judaism at the time of the Christian beginnings. Although quite aware of the Jewish origin of Jesus, of his followers, and of the religion that resulted from his brief time among men, they were convinced that what had been a religion of strength and promise, with the timeless challenge of the prophets heralding for all time God's unalterable will and pleasure, had sadly decayed or deteriorated into an arid and barren legalism, under which Jesus had suffered and against which Paul had fulminated. God had been driven from his world; had been so highly elevated that he had become aloof. Like an eastern monarch—these interpreters were not uninfluenced by the recent burgeoning into importance of the Near East: ancient history was no longer to be restricted to the chronicle of Greece and Rome—God had become isolated on his lofty supramundane throne so that even angels and archangels had difficulty gaining access to him; for mortals he had become utterly remote. He was to be obeyed; his laws kept in literal and blind obedience. It was from this sad decay of what had once been a noble religion that, like a fragrant lily amazingly blooming from the muddy bottom of a stagnant lake, Jesus had appeared "in the fullness of time," to stand in absolute contrast to this rigid and intolerable system. His attempt was to lift the crushing yoke of the law from the necks of the suffering people and to protest the constant addition of extra weight added by those who arrogantly claimed to be the only true religious, the "scribes and Pharisees," whose daily aim it seemed to be to find new restrictions, new "thou shalt not's," to add to the hopeless fate of the pious poor.

For, and this was the worst of it, these professional men of devotion, the Pharisees, themselves would not wear this yoke, but were content to demand from others what they would not, could not, did not do themselves. Thus the byword "Pharisee"—to Abrahams and his fellow Jews the designation of those of old who had been the flower of Jewish development, who alone had a wise and compelling word for the people, who alone remained unscathed and unafraid when the walls of Jerusalem fell before the forces of Titus and the temple of God was destroyed, never to be rebuilt—had become synonymous with "hypocrite." Jesus had so employed it as the gospels manifestly proved.

Such was essentially the contention of such weighty and influential writers as Ferdinand Weber,[3] Emil Schürer,[4] and Wilhelm Bousset.[5] All of their volumes, while containing much of lasting value, sounded the same essential note: the Judaism of Jesus' day had become synonymous with legalism. The crude and fanatic charges of J. Eisenmenger,[6] who, as G. F. Moore properly remarked, was the "notorious source of almost everything that has been written since his time in defamation of the Talmud or in derision of Jewish superstitions,"[7] were for the most part absent from or greatly modified in the studies of these writers who were scholars, not mudslingers. Nonetheless the picture they drew was a sorry caricature of the facts as seen by Jewish scholars like Abrahams and his lifelong friend and colleague Claude G. Montefiore and to Christian scholars like R. T. Herford and George Foot Moore.

It was not the purpose of Schürer to write a history of Judaism; rather he had sought to furnish students with the various sorts of knowledge necessary to an understanding of the New Testament. To him, as to Weber, Judaism was synonymous with legalism, and legalism was his most cultivated antipathy. His lengthy discussion of "Life under the Law" was definitely a work of Christian apologetic, in no sense an impartial survey of Judaism. For him, as for Weber, legalism was the sum and substance of Judaism, with its one requirement, behavior before a supramundane God who had become in consequence of his isolated grandeur quite inaccessible; for Christians, in contrast, religion was communion with a God who stood ever ready to hearken and to aid.

Like Schürer, Bousset's real interest in Judaism was in terms of the light it threw upon Christianity. In one of his earlier writings, *Jesu Predigt in ihrem Gegensatz zum Judentum: ein religionsgeschichtlicher Vergleich,* which appeared a decade before his *Die Religion des Judentums,* he had stressed, as the title indicates, the antithesis between Jesus and Judaism at every point of consequence. This fundamental cleavage between Jesus and Judaism, so stressed by Bousset, lay in their almost diametrically opposed view of God and feeling toward him. "God is no more in the world, the world no more in God." This, Bousset insisted, was the view of Jewry; it was the inevitable consequence of the earlier prophetic insistence on the exaltation and uniqueness of God, which had become frozen into the "dogma of an abstract, transcendent monotheism." "The later Judaism [*sc.* in the days of Jesus] had neither in name nor in fact the faith of the Father-God; it could not possibly rise to it." In Jesus is to be seen a wholly new and different "piety."

For Bousset this essential center of difference between Jesus and the Judaism to which he stood in uncompromising protest is to be found in his teaching. Unlike earlier treatments which had centered their attention upon the traditional person and work of Christ, Bousset's contention was that this new emphasis on the Fatherhood of God was not only the sum and substance of Jesus' proclamation, but that it at once became the central doctrine of early Christianity.

For this picture of contrast—Jesus and his successors *vs.* the Judaism which had strangely given birth to its severest critic—which was doubly wrong, for it misrepresented early Christianity as certainly as it did Judaism, Bousset was heavily dependent upon Wilhelm Baldensperger[8] and Johannes Weiss[9] and, via them, upon the apocalyptic literature which had been produced in such lavish abundance during the three centuries between Antiochus Epiphanes and Hadrian.

In their criticism of both Schürer's and Bousset's pronouncements, Jewish scholars insisted that this gross distortion was in no small measure due to their improper limitation of sources. To use as primary sources for any reconstruction of the Judaism of the day of Jesus the Apocrypha and Pseudepigrapha was utterly unwarranted. In his review of Bousset's *Die Religion des Judentums* Felix Perles quoted the earlier protest of D. A. Chwolson:

> *So wenig man das Wesen des Christenthums aus der Apocalypse Johannis oder aus apokryphischen Evangelien kennen lernen kann, ebensowenig kann man das Judenthum zur Zeit Christi aus dem Buche Enoch, dem Buche der Jubiläen und ähnlichen Schriften erforschen.*[10]

The criticism was warranted, for the rabbinic sources which Abrahams and G. F. Moore were to insist were indispensable tools for any proper study of the subject, were largely ignored by these earlier writers. None of them was at home in the field of rabbinics. Schürer had made, at second hand, some use of quotations from the Mishnah; Bousset was content to depend upon quotations in translation cited by others for his utilization of what he styled "die späterer Litteratur." For his picture of Judaism as a somber background for the radically different Jesus, the dates of his sources were to him the significant thing. Thus writings which he employed, he insisted, were contemporary with Jesus and the resulting gospels. The rabbinic materials came generations later, after the disastrous outbreaks against Rome in the days of Vespasian and Hadrian, and thus threw little or no light on earlier belief and practice. The possibility that in this "later literature" was preserved unchanged much material from the days under portrayal was conveniently overlooked or disregarded.

It was against this portrayal of Judaism and its Pharisees, which seemed a sorry misunderstanding if not a deliberately perverse caricature, that Israel Abrahams spoke out. Always with a restraint prompted by dignity and understanding, and devoid of anything smacking of pugnacious challenge—not, as one American critic strangely believed, because he found nothing he could challenge, for the picture had been warranted!—he corrected what to him appeared to be mistaken. Some of these were in the form of reviews and evaluations, notably the paper read before the Society of Historical Theology at Oxford, "Professor Schürer on Life under Jewish Law," and printed the same year in the *Jewish Quarterly Review*,[11] which for twenty years he edited, together with his friend and colleague, Claude G. Montefiore; many more were in the form of expositions and descriptions of what this aspect of Judaism was or was not, buttressed by his profound and exact familiarity with the texts which were to him fundamental to a true evaluation of Judaism and which too often were unknown not alone to non-Jews but to many Jews unable to appreciate and evaluate their heritage.

Together with his continued protest—at times in the form of direct refutation; at times in a skillful correction and re-evaluation—against misinterpretations which were constantly being repeated by those who sought to illumine and justify their certainty that everything which Jesus said, as faithfully recorded in the gospels, was an attack upon the Pharisees and that Paul's words about the Law were additional proof of the intolerable yoke of slavery which the Pharisees were constantly making more burdensome and from which Christ had died in his effort to set men free—was another basic concern, the desire to appraise more adequately the beginnings of the Christian movement and to illumine what had seemed to him obscure. In the preface to this First Series of essays he indicated this concern:

> *Jewish students of the Old Testament have gained much from the researches made by Christian scholars, not merely philologically and in the archaelogical field, but also theologically. For the Jew has so ingrained a belief in the organic union of ritual with religion, is so convinced that the antithesis of letter and spirit is mistaken psychologically, that he needed the analytical criticism to enable him to appreciate historically the difference between the prophetic and the priestly strata in the Hebrew Bible, between the abiding principles and Messianic dreams of religion and those detailed rules of ritual and maxims of conduct by which it is sought to realize those principles and dreams in actual*

> *life. But it is just because of this that the Jew may be able to return the compliment, and help Christians to understand certain phases of the Gospels.*[12]

In these two volumes of essays and notes he has addressed himself to this task for which he was eminently suited and equipped, but which had not hitherto received much direct attention. Not infrequently he had touched upon this phase or that of early Christianity in communications in the pages of *Jewish Quarterly Review,* in his many studies of biblical and rabbinic thought, and in his critical reviews and appraisals of current books and articles, both Jewish and Christian, in the *Jewish Chronicle,* to which he had been a regular contributor for over thirty years.[13] But these excursions had been for the most part incidental, almost peripheral, and the by-product of other concerns. It was in no small part due to Claude G. Montefiore that he concerned himself directly with studies which were prompted by phrases or implications in the gospels and upon which he sought to throw light in terms of contemporary Jewish thinking. In October 1888 he had joined with Montefiore in establishing a new journal, *Jewish Quarterly Review.* In the Introductory to the first issue the editors had stated their aim:

> *One prominent portion of our new quarterly . . . will be devoted to the past—to the better knowledge of Jewish history, literature, and theology in bygone days. And here, while the fare we offer will, we hope, be attractive and valuable to the pure scholar, it will also mostly be presented—at least that is the editorial desire—in such a form as to prove interesting as well as novel to the "general reader." These two objects are not by any means necessarily inconsistent.*[14]

For twenty years this journal under their joint editorship proved that the "two objects" were far from inconsistent, with many articles by both Jewish and Christian scholars making lasting contributions to biblical and historical problems; with others devoted to contemporary issues, many of which are of a sort to prove revealing and significant for modern readers today, for whom last year this significant twenty-volume thesaurus of sound scholarship has been made once more available in a sumptuous republication.

Seven years after the birth of *Jewish Quarterly Review* the two editors produced jointly the volume *Aspects of Judaism.* In 1909, a year after the last issue of the *Journal,* Montefiore published his two-volume magnum opus, *The Synoptic Gospels.* The work was in a very real sense, as he himself styled it, "a pioneer." There had been no serious—not to say impartial—Jewish examination of the gospels. As Montefiore candidly admitted:

> *The teaching of Jesus has not been much discussed and appraised as a whole. And when it has been so discussed, the line has been rather to depreciate or to cheapen. Jewish writers have either looked for parallels or for defects. Considering what Judaism and the Jews have had to suffer at Christian hands, this Jewish treatment of the Gospels is not astonishing. . . . No wonder that they should desire to defend the excellence of their own religious writings and of their own religion, which have been so constantly depreciated and misunderstood by Christian writers. All this is quite human, quite natural.*[15]

This Jewish prejudice and misunderstanding, against which Montefiore sought, and successfully, to direct his volumes, was not unlike the corresponding misunderstanding so evident in Weber, Schürer, and Bousset, against which both Montefiore and Abrahams had written.

This work, like the earlier *Aspects of Judaism,* was conceived as a joint work:

> *It had been for many years the desire of my friend Mr Israel Abrahams, Reader in Talmudic and Rabbinic Literature in the University of Cambridge, and myself to join together in some work upon the New Testament. The Additional Notes which he is going to contribute to the present book will be a partial fulfilment of our old desire. I had greatly hoped that these Notes, in which Mr Abrahams' wealth of Rabbinic learning will be used to illustrate and explain the Gospel text, would have appeared together with my own commentary. I keenly trust, though this hope has been, to my deep regret, disappointed, that they will appear (as the third and concluding volume of the work) before the edition of 1910.*[16]

In accord with this hope the title page of the first edition reads

THE SYNOPTIC GOSPELS
edited with
An Introduction And A Commentary
by
C. G. MONTEFIORE
Together With A Series of
Additional Notes
by
I. ABRAHAMS
In Three Volumes

On pp. 41 ff., as a part of his treatment of a theme, are the words: "For the Rabbinic use of the word 'Christ' or 'Messiah,' as a personal name, see Additional Notes 1." Throughout the two volumes this is steadily repeated, with no less than fifty-seven such Additional Notes called for. Not only was his earlier hope that these notes would appear at the same time as the commentary, disappointed, as he had remarked, but Volume 3 never appeared. When in 1927 a second edition of *The Synoptic Gospels* appeared, all reference to Additional Notes and Volume 3 has vanished from the title page, and the series of "For the Rabbinic use . . . see Additional Note xy" has been removed. In the preface to the new edition stand the words:

> *It was a very great disappointment to me (as I know it was also to many others) that the Additional Notes, some sixty in number, which my dear friend, the late Dr. Israel Abrahams, for many years Reader in Talmudic and Rabbinic Literature in the University of Cambridge, had intended to write, were never completed. These Notes were to have formed the third volume of the Commentary. I am well aware how many persons looked forward, very justifiably, to this volume as sure to prove much the most valuable section of the whole. For various reasons Dr. Abrahams found himself unable to write most of the notes; some of them, with other important essays and material, were published separately as* Studies in Pharisaism and the Gospels *(First Series, 1917; Second Series, 1924), a work to which I constantly refer in the course of my Commentary. Dr. Abrahams knew how sad I felt that he was unavoidably prevented from carrying out his original intention, and in order that my second edition should, at all events, contain something from his pen, he wrote for me, when already ill, at considerable sacrifice, an important essay upon that very obscure person, the* 'Am-ha-'Areç. *He gave me the MS. not many months before his death (October 1925), and he asked that I should return it for revision just before it was wanted for press. This essay, which is printed at the end of Vol. II., was therefore never revised by its author.*[17]

Constantly in this second edition, in buttress or reference to a point under discussion occur the words, "See Abrahams, Studies, I or II, chap. ........"[18]

Eight years after Montefiore's first edition of the Commentary had appeared Abrahams published the First Series of *Studies in Pharisaism and the Gospels,* which he styled "designed as an Appendix to Mr. Montefiore's work." Most of the twenty-one articles in this first volume were written between the years 1908-1911 and were in type the following year. Apparently the delay in publication was in part due to his hope to make them more in accord with the earlier plan, for they correspond to but twenty-three of the fifty-seven "See Additional Note's" in Montefiore's two volumes. One of them (IX), "First Century Divorce," while corresponding to Montefiore's reference to forthcoming "Additional Note 18," was actually written at the urgent request of the Royal Commission on Divorce and Matrimonial Causes and is published essentially without change. In it he refers appreciatively to Montefiore's treatment of various passages in the gospels on divorce. While these twenty-one chapters in the First Series embrace substantially the first twenty-five of the themes which Montefiore expected would be amplified,[19] in the Second Series only eight of the sixteen essays and twenty-six miscellaneous notes are on themes which Montefiore had hoped would be treated in the expected "third volume."

This connection with Montefiore's volumes accounts for the form of many of these studies by Abrahams, which, as he candidly recognizes, "though possibly they might pass as exegetical comments, are quite inadequate as essays." At the time the First Series appeared he was contemplating a Second Series in which he might be able to treat more of the themes which he and his colleague had considered. He actually lists the titles of several such which were "either practically written" or "definitely planned." Several of these did appear in the subsequent Second Series and one, as already remarked, "The 'Am ha- 'Arec," comprises the final pages of Montefiore's revised edition of *The Synoptic Gospels.* One conspicuous absence is to be noted. The essay, "Life under the Law," which he mentions as one of the expected chapters, was never produced, at least under that title, although he has expressed very definitely his views on that controverted subject in many of his treatments of related themes. He was so constantly confronted with rival demands upon his time, each insistently claiming priority, that occasionally, when queried by not too placid publishers long awaiting promised copy, he may well have remembered the word of the disguised prophet to the indignant Ahab, "Thy servant was so busy here and there that the man got away."

While these two volumes did not constitute the earlier expected Volume 3 to Montefiore's Commentary, and while less than half of the anticipated Additional Notes were produced, their present form clearly indicates the earlier expectation. In no sense are they a connected study—not to mention history—of Pharisaism. Nor are they a connected study or even a survey of the gospels, of Jesus, or of early Christianity. Rather they are a series of essays—some long, some very brief critical notes—

of a sort to illumine both. Through them all, be they very technical as some are, with constant quotations from the rabbinic texts, frequently untranslated, or winsomely simple—"popular" in the best sense of that abused word—as the charming essay, "Pharisaic Delicacies" (II, xiii), is to be discerned one constant note, almost the leit motif: Pharisaism grew weeds; it also grew flowers. Pharisaism will never be understood by those who view everything that is recorded in the gospels as said by Jesus as a deliberate attack on Pharisaism *per se.* There is no need to darken the one to enhance the beauty of the other.

To this extent, and it is a real extent—far greater than apparently Abrahams realized—his volumes are apologetic. But this is by no means an indication of either weakness or bias. As William Sanday wrote, in a paragraph which later Abrahams quoted with satisfaction:

> *We see the spirit of true scholarship at work. It is scholarship to which I should be inclined to attach somewhat preeminently the epithet 'humane.' The writer before all things is a 'humanist,' and that in a field where in the past 'humanism' has been too much wanting. Perhaps there is a little more of apology than he thinks in what he writes. But it is at least amiable apology, intent on bringing out really good things, and free from carping disparagement of the other side.*[20]

Against the double temptation, on the one hand for Christians to darken the colors in which they draw the picture of the contemporaries and opponents of Jesus, and on the other, for Jews to minimize the originality of the one destined to be, if not the founder, certainly the foundation stone of Christianity—against this double temptation Abrahams was unalterably opposed. In the two sets of *Studies* it is not surprising that it is against the first temptation that his warnings are more noticeable, at least to Christian eyes.

While, as has been remarked, the studies are not designed as consecutive chapters in a history or complete survey of either Pharisaism or the gospels, they are of a nature to make both more understandable. A glance at the titles of the *Studies* reveals the comprehensiveness attempted. All, in a very real sense, are intended to clarify or throw light upon topics or words in the several gospels. Thus some seek to illumine this or that saying of Jesus: "Thou hast said," "Let the dead bury their dead," "The kingdom of God is within you," "The light of the world," "Why callest thou me good?" "Truth shall make you free," "Love thy neighbour," "They make broad their phylacteries," "Give unto Caesar." Some are very short and crisp. Others are longer and detailed, not infrequently leading into subjects somewhat remote from the one supposedly under consideration. "The Imitation of God" runs forty-five pages, but actually is made up of an address which he had delivered as president of the Oxford Society of Historical Theology three years before and which is printed as delivered. This seventeen-page address, however, is here followed by twenty-four notes, all long, technical, and ranging from Pythagoras and Plato to Philo and Maimonides. Others treat such themes as "John the Baptist," "Barabbas," "The Dove and the Voice," "Parables," "The Cleansing of the Temple," "Disease and Miracle," "The Lord's Prayer," "The Good Samaritan." Several seek to find in the rabbinic texts, which are for him—*pace* Schürer and Bousset, not to mention some more recent investigators who reach similar conclusions, but by following other paths—the repository of views of the Pharisees of Jesus' day, sentiments, doctrines, and the like which are analogous to, at least suggested by, those occurring in the gospels: "The Yoke," "The High Priest's Confession," "Whited Sepulchres," "The Second Death," "Some Rabbinic Ideas on Prayer," "The Cessation of Prophecy," "First Century Divorce," "Poverty and Wealth," "The Sabbath," "Life of the Resurrection."

Abrahams' familiarity with rabbinic literature, which had made him the natural successor to Solomon Schechter as Reader in Rabbinic and Talmudic Literature at Cambridge, was but one of his many accomplishments. As his longtime colleague Montefiore wrote of him in his cameolike memorial, "His range was prodigious. Jewish literature of all sorts, Jewish history of all periods, Jewish poetry, Jewish mysticism; he was everywhere at home."[21] All this is evident in these two volumes which are properly regarded his greatest work.

This judgment by his fellow religionist and colleague had been expressed by the reviewer in the London *Times* when the Second Series appeared:

> *The Christian reader will find much in this work to give a truer and deeper meaning to many passages in the New Testament. Turn, for instance, to the note on "the Light of the World," or the exposition of the Parable of the Good Samaritan. They not only suggest points of view which give added force to well-known passages in the Gospel, but they also save us from putting into the narratives more than they ought to bear. In dealing with "Some Rabbinic Ideas of Prayer," Mr. Abrahams is less concerned to trace the steps by which they were evolved than to explain the developed conception of prayer presented in rabbinic teaching. This is just the sort of study that we need to-day. Every*

*one of the chapters is the work of a learned and cultured man whose devotion to Judaism becomes all the more plain by his readiness to appreciate whatever truth he has found in the New Testament, and to expound it in the light of his wide knowledge of rabbinical literature.*[22]

This appraisal was widely shared by the critical press.[23] More significant, however, than the many favorable reviews is the regularity with which these *Studies* have been cited with approval and used for footnote support of subsequent studies concerned with the beginnings of Christianity and its central figure.

Of course Abrahams was not alone. In addition to the writings of his colleague Montefiore, whose *The Synoptic Gospels* and Jowett Lectures for 1900, *Some Elements of the Religious Teaching of Jesus,* sounded essentially the same note as did Abrahams' gathered notes and articles, but with the emphasis essentially reversed so as to consider Jesus in the light of his relationship to his opponents, rather than the Pharisees in the light of words attributed to Jesus, R. T. Herford published in 1913 his important volume, *The Pharisees,* and eleven years later the second and greatly enlarged edition, in which he accepted and stressed Lauterbach's[24] contention that the distinguishing mark between Pharisees and Sadducees was their respective attitude to the oral tradition—eventually resulting in the rabbinical writings—in its application to Torah. This essential difference, mentioned by Josephus,[25] but only incidentally, was basic and far-reaching. This same note was subsequently stressed by George Foot Moore in his three-volume *Judaism.*[26] Both Herford and Moore—the former directly, the latter more incidentally but none the less effectively—were weighty correctives to the out-of-balance representations of Pharisaism against which Abrahams had so constantly stood.

One very practical result of this common front held by these scholars whose knowledge none disputed, both Jewish and Christian, has been the conspicuous change of tone in subsequent studies of Jesus and of the nature of the Jewish background in which he lived and spoke. New Testament Introductions written subsequent to the appearance of these several volumes have been markedly free from what a contemporary Jewish scholar has properly styled the former "hostile and condescending attitude found in those written before" and which led him to conclude: "I know of no area where anti-Jewish feeling, both toward Jews and toward Judaism, is now as rare as it is in the domain of Christian Bible scholars.[27]

Since the appearance of the Second Series in 1924 and the death of Abrahams in early October of the following year[28] many volumes on both Pharisaism and the gospels have appeared. The first part of the huge five-volume compilation of rabbinic parallels and similarities to New Testament utterances assembled by Paul Billerbeck (and graced on the title page with the name of Hermann L. Strack) under the title *Kommentar zum Neuen Testament aus Talmud und Midrasch*[29] had appeared in 1922, and is referred to by Abrahams in the preface to his Second Series. This colossal work has been of very great value in making available materials of what was virtually *terra incognita* to many earlier writers to whom Abrahams had constantly, if courteously, protested and against whom both Herford and Moore had launched their broadsides. No scholar will deny the very great value of this huge anthology, although the criticism is easy and warranted that because of the straining of the compiler(s) for completeness a host of irrelevances had been included.[30] Other studies of lasting importance include Louis Finkelstein's *The Pharisees,* which apppeared in 1938, following his lengthy article under the same title in the *Harvard Theological Review,*[31] in which the author propounded and argued his thesis that the Pharisees were an urban group, unlike their opponents the Sadducees, and in consequence definitely more open to modifications and changes. One of the many values of this work is the lengthy bibliography: A. "Literature on the Pharisees" (8 pp.) and B. "General Bibliography" (33 pp.), which includes everything of significance written prior to 1938. Three other works of more than incidental importance in connection with Abrahams' *Studies* are J. Lauterbach's "The Pharisees and Their Teachings,"[32] Solomon Zeitlin's "The Pharisees and the Gospels,"[33] and D. Daube's *The New Testament and Rabbinic Judaism.*[34]

That Abrahams and his fellow contenders made their point, namely, that rabbinic Judaism was far from the barren legalism that had been chromoed by scholars both ignorant of and indifferent to the Hebrew and Aramaic writings which they neglected and distorted, is today almost universally agreed. There has been, however, an increasing feeling among some, who would without question agree with the statement in the preceding sentence, that this rabbinic Judaism, found in the Mishnah and the Talmuds, is not the same as the Pharisaism of the day of Jesus and his earliest followers.

This growing feeling, conspicuously the thesis of the late Erwin R. Goodenough and harped upon in his twelve-volume *Jewish Symbols,*[35] namely, that there were many variations in the days of Jesus from this one type of Judaism and that the picture thus presented of Judaism ("Pharisaism") in the days of Jesus is at best but partial since it fails to include those other phases, notably "Hellenistic Judaism," certainly existent, while this rabbinic Judaism may well be a later development mistakenly read back—this critique was really developed more against the contention of George Foot Moore than that of Abrahams.

In his impressive study *Judaism,* Moore, it was alleged, had made unduly central, even all-else-eclipsing, what he styled "normative Judaism." By his very choice of that descriptive "normative" he had suggested that all other phases were at least peripheral and inconsequential. Thus the apocalyptic writings which had flourished for three centuries (175 B.C.-A.D. 125) were utterly disregarded as of no real consequence because of the absence of any reference to them in the rabbinical writings. Philo, who could not be disregarded, was to all intents a lone mountain peak, not only quite apart from the thought and life of Palestinian Jewry but with presumably little if any influence upon his fellow Jews.

Over against that fictional "normative" Judaism, Goodenough and his followers—many of whom were far from sharing in full his at times very daring and unsupported conclusions, based in part on archeological evidence, in part upon intuition—saw a mystic Judaism greatly influenced by the hellenistic world in which they were at home and from which they had borrowed much. Religious symbols were to Goodenough of prime importance in appraising the nature of the Judaism which utilized them. True, they were for the most part not to be found in the rabbinic writings, for the rabbis were both anti-iconic and hostile to mysticism. The rarity of material decorations in Palestine prior to A.D. 70 were seen by him as a consequence of the local influence of the Pharisees; the great increase of decoration after 70 was to him evidence of the decline of this "pharisaic-rabbinic" influnce. Thus in contrast to Moore's "normative Judaism" and essential neglect of any other phases as inconsequential, Goodenough saw a sharp cleavage between "rabbinic and antirabbinic" Judaism, substituting a single antirabbinic mystical Judaism for what many of his partway followers preferred to see as an "enormous variety of personal, doctrinal, political, and cultural divergences which the rabbinic and other evidence reveals."[36]

Both Moore and Abrahams—the former by direct assertion, the latter by implication—felt that the rabbinical Judaism found in the Mishnah and related writings was essentially the outgrowth and development of the life and thought of the previous century, that is, that by the days of the Christian beginnings the tracks had been laid on which later rabbinic trains ran. Thus the normative Judaism which Moore described, and with which Abrahams would most certainly have agreed in essence, was no new second- or third-century about-face. Both Abrahams and

Moore were, however, very careful—as too often modern critics fail to note—to distinguish between the utterances of later Tannaim, not to mention Amoraim, and those of an earlier date. Thus both escape entirely the frequent charge of using far later material unwarrantably, a danger which Bousset feared and accordingly sought to excuse himself for using "contemporary Jewish material"—the apocalypses—in place of what he regarded century-later writings.

In the writings of neither Abrahams nor Moore is much attention paid to the apocalyptic literature. Both make occasional reference to these wildfire productions, but obviously they are considered of minor importance. They are entirely unmentioned in the writings of the rabbis. This might well have seemed to Moore adequate reason for ignoring them, especially as his work was specifically concerned with Palestinian Judaism as reflected in the Tannaite sources of the second century, as his too-often ignored subtitle "The Age of the Tannaim" makes clear. He was not principally concerned with "Jews in their wide dispersion" or with Judaism in the time of the New Testament. Thus much of the criticism of his use of the term "normative Judaism" would be tempered were his critics to read the preface to his third volume. Abrahams was directly concerned, as for the most part Moore was not, with materials which parallel and illuminate aspects of and utterances in the gospels. He was equally cautious, however, in his use of illustrative rabbinic material, always refraining from implying that everything in the Mishnah and later codifications was of a date or nature to make a comparison warrantable. It is precisely at this spot that he guards himself as Strack and Billerbeck's huge anthology fails so often to do.

With these restrictions and qualifications in clear mind, the question remains: Even though in the work of both Abrahams and Moore detailed consideration of these wildfire writings, the apocalypses, did not seem warranted or germane—and both criticized Bousset and R. H. Charles for what seemed to them unbalanced use of these materials and for constantly discerning in them Pharisaic emphases if not actual authorship—must not these writings be considered in any sober and complete study of the sort of Judaism from which early Christianity emerged and in which Jesus had been nurtured and lived? It is true that they left no trace in later records of Jewish thinking, but did not many Jews in the days of Jesus prize and use them? Later Christians did use them and added many to those already produced, but nonetheless this cannot be regarded as any new gentile trait or innovation, but a definite carry-over from popular Judaism, not that, admittedly, of the scribal Pharisees, whom Abrahams rightly saw substantially of a mind with the Judaism of the Mishnah. For this latter type of Judaism there was no place for this sort of revelation. God had revealed his complete will in the Torah. This was his one avenue of revelation. It was this insistence—no new emphasis in post-Christian centuries as many modern enthusiasts insist—which had centuries earlier meant the end of prophecy. Nor is it surprising that the more rigidly conservative Jews, of whom the Sadducees may be seen as an example, had little use for this new development which they not only properly failed to find in the Scriptures but which was cluttered up with angels and nonscriptural aberrations like resurrection. What was good enough for Moses, was good enough for them. Thus their ear too was deaf.

In Christian circles these views—and presumably these writings—were from the start highly popular, which indisputable fact is enough to suggest that the popularity was no new gentile importation but a carry-over from popular Judaism. That Jesus found this sort of expectation highly congenial—and attempts to account for this fact in terms of his supposed cleavage from his native or "official" Judaism, while occasionally championed today, seems quite mistaken—is not to be overlooked in accountting for the Christian views of his earliest followers. It is quite unlikely that their convictions about him and his message, which led them so speedily to apotheosize him, were accompanied by a rejection or total reslanting of his basic notions and insistence. Rather, the expectation of a sudden cataclysmic end of the present age and the dawn of a new—the kingdom of God momentarily to appear—which was the mainspring of the early Christian movement, is most naturally explained as their unaltered, inheritance from the crucified prophet whose tragic death was heightened by the failure of the kingdom to come in his own lifetime as he had so passionately believed and predicted.

Nor was Jesus alone in this thinking. The largest fellowship which he had—minimized as it is in the gospel accounts—which made his presence in Jerusalem of such menace in the eyes of the authorities, fearing lest it spark a popular disastrous uprising, suggests very definitely that Sadducees and Pharisees—of the latter, at least those of a sort akin to the ones who subsequently established at Jamnia the famous Beth Din, which speedily came to believe itself to be the continuum of the previous Sanhedrin—were far from being the only group of any consequence in Palestine. Thus it has become increasingly common today to insist, in counter to what is popularly believed implied by Moore's "normative Judaism," that Pharisees, at least of the rabbinic strain, were but one of several far from-uniform groups. And the term "apocalyptic" is now unhesitatingly employed as a descriptive adjective modifying many Pharisees of the days of Jesus.[37]

Another emphasis, constantly made by both Abrahams and Montefiore, was the danger of seeing all that Jesus said in the nature of a direct attack upon the Pharisees. In the half century that has elapsed since their repeated, at times heated, protest, at this misreading of history their insistence has actually become a part of Christian (critical) orthodoxy, due in no small part to the recognition that the gospels—the synoptics as well as John—are comparatively late books and, while preserving materials from the days they purport to depict, reflect the point of view and outlook of the age and thinking which gave them birth. As the movement gradually coming to be known as "Christian" moved farther and farther away from Jewry, the opposition heightened and became increasingly intense and vocal. The extent to which Pharisees of the rabbinic sort dominated the picture in the "fifteenth year of Tiberius" may be open to some doubt, and accordingly the notion that they were the chief offenders lashed by Jesus; that after the destruction of Jerusalem, the end of the Sanhedrin as an effectual instrument of government, and the birth of rabbinic schools at Jamnia and Tiberias, the hostility became open and often virulent is beyond question. And Pharisees were the one group which had weathered the disaster of A.D. 66-73. However many other groups there had been, and regardless of their earlier influence, which many modern investigators today tend to overstress, as in their hankering after the bizarre they have sought to prove that every Jew was either a hellenist or a gnostic or a devotee of some other exotic group as that which it is fancied lived in the cliffs in and near Qumran, west of the Dead Sea, these had their day and ceased to be. When Jerusalem fell, they fell with it. Only the Pharisee, who alone had sought to solve the baffling problem of an old and unchanging law and a new society, survived. In consequence, it was they whom the early Christians found their greatest opponents. Despite the manifestly apologetic cast of the book of Acts, the emphasis is seemingly solid and adequately buttressed by other writings—both Christian and "pagan"—that the Jews were the Christians' chief opponents. Thus it is not strange that early words of controversy should be repeated and intensified. The group whom they were finding their chief opponents—not others which had long ceased to be—were their natural target, and the gospels which they produced not unnaturally tended to center their attack not upon groups no longer of concern but upon those who were continuing the hostility which tradition told them had opposed their crucified Lord.

It is interesting to conjecture what conclusions would have been reached by either Abrahams and Montefiore on the one hand and G. F. Moore on the other had the announcements of the finds at Qumran and the bedlam of contradictory, almost pontifical, pronouncements as to their date and value been noised abroad in their day. It is intriguing but idle to guess. In view of their sobriety and cautious appraisal of evidence it would appear probable that, at least in substance, they would have concluded, as an increasing number of their colleagues seem inclined today, to see the principal value of these scrolls, whatever their very uncertain date, as resident in themselves, and not to regard them as sources of new and revolutionizing knowledge of either the Pharisees, for here their contents are seemingly negative, or of Christianity where their value as sources is certainly nil.

To what extent, were Israel Abrahams alive today, he would have modified essentially his findings at this time when once more they are to be available for study and reflection, is most uncertain. While profoundly interested in the subject of the gospels, this was not his prime concern, nor would he have styled himself in any sense an expert in this field. The past fifty years have resulted in some definite modifications and changes of emphasis in gospel analysis and interpretation. But these changes would not essentially alter the problem he faced and sought to illumine, and his insights are for the most part as timely now as they were when he put them into print. Much the same may be said of his picture of rabbinic Judaism. To what extent he would have inclined to have increased his stress upon other groups in the Judaism of Jesus' day is at best uncertain. But he might well have considered the wisdom of greater stress upon other groups without in the slightest invalidating what he did say of the Pharisees themselves. His picture of rabbinic Judaism—of whom the Pharisees were the best example—stands unaltered, quite regardless of what other groups there may have been at that time, both in Palestine and out. Thus these essays and notes—both long and short: some technical and demanding a more than general interest and glib readiness to locate this expression or that of an insight of the past as being "in the Talmud"; others which require no advanced study or knowledge of the language of the rabbis—are still a veritable treasure chest for those who have the insight to realize, be they Jews or Christians, that if they would know their own religion in its real depths they must view with understanding and respect that of their fellows. None knew this better or sought more wholeheartedly to teach it than did Israel Abrahams.

*Quicquid ex Abrahams amavimus, quicquid mirati sumus, manet mansurumque est in animis hominum, in aeternitate temporum, in fama rerum.*[38]

MORTON S. ENSLIN

# ERRATA

Since the text of these *Studies* is reissued without internal change, the following minor typeslips may be noted:

I. p. 42, line 25: read "pp. 213 ff." *pro* "p. 181."
   p. 55, line 7 (from bottom): read "Rabbis."
   p. 86, line 17: read "Shequalim i, 3."
   p. 107, line 7: read "difficult" *pro* "different."
   p. 145, line 27: read "emphatic infinitive" *pro* "infinite."
   p. 163, line 12: read "injurer" *pro* second "injured."

II. p. 9, line 11: read "Why" *pro* "Who."
   p. 19, line: read "Yea."
   p. 54, line 16: read "Revelation" *pro* "Revelations."
   p. 60, line 5 (from bottom): *διεπέμψαντο.*
   p. 83, n.2: read "Isaiah xlvi.12."
   p. 89, line 21: read "Rabbinic."
   p. 123, n.3 This note can be misleading. "Mishnah Aboth, ch. v end" is the source of the quotation "Be bold as a leopard . . . in Heaven"; "T.B. Sabbath 31a" of the word of Jannai. (Actually this latter is 31b; it is also quoted in T.B. Yoma 71b.)
   p. 137, line 4 (from bottom): read "Sanh. iv, 1-3" *pro* "iv, 13 end."
   p. 155, line 9 (from bottom): probably read "Prov. xxviii, 18" *pro* "xxi. 10."
   p. 186, line 10: The passage mentioned by Dalman and quoted by Abrahams (without indicating its location) is T.B. Taanith 24b.
   p. 198, lines 33f. This reference to (Justin M.) "Dialogue xxii and lxviii" is surely in error, apparently a typeslip for "xli and cxvii," which are seemingly the passage Abrahams had in mind.

# NOTES

[1] *American Jewish Year Book,* 28 (1926), pp. 230-231.

[2] Psalm 18:29.

[3] *System der altsynagogalen palästinischen Theologie* (1880).

[4] *Lehrbuch der neutestamentlichen Zeitgeschichte,* as it was titled when it first appeared in 1874. Subsequent greatly enlarged editions appeared under the caption *Geschichte des jüdischen Volkes im Zeitalter Jesu Christ.* The English translation of this thesaurus of information appeared im 1901, under the title *A History of the Jewish People in the Time of Jesus Christ.*

[5] *Die Religion des Judentums im neutestamentalichen Zeitalter* (1903).

[6] *Entdecktes Judenthum* (1700).

[7] "Christian Writers on Judaism," in *Harvard Theological Review,* 14 (1921), p. 214. This detailed survey and appraisal (pp. 197-254), to which I am much indebted, together with his monumental *Judaism in the First Centuries of the Christian Era: The Age of the Tannaim* (1927 and 1930), had much to do with the change of tone in Introductions to the New Testament and other volumes dealing with Judaism at the time of the Christian Beginnings. Like Abrahams, Moore's knowledge was encyclopedic; unlike his British colleague, with whom he had much in common, his criticism of the spurious or to him mistaken scholarship was devasting, at times blistering.

[8] *Das Selbstbewusstsein Jesu im Lichte der messianischen Hoffnungen seiner Zeit* (1888).

[9] *Die Predigt Jesu vom Reiche Gottes* (1890). This short study, later rewritten and greatly enlarged, sounded the note later to be expanded and capitalized by A. Schweitzer in his insistence upon thoroughgoing eschatology as the sole trustworthy avenue to the Jesus long lost in the fogs of historical search.

[10] D. A. Chwolson, *Das letzte Passamahl Christi* (1892), p. 71.

[11] *Jewish Quarterly Review,* 11 (1899), pp. 626-642. In this analysis of Schürer's work he stresses the one fundamental weakness in a work from which (he confesses) he had learned much and of which he regrets being forced to speak adversely, for he is well aware of the rabbinic proverb, "Into a well from which thou hast drunk water, cast no stone"; viz., Schürer's unfamiliarity with the sources which at second hand he seeks to use and abuse.

[12] I, p. vii.

[13] The column "Books and Bookmen" in this journal was his own creation, and to it he contributed almost weekly from August 26, 1892 to April 13, 1917.

[14] *Jewish Quarterly Review,* 1 (Oct. 1888), p. 1.

[15] *The Synoptic Gospels* (1909), I, pp. xvii f.

[16] *Ibid.,* p. vii.

[17] *The Synoptic Gospels*[2] (1927), I, pp. vii f.

[18] In his popular volume, *Some Elements of the Religious-Teaching of Jesus* (1910), Montefiore refers to several of these Additional Notes as if he had already seen them. One of these, on the "Rabbinic conceptions and laws of clean and unclean and their application in everyday life," is referred to as "additional note 10 by Mr. Israel Abrahams in vol. iii of my *Commentary upon the Synoptic Gospels* (to be published shortly)," and is three times mentioned in the first edition of the *Commentary* itself (pp. 86, 167, 171) with the words "as Additional Note 10 explains," which surely suggests that it had already been written. It never appeared, and in the revised edition he completely rewrote his earlier text and himself discussed in detail this point.

[19] There are two omissions: the "Rabbinic doctrine of 'the Kingdom' " ("Additional Note 5," Montefiore, p. 57) and " 'ceremonial defilement' in eating" ("Additional Note 10." Montefiore, p. 86). In addition, Abrahams' XIV ("Poverty and Wealth") would scarcely correspond to Montefiore's anticipation (p. 125) of Note 15 on the first persecutions of Christians by Jews, as would be expected from the list of correspondences which stands facing p. 1 in the First Series of *Studies.* Actually this theme was treated by Abrahams in his tenth essay in the Second Series. To this, however, Montefiore makes no reference in the completely rewritten section in his second edition.

[20] William Sanday, "The Language of Vindictiveness in the Prayer Book, in the Bible, and in Modern Life," in *The Use of the Psalter* (Tracts on Common Prayer, No. 2), 1918, p. 61.

[21] "Necrology" in *Publications of the American Jewish Historical Society,* 31 (1928), pp. 249 f. For further evidence of the regard and appreciation with which this devoted scholar was regarded by his colleagues one may read such other tributes

as now stand as early chapters in the Festschrift *(vide infra)* by Stephen S. Wise, F. J. Foakes Jackson, Nathan Krass, and Claude G. Montefiore. To these should be added the moving "character sketch" by Herbert Loewe which appeared in the *American Jewish Year Book*, 28 (1926), pp. 219-234.

There is no definitive list of the writings of Dr. Abrahams, but the Select Bibliography compiled by Dudley Wright for the Festschrift *Jewish Studies in Memory of Israel Abrahams* (1927) is an indication of his productivity. This list covers twenty-nine pages (xix-xlvii) and is arranged in five parts:

I. Contributions to *Jewish Chronicle.*
II. Contributions to *Jewish Guardian.*
III. Contributions to *Encyclopaedias* of *Religion and Ethics; Biblica* and *Britannica.*
IV. Contributions to *Transactions Jewish Historical Society, Jewish Quarterly Review,* &c.
V. Other Works.

Of these "other works," the following books may be listed as partial evidence of his breadth of coverage and concern:

*Aspects of Judaism* (1895); *Jewish Life in the Middle Ages* (1896); *Chapters on Jewish Literature* (1899); *Maimonides* (with D. Yellin, 1903); *Judaism* (1907); *Literary Remains* of S. Singer, 3 vols., edited by *Abrahams* (1908); *The Book of Delight and other Essays* (1913); *Annotated Edition of the Authorized Daily Prayer Book* (1914); *Studies in Pharisaism and the Gospels,* First Series (1917); *By-paths in Hebraic Bookland* (1920); *Permanent Values in Judaism* (1923); *The Glory of God* (1925); *Studies in Pharisaism and the Gospels,* Second Series (1924); *Hebrew Ethical Wills,* 2 vols. (posthumously, 1926); *Campaigns in Palestine from Alexander the Great* (Schweich Lectures, 1922; publ. posthumously, 1927).

[22] London *Times,* Literary Supplement, 23 (April 24, 1924), p. 248.

[23] *Expository Times,* 35 (1923-24), pp. 445 f.; *Journal of Religion,* 4 (1924), p. 444: *Journal of Theological Studies,* 26 (1924-25), pp. 92 f.; *Nieuwe Theologische Studiën,* 1 (1918), pp. 25 f.; *Orientalische Literaturzeitung,* 24 (1919), p. 93, *Recherches de Science Religieuse,* 14 (1924), pp. 327 f.; *Revue des Sciences Philosophiques et Théologiques,* 14 (1924), p. 110; *Theology,* 9 (1924), p. 120.

[24] Jacob Z. Lauterbach, "The Sadducees and the Pharisees," in *Studies in Jewish Literature Issued in Honor of Kaufmann Kohler* (1913), pp. 177-178.

[25] Josephus, *Antt.* 13, 10, 6 (§§ 297 f.); *Wars* 1, 5, 2 (§ 110).

[26] *Judaism in the First Centuries of the Christian Era: The Age of the Tannaim* (1927-1930).

[27] Samuel Sandmel, *We Jews and Jesus* (1965), p. 101.

[28] October 6, 1925.

[29] 1922-1928.

[30] For a survey and critique of this aspect of this work see S. Sandmel, "Parallelomania," delivered as his presidential address before the Society of Biblical Literature in 1961 and published in *Journal of Biblical Literature,* 81 (1962), pp. 1-13; esp. pp. 8ff.

[31] *Harvard Theological Review,* 22 (1929), pp. 185-261.

[32] *Hebrew Union College Annual,* 6 (1929), pp. 176-198.

[33] In *Essays and Studies in Memory of Linda R. Miller* (1938), pp. 235-286. And see now Zeitlin's treatment of the subject at large in volume II of his monumental work, *The Rise and Fall of the Judaean State* (1967).

[34] London, 1956.

[35] Erwin R. Goodenough, *Jewish Symbols in the Greco-Roman Period,* 12 vols. (1953-1964).

[36] For a detailed survey and critique of Goodenough's position, with a full listing of all the reviews and appraisals his 12-vol. work produced, see the article by Morton Smith, "Goodenough's *Jewish Symbols* in Retrospect," *Journal of Biblical Literature,* 86 (1967), pp. 53-68.

[37] W. D. Davies, who shares this view, but with a restraint in marked contrast to some of its proponents, has long argued that many Pharisees were greatly attracted to apocalyptic speculations, standing midway between the Sadducees, who regarded this thinking as not only bizarre and unbiblical but as definitely a menace to the status quo, and the "Zealots," to whom it was the "breath of life." See his article "Apocalyptic and Pharisaism" in the *Expository Times,* 59 (July 1948), pp. 233-237; his *Christian Origins and Judaism;* and his recently (1967) reprinted study *Introduction to Pharisaism.* Many others, including the late Ralph Marcus, share this same view.

[38] Tacitus, *Agricola* 46.

# PREFACE

IN 1909 Mr C. G. Montefiore published what may without exaggeration be termed an epoch-making Commentary on the Synoptic Gospels in two volumes. It was intended that I should have the honour of contributing a third volume, containing Additional Notes. This plan has not been fulfilled. The reason is simple. I had promised more than I could perform. The problems proved so many, so intricate, that I have found it beyond my capacity to deal with them all.

But if the original design could not be fully carried out, neither was it entirely abandoned. A saying of Rabbi Tarphon seemed appropriate to the situation. "It is not thy part to complete the work, yet art thou not altogether free to desist from it." On this principle, Notes were from time to time written and printed, until by the year 1912 the contents of the present book were in type. Most of the Notes were actually written between the years 1908–1911. I have recently gone through the proofs carefully, and have added some references to later literature, but substantially the Notes remain as they were written several years ago. The abandonment, for the present at least, of the hope to do much more has impelled me to publish what I have been able to do.

The circumstance that this volume was designed as an Appendix to Mr Montefiore's work accounts for the inclusion of subjects of unequal importance. Certain Notes, natural and necessary to a consecutive Commentary, would hardly have suggested themselves for a series of independent Studies. Moreover, some of the Chapters in the present book, though possibly they might pass as exegetical comments, are quite inadequate as essays. It must be remembered that it was purposed to supplement several of these Notes by further Notes on other aspects of the same problems as they presented themselves in the course of the Synoptic narratives. The author is not without hope that he may be able before long to issue a second series of Studies in which some of the omissions are rectified. In point of fact several Studies on other matters are practically written, and others definitely planned. Among the subjects to be discussed in this second Series would be: certain aspects of "Life under the Law," the "Yoke of the Commandments," "Ritual Purity," the "Traditions of the Elders," the "Last Supper," "Rabbinic Conceptions of Sacrifice and Prayer," the "Trial of Jesus," the "Am Ha-areṣ," the "Two Ways," the "Psychology and Liturgy of Confession," and above all the "Kingdom of God," "Pharisaic Eschatology," and the "Jewish Apocalypses."

This being the case, I have deferred for a later occasion any general appreciation of the Gospel teachings. Nor do I think it necessary to justify at any length the intrusion of a Jewish student into the discussion of the Synoptic problem. Mr Montefiore, as is admitted on all hands, rendered a conspicuous service both to Jewish and Christian scholars by his frank and masterly examination of the Gospels from a professedly Jewish stand-point. Undoubtedly *a* (though not *the*) real Synoptic problem is: how to hold the balance truly between the teaching of Jesus on the one hand and of Pharisaic Judaism on the other. Obviously, then, Jewish students have both the right and the duty to attempt a contribution to this balanced judgment. Apart from the fact that their studies in Pharisaic literature are inevitably more intimate, there is another very important consideration. Pharisaism was not a mere historical phase; it has remained a vital force, it has gone on without a moment's break from the centuries before the Christian era to the twentieth century of that era. It has been put to the test of time and of life. It has survived throughout an experience, such as no other religious system has undergone. Hence the Jewish student is able to apply to current criticisms of Pharisaism not merely literary tests, but also the touchstone and possibly the corrective of actual experience.

There is perhaps room for yet another suggestion. Jewish students of the Old Testament have gained much from the researches made by Christian scholars, not merely philologically and in the archaeological field, but also theologically. For the Jew has so ingrained a belief in the organic union of ritual with religion, is so convinced that the antithesis of letter and spirit is mistaken psychologically, that he needed the analytical criticism to enable him to appreciate historically the difference between the prophetic and the priestly strata in the Hebrew Bible, between the abiding principles and Messianic dreams of religion and those detailed rules of ritual and maxims of conduct by which it is sought to realize those principles and dreams in actual life. But it is just because of this that the Jew may be able to return the compliment, and help Christians to understand certain phases of the Gospels. Many modern Christians seem torn between two sides of the teaching of Jesus—his prophetic-apocalyptic visions of the Kingdom and his prophetic-priestly concern in the moral and even ritual life of his day, in which he wished to see the Law maintained in so far as it could be applied under existing circumstances. The Christian scholar, impregnated with Paulinism, sometimes appears to find these two aspects of the Gospel teachings inconsistent. Hence we have the disturbing phenomenon of waves in Christian thought, the humanists who regard Jesus as almost exclusively a moralist, and the apocalyptists who treat him as almost exclusively a visionary. The Jew sees nothing inconsistent in these two aspects. The very causes which make Christian commentaries useful for the Jew if he would understand the Old Testament, may make Jewish commentaries helpful to the Christian for understanding some aspects of the New Testament.

I am well aware of the many imperfections of the Studies here presented. But I do claim that I have not written apologetically. Still less have I been moved by controversial aims. Only on rare occasions have I directly challenged the picture of Pharisaism drawn in Germany by Prof. Schürer and in England by Canon Charles. I have preferred to supplement their views by a positive presentation of another view. In this sense only are these Studies apologetic and controversial. At all events, though I acknowledge that I have fallen far below Mr Montefiore in the faculty of unprejudiced judgment, I have never consciously suppressed defects in the Pharisaic position, nor have I asserted in behalf of it more than the facts, as known to me, have demanded. I am confident that those who are best acquainted with the difficulties of the problems discussed will be the most lenient critics of my errors and misconceptions.

I. A.

*December*, 1916.

# CONTENTS

It may be well to indicate the relation of the present Chapters to the Additional Notes referred to in Mr Montefiore's work. The correspondence is as follows:

| Additional Notes in Mr Montefiore's work. | Chapters in the present volume. |
|---|---|
| 1 | xviii. |
| 2 | iii. |
| 3 | iv. |
| 4 | v. |
| 6 | i. |
| 7 | xiii. |
| 8 | xix., xx. |
| 9 | vii. |
| 11 | vii. |
| 12 | xvi. |
| 13 | xvii. |
| 14 | xii. |
| 15 | xiv. |
| 16 | xiv. |
| 17 | vi. |
| 18 | ix. |
| 19 | xv. |
| 20 | xiv. |
| 21 | xi. |
| 22 | viii. |
| 23 | xxi. |
| 24 | ii. |
| 25 | x. |

## I. THE FREEDOM OF THE SYNAGOGUE.

The Synagogue,—that most gracious product of Jewish legalism—cannot have been the invention of the Hellenistic diaspora (as is maintained, without adequate evidence, by M. Friedländer, Introd. to *Synagoge und Kirche*, 1908). If it was due to a diaspora at all, it must be attributed to the exile in Babylon. This is no modern guess, for we have the statement of Justin (Dialogue with Trypho 17) that Jews applied Malachi i. 11, 12 to the prayers of the Israelites *then* in dispersion. We may confidently assert (with W. Bacher, Hastings' *Dictionary of the Bible*, s.v.; G. A. Smith, *Jerusalem* I. 364) that the Synagogue was a Palestinian institution of the Persian period. It was an institution momentous for the history of religion. "Their (the Jews') genius for the organisation of public religion appears in the fact that the form of communal worship devised by them was adopted by Christianity and Islam, and in its general outline still exists in the Christian and Moslem worlds" (C. Toy, *Introduction to the History of Religions*, 1913, p. 546).

In the Greek diaspora the Synagogue undoubtedly became of special importance. But its connection with Palestinian models is clear. Philo's account of the services in the Greek synagogues points to the two features which distinguished the Palestinian system; the reading and interpretation of the Scriptures, and the recitation of passages to which the assembly responded by terms of liturgical assent (cf. *Cambridge Biblical Essays*, 1909, p. 190). These features are shown in Ezra and Chronicles, and in all the Palestinian records that have come down to us (as in Sirach). True, the Maccabean history makes no direct reference to the Synagogue, but the main interest in that history was Jerusalem and the Temple. None the less, the books of the Maccabees prove most clearly that the people were in possession of copies of the Scroll of the law from which they read publicly (1 Macc. i. 57, iii. 48), were in the habit of gathering for prayer (iii. 44), and above all of singing hymns with such refrains as "His mercy is good, and endureth for ever" (iv. 24).

That there is little allusion in the Books of the Maccabees to places of worship is intelligible—though the silence is not absolute. It must not be overlooked that (iii. 46) Mizpah is described not as an ancient shrine or altar but as "a place of prayer" (τόπος προσευχῆς). But the fact seems to be that the institution of the Synagogue was earlier than the erection of places of worship. In the Temple itself, the reading of the Law was conducted by Ezra in the open courts, which remained the scene of the prayer-meetings to the end, as the Rabbinic sources amply demonstrate (e.g. Mishnah Sukkah chs. iv—v; cf. Sirach l. 5—21; 1 Macc. iv. 55). So, too, with the first prayer-meetings in the "provinces." The meetings were probably held in the open air; and that this was the most primitive form is shown by the fact that the assemblies on occasions of national stress, even in the last decades of the existence of the temple, were held in the public thoroughfares (Mishnah Taanith ii. 1). By the first century A.D. Synagogue buildings were plentiful both in the capital and the provinces. They probably came into being under the favourable rule of Simon. It must always, however, be remembered that Synagogue buildings in various parts of Palestine are possibly referred to in Psalm lxxiv. 8, usually assigned to the early years of the Maccabean age.

This is not the place to discuss the whole question, but one supreme fact must not be omitted. From first to last, there was an organic relation between Temple and Synagogue (though Friedländer, *loc. cit.*, denies this). That there were prayers in the Temple is of course certain (Mishnah Tamid v; Philo on Monarchy vi). Isaiah's phrase (lvi. 7) a "house of prayer" (LXX. οἶκος προσευχῆς) applied to the Temple was fulfilled to the letter. It is probable that *all* the Greek words used in the diaspora for the Synagogue (that word itself, Proseuche and place of instruction,—the last occurs in the Hebrew Sirach) were derived from Hebrew or Aramaic equivalents. Certain is it that, in Palestine, no Greek terms were imported to describe the Synagogue. The real model for Palestine and the diaspora was the Temple. It was a true instinct, therefore, which identified the "smaller sanctuary" of Ezekiel xi. 16 with the Synagogue (T. B. Megillah 29 b). The very word *Abodah* used of the Temple *service* became an epithet for the service of prayer (the "Abodah of the heart," Sifrê Deut. § 41). The link between Temple and Synagogue was established in Palestine by the system in accordance with which local delegacies accompanied the priests during their course of service in Jerusalem, while at home there were simultaneously held public readings of the law (Mishnah Taanith iv. 2).

The evidence from the Greek sources points in the same direction. Agatharchides of Cnidos (second century B.C.) records how the Jews spend their Sabbath in rest, and "spread out their hands and *pray* (εὔχεσθαι) till the evening." The whole context of the passage (as cited in Josephus *Against Apion* I. 22) shows that Agatharchides was referring to Jerusalem. That, however, in Egypt the Synagogue imitated the Palestinian methods is clear from Philo. Even Philo's Egyptian Therapeutae have their analogue, and possibly exemplar, in the Palestinian Essenes. As regards Alexandria, Philo gives unmistakable proof of the dependence of the Synagogue on the Temple method. His account, though its force has not been adequately realized, entirely depends on the Palestinian model. He tells us how (II. 630) "the multitude listens in silence, except when it is customary to say words of good omen by way of assent to what is read." This can only refer to the recitation of passages (chiefly no doubt Psalms) by one while the rest answer by "Amen" and similar ancient liturgical responses, such as were used in the Temple. That this must refer to prayers and not to reading the law is certain, for Philo then *proceeds* to describe the Scriptural readings and the expositions. Very instructive as to the connection between the Synagogues of the diaspora and the Temple is Philo's further statement that the exposition of the Scriptures was delivered by *one of the priests who happened to be present* (τῶν ἱερῶν δέ τις ὁ παρὼν) or by one of the elders (ἢ τῶν γερόντων).

This picture of the activity of the priests in teaching the law is a remarkable testimony to the truth that though the Temple was essentially the home of the sacrificial ritual, its influence on life, was far-reaching and beneficial. Had it been otherwise, Philo would not have eulogised the Temple and priesthood—as he does in many places. Perhaps nothing could more piquantly show how completely Jerusalem, its Temple and its services, contrived to harmonise sacrificial ritual with prayer and a manifold activity, than the quaint report given by one who lived in Jerusalem during the existence of the Temple and survived its fall. R. Joshua b. Ḥananya said: "When we rejoiced (during Tabernacles) at the Joy of the Water-drawing we saw no sleep with our eyes. How so? The first hour, the morning Tamid (sacrifice), and thence to the prayer; thence to the musaph (additional) offering, thence to the musaph prayer; thence to the House of Study, thence to the meal; thence to the afternoon prayer, thence to the evening Tamid; thence onwards to the joy of the water-drawing" (T. B. Sukkah 53 a).

The Synoptists draw a pleasing picture of the freedom of teaching permitted by the Synagogue. Jesus performed this function throughout Galilee. The Fourth Gospel and Acts confirm the Synoptic record as to the readiness of the "rulers of the Synagogue" to call upon any competent worshipper to interpret and expound the Scriptures that had been read. Such instruction was usual in the Synagogue long before the time of Jesus as Zunz has shown (*Die gottesdienstlichen Vorträge der Juden*, ch. xx.), and the evidence is admirably marshalled and supplemented by Schürer (*Geschichte des jüdischen Volkes* etc. II[4]. pp. 498 seq.). Philo (II. 458) describes how one would read from the book, while another, "one of the more experienced" (τῶν ἐμπειροτάτων), expounded. In Palestine, too, the only qualification was competence, just as for leading the services experience (cf. the רגיל of the Mishnah Taanith ii. 2) was a chief requisite. As the discourses grew in length the *locale* for the sermon seems to have been transferred from Synagogue to School, and the *time* sometimes changed from the morning to the afternoon or previous evening. We find later on both customs in force together (T.J. *Taanith*, i. § 2 etc.). But at the earlier period, when the discourse was brief, it must have been spoken in the Synagogue, and immediately after the lesson from the Prophets.

The only two occasions of which we have a definite account of teaching in the Synagogue are, curiously enough, treated by Schürer (II[4]. 533 n. 123) as exceptions. His reason for doing so is derived from a purely philological argument. In the two cases, Luke iv. 17 and Acts xiii. 15, it is specifically recorded that the address followed the reading from the Prophets. In the first instance Jesus speaks after reading a couple of verses from Isaiah; in the second, we are explicitly told that in the Synagogue of Antioch, after the reading of the Law and the Prophets, the rulers of the Synagogue sent to them [Paul and his company], saying, "Brethren, if ye have any word of exhortation for the people, say on." We may note in passing that whereas Jesus both reads the lesson and expounds it, Paul does not seem to have read the lesson. This indicates an interesting difference in practice, for which there is other evidence. Rapoport (*Erech Millin*, 168) concludes from various Rabbinical passages that in the second century the reader of the Prophetical lesson was, in general, one who was able also to preach.

It may be that this custom existed side by side with another method which encouraged the *children* to read the lessons in Synagogue (cf.

Blau, *Revue des Etudes juives*, LV. 218). The two customs can be reconciled by the supposition (based on *Soferim*, xii. 7, xiv. 2) that when a preacher was present, he read the Prophetical lesson, and in the absence of such a one the children read it, perhaps at greater length. For the Prophetical reading was by nature a sermon, and as the service concluded with a sermon, the Prophetical lesson concluded the service when no preacher was present. It is clear from the narrative in T.B. *Beza*, 15 b, that the homily of the Rabbi was the end of the service, and it follows that the homily was given after the reading from the Prophets. But Schürer holds that as a general rule the discourse followed on the Pentateuchal lesson, and that the Prophetical reading without explanation concluded the service. True it is that the Prophetical lesson was named *haftara* (הפטרה or אפטרה), a word corresponding to *demissio*, i.e. the people was dismissed with or after the reading from the Prophets. But this surely is quite compatible with a short discourse, and the dismissal of the people might still be described as following the Prophetical lesson. Moreover, it may well be that the term *haftara* refers to the conclusion not of the whole services but of the Scriptural readings, the Prophetical passage being the *complement* of the Pentateuchal section. This was the view of various medieval authorities as cited in Abudarham and other liturgists. (It is accepted by I. Elbogen in his treatise *Der jüdische Gottesdienst in seiner geschichtlichen Entwicklung*, Leipzig, 1913, p. 175).

The oldest Prophetical lessons were most probably introduced for festivals and the special four or five Sabbaths in order to reinforce and interpret the Pentateuchal lessons, and (in the view of some) to oppose the views of schismatics. The Pharisees, owing to the conflicting theories of the Sadducees, attached to the sections from the Law such readings from the other Scriptures (particularly the "Earlier Prophets" who offered historical statements) as supported the Pharisaic exposition of the festival laws. (Cf. Büchler, *J. E.*, VI. 136 a. The same writer there cites T.B. *Megilla*, 25 b, T.J. *Megilla*, iv. 75 c, *Tosefta*, iv. 34 as Talmudic evidence that the reading of the haftara on the Sabbath had already been instituted in the first century of the common era). According to Abudarham, the author of a famous fourteenth century commentary on the Synagogue liturgy, the Prophetic readings grew up in a time of persecution, and were a substitute for the Pentateuchal readings when these were interdicted. On the other hand, L. Venetianer has lately suggested (*Z. D. M. G.* vol. 63, p. 103) that there were no specific readings from the Prophets till the end of the second century, and that the Prophetical lectionaries were chosen polemically in reply to lectionaries and homilies in the early Christian Church. But it seems far more probable that the haftaras were chosen for other reasons: (*a*) to include some of the most beautiful parts of the Scriptures, (*b*) to reinforce the message of the Pentateuch, and (*c*) to establish firmly the conviction that the whole of the canonical Scriptures (which, when the haftaras were first appointed, did not yet include the hagiographa) were a *unity*. (Cf. Bacher, *Die Proömien der alten jüdischen Homilie*, 1913, Introduction.)

There does not seem to have been any interval between the two readings, in fact the reciter of the haftara previously read a few verses from the Pentateuchal lesson (T.B. *Megilla*, 23 a). The sermon often dealt with the substance of the Pentateuchal lesson, and the preacher frequently took his text from it. But it is initially unlikely that the sermon should precede the haftara, seeing that the latter was introduced to help the understanding of the Law. We are not, however, left to conjecture. For we possess a large number of discourses which were specifically composed round the haftara. Many of the homilies in the *Pesiqta Rabbathi* are of this class; they are of course not, as they now stand, so early as the first century, but they represent a custom so well established as to point to antiquity of origin. The famous fast-day discourse reported in the Mishnah Taanith ii. 1 is based on two texts from the prophets (Jonah iii. 10 and Joel ii. 13), —both of which passages were eminently suitable as the lesson for such an occasion. Of the forty-seven chapters in the Pesiqta (most of which are compounded of many discourses) in Friedmann's edition, more than twenty are based on haftaras; in the *Pesiqta of R. Cahana* there are eleven such chapters. That these discourses *followed* the reading from the Prophets is shown by the recurrence of such a phrase as: "As he has read as *haftara* in the Prophet" (מה שהשלים בנביא Friedmann, 1 b) when quoting the text expounded. (The verb שלם is equivalent in this context to אפטר, just as שלמתא is another word for הפטרה, and it must signify to *complete* the lesson rather than to *dismiss* the congregation.) Similar evidence that the discourse was preceded by the actual reading of the *haftara* is derivable from Friedmann's edition, pp. 29 a, 42 a (ממה שהשלים הנביא), 54 a, 142 b (ממה שכתב בעניין "As he has written in the passage read"), 149 b (ממה שקראו בעניין הנביא), 179 a (ממה שקרינן בענין). Perhaps the most instructive passage of all is on 172 a. Here the discourse is on the Pentateuchal text Leviticus xxiii. 24 read on the New Year festival: "In the seventh month, in the first day of the month, shall be a solemn rest unto you, a memorial of blowing of trumpets." At the end of the last Pisqa the homily runs: "Says the Holy One, blessed be He, in this world, through the trumpet (shofar) I have had compassion on you, and so in time to come I will be merciful to you through the trumpet (shofar) and bring near your redemption. Whence? From what we have read in the lesson of the Prophet (מניין? ממה שקראו בעניין בנביא): Blow ye the trumpet in Zion...for the day of the Lord cometh (Joel ii. 1)." In this case it is quite clear that the discourse on the Pentateuchal text *followed* the *haftara*.

I have been at some pains to show that the New Testament accounts of the preaching in the Synagogues refer to the normal and not to the exceptional, because these accounts are the most precise we possess and it is important to know that we may rely on them completely. What then can we exactly infer as to the extent of freedom which the worshippers enjoyed not only with regard to teaching but also with regard to the selection of passages on which to speak? I do not find it possible to accept the view that the homilist was allowed a *perfectly* free hand, that he might open the Prophet or Prophets where he willed, read a verse or two and then address the congregation. That the readings from the Law and the Prophets were in the time of Jesus very short is fairly certain. The rule that at least 21 verses were read from the Law and the Prophets was, as Büchler shows (*J. Q. R.*, v. 464 seq.; VI. 14 seq., 45), late. In the Massoretic divisions we find Sabbath lessons (Sedarim) which contain seven, eight and nine verses, and there are many indications that the oldest *haftara* often comprised very few verses. This follows indeed from the very nature of the *haftara*. It originally corresponded in substance with, and agreed often in its opening word with the opening word of, the Pentateuchal lesson. But this correspondence mostly only concerns a single verse or two, not long passages. Thus the reading Isaiah lxi. 1—2 (Luke iv. 16) was possibly the whole of the *haftara*. Later on, it became usual to round off the reading by *skipping* until a suitable terminating verse was reached.

Let us try to define exactly what it is that Luke describes. Jesus stood up to read. Then "there was delivered unto him a book of the prophet Isaiah." The verb used for "delivered up" (ἐπεδόθη) might be interpreted "was delivered unto him in addition." In that case Jesus would have first read a verse of the Pentateuchal lesson (perhaps Deut. xv. 7) and then proceeded with the *haftara*. But it is impossible to press the Greek verb in this way. Yet it is at all events clear that the *prophet* was not Jesus' choice; it was handed to him. Moreover, the wording in Luke makes it almost certain that just as the book of Isaiah was not Jesus' own choice, so the passage from Isaiah was not chosen by Jesus himself. "He opened the book and found the place where it was written." The word "found" (εὗρεν) does not mean he looked for it and chose it, but he "found" it ready. This is implied by a change in the verbs which has I think been overlooked. We are simply told that Jesus "opened" (ἀνοίξας) the book. Jesus does not unroll it, as he would have done had he searched for a text. (The reading ἀναπτύξας is rejected by W.H., Nestle etc.) Luke on the other hand tells us that when he had finished the reading he "rolled it up." The A.V. "he closed the book" does not give the force of the Greek (πτύξας). Thus when he has finished Jesus rolls up the scroll which he did not unroll, for it was given to him already unrolled, so that he only opened it at the place already selected and found the passage in Isaiah ready for him to read. In fact, while the Pentateuch was read in an unbroken order, the *haftara* might be derived from any part of the Prophets, provided always that one condition was fulfilled: the passage was bound to resemble in subject-matter the Torah portion just read. As Dr Büchler well puts it: "This is clear from the origin of the institution itself; and moreover the examples quoted by the Mishna, Boraitha and Tosefta, bear unmistakable testimony to the existence of this condition" (*J. Q. R.*, VI. 12).

It has often been pointed out that Jesus sat down (Luke iv. 20) to expound the Scriptures, and that this accords with Rabbinic custom. There is no contradiction in Acts xiii. 16, where "Paul stood up." Though Paul's exhortation follows Jewish lines in its structure, it is not an explanation of the Law. For, though the address may be due more to Luke's hand than to Paul's, it resembles the exhortations in the Books of the Maccabees; and, at all events, so far from expounding the Law, it is an ingenious eulogy of it up to a point, and thence an argument against its sufficiency. The climax of Paul's whole speech is reached in verse 39, and the opposition which followed, from those who venerated the Law against one who proclaimed its insufficiency, cannot be regarded as any breach in that freedom of the Synagogue which he had previously enjoyed. On the other hand, Jesus expounded the Scriptures, applying Isaiah lxi. 1, 2 to himself. He seems to have combined lviii. 6 with lxi. 1. The right to "skip" while reading the

Prophets was well attested (Mishnah *Megilla* iv. 4). Being written on a Scroll, the two passages might easily be open together, and Jesus, in accordance with what at all events became a usual Rabbinic device, intended to use both texts as the key to his exposition. Such skipping to suitable passages may be noted in the Geniza fragments of haftaras in the triennial cycle.

If the view here taken of the incident in Luke be correct, then we have distinctly gained evidence that, at the opening of the public teaching of Jesus, the Synagogue lectionary was becoming fixed at all events in its main principles. That this was the case with the essential elements of the service is very probable. There is no reason whatever to doubt the tradition (T.B. *Berachoth*, 33 a) which ascribed the beginnings of the order of service to the "Men of the Great Synod," the successors of the three post-exilic prophets, Haggai, Zechariah, and Malachi. The doubts which Kuenen threw on the reality of this body—doubts which for a generation caused the "Great Synod" to be dismissed as a myth—are no longer generally shared, and Dr G. Adam Smith in his *Jerusalem* has fairly faced the absurd position in which we are placed if we deny, to a highly organised community such as Ezra left behind him, some central legislative and spiritual authorities in the Persian and Greek periods. The two functions were afterwards separated, and it may well be (Büchler *Das Synhedrium in Jerusalem*, 1902) that two distinct Synhedria, one with civil the other with religious jurisdiction, existed in the last period before the fall of the Temple. As regards the Synagogue service, it probably opened with an invocation to prayer, must have included the *Shema* (Deut. vi. 4—9, xi. 13—21; to which was added later Numbers xv. 37—41), a doxology and confession of faith, the eighteen benedictions in a primitive form, readings from Pentateuch and Prophets, and certain communal responses. With this Schürer (*loc. cit.*) is in substantial agreement. The actual contents of the liturgy long remained fluid; the fixation of the Synagogue prayers was the work of the post-Talmudic Gaonim of the seventh century onwards.

Attention should be paid to a remarkable difference of language with regard to prayer and study of the Law. Nothing better brings out the real character of Pharisaism. It relied on rule and based much confidence on the effect of good habits. But it left free the springs of emotion and the source of communion. While, then, Shammai urged (Aboth i. 15) "Make thy *Torah* a fixed thing" (עשה תורתך קבע), Simon—a disciple of Joḥanan b. Zakkai—proclaimed (*ib.* ii. 18) "Make not thy *prayer* a fixed thing" (אל תעש תפלתך קבע). Study was to be a habit, prayer a free emotion. The true tradition of Pharisaism from beginning to end of the first century is seen from Hillel, through Joḥanan, to his disciples—one of whom in answer to Joḥanan's problem: "Go forth and see which is the good way to which a man should cleave" said: "A good heart." And the master approved this solution as the right one (Aboth ii. 13). No fixation of a liturgy changed this attitude. Prayer might be, as time progressed, ordained to follow certain forms, but within those forms freedom prevailed, as it still prevails in the most conservative Jewish rituals.

With regard to reciting the Scriptures, the public reading of the Law for occasions was certainly instituted by Ezra, and continued by his successors in authority; the passages read were translated into the vernacular Aramaic (Targum). We know that the Palestinian custom, when finally organised, provided for a cycle of Sabbath lessons which completed a continuous reading of the Pentateuch once in every three years (T.B. *Megillah*, 29 b). As to the antiquity of the beginnings of this Triennial Cycle Dr Büchler's epoch-making Essays leave no doubt (*J. Q. R.*, v. 420, vi. 1). The strongest argument for this supposition is of a general character, but it is reinforced by many particular facts. Many events in the Pentateuch which are left undated in the original are dated with exactitude in the Rabbinic tradition. This is amply accounted for by the simple fact that these events are contained in the Sabbath lessons which fell normally to be read on certain dates, which Tannaitic tradition thereupon associated with those events. This argument enables us to work backwards and assume a somewhat early origin for the fixation of the readings on those particular dates.

It may here be of interest to interpolate one or two instances of the light thrown on passages in the N.T. by the Cycle of lessons. Dr King (*Journal of Theological Studies*, Jan. 1904) has ingeniously shown that the association (in the second chapter of the Acts) of the Gift of Tongues with Pentecost falls in admirably with the Triennial Cycle. The first year of the Cycle began on Nisan 1, and the opening verses of Genesis were then read. The eleventh chapter of Genesis was reached at the season of Pentecost. This chapter narrated the story of Babel, i.e. the Confusion of Tongues. The Gift of the Spirit is a "reversal of the curse of Babel." A second instance may be found in the Fourth Gospel. The discourse of Jesus regarding the Manna must have occurred in the spring, although the date "the Passover was near" (John vi. 4) is justly held to be a suspicious reading. But the note of time "there was much grass in the place" (verse 10) is confirmed by the "green grass" of Mark vi. 39. John particularly specifies that the five loaves were made of "barley" (verses 9, 13). The new barley would certainly not be available till a few weeks after the Passover, and the poor would not have possessed a store of the old barley so late as the spring. Everything points, then, to a date soon after the Passover. Now in the second year of the Triennial Cycle the lessons for the first weeks in Iyyar (end of April or beginning of May) were taken from Exodus xvi., the very chapter in which the miracle of the Manna is reported. Of course the dates of both Acts and the Fourth Gospel are uncertain. But such coincidences as these (to which others could easily be added) point to the use of good and old sources, and they at least confirm the view that, in its initial stages, a Cycle of lessons may have been already in vogue in the first century.

Some obscure arguments in the Gospels might lose their difficulty if we were acquainted with the Scriptural readings with which they were possibly associated. Thus in the Sabbath incident (Matthew xii.), the argument would be more logical if Numbers xxviii. 9—10 and 1 Sam. xxi. 1—10 had been recently read in the Synagogues. "Have ye not read what David did?" and "Have ye not read in the Law?" (Matthew xii. 3, 5) would have a sharp sarcastic point in that case. It may well be, again, that the Parable of the Prodigal Son was spoken during the weeks when Genesis xxv. onwards formed the Sabbath lessons. There is distinct indication from Philo (see below Note on Parables) that the idea conveyed in the Parable alluded to was connected with the story of Esau and Jacob. Another instance is yet clearer. The discourse in the Fourth Gospel (vii. 37, 8) belongs to Tabernacles. "As the scripture hath said, out of his belly shall flow rivers of living waters. But this spake he of the Spirit." The reference probably is to Zechariah xiv. 8 (now read in the Synagogues on the first day of Tabernacles, possibly under the Triennial Cycle read later in the festival week). Zechariah indeed has: "living waters shall go out *from Jerusalem*." But as in Rabbinic tradition (T. B. Sanhedrin 37 a, Ezekiel xxxviii. 8, Jubilees viii.) Jerusalem was situated in the *navel* of the earth, John may be using *belly* as a synonym for Jerusalem. Even more significant are the words that follow: "But this spake he of the Spirit." The Ceremony of the Water-drawing (already referred to above), which occurred on Tabernacles, was interpreted to mean the draught of the Holy Spirit (Genesis Rabba, ch. 70). Some far-reaching suggestions as to the nature of the teaching of Jesus, as found in the Fourth Gospel, in relation to the ideas of the *Doreshe Reshumoth* (on whom see a later Note), may be found in G. Klein's *Der älteste christliche Katechismus und die jüdische Propaganda-Literatur* (Berlin 1909). See especially the section (pp. 49—61) entitled "Jesu Predigt nach Johannes." My own general impression, without asserting an early date for the Fourth Gospel, is that that Gospel enshrines a genuine tradition of an aspect of Jesus' teaching which has not found a place in the Synoptics.

There is no reason to suppose that the freedom of teaching in the Galilean Synagogues was ever denied to Jesus. So important and dramatic an incident as such a denial must have found a mention in the Synoptists. Yet they are agreed in their silence as to an event of that nature; of course John (xviii. 20) represents Jesus as throughout, and to the last, teaching in synagogue. The cessation of references to such teaching in Mark after the sixth chapter may be best explained on the supposition that Jesus voluntarily changed his method when he found that he no longer carried the Synagogue audiences with him. The turning point is clearly given by Mark in his account of the experience of Jesus at Nazareth. The prophet found no honour in his own country, and this loss of sympathy appears to have induced Jesus to abandon the Synagogue discourses in favour of more informal teaching in the villages and in the open air, reverting indeed to the older practice. Prof. Burkitt (*The Gospel History and its Transmission*, p. 68) holds that the final rupture occurred with the religious authorities in Galilee in consequence of the healing of the man with a withered hand in the Synagogue on a Sabbath (Mark iii. 1). The Pharisees are said thereupon to have taken counsel with the Herodians to accuse and destroy Jesus. This was the definite breach (iii. 6). Prof. Burkitt with brilliant skill works out a scheme which accounts for Jesus spending the eight months in territory in which the jurisdiction of Herod Antipas did not run. During the greater part of the year before the last Passover Jesus "lives a wandering life in exile from Galilee or in concealment, and his chief work is no longer that of Revivalist but of the *Pastor pastorum*" (*op. cit.*, p. 89). This theory makes it necessary to explain as exceptional not only the later attempts to teach in the Nazareth Synagogue (where the failure is certainly not due to Pharisaic hostility), but also the subsequent teaching in the villages recorded in general terms (Mark vi. 6 "And he went round about the villages teaching"; cf. the parallels in Matthew and Luke) and the teaching of the crowd (Mark vi. 34). Moreover the language of Mark viii. 27 points to public teaching (outside Galilee), and (x. 1) where he enters the borders of Judæa "multitudes come together unto him again, and *as he was wont* he taught them again." That the death of John the Baptist greatly influenced Jesus in avoiding Galilee is highly probable; and there may have been some growing suspicion of him in the official circles of the Synagogues. But it cannot be said that there is any evidence at all that Jesus ever attempted to teach in any synagogue and was met with a refusal.

Still less is there any ground for holding that "the influence of the Sanhedrin everywhere haunted" Jesus and his disciples. Prof. G. A. Smith (*Jerusalem*, I. 416–7) strongly maintains that this was so, though Schweitzer, *Quest.* p. 362, is of another opinion. My own conviction is that most of the controversies between Jesus and the Pharisees occurred in Jerusalem and not in Galilee. If the tradition of the Galilean scene be authentic, the Pharisees were Priests who had been in Jerusalem and had returned to their Galilean homes after serving their regular course. The references to Pharisees or scribes who came from Jerusalem (Mark iii. 22, Matthew xv. 1) do not point to deputations from the capital. The language of Mark vii. 1 is the most explicit: "And there were gathered together unto him the Pharisees and certain of the scribes which had come from Jerusalem and had seen that some of his disciples ate their bread with defiled, that is unwashen hands." This looks very much as though the Pharisees were there in quite a normal manner; it is forcing the words, here and in the other passages cited, to represent them as "deputations" or as dogging the footsteps of Jesus. Herod Antipas may have had some such designs, but the Sanhedrin of Jerusalem had neither power nor motive to take action until the scene was transferred to the capital.

With regard to the *effect* of Jesus' discourses in the Synagogues, we are told that "he taught as one having authority" (Mk i. 22; Mt. vii. 29; Luke iv. 32). If the only version of this record were Luke's, the reference would obviously be to the authority with which the words of Jesus "came home to the consciences of his hearers" (Plummer). But the other two Synoptists agree in contrasting this "authority" with the manner of the Scribes. H. P. Chajes suggests that the real meaning is that Jesus taught in Parables (see Note on Parables below).

This would possibly have to be compared with Philo's remark that the teaching in the Alexandrian Synagogues was by way of allegory (διὰ συμβόλων II. 630). More acceptable is A. Wünsche's explanation of the claim that Jesus spoke ὡς ἐξουσίαν ἔχων (*Neue Beiträge zur Erlaüterung der Evangelien*, Göttingen, 1878, p. 110). The phrase recalls the Rabbinic idiom of speaking "from the mouth of power" (מפי הגבורה), connoting the possession of direct divine inspiration. The Pharisaic teachers certainly laid no general claim to the dignity. But the remark "he taught as one having authority" is usually explained by referring to the Rabbinical method as unfolded in the Talmud—with all its scholastic adhesion to precedents, and its technical and complicated casuistry. But this reference is not quite relevant.

For the Talmudical method was the result of long development after the age of Jesus, and the question is: to what extent can we reasonably assert that the method was already prevalent before the destruction of the Temple and the failure of the Bar Cochba War of Independence (135 A.D.) drove the Rabbis into their characteristic scholasticism? There was, moreover, all along a *popular* exegesis besides the *scholastic*, a form of homily specially intended for the edification and instruction of the simple and unlearned; and it would thus be improper to contrast the simplicity and directness of Jesus with the sophistication and precedent citations of the Rabbis even if the latter features were earlier than we have evidence of. Hillel, the greatest of the predecessors of Jesus, taught almost without reference to precedent; he only once cites an earlier authority. Hillel's most characteristic utterances are as free as are those of Jesus from the bonds of scholastic tradition. He, too, exemplifies the prophetic independence of conventions. Naturally, the appeal to and reliance on precedents presupposes an accumulation of precedents to appeal to and rely on. Such a mass of previous rule and doctrine would only be built up gradually. (See T. J. Pesaḥim 39 a, where Hillel cites his teachers. In the Babylonian Talmud Pesaḥ. 66 the citation, however, is omitted. Cf. Bacher *Tradition und Tradenten in den Schulen Palästinas und Babyloniens*, Leipzig, 1914, p. 55.) It was mainly the Amoraim of the third century onwards that made the appeal to precedent, and naturally as the precedents accumulated so appeal to them would increase, as in the modern English legal experience with regard to the citation of illustrative "cases." The earlier Jewish teaching certainly goes to the Scriptures, but so does Jesus; and this earlier teaching (like that of Jesus) uses the Scriptures as a general inspiration. It is only later (in the middle of the second century) that we find a strict technical reliance on chapter and verse, and in point of fact Jesus (in the Synoptists) appeals in this way to Scripture quite as much as does any of the earlier Rabbis. It was perhaps just his eclecticism, his independence of any particular school, that is implied by the contrast between Jesus' teaching and that of the Scribes.

The solution may be found in the supposition that Jesus taught at a transition period, when the formation of schools of exegesis was in process of development. Hillel's famous contemporary, Shammai, does seem to have been a stickler for precedent, and his school was certainly distinguished from that of Hillel by this very characteristic. If it be the truth, further, that Shammai (as Dr Büchler conjectures) was a Galilean, then it is possible that especially in Galilee there was growing up in the age of Jesus a school which taught with close reference to particular rules and views with which Jesus had little in common. The ordinary Galilean Jew would then feel that there was a difference between the conventional style of the local scribes and that of Jesus, who did not associate himself with any particular school. On some points, however, such as his view of divorce, Jesus (if the text of Matthew xix. 9 be authentic) appears to have been a Shammaite. It is by no means improbable (Bloch, *Memorial Volume*, ספר היובל Hebrew Section, pp. 21 seq.) that at the time of Jesus the views of Shammai were quite generally predominant, the school of Hillel only gaining supremacy in Jewish law and custom after the fall of the Temple. If that be so, Jesus, in departing from the Shammaite method, might well seem to be one who taught with authority and not as one of the Scribes. At a later period the question as to the school to which a scholar belonged would no doubt influence his admissibility as preacher in a particular place.

Jesus spoke without reference to any mediate authority. To the Scribes it became an ever more sacred duty to cite the original authority for any saying, if it were consciously derived from another teacher. Such reference was an obligation which attained even Messianic import. "He who says a word in the name of its author brings Redemption to the world" (Aboth—Chapter of R. Meir—VI., *Megilla* 15 a). Verify your quotations, is C. Taylor's comment (*Sayings of the Jewish Fathers*, 1897, Additional Note 54). The saving-power of literary and legal frankness goes deeper than that. Such punctiliousness assuredly cannot be attributed to the Scribes as aught but a virtue, which if it encouraged scholasticism, also encouraged honesty. It did more. It promoted the conception of a continuous tradition, which conception while it obscured the facts of history, and required constant criticism by those facts and also by appeal to ultimate principles as distinct from derived rules, nevertheless gave harmony to the scheme of doctrine.

The view that Jesus was an original eclectic, that like Horace—though in a far from Horatian sense—he was "nullius addictus jurare in verba magistri," is confirmed by the difficulty of "placing" Jesus with regard to the schools of his age. The fact is not to be minimised that we are imperfectly acquainted with those schools; we have only the sure knowledge (which is derivable from Philo and Josephus) that an amazing variety of religious grouping was in progress in the first century. But even as far as we know these schools Jesus seems to belong to none of them. It is undeniable that certain features of his teaching are Essenic. But he did not share the Essenic devotion to ceremonial ablutions. Further, he was an Apocalyptic, but he was also a powerful advocate of the Prophetic Judaism. Then, again, it is plausible to explain much of the gospel attack on the Scribes as due to contempt of the Sadducean priesthood. But R. Leszynsky (*Die Sadducäer*, Berlin 1912, ch. III.) finds it possible to claim Jesus as a Sadducee!

It is sometimes thought that the teaching with authority is shown by Jesus' frequent phrase "but I say unto you" (J. Weiss on Mk i. 21). But this use of the phrase needs interpretation. The most interesting passage in which it occurs is Mt. v. 43—4: "Ye have heard that it was said, Thou shalt love thy neighbour and hate thine enemy, but I say unto you, Love your enemies." Now it is obvious that nowhere in the O.T. are men told to hate their enemies. But in the exegetical terminology of R. Ishmael (end of first century) there is a constantly recurring phrase which runs thus: "The text reads so and so. I *hear* from it so and so: *but* other texts prove that this is not its true meaning" (שומע אני...תלמוד לומר). If this as Schechter (*Studies in Judaism*) suggests (though Bacher *Die älteste Terminologie der jüdischen Schriftauslegung*, I. 190 dissents on inadequate grounds), underlies the passage just cited from Matthew, then Jesus' phrase: "Ye have *heard*... but I say unto you" would be parallel to the Rabbinic idiom. It removes the main difficulty in regard to the hating of one's enemy, for Jesus would not be referring to any text enjoining hatred, but to a possible narrowing of the meaning of the text enjoining love. In that case, Jesus' "but I say unto you" differs from the usual Rabbinical formula in that it introduces a personal element, but as with them,

Jesus' exegesis really leads up to the citation and interpretation of another text (in this case: '"Ye shall be perfect as your heavenly father is perfect"') which takes a wider sweep and illumines the particular matter under discussion. This is in full conformity with the Rabbinic method. They, too, derived the ideal of man's character from the character of God. "Be ye holy for I the Lord am holy" (Leviticus xix. 2, of which the turn in Matthew is a reminiscence) was with the Rabbis the ground text of the idea of the *Imitation of God*. It was with them the highest motive for lovingkindness and charity. (Sifrâ on Levit. xix. 2).

## II. THE GREATEST COMMANDMENT.

The combination of the commandments to love God and to love one's neighbour is "highly striking and suggestive." Commentators rightly see that the Scribe's question as to the Greatest Commandment was not captious, but (as Gould puts it) the Pharisee thought: "Here is possibly an opportunity to get an answer to our standing question, about the first commandment." For practical purposes of ethical monition, the enunciation both of Love God and Love thy fellow man is necessary. But on a profounder analysis the second is included in the first, as is shown in the Midrash. Man being made in the image of God, any misprision of man by man implies disregard of Him in whose image man is made (*Genesis Rabbah* xxiv. last words). It therefore is not at all unlikely that such combinations as we find in the Synoptics were a common-place of Pharisaic teaching. It is true that Wellhausen—oblivious of the occurrence of the combination in the Testament of the Twelve Patriarchs (Isaachar v. 2, vii. 5, Dan v. 3)—holds that "the combination of commandments was first effected in this way by Jesus." That excellent student of Rabbinics, Dr C. Taylor, was not so certain on this point. It will perhaps be interesting to cite what he says on the subject in one of his earlier works (*The Gospel in the Law*, 1869, p. 276):—

It might seem that our Lord's teaching was novel in respect of its exhibiting the twofold Law of Love as the sum of Old Testament morality. Thus, in Matt. xxii. 40, Christ is represented as answering to the lawyer's question: 'Thou shalt love the Lord thy God with all thy heart, and with all thy soul, and with all thy mind. This is the first and great commandment. And the second is like unto it, Thou shalt love thy neighbour as thyself. *On these two commandments hang all the law and the prophets.*' But the addition in St Mark's account (xii. 32): 'Master, Thou hast said the truth,' might imply that the answer to that oft-mooted question was no new one, but rather that which was *recognised* as true. In another passage—introductory to the Parable of the Good Samaritan—'a certain Lawyer' gives the two commandments, *To love God*, and, *To love one's neighbour*, as a summary of the law. He is asked: 'What is written in the law? how readest thou?' And he answers: 'Thou shalt love the Lord thy God with all thy heart, and with all thy soul, and with all thy strength, and with all thy mind; and thy neighbour as thyself' (Luke x. 26, 27). But the fact that St Paul grounds this equivalence on reason solely, goes far to prove that he did not regard the mere statement of it as a characteristic novelty in the Christian scheme. 'Love,' writes the Apostle, 'worketh no ill to his neighbour: *therefore* love is the fulfilling of the law' (Rom. xiii. 10). In John xiii. 34 the words, 'A *new* commandment I give unto you, That ye love one another,' might seem to imply that the law of mutual love was put forward as new. But the words following explain wherein lay the novelty: '*As I have loved you*, etc.'

It is not clear why a "lawyer" (νομικός) is introduced in Matthew; Luke's frequent use of the word is more intelligible. But it seems probable that the word had become acclimatised in Hebrew—though there is only one instance recorded of it. Jose b. Ḥalafta (second century) was so famed as a profound and ready exponent of the Law that it was said of him "his information as to the Law is ever with him" (נמוקו עמו), where several authorities see the Greek νομική (sc. ἐπιστήμη). Cf. Levy and Krauss s.v.; Bacher *Agada der Tannaiten* ii. 155. Jastrow s.v. takes another view. In support of the identification, it may be pointed out that Νομικός had become a proper name in the first century. Joesdros, son of Nomikos, was one of the four orators who were sent to attack Josephus (2 *War*, xxi. 7). For the suggestion that the νομικός of the Synoptics was a Sadducean lawyer, see J. Mann in *J.Q.R.* Jan. 1916, p. 419. Possibly the use of the term should be sought in another direction. In the primitive account of the incident, the questioner may have been, not a born Jew, but a Gentile νομικός inclined to become, or who had recently become, a proselyte to Judaism. As will be shown, at the end of this note, such summaries of the Law were naturally made in the literature of propaganda or catechism.

Aqiba attached, as every Jew did, the highest importance to the text in Deut. vi. 4, and he died with it on his lips (T.B. *Berachoth* 61 b). He further saw in martyrdom the fulfilment of the law bidding Israel love God with all his soul or life. The various terms of this law are differently rendered in the LXX, Deut. vi. 5 and 2 Kings xxiii. 25, and this fact goes far to explain the dissimilar versions of the Deuteronomic text in the three Synoptics. Chajes aptly suggests (*Markus-Studien* p. 67) that the LXX in Deut. was influenced by Rabbinic exegesis. It there uses διανοίας for καρδίας, and it elsewhere employs the former word in rendering yeṣer (Gen. viii. 21 כי יצר לב האדם רע, ὅτι ἔγκειται ἡ διάνοια τοῦ, 1 Chr. xxix. 18 ליצר מחשבות לבב, ἐν διανοίᾳ καρδίας, Gen. vi. 5 וכל יצר מחשבות לבו, καὶ πᾶς τις διανοεῖται ἐν τῇ *καρδίᾳ αὐτοῦ*). Now the Rabbinic interpretation of Deut. vi. 5 also introduced the yeṣer (בכל לבבך: "With all thy heart," i.e. with thy two yeṣers, בשני יצריך, Sifre on Deut. vi. 5, ed. Friedmann 73 a). Similarly though in 2 Kings xxiii. 25 the LXX renders מאדו by *ἰσχύς* in Deut. vi. 5 it uses the term *δύναμις*, a word which, as the LXX of Ezek. xvii. 18, 27 shows, may correspond to the sense *substance* (הון), which was precisely the Rabbinic interpretation of מאדך in Deut. vi. 5 (Sifre, *loc. cit.*; *Ber.* 61 b).

A well-known passage of the Sifra (on Leviticus xix. 18, ed. Weiss, p. 89 a) runs thus: "*Thou shalt love thy neighbour as thyself*: R. Aqiba said, This is the greatest general principle in the Law (זה כלל גדול בתורה). Ben Azzai said: *This is the book of the generations of man* (Genesis v. 1) is a greater principle than that (כלל גדול מזה)." There is no difference between these Tannaim on the question itself: love of one's fellow-man is fundamental, but while Aqiba derives the conclusion from Leviticus xix. 18, Ben Azzai points back to the story of the creation, to *the book of the generations of man*, as the basis of the solidarity of the human race, and the obligation that accrues to every man to love his fellow. Aqiba himself elsewhere traces the same duty to another phrase in the Genesis story (Mishnah, *Aboth* iii. 14, in Taylor iii. 21): "Beloved is man in that he was created in the image of God" (Genesis ix. 6, cf. the quotation from *Genesis Rabbah* above). As Taylor remarks on this last passage in the Mishnah (*Sayings of the Jewish Fathers*, ed. 2, p. 56): "Man is beloved by God in whose image or likeness he was created; and he should be beloved by his fellow-men as a consequence of this love towards God himself." The text cited (Genesis ix. 6) runs in full: "Whoso sheddeth man's blood, by man shall his blood be shed: for in the image of God made he man." As R. Aqiba comments (*Genesis Rabba* xxxiv.): "If one sheds blood it is accounted to him as though he diminished the likeness." The same idea is also attributed (*Aboth d. R. Nathan*, xxxix. ed. Schechter, p. 118) to one of Aqiba's most noted disciples—Meir—while another of his disciples—Nehemiah—(*op. cit.* xxxi. p. מו), on the basis of Genesis v. 1, declares "A single human life is equal to the whole work of creation," אדם אחד שקול כנגד כל מעשה בראשית (with Aqiba's saying in *Aboth* iii. 14, especially the latter part of the Mishnah, cf. 1 Ep. John iii. 1).

These citations, it will be observed, are from Jewish authorities of the end of the first or the beginning of the second century. But, as is well known, the idea that forbearance to one's fellow-man is the basis of the Mosaic law goes back to Hillel (T.B. *Sabbath* 31 a; *Aboth de R. Nathan* ii. 26). The mere formulation of the "Golden Rule" in the negative version is far older than Hillel. So far as Jewish sages are concerned it may ultimately rest on such phrases as Psalm xv. 3, where the man who sojourns in the Lord's tent is he that doeth no evil to his neighbour (לא עשה לרעהו רעה). The actual maxim of Hillel is found in Tobit iv. 15 (*ὃ μισεῖς μηδενὶ ποιήσῃς*). This version points to the conclusion that when Hillel used the word לחברך (דעלך סני לחברך לא תעבד, "What-to-thyself is-hateful to-thy-fellow thou shalt not do"), he meant by it *fellow man*. In the Aramaic text of Tobit (Neubauer, Oxford, 1878, p. 8) the reading is ודסאני לך לחורני לא תעביד (the Hebrew text, *ibid.* p. 24, runs ואשר תשנא לנפשך לא תעשה לאחרים). Hillel elsewhere (*Aboth* i. 12) uses the widest possible term: he speaks of love for one's fellow-creatures (אוהב את הבריות). As is well known, the negative form of the Golden Rule not only preceded Jesus it survived him. It underlies Romans xiii. 10. St Paul's remark runs: *ἀγαπήσεις τὸν πλησίον σου ὡς σεαυτόν. ἡ ἀγάπη τῷ πλησίον κακὸν οὐκ ἐργάζεται*—thus the Apostle explains or rather justifies Leviticus xix. 18 by the negative form of the Golden Rule (practically as in Ps. xv. 3). Curiously enough this is paralleled by the Targum Jer. on Leviticus xix. 18 (ed. Ginsburger, p. 206), for the Targum actually inserts the negative Rule as an explanation of "thou shalt love thy neighbour as thyself" (לא תהוון נקמין ולא נטרין דבבו לבני עמך ותרחמיה לחברך דמן אנת סני לך לא תעביד ליה אנא יי) Philo (ap. Eusebius, P. viii. 7), too, has the negative Rule, though his phraseology (*ἅ τις παθεῖν ἐχθαίρει, μὴ ποιεῖν αὐτόν*) is not verbally derived either from Tobit or from the source employed in the Didache (*πάντα δὲ ὅσα ἐὰν θελήσῃς μὴ γίνεσθαί σοι, καὶ σὺ ἄλλῳ μὴ ποίει*). But Philo's source can easily be suggested. It is not Jewish at all. Isocrates (*Nicocles* 39 c) has the maxim: *ἃ πάσχοντες ὑφ' ἑτέρων ὀργίζεσθε, ταῦτα τοῖς ἄλλοις μὴ ποιεῖτε.* Moreover, a similar saying is quoted from the Confucian Analects (Legge, *Chinese Classics* I. Bk. xv. 23). Jacob Bernays, on the other hand, holds that Isocrates had no thought of a general moral application of the principle, and believes that Philo was drawing on a Jewish source (*Gesammelte Abhandlungen*, Berlin, 1885, Vol. I. ch. xx.). Bernays cites Gibbon's quotation of Isocrates in his account of the Calvin-Servetus episode (*Decline and Fall*, ch. liv. n. 36).

Here it may be pointed out that the contrasts drawn between the negative and positive forms of the Golden Rule are not well founded. One cannot share the opinion of some Jewish scholars (such as

Hamburger) that there is *no* difference between the negative and positive formulations. But Bischoff (*Jesus und die Rabbinen*, p. 93) is equally wrong in asserting that Hillel's maxim differs from that of Jesus just as "Neminem laede" differs from "Omnes juva," or as Clough puts it in his fine satirical version of the Decalogue: "Thou shalt not kill, but needst not strive officiously to keep alive." Augustine (*Confessions* I. xviii.) saw no objection to paraphrase the positive of Matthew vii. 11 into the negative *id se alteri facere quod nolit pati*. For the Old Testament commands in "thou shalt love thy neighbour as thyself" (Leviticus xix. 18) and "ye shall love the stranger" (Deut. x. 19) are positive enough, and Hillel himself elsewhere (*Aboth* i. 12), as already cited, uses a quite positive (and general) phrase when he accounts as one of the marks of the peace-loving disciples of Aaron "love for fellow creatures." It would be absurd to maintain that Philo, who also, as has been seen uses the negative form, teaches a negative morality. Similarly with Tobit. The negative rule occurs in a chapter full of positive rules of benevolence: Give alms of thy substance; Love thy brethren; Give of thy bread to the hungry, and of thy garments to them that are naked; bless the Lord thy God always—and so forth. Why should Hillel not have satisfied himself with citing the text of Leviticus xix. 18? One suggestion is given below. But a profounder answer may lie in the thought that the negative form is the more fundamental of the two, though the positive form is the fuller expression of practical morality. Hillel was asked to summarise the Torah, and he used that form of the Golden Rule from which the Golden Rule itself is a deduction. The axiomatic truth on which the moral life of *society* is based is the right of the unimpeded use of the individual's powers, the peaceful enjoyment of the fruit of his labours, in short, the claim of each to be free from his fellow-man's injury. When we remember how great is our power of evil, how relatively small our power for good, how in Sir Thomas Browne's words, "we are beholden to every man we meet that he doth not kill us," how "the evil that men do lives after them, the good is oft interred with their bones," it is at least a tenable theory that the negative Rule goes deeper into the heart of the problem. "Do as you would be done by" is less fundamental than Hillel's maxim, just as it is less full than the Levitical law of neighbourly love, for love is greater than doing (cf. the writer's remarks in *Aspects of Judaism*, ch. VI). This criticism does not dispute, however, that the Gospel form is a splendid working principle which has wrought incalculable good to humanity. The persistence, however, of the negative after the pronouncement of the positive form, itself argues that the former is more basic.

But neither Tobit nor Philo, nor any other sources cited, do more than formulate the Golden Rule. Hillel not only formulates it, he describes it as the essence of the Torah, *Sabb.* 31 a: זו היא כל התורה כולה ("this is the whole law") and in the *Aboth d. R. Nathan, loc. cit.*: הוא כללה של תורה מה דאת סני לגרמך לחברך לא תעבד ("This is the principle, substance, of the law: what thou hatest for thyself do not to thy fellow"). This is on the same line with the famous saying of R. Simlai (third century), but it goes beyond it. Simlai said (T.B. *Makkoth* 23 b—24 a): "Six hundred and thirteen precepts were imparted to Moses, three hundred and sixty-five negative (in correspondence with the days of the solar year) and two hundred and forty-eight positive (in correspondence with the number of a man's limbs). David came and established them (lit. *made them stand, based them,* העמידן) as eleven, as it is written (Ps. xv.): Lord, who shall sojourn in thy tent, who shall dwell in thy holy mountain? (i) He that walketh uprightly and (ii) worketh righteousness and (iii) speaketh the truth in his heart. (iv) He that backbiteth not with his tongue, (v) nor doeth evil to his neighbour, (vi) nor taketh up a reproach against another; (vii) in whose eyes a reprobate is despised, (viii) but who honoureth them that fear the Lord. (ix) He that sweareth to his own hurt, and changeth not; (x) he that putteth not out his money to usury, (xi) nor taketh a bribe against the innocent. He that doeth these things shall never be moved. Thus David reduced the Law to *eleven* principles. Then Isaiah came and established them as *six* (xxxiii. 15): (i) He that walketh in righteousness and (ii) speaketh uprightly; (iii) he that despiseth the gain of deceits, (iv) that shaketh his hands from holding of bribes, (v) that stoppeth his ears from hearing of blood, and (vi) shutteth his eyes from looking upon evil. Then came Micah and established them as *three* (Micah vi. 8): What doth the Lord require of thee but (i) to do justice, (ii) to love mercy, and (iii) to walk humbly with thy God? Once more Isaiah established them as *two* (Is. lvi. 1): Thus saith the Lord: (i) Keep ye judgement, and (ii) do righteousness. Then came Amos and established them as *one* (Amos v. 4): Thus saith the Lord, Seek ye me and ye shall live, or (as R. Naḥman b. Isaac preferred): Habakkuk came and made the whole Law stand on one fundamental idea (Habakkuk ii. 4): The righteous man liveth by his faith."

Such attempts to find a basic principle for the whole of the Law can thus be traced clearly from Hillel through Aqiba to the days of Simlai. Simlai, it will be observed, quotes the prophets as the authors of attempts in this direction, and it is interesting to note (cf. Güdemann, *Nächstenliebe*, Vienna, 1890, p. 23) that while Hillel contents himself with concluding "this is the whole Law," Jesus (Matthew xxii. 40) adds the words "and the prophets." Naturally there was no intention in the Pharisaic authorities who thus reduced the Law to a few general rules, to deny the obligation to fulfil the rest of the law. Hillel's reply to the would-be proselyte, who asked to be taught the Law while he stood on one foot, runs: "That which thou hatest (to be done to thyself) do not to thy fellow; this is the whole law; the rest is commentary; go and learn it." Yet, the person so addressed might omit to go and learn it. Hence in Jewish theology an objection was raised to such summaries just because they would tend to throw stress on part of the Torah to the relative detriment of the rest. This feeling has always lain at the back of the reluctance to formulate a Jewish creed; even the famous attempt of Maimonides failed to effect that end. Could the legalistic spirit of an earlier period permit a thoroughgoing distinction between important and unimportant laws? When Aqiba and Ben Azzai spoke of neighbourly love as the greatest fundamental law (כלל גדול) they meant such a general or basic command from which all the other commands could be deduced. Thus (as Güdemann rightly argues, *op. cit.* p. 21), the Tannaitic Hebrew (כלל גדול) does not correspond to the Synoptic Greek (μεγάλη ἐντολή). The Rabbi was not discriminating between the importance or unimportance of laws so much as between their fundamental or derivative character. This is probably what Jesus was asked to do or what he did; the Greek obscures the exact sense both of question and answer. That a Hebrew original underlies the Greek is probable from the use of the positive: ποία ἐντολὴ μεγάλη ἐν τῷ νόμῳ? It is more natural in Hebrew (cf. Güdemann, *op. cit.* p. 23) to find the positive thus used as superlative (Aqiba's כלל גדול בתורה = the greatest fundamental law in the Torah). But the passage from the one idea to the other is easy. Easy, but not inevitable, whether by the logic of thought or the ethics of conduct. For Pharisaism created just that type of character to which *do these and leave not the others undone* (Matthew xxiii. 23) admirably applies—a type which against all logic effected a harmony between legislative punctiliousness as to detailed rules and the prophetic appeal to great principles. The same second century Rabbi (Ben Azzai) who said (*Aboth*, iv. 5) "Hasten to a light precept" also maintained that the text relating the common origin of all the human kind was the fundamental text of the Torah (*Sifra* ed. Weiss, p. 89 a) and that the love of God was to be shown even unto death (*Sifre*, Deut. § 32). The Hebrew prophets, however, did discriminate between the moral importance of various sides of the religious and social life, and there may have been those who in Jesus' day desired such a discrimination, and welcomed its reiteration by Jesus.

In a sense, estimations of the varying importance attaching to precepts must have been in vogue at the beginning of the Christian era. If Matthew v. 19—20 be admitted as genuine, Jesus differentiated the precepts in this way ("one of the least of these commandments"), while exhorting obedience to all precepts alike. Philo in the context already quoted (Eusebius *P. E.* viii. 7) very distinctly occupies the same position (Gifford's translation, p. 389).

But look at other precepts besides these. Separate not parents from children, not even if they are captives; nor wife from husband, even if thou art their master by lawful purchase. These, doubtless, are very grave and important commandments; but there are others of a trifling and ordinary character. Rifle not the bird's nest under thy roof: reject not the supplication of animals which flee as it were sometimes for protection: abstain from any harm that may be even less than these. You may say that these are matters of no importance; but at all events the law which governs them is important, and is the cause of very careful observance; the warnings also are important, and the imprecations of utter destruction, and God's oversight of such matters, and his presence as an avenger in every place.

Some aspects of this problem—especially with regard to the lawfulness and even obligation to sacrifice some precept in the interests of fulfilling others—will be discussed later in the Note on the Sabbath. Here it must be enough to point out the continuity of the theory, that while the precepts could be divided between 'light' and 'heavy,' obedience to all was equally binding. While, however, Philo bases this general obligation on the punishment for disobedience, the Pharisaic tradition rested on the reward for obedience, and placed that reward in the life after this (much as in Matthew v. 19). When we reach the latter part of the second century, we find R. Jehuda Ha-nasi definitely teaching: "Be heedful of a light precept as of a grave one, for thou knowest not the grant of reward for each precept" (Aboth, ii. 1). But the very terms of the caution that one commandment is light (קלה) while another is heavy (חמורה), admit the differentiation. Rabbi Jehuda, it will be noted, asserts that *all* the commandments must be equally observed, because the reward for each is unknown.

This last clause is to be explained by the parable which is to be found in Debarim Rabba, ch. vi. and in parallel Midrashim (on the text, Deut. xxii. 7).

A King hired some labourers and sent them into his Pardes (garden, estate). At eve, he inquired as to the work of each. He summoned one. "Under which tree didst thou labour?"—"Under this."—"It is a pepper plant, the wage is a gold piece." He summoned another. "Under which tree didst thou labour?"—"Under this."—"It is a white-flowered tree (almond), the wage is half a gold piece." He summoned a third. "Under which tree didst thou labour?"—"Under this."—"It is an olive tree, the wage is two hundred zuzim." They said: "Shouldst thou not have informed us which tree would earn the greatest reward, that we might work under it?" The King answered: "Had I so informed you, how would my whole Pardes have been worked?" Thus the Holy One did not reveal the reward except of two commandments, one the weightiest of the weighty—honour of parents (Exod. xx. 12), the other the lightest of the light—letting the mother-bird go (Deut. xxii. 7) [note the parallel here with Philo], in both of which is assigned the reward, length of days.

Underlying the parable (as indeed is to some extent implied by the form of the Parable in the Tanḥuma) must have been a more primitive one in which all the labourers receive the same reward (cf. Matt. xx. 10), in accordance with the famous saying (end of T.B. Menaḥoth), that not the amount of service but its motive is the decisive quality. So, too, with regard to the very two precepts alluded to in the Parable, we have the view of R. Jacob (middle of the second century) as given in the Talmud (Qiddushin, 39 b).

R. Jacob held that the reward for the performance of the precepts is not in this world. For he taught: Whenever, side by side with a Precept written in the Torah, the reward is stated, the future life (resurrection) is concerned. Of the honour to father and mother it is written (Deut. v. 16) "that thy days may be prolonged and that it may be well with thee." Of the letting go of the mother-bird it is written "that it may be well with thee, and that thou mayest prolong thy days" (Deut. xxii. 7). Behold, a father bade his son, Ascend the tower (*birah*) and bring me some young birds. The son ascended, let the mother go, and took the young. In the act of descending, he fell and died. How was it well with him, and where his length of days? But the meaning is, that it may be well with thee in the world which is all good, and that thy days may be prolonged in a world whose duration is eternal.

Gradation of precepts was, nevertheless, admitted. Certain of them were described as *essential*, *corpora legis* (גופי תורה, Aboth end of ch. iii., Ḥagigah i. 8, see Dictionaries, s.v. גוף), others as less essential. This difference perhaps concerned rather the question as to the ease or difficulty of arriving at the Scriptural basis. Certain of these essentials related to the ritual laws committed to the (Aaronite?) Am-haareṣ (T.B. Sabbath, 32). Other views of gradation concerned the moral laws: thus in one famous enumeration (1) the most important rewardable performances were honouring parents, the exercise of loving-kindness, effecting reconciliation between man and his fellow, and the study of the Torah; and (2) the most serious punishable offences were idolatry, incest, bloodshedding, and slander; for the former there was reward, for the latter punishment, in this world and in the next (*Aboth de R. Nathan*, I. ch. xl., ed. Schechter, p. 120). Again, the seven "Noachide" precepts were regarded as the fundamental demands of ethics (on these see *Jewish Encyclopedia*, vol. vii. p. 648). Further, the obligation of the priest to disregard the laws of ritual purity when engaging in the burial of the dead for whose obsequies no one else was available (מת מצוה, on which see J. Mann, *loc. cit.*); the discussions as to the relative worth of studying the Torah and of performing the commandments; the evaluation of the import of *fear of sin* and *wisdom*; the supersession of the honour of parents by the higher law of reverencing God when the parents urged actions opposed to that reverence; the metaphorical contrast of *root* and *branch*, meet us throughout the first and second centuries (cf. several citations in Mishnah Aboth, and Sifra on Leviticus xix.). This range of ideas reaches its culmination in the decision made by the famous assembly at Lydda after the Hadrianic persecutions of 135. What were the limits of conformity to the Roman demands? Rather than commit idolatry, murder, or incest a Jew must die! (T.B. Sanhedrin, 74 a).

We may suppose, however, that just as there were scruples in later ages (Ḥagigah 11 b), so not everyone in the age of Jesus was willing to admit these gradations. As Güdemann writes: "If it be asked how it came about that a Scribe should need to ask the question of Jesus, it may be rejoined that the endeavour to bring Judaism within one or a few formulas would certainly not have been agreeable to the supporters of the Zealot party. They might perceive in such an endeavour a connivance towards what we should nowadays term the liberal position, and it is undeniable that every generalisation easily renders the particulars volatile. The ignorant, the Am-haareṣ, might, if he heard speak of a few fundamental rules, readily persuade himself that these alone—as Hillel and similarly after him Jesus expressed themselves—comprised the 'whole Law'; while the demand of Hillel to regard 'the rest' as 'commentary' and to 'learn it' would be altogether ignored." The questioner of Jesus desired an opinion as to whether Jesus did or did not share this fear of reducing the Law to fundamental rules. At the same time, Jesus may well have been attaching himself to Hillel's example, while at the same time implying a moral discrimination between law and law. Yet this last point is not certain. In the Palestinian Talmud (*Berachoth* i. 8 [5]), R. Levi, a pupil of Aqiba, cites the Shema (Deut. vi. 4 *seq.*) as fundamental because the Decalogue is included within it (מפני שעשרת הדברות כלולות בהם; on the connection between the Shema and the Decalogue see Taylor, *Sayings of the Jewish Fathers*, Excursus IV.). It is noticeable (cf. Güdemann, *op. cit.* p. 22) that in Mark (xii. 29) the answer of Jesus begins with the Shema, Deut. vi. 4 (שמע ישראל), though in Matthew the verse is wrongly omitted. It does not seem that in any extant Rabbinic text, outside the *Testaments of the Twelve Patriarchs*, the Shema and the love of one's neighbour are associated, though there is mention of a passage in which this combination was effected by Ben Zoma and Ben Nanas with the strange addition that greater than any of these texts was Numb. xxviii. 4, possibly because of the atoning function of the daily sacrifices, or because of the association of God, Exod. xxv. 9 etc., with the Sanctuary, the divine dwelling place on earth (Introd. to the *En Jacob*; see Güdemann, *loc. cit.*, Theodor, *Genesis Rabba*, p. 237). In the Nash Papyrus the Decalogue is followed by the Shema; the two passages indeed stand close together (the Decalogue in Deut. v. 6—18, the Shema in vi. 4—9). The Didache (ch. i.) associates the combination as found in the Synoptics also with the negative form of the Golden Rule: "There are two ways, one of life and one of death, and there is much difference between the two ways. Now the way of life is this: First, thou shalt love God that made thee; secondly thy neighbour as thyself; and all things whatsoever thou wouldest should not happen to thee, neither do thou to another." The Decalogue follows. The Jewish provenance of this passage is indisputable. Taylor (*Teaching of the Twelve Apostles*) suggests that the negative rule grew out of the Decalogue, with its many *do nots.* What is the general principle of the things not to do to one's neighbour? Answer: "What-to-thyself is-hateful" (the דעלך סני of Hillel). Hence its description by Hillel as the sum total of the Law. One further point only calls for remark here. It is quite natural that simplifications or systematisations of the Law would be most required for proselytising propaganda. It would be necessary to present Judaism in as concise a form as possible for such purposes. Hence it is not surprising on the one hand that it is to a would-be proselyte that Hillel's summary as well as a similar citation of the principle by Aqiba

(*Aboth de R. Nathan*, ed. Schechter, p. 53) is addressed and on the other that we find it in the *Didache* and in connection with the doctrine of the two ways. Nor is it without significance that Philo's citation of the negative rule occurs in a passage in which he is selecting just those elements of the Jewish Law which were worthy of commendation and acceptance by the Greek world. (Cf. on these and several other matters the interesting work of G. Klein, *Der Aelteste Christliche Katechismus und die Jüdische Propaganda-Literatur*, Berlin, 1909, p. 85, and K. Kohler in *Judaica*, Berlin, 1912, pp. 469 seq. The latter points to the old Jewish Didaskalia, in his view enshrining the ethics of the Essenes.)

## III. JOHN THE BAPTIST.

The Rabbinic literature contains no reference to John the Baptist. There is, however, an interesting passage on the subject in Josephus (*Antiquities*, XVIII., v. § 2). Some doubt has been thrown on the authenticity of this passage, but the suspicion has no firm basis.

Josephus gives a favourable account of John and his work. This is *à priori* what we should expect, for John has decidedly Essenic leanings and the Essenes were favourites with the Jewish historian. John, says Josephus, was "a good man who exhorted the Jews to exercise virtue (ἀρετή), both as to justice (δικαιοσύνη) towards one another and piety (εὐσέβεια) towards God, and to come to baptism (βαπτισμῷ συνιέναι). For baptism (τὴν βάπτισιν) would be acceptable to God thus (οὕτω), if they used it, not for the pardon of certain sins, but for the purification of the body, provided that the soul had been thoroughly purified beforehand by righteousness" (μὴ ἐπὶ τινῶν ἁμαρτάδων παραιτήσει χρωμένων, ἀλλ' ἐφ' ἁγνείᾳ τοῦ σώματος, ἅτε δὴ καὶ τῆς ψυχῆς δικαιοσύνῃ προεκκεκαθαρμένης). People, continues Josephus, flocked to him in crowds, were stirred by his addresses, and seemed willing to follow him in all things. Herod Antipas, fearing a popular rising, seized John, sent him in chains to Machaerus, and had him put to death there. When Herod's army suffered a reverse, the people attributed the king's misfortune to God's displeasure at the ill-treatment of John.

Both the recent editors of Josephus (Niese and Naber) admit this passage without question. There is a natural reluctance on the part of cautious scholars to pronounce unreservedly in its favour, mainly because of the fact that elsewhere the text of Josephus has been tampered with in a similar context. Thus Schürer (I[3]. 438), after presenting a forcible though incomplete argument in favour of the passage, adds: "Since, however, Josephus in other places was certainly subjected to interpolation by a Christian hand, one must not here place too absolute a reliance on the authenticity of the text." On the Jewish side, though his leanings are in favour of the authenticity, S. Krauss (*Das Leben Jesu nach jüdischen Quellen*, Berlin, 1902, p. 257) remarks: "The question as to the genuineness of the John-passage has not yet been decisively settled; the passage is anyhow open to suspicion." But, on the whole, the authenticity of the reference is accepted by scholars, Jewish and Christian. Thus to cite only two instances, H. St J. Thackeray (*Dictionary of the Bible*, Extra Volume, p. 471) passes judgment in these words: "There is no reason why it should not be accepted as genuine"; and K. Kohler (*Jewish Encyclopedia* VII. p. 218) does not even mention the controversy, but uses the passage without any question. The passage in Josephus referring to John the Baptist rests, of course, on a different footing to the "testimony to Christ" (Josephus, *Antiq.* XVIII. iii. § 3). The authenticity of the latter has been recently maintained with much plausibility by Profs. F. C. Burkitt (*Theologisch Tijdschrift*, 1913, xlvii. pp. 135–144), A. Harnack (*Internationale Monatsschrift*, June, 1913, pp. 1038–1067), and W. E. Barnes (*Companion to Biblical Studies*, 1916, p. 34). But it remains very difficult to accept Josephus' "testimony to Christ" as genuine, at all events as it stands; the reference to John the Baptist may well be so.

It seems to me that a Christian interpolator must have brought that passage into closer accord with the Gospels. I do not refer merely to such differences as the motive assigned for putting John to death. Josephus assigns fear of political unrest; the Gospels, the personal animosity of Herodias. But, as Schürer is careful to point out, these motives are not absolutely incompatible. Much more significant is the silence of Josephus as to any connection between John and Jesus. This, of itself, is almost enough to authenticate the passage. Gerlach has called attention to this fact in his book *Die Weissagungen des Alten Testaments in den Schriften des Flavius Josephus* (Berlin, 1863, p. 113) and Origen had long ago done the same thing. Origen (*c. Celsum* I. xlviii.) says: "The Jews do not associate John with Jesus." Gerlach misuses this statement, for Origen is not making an independent assertion, but (as the context shows, cf. *op. cit.* xlvii.) is basing his generalisation on the passage in Josephus. Origen, by the way, who cites this passage, has no knowledge of the supposed "testimony to Christ" (see, however, Burkitt, as already cited); the two passages stand, as said above, on quite different footings. That Jews other than Josephus may have taken a favourable view of John's work is indicated also by several passages in the Gospels. Luke, it is true, asserts (vii. 30) that the Pharisees and the lawyers (scribes) rejected John, and refused to accept his baptism. But this is in opposition to the statement of Matthew (iii. 7): "[John] saw many of the Pharisees and Sadducees coming to his baptism," and Mark (i. 5) implies no Jewish opposition to his call to baptism. Moreover, all three Synoptics (Mark ii. 18; Matthew ix. 14; Luke v. 33) represent the disciples of John as associated with the Pharisees in fasting. Thus just as Josephus assures us that the Pharisees were not opponents of the Essenes (as they were of the Sadducees) so there was no violent division between John and the Pharisees; the assumption that the Jews rejected John belongs to the later conception (whether originating with John himself or not) that John was the forerunner of Jesus. That John's own disciples did not accept this conception is thus asserted by Prof. Adeney (*The Century Bible*, St Luke, p. 185): "These [the disciples of John] then hold together and keep up their customs after their master has been removed from them, and in spite of the appearance of the new Prophet, thus declining to follow John's own teaching in pointing on to Christ. We meet such later at Ephesus (see Acts xviii. 25, xix. 3)." Cf. also the remarks of Prof. Lake, *The Earliest Epistles of St Paul*, 1911, pp. 108, etc.

Still more important is another point to which Gerlach called attention, and to which Naber has more recently again referred. There is a real difference between the nature of John's baptism as described by Josephus and the Gospels. Mark (i. 4) introduces John as proclaiming a "baptism of repentance for remission of sins" (*βάπτισμα μετανοίας εἰς ἄφεσιν ἁμαρτιῶν*). But in Josephus this significance of baptism is specifically dissociated from John. Not only is this deliberate, it is clearly controversial. As Naber argues (*Mnemosyne* XIII. 281), it is scarcely credible that Josephus was ignorant of the Christian baptism which *was* "for the remission of sins." Naber suggests, then, that in the passage in which Josephus refers to Jesus, the historian cited the Christian baptism with expressions of disapproval, and as this was displeasing to Christian readers, the passage was altered. On the other hand the John passage was left standing, and the controversial *μὴ ἐπὶ τινῶν ἁμαρτάδων παραιτήσει χρωμένων* remained. If this be so, it may well be that Josephus really has preserved for us the exact nature of John's baptism. But before saying a word on that, it is necessary to turn to a question of language.

In his first editions Graetz accepted Josephus' account of John as authentic. But in his later editions of the *Geschichte der Juden* he strongly contends that the passage is spurious. He urges that Josephus would not have described John as the "Baptist" (τοῦ ἐπικαλουμένου βαπτιστοῦ) without further explanation. Graetz does not see that it is possible to regard these three words as an interpolation in a passage otherwise authentic. But it is not necessary to make this supposition. For it is quite in Josephus' manner to use designations for which he offers no explanation (cf. e.g. the term "Essene"). And the meaning of "Baptist" is fully explained in the following sentence, Josephus using the nouns βάπτισις and βαπτισμός to describe John's activity. The terminology of Josephus, I would urge, makes it quite unlikely that the passage is an interpolation. For, it will be noted (*a*) Josephus does not use βάπτισμα which is the usual N.T. form; (*b*) he does use the form βάπτισις which is unknown to the N.T.; (*c*) he uses βαπτισμός in a way quite unlike the use of the word when it does occur in Mark (vii. 4) or even in Hebrews (ix. 10). It is in fact Josephus alone who applies the word βαπτισμός to John's baptism. Except then that Josephus used the epithet βαπτιστής (which may be interpolated) his terminology is quite independent of N.T. usage. It is true that Josephus uses the common LXX. word λούω when describing the lustrations of the Essenes, but the verb βαπτίζω was quite familiar to Jewish writers. It is rare in LXX. but is curiously enough found precisely where bathing in the Jordan is referred to, in the significant passage 2 Kings v. 14: "Then went he down and dipped himself (ἐβαπτίσατο) seven times in Jordan[1]." Significant, too, is the fact that Aquila, who translated under Aqiba's influence, uses βαπτίζω where the LXX. uses βάπτω (Job ix. 31; Psalm lviii. 3). In the latter place the verb is also used by Symmachus, who further introduces it into Jer. (xxxviii. 22). To Josephus himself the verb was so familiar that he even makes a metaphorical use of it. In describing the masses of people "flocking into the city" he says ἐβάπτισαν τὴν πόλιν.

Another point on which a few words are necessary is John's relation

[1] Cheyne, *Encycl. Biblica* col. 2499, represents John the Baptist "who was no formalist" as using the Jordan in spite of the Rabbinic opinion that "the waters of the Jordan were not pure enough for sacred uses." But the Jordan water was only held insufficiently clean for one specific purpose: the ceremony of the Red Heifer (Parah viii. 9). No Rabbi ever dreamed of pronouncing the Jordan unfit for the rite of baptism.

to the Essenes. That Josephus means to identify him with that sect is clear. For the very words he uses of John are the terms of entry to the Essenic confraternity. In *Wars* II. viii. § 7 Josephus reports: "If he then appears to be worthy, they then [after long probation] admit him into their society. And before he is allowed to touch their common food, he is obliged to take tremendous oaths, in the first place that he will exercise piety towards God, and next that he will observe justice towards men" (πρῶτον μὲν εὐσεβήσειν τὸ θεῖον, ἔπειτα τὰ πρὸς ἀνθρώπους δίκαια διαφυλάξειν). The other terms used of John by Josephus (ἀρετή, ἁγνεία) are also used by him of the Essenes. The Gospels attribute to John Essenic characteristics. The account of John in Mark i. is more than merely illustrated by what Josephus says in his Life § ii.: "When I was informed that a certain Bannos lived in the desert, who used no other clothing than grew on trees, and had no other food than what grew of its own accord, and bathed himself in cold water frequently, both by day and by night, in order to preserve purity (πρὸς ἁγνείαν), I became a follower of his." John's asceticism is not identical with this, but it belongs to the same order. It is quite untenable to attempt, as many are now tending to do, to dissociate John altogether from Essenism. Graetz seems right in holding that John made a wider appeal than the Essenes did by relaxing some of the Essenian stringency: their communism, their residence in separate colonies, their rigid asceticism. John, like another Elijah, takes up the prophetic rôle. He calls to the Jews to repent, in expectation of the Messianic judgment perhaps. Pharisaic eschatology, in one of its tendencies, which rising in the first century became dominant in the third, connects the Messianic age with repentance. There is, however, this difference. The formula of John (or Jesus) was: Repent *for* the Kingdom is at hand. The Pharisaic formula was: Repent *and* the Kingdom is at hand. Pharisaic eschatology did not, however, ally this formula to the baptismal rite. John associates his prophetic call with baptism, partly no doubt in relation to the metaphorical use of the rite in many parts of the O.T., but partly also in direct relation to the Essenic practices. He treats baptism as a bodily purification corresponding to an inward change, not as a means of remitting sins. Cheyne, who takes a different view as to the Essenic connection of John, expresses the truth, I think, when he writes as follows (*Encyclopaedia Biblica*, col. 2499): "He led them [his followers] to the Jordan, there to give them as representatives of a regenerate people the final purification which attested the reality of their inward change." Then he adds in a note: "No other exegesis seems reasonable; Josephus, as we have seen, sanctions it. The true baptism is spiritual (Psalm li. 7 [9]). But it needs an outward symbol, and Johanan [John], remembering Ezekiel xxxvi. 25, and having prophetic authority, called those who would know themselves to be purified to baptism. It is no doubt true that baptism was regularly required of Gentile proselytes, but Johanan's baptism had no connection with ceremonial uncleanness." It is interesting to note the use made in Pharisaic circles of this same text in Ezekiel. "Said R. Aqiba [end of first and beginning of second century A.D.]: Happy are ye, O Israel! Before whom do you cleanse yourselves? Who cleanseth you? Your Father who is in Heaven! As it is written, And I will sprinkle clean water upon you and ye shall be clean."

On the question of Baptism in general see next Note. On John's references to the Pharisees see note on Pharisees. John we are told in a difficult passage (Matt. xi. 13; Luke xvi. 16) was the end of the Law and the Prophets. He certainly was faithful to the Law and a worthy upholder of the olden Prophetic spirit. But except in the sense that, in the Christian view, he was the last to prophesy the Kingdom in the spirit of the Law and the Prophets, John was the end of neither. When John died the 'Law' was only in the first stages of its Rabbinical development. And from that day to this there have never been lacking in the Jewish fold men who, in accord with the Prophetic spirit, have made a direct appeal to the hearts of their brethren on behalf of repentance and inward virtue.

# IV. PHARISAIC BAPTISM.

Unnecessary doubt has been thrown on the prevalence of baptism as an initiatory rite in the reception of proselytes during Temple times. Schürer, while exaggerating the number of ablutions prescribed by Pharisaic Judaism, rightly insists (III³. 131) that both *à priori*, and from the implications of the Mishnah (*Pesaḥim*, viii. 8), proselytes must have been baptised in the time of Jesus. The heathen was in a state of uncleanness and must, at least as emphatically as the Jew in a similar state, have undergone the ritual of bathing. Only in a state of ritual cleanness could the new-comer be received "under the Wings of the Divine Presence"—a common Rabbinic phrase for proselytism (e.g. T.B. *Yebamoth*, 46 b) directly derived from the beautiful terms of Boaz' greeting to Ruth, the ideal type of all sincere proselytes: "The Lord recompense thy work, and a full reward be given thee of the Lord God of Israel, under whose wings thou art come to trust." So, too, Jesus, after his baptism, sees the spirit of God descending as a dove. The symbolism of the Holy Spirit by a dove is a notion found in Rabbinic books (see below note on "the Dove and the Voice"). But I think it is more fully explained when it is brought into connection with the figure that the proselyte comes under the Wings of the Divine Presence. Thus the fact that, in the Gospels, baptism precedes the metaphorical reference to the bird, strengthens the argument in favour of the early prevalence of the baptism of proselytes.

Yet it can hardly be said that the evidence so far adduced *proves* the case. Schürer (*loc. cit.*) and Edersheim (II. Appendix XII.) think that the Mishnah (cited above) does establish the point. But Dr Plummer, while conceding that "the fact is not really doubtful," asserts that "direct evidence is not forthcoming" (Hastings, *Dictionary of the Bible*, I. 239). The Mishnah cited (to which *Eduyoth*, v. 2 is parallel) describes a difference of view between the schools of Hillel and Shammai. If a man has "been made a proselyte" on the fourteenth of Nisan and has then been baptised, (must he wait seven days before he is regarded as "clean" or) may he eat the Paschal lamb the same evening? (The suggestion of Bengel, *Ueber das Alter der jud. Proselyten-taufe*, p. 90, that the bath was not a proselyte-bath is groundless.) This Mishnah certainly implies that the baptism of proselytes occurred while the Paschal lamb was still being offered, i.e. during Temple times. But the passage does not quite prove this, for it is just possible that the discussion is merely scholastic. On turning, however, as neither Schürer nor Edersheim has done, to the Jerusalem Talmud and the Tosefta, it becomes certain that we are dealing with historical fact and not with dialectics. (See T.J. *Pesaḥim*, viii. last lines; Tosefta, *Pesaḥim*, vii. 13, ed. Zuckermandel, p. 167.) "Rabbi Eleazar ben Jacob says: Soldiers were Guards of the Gates in Jerusalem; they were baptised and ate their Paschal lambs in the evening." Here we have an actual record of the conversion of Roman soldiers to Judaism on the day before the Passover (an altogether probable occasion for such a step), and of their reception by means of baptism. This Eleazar ben Jacob the Elder is one of the most trustworthy reporters of Temple events and rites, which he knew from personal experience. (Cf. Bacher, *Die Agada der Tannaiten*, $1^2$. p. 63.) "The Mishnah of R. Eleazar is a small measure, but it contains fine flour" (T.B. *Yebamoth*, 49 b) was the traditional estimate of the value of this Rabbi's traditions. The exact date of this incident cannot be fixed. Graetz places it in the year 67 A.D. If that be so, then we are still without direct evidence that proselytes were baptised half a century earlier. But the probability is greatly increased by this historical record.

It is noteworthy that, according to Bacher's reading of this account, baptism without previous circumcision seems sufficient to qualify the heathen proselyte to eat the Paschal lamb. This is directly opposed to the Law (Exodus xii. 48). Later on there was indeed found an advocate for the view that baptism was sufficient (without circumcision) to constitute a proselyte (T.B. *Yebamoth*, 46 a). But it seems more reasonable to suppose that R. Eleazar ben Jacob takes it for granted that the Roman soldiers were circumcised before baptism. In the corresponding Mishnah, and in the whole context in the Tosefta, this is certainly presupposed. The predominant and almost universal view was that in Temple times three rites accompanied the reception of proselytes: circumcision, baptism, and sacrifice (T.B. *Kerithoth*, 81 a). After the fall of the Temple the first two of these three rites were necessary (*ibid.* 9 b). In the case of women, when sacrifices could not any longer be brought, the sole initiatory rite was baptism. It may be that as women were of old, as now, the more numerous proselytes, baptism came to be thought by outside observers as the only rite in all cases. Thus Arrian, in the second century, names baptism as the one sufficing ceremony which completely turns a heathen into a Jew (*Dissert. Epictet.* II. 9).

The baptism by John resembles the baptism of proselytes in several points, among others in the fact that both forms of baptism are *administered*, not performed by the subject himself. At all events, the proselyte's bath needed witnessing.

In Mark i. 9 the repentant are baptized ὑπὸ Ἰωάννου. But in Luke iii. 7, where the ordinary text (and Westcott and Hort) has βαπτισθῆναι ὑπ' αὐτοῦ, the Western text has βαπτισθῆναι ἐνώπιον αὐτοῦ (probably as Prof. Burkitt has suggested to me = קדמוהי). In the Pharisaic baptism of proselytes, at all events, the presence of others was entirely due to the necessity of witnessing (*Yebamoth*, 47 a). Sometimes a causative form, sometimes the *kal* form, of the verb *ṭabal* is used in the Rabbinic texts; but in the case of male proselytes there seems to have been no act on the part of the witnesses. In the case of women, the witnesses (three *dayanim*) stood outside, and other women "caused her to sit down" (i.e. supported her) in the bath up to her neck. The male proselyte stood, with the water up to his waist (*Yebamoth*, 46–48; *Gerim*, ch. i.). In all cases, the bathing was most probably by total immersion (for the evidence see the writer's article in the *Journal of Theological Studies*, XII. 609, with the interesting contributions by the Rev. C. F. Rogers in the same periodical, XII. 437, XIII. 411). Total immersion is clearly implied by the Zadokite Fragment (edited by Schechter, 1910, ch. xii.). If that fragment be a genuine document of the second century B.C., its evidence for the total immersion of the priests is of great weight. In the Talmud the bath in such a case had to be at least of the dimensions 1 × 1 × 3 cubits, sufficient for total immersion (שכל גופו עולה בהם, *Erubin*, 46). The bathing of the *niddah* (menstrual woman) was by total immersion, and we have the definite statement of a baraitha (*Yebamoth*, 47 b) that the rules for the bathing of proselytes (male and female) were the same as for the *niddah*. In only one case of baptism did the bystander participate actively. On entering Jewish service, a heathen slave was baptised. If he claimed that such baptism was for complete proselytism (לשם גירות) he became free. But in order to make it clear that the baptism was not for this purpose, the owner of the slave was required to seize hold of him while in the water (לתקפו במים), as a clear indication that the baptism was not a complete proselytism (*Yebamoth*, 46 a). Obviously in cases of proselytes the baptism would be the perfectly free, unfettered and unaided act of the proselyte himself.

But there is, it is often said, this difference between Johannine and Pharisaic baptism: the former was a moral, the latter a physical purification. Josephus, it has been shown, hardly regarded this contrast as essential. Nor, in the case of the proselyte-bath, can it be doubted that the two ideas are welded together. In the older Rabbinical literature we do not, it is true, find any specific reference to a baptism of repentance. The phrase first meets us in the Middle Ages. A thirteenth century authority for the first time distinctly speaks of the man who bathes for penitence' sake (טובל לשם תשובה), and of bathing in general, as an essential of repentance (שכל השבים חייבים בטבילה). See *Shibbole Halleket*, § 93 (ed. Venice, fol. 41 a). Apparently this rule that "all penitents are baptised" is traced to a passage in the *Aboth de R. Nathan* (see the *Tanya*, § 72; ed. Venice, p. 102 b). But though the passage in the *Aboth* (ch. viii.) does not easily bear this implication (the text as we have it is certainly corrupt), we can carry the evidence five hundred years further back than the thirteenth century. In the Palestinian Midrash *Pirke de R. Eleazar*, compiled about 830, Adam's repentance after expulsion from Eden consists of bathing, fasting and confession (*op. cit.* ch. xx.). Older still is the passage in the Apocryphal (and not obviously Christian) *Life of Adam and Eve*, which represents the repentant Adam as standing for forty days in the Jordan (Kautzsch, *Pseudepigraphen zum Alten Testament*, p. 512; Charles, *Apocrypha and Pseudepigrapha of the Old Testament*, Oxford, 1913, p. 134).

Earlier still is (probably) the famous passage in the fourth Sibylline Oracle (iv. 165 seq.) which, even in its present form, must belong to the first Christian century (c. 80 A.D.). In iii. 592 there is a reference to the morning lustrations (cf. the *morning bathers* of T.B. *Berachoth*, 22 a. On this and other allied points see S. Krauss, *Talmudische Archäologie*, Leipzig, 1910–1912, I. pp. 211, 217, 229, 669; II. p. 100; III. p. 360). But in iv. 165 there is a direct association of repentance with bathing. I quote Terry's rendering with some emendations:

> Ah! miserable mortals, change these things,
> Nor lead the mighty God to wrath extreme;
> But giving up your swords and pointed knives,

And homicides and wanton violence,
Wash your whole body in perennial streams,
And lifting up your hands to heaven seek pardon
For former deeds and expiate with praise
Bitter impiety; and God will give
Repentance; he will not destroy; and wrath
Will he again restrain, if in your hearts
Ye all will practise precious godliness.

This, it will be noted, is an appeal to the heathen world. It falls well within the range of the Jewish Hellenistic literature, and there is no necessity for assuming a Christian authorship.

Water was a *symbol* of repentance still earlier. The Targum to 1 Samuel vii. 6 (cf. Midrash, *Samuel* and *Yalkut*, ad loc., and T.J. *Taanith*, ii. § 7) explains the action of Israel at Mizpah in that sense. The text does indeed associate in a remarkable way a water-rite (of which nothing else is known), fasting, and confession as elements in repentance: "And they gathered together to Mizpah, and drew water and poured it out before the Lord, and fasted on that day, and said there, We have sinned against the Lord." Ascetic rites (such as fasting) were ancient accompaniments of the confession of sin, as in the ritual of the day of Atonement; and the association of asceticism with cold bathing is at least as old in Judaism as the Essenes. In the *Didache* fasting precedes baptism (vii. 4), but it is not clear how early the Synagogue introduced the now wide-spread custom of bathing on the Eve of the Day of Atonement in connection with the confession of sins. Talmudic is the rule "A man is bound to purify himself at the festivals" (T.B. *Rosh Hashana*, 16 b), no doubt with reference to ceremonial uncleanness. But Leviticus (xvi. 30) lays it down: "From all your sins before the Lord ye shall be clean" on the Day of Atonement, and the same word (טהור) which here means spiritually clean also signifies physically and ritually clean. "Wash you, make you clean, put away the evil of your doings" (Isaiah i. 16) is one characteristic text of many in which the prophets make play with the metaphor. The Sibylline call to actual baptism of the sinning Greek world is obviously based on this very passage. Another passage, to which great importance was justly attached in Rabbinical thought, is Ezekiel xxxvi. 25—27: "I will sprinkle pure water upon you, and ye shall be clean; from all your filthiness and from all your idols will I cleanse you. A new heart also will I give you, and a new spirit will I put within you; and I will take away the stony heart out of your flesh, and I will give you an heart of flesh. And

I will put my spirit within you, and cause you to walk in my statutes, and ye shall keep my judgments and do them." Here we have, together, all the main ideas of Pharisaic baptism; and it is noteworthy that this passage from Ezekiel is extensively used in Rabbinic homilies.

Such passages as these attest the early association between physical and moral purification, such as meets us in the Johannine baptism. And the ideas are close. Whoever invented the epigram "Cleanliness is next to Godliness," it is a fair summary of Pharisaic conceptions on the subject under discussion. Throughout the *Psalms of Solomon* "to be clean" is identical with "to be forgiven." In Rabbinic Hebrew, as in Biblical, the same word means physically and spiritually clean. To "repent" is to "be purified." (Cf. the הבא ליטהר of T.B. *Yoma*, 38 b, and the phrase "before whom do you cleanse yourselves?" i.e. repent of your sins, of the previous Note.) Sin is, conversely, uncleanness. There is no need to quote Biblical instances of the use. In Rabbinic Hebrew the very strong word (סרח) which literally means "to be putrid" is a common term for "to sin." A very remarkable figure of speech is attributed to Hillel. He bathed his body to keep clean that which was made in the image of God (*Levit. Rabba*, xxxv.). The connection between sin and atonement by bathing is brought out in the Midrash on Ps. li. 4 on the text, "Wash me thoroughly from mine iniquity." The Midrash comments: "Hence, whoever commits a transgression is as though he was defiled by contact with a dead body," and he needs sprinkling with hyssop. Here the reference is clearly to moral not to ritual transgression. In 2 Kings v. 14 we are told of Naaman that after his leprosy was healed "his flesh came again like the flesh of a little child"; and so the proselyte on his baptism "became like a little child" (T.B. *Yebamoth*, 22 a, 48 b). On the text "Be thou a blessing" (Gen. xii. 2) the Midrash (playing on the similar words ברכה "blessing" and בריכה "pool") comments: "As yonder pool purifies the unclean, so thou bringest near the far off and purifiest them to their Father in Heaven" (*Genesis Rabba*, xxxix. § 11). And those thus brought near are created anew. "He who makes a proselyte is as though he created him" (*ibid.* § 14)—thus conversion is a re-birth. In this sense the lustrations of Exodus xix. 10 were regarded as physical accompaniments of the approaching revelation on Sinai, when all the world was made anew. Man's repentance is the cause, too, of the creation of the new heavens and the new earth of Isaiah lxvi. (*Yalkut*, Isaiah, § 372). There are shades of difference in this idea of renewal, especially as concerns the nature of man. John's baptism seems to have this point in common with the Pharisaic baptism of proselytes—it was a baptism once for all. For the proselyte had, in the Pharisaic view, adopted Judaism completely; and, like one born physically a Jew, he could not thereafter evade the responsibilities of the religion which he had freely accepted, just as he shared its hopes. Benedictions usually *preceded* the performance of precepts. Not so with the ṭebilah, baptism, of the proselyte. It was only as he ascended from the bath that he said: "Blessed art thou who hast sanctified us by thy commandment and commanded us concerning ṭebilah" (T.B. Pesaḥim 6 b). It may well be, as Bousset states (*Die Religion des Judenthums im neutestamentliche Zeitalter* ed. 2, 1906, p. 230) that there was nothing sacramental in Pharisaic baptism. But, like the performance of the whole Law, it was a consecration.

Pharisaic baptism, then, agreed with what seems to have been the primitive Christian view that it was once for all, though in the case of a revert, and of a slave seeking freedom, ṭebilah would be again necessary. Ṭebilah, however, did not ensure sinlessness, or the abrogation of the power to sin. That consummation was reserved for the Messianic age. If, however, Christian baptism was the introduction to the Kingdom, then no doubt baptism would carry with it the hope of sinlessness. (On the problem of sin after Christian baptism, and the apparent reversion to the Jewish theory of repentance, see Prof. K. Lake, *The Stewardship of Faith*, London, 1915, p. 181). John seems to imply also that the consequent change of mind (μετάνοια) was also "once for all." In the Rabbinic theology such a permanent amelioration of the human character was not possible, at least in the earthly life. Men might move the stone from the mouth of the well, but it had to be replaced, and the "evil inclination" (*Yeṣer hara*) returned to where it had been and needed expulsion again and again (*Genesis Rabba*, lxx. § 8). God will in the end destroy the evil Yeṣer, but in human life the struggle is incessant and the Yeṣer leads to sin daily (T.B. *Qiddushin*, 30 b). "In this world," says God to Israel, "ye become clean and again unclean; but in the time to come I will purify you that ye never again become unclean" (Midrash, *Tanḥuma*, Meṣora, §§ 17—18). Contrariwise (as perhaps John's baptism intends), repentance brings the Messiah near (T.B. *Yoma*, 86 a, b. Cf. Montefiore, *Jewish Quarterly Review*, XVI. p. 236 and references there given). The renewal of man's nature by repentance, unlike the re-birth by conversion, is continuous and constant. It is a regular process, not a catastrophe. Israel is compared to the Angelic hosts. "As they are renewed day by day, and return, after they have praised God, to the fire from which they issued, so too the Israelites, if their evil passions ensnare them in sin, and they repent, are forgiven by God year by year and granted a new heart with which to fear him" (Midrash, *Rabba*, Shemoth xv. § 6; *Echa* on v. 5).

In Ezekiel's phrase, God sprinkles pure water on Israel and puts His spirit within him. By the middle of the second century the "last of the Essenes," Phineas ben Jair, treats "purification" as what Dr Schechter well calls "one of the higher rungs of the ladder leading to the attainment of the holy spirit" (*Studies in Judaism* II. p. 110). But the connection between water and the Holy Spirit can be traced much closer than this. In the Hebrew Bible the word "to pour out" (שפך), properly applicable only to liquids, is applied to the Divine Spirit. "In those days I will pour out my spirit on all flesh" (Joel iii. 1 [ii. 28]; cf. Ezekiel xxxix. 29). In Rabbinic Hebrew the word which means "to draw" liquids (שאב) is often used of drawing the holy spirit. In Isaiah xii. 3 we have the beautiful image: "With joy shall ye draw water from the wells of salvation." With all of this compare *Genesis Rabba*, lxx. § 8 (on Genesis xxix. 2 seq.). "*Behold there was a well in the field*: that is Zion; *lo there were three flocks of sheep*: these are the three pilgrim feasts; *from out of that well they drew water*: from thence they drew the holy spirit." Similarly the "Place of the Water-drawing," referred to above in Note I., is explained as the place whence "they drew the holy spirit" (T.J. *Sukkah*, v. § 1).

There is no ground then for the emphatic statement of Dr S. Krauss (*Jewish Encyclopedia*, II. 499) that "The only conception of Baptism at variance with Jewish ideas is displayed in the declaration of John that the one who would come after him would not baptise with water but with the Holy Ghost." The idea must have seemed quite natural to Jewish ears, as is evident from the parallels quoted above. It must be understood that some of these parallels (especially the last, which is not older than the third century) are cited not as giving the origin of the phrase in the Gospels, but as illustrating it. Such illustrations may be used irrespective of their date in order to discriminate from specifically un-Jewish ideas, those ideas which are found in the New Testament, and are found again in Jewish circles later on. It is important to know the ideas that recur. And, of course, the parallels may often be older than the first citation in which they are now to be found. On the other hand, some borrowing from the Gospels must not be dismissed as impossible or unlikely. An idea once set in circulation would become general property, and if it fitted in with other Jewish ideas might find a ready hospitality. It is well to make this plain, though I do not for a moment think that in baptism we have a case in point. The Rabbis have no hesitation in saying that prayer replaced sacrifice, but they never hint at the thought that baptism replaced the proselyte's sacrifice, as some writers suggest. My main contention is that the recurrence or non-recurrence of New Testament ideas and expressions is the surest test we have of their essential Jewishness or non-Jewishness. The test is not perfect, for parallels are occasionally missing to very Judaic ideas, and on the other hand alien ideas did occasionally creep into the theology of Judaism inadvertently. Often again, the usages and ideas of the New Testament stand *between* Old Testament usages and later Rabbinic; in such cases they are valuable links in the chain. This is emphatically the case with the New Testament references to Synagogue customs.

A good instance is also the metaphor of baptism with fire which, though absent from Mark, occurs in both Matthew and Luke. Fire in the Old Testament is not only capable of being "poured out" like water, but its capacity in this respect becomes the basis of a second derived metaphor: "He hath poured out his fury like fire" (Lamentations ii. 4). Fire is the natural element for purging, and is frequently used in the Old Testament in the two senses of punishing and refining. In the phrase "baptism by fire" we have thus two Old Testament ideas combined; fire is poured out, and it is used as a purifying and punitive agent. Some see in the baptism by fire an allusion to illumination. The light of day was removed by Adam's sin and restored on his repentance (*Genesis Rabba*, xi.; T.B. *Aboda Zara*, 8 a). The illuminative power of repentance is already found in Philo (Cohn and Wendland, § 179): "From the deepest darkness the repentant behold the most brilliant light." In the Testament of Gad (v. 7, ed. Charles, p. 154) we read: "For true repentance after a godly sort driveth away the darkness and enlighteneth the eyes." The same illuminating function is (on the basis of Psalm xix. 8) often ascribed, of course, to the Law, which further (with reference to Deut. xxxiii. 2) is also typified by fire. But the context in which baptism by fire occurs in the Gospels precludes all thought of fire as an illuminant. In the Sibylline passage quoted above, the gracious promise of pardon after true repentance on immersion in water has a harsher sequel. If there be no repentance with baptism, there shall be destruction by fire. For the Oracle continues (iv. 70):

> But if, ill-disposed, ye obey me not,
> But with a fondness for strange lack of sense
> Receive all these things with an evil ear,
> There shall be over all the world a fire
> And greatest omen with sword and with trump
> At sunrise; the whole world shall hear the roar
> And mighty sound. And he shall burn all earth,
> And destroy the whole race of men, and all
> The cities and the rivers and the sea;
> All things he'll burn, and it shall be black dust.

Fiery baptism is a purging process, and in Luke (iii. 17) is associated with the winnowing fan ("but the chaff he will burn"). The context is equally clear in Matthew (iii. 12). This is a frequent Old Testament usage. The idea is carried out most fully in a saying of Abbahu (end of third century). Schöttgen has already cited this parallel from T.B. *Sanhedrin*, 39 a. Abbahu explains that when God buried Moses, he bathed himself in fire, as it is written: "For behold the Lord will come with fire" (Isaiah lxvi. 15). Abbahu goes on to say, "By fire is the essential baptism," and he quotes: "All that abideth not the fire ye shall make to go through the water" (Num. xxxi. 23). Thus baptism by fire is the divine analogue to man's baptism by water. Man could not bear the more searching test.

One other phrase needs annotation: baptising in or into the name of Christ. It is a difficult expression, but so are all the Rabbinic metaphors in which the word "name" occurs. (Cf. my article on "Name of God" in Hastings, *Dictionary of Religion and Ethics*, vol. IX.) Part of the significance of the Gospel expression is seen from the corresponding late Hebrew (Gerim i. 7): "Whoever is not a proselyte to (or in) the name of heaven (לשם שמים) is no proselyte." (Cf. for the phrase, *Koheleth Rabbah* on Eccles. vii. 8 end.) In this context the meaning is that the true proselyte is baptised for God's sake, and for no personal motive. It is a pure, unselfish act of submission to the true God. But in the Talmud (e.g. T.B. *Yebamoth*, 45 b, 47 b last lines) there is another phrase, which throws light on this. Slaves, on rising to the rank of freemen, were re-baptised, and this slave baptism was termed a baptism to or in the name of freedom (לשם שחרור or לשם בן חורין). A fine contrast and complement of baptism *in the name of freedom* is the proselyte's baptism *in the name of heaven*, or in its Gospel form—baptism in the name of Christ. The Christian phrase, it is strongly contended by many, has a magical connotation. But if so, (and it is hardly the case unless magical be interpreted as equivalent to mystical), it was an acquired rather than a primitive connotation. The explanation suggested comes near that which regards baptism *into the name* as a Roman legal term, implying that the newcomer is admitted on the roll of the patron's clients or dependents. Never, surely, was a legal term more transfigured, both in Church and Synagogue.

## V. THE DOVE AND THE VOICE.

From two opposite sides the Rabbinic parallels to the Dove have been minimised, by Dr Edersheim and Dr Abbott. The former, in order to expose the "mythical theory," insists with "warmth of language" that the whole circumstances connected with the baptism of Jesus "had no basis in existing Jewish belief." The latter, in pursuance of his view that the "Dove" arose from a textual misunderstanding, argues equally that there was no extant Jewish symbolism which could justify the figure.

But the doubt would have been scarcely possible had the two ideas, the Dove and the Heavenly Voice, been treated together. It must not be overlooked that in several passages the Heavenly Voice (Heb. *Bath-Qol*, Daughter of the Voice) is represented as piping or chirping like a bird. The notes of a bird coming from aloft often unseen would naturally enough lend themselves to mystic symbolism in connection with the communication of a divine message. There are two clear instances of this use of the verb "chirp" with regard to the *Bath-Qol* in the Midrash Qoheleth Rabbah. In one (on Eccles. vii. 9) we read: "I heard the Daughter of the Voice chirping (מצפצפת) and saying: Return O back-sliding children (Jer. iii. 14)." Even clearer is the second passage on Eccles. xii. 7, though the text explained is verse 4 of the same chapter: "*And one shall rise up at the voice of a bird.* Said R. Levi, For 18 years a Daughter of the Voice was making announcement and chirping (מצפצפת) concerning Nebuchadnezzar." (It is possible that in the Jerusalem Talmud, *Sabbath* vi. 9, we have another instance, and that we should correct מפוצצת, which is the reading of the text there, to מצפצפת). The evidence goes further. For while in these passages the Heavenly voice is likened to the soft muttering of a bird, in one place the *Bath-Qol* is actually compared to a *dove*. This occurs in the Babylonian Talmud, *Berachoth* fol. 3 a): "I heard a *Bath-Qol moaning as a dove* and saying: Woe to the children through whose iniquities I laid waste My Temple."

It is this association of the bird and the heavenly voice that may underlie the Gospel narrative of the baptism, and at once illustrate and authenticate the symbolism of the Synoptists. There is no need to enter here at length into the question of the *Bath-Qol*, for Dr Abbott (*From Letter to Spirit*, Book II. and Appendix IV.) has admirably collected the materials. It is surely supercritical to question the antiquity of the *Bath-Qol* in face of the evidence of Josephus (*Antiquities*, XIII. x. 3) and of the Rabbinic tradition concerning Hillel: "There came forth a *Bath-Qol* and said: There is among you a certain man worthy of the Holy Spirit, but the generation is not worthy thereof" (Jer. *Soṭa* ix. 12, otherwise 13). Dr Abbott aptly compares Mark i. 7. The whole passage in Mark fits in with the belief that in the absence of the direct inspiration of prophets by the Holy Spirit (after the death of Haggai, Zechariah and Malachi), the *Bath-Qol* took its place (*loc. cit.*). The Synoptists, like the Rabbis, never report a direct message from God.

In the Rabbinic literature the dove is for the most part an emblem of Israel, its gentleness, fidelity, its persecution, its submission (H. J. Holtzmann, *Die Synoptiker*, ed. 3, p. 44, has collected some useful materials on the symbolism of the Dove in other literatures). Here is a characteristic Rabbinic passage (Midrash Tanḥuma, p. Teṣave: cf. ed. Buber, *Exod.* p. 96), "Israel is compared to a dove (Canticles i.). As the dove knows her mate and never forsakes him, so Israel, once recognising the Holy One as God, never proves faithless to him. All other birds, when they are about to be slaughtered, wince, but the dove holds out its neck to the slayer. So there is no people so willing as Israel to lay down its life for God. Just as the dove (after the flood) brought light to the world, so God said unto Israel, who are likened to the dove, Take olive oil and light my lamp before me." It has been suggested (R. Eisler in the *Quest*, July 1912) that the Jews expected the Messiah to be a second Noah, and that he would inaugurate the era by a punishment and a purification by a new flood. If the evidence were sufficient to support this view (Eisler quotes Zech. xiv. 2, Joel iii. [iv.] 18, and Ezekiel xlvii. 1) we might see a Messianic reminiscence of Noah's dove. Elsewhere other points of comparison are made (*Berachoth* 53b, etc.). As "the wings of a dove covered with silver and her feathers with yellow gold" (Ps. lxviii. 13) are the bird's means of escape from danger, so is Israel saved by the Law, the pure words of the Lord which are "as silver tried in a furnace of earth, purified seven times" (Ps. xii. 7). But, as Wünsche well remarks (*Neue Beiträge*, p. 501) the very comparison of suffering Israel to a dove may have influenced the growth of the metaphor as applied to the Messiah, whose function it was to save Israel. The "Spirit of God" of the Cosmogony in Genesis is thus sometimes (as we shall see later) compared to a dove, sometimes to the spirit of the Messiah, who will not come until Israel deserves the boon by Repentance (Genesis Rabba, ch. ii., ed. Theodor, p. 17; *Yalquṭ* on Gen. i. 2). The identity is carried farther. In the Bible God is said to have borne Israel on Eagle's wings, to protect Israel as a parent bird protects its nest (Deut. xxxii. 11); more generally (Isaiah xxxi. 5): "as birds flying so will the Lord of hosts protect Jerusalem." Nay more, just as the Divine Presence goes into exile with Israel, so God himself is, with Israel, compared to a troubled bird (though not a dove), driven from its nest (the Temple) while the wicked prevail on earth (Midrash on Ps. lxxxix., *Yalquṭ* § 833). It is quite in keeping with this whole range of ideas to find the Targum (Canticles ii. 12, etc.) interpreting as the "voice of the Holy Spirit of Salvation" the text, the "voice of the turtle-dove is heard in our land." (Cf. alfo *Sifre* on Deut. § 314, with reference to Canticles ii. 8.)

Now it is obviously near at hand to find the main source of the comparison of the Holy Spirit to a bird in Genesis i. 2, "And the Spirit of God brooded (as a bird) upon the face of the waters." We are happily not called upon to discuss the origin of the idea in Genesis itself and its relation to the "world-egg." The Jewish commentators (even on Jeremiah xxiii. 9) recognise no other meaning for the verb used in Genesis (רחף), except brooding or moving as a bird. It is well here to cite Rashi's note on the Genesis passage: "The Spirit of God was moving: the Throne of Glory was standing in the air and moving on the face of the waters by the Spirit of the Mouth of the Holy One blessed be he, and by his Word like a dove that broods on the nest, in French *acoveter*." This idea is derived by the commentator partly from the Midrash Cōnēn (Jellinek, *Bet Hamidrash*, ii. 24: "And the holy spirit and the holy Presence was moving and breathing on the water"), but chiefly from the famous incident concerning Ben Zoma, a younger contemporary of the Apostles. I have cited Rashi's adoption of it to prove that some moderns have misread the Talmud when they regard the Rabbis as deprecating Ben Zoma's idea. If anyone understood the spirit of the Talmud it was Rashi, and the fact that he (like other Jewish commentators) adopts the simile of the dove is of itself enough to show that Ben Zoma's simile was not considered objectionable. Moreover, the passage relating to Ben Zoma is too frequently reproduced in the Rabbinical sources for it to have been held in the disrepute which has strangely been assigned to it by those who would like to expunge this very clear parallel to the dove of the Synoptists, for it is obvious that we have not only a comparison to the dove, but also to its appearance "on the face of the waters," which fits in so well with the baptismal scene at the Jordan, the dove descending as "Jesus, when he was baptised, went up straightway from the water." Even without the Ben Zoma analogue one could hardly doubt that the Synoptists must have had Genesis i. 2 in mind.

The Ben Zoma incident is reported in the Talmud (Ḥagiga 15a) as follows: "Rabbi Joshua the son of Ḥananiah was standing on an ascent in the Temple Mount, and Ben Zoma saw him but did not stand before him. He said to him: Whence comest thou and whither go thy thoughts, Ben Zoma? He replied, I was considering the space between the upper waters and the lower waters, and there is only between them a mere three fingers' breadth, as it is said, and the Spirit of God was brooding on the face of the waters like a dove which broods over her young but does not touch them. Rabbi Joshua said to his disciples, Ben Zoma is still outside; for, 'and the Spirit of God was hovering'—when was this? On the first day. But the separation was on the second day." There are several variants of the passage, but this on the whole seems to me the most original in the important reference to the dove. (Bacher, *Agada der Tanaiten*, ed. 2, Vol. I., p. 423, holds the Tosefta Ḥagiga ii. 5 and Jer. Talm. Ḥagiga reading more original because the allusion to the Temple is an anachronism.) Some of the variants either suppress the dove or replace it by an eagle, citing Deut. xxxii. 11 (where the same verb רחף is used of an eagle). Such a harmonisation shows the hand of an editor, and the dove would not have been introduced later. Dr Schechter (*Studies in Judaism*, II. p. 113) is convinced that the *dove* is the original reading. Now the theory that by the phrase "Ben Zoma is still outside" it was implied in this "fragment of a Jewish Gnosis" (as L. Löw, *Lebensalter*, p. 58 suggests) that he had not yet returned to the orthodox path is quite untenable. Other passages show that the meaning is: Ben Zoma is still out of his senses. He had pried too closely into the problems of creation, and had fallen into such perplexity that he confused the work of the first with that of the second day. At all events, the figure of the dove is not asserted to have originated with Ben Zoma, there is nothing in the passage to imply that it was regarded as an innovation, or that Ben Zoma's idea was unorthodox or heretical. Of course it is quite true, as Dr Abbott urges, that the Rabbinic figure does not imply that the Holy Spirit appeared visibly as a dove, but that the motion and action of the Spirit were comparable to the motion of a dove over her young.

## VI. LEAVEN.

The term leaven (שְׂאֹר = Gk. ζύμη) is used in N.T. as a symbol of "corruption." Something of the same idea is found in a well-known Rabbinic passage to be discussed later. As to the O.T. conception of leaven, an excellent account is given by A. R. S. Kennedy in *Encyclopaedia Biblica*, col. 2754, "In the view of all antiquity, Semitic and non-Semitic, panary fermentation represented a process of corruption and putrefaction in the mass of the dough." Plutarch (*Quaest. Rom.* 109) has the same idea. Philo, on the other hand, has the idea with a somewhat different *nuance*. To him, leaven symbolises the puffing-up of vain self-conceit (Frag. on Exod. xxiii. 18), or the vice of insolence (on Levit. ii. 11, *de offer.* vi., Mangey II. 255). It is probable, too, that the Roman satirist Persius (I. 24) also implies by *fermentum* "vanity" rather than "corruption."

Later Jewish moralists (cf. Zohar on Gen. xlvii. 31) have made extensive use of the leaven metaphor (especially with reference to the prohibition of leavened bread חמין on Passover). As, however, "leavened" bread was in itself more palatable as an article of food than unleavened, the metaphorical use of "leaven" sometimes expresses an improving process. Kennedy (*loc. cit.*) puts it rather differently: "In the N.T. leaven supplies two sets of figures, one taken from the mode, the other from the result, of the process of fermentation. Thus Jesus likened the silent but effective growth of the 'Kingdom' in the mass of humanity to the hidden but pervasive action of leaven in the midst of the dough" (Mt. xiii. 33). It is probable, however, that the parable also takes account of the result; the leavened mass of humanity, through intrusion of the leaven, attains a superior moral condition, just as the leavened bread is a more perfect food than unleavened. Paul applies the process in the opposite sense. Just as "evil company doth corrupt good manners" (1 Cor. xv. 33), so "a little leaven leaveneth the whole lump" (1 Cor. v. 6; Gal. v. 9). The latter idea is Rabbinic (Succah 56 b) both on this side (*Woe to the wicked, woe to his neighbour*

אוי לרשע אוי לשכינו) and on the reverse side, for the righteous extends virtue and its consequences to his neighbour (*Happy the righteous, happy his neighbour* טוב לצדיק טוב לשכינו). But the Rabbinic idea does not associate itself with leaven, but with the plague-spot, which appearing in one house, compels the demolition of the next house (Mishna, Negaim xii. 6; Sifra on Levit. xiv. 40; Weiss 73 b). A very close parallel to Paul's proverb (μικρὰ ζύμη ὅλον τὸ φύραμα ζυμοῖ) is found in Hebrew (כאשר השאור המועט מחמיץ עסה גדולה), but this occurs in a fifteenth century book (Abraham Shalom b. Isaac's *neve shalom* xi. 2), and is possibly a reminiscence of 1 Cor. But the sentence is not very recondite, and may be independent of Paul. The permanence of the effect of leaven in the mass is found in Yalquṭ Ruth § 601, where the leaven is said to cling to proselytes up to 24 generations.

Most notable of all metaphorical applications of leaven is its association with man's evil tendencies or inclinations (יצר הרע). The chief references in Rabbinic thought are two, both of which are alluded to in the passage about to be quoted from Weber. The latter (in his *Jüdische Theologie*) identified the evil inclination with the *body*. On p. 221 (ed. 2 p. 229) he writes:

That the body is impure, not merely as perishable, but because it is the *seat of the evil impulse*, we see from what is said in Num. Rabba xiii. (Wünsche p. 312): God knew before he created man that the desire of his heart would be evil from his youth (Gen. viii. 21). "Woe to the dough of which the baker must himself testify that it is bad." This Jewish proverb can be applied to the Jewish doctrine of man. Then the dough is the body, which God (the baker) worked and shaped, and the impurity of the body is grounded in the fact that it is the seat of the *yeṣer hara'*, which is in the body that which the leaven is in the dough (שאור שבעיסה), a fermenting, impelling force (Berachoth 17 a).

But, as Prof. F. C. Porter rightly comments, Weber's view is not well founded. This is Prof. Porter's criticism ("The Yeçer Hara," in *Yale Biblical and Semitic Studies*, p. 104).

Here the identification of the dough with the body, in distinction from the soul, is mistaken. The dualistic psychology is supplied by Weber, not suggested by the source. God's judgment upon man in Gen. viii. 21 is likened to a baker's condemnation of his own dough. The proverb is also found in Gen. Rabba xxxiv. (Wünsche, p. 152) as a saying of R. Hiyya the Great (Bacher, *Agada der Tannaiten* II. 530). The comparison of the evil impulse with leaven is an entirely different saying, which should not be connected with the other. But in this case also the dough is man, human nature, not the body. It is the prayer of R. Alexander (Berach. 17 a): "It is revealed and known before thee that our will is to do thy will. And what hinders? The leaven that is in the dough and servitude to the Kingdoms. May it be thy will to deliver us from their hand."

Matthew (xvi. 12) interprets the "leaven of the Pharisees" to mean "teaching of the Pharisees," an interpretation which Allen (p. 175) rightly rejects. Luke (xii. 1) interprets it of "hypocrisy." Mark (viii. 14–21) gives no explanation, but reads "beware of the leaven of the Pharisees and the leaven of Herod." It will be seen that this reading strangely agrees with the words of R. Alexander's prayer: "the leaven that is in the dough (= the leaven of the Pharisees) and servitude to the Kingdoms (= the leaven of Herod)." Two things impede man: the evil *yeṣer* and the interference of alien rule. Both these preventives to man's advance will vanish with the coming of the Kingdom. With the advent of the Messiah the evil *yeṣer* will be finally slain (see refs. in Schechter, *Aspects of Rabbinic Theology*, p. 290); and in the second place with the Kingdom of heaven Israel triumphs over Rome (Pesiqta K. 50 a; Pesiqta R. 75 a).

There is a striking saying attributed to R. Joshua b. Levi, who belongs to the first half of the third century. It is obvious that the parable of the leaven requires a favourable application of the symbol. R. Joshua carries this application to the extent of likening leaven to peace. "Great is peace, in that peace is to the earth as leaven to dough; for had not God set peace in the earth the sword and the wild-beast would have depopulated it" (Pereq ha-Shalom, beginning; Bacher, *Agada der Palästinensischen Amoräer* I. 136). The exact force of R. Joshua's comparison is not clear. He bases his idea on Leviticus xxvi. 6: and it is possible that he had in mind the thought found in the Sifra on that text (ed. Weiss, p. 111 a). "I will give peace in the land" and (in the usual translation) "I will make evil beasts to cease." So R. Judah interprets. But according to R. Simeon the meaning is that God will not destroy evil beasts, but will render them innocuous; for "the divine power is better seen when there are in existence evils which do not injure" (comparing Isaiah xi. 6—8). In this sense, peace would be not inert, but an active agency; a ferment of the good against the evil. The idea of stirring, agitating (רגז and כעס), is not only applied to the evil *yeṣer*. It is also used of the good *yeṣer*. "Let a man stir up his good *yeṣer* against his bad" (T. B. Berachoth, 5 *a*); "rouse thy [good] *yeṣer* and thou wilt not sin" (Ruth Rabbah, towards end). Peace is thus the leaven, stirring up the good yeṣer, to strive against hostile forces. If Peace is to have her victories, she must fight for them.

## VII. PUBLICANS AND SINNERS.

The Roman taxes and custom duties and their mode of collection are admirably described by Schürer (I. § 17) and Herzfeld (*Handelsgeschichte der Juden des Alterthums*, § 47). The taxes proper were in Roman times collected by state officials, but the customs were farmed out to *publicani*. In maritime places these were particularly onerous, and Herzfeld ingeniously cites the proverbial maxim ('Aboda Zara, 10 *b*) "Woe to the ship which sails without paying its dues" in illustration of Matthew ix. 9, 10. That the demands of the *publicani* and their underlings were often excessive is natural enough, and—especially when the officials were native Jews (*cp.* Büchler, *Sepphoris*, pp. 13, 40, etc.)—the class was consequently the object of popular resentment. It is not the case (as Schürer assumes) that the Jewish authorities connived at frauds on the regular revenue. At all events the trick permitted in the Mishnah (Nedarim, iii. 4) was interpreted by the Talmud (Nedarim, 28 *a*) as having reference not to the authorised taxes but to the arbitrary demands of unscrupulous extorters or inventors of dues. "The law of the Government is law"—on which see Note VIII—is used on the Talmudic folio just quoted as making it impossible that the Mishnah (which permits one to evade "murderers, robbers, confiscators and tax-gatherers" by falsely declaring the property coveted to be sacerdotal or royal property) can refer to lawful taxes.

We have already seen that the tax-gatherers are associated with robbers and murderers (*cp.* also Baba Qama, 113 *a*). Hence they were regarded as unfit to act as judges or to be admitted as witnesses (Sanhedrin, 25 *b*). An early baraitha made a tax-gatherer ineligible as ḥaber; in the older period the disqualification did not cease with the abandonment of the occupation, afterwards this particular severity was mitigated (Bechoroth, 31 *a*). It is clear from the last quotation that the publican might sometimes be a man of learning. Yet this condemnation was not universal. Baya (or Mayan) the tax-gatherer (or his son), who was charitable to the poor, was publicly mourned and honoured at his death (Sanhedrin, 44 *b*; J. Ḥagiga, ii. 2). So, concerning the father of Ze'ira (Sanhedrin, 25 *b*) a favourable report is made. There is also a (late) story of Aqiba (or in another version Joḥanan b. Zakkai), telling how the Rabbi with eagerness reclaimed the son of an oppressive tax-gatherer, teaching him the Law, and bringing peace to the father's soul (Kallah, ed. Coronel, 4 *b*. For other references see *Jewish Encyclopedia*, vol. I. p. 310).

The association in the Gospels of the two expressions Publicans and Sinners is parallel to the combination of "publicans and robbers" in the Rabbinic literature. The "sinners" were thus not those who neglected the rules of ritual piety, but were persons of immoral life, men of proved dishonesty or followers of suspected and degrading occupations. The Rabbis would have been chary of intercourse with such men at all times, but especially at meals. For the meal was not regarded simply as a satisfaction of physical needs. It was a service as well, consecrated by benedictions; it was also a feast of reason. The keynote of this is struck in the saying of R. Simeon (Aboth, iii. 3): "Three who have eaten at one table and have not said over it words of Torah, are as if they had eaten sacrifices of the dead (idols), for it is said: All tables are full of vomit and filthiness without *place* (*Maqom*)." This last word is taken in its secondary sense to mean the Omnipresent, God. "But," continues R. Simeon, "three who have eaten at one table, and have said over it words of Torah, are as if they had eaten of the table of God (*Maqom*), blessed be he, for it is said: This is the table that is before the Lord" (Ezekiel xli. 22). This conception is exemplified also in the table-discourses of Jesus to his disciples, and lies, to some extent, at the bottom of institution of the Eucharistic meal. In Jewish life this idea that the table is an altar gained a firm hold and led to a whole system of learned readings, devotions, and most remarkably, of hymns during meals, the Passover home-rites being but a conspicuous example of a daily Jewish usage. Just, then, as later on Christians would not share the Eucharistic meal with notorious evil-livers, so the Jewish Rabbi at various periods would (with less consistent rigidity) have objected to partake of any meal with men of low morals. So, also, Jesus' disciples are exhorted (Matthew xviii. 17) to treat certain offenders as "the Gentile and the Publican" with whom common meals would be impossible. The Essenes held a similar view as to the exclusion from their table of those who did not share the Essenic principles.

When, then, we find that the "pure-minded in Jerusalem would not sit down to a meal unless they knew who their table-companions were to be" (Sanhedrin, 23 *a*), the motive was neither pride nor exclusiveness, but a desire that the meal should not degenerate into mere eating and drinking. They would wish to be assured of the presence of fit comrades for learned and edifying discourse. They would not readily accept invitations to banquets at all, "the student who is always found at other people's tables profanes the name of God" (Yoma, 86 *b*, *Aboth de R. Nathan*, I. xxvi.). The Rabbis were convivial, but not gluttons; and many of them would never eat outside their own homes except at a "meal of duty," i.e. a semi-religious function, such as a marriage festivity. Instructive is the incident recorded as having occurred in Jerusalem c. 65 A.D. At the feast held on the circumcision of Elishah b. Abuyah, among those present were Eleazar b. Hyrqanos and Joshua b. Ḥananyah. While the other guests were partaking of meat and wine, these two sat "stringing together," like pearls on a cord, the words of the Scriptures. (Qoh. R. on viii. 8; see Bacher, *Prooemien* etc., p. 9.) To such men, a meal was not a mere occasion for eating and drinking. The reluctance to eat with the 'Am ha-areṣ was of a different origin; fears as to neglected tithes etc. arose (cf. Büchler, *Der Galiläisch Am-haareṣ* 162, 208). Similarly, with regard to joining the heathen at table, fear of mixed marriage came to the fore (cf. A. Wiener, *Die jüdischen Speisegesetze*, Breslau 1895, pp. 430 seq.; W. Elmslie on 'Abodah Zarah v. 5, with references there given). It is clear from the context that such joint meals did take place. But with all this there went a unique sense of obligation to the poor and the miserable. Isaiah (lviii. 7) had spoken of the duty "to bring the poor that are cast out to thy house," and from the middle of the second century B.C. it was laid down as a duty to entertain at meals "the children of the poor" (Aboth, i. 5), to which category were later added "those who were distressed in soul" (*Aboth de R. Nathan*, II. xiv.). It is not at all the case that a Pharisee would have declined to receive even "sinners" *at his own table*. But he might have refused an invitation to join them at *their* table, where the ritual and atmosphere could hardly fail to be uncongenial.

Probably the Pharisees exaggerated the force of evil example (cf. Hermas Mand. x. i. 4 against φιλίαις ἐθνικαῖς). We frequently find in the second and third centuries regulations due to a sensitive repugnance to placing oneself in a position of suspicion. (This is the meaning of some passages quoted by Dr Büchler in his essay on

"The Political and Social Leaders of the Jewish Community of Sepphoris," ch. iii. § 5.) On the other hand especial eulogy was expressed of those who defied suspicion and remained untainted in an environment of temptation (Pesachim, 113 *a*). But for the most part the Pharisees entertained an exaggerated fear both of the danger of actual moral lapse, and even more of the loss of repute from suspicion of such lapse, likely to be incurred by association with dishonest men or unchaste women. It was, however, a defensible theory of conduct, and one which most educationalists of the present day accept. We sometimes find Rabbis prepared to defy suspicion and temptation when engaged in what we now call rescue work, but such cases are rare. Moreover, as the women who were the unchaste associates of unchaste men were chiefly foreigners, the Rabbis felt no strong impulse towards putting their heads in the lions' dens.

But, to return to my main point, it is unnecessary to cite the Rabbinic passages in which men are warned of the personal dangers of associating with men or women of low morals. Some passages have already been quoted in Note VI. (Cf. also C. Taylor's Note on Aboth i. 8 [7].) Another common saying was that though the evil yeṣer of idolatry had been slain, the evil yeṣer of unchastity was very much alive (Yoma, 69 *b*; 'Aboda Zara, 17 *b*). There was much lack of courage, but less taint of self-righteousness, in the efforts of the moralist to preserve men from temptation and contagion. Luke's Pharisee who thanked God that he was not as the Publican (Luke xviii. 11) must have been an exceptional case, one of the weeds of ritualism, not one of its ordinary or natural fruits. "A familiar saying in the mouth of the Rabbis of Jabneh," says the Talmud (Berachoth, 17 *a*), "was this: I (who study the Law) am a creature (of God), and my fellow man is a creature (of God). My work is in the city, his in the field; I rise early to my work, he rises early to his. Just as he cannot excel in my work, so I cannot excel in his. Perhaps thou wilt say: I do much and he does little (for the Torah). But we have learned (Menaḥot, 110 *a*), He who offers much and he who offers little are equal, provided that each directs his heart to Heaven." The penitent publican's prayer "God be merciful to me a sinner," as well as his gesture ("he smote upon his breast") are essentially Pharisaic; it is interesting to see Luke introducing this last ritualistic touch in an attack on ritualism. The Pharisee placed the repentant sinner on a higher pedestal than the out-and-out saint (Berachoth, 34 *b*). This was expressed in another way by saying that God honours the repentant. Again, "Broken vessels are a disgrace for a man to use, but God loves the broken heart" (Midrash, Levit. Rabba, vii. 2; Mid. Tehillim on xviii. 2). A penitent publican, like any other repentant sinner (cf. the fine passage on the harlot in Philo, *On Monarchy* ii. 8), would find a ready welcome to the arms of the Rabbi. True it was held difficult for a publican to repent (Baba Qama, 94 *b*), but by *repent* is meant in the context *to make restitution.* The victims of the publican's oppression were not easily identifiable, and it was not in the sinner's power to undo the wrong which he had inflicted. Besides, the community must not connive at such plundering by manifesting over-readiness to take back payment from ill-gotten gains. The Rabbis would have scornfully rejected the cynical principle *pecunia non olet.* But though the community might decline the proferred restitution, God would accept; man might justly reject, yet the sinner must do restitution (anonymously) for God's sake. On the basis of this same passage (Baba Qama, 94—95) Maimonides thus accurately sums up the position: "If the robber wished to repent, and the thing actually stolen being no longer in existence, offered to repay the value of the stolen thing, it is an ordinance of the sages that they must not accept the money, but they *help him and pardon him,* so as to make near unto the penitent the right way; yet if one received the money from him he would not forfeit the approval of the sages" (Hilchoth גזילה, i. 13). And even though the Scripture says the opposite (Proverbs xxi. 27: "The sacrifice of the wicked is an abomination"), the gift-offerings of sinners were accepted in the Temple in order to encourage them to repent (Ḥullin, 5 *a*; Pesikta R., 192 *a*).

There was in the Pharisaism of all ages a real anxiety to make the return of the sinner easy. It was inclined to leave the initiative to the sinner, except that it always maintained *God's* readiness to take the first step. Jesus in his attitude towards sin and sinners was more inclined to take the initiative. Yet, until the modern epoch of a new humanism, society has worked by reprobation rather than attraction, and the practical methods of Western communities in dealing with criminals have been as harsh as the methods of any other system. And Rabbis did often act in the same spirit as Jesus. In the first place if a genuine Pharisee ever thanked God that he was not as the publican, he would only have done so in the spirit of the famous utterance: "There, but for the grace of God, goes John Baxter." Thus a first century Rabbi (Neḥunya ben Haqana) utters a prayer in which he contrasts the happier lot of the speaker—who frequents the house of study—and the less happy lot of someone else—who frequents theatre and circus (Berachoth, 28 *a*). This prayer is simply a grateful recognition for good fortune; it in no sense implies (except quite indirectly) that the speaker prides himself on being a better man. His lines have been cast in happier places. Such prayers and such an attitude are moreover an encouragement to right living. They aim at showing that virtue has its abundant reward in a sense of duty done and in the confident hope of future bliss. And here arises the real difficulty. Praying *for* sinners (i.e. for other people), fussy efforts at rescuing outcasts (i.e., again, other people) may come very close indeed to "pharisaic" self-righteousness. These psychological problems are so complex that they transcend the grasp of most theologians, and the latter are driven to look at the problems incompletely and therefore erroneously. One might put it generally by asserting that the Rabbis attacked vice from the preventive side; they aimed at keeping men and women honest and chaste. Jesus approached it from the curative side; he aimed at saving the dishonest and the unchaste.

The Rabbis thought that God loves the prayers of the righteous; they held that *all* the divine sympathy was not expended on the petitions of the sinner. But the association of the sinner with the righteous—in prayer and fasting—was necessary to make religion a real thing (Kerithoth, 6 *b*). And as regards actual, practical intrusion into the life of the sinner, there is much in the Rabbinic literature urging men to seek the active reclamation of the erring. "He who does not pray for his neighbour or bring him to penitence himself will suffer" (Midrash Jonah). As Maimonides puts it (on the basis of several Talmudic passages, Ber. 12 *b* etc.): "Whoever has it in his power to prevent others from sinning, yet leaves them in their stumbling, has no forgiveness" (Teshuba, iv. 2; Deoth vi.). So far does this counsel go, that the Israelite is required to press his reproof and his efforts at reclamation on the sinner though the latter revile and even strike his monitor (Erachin, 16 *b*). Thoroughly in accord with Rabbinic teaching (Sifra on Leviticus xix. 17) is the Targum rendering of that same text: "Thou shalt rebuke thy neighbour and not receive punishment for his sin" which your active reproof might have prevented. *His* sin becomes *your* sin. The parable of Moses and the stray sheep which he seeks in the desert and bears in his bosom (Midrash, Shemoth Rabba, ch. ii.) points the same moral. This idea is already found in the Psalter, "I have gone astray like a lost sheep; *seek* thy servant" (Ps. cxix. 176). So, Ps. xxxiv. 14, "Seek peace and pursue it," was held by the Rabbis to compel men to go about the world as peace-makers. Perhaps the most apt citation in this connection (the subject is further discussed in the note on Forgiveness) is the manner in which Jewish homilists set up Aaron as an ideal character. There can be no question here but that this idealisation is earlier than the Gospel criticism of the Pharisaic indifference to "sinners." We meet with its germ in Malachi ii. 6, where Levi is eulogised in the words "he did turn away many from iniquity." These words were applied specifically to Aaron (*Aboth de R. Nathan*, I. xii.), and Hillel already has the saying: "Be of the disciples of Aaron, loving peace and pursuing peace, *loving mankind, and bringing them near to the Torah*" (Mishnah Aboth, i. 12). Here is the same spirit as "the light of the law which was given to lighten every man" (*Testament of Levi*, xiv.). This "bringing men near" applies to proselytism, but in Rabbinical literature it is again and again used of active labour in rescuing sinners. Nitai the Arbelite cautioned against association with the wicked (Aboth, i. 7, on the relation between this and i. 12 see Jewish commentaries). But this was not the only view held. Aaron, we are told, would offer friendly greetings to the wicked (Joḥanan b. Zakkai, we are told, Ber. 17 *a*, punctiliously greeted heathens in the market-place), who would thus be shamed from their sin (*Aboth de R. Nathan, loc. cit.*); he would go out on the roads at night, intercept those who were about to transgress, and with soft, affectionate words of intimate comradeship, would divert them from their intention (Buber Tanḥuma, Numbers, p. 10), and thus "all Israel loved Aaron, men and women." To "bring another man near" to the Torah was to create a soul (*Aboth de R. Nathan*, II. xxvi.). This ideal, pre-Christian in Rabbinic literature, was also post-Christian. There is the oft-cited case of R. Meir (to whom was due a first draft of the Mishnah). Hard by his abode lived men who were violent criminals, and they so troubled Meir that he prayed for their extinction. But his wife Beruria checked him, and at her instigation he admitted that it was better to pray for their conversion (Berachoth, 10 *a*). Meir, it will be remembered, was noted for his persistent friendship to his heretic and sinful master and friend, Elisha ben Abuya, for whose return to the fold he so tenderly exerted himself. Even more to the present point is the conduct of R. Ze'ira. In his neighbourhood were robbers and highwaymen, but Ze'ira showed them intimate friendship, so that they might be brought to penitence, which indeed came about in their sorrow at the Rabbi's death (Sanhedrin, 37 *a*). Pathetic, too, is the idea of

R. Joshua ben Levi that the Messiah would eventually be found at the gates of Rome, among the sick poor, binding up their wounds (Sanhedrin, 98).

And so the story might be continued. The Rabbis could see the good in all men, and might exalt above those of spotless reputation one engaged in what they considered unsavoury and demoralising occupations. Gazing over the crowd, Elijah picked out as assured of the future life a jailor, who had cared for the morals of his prisoners (Ta'anith, 22 *a*). On occasion of a drought in Judæa, people reported to Abbahu that they knew a man whose prayers for rain were infallible. His popular name was Pentekaka (*lit.* the man of *Five Sins*). R. Abbahu interviewed him, inquired as to his means of livelihood, whereupon Pentekaka said that his name corresponded to his profession. "I am occupied with harlots, I clean the theatre, I carry the vessels to the bath, I amuse the bathers with my jokes, and I play the flute." But, asked the Rabbi: "Have you ever done a good thing in your life?" Pentekaka answered: "Once I was sweeping out the theatre and I saw a woman standing between the pillars, bitterly weeping. I spoke to her and ascertained that her husband was a prisoner, and she could only buy his freedom by sacrificing her chastity. So I sold my bed and my pillow and all my possessions, and I gave the money to her, bidding her go ransom her husband and not sell her honour to strangers." Hearing such words from such a man, Abbahu exclaimed: "Thou art the man fit to pray for us in our hour of trouble" (Talmud Jer. Ta'anith, i. 2).

## VIII. "GIVE UNTO CAESAR."

To Samuel of Nehardea (c. 165—c. 257 A.D.) belongs the honour of formulating the principle which made it possible for Jews from the early middle ages onwards to live under alien laws. Jeremiah had admonished his exiled brothers: "Seek ye the peace of the city whither I have caused you to be carried away captives, and pray unto the Lord for it; for in the peace thereof shall ye have peace." It grew necessary to become more explicit, and the Rabbis proclaimed a principle which was as influential with the synagogue as "Give unto Caesar that which is Caesar's" became with the Church. "The law of the government is law" (*dina d'malchutha dina*, T.B. *Baba Qama* 113 b; *Baba Bathra* 54 a; *Giṭṭin* 10 b; *Nedarim* 28 a) said Samuel, and ever since it has been a religious duty for the Jews to obey and accommodate themselves as far as possible to the laws of the country in which they are settled or reside (cf. my remarks in *Encyclopaedia Britannica*, ed. 11, vol. xv. p. 404). "To Jeremiah and Mar Samuel," says Graetz, "Judaism owes its possibility of existence in a foreign country" (*Geschichte der Juden*, IV. 2, iii.).

What Mar Samuel, however, did was not to devise a new principle, but to give that principle the precision of law. Very much in the history of civilization has depended on the power of moralists to concentrate a theory into an epigram; the sayings of Jesus and Samuel are apt illustrations. Long before Samuel, however, the same attitude prevailed. At the period of the disastrous Bar Cochba insurrection, when Roman law and Roman administration were bitterly resented, the Rabbinic teachers impressed on their brethren the absolute duty of paying the taxes imposed by the Government. According to the statement of Johanan ben Zakkai (Mechilta on Exodus xix. 1, ed. Friedmann, p. 61 b top) the Romans, after the destruction of the Temple, imposed the enormous tax of fifteen shekels; and though the exact significance of this is doubtful, it may have been a tax on leases; we know that the Roman imposts were very considerable (cf. Büchler, *The Economic Conditions of Judæa after the destruction of the Second Temple*, 1912, pp. 62 seq.). Yet it was held obligatory to pay these taxes with the utmost scrupulosity, in so far as they were lawfully imposed, and were not the whimsical exactions of the publicans (T.B. *Baba Qama* 113 a; *Nedarim* 28 a; Tosefta, *Nedarim* iii. 4; *Semaḥ* ii. 9 where evasion of taxation is denounced as equivalent even to murder, idolatry, incest, and profanation of the Sabbath).

Nor does the evidence extend only to the Hadrianic period. It goes back even further. On the text in Ecclesiastes viii. 2 ("I counsel thee, Keep the king's command, and that in regard of the oath of God"), the Midrash (Tanḥuma on Genesis viii. 16, *Noah* § 10; ed. Buber, p. 33) comments thus: "The Holy One said unto Israel, I adjure you that even though the (Roman) Government decrees against you harsh decrees ye shall not rebel against it for anything that it decrees, but keep the king's command. But if it decrees against you to abandon the Torah and the commandments and deny God, then do not obey it, but say unto it: I keep the king's laws only in those things which are necessary for the government." The Midrash goes on to cite the conduct of Daniel's three friends who assure Nebuchadnezzar: "In so far as duties and taxes are concerned, in all that thou decreest upon us, we will obey, and thou art our king, but to deny God—we have no need to answer thee in this matter...we will not serve thy gods, nor worship the golden image which thou hast set up" (Daniel viii. 16). The difficulty of this compromise was twofold. First, bad government is incompatible with the Kingdom of God (Schechter, *Some Aspects of Rabbinic Theology*, p. 106), and the Roman Government was often deserving of inclusion in the category of bad government. Secondly, the tendency of Roman emperors to assert their divine status, and to found their authority on a theory somewhat approaching that of divine right, made Roman rule in general obnoxious to Jewish sentiment. Nevertheless, as Tacitus admits, the Jews were long patient under the irritation; they rebelled only when chronic irritation was transformed into specific provocation: "Duravit tamen patientia Judæis usque ad Gessium Florum procuratorem; sub eo bellum ortum." That occurred in the spring of 66 A.D. Some of the previous procurators had so far studied Jewish susceptibilities as to strike (probably employing Jewish workmen) coins of special designs for local circulation in Judæa. There were on these no figures of animate objects, but only ears of corn, palm-trees or branches (?), the cornucopia, diota, covered vase, or wreath. In 35 A.D. Pontius Pilate struck coins decorated simply with the laurel wreath and the lituus or augur's wand (T. Reinach, *Jewish Coins*, ed. Hill, p. 41). At a much later period we find a Rabbi (Naḥum b. Simai) described as remarkable for his "holiness" because "he never looked upon the form of a coin" (*Pesaḥim* 104a and parallels in Bacher, *Agada der Palästinensischen Amoräer* III. 616); this probably refers, however, to coins on which were figures of the emperors.

Very clearly belonging to the period of the Vespasian war is the saying recorded in the Mishnah, *Aboth* iii. 2. The authority cited is Ḥaninah (Ḥananiah), the prefect of the priests, who was a contemporary of Joḥanan ben Zakkai, and like him a member of the peace party. "Pray for the peace of the kingdom," said Ḥaninah, "since but for the fear thereof men would swallow one another alive." This may allude specifically to public prayer on behalf of the ruler (see Ezra vi. 10; Baruch i. 11; I. Macc. vii. 33; Philo, *Leg. ad Caium*, xxiii., xlv.; Josephus, *War* II. x. 4; T.B. *Yoma* 69a; I. Timothy ii. 1, 2, and cf. Schürer ii. § 24; Singer, *Transactions of the Jewish Historical Society of England* iv. 103). It is interesting to add a conjecture made by Dr Bacher. We have no record of the precise liturgical phraseology of the prayer for the Government unless Dr Bacher has discovered it in the *Aboth de Rabbi Nathan* (II. ch. xxxi. p. 68, ed. Schechter). By a slight emendation of the text, the words of the prayer would be: "May it (the Roman Government) rule over us for all time" (שתהא שולטת בנו כל הימים Bacher, *Agada der Tannaiten*, ed. 2, vol. i. p. 52).

But though thus prepared to obey Rome and abide by all its lawful regulations, there was to be no compromise when Caesar infringed the sphere which appertained to God. This distinction we have already seen in the Midrash, but we find the same very clearly expressed in the pages of history. Josephus records several instances of the readiness of the Jews to suffer death rather than admit the images of Caesar (e.g. *War* II. ix. 3). Most nearly illustrative of the subject before us is the passage in which the historian describes what took place when Caius Caesar (who succeeded Tiberius as emperor in 37 A.D.) sent Petronius with an army to Jerusalem to place his statues in the Temple; he was to slay any who opposed this step, and to enslave the rest of the nation (*War* II. x. 1). Petronius marched from Antioch southwards towards Judæa; but when he reached Ptolemais in Galilee he was met by a deputation of Jews. Prevailed upon by the multitude of the supplicants, he summoned a meeting of all the men of note to Tiberias, where he declared unto them the power of the Romans and the threatenings of Caius, and also pronounced their petition unreasonable. "For as all the nations subject to Rome had placed the images of the emperor in their several cities among the rest of their gods, for them alone to oppose it was like the behaviour of rebels, and was insulting to the emperor." Josephus then proceeds as follows, and the passage may usefully be cited in full (§§ 4, 5):—

And when they insisted on their law, and the custom of their country, and how it was not lawful for them to put even an image of God, much less of a man, in any profane part of their country, much less in the Temple, Petronius replied, "And am I not also bound to keep the law of my lord? For, if I transgress it and spare you, I shall justly perish. And he that sent me, and not I, will war against you; for I am under command as well as you." Thereupon the whole multitude cried out that "they were ready to suffer for their Law." Petronius then tried to quiet their noise, and said to them, "Will you then make war against the Emperor?" The Jews said that they offered sacrifices twice every day for the emperor and the Roman people; but if he would set up his statues, he must first sacrifice the whole Jewish nation; and they were ready to expose themselves to be slain with their children and wives. At this Petronius felt both astonishment and pity on account of their invincible regard to their religion, and their courage which made them ready to die for it.

Petronius yielded, and incurred the censure of Caius, but the latter's death in 41 intervened to save him from the consequences of his complacency to the Jewish steadfastness towards their God, and his own disobedience towards Caesar. Philo (*Leg. ad Caium* xxxii., xxxvi.) narrates the same circumstances at greater length; but he, too, records that the Jews willingly and even enthusiastically accepted the sovereignty of Caius, in all matters except the proposed "innovations in respect of our Temple;...the honour of the emperor is not identical with dishonour to the ancient laws (of Judaism)." Caius well represents the opposite case when he retorts (xliv.): "Ye are haters of God, in that ye deny me the appellation of a god," though he was generous enough to attribute this blindness to the Jews as a misfortune rather than as a fault: "These men do not appear to me to be wicked so much as unfortunate and foolish, in not believing that I have been endowed with the nature of God." This misfortune and unwisdom the Jews never abandoned, and thus were always protagonists in the refusal to give unto Caesar that which is God's.

## IX. JEWISH DIVORCE IN THE FIRST CENTURY[1].

Social conditions in Palestine at the beginning of the Christian era were bewilderingly complex. Restricting our attention to the question of marriage, we find at the one extreme a sect (the Essenes) which advocated celibacy, and possibly at the other a sect (the Zadokites) which forbade divorce, or at all events remarriage. Then there were the aristocrats of the court circle who had adopted Roman ways. For instance, Josephus records two instances in which women of the Herodian house (Salome, 25 B.C., and Herodias, contemporary with John the Baptist) divorced their husbands, and paralleled the excesses denounced by Juvenal in his sixth satire (Mark x. 12 may be directed against such licentiousness). The Pharisaic Judaism of the same period regarded marriage as the ideal state, yet freely permitted divorce. If the ideal were shattered it seemed to accord best with the interests of morality to admit this, and afford both parties to the calamity a second chance of lawful happiness. The marriage bond should be inviolable, but must not be indissoluble.

The progress of law and custom in Jewry tended not to modify the theoretical ease of divorce, but to increase its practical difficulties. The Gospel view was that the Deuteronomic divorce was a concession to human weakness, a lowering of the earlier standards of Genesis which held marriage to be indissoluble. The Rabbinic reading of history was different. The Pentateuch introduced the formality of the written

[1] This Note was written at short notice, to comply with the urgent request of the late Lord Gorell, Chairman of the Royal Commission on Divorce and Matrimonial Causes. The Note was presented to the Commission, and the author was examined on November 21, 1910. I received valuable help from Dr M. Berlin. For various reasons it seems best to leave the Note without substantial change. Hence it is impossible to allude to the interesting views of Prof. L. Blau published in 1911—1912. In his *Jüdische Ehescheidung und der jüdische Scheidebrief*, pages 45—72 of Part I are devoted to an exposition of the New Testament passages on Divorce, with Rabbinic and other parallels.

Letter of Divorce, and Rabbinism regarded this as an advance in civilization, not a retrogression. The Deuteronomic divorce was a restriction of the earlier right or power of the husband to discard his wife at will and with scant ceremony. Rabbinism contrasted the decent formalities of the Mosaic Code with the arbitrary indelicacy of primitive custom (Genesis Rabba ch. xviii.).

The Pentateuch, however, contemplates the husband as alone having the right to effect a divorce. In the Babylonian Code of Hammurabi the wife had some power of initiative, and when recently the Egyptian papyri of the fifth century B.C. were discovered, it was thought that these Aramaic documents showed the Jewish woman in possession of the same status as man in regard to initiating divorce. Closer study, however, shows that at most the woman of the papyri could *claim* a divorce, she could not *declare* one. This condition remained unaltered in the first Christian century. Josephus (*Antiq.* xv. viii. 7) distinctly asserts: "With us it is lawful for the husband to do so (*i.e.* dissolve a marriage), but a wife, if she departs from her husband, cannot marry another, unless her former husband put her away." In two cases the husband's right of divorce was abrogated by the Pentateuch (Deut. xxii.), if he ravished a virgin or if he falsely accused his wife of ante-nuptial incontinence. In the first case the man was compelled to wed the woman in an indissoluble union, in the second case he could not divorce his wife. In later Rabbinic law a divorce if pronounced was technically valid; the Biblical law, however, does not deal with such a case, and the wife was immune from divorce. But what was her position? The option rested with her. She could compel her husband to retain her, or she could accept a divorce. Philo declares (ii. 313 καὶ μένειν τε ἀπαλλάττεσθαι, this last word being Philonean for divorce) that she could divorce him, but it is not probable that the law ever agreed with Philo's view. At most the injured wife may have been entitled to move the court to compel her husband to write her a Letter of Divorce. The situation reminds one of Meredith's *Diana of the Crossways.*

We are in possession of a clear piece of evidence as to the Jewish progress in divorce law in the period preceding the Christian era. In Matthew xix. 10 the disciples after hearing Jesus' declaration on the indissolubility of marriage, object: "If the case of the man is so with his wife, it is not expedient to marry." Here, the difficulty of divorce is treated as a bar to wedlock. This is the man's point of view. What of the woman's? Now in the first century B.C. it would seem that,

5—2

from the woman's side, the facility of divorce was a bar. In face of the ease with which a husband could whistle off his wife, women refused to contract marriages, and men grew grey and celibate (T. J. Kethuboth, end of ch. viii.; T. B. Kethuboth 82b, Tosefta xii.). Thereupon the Pharisaic leader, Simon b. Sheṭaḥ, the reputed brother of Queen Alexandra, enacted that the wife's *Kethubah* or marriage settlement was to be merged in the husband's estate, that he might use it as capital, but that his entire fortune, even such property of his as had passed into other hands, should be held liable for it. This effectively checked hasty divorce (cf. 'Erubin 41 b), and indeed the rights of wives under the Kethubah were throughout the ages a genuine safeguard to their marital security. In respect to holding property and possessing independent estate the Jewish wife was in a position far superior to that of English wives before the enactment of recent legislation.

Another point of great importance was this. Jewish sentiment was strongly opposed to the divorce of the wife of a man's youth, and men almost invariably married young. The facilities for divorce seem mostly to have been applied or taken advantage of in the case of a widower's second marriage (a widower was expected to remarry). "What the Lord hath joined, let no man put asunder" represented the spirit of the Pharisaic practice in the age of Jesus, at all events with regard to a man's first marriage. It is rather curious that while in the Gospel so much use is made of the phrase of Genesis "one flesh" to prove marriage indissoluble, no reference is made to another verse in the same context "It is not good that the man should be alone" which obviously requires marriage and not celibacy. It may be that Jesus, anticipating the near approach of the Kingdom, was teaching an "interim" ethic, which would have no relation to ordinary conditions of life (cf. the view that Angels do not marry Enoch xv. 3—7, Mark xii. 25 and the later Rabbinic maxim that in the world to come there is no procreation (Berachoth 17a)). But it is more likely that he was laying down a rule of conduct only for his own immediate disciples, declaring that "all men cannot receive this saying." That, however, a belief in the divinity of the marriage tie was compatible with a belief that the tie could be loosened, is shown by the course of Jewish opinion. The Rabbis held with Jesus that marriages are made in heaven (see *Jewish Quarterly Review*, II. 172), and several Old Testament phrases point to the same roseate view. Of the marriage of Isaac and Rebecca it is written "the thing proceedeth from the Lord" (Gen. xxiv. 50). "Houses and Riches are the inheritance of fathers," says the author of Proverbs

(xix. 14), "but a prudent wife is from the Lord." Again, "Fear not," said the Angel to Tobias (Tobit vi. 17), "for she was prepared for thee from the beginning." The Pharisees fully accepted this amiable theory of divine fatalism. "God," said the Rabbi, "sitteth in heaven arranging marriages." Or it was more crudely put thus: "Forty days before the child is formed a heavenly voice proclaims its mate" (T. B. Moed Qaton 18b; Soṭa 2a). In the Middle Ages, belief in the divine arrangement of marriage affected the liturgy, and on the sabbath following a wedding, the bridegroom proceeded to the synagogue with a joyous retinue, and the congregation chanted the chapter of Genesis (xxiv.) in which, as shown above, the patriarch's marriage was declared as ordained by God. Naturally this belief in the pre-ordainment of marriage must have strengthened the Jewish objection to divorce. "For I hate divorce, saith the Lord" (Malachi ii. 16) was a verse much honoured in Pharisaic thought, and Malachi's protest gave rise to the pathetic saying: "The very altar sheds tears when a man divorces the wife of his youth," and to the sterner paraphrase "He that putteth her away is hated of the Lord" (T. B. Giṭṭin 90. Cf. Prov. v. 19; Eccles. ix. 9; Ecclus. vii. 26, yet see also xxv. 26).

But though divorce is hateful, continuance of the marriage bond may be more hateful still. Perfect human nature could do without divorce, but it could also do without marriage. Adam and Eve, it has been well said, went through no marriage ceremony. The formalities of marriage are not less the result of human imperfection than is the need of divorce. Were it not for the evil in human nature, said the Rabbis (Gen. Rab. ix.; Eccles. R. iii. 11), a man would not marry a wife—not that the married state was evil, on the contrary, it was held to be the highest moral condition—but the passions which are expressed in the marital relationship are also expressed in the lower lusts. We may also perhaps read another idea into this Rabbinic conception. X needed the marriage bond to limit his own lusts and also to ward off Y. And just as, in this sense, man's evil side requires a marriage contract, so in another sense his good side demands the cancellation of the contract, if its continuance be degrading or inharmonious.

Hence, though the strongest moral objection was felt against divorce, and though the vast majority of Jewish marriages were terminated only by death, the Pharisaic law raised no bar to divorce by mutual consent of the parties, just as marriage, despite its sacred associations, was itself a matter of mutual consent. It should be remembered that in the Jewish document of divorce no ground for the act is defined, the husband simply declares his wife thenceforth *sui juris* and free to re-marry. She could, and often did, re-marry her husband, unless he had divorced her for unchastity, or unless she had in the meantime contracted another marriage. In the time of Jesus it was not necessary for a divorce by mutual consent to come before a regular court or Beth Din of three Rabbis, as later became the practice. The whole ceremony could, at the earlier period, be gone through privately, in the presence of two witnesses. An expert Rabbi was, however, probably required to ensure the proper drawing up of the document, and the due fulfilment of the legal delivery to, and acceptance by, the wife. Thus if Joseph of Nazareth and his betrothed bride had mutually consented to a divorce, there is no reason in Jewish law why he should not have "put her away privily" (Matthew i. 19). There is little ground for thinking that such divorces by mutual consent were either frequent or productive of social evils, though it may be that the woman's assent was occasionally extorted by harsh measures. But though the Rabbis could oppose no legal bar to divorce by mutual consent, it was their duty to exhaust every possible expedient of moral dissuasion. Aaron, in Hillel's phrase (Aboth i. 12), was the type of the peace-maker, and this was traditionally explained (Aboth de R. Nathan, ch. xii.) to mean that his life-work was, in part, the reconciliation of estranged husbands and wives (see above, Note VII).

But the case was different when one of the parties to the divorce was unwilling to assent, or when one party had something to gain by treating the other party as unwilling. From the eleventh century it has been customary in Jewish law to require that in all cases the wife shall assent to the divorce, except where her misconduct or failure could be shown to be sufficient cause why the marriage might be forcibly dissolved by the husband. But this condition of the woman's assent was not necessary at the beginning of the Christian era, when neither Rabbinic sanction nor the wife's consent was obligatory. The rule in the first century was (Yebamoth xiv. 1): "A woman may be divorced with or without her will, but a man only with his will." If, however, the wife contested the divorce, it is highly probable that the husband had to specify his reasons and bring the matter before a regularly constituted Beth Din. This was certainly the case if he suspected her of adultery (Sota i. 3—4). The accusing husband took his wife before the local Beth Din or court of three, and after a first hearing two Rabbis would conduct the accused to the Supreme Court in Jerusalem, which alone could deal finally with such charges. If she confessed, she forfeited her marriage settlement and was divorced; otherwise the ordeal of the waters (Numbers v.) was applied. We may well suppose that in other cases, especially such as involved a stigma on the wife, the matter would be made a matter of public inquiry if she so claimed. It is only thus that we can fully explain the different views taken at the early period as to lawful grounds of divorce. The schools of Hillel and Shammai differed materially (Giṭṭin, end): the former gave the husband the legal right to divorce his wife for any cause. Cf. Matthew xix. 3, Josephus *Antiq.* IV. viii. 23 ("for any cause whatsoever"). Philo uses similar language (Spec. Laws, Adultery, ch. v.). The school of Shammai limited the right to the case in which the wife was unchaste. The "schools" or "houses" of Hillel and Shammai belong to the first century. It is uncertain whether this particular difference of opinion on divorce goes back to Hillel and Shammai themselves, and thus to the very beginning of the Christian era. It is barely possible that the teaching of Jesus on the subject led to further discussion in the Pharisaic schools, and that the rigid attitude of Jesus influenced the school of Shammai. This, however, is altogether improbable, for the view of the latter school is derived from Deuteronomy (xxiv. 1) by a process which closely accords with the usual exegetical methods of the Shammaites. Matthew v. 32 (as the text now stands) with its λόγου πορνείας is certainly derived from the school of Shammai, for the text of Deut. xxiv. 1 reads ערות דבר, and it was the school of Shammai who turned the words round into דבר ערוה (Giṭṭin ix: 10), which corresponds in order with the text of Matthew. Hillel's language: "even if she spoiled his food," is of course figurative, and may point to indecent conduct, a sense which similar metaphors sometimes bear. Hillel was a teacher noted for his tender humaneness; it was he who popularised in Pharisaic circles the negative form of the Golden Rule before Jesus stated it positively. Hence, it is not just to speak of his view on divorce as "lax" or "low," even if (as no doubt later Rabbinic authority assumed) Hillel used this forcible language to preserve as inalienable the ancient norm that a husband possessed complete right to divorce his wife for any cause. For it must be observed that his "lax" and "low" view of divorce was also a more rigid and elevated view as to the necessity of absolute harmony in the marriage state. Still, his view (or its interpretation) did produce a condition of subjection in the woman's status, and left room for much arbitrariness on the part of the husband. Yet 'Aqiba who went beyond Hillel in maintaining the husband's arbitrary powers ("even if he find another woman more beautiful"), was in fact no friend of divorce, for he applied the severest rules in estimating the pecuniary rights of the wife under the marriage settlement. "Sell the hair of your head to pay it," said 'Aqiba (Nedarim ix. 5) to a would-be divorcer who complained that the payment of the heavy demands of the settlement would impoverish him. As D. Amram in his excellent book on the subject of *The Jewish Law of Divorce* (Philadelphia, 1896) puts it, neither Hillel nor 'Aqiba was making law, they were stating it, "regardless of their personal views or opinions" (p. 37). It is true, however, that their statement of the law helped to make and perpetuate it for future times. The injurious effect was much mitigated, though never theoretically removed, by subsequent modifications. We can trace the gradual incidence of restraining enactments and customs. Already in the year 40 A.D. we find various reforms introduced by Gamaliel, who ordained *e.g.* that the *Geṭ* or divorce letter must be subscribed by the witnesses, and withdrew from the husband the right to cancel the *Geṭ* unless the wife or her attorney were present (Giṭṭin iv. 2). Such cancellation was made before Gamaliel's reform; the husband would locally constitute a Beth-din of three Rabbis *ad hoc*. Though, as stated above, the divorce itself needed no Court, many questions (as to settlements etc.) arising out of the divorce would have to be brought before the Beth-din.

There were, indeed, certain grounds on which husband or wife could claim the help of the Court in effecting a divorce against the other's will. In all such cases, where the wife was concerned as the moving party, she could only demand that her husband should divorce her; the divorce was always, from first to last, in Jewish law the husband's act. The matter was not, however, always left to the parties themselves. "Joseph being a righteous man, and not willing to expose her to shame, determined to divorce her secretly." This implies that Joseph had no option as to discarding his wife. Cf. Montefiore, *Synoptic Gospels*, p. 454. This work contains an excellent analysis of the various Gospel passages on divorce, see pages 235—242, 454, 508—510, 688—692, 1000—1. To return, if the husband suspected his wife of unchastity while betrothed to him, he was compelled, as a "righteous man," to divorce her (betrothal was so binding that divorce was necessary to free a betrothed couple). His only option was between divorcing his bride privately with her consent, or formulating a charge of infidelity against her, thus subjecting her to public disgrace as well as divorce. Divorce was not in itself a disgrace, seeing that it might occur on grounds involving no moral stigma. The case was aggravated by the circumstance that Mary was with child, until Joseph, in Matthew's account, received the assurance that his whole suspicion was erroneous. The wisdom books and the Rabbinic doctors agreed in regarding adultery as peculiarly heinous when it resulted in the birth of a child (Ecclus. xxiii. 23, Ḥagiga i. 7). The offence was a three-fold sin: against God, against the husband, against the family (Hamburger, *Real-Encyclopädie des Judenthums* I. 258). In Jewish law adultery was the intercourse of a married woman with *any* man other than her husband. Though his conduct was severely reprobated, and at all events in later centuries gave his wife a right to claim a divorce, a man was not regarded as guilty of adultery unless he had intercourse with a *married* woman other than his wife. For though monogamy had become the prevalent custom in Jewish life long before the Christian era (cf. *Jewish Encyclopedia*, VIII. p. 657), the man could legally marry several wives, and sometimes did so. Thus an unmarried and unbetrothed woman with whom a married man had intercourse might become his wife; indeed such intercourse could be legally construed into a marriage. By the Pentateuchal law the penalty for adultery was death.

But this law can never have been frequently enforced. It needed eye-witnesses (hence the "taken in the very act" of John viii. 4). Moreover, as Dr Büchler has pointed out, the husband would hesitate to charge his wife, and the detected adulterer would offer heavy compensation to save his own life which was forfeit. The husband could privately divorce his wife, she naturally losing all her rights under the marriage settlement. A charge of adultery would have to be public, and tried before the central court. It is not probable that the death penalty for adultery was inflicted at all in the age of Jesus. The Jewish courts had lost the general power of capital punishment in the year 30 A.D. (T. J. Sanh. 18 a, T.B. 41 a). The Mishnah cites a single case which would fall within the age of Jesus, but it does so doubtfully (Sanh. vii. 2), and Josephus' casual assertion that the penalty for adultery was death is rather an antiquarian note than a record of experience (Apion ii. 25). On the other hand it would seem that the ordeal of the bitter waters, as applied in case of suspected adultery of the wife, was still prevalent, for the Mishnah records (Soṭa ix. 9) that the ceremony was only abolished during the Roman invasion (circa 70 A.D.), though Queen Helena of Adiabene—a proselyte to Judaism in the first century A.D.—sought to restore the practice (Yoma iii. 10, Tosefta Yoma ii. 3). It is interesting to note that 'Aqiba—whose view on divorce was so "lax"—nobly said of the ordeal: "Only when the (accusing) husband is himself free from guilt will the waters be an effective test of his wife's guilt or innocence" (Sifre, Nasô 21; Soṭa 47 b). With this may be usefully compared the fine utterance (John viii. 7): "He that is without sin among you, let him first cast a stone at her" (*Jewish Encyclopedia*, I. 217; Hastings, *Encyclopaedia of Religion*, I. 130, from my article there I have taken some passages). The abolition of the ordeal is attributed by the Mishnah to the great prevalence of adultery, and it may be that, just as on the inroad of Hellenism some unsettlement of native morals occurred in the towns and among the wealthy (this being all that the attacks on harlotry and unchastity in the Wisdom Literature implies), so in the disturbed conditions due to the Roman régime a temporary laxity of morals intruded itself. The Rabbis held adultery in the utmost detestation. Not all a man's other virtues could save the adulterer from Gehenna (T. B. Soṭa 4 b). Unchastity drives away from man the Divine Presence which dwells only in the chaste soul. It is impossible, however, to attempt to collect here the mass of Pharisaic maxims against such offences. In the year 135 A.D., at the crisis of the disastrous revolt against Hadrian, a meeting was held at Lydda. The assembly was attended by several famous Rabbis (including 'Aqiba), and the question was discussed as to the extent of conformity with Roman demands which might justifiably be made rather than face the alternative of death. The result is a remarkable testimony to Jewish abhorrence of unchastity. It was decided (Sanh. 74 a) that every Jew must surrender his life rather than commit any of the three offences: idolatry, murder, or *gillui 'arāyoth*, a phrase which includes both adultery and incest.

The penalty for proven adultery, when the capital punishment was abolished, was mitigated into the divorce of the woman (the husband having no option); the wife also lost all her rights under the marriage contract, and was not permitted to marry her paramour (Soṭa v. 1). The husband could, nay must, divorce her on suspicion, but her settlements would be intact. It would therefore be to his advantage sometimes to prefer a public charge against her. The male adulterer was scourged, but was not compelled to divorce his own wife unless she insisted. In general, when the Mishnah speaks of "compelling" the husband to execute a Bill of Divorce, the Court could scourge, fine, imprison, and excommunicate him, and had practically unlimited power to force him to deliver the necessary document freeing his wife. By a legal fiction which undeniably had moral justification, the act would still be described as voluntary on the husband's part. But in case of his determined contumely, there would be no redress, as the Court could not of its own motion dissolve a marriage, though it could pronounce a marriage *ab initio* void. The secular courts might be used to enforce the desire of the Beth-din (Giṭṭin ix. 8). But the Beth-din could not be induced to return the compliment, and validate a divorce pronounced in a Roman Court (Giṭṭin i. 5). For the whole tenour of Jewish divorce depended on the theory that divorce was the act only and solely of the husband, and no Beth-din could validate a divorce which was the act of any court, and not of the husband, in the prescribed forms. Moreover, on matters affecting marriage and divorce the Jewish courts would be most jealous of external interference. In modern times, however, the London Beth-din would refuse to sanction or validate a divorce which had not been previously effected in the civil courts of the country.

Other consequences followed from the theory that divorce was the willing act of the husband. The divorce of the insane husband of a sane wife would be impossible (Yebamoth xiv. 1), as he could not execute the deed of divorce. Nor could the insane wife of a sane husband be divorced by him, because she stood in all the greater need of his protection. (If the insanity were proved to have existed before marriage, the marriage could be pronounced initially void, for the marriage of the insane was illegal.) It should here be pointed out that though the sane husband could divorce his sane wife on a variety of grounds, and in the first century could do so without the intermediation of a Court, he could not secure himself against the divorced wife's claims for maintenance unless he satisfied the Court that the divorce had been properly executed, and that the wife's just rights had been satisfied. In that sense, the Courts would have a power to revise his personal acts, even in the early period under review. Apart also from legal duties, the husband was expected to show every possible considerateness to his divorced wife. She was, of course, no longer under his jurisdiction, she was *sui juris*, and her husband lost the usufruct of her estate. This last fact was a constant preventive of arbitrary divorce (T. B. Pesahim 113 b). But the husband was expected, as a humane son of Israel, to save his divorced wife from penury. "It is related of Rabbi José the Galilean (about 100 A.D.), that after his divorced wife had remarried and was reduced to poverty, he invited her and her husband into his house and supported them, although when she was his wife she had made his life miserable, and his conduct is the subject of Rabbinical laudation. 'Do not withdraw from thy flesh,' said Isaiah (lviii. 7); this, Rabbi Jacob bar Aḥa interpreted to mean, 'Do not withdraw help from thy divorced wife'" (Amram, *op. cit.* p. 110). If the divorced woman retained charge of infant children, the former husband not only had to maintain her, but he was also required to pay her for her services. But, in general, as to the custody of the children, the regulations were extremely favourable to the wife, who was treated with every conceivable generosity. These regulations, however, except as concerned the infant up to the time of weaning, were not formulated so early as the first century. It is clear that a husband was very reluctant to divorce his wife if she were also the mother of his children. Though it was held a duty to divorce an "evil woman"—an incurable scold and disturber of the domestic peace—nevertheless if she were a mother, the husband would waive his right and endure his fate as best he might ('Erubin 41 b).

We have already seen that the insane husband was incompetent to deliver a Bill of Divorce. In certain other cases of disease—though not of mere infirmity—the wife could claim a divorce. If she became deaf-mute after the marriage, he could divorce her; if he contracted the same defects he could not divorce her (Yebamoth xiv.). If the husband fell a victim to leprosy the wife could claim a divorce, and in the second century the Courts could enforce a separation in such cases against the will of the parties, unless the latter satisfied the authorities that there would be no continuance of sexual intercourse. The wife could claim a divorce in other cases of loathsome disease, as well as when the husband engaged in unsavoury occupations which rendered cohabitation unreasonably irksome (Kethuboth vii. 9). In those cases the wife retained her settlements. The husband could divorce the wife with loss of her settlements if she transgressed against the moral and ritual laws of Judaism, and some Rabbis of the first century held that the same rule applied if the wife made herself notorious by her indelicate conduct in public. If he became impoverished and unable, or if he were unwilling, to support her adequately, if he denied to her conjugal rights, she could by rules adopted at various times claim the right to her freedom (Kethuboth v. 8—9), indeed such treatment on his part was a breach of the contract made in the marriage deed. Similar rights accrued to the wife—some of these concessions belong to a considerably later period—if he restricted her liberty, if he became an apostate, if he committed a crime which compelled him to fly the country, if he violently and persistently ill-treated her, if he refused marital rights, and if he were openly licentious in his life. In case of desertion, the wife could not obtain a divorce; though, in order to presume his death, the Court would waive some of its usual strictness as to the reception of evidence. If the whereabouts of the husband were known, the local Court would use every effort to compel him to return or grant a divorce. The excellence of intercommunication between Jewish settlements would enable the Court to trace him. But the Court could not grant a divorce to the wife if the husband had merely vanished and left no trace, unless they saw valid ground for presuming death. The persecutions, to which the Jews were subjected, compelled many men to leave home in search of a livelihood, and in the Middle Ages, out of love and consideration for his wife, the husband would sometimes give her a *conditional* divorce which would become effective if he failed to appear within a stated term. It is said that in ancient times a Jewish soldier, on going to active service, delivered such a divorce which would be valid if he died on the field. The effect would be to save his widow from the levirate marriage, from which as a divorcee she was free. In course of time the position of the woman was continuously improved, generation after generation of Rabbinical jurists endeavouring to secure to her an ever greater measure of justice and generosity.

The wife's barrenness, after ten years' married life, was a ground for divorce (Yebamoth 64 a); later on it was disputed whether the Court should leave the man to follow his own feeling in the matter, or whether it should *compel* him to divorce his wife, or alternatively (in countries where monogamy was not demanded by law) marry an additional wife. Philo gives us reason to think that at the earlier period husbands were reluctant to make use of their power to divorce a barren wife. But childless marriages were regarded as a failure, and the point gave much trouble at various epochs. It was a religious duty to beget offspring, this was the fundamental purpose of marriage. We very rarely come across a celibate among the well-known Pharisees. Ben-'Azzai (Tos. Yebamoth viii. 4, Soṭa 4 b etc., cf. *J. E.* II. 672) was a rare exception. He belongs to the beginning of the second century, and he remained unmarried though he denounced celibacy. When a colleague remonstrated with him, pointing out the inconsistency between his conduct and his doctrine, Ben-'Azzai replied: "What shall I do? My soul clings in love to the Torah (Law); let others contribute to the preservation of the race." But it was not believed that this prime duty to society could be vicariously performed, and every Jew was expected to be a father. The act of sexual intercourse was consciously elevated by this view from an animal function to a fulfilment of the divine plan announced at the Creation.

From this brief summary it will be seen that the Jewish law of divorce must be judged in relation to the general principles of social and domestic ethics. Rules for marriage and divorce cannot be appreciated apart from many other factors. Jewish teaching and training were directed towards producing moral sobriety, continence, purity. It did this by word and deed, by formulating moral maxims and fostering moral habits. Society usually attacks the problem at the wrong end; it penalises marital offences instead of making those offences rare. The ancient Synagogue dealt with the youth and maid in the formative period of their lives. The Jewish law of divorce applied to a society of firm domestic solidarity, it was the law of a society in which young marriages predominated, and the contracting parties entered into a life-long wedlock straight from a pious and virtuous home, a home in which harmony and happiness were the rule, and the relations between husband, wife and children were distinguished by a rarely equalled and never surpassed serenity and reverence. As a saying (certainly not later than the first century) runs (Yebamoth 62 b): "Our masters have taught, He who loves his wife as himself, and honours her more than himself; who leads his sons and daughters in the straight path, and marries them near their time of maturity;—to his house the words of Job apply (v. 24): Thou shalt know that thy tent is in peace." With much of this ideal the modern world has lost sympathy, but the Judaism of the first century maintained it, and built on it a moral structure which stands high among the manifold attempts to erect an effective discipline of life.

## X. WIDOWS' HOUSES.

That in all ages, and not inconspicuously in our own, men are tempted to make undue use of their influence over wealthy women in the cause of religious institutions is a familiar fact. In the second century, in Sepphoris, the women resented the duty of supporting scholars (*Baraitha* in *Pesaḥim* 49 b). But, on the other hand, we have the testimony of Jerome that Jewish women were not only among the regular performers of this obligation, but were eulogised by him on this very ground, "Ex quo apparet eum de aliis sanctis dixisse mulieribus, quae *juxta morem Judaicum* magistris de sua substantia ministrabant, sicut legimus ipsi quoque Domino factitatum" (*Adversus Jovinianum* i. 277; cf. A. Büchler, *Sepphoris*, p. 75).

These last words of Jerome are a striking reminder of the unequal measure with which the Pharisees and their opponents are judged, not by Jerome but by more recent writers. The influence exercised by the early preachers of the Gospel over women is well attested, and held the reverse of blameworthy. When, then, Josephus complains of the "great influence over women" which a certain Pharisaic faction possessed (*Antiq.* XVII. ii. 4), it is scarcely just to endorse his condemnation, or to forget two points: (*a*) he distinctly speaks of a faction only (μόριον), carefully avoiding the word by which he usually designates the main body of the Pharisees (αἱρέσεις); (*b*) his animosity is directed against the *political* activity of this faction, who committed what to Josephus was the height of iniquity, in that "when all the rest of the people gave assurance by oath of their good-will to the Emperor and to the King's government, these very men would not swear, who were more than 6000; and when the King imposed a fine upon them, Pheroras' wife paid the fine for them."

Moreover, it must be remembered that such charges were part of the ordinary invective of controversy. In the Psalms of Solomon (see particularly Ps. iv.) the Pharisees themselves make a very similar attack on the Sadducees. In the Assumption of Moses, again, the Pharisaic author (vii. 6) assails either the zealots of his own order or the priestly caste in the words that they are "devourers of the goods of the poor," saying they do so out of mercy (misericordiam, according to Charles the word means *justice*). Colani's contention that this last phrase is to be explained by the decree of the Sanhedrin (Kethuboth 50 a) in the second century forbidding a man to give more than one-fifth of his fortune and income to the poor is monstrous. The decree of the Sanhedrin was due to the excessive generosity which led men to impoverish themselves in the cause of charity, with perhaps (as Dr Kohler ingeniously suggests) some intentional opposition to the Essenic communism and to such ideas as Matthew xix. 21 (*J. E.* III. p. 668). The Talmûd gives the former reason, and in any event the expression "devourers of the goods of the poor" cannot be explained by any such incident. Dr Charles thinks the Sadducees are attacked; if so, one must not assume that the attack of their critics was just. The poor no doubt often felt the pressure of the taxes imposed on them, and there is a late Midrash (Shoḥar Ṭob on Ps. i., cf. Yalquṭ) in which a biting satire is put into the mouth of Korah. He adduces the case of a widow who is deprived of her crops and sheep by the many demands made on her slender resources by the priests. Certainly the Pharisees were themselves the most severe critics of the possible abuses of their own system. When, however, M. Friedländer remarks (*Die religiösen Bewegungen innerhalb des Judentums im Zeitalter Jesu*, p. 112) that the Pharisees themselves said quite as severe things as did Jesus about certain abuses ("schlimmeres wahrlich hat auch Jesus nicht von diesen Weltverderbern ausgesagt"), he misses the significance of this fact. If the Pharisees were thus critical, then it is manifestly unjust to treat the criticism as though it could apply against Pharisaism as a whole.

To justify the words "which devour widows' houses" as a description of average scribes, would require much more evidence than has ever been adduced. "Widows were known there (in Jerusalem), it appears, who had been reduced from comfort to beggary by giving up their means to religious uses at the suggestion of scribes" (Menzies on Mk xii. 38, p. 229). The text hardly requires us to make this assumption. But then there comes the incident of the Widow's mites. "She of her want did cast in all that she had, even all her living" (Mk xii. 43). This sacrifice is eulogised, and justly. Yet the acceptance of such a gift might be denounced by a hostile critic as a "devouring" of the widow's substance. Jesus, however, praises it, just as the

Pharisaic Scribe does in the story (cited by Schöttgen). A priest who had scorned a certain woman's handful of flour was rebuked in a vision overnight: "Despise her not; it is as though she offered her life" (*Leviticus Rabba* iii. § 5). It need hardly be added that the Pharisees attached much importance to the exiguous gifts of the poor (cf. the passages adduced by Schöttgen on Mark, p. 251; *Baba Bathra* 10 a; *Leviticus Rabba* iii., where the poor's offering of two doves is preferred to King Agrippa's thousand sacrifices קרבן של עני קדמך; see also Wünsche, p. 402, he quotes: *Numbers Rabba* xiv., Mishnah, *Menaḥoth* xiii. 1; and add *Pesaḥim* 118 a). On the other hand, Gould (Mark xii. 40) suggests that "the devouring of widows' houses would be under the forms of civil law, but in contravention of the Divine law of love."

But the forms of civil law were by no means harsh on widows. The prevalent custom in Jerusalem and Galilee was to allow a widow to remain in her husband's house, and be maintained from his estate during the days of her widowhood (Mishnah, *Kethuboth* iv. 12). In Judæa (apart from Jerusalem) the widow might be compelled to receive her settlement, and then leave the house. Such a rule might have pressed hard in certain cases. Strong language is used in a late passage in the Palestinian Talmud against those who help the "orphans" to take this harsh course against "widows" (T.J. *Soṭa* on iii. 4). But on the whole the widow was well protected by the Jewish civil law (see L. N. Dembitz in the *Jewish Encyclopedia*, xii. p. 514). The example of the widow of Zarephath was held up for imitation (*Cant. R.* ii. 5, § 3) and Jerome's praise would well apply to such a case. But to "devour widows' houses" was no common failing of those who based their lives as the Pharisees did on the Scriptures which so often and so pathetically plead the widow's cause. Moralists in all ages have had to repeat this urgent appeal, and there was no doubt adequate ground for such a homily in the age of Jesus. But the Pharisaic teachers were keenly alive to their duty in all periods to take up the cause of the widow. And they expressed themselves emphatically on the subject again and again; nowhere, perhaps more forcibly than in their saying *Exodus R.* ch. xxx. (כל הגוזלן כאלו גוזל להק"ב), "He who robs the widow and orphans is as though he robbed God himself."

## XI. THE CLEANSING OF THE TEMPLE.

From a not unreasonable point of view the dignity and worth of the Temple in relation to national life must be considered as enhanced and not diminished by the association of that life with the Temple environment. The sacro-sanctity of the inner courts would be, as it were, humanised by the secularisation of the more remote precincts. To many a modern mind it is attractive rather than repellent to read of the popular uses to which the Temple was sometimes devoted. The famous celebration of the semi-religious function of the Water-Drawing, during the Feast of Tabernacles, with its deep spiritual significance allied to merry, carnival-like rites, is a case in point. Modern writers are too apt to confuse Pharisaism with Puritanism; more than half of the contrasts imagined between Hellenism and Hebraism arise from this same confusion. Josephus, moreover, records the holding of even more pronouncedly secular assemblages within or close to the Temple precincts (*War* I. xx; II. i, xvi; V. v). The tendency to treat the modern Synagogue as a place formally restricted to purposes of worship was a reaction which is happily breaking down, especially in America, where so many of the so-called Jewish reforms are reversions to ancient traditions.

"But indeed in those days nearly every priest must have been a trader." With these words Dr G. A. Smith concludes his brilliant account of the Temple Revenues, Properties and Finance in the first century of the Christian era (*Jerusalem*, Vol. I. p. 366). But surely the same might be said with equal validity of the governing bodies of many a Church and University in our own times, without implying that the financial side of these institutions was unduly prominent. The question always is: what is the implication? There is little ground for the supposition that the people were, in general, oppressed by the Temple financial arrangements. The Temple, again, was made a place of safe deposit for private money, but no trading was involved, and the authorities who speak of these deposits in the Temple almost explicitly state this. Thus the stores alluded to in II. Maccs. iii. were, as Dr Smith points out, "laid up for the relief of widows and fatherless children," and in part belonged to Hyrcanus son of Tobias. "It was," writes the same authority (II. Maccs. iii. 12), "altogether impossible that [by confiscating this money] such wrongs should be done unto them that had committed it to the holiness of the place, and to the majesty and inviolable sanctity of the Temple, honoured over all the world." The priests would clearly have no financial operations at all in relation to such funds, while Josephus (*War* VI. v. 2) when he says that in the Temple treasuries "the rich had built themselves store-chambers there" refers to a time of stress, when the Temple would, as a fortified place, be an obvious asylum. Again, here, however, the language of Josephus does not suggest that the priests in any way traded with the money. From the same historian's earlier account of the Parthian raid on Jerusalem (*War* I. xiii. 9) it may be gathered that private persons were not in normal times in the habit of using the Temple treasury as the store-house of their property. It is scarcely worth while citing the mass of facts available to show that sacred edifices have in many ages been used as safe-deposits, without necessarily incurring any suspicion of the taint of commercialism.

The presence in the Temple precincts of money-changers—for a full account of whose operations see S. Krauss, *Talmudische Archäologie*, 1911, II. 411—is generally conceded to have been an arrangement designed for the advantage of the pilgrims. The Temple-tax of half a shekel had to be paid in definite coinage. It could not be paid in ingots, but only in stamped coins (T.B. *Berachoth* 47 b with reference to Deut. xiv. 25; cf. *Sifrê* ad loc.). It must not be paid in inferior alloy but in high grained silver (T.B. *Bechoroth* 51 a). Again and again we are informed that the only coins accepted were *Tyrian* (Mishnah, *Bechoroth* viii. 7; Tosefta, *Kethuboth* xiii. 3, ed. Zuck. p. 275), which indeed were so emphatically the legal tender in the Temple that they were termed Jerusalemite as well as Tyrian. But it is not quite clear which Tyrian coins were meant. T. Reinach points out that among the conditions imposed on the vanquished Jews by Antiochus Sidetes was the withdrawal of the right of coining silver, though the striking of small bronze coins, intended for local circulation, was intermittently continued. This was in 134 B.C. But "very few years after the surrender of Jerusalem, in 126 B.C., when the civil war was waging between the sons of Demetrius II and the usurper Alexander Zebinas, the wealthy town of Tyre seems to have snatched from one of the pretenders to the throne the practical acknowledgment of its independence and the right to issue a silver coinage of its own. The Tyrian coinage, which lasted for almost two centuries, consists mostly of shekels (staters), bearing as types the head of the town God Heracles and the Ptolemaic eagle; their legend *Tyre the holy and inviolable* (Τύρου ἱερὸν καὶ ἄσυλον) seems to be imitated from the *Yerushalem Kedoshah* of Simon's shekels. The dates are reckoned from the new era of 126 B.C. These coins, notwithstanding their heathen types and Greek lettering, were of so exact a weight and so good an alloy that they enjoyed a large circulation in Judæa, and were even officially adopted as sacred money, that is to say the Rabbis decided that the annual head-tax of one [half-]shekel due from every Israelite to the Temple treasury was to be paid in Tyrian money." It is strange enough that while the bronze coins circulated in Judæa should conform scrupulously to the tradition and represent nothing but inanimate objects, the payment of Temple dues should not only be accepted but required in coins containing figures on them. Reinach meets this objection by the suggestion that "once thrown into the Temple treasury, all gold and silver coins were melted down and transformed into ingots" (T. Reinach, *Jewish Coins*, ed. Hill, 1903, pp. 20—23). At all events, while the coins most current in Syria were the Roman tetradrachms and denarii (such a silver denarius is referred to in Matthew xxii. 15), the Temple demanded payment on the Phoenician standard (cf. Krauss, *op. cit.*, p. 405), and the money-changer for this (and for other reasons) was therefore an actual necessity.

In passing it may be remarked that there is no ground for supposing that the ordinary business of money-changing went on in the Temple. In the N.T. the word κολλυβιστής is always used in describing the scene of the cleansing of the Temple, and it must be interpreted to mean the receiver of the *qolbon* (קולבון), or fee for changing other currencies into Temple currency and exclusively for Temple use. When Mark (xi. 16) adds the detail that Jesus "would not allow any one to carry a vessel through the Temple," the meaning no doubt is that he sided with those who ordained that the Temple must not be made a public thoroughfare (T.B. *Yebamoth* 6 b). Others went further, and forbade frivolous behaviour outside the Temple precincts and in the neighbourhood of the Eastern Gate (*Berachoth* 54 a). Similar rules were applied to the Synagogues (*Megillah* 27—28), and one may cite the regulation in Cambridge against carrying trade parcels through the College precincts. That Jesus is applying an established rule and not innovating is confirmed by the fact that he cites old prophetic texts (Isaiah lvi. 7, Jer. vii. 11) in support of his attitude.

Granting, then, that certain commercial operations were necessary for the maintenance of the Temple or convenient for those who had occasion to present themselves in its courts, there was nothing in such circumstances inherently censurable. If there was a sort of market within the Temple enclosure, it is impossible to assent to Dr Edersheim's easy conclusion: "It needs no comment to show how utterly the Temple would be profaned by such traffic." On the contrary, it needs much comment to show this. Equally exaggerated is Lightfoot's characterisation of the money-changer's profit as "unholy gain." Gould, in his note on Mark xi. 17, clearly sees that such attacks imply not merely an invective against an illegitimate use of the Temple, but a thorough-going antipathy to trade as such. Yet if the money-changer were necessary his profits were not "unholy." The labourer is worthy of his hire. Thus, there was considerable labour, and that of an expert kind, involved in the examination of animals to pronounce them perfect or blemished, and a fee was naturally charged (Mishnah, *Bechoroth* iv. 5). These fees as well as the profits of the money-changers were strictly limited by law and usage. Dr Edersheim seriously overestimated the gain. "If we compute the annual Temple-tribute at about £75,000, the bankers' profits may have amounted to from £8000 to £9000, an immense sum in the circumstances of the country." We have, on the other hand, the clear statement that the profit was only one in twenty-four or one in forty-eight (Tosefta, *Sheqalim* i. 8, ed. Zuck. p. 174; Maimonides, *Sheqalim* iii. 7; Krauss, *Talmudische Archäologie* II. 413). Even if we take the higher estimate, that of Rabbi Meir, Edersheim has overrated the changer's earnings by three to one.

Nor is it at all certain that this profit found its way regularly into private pockets. The Babylonian Talmud (*Menaḥoth* 108 a) has no suggestion of the secular destination of the changer's gain. Maimonides (*loc. cit.*) decides that the profit was used for the Temple purposes. Here he was following the tradition of Meir. In the Jer. Talmud there is indeed an opinion expressed that the money-changer himself took the profit. But this opinion is only one among several, and very probably refers to the provincial money-changers and not to those in the Temple. From the fifteenth to the twenty-fifth of Adar the money-changers set up their "tables" in every country place (Mishnah,

*Sheqalim* i. 3), and it is probable that the banker received the commission of one in twenty-four for himself. Schwab, in his French translation of the Palestinian Talmud (Vol. v. p. 268) inserts the words "en province," which is a manifest impropriety, for though this may be the sense, the words do not occur in the text, which runs as follows:—"To what use were the qolbons turned? R. Meir says, they were added to the fund of the sheqalim; R. Lazar says, they were employed for free-will offerings—nedabah; R. Simeon of Shizur (Saijur) says, they provided with them gold-plates and covering for the Holy of Holies; Ben Azzai says, the bankers took them as their profit; and some say they used them for the expense of keeping the roads in repair" (T.J. *Sheqalim*, chapter i. last lines). The roads were put in order at the beginning of Adar (Mishnah, *Sheqalim* i. 1). This association of the repair of the roads with Ben Azzai's view may justify the conclusion that he was referring to provincial and not Jerusalem transactions (the scene of the money-changing was transferred to the Temple on Adar the twenty-fifth; Mishnah, *Sheqalim* i. 2). In the parallel passage in the Tosefta, however, the words about the repair of the roads are wanting. Nevertheless, the weight of evidence is in favour of the verdict that the gains of the exchange were devoted to public and not to private ends. When once the money had been paid over to the Temple treasury, it was held unlawful to use it to gain profit even for the Sanctuary (at least this was Aqiba's view, Mishnah, *Sheqalim* iv. 3); but as the qolbons were paid before the money was actually received by the Sanctuary, they would not be profit directly made by the use of the sacred funds as capital.

We may conclude that besides the ordinary traders in money-changing, there were also operators of a less commercial type. The former would not have been permitted to carry on their trade in the Temple precincts; the latter were only authorised in the outer Court of the Temple between the 25th of Adar and the 1st of Nisan, an interval of about one week (Mishnah, *Sheqalim* i. 3. Cf. D. Oppenheim, *Literaturblatt des Orients*, Vol. x. 1849, p. 555). As, in this case, the profits were destined for public and sacred uses, and the operator received no gain from the transactions, it would seem likely that the money-changing for purposes of the Temple-tax was performed by officials of the Temple, that is by the priests. This would ensure that in normal circumstances the people would be fairly treated, and it was only under the aristocratic régime of the Temple's last decades that we hear of oppression. This occurred less with regard to the money-changing than with regard to the prices of pigeons and so forth for the sacrifices, the actual buying and selling of which moreover do not seem to have been normally carried on within the Temple precincts (cf. Oppenheim, *op. cit.* p. 556). When oppression occurred, the popular defenders of the people in such cases were the Pharisaic leaders. We find on record the action of various Rabbis which lowered the prices of pigeons even to the point of modifying the law on the subject (Mishnah, *Kerithoth* i. 7, where by reducing the number of pigeons to be brought by women the price of the birds was lowered by Simeon ben Gamliel from a gold denarius to half a silver denarius—that is to one-fiftieth of the original price). An earlier Rabbi (Baba ben Buta, contemporary with Herod) actually brought in 3000 sheep so that offerers might have animals for use. But Edersheim adds to the latter story a detail absent from the source he quotes (T.J. *Ḥagigah* ii. 3). Baba ben Buta found the Temple desolated as he termed it, but not because the grasping priests had limited the supply to maintain a high price, but because it was a festival and the ruling priests held that it was not lawful for private offerings to be brought on a holy day. The question was one at issue between the Schools of Hillel and Shammai, and Baba ben Buta, though a disciple of the latter, in this detail followed the decision of the former. But there is evidence enough that certain rapacious priestly families were detested by the people (witness the case of the House of Ḥanan) and that the Pharisees themselves denounced such practices (T.B. *Pesaḥim* 57 a). While, then, it is impossible to agree that the whole of "this traffic, money-changing, selling of doves, and market for sheep and oxen was in itself, and from its attendant circumstances, a terrible desecration" (Edersheim), there might well have been occasions on which indignation such as that of Jesus would be justified. But we must not magnify an exception into the rule.

The danger always lies in this tendency to confuse a system with its abuses. This, as it seems to me, is an error made by many commentators on the Gospels, who seek to expand the often-enough just criticism of Jesus against abuses, into an unjust condemnation of the whole Pharisaic system. It is fair enough for the anti-Nomists to criticise and judge Pharisaism as a religion based on Law; but there is no justice in refusing to consider the legalistic point of view and its possible merits. Still less is it fair to confuse legalism with externalism, or to assume without close examination of each instance that the moral abuses, which seem superficially inherent in a legalistic system, were really the logical result of the system, or did actually occur in

Pharisaism as lived by those who believed and rejoiced in it. (R. Travers Herford's *Pharisaism, its Aim and its Method*, London 1912, appeared after the present volume was mostly in type. Otherwise frequent reference would have been made to this brilliant and successful attempt to do justice both to Jesus and to the Pharisees.) The Cleansing of the Temple is a good case in point. And, therefore, I venture to repeat here what I wrote at an earlier date, when pleading for a revision of this tendency where the judgment on Pharisaism is concerned (*Jewish Quarterly Review*, 1899, p. 641). "Externalism needs the most careful watching, and ritual is always in need of freshening under the inspiration of the ideas which lie behind it. But Pharisaism was not ritualism. I, and many Jews with me, have no resentment whatever against the general spirit of the criticism to which the Law was subjected by Jesus, against his healthy onslaught against externalism. When Jesus overturned the money-changers and ejected the sellers of doves from the Temple he did a service to Judaism.... But were the money-changers and the dove-sellers the only people who visited the Temple? And was everyone who bought or sold a dove a mere formalist? Last Easter I was in Jerusalem, and along the façade of the Church of the Holy Sepulchre I saw the stalls of the vendors of sacred relics, of painted beads and inscribed ribbons, of coloured candles, gilded crucifixes, and bottles of Jordan water. There these Christians babbled and swayed and bargained, a crowd of buyers and sellers in front of the Church sacred to the memory of Jesus. Would, I thought, that Jesus were come again to overthrow these false servants of his, even as he overthrew his false brothers in Israel long ago. But I will also tell you what I did not think. I did not think that the buying and selling of sacred relics was the sole motive which brought thousands of pilgrims to Jerusalem; I did not say: Here is the whole of the Gospel, this is its inevitable end, its sure outcome. I knew that there is more in Christianity than this, that there are other Christians than these. Nay, as I turned away, I thought that perhaps if I had the insight to track a dealer in relics to his inmost soul, I might after all find there a heart warm with the love of Christ."

It must finally be remembered that the payment of the Temple-tax was a privilege as well as a burden. It was the typical illustration of the democratic basis of Jewish life. The daily sacrifices being for all Israel were paid for by all Israel. "All Israel were partners in this" (*Pesiqta Rabbathi* x, ed. Friedmann, p. 33 b). An individual might not claim the privilege to pay for the whole cost of the continual offerings (see Friedmann's note *ad loc.*): all Israel must share in the burden and the privilege. In estimating the effect of the Temple dues on the popular life this element must not be overlooked. It colours the whole estimate we have to form of the system. There were amenities as well as sacrifices involved in the sacrificial institution. It was not founded on exaction nor corrupted by peculation. These were the occasional abuses of a régime which, on the whole, secured popular enthusiasm for a beloved tradition.

## XII. THE PARABLES.

"The parable became a truth, proved upon the pulses of men." These words, used by a modern writer in another connection, aptly characterise the abiding significance of the New Testament Parables. A vast amount of religious and literary genius has been directed, throughout the ages, to the worthy object of extracting the fullest meaning from the Parables attributed to Jesus. But far more effective has been the process by which these Parables have been "proved upon the pulses of men."

It is generally felt that Jesus was not the originator of the method of teaching by Parables. Even Jülicher, who advances so strenuous a plea for the originality of the *contents* of the New Testament Parables, does not claim—of course in presence of the Old Testament Parables cannot claim—that the method was a new creation (*Die Gleichnisreden Jesu*, I. 164). Bousset roundly asserts that, though as an exponent of the Parabolic art Jesus "spoke" while the Rabbis "stammered," nevertheless "Jesus owed the vehicle on which he mainly relied in his popular preaching—the Parable—to the Synagogue and the Scribes" (*Jesus*, p. 30). And, again, "There can be no doubt that he first learned such a manner of teaching in the Synagogue. All that has come down to us in the way of Parables from Rabbinic tradition—later though they undoubtedly are—bears so close a resemblance both in form and matter to the Parables of Jesus, that no idea of accident can be entertained. And *since any influence of Jesus upon the later Jewish Rabbinism is out of the question*, we can only assume that Jesus caught the form of his Parabolic speech from the Scribes in the Synagogue" (*op. cit.* p. 43). On both the points raised in this last sentence Bousset is probably right, but he has gone beyond the evidence in the vigour of his statement, for we know very little as to the contemporary style of Synagogue homily. It is, however, true that just in the case of ideas which affect the folk influence is most likely to be exercised without the consciousness of imitation. Ziegler (*Die Königsgleichnisse des Midrasch*, 1903, Introduction) rightly maintains that many Parables must have been part of the common fund (*Gemeingut*) of the people, and that Jesus may have drawn upon and added to this common fund. Jesus had no need to take his Parables from other Agadists, just as other Agadists had no need to take their Parables from Jesus. But as Ziegler judiciously sums up the matter, p. xxii: "It is indeed conceivable that Jesus employed much that he had heard from his teachers; it is also possible that sundry Parables of Jesus became popular, lived on in the mouth of the folk, and thence were taken over by later Agadists, without the least inkling on their part as to the identity of their author, just as to-day Heine is inadvertently quoted by the most pronounced Heine-phobes—yet it is out of the question to assert anything like a systematic influence of one side on the other." There must have been a large Jewish stock of fables and parables floating about long before they were set down in writing (Fiebig, *Altjüdische Gleichnisse und die Gleichnisse Jesu*, 1904, 25), and it is possible that both the Tannaim and Evangelists drew from the stock.

Close comparison of the Gospel Parables with the most similar of the Rabbinic nearly always reveals dissimilarity amid the similarity. Though in his earlier work just cited, Fiebig falls short of justice to the Rabbinic Parables as a whole, I fully agree with a conclusion which he reaches in his later work (*Die Gleichnisreden Jesu*, Tübingen, Mohr 1912), which appeared after this Note was in type. Fiebig is clearly right when he claims that the Gospel Parables are marked by characteristic features which testify to an original and exalted personality in their authorship, or at least in their adaptation. Yet the hand of the editor has been at work, and it is scarcely possible to formulate canons of criticism by which the genuine Parables of Jesus may be distinguished from the rest. It would be delightful could we accept fully the view of the Rev. J. W. Hunkin (*Journal of Theological Studies*, XVI. 381) that "the parables have been transmitted in the Synoptic tradition very nearly in the form in which they were spoken by Jesus." But without going this length, it is obvious that some of the Synoptic Parables point to a strong personality. And the same is true of the Rabbinic Parables. Amid the sameness one detects individualities. Hillel, Aqiba, Meir, Joshua b. Levi, Abbahu, are to a certain extent as distinct in their Parables and Similes as in their doctrines, and if they drew on the common stock of their people's lore, reinforced as that stock was by accretions from the lores of other folk, they made their borrowings, as their inventions were, personal by the genius with which they applied them to living issues.

All authorities are agreed that there can have been no direct, literary borrowing by the later Rabbis from the books of the New Testament. Thus Prof. Burkitt suggests (*J. T. S.* xv. 618) that Matthew vii. 24—7 is the ultimate source of the Rabbinic contrast of two forms of building in *Aboth de Rabbi Nathan* xxiv. The parallel is not close in detail, and an examination of the variant in the second recension of the *Aboth* xxxv. renders it remotely possible that we have here a confused reminiscence of some Philonean ideas on the Tower of Babel (Mangey, I. 420). The Rabbis were, moreover, fond of comparing the various aspects of the study and performance of Law to firm and infirm structure such as a tree with many and few roots (Mishnah, *Aboth* iii. 22). But if there were borrowing in the particular case before us, Prof. Burkitt is clearly right in holding that "it was probably second-hand, i.e. from one of the Minim," and that the Midrash "put it down to Elisha ben Abuya [the heretic] to avoid offence." Similarly, if it be the case that the Talmud (*Me'ilah* 17 b) borrowed from a Christian source the story of an exorcism, the borrowing must have been unconscious. (But see on this interesting point the discussion in the *Revue des Études Juives* vii. 200, x. 60, 66, xxxv. 285.)

Another instance of greater curiosity concerns the Parable of the Prodigal Son. In the literary sense this is original to Luke. But some of the phraseology seems traceable to Aḥiqar, and the root idea is Philonean (G. Friedländer, *The Grace of God*, 1910). Now, the text of the Talmud must at one time have contained a passage reminiscent of the Parable. For in a Genizah MS. (published by L. Ginzberg in *Gaonica*, New York, 1909, ii. 377) Aḥa, the famous eighth century Gaon, quotes *Sanhedrin* 99 a in a version no longer fully extant in the Talmud texts. To illustrate the Pharisaic principle that the penitent sinner stands on a higher level than the completely righteous, Abbahu cites the parable of "a king who had two sons, one of whom ordered his way well, while the other went out to depraved living"

למלך שהיו לא [לו] שני בנים אחד הלך בטוב ואחד יצא לתרבות רעה

This looks like a reminiscence of Luke's Parable, and it may have been removed from the Talmud text by scribes more cognisant than Abbahu was of the source of the story. Dr Ginzberg, who recognised the similarity, takes another view. His words (*op. cit.* p. 351) are: "The source for the parable...is not known to me. Obviously R. Aḥa must have had it in his text of the Talmud....In any event, it is the short, original form of the New Testament parable of the prodigal son."

And here reference may be made to another instance. The Gospel Parable of the Sower is introduced by the medieval Jewish adapter of the Barlaam and Josaphat romance. Abraham b. Ḥisdai wrote his Hebrew version (*Ben ha-melech we-hanazir*) under the title "King's Son and Nazirite," or as moderns prefer to render the Hebrew title "Prince and Dervish," in the thirteenth century. The tenth chapter contains the Parable of the Sower at great length. The main idea, comparing the propagation of Wisdom to the Sower, must have occurred in the original Indian of Barlaam (J. Jacobs, *Barlaam and Josaphat*, 1896, p. cxi). A well-known Indian parallel, moreover, is found in the Sutta Nihata (cf. P. Carus, *Gospel of Buddha* § 74); this is clearly more primitive than the Gospel version. Yet Abraham b. Ḥisdai gives us a form, the details of which are for the most part bodily derived from the New Testament, a fact of which he was assuredly unaware. The over-working of the Indian original of Barlaam by a Christian redactor must have already occurred in the recension of the romance used by the Hebrew translator as his base. (On the problem of the relation of the Hebrew to other versions of Barlaam see M. Steinschneider, *Die hebraeischen Uebersetzungen des Mittelalters*, Berlin, 1893, § 532.) With regard to another suggestion of Rabbinic borrowing, the case is different. It has been argued that the beautiful Parable of the Blind and Lame (see below) is not Rabbinic, but Indian. The Indian parallels cannot, however, be the source of the Rabbinic Parable as it now stands. In the Indian (E. Leumann, *Die Avasyaka-Erzählungen*, Leipzig, 1897, p. 19) a lame man gets on a blind man's back and together they escape from a forest fire. This is not a *source* for the Rabbinic Parable, which differs totally in idea. Nor can I be persuaded by Dr M. James (*J.T.S.* xv. 236) that the version of the Parable (much closer to the Rabbinic than the Indian is) found in Epiphanius (ed. Dindorf, II. 683) is older than the Rabbinic. The Christian form seems to me derived from the latter. Finally I may refer to the Parable of the Three Rings, made famous by Lessing in his *Nathan der Weise*. There are many parallels to this, some using it as a vindication of Christianity, others of Italian scepticism. In the Hebrew Chronicle of Solomon ibn Verga, it is a pathetic plea for tolerance by an oppressed faith, and M. Gaston Paris firmly maintains that if not originally Jewish, the Parable is presented in its original form by the Hebrew Chronicler (*Revue des Études Juives* xi. 5).

Naturally, the preceding jottings—to which others might be added—are not designed as a formal discussion of the problem of borrowing. They may, however, serve as an indication of the vast amount of research, literary and historical, yet remaining to be undertaken before the problem can be seriously considered. One thing is clear; the result cannot but be a triumph for humanism. That Buddha could be made a hero for Christian and Jew is not the least of the episodes in that triumph.

Free trade in good stories corresponds to the common experience and common aspiration of mankind. We have, in the readiness of men to adopt other men's superstitions, a sad comment on the universality of the lower elements in human nature. But the adoption by one and all from one and all of beautiful Parables is a mark of the universality of the higher elements. It is of itself a beautiful Parable "to preach the simple brotherhood of souls that seek the highest good."

We must try to get closer to another aspect of the historical problem. The Parable was used by Old Testament writers with perfection of art. The Tannaim, from the latter part of the first Christian century onwards, make a far more extensive use of the method. But, in between, the later Biblical writers, the authors of the Pre-Christian Jewish Apocalypses (with the possible exception of Enoch) and such a representative Alexandrian as Philo have no parables. In one of his early works (*Markus-Studien*, 1899, p. 11), an able Jewish scholar, H. P. Chajes, concludes that in the age of Jesus the Parable was an unusual device, and that it had not yet won the place which it afterwards filled in the Rabbinic method of popular instruction. He even suggests that this is the original meaning of the Evangelists' discrimination between the teaching of Jesus and that of the Scribes. "He taught as one having authority" should read "he spoke in Parable." (Underlying the Greek text ὡς ἐξουσίαν ἔχων is the Hebrew *Ke-moshel*—כְּמוֹשֵׁל—which Dr Chajes would emend to *be-mashal*—בְּמָשָׁל.) Dr Chajes proceeds (p. 12): It will easily be retorted, How could the mere use of Parables have made so striking a sensation, seeing that the *Mashal* (Parable) plays so prominent a rôle among the Rabbis? Yes, among the Rabbis; but it is extremely doubtful whether this was yet the case in the age of Jesus. A real Agadic activity cannot be posited before the epoch of Hillel, and no Parable can with certainty be assigned to that teacher.

It was only at a later period, after the destruction of the Temple, that the Parable attained high honour, as we already find it to be the case with Joḥanan ben Zakkai, Joshua ben Ḥananya, and especially Meir (cf. Mishnah, *Sota*, ix. 15; T. B. *Sanhedrin*, 38 b, last lines).

This argument scarcely survives examination. One Rabbinic source ascribes to Hillel (and, in some readings, also to his contemporary Shammai) a mystic knowledge of the language of the hills, the trees, the beasts and the demons, and a special predilection for parables or fables (*Soferim*, xvi. 9). The authenticity of this ascription is doubted by Bacher (*Agada der Tannaiten*, I. 10, notes 3—5). But the *only* ground for this suspicion is the fact that the Talmud (T. B. *Sukkah*, 25 a) makes the same remark concerning Joḥanan ben Zakkai. *Soferim* seems to present the older tradition, for while it equally ascribes this knowledge to Joḥanan, it also carries the statement back to Hillel, whose disciple Joḥanan was. Weiss, the author of the History of Jewish Tradition (in Hebrew) *Dor dor vedorashav*, i. 157, throws no doubt on the trustworthiness of the passage in *Soferim*. That Hillel's thought sometimes ran in the direction indicated appears also from the Mishnah (*Aboth*, iv. 8), for Hillel said: "The more women, the more witchcraft"—he may therefore have had an academic interest in demonology as *Soferim* asserts. And it is otherwise quite clear that at all events part of the statement in *Soferim* must be true, for we have abundant evidence that Hillel was fond of Parabolical forms of speech (cf. Weiss, *op. cit.* pp. 160 seq.). That Hillel was interested in folk-lore is demonstrated by the anecdotes told of him (T.B. *Sabbath* 31 a, *Aboth de R. Nathan* xv.). Again, in the last reference, in his interview with a would-be proselyte, Hillel is recorded to have compared the study of the details of the Temple service to the etiquette at an earthly Court. This comes very near an actual Parable. So, too, there is a compressed Parable in Hillel's striking enunciation of the doctrine of retribution: "He saw a skull which floated on the face of the water, and he said to it, Because thou didst drown (others) they drowned thee, and in the end they that drowned thee shall be drowned" (Mishnah, *Aboth*, ii. 7). Another of Hillel's phrases: "He who serves himself with the tiara perishes" (*ib.*) is a figurative condemnation of the self-seeker's appropriation of the Crown of the Torah. Illustrating the covenant of love between God and Israel Hillel said: "To the place that my heart loves my feet carry me. If thou comest to My house, I will come to thine; but if thou comest not to My house I will not come to thine"

(Tosefta, *Sukkah*, iv. 3). There are several other such sayings recorded of Hillel; and frequent mention is made of his wide acquaintance with popular lore as well as his readiness to enter into familiar conversation with the common folk. All of this goes to confirm the authenticity of the tradition reported in *Soferim* as cited above. Besides this, there are quoted in Hillel's name two actual Parables—rudimentary, but bearing unmistakably the Parabolical stamp. Bacher fully accepts the authenticity of these Parables though they occur in a somewhat late Midrash (Leviticus *Rabba*, lxxxiv.). Chajes adduces no adequate ground for suspicion. The first of the two Parables referred to is as follows: Hillel's disciples were walking with him on a certain occasion, and when he departed from their company they enquired "Whither goest thou?" He answered, "I go to fulfil a religious duty."—"What duty?"—"To bathe in the bath-house."—"Is this, then, a duty?"—"Ay," replied Hillel; "the statues of kings which are set in theatres and circuses—he who is appointed concerning them cleanses and polishes them; he is sustained for the purpose, and he grows great through intercourse with the great ones of the kingdom. I, created in the image and likeness of God, how much more must I keep my body clean and untainted." Ziegler (*op. cit.* p. 17) agrees with Weiss and Bacher in holding this passage a genuine saying. The authenticity is guaranteed (as Bacher argues) on linguistic grounds, for whereas the preceding passage is in Hebrew, the second Parable which immediately follows is in Aramaic, and this very intermixture and interchange of Hebrew and Aramaic is characteristic of several of Hillel's best authenticated utterances. The second Parable is this: again Hillel is walking with his disciples (the parallel to the journeys of Jesus in the company of his disciples may be noted); he turns to part from them, and they ask his destination. "I go home," said Hillel, "to render loving service to a certain guest who sojourns in my house."—"Hast thou then a guest ever in thy house?"—"Is not the unhappy soul a sojourner within the body? To-day it is here, and to morrow it is gone!"

At this point a general remark may be interpolated. While rendering these and other Rabbinic Parables, the translator feels himself severely handicapped. Not only were the New Testament Parables elaborated by the Evangelists far more than the Talmudic were by the Rabbis, but the former have been rendered with inimitable skill and felicity, while the latter have received no such accession of charm. Even Herder's paraphrases of Midrashim are turgid when compared with the chaste simplicity of style and form under which the New Testament Parables appear in the Vulgate, and even more conspicuously in Luther's Bible and the Anglican versions. These versions are, from the point of view of literary beauty, actually improvements on the Greek, just as the Hebrew of the twenty-third Psalm has gained an added grace in the incomparable English rendering with which we are all familiar. No one has done as much for the gems of Rabbinic fancy. They have remained from first to last rough jewels; successive generations of artists have not provided increasingly becoming settings to enhance their splendour. But even so some modern writers have been unfairly depreciatory of the Rabbinic Parables, for while there is a considerable number of no great significance, there are some which are closely parallel to those of the New Testament, and some others which may be justly placed on the same high level. There are no more beautiful Parables than that of the blind and the lame (*Sanhedrin*, 91 a—b, Mechilta, בשלח ii.), which may be summarised thus:

A human King had a beautiful garden in which were some fine early figs. He set in it two watchmen, one lame and the other blind. Said the lame man to the blind, "I see some fine figs, carry me on your shoulders and we will get the fruit and eat it." After a time the owner of the garden came and asked after his missing figs. The lame man protested that he could not walk, the blind that he could not see. So the master put the lame man on the blind man's back and judged them together. So God brings the soul and casts it in the body (after death) and judges them together.

It is difficult to understand why the excellence of such Parables should be contested. Fiebig (p. 88) objects that it is very improbable that a king should employ the lame and the blind as watchmen. One wonders why not, seeing that in the East particularly the old and the decrepit are much used for such sedentary work. It may be that the difficult passage II. Samuel v. 6 implies the employment of the blind and lame as sentinels of the citadel. Undoubtedly the idea of the *watchmen* is necessary for the Rabbinic Parable—which is not a mere adaptation of the Parable which Dr James cites. In the Epiphanius parallel (*J.T.S. loc. cit.*) the King is described as possessing among all his subjects *only two* men unfit for military service, this is surely not less improbable than the lame and blind watchmen. Besides, there are many improbabilities in the New Testament Parables also (as e.g. the refusal of a king's invitation to a banquet, Matt. xxii. 2; in Luke xiv. 16 the banquet however is given not by a king but by "a certain man"). Such improbabilities are not defects in Parables at all. We might have been spared some inept criticism of the New Testament Parables, had due notice been taken of the wise Rabbinic maxim: Do not apply your logic to a Midrash. Again, it is sometimes said that the Rabbinic Parables fall below those of the New Testament in that the latter deal with far greater subjects, Sin and Grace, Prayer, Mercy, Love, the Kingdom of Heaven (Fiebig, p. 105). That in the enormous mass of Rabbinic Parables many treat of trivialities in a trivial fashion is true; but simplicity must not be confused with insignificance. There is a quality of homeliness about many of the Rabbinic Parables, a quality inherited from the Bible, with its Ewe-lamb and its Song of the Vineyard. It is this quality that distinguishes the Jewish from the ordinary Eastern Parable; the former, far less than the latter, merely illustrates a maxim. Many Oriental Parables are expanded Proverbs, but the Rabbinic Parables cannot as a rule be compressed into a Proverb. As to subject matter, very many of them are directed to most of the subjects which Fiebig enumerates, and to other fundamental problems of life and death and the hereafter. Thus the Parable quoted above of the lame and the blind expresses the unity of body and soul, or rather the truth that a man is a single product of dust and spirit. The persistence in later Jewish thought of the belief in the bodily resurrection was in part, at least, due to the impossibility of separating body and soul, even in the aspect of immortality.

The following summary from the excellent article by Dr J. Z. Lauterbach (*Jewish Encyclopedia*, IX. 513 a) is a just though of course incomplete statement of the subjects of the Rabbinic Parables:

In the Talmud and Midrash almost every religious idea, moral maxim, or ethical requirement is accompanied by a Parable which illustrates it. Among the religious and moral tenets which are thus explained may be mentioned the following: the existence of God (Gen. R. xxxiv. 1); his manner of retribution, and of punishing sins both in this world and the next ('Ab. Zarah, 4 a, Yalq. Lev. 464, Sabb. 152 a); his faithful governance ('Ab. Zarah, 55 a, Sanh. 108 a); his impatience of injustice (Suk. 30 a); his paternal leniency (Ex. R. xlvi. 6) and his relation to Israel (*ib.* xlvi. 4, Ber. 32 a); Israel's sufferings (Ber. 13 a); the folly of idolatry ('Ab. Zarah, 54 b—55 a); the Law as the guardian and faithful protector in life (Soṭah, 21 a); the sin of murder (Mechilta, יתרו, 8); the resurrection (Sabb. 91 a); the value of benevolence (B. B., 10 a); the worth of a just man for his contemporaries (Meg. 15 a); the failure of popularity as a proof of intrinsic value (Soṭah, 40 a); the evil tendency of freedom from anxiety (Ber. 32 a); the limitations of human knowledge and understanding (Sanh. 39 a); the advantage frequently resulting from what seems to be evil (Niddah, 31 a); conversion (Sabb. 153 a); purity of soul and its reward (*ib.* 152 b).

This list could be much extended, but it suffices to demonstrate that the depreciation of the Rabbinic Parables, on the ground of triviality of motive, is a mere aberration of criticism. It can, therefore, hardly be maintained with Fiebig (*op. cit.* p. 87), that "the manifold situations of human life are only sparingly and pallidly depicted" in the Rabbinic Parables. It is, on the other hand, a sound discrimination (p. 83) that there are in the Rabbinic literature a vast number of royal Parables. Hillel and Joḥanan b. Zakkai present some examples (Bacher, *Agada der Tannaiten*, I. 73, 81). Most of the royal Parables, however, belong to the period later than the fall of Bethar in 135, and they only begin to predominate with Domitian in the hands of Agadists like Meir and Simon b. Yoḥai (Ziegler, p. xxiii). By that time the interest of Jewish moralists in good government as part of the idea of the Kingdom of God (cf. Schechter, *Aspects of Rabbinic Theology*, ch. vii.) led them to portray under royal metaphors the relations of God to man, and they did this both by way of contrast and similitude. Some of the oldest Parables in which the heroes are *kings*, perhaps dealt in their original forms with ordinary *men*, and *kings* was probably substituted for *men* in some of them (both Rabbinic and Synoptic) by later redactors.

One point deserves close attention. It is not possible to assent to Fiebig's characterisation that "in comparison with the Synoptic Parables, it strikes one that the processes of Nature—sowing and harvest, growing, flowering and fruitage, were taken little account of [in the Rabbinic Parables]." In the latter, besides many Parables treating of trades, handicrafts, seafaring, school-life, domestic affairs, there are many comparisons drawn from the fields, vineyards, streams, flowers, trees, fruits, birds, beasts, and other natural objects. This is perhaps more noticeable in those phases of the Agada which do not assume the form of narrative Parables, but it is frequent in the latter also, and the Rabbinic examples agree with the Synoptic in treating of nature under cultivation rather than in a wild state. With regard to the *harvest*, Schweitzer holds that the reference in the New Testament Parables is eschatological, pointing at all events to a definite note of time; *this* particular harvest in the last year of Jesus' life is to be the last harvest on earth, and the Kingdom is to follow it immediately. In Joel iii. 13, Isaiah xvii. 5—11, as well as in the Jewish Apocalypses (e.g. Baruch lxx.), the harvest is synonymous with the judgment. This is not altogether convincing, for it is curious that the images of the sower and the mustard seed—the harvest and the full-grown tree, processes of long maturation—should express the idea of a sudden consummation and nothing more.

The idea of the harvest in the Synoptics is probably a composite one, the standing corn is regarded as food for the sickle, whether it be the sickle of an angry Master or of the human reaper of the accumulated reward of long drawn out endeavour. If the expression "the harvest is large but the labourers are few" (Matt. ix. 37—38, Luke x. 2; cf. John iv. 36) were the authentic exordium to the mandate to the disciples in Q, we have here the harvest used in quite a different sense from the Apocalyptic. Both these uses meet us in Rabbinic. In the first place, with regard to the passage just cited, there is a Rabbinic parallel nearer than is generally supposed, though so long ago as 1847 Zipser suggested it (*Literaturblatt des Orients*, 1847, col. 752). In the Mishnah, *Aboth* ii. 19 (20), occurs a saying which in Dr Taylor's rendering runs thus: "R. Tarphon said, 'The day is short, and the task is great, and the workmen are sluggish, and the reward is much, and the Master of the house is urgent. He said, It is not for thee to finish the work, nor art thou free to desist therefrom; if thou hast learned much Torah, they give thee much reward; and faithful is the Master of thy work, who will pay thee the reward of thy work, and know that the recompence of the reward of the righteous is for the time to come.'" Dr Taylor sees in this Mishnah points of contact with the Parable of the Vineyard in Matt. xx., "where the *οἰκοδεσπότης* (Master of the house) says to the labourers whom he finds unemployed, *Τί ὧδε ἑστήκατε ὅλην τὴν ἡμέραν ἀργοί;* ('Why stand ye here all day idle?')." The first part of this Mishnah is usually taken to correspond to the "ars longa vita brevis" of Hippocrates. But it is a very plausible suggestion of Zipser's that the first clause of the Hebrew has been wrongly punctuated. It is commonly read הַיּוֹם קָצֵר ("the day is short"), whereas the true reading should be הָיּוֹם קָצִר ("to-day is harvest"—there is no need to emend to קָצִיר as the Gezer Calendar Stone, published in the *Quarterly Statement* of the P. E. F., Jan. 1909, gives us several times over the spelling קצר for "harvest"). This is confirmed by another word in the saying, "Master of the House," for the Hebrew equivalent בעל הבית often means "landowner" (cf. Dr A. Büchler, *Sepphoris*, p. 38, etc.) just as the *οἰκοδεσπότης* of Matthew does (this equivalence of the Hebrew and Greek just quoted was noted by Dr Taylor, and has been elaborated I think by Dr Nestle). The whole of Tarphon's saying would thus have an agricultural setting. It may be pointed out in passing that this is not the only parallel between sayings of Tarphon and the New Testament. Compare the "mote" and "beam" of *'Arachin*, 16 b with Matt. vii. 3 (there seems no reason for doubting with Bacher, *Agada der Tannaiten*, I. 351 n., the authenticity of this saying as one of Tarphon's). Tarphon lived during the existence of the Temple (T. J. *Yoma*, iii. § 7, 38 d), and was thus a contemporary of the Apostles. He was a strong opponent of the Jewish Christians (*Sabbath*, 116 a), and hence his name was used by Justin Martyr (whose Tryphon = Tarphon) as a typical antagonist. It is impossible that Tarphon would have taken his similes from Christian sayings, and the parallels point unmistakably to the existence of a common and ancient source. The whole Mishnah is more elaborate than most of the passages in *Aboth* and we may conclude that Tarphon is not the author of the opening clauses but only of their interpretation in terms of studying the Law.

These opening clauses however, when juxtaposed with Matt. ix. 37--8, present under the figure of the harvest a very different idea from the Judgment. It is the goal of effort rather than the starting point of doom, the reward of life rather than the precursor of death. There is nothing apocalyptic about this, nothing catastrophic. "The king does not stand (in satisfaction) by his field when it is ploughed, or when it is hoed, or when it is sown, but he stands by it when it is full of corn for the granary," said R. Simon (Tanḥuma Miqeṣ on Gen. xxviii. 13). On the other hand there are some Rabbinic passages in which the harvest is a type of the Judgment in the sterner sense (Leviticus *Rabba*, xviii. § 3).

Several of the New Testament Parables are clearly inconsistent with a firm belief in the immediate approach of the end; there is no "interim morality" in the Parable of the Talents (Matt. xxv. 14—30, Luke xix. 12—27, cf. Mark xiii. 34—37). It is improbable, however, that the same Jesus who said "Be not therefore anxious for the morrow" (Matt. vi. 34), and "Sell all thou hast" (*ib.* xix. 21), should have cried "Well done, good and faithful servant" to those who had traded with their capital. To the idea of this story we have a Rabbinic parallel, but not in Parable form; it is cited as an incident (*Debarim Rabba*, III. § 3), and in some particulars the moral is other than in the New Testament. For, after all, the five and the two talents were risked, and might have been lost in the trade. In the Midrash incident this objection does not suggest itself. This is the incident referred to: "R. Phineas ben Jair [second half of second century] lived in a certain city of the South [Lydda?], and certain men went to support themselves there. They had in their possession two seahs of barley, which they deposited with him. These they forgot and left the place. And R. Phineas ben Jair went on sowing them year by year; he made a granary for them, and stored them. After seven years these companions returned to claim their seahs. Immediately R. Phineas ben Jair recognised them, and he said to them, Come, take your stores. Lo, from the faithfulness of flesh and blood thou recognizest the faithfulness of the Holy One, blessed be He." (This last clause reminds one of the "faithful servant.")

In Rabbinic parallels to several others of the Synoptic Parables the inferiority is not always on the Rabbinic side as Jülicher in particular thinks. In the first place the parallels sometimes strike a note which finds no exact echo in the Synoptic examples. It is strange that Fiebig can cite (from Mechilta *Beshallaḥ*, ed. Friedmann, 29 b) the following as he does (*op. cit.* p. 34) without noting that it is a somewhat unique expression of the relation between God and man.

Rabbi Absolom the Elder says: A Parable. To what is the matter like? To a man who was angry with his son, and banished him from his home. His friend went to beg him to restore his son to his house. The father replied: Thou askest of me nothing except on behalf of my son? *I am already reconciled with my son.* So the Omnipresent said unto him (Moses), "Wherefore criest thou unto me?" (Exodus xiv. 15). Long ago have I become well disposed to him (Israel).

Here then we have the idea that the Father is reconciled to his erring son even before the latter or any intercessor makes appeal, in accordance with the text: "Before they call I will answer" (Isaiah lxv. 24). Compare also the similar idea in the *Pesiqta Rabbathi* ch. v. (ed. Friedmann, p. 17 b); these expressions of the Father's love seem to go even beyond the beautiful pathos of Luke xv. 20.

A King ordered the men of a certain district to build a palace. They built it. Then they stood by the gate and proclaimed: Let the King come in! But what did the King do? He entered by a wicket door, and sent a herald to announce: Shout not, for I have already come to the palace. So, when the Tabernacle was erected, Israel said: Let my Beloved come to his garden! The Holy One sent and said unto them: Why are ye anxious? Already have I come into my garden, my sister, my bride.

So, too, the medieval poet Jehuda Halevi sang, though he was thinking more of the divine omnipresence:

> Longing I sought Thy presence,
> Lord, with my whole heart did I call and pray;
> And going out toward Thee,
> I found Thee coming to me on the way.

Another note of the Rabbinic Parables (which has I think no echo in the Synoptics) is the idea of "Chastisements of love" (*Berachoth* 5 a) which finds expression in many comparisons, among which perhaps the following is the most characteristic (Exodus *Rabba*, xxi. § 5). The Midrash very pathetically puts it that God wishes Israel to cry to him, he longs to hear Israel's voice raised in filial supplication. Just as he chastises Israel to discipline him, so he tortures Israel to force from him the prayer which Israel refuses to yield while free from racking pain. The divine ear yearns for the human voice. This profound, mystical thought, is expressed with both quaintness and tenderness in the following Parable:

Why did God bring Israel into the extremity of danger at the Red Sea before saving him? Because he longed to hear Israel's prayer. Said R. Joshua ben Levi, To what is the matter like? To a king who was once travelling on the way, and a daughter of kings cried to him: "I pray thee, deliver me out of the hand of these robbers!" The king obeyed and rescued her. After a while he wished to make her his wife; he longed to hear her sweet accents again, but she was silent. What did the king do? He hired the robbers again to set upon the princess, to cause her again to cry out, that he might hear her voice. So soon as the robbers came upon her, she began to cry for the king. And he, hastening to her side, said: "This is what I yearned for, to hear thy voice." Thus was it with Israel. When they were in Egypt, enslaved, they began to cry out, and hang their eyes on God, as it is written "And it came to pass...that the children of Israel sighed because of their bondage...and they cried..." Then it immediately follows: "And God looked upon the Children of Israel." He began to take them forth thence with a strong hand and an outstretched arm. And God wished to hear their voice a second time, but they were unwilling. What did God do? He incited Pharaoh to pursue after them, as it is said, "And he drew Pharaoh near." Immediately the children of Israel cried unto the Lord. In that hour God said: "For this I have been seeking, to hear your voice, as it is written in the Song of Songs, My dove in the clefts of the rocks, let me hear thy voice; thy voice, the same voice which I first heard in Egypt.

Again, the following is a gracious Parable, which, were one on the look-out for Rabbinic foils to the Gospels, might be contrasted with Matthew xxi. 9.

When R. Isaac parted from R. Naḥman, the latter asked for a blessing. Said R. Isaac: I will tell thee a Parable. A traveller was passing through a desert, and he was hungry, faint, and thirsty. He found a tree, whose fruit was sweet, whose shade was pleasant, and at whose foot there flowed a stream. He ate of the fruit, drank of the water, and sat in the shade. On his departure he said: O tree, O tree, how shall I bless thee? If I say to thee, May thy fruit be sweet, lo thy fruit is sweet already; that thy shade shall be pleasant, lo it is pleasant now; that a stream shall water thee, lo this boon is thine at present. But I will say: May all the saplings planted from thee be like thyself! So, thou, How shall I bless thee? With Torah? Torah is thine. With wealth? Wealth is thine. With children? Children are thine. But I say: God grant that thy offspring may be like thyself! (*Ta'anith* 6 a).

Or, to turn to another idea, the following is an original note, at all events there is no full Synoptic parallel. The citation of the passage will serve also a secondary purpose; it will again illustrate the frequent Rabbinic habit of syncretising the Parable of idea with the application of historical incident.

R. Hanina bar Idi said: Why are the words of the Torah (Scriptures) likened unto water, as it is written (Isaiah lv. 1) *Ho every one that thirsteth come ye to the water*? To say unto thee: Just as water forsakes a high place and goes to a low place, so the words of the Torah find a resting-place only in a man whose character is lowly. R. Oshaya also said: Why are the words of the Torah likened to these particular liquids, water, wine, and milk, for the text continues: *Come ye, buy wine and milk without money*? To say unto thee: Just as these three liquids are kept only in the simplest of vessels, so the words of the Torah are only preserved in a man of humble spirit. It is as once the Emperor's daughter jeeringly said to R. Joshua b. Ḥananya: "Ho! Glorious Wisdom in a foul vessel!" He replied: "Ho! daughter of him who keeps wine in an earthen pitcher!"—"In what sort of vessel should wine be kept, then?" asked the princess.—"Important people like you should store their wine in pitchers of gold and silver."—She persuaded the Emperor to follow this course, but soon men came to him to report that the wine had turned sour. "My daughter," said the Emperor, "who told you to suggest this thing?"—She replied that her adviser was R. Joshua b. Ḥananya. The latter was called, and in answer to the Emperor's questions replied: "As she spake to me, so spake I unto her." (*Taanith*, 7 a; *Nedarim*, 50 b).

Various Rabbinic parallels to New Testament Parables have been detected by various scholars. One must here remark that the similarity of *idea* must not be confused with identity of Parabolical treatment. Philo has no true Parables, but several of his ideas are found later on developed into that literary type. For instance, what became a favourite Rabbinic Parable, the comparison of the creation of the world to the planning of a palace (Genesis *Rabba*, i.), a comparison associated by Bacher with the schools of Hillel and Shammai, is already found fully developed in Philo (*de opif. mundi*, 4, 5).

Leaving the study of parallels, if the Rabbinic Parables are considered absolutely, without comparative reference to those of the New Testament, it is clear that they must be allowed to rank high in literature of the kind. The Parable took a very firm root in the Jewish consciousness, though for some centuries it was not transplanted from its native soil—Palestine—to Babylonia, and Rab (died 247) scarcely presents any instances of the *Mashal* (Bacher, *Agada der babylonischen Amoräer*, 1878, p. 31). But the influence of the Palestinian Midrash prevailed, and throughout the middle ages and the modern epoch, Jewish homilies have been consistently illustrated by Parables. Now, as of old, the Parable was the instrument for popularising truths which in an abstract form were not so easily apprehensible.

Professor Bacher elsewhere describes the *Mashal* (Parable) as "one of the most important elements of the Agada." Agada must here be understood in its widest signification: the exposition of Scripture and the application of the precepts of the Law to the elucidation of principle and the regulation of conduct. The utility and even necessity of the Mashal for understanding the Torah are variously enunciated in a series of fine similes in the Midrash, and the passage (Canticles *Rabba*, I. i. 8; Genesis *Rabba*, xii. 1; Eccles. *Rabba* on ii. 11; T. B. *Erubin*, 21 b footnote) may here be paraphrased in full: "R. Naḥman said: A great palace had many doors, and whoever entered within it strayed and lost his direction (for the return). There came one of bright intelligence who [cf. Ariadne] took a clue of rope and tied one end of it to the entrance, and went in and out along the rope. Thus before Solomon arose no man could understand the words of the Torah, but all found it intelligible after the rise of this King." Further, said R. Naḥman, "It is like a wild thicket of reeds, into which no man could penetrate. But there came a clever wight who seized a scythe and cut a path, through which all men could come and go. Thus was it with Solomon." R. Jose said: "it is comparable to a great case full of fruits, but the case had no handles and no one could move it. Then there came one who made handles, and everyone could move it." R. Shila likened Solomon's service to that of a man who provided a handle to a huge cask full of hot liquid. R. Ḥanina put the same thought in these terms: "It was like a deep well, full of water, and the water was cool, sweet and wholesome, but no creature could reach it to drink. A certain one came and joined rope to rope and cord to cord; he drew water from the well and drank. Then, for the first time, all could draw and drink. Thus from word to word, from Mashal to Mashal, Solomon reached the uttermost secret of the Torah. And this he did by means of the Mashal." So, the passage continues, "The Rabbis said, Let not the Mashal be light in thine eyes, for by means of the Mashal a man can stand in the words of the Law, for it is comparable to a king who lost gold from his house, or a precious pearl, and found it by means of a clue worth a Roman *as*." There is in all this a two-fold meaning. Solomon added certain things to the Law, the Rabbis assigned to him a number of takkanoth or new regulations which made the Law practically usable; he also popularised the Law, making it accessible to the masses by means of the Mashal. As the Midrash continues, Solomon by means of the Mashal attained to a knowledge of legal minutiae; he also made the Law popular. "Rabbi Judan said, Whoever speaks words of Law in public (among the many) is worthy that the Holy Spirit should rest upon him, and this thou learnest from Solomon."

In this analytical passage, the term *Mashal* is used in a very wide sense, and includes all forms of applied morality. Parable thus becomes part and parcel of the instrument for arriving at truth and for making truth prevail. Truth, to Pharisee and Evangelist alike, is the will of God, and the Parable was at its highest when seeking to understand and to do that will. The Parables of Talmud and Gospels are (so Zipser put it) derived from a common source, the systematised teaching of Hillel and Shammai. Parables were not merely an entertainment, they were not merely designed to interest the people. They were the method by which the mysteries of providence and the incidences of duty were posted and illustrated. Sometimes these mysteries and incidences are beyond understanding and when then Mark (iv. 11) describes the Parable as actually employed by Jesus to prevent men from understanding, the description is happily characterised by Bousset when he calls it "preposterous," and dismisses it as "the dogmatic pedantry of a later age." The same idea is found in all the Synoptics and cannot be dismissed in this easy way. What is "preposterous" is the supposition that Jesus taught in Parable *in order* that men might misunderstand. This is to mistake an Oriental process of thought by which consequences are often confused with motives. (Cf. Skinner on Isaiah vi. 10.) The Parable has this danger that it may imply more than it says, and may leave behind it more puzzles than it solves. It is not an exact instrument; it works without precision. The *consequence* of a Parable may be misunderstanding, or what is equivalent, partial understanding, and it is certain from the language of the evangelists that the Parables ascribed to Jesus were liable to this consequence. Hence, as it was improper to admit that Jesus used an imperfect form imperfectly, consequence was translated into intention, and the misunderstanding was described as designed in order to prevent the Jews from turning and finding forgiveness. Later on, when the eschatological element in the teaching of Jesus was forced into greater prominence, the supposition that the Parable was used in order to veil a Messianic secret may easily have arisen. The latter, however, cannot be the original force of the reference, for it is plain enough that many of the New Testament Parables, different though they be to explain in all their details, are absolutely simple inculcations of moral and religious truths, profound but not mysterious.

## XIII. DISEASE AND MIRACLE.

Rabbinic Judaism took over from the Old Testament a belief that disease was a consequence of sin (Leviticus xxvi. and parallels in Deuteronomy). This theory was especially held to explain general epidemics, and also those afflictions the origin of which was at once most obscure and their effects most dreaded—such as leprosy. It is not necessary to do more than recall the cases of Miriam, Joab, Gehazi, and Job.

The Rabbinic sources contain many assertions as to the relation between sin and disease. (Cf. the valuable discussion in the Tosafoth to Aboth iv. 11.) "Measure for Measure" applied here as in other aspects of Rabbinic theology (Mishnah, Aboth v. 11—14). R. Ammi (of the third century, but his view was shared by earlier authorities) asserted *sans phrase* that there was no affliction without previous sin (Sabbath, 55 a). R. Jonathan said: "Diseases (נגעים) come for seven sins: for slander, shedding blood, false oaths, unchastity, arrogance, robbery, and envy" ('Erachin, 16 a). In particular leprosy was the result of slander (Leviticus Rabba, xviii. § 4). On the other hand, "When Israel stood round Sinai and said, All that the Lord has spoken we will do, there was among the people no one who was a leper, or blind, or halt, or deaf," and so forth (*ibid.*; Sifrê 1 b, the sin of the golden calf, like other acts of rebellion, caused leprosy and other diseases, Pesiqta Rabbathi vii., ed. Friedmann p. 28). Thus obedience prevented disease, just as disobedience produced it. This, to a large extent, moralised the idea: it set up the moral life as the real prophylactic. In general the principle enunciated in Exodus xv. 26 was adopted by the Rabbis, though it must be remembered that so great an authority as R. Meir altogether disputed the theory as to the connection between suffering and transgression. God's dealing with men, he held, was an unfathomable mystery. Leprosy, again, like other diseases might, in another view, merely be the beneficent earthly penalty designed to save the sufferer from tribulations in the future (Lev. R. xvii.).

To exemplify the application of the "Measure for Measure" idea, the case of blindness will suffice. Naḥum of Gimzu (first century) explained his blindness as the consequence of his inhumanity to a poor sufferer (Ta'anith, 21 a). The man who accepted bribery and perverted justice would not pass from the world unless he suffered the infliction of physical blindness corresponding to his moral lapse (Mechilta, Mishpaṭim, § 20, p. 100 a, Sifrê, on Deuteronomy, § 144). The case of one blind from birth was more difficult to fit into the theory, and in John ix. 1 Jesus denies that such an affliction was due to sin at all. It is there explained that the congenital blindness had been imposed that it might be cured, so "that the works of God should be made manifest in him." This explanation is identical with that of Ecclesiasticus xxxviii, except that Sirach applies it to the doctor's art. "The Lord hath given men skill, that he might be honoured in his miraculous works." Disease—more particularly pestilence—was ascribed also to sins which were not punished by human tribunals. In general it was thought that sin left its material impress, and the later mystics put it that it disfigured the image of God (Schechter, *Studies in Judaism*, II. 274).

Two points only must be further indicated; the legal position of the leper in Rabbinic law is sufficiently indicated in the *Jewish Encyclopedia* VIII, 10 a. ("Leprosy was not considered contagious.") The first point is that the moral stigma attaching to disease soon took a more amiable form. As Dr Schechter well puts it (*Studies in Judaism*, I. 269): 'The only practical conclusion that the Rabbis drew from such theories as identify suffering with sin was for the sufferer himself, who otherwise might be inclined to blame Providence, or even to blaspheme, but would now look upon his affliction as a reminder from heaven that there is something wrong in his moral state. Thus we read in tractate Berachoth (5 a): "If a man sees that affliction comes upon him, he ought to inquire into his actions, as it is said, Let us search and try our ways, and turn again to the Lord (Lam. iii. 40). This means to say that the sufferer will find that he has been guilty of some offence."'

The second point is that though leprosy was regarded as the punishment for the worst crimes, it was not thought lawful or right to leave the leper to his fate. Sympathy with suffering was not diminished by any theories as to the origin of the suffering. In Ecclesiasticus Rabba (on ix. 7) is told the touching story of Abba Taḥna. As the sun was near its setting on a Friday afternoon, Abba Taḥna was going home with all his worldly goods in a bag on his shoulders. At the cross-road he saw a man smitten with leprosy. The latter entreated the Rabbi in these terms: "My master, show me charity and carry me to the city." The perplexed Rabbi said: "If I leave my goods, how shall I sustain myself and my household? and if I leave this leper I shall commit a mortal sin." Abba Taḥna conquered the suggestion of his evil inclination, left his bag, and bore the leper into the town. In the end he did not suffer for his action. But the whole passage is an effective comment on Luke x. 30.

Demoniac "possession" as a cause of disease, and "exorcism" as its cure, were well known to the Rabbis. But it is certain that these beliefs and practices were uncommon in Palestine at the time of Jesus. The easy assumption to the contrary has no foundation. Though the Enoch and other apocalyptic literature has a developed demonology, and Acts xxiii. 8 implies a Pharisaic angelology, there is a remarkable infrequency of references to the subject in the Mishnah and the Tannaite literature (L. Blau, *Das altjüdische Zauberwesen*, p. 23). Quite early was the power attached to prayers for rain. The fact that Onias (on whom see *Jewish Encyclopedia* IX. 410 and refs.) stood in a ring while praying for rain has a "magical" look, but it is not clearly a charm. There is nothing of the magician or spell-worker in the picture of Onias drawn in Josephus (*Antiq.* XIV. 2, 1). Hillel (p. 95 above) was a student of demon-lore, perhaps under Parsic influence—he was by birth Babylonian. Compare the prayer cures of Ḥaninah b. Dosa (first century)—he had magical leanings (see *J.E.* VI. 214), but the female demon Agrat mentioned in his case was Persian. Persian influence reached Palestine in the first century (Darmesteter in *Revue des Etudes Juives* I. 195) but became more pronounced after the Palestinian schools were superseded by the Babylonian early in the third century. Members of the Sanhedrin were expected to understand magic in order to deal with causes in which the question arose (Sanhedrin 17 a. See refs. in Taylor, *Aboth* V. 9). The same Mishnah (v. 9) refers to demons, but this like Ḥagigah 16 a apparently belongs to the late second century. It is in the Babylonian Talmud that we find an appalling mass of demonology which, though it stands in relation to earlier beliefs,—Biblical, Apocalyptic and Rabbinical—cannot properly be cited as applicable to the time of Jesus in the Holy Land

(Perles on Bousset, p. 35. Bousset frankly admits the validity of Perles' objection in the second edition of his *Religion des Judentums*, p. 388, n. 4, but hardly corrects his general statements in accordance with the admission). Probably, therefore, the Pharisees were amazed at the attitude and actions of Jesus, so that it is intelligible that Jesus was afterwards called a "magician" (Sabbath, 104 b), though subsequent schools of Pharisaism would have been less amazed than his contemporaries were. It may be, indeed, the fact that the Essenes were (as Geiger supposes) "healers," in which case we should have a further bond between Jesus and this sect. There was between the years 150 and 450 a great increase in Jewish circles in the belief in demons and their influence. (Cf. Conybeare, *Jewish Quarterly Review*, ix. 87.) It is undeniable, however, that some cases of exorcism are recorded earlier. But it is curious that they are all associated with the Roman imperial family. Josephus, who makes indeed a general assertion as to demoniac possession (*Wars* VII. vi. 3), only recites an actual cure by exorcism performed in the presence of Vespasian (*Antiquities* VIII. ii. 5). So, too, the notorious instance of exorcism reported of a second century Rabbi, Simon b. Yoḥai, was not only performed in the case of a Roman lady of the imperial family, but actually occurred in Rome, if it be not indeed a mere reproduction of a Christian story (see p. 92 above). Again, though the Jewish exorcists (Acts xix. 13) were "strollers," yet the scene of their exploits is not Judæa but Ephesus and the impression conveyed is that they were playing with foreign fire. It does not seem, therefore, appropriate to the purpose of these Notes to enter at large into the Rabbinic parallels to New Testament ideas on demonology. (See, besides the literature already referred to, Kohler in *Jewish Encyclopedia*, IV. 517 b.)

In the earlier period we find the physician held in high repute (Ecclus. xxxviii. 1 seq.), though Sirach accepts the theory that disease is connected with sin. The "confections" of the apothecary are associated with prayer in effecting a cure. Moses prays for Miriam's relief, and God is the "Healer." The prayer for such divine healing found a place in the oldest part of the Synagogue liturgy, the eighteen benedictions, the words used being derived in part from Jeremiah xvii. 14. This two-fold conception always finds expression in Jewish thought. Prayers for the sick go side by side with the demand that every community shall have its doctors (Sanhedrin, 17; Maimonides

Sanh. i. 10). Rabbinic "medicine" has very much of the "sympathetic" and the folk-cure and the exorcist about it, but there is no ground whatever for Bousset's assumption that the Rabbinic demonology arose from any supposed surrender of the divine omnipotence, and the yielding of part of his powers to demons and the like. The Rabbis considered, in one sense, every recovery from sickness as a "miracle." Said they: "Greater is the miracle that occurs when a sick person escapes from a perilous disease than that which happened when Hananiah, Mishael and Azariah escaped from the fiery furnace" (Nedarim, 41 a).

## XIV. POVERTY AND WEALTH.

The twelve were sent forth "two by two," just as was the rule with the Jewish collectors of alms (T.B. *B. Bathra* 8 b); indeed *solitary* travelling, especially at night, was altogether antipathetic to Jewish feeling. According to all three synoptics (Mark vi. 7, Matt. x. 10, Luke ix. 3) the disciples were to take nothing for their journey, no provisions, no wallet, no money. Even so did the Essenes travel, according to the report of Josephus (*War* II. viii. 4): "They carry nothing at all with them when they travel." The twelve were to accept hospitality wherever it was offered, and the Essenes "go (on their journeys) into the houses of those whom they never knew before," the houses, however, belong to brother Essenes. The Essenes carried weapons with them, while Matthew and Luke distinctly assert that the twelve were not even to carry a staff. This seems an improbable restriction, for the staff (ῥάβδος) was a common necessary for the traveller, serving at the same time as a help to walking and as a weapon. The ordinary Jewish traveller carried a staff and a bag (see Dictionaries s.v. תרמיל). Mark distinctly states that the twelve *were* to carry a staff (εἰ μὴ ῥάβδον μόνον), and later on we find one or two of the disciples in possession of weapons (Mk xiv. 47, Matt. xxvi. 51). Luke (xxii. 38) reports that there were two swords. Luke seems to feel the contradiction between the earlier commission and this, and so inserts the passage (xxii. 35, 36) to explain the divergence.

The Essenes were "despisers of riches" (Josephus, *loc. cit.* § 3) but they were not worshippers of poverty. "Among them all there is no appearance of abject poverty, or excess of riches," says Josephus. Theirs was a rule of equality, a régime of simple sufficiency not of common insufficiency. A life of such poverty was the natural corollary of life in a society aiming at a holy life, and we find a similar rule among the Therapeutae described by Philo; though the Therapeutae were closer to the later Christian monastics than were the Essenes.

That the pursuit of certain ideals was incompatible with the desire to amass material wealth is, however, a common thought of the Rabbis: "This is the path to the Torah: A morsel with salt shalt thou eat, thou shalt drink also water by measure, and shalt sleep upon the ground, and live a life of trouble the while thou toilest in the Torah. If thou doest this, happy shalt thou be and it shall be well with thee (Ps. cxxviii. 2); happy shalt thou be in this world, and it shall be well with thee in the world to come" (Mishnah, *Aboth* vi. 4).

But this implies no cult of poverty. Among the blessings prayed for by Abba Areka were "wealth and honour" (*Berachoth* 16 b). From time to time, ascetic movements have arisen in Judaism (cf. *Jewish Encyclopedia* ii. 167), and the value of such movements cannot be denied (cf. C. G. Montefiore *Truth in Religion* pp. 191 seq.). On the whole, however, Pharisaic Judaism had, on the one hand, too full a belief in calm joyousness as a fundamental and generally attainable ideal of life, and on the other hand too acute and recurrent an experience of the actualities of destitution, for it to regard poverty as in itself a good. (Cf. Note XVI below.) Even in the pursuit of the Torah, there comes a point where poverty is a preventive rather than a help. Eleazar ben 'Azariah, who succeeded the second Gamaliel as President of the Sanhedrin, and was himself wealthy (*Qiddushin* 49 b), summed the truth up in his epigram: "Without food, no Torah; without Torah, no food" (*Aboth* iii. 26). That destitution may be a bar to the ideal is an experience of many an idealist. After the Bar Cochba war, there was so general an impoverishment in Palestine, that the study of the Torah was intermitted. (Cf. the lurid picture drawn by Dr A. Büchler in his essay on *Sepphoris in the Second and Third Centuries*, pp. 70 seq.) "God weeps daily alike over the man who could study Torah but omits to seize his opportunity, and over the man who cannot study yet continues to do it" (T.B. *Ḥagigah* 5 b). In other ways, too, the Rabbis recognised that poverty was an evil. "Poverty in the house of a man is more distressful than fifty plagues" (T.B. *Baba Bathra* 116). The sufferings endured are so intense that they save a man from seeing Gehinnom (*'Erub.* 41 b, cf. *Yebamoth* 102 b). Poverty is an affliction equal in severity to all the curses in Deuteronomy combined (*Exod. Rabba* xxxi.). The contrast between the earthly lot of rich and poor is found in well-known passages of the Wisdom literature. Very pregnant is the saying attributed in the Talmud to Sirach, though the passage is not found in any known text of the apocryphal book. It runs thus (*Sanh.* 100 b):

"All the days of the poor are evil (Prov. xv. 5): Ben Sira said, the nights also. The lowest roof is his roof, and on the highest hill is his vineyard. The rain off (other) roofs (falls) on his roof, and the soil from his vineyard on (other) vineyards"—another illustration of the truth that to him that hath shall be given, and from him that hath not even his little shall be taken away. Poverty dogs the footsteps of the poor, putting him at a constant disadvantage (T.B. *Baba Qama* 92 a). Poverty even affects the personal appearance. "Beautiful are the daughters of Israel, but poverty mars their face" (*Nedarim* 66 a).

But though an evil, poverty was not the consequence of sin, unless that sin be the misuse of wealth (*Leviticus R.* xxxiv.). There is a wheel revolving in the world, and wealth ill-spent ends in poverty (*Exod. Rabba* xxxi.; T.B. *Sabbath* 151 b). But the poor though deserving of human pity have no right to complain of the Divine justice. As Philo says: "Poverty by itself claims compassion, in order to correct its deficiencies, but when it comes to judgment...the judgment of God is just" (*Fragments*, Mang. II. 678). In fact the Rabbinic analysis goes deeper, and makes it necessary for us to qualify the general statement that Poverty is an evil. "There is no destitution but poverty of mind" (אין עני אלא בדיעה *Nedarim* 41 a). Compare with this the sarcastic allusion to "the poor man who hungers but knows not whether he is hungry or not" (*Megillah* 16)—this is the real poverty, the lack of original insight, the absence of self-sufficiency in character. Poverty, as we have seen, may be so crushing as to destroy the victim's ideals. Far be it for an arm-chair moralist to inveigh against those who listen not to a Moses because the iron of misery has entered into their souls, so that they cannot hear for anguish of spirit, and for cruel bondage. But the excuse cannot be accepted. There was none so poor as Hillel, yet he worked for a half-dinar a day and paid a moiety to the door-keeper for admission to the house of study, sometimes braving the winter snow. Thus the cares of poverty are no defence against the charge of neglecting the Torah. And, continues the same Talmudic passage (T.B. *Yoma* 25 b), there was none so wealthy as R. Eleazar ben Ḥarsom, yet he forsook his wealth, and with a skin of flour spent his days in the house of study. The cares of wealth are no defence. Man must rise superior to either. As the Midrash puts it (*Exod. R.* xxxi.): Happy is the man that can endure his trial, for there is none whom the Holy One trieth not. The rich God tries whether his hand be open to the poor, the poor He tries whether he can calmly endure affliction. If the rich man sustain his trial, and worketh righteousness, lo, he eateth his money in this world and the capital endureth for the world to come and God delivereth him from Gehinnom. And if the poor man sustain his trial and kick not against it, lo! he receives a double portion in the world to come. Then the Midrash proceeds to distinguish between the wealth which doeth evil to its owner and the wealth that doeth good to him, and so with the qualities of strength and wisdom. Suffering, indeed, was the lot of rich and poor alike. A life of unbroken prosperity was the reverse of a boon. An old baraitha (of the school of R. Ishmael) asserts that "he who has passed forty days without adversity has already received his world in this life" (*'Erachin* 16 b foot); one who was not afflicted would not belong to the category of Israel at all (*Ḥagiga* 5 a). Here we read the note of experience. It was Israel's lot so to suffer that it was forced to fall back on the theory that only by "chastisements of love" (*Berachoth* 5 a) might he obtain purification and atonement (Sifrê 73 b). So, too, in another sense, the difference between men's condition—not an absolute difference, for wealth was accessible to all possessed of knowledge, i.e. virtue (*Sanhedrin* 92 a on the basis of Proverbs xxiv. 4), while there was a ladder in men's affairs up which the poor rise and the rich descend (*Pesiqta* ed. Buber 12 a) or a wheel revolving to similar effect (*Sabbath* 151 b)—was a means of atonement when sacrifices ceased (see quotations p. 128 below).

There is no cult of poverty neither is there a cult of wealth. Both are conditions of good and ill rather than good or ill themselves. Not the possession of wealth but too absolute a devotion to its acquisition and too ready a surrender to its temptations were feared. It was the gold and silver showered on Israel by a bountiful God that provided the material for the golden calf (*Berachoth* 32 a). Hillel held that increase of property meant increase of anxiety (*Aboth* ii. 7). Yet Rabbi Judah honoured the rich, and so did Aqiba (T.B. *'Erubin* 86 a), for the rich maintain the order of the world when they turn their possessions to the service of their fellows: the rich support the poor, and the poor support the world, says the Talmud (*loc. cit.*)—a not inept statement of the relations between capital and labour as understood until the inroad of recent economic theories. Equality, whether in the degree of wealth or poverty, was regarded as destructive of the virtue of charity. If all men were equal, all rich or all poor, who would perform *the loving kindness of truth* of Psalm lxi.?

(Tanḥuma, Mishpaṭim ix. אם אעשה עולמי שוה חסד ואמת מן יוצרוהו)

Thus, there must be inequality. This theory, that the poor are necessary to the rich, runs through the Jewish theory of alms-giving and charity in all subsequent ages. Wealth becomes an evil when it is made the instrument of oppression (*Aboth de R. Nathan* II. xxxi.), or when the acquisition of it leads to the neglect of the Torah. The poor are God's people (*Exod. R. loc. cit.*) and "poverty becomes Israel as a red halter a white horse" (*Ḥagiga* 9 b)—it sets off and augments the beauty in each case. And it moreover acts as a restraint against the abuses which luxury may induce. Extreme wealth is hard to bear (*Giṭṭin* 70 a), yet charity is its salt (*Kethuboth* 66 b), and is more efficacious than any of the sacrifices (*Succah* 29 b). Yet, if wealth often leads to a materialistic life, poverty may impel to unworthy pursuits (*Kiddushin* 40 a). The wealthy man may win Paradise like Monobazus, storing up wealth in heaven by generous use of his riches on earth (T.B. *Baba Bathra* 11 a). The poor man is equally able to attain bliss. Most of the Rabbis were poor artizans, but some were rich (*Nedarim* 50 a seq.). The wealthy among them scorned the idea that wealth, as such, made up any part of the man's real account (*Pesaḥim* 50 a).

For, "when Solomon built the Temple, he said to the Holy One in his prayer: Master of the Universe, if a man pray to thee for wealth, and thou knowest that it would be bad for him, give it not. But if thou seest that the man would be comely in his wealth (נאה בעשרו), grant wealth unto him" (*Exodus Rabba* xxxi. § 5). To sum, again, poverty and wealth are conditions not ends. Hence the test of wealth is subjective, not objective. Who is rich? In the Mishnah (*Aboth* iii. 3), contentment is the definition of wealth. "Who is rich? he who is contented with (literally, he who rejoices in) his lot; for it is said, when thou eatest the labour of thine hands, happy art thou, and it shall be well with thee (Ps. cxxviii. 2), happy art thou in this world and it shall be well with thee in the world to come." It may be difficult but it is not impossible for one and the same person to eat at the two tables.

## XV. THE CHILDREN.

The passages depicting Jesus' love for children are marked by a singular tenderness and beauty. In several points there is contact here with the stories of Elijah and Elisha. There is, however, a painful contrast between the Synoptics (Mark x. 13—16 and parallels) and the incident of Elisha and the bears (2 Kings ii. 23). But this is a good illustration of the need to examine the judgment passed by the Pharisees on certain Old Testament incidents. What did the Pharisees make of Elisha's conduct? From the text (2 Kings xiii. 14), "Now Elisha fell sick of the disease *of which he died*," the inference was drawn that the prophet must previously have suffered from diseases of which he did *not* die. "The Rabbis have taught (in a baraitha), Elisha suffered three illnesses, one because he thrust Gehazi off with both his hands, *one because he incited the bears against the children*, and the one of which he died" (T.B. *Soṭa* 47 a, *Baba Mezia* 87 a).

Simplicity of faith, such as characterises the child's confidence in its parent, is the motive of Psalm cxxxi. "Lord, my heart is not haughty...Surely I have stilled and quieted my soul like a weaned child with his mother." The weaned child in the Orient would be old enough to run alone. Cf. I. Samuel i. 22. In 2 Macc. vii. 27 the mother of the seven martyrs speaks of suckling her child for three years, and in the Rabbinic period the average age for weaning was between the second and third year (cf. Krauss *Talmudische Archäologie* ii. p. 9 and notes p. 436). Young pupils were termed sucklings (Taanith 9 a). Hence the Psalmist's point of comparison is not the helplessness of the child, nor its contentment in spite of the loss of what once seemed indispensable; but its natural readiness to return to its mother despite the fact that it no longer needed her. This Psalm (though the particular metaphor is differently explained) is thus the model for man's attitude towards God (Midrash on the Psalm quoted). David made it the guide of his life in all his vicissitudes (*ibid.*; cf.

T.B. *Soṭa* 10 b). Just as only the man could enter the Kingdom who sought it as a child (Mark x. 15), so he who makes himself small (perhaps as a child המקטין) in this world is made great (perhaps "grown up" גדול) in the world to come, and he who holds himself as a slave for the Torah here is made free hereafter (*Baba Mezia* 85 b). In the Old Testament God's relation to Israel is compared to the relation between a father and his young child. This relation was much treasured in the Midrash (see *Yalquṭ* on Jeremiah i. 5 and Hosea xi. 3 and parallels). God's nearness to the child is expressed also by the thoughts (1) that the young is without sin (בן שנה שלא טעם טעם חטא *Yoma* 22 b, cf. *Niddah* 30 b, Löw *Lebensalter* p. 65); and (2) that the Shechinah is with the young. The whole passage which follows has several other striking ideas which lead up to the most striking of all: "Rabbi used to despatch R. Assi and R. Ammi to visit the towns of Palestine in order to see that local affairs were well ordered. Once they went to a place and asked to see its Guardians. They were confronted with the Chiefs of the Soldiery. These, said the Rabbis, are not the Guardians of the town, they are its destroyers.—Who, then, are the true Guardians?—The teachers of the children....The nations asked, Can we prevail against Israel? The answer was given, Not if you hear the voices of the children babbling over their books in the Synagogues...See how deeply loved of God the children are. The Sanhedrin was exiled, but the Shechinah (Divine Presence) did not accompany its members into exile; the Priests were exiled, but still the Shechinah remained behind. But when the children were exiled, forth went the Shechinah with them. For it is written (Lam. i. 5): Her children are gone into captivity, and immediately afterwards: And from the daughter of Zion all her beauty is departed" (*Echa Rabba* Introd. and 1, 32).

The antiquity of the custom of blessing children by laying on of hands is attested by Genesis xlviii. 14. The same passage (the very words of verse 21 are used) was the source of the modern Jewish custom of blessing the children especially in the home and on the Sabbath eve. "Before the children can walk, they should be carried on Sabbaths and holidays to the father and mother to be blessed; after they are able to walk they shall go of their own accord with bowed body and shall incline their heads and receive the blessing." This is from a book published in 1602 (Moses Henochs' *Brautspiegel* ch. xliii.). Similarly the children are taken to the Rabbi, who places his hand on the head of the children in the Synagogue and blesses them, especially on Friday nights. It is not easy to say how old these customs are. From Biblical times onwards the teacher regarded his pupils as his children, and constantly called them so. (For the part assigned to children in public worship see p. 4 above, and my *Jewish Life in the Middle Ages*, pp. 31–2. Very beautiful is the passage in *Soṭa* 30 b, in which is related how the infant on its mother's knee, and the babe at the breast, no sooner saw the Shechinah at the Red Sea, than the one raised its head, the other took its lips from the breast and exclaimed: This is my God and I will glorify him.) Such customs as just described do not always find their way into literature (cf. D. Philipson in *Jewish Encyclopedia* iii. p. 243), and they are often far older than their earliest record. They suffice to show how fully in accord with the Jewish spirit was Jesus' loving regard for the young. In olden times, the Jewish child began to learn the Pentateuch with the Book of Leviticus. Why? Because the sacrifices are pure and the children are pure. Said R. Assi, "Let the pure come and occupy themselves with what is pure" (*Leviticus Rabba* vii.).

## XVI. FASTING.

Philo did not represent Pharisaic teaching as to the relation between body and soul; he held that they formed a dualism, while the Rabbinic view was that they constituted a unity. "Righteousness," he says, "and every virtue love the soul, unrighteousness and every vice the body" (I. 507; cf. Drummond, *Philo-Judaeus* i. 23). Pharisaism, on the other hand, placed the seat of good and evil, virtue and vice, equally in the heart (cf. Porter, *op. cit.* p. 52 above). But on the subject of asceticism Philo and the Rabbis were at one. His theory would naturally lead, on the contemplative side, to such developments as the societies of the Essenes and Therapeutae, which belong, just as the medieval and modern Ḥassidic asceticisms belong, to Judaism quite as much as do any of its more normal institutions. Yet, despite his admiration for these societies, Philo steered a sane course between extremes, and so on the whole did Pharisaism. He, like them, had no love for excesses in table luxury; he, like them, thought that enjoyment was possible and laudable without excess. Philo disapproved of the sumptuous Alexandrian banquets which took toll of the world to supply rare dainties (I. 81), but, he adds, "Do not turn to the opposite course and immediately pursue poverty and abasement, and an austere and solitary life." And, as Drummond (i. 24) summarises Philo's conclusion (on the basis of the passages quoted and of I. 549—51), the philosopher counselled: "On the contrary, show how wealth ought to be used for the benefit of others; accept posts of honour and distinction, and take advantage of your position to share your glory with those who are worthy, to provide safety for the good, and to improve the bad by admonition; and instead of fleeing from the banquet-table exhibit there the virtue of temperance." Cf. F. C. Conybeare, *Philo about the Contemplative Life*, 1895, p. 270. This became precisely the predominant Jewish view. Maimonides (*Eight Chapters* iv., ed. Gorfinkle, pp. 62, 65) concedes that Jewish pietists at various periods deviated into extremes of asceticism, but he diagnoses their conduct as a medicine against disease, the medicine being noxious to the healthy. "The perfect Law which leads to perfection recommends none of these things. It rather aims at man's following the path of moderation"; but in order "that we should keep entirely from the extreme of the inordinate indulgence of the passions, we should depart from the exact medium, inclining somewhat towards self-denial, so that there may be firmly rooted in our souls the disposition for moderation" (cf. *Guide* iii. 35). Self-discipline is not self-torture, and man's right and duty to participate in all lawful happiness is illustrated in such remarks as that of Abba Areka in the famous Talmudic passage: "On the day of reckoning man will have to give account for every good which his eyes beheld and which he did not enjoy" (T.J. *Qiddushin*, last lines).

In the first century we find, however, an unsettled condition of opinion. Whether or not it belong to the original source (it is absent from Mark), yet the outburst in Matt. xi. 18, Luke vii. 33 is an apt summary of the conflict of views. John was addicted to fasting—he had a devil!; Jesus was not so ascetic, therefore he was a glutton and a wine-bibber! These passages suggest also another contrast, that presented by II. Samuel xii. 21—23, and Mark ii. 19, 20 (incidentally it may be remarked that the custom of a bridal pair fasting on the wedding-morn is only imperfectly traceable to a baraitha in T.J. *Bikkurim* iii. 65 c).

| II. Samuel xii. 21—23. | Mark ii. 19, 20. |
|---|---|
| Then said his servants unto him [David], What thing is this that thou hast done? thou didst fast and weep for the child, while it was alive; but when the child was dead, thou didst rise and eat bread. And he said, While the child was yet alive, I fasted and wept, for I said, Who knoweth whether the Lord will not be gracious unto me, that the child may live? *But now he is dead, wherefore should I fast?* can I bring him back again? I shall go to him, but he shall not return to me. | And John's disciples and the Pharisees were fasting: and they come and say unto him, Why do John's disciples and the disciples of the Pharisees fast, but thy disciples fast not? And Jesus said unto them, Can the sons of the bride-chamber fast, while the bridegroom is with them? as long as they have the bridegroom with them they cannot fast. But the days will come *when the bridegroom shall be taken from them, and then will they fast* in that day. |

These passages are interesting from another point of view. They suggest (in David's saying) the addiction to fasting as a form of supplication, and (in the saying of Jesus) as a form of mourning. Both of these ideas are abundantly illustrated by the Old and New Testaments, and also by other evidence available from the beginning of the Christian era. Thus R. Zadok fasted for forty years to ward off the destruction of the Temple (T.B. *Giṭṭin* 56 a). Fasting was always thought one of the means of causing an alleviation of calamity (T.J. *Ta'anith* ii. 65 b top; cf. Mishnah, *Aboth* iv. 11), but this, as we shall see, was only admitted by the moralists with the condition that such fasting be associated with true repentance. In time of drought and other exceptional natural visitations public fasts were decreed during Temple times (see Mishnah, *Ta'anith* passim; the rule was not, however, continued in Babylonia, T.B. *Pesaḥim* 54 b), just as was done in the Maccabean age under the stress of political crises (I. Macc. iii. 47; II. Macc. xiii. 12, cf. the Elephantine Papyrus ed. Sachau i. 15, p. 7). Before starting on his journey from Babylon to Jerusalem, a journey likely to be attended with danger, Ezra, thinking it unbecoming to ask for a mounted guard, calls a fast, and this is efficacious as protection (Ezra viii. 23). Such examples would naturally be long imitated. When, at the beginning of the fourth century A.D., Zeira was about to travel also from Babylon to Palestine, he fasted 100 days (T.B. *Baba Mezi'a* 85 a. The number is no doubt exaggerated, the Jerusalem Talmud, *Ta'anith* 66 a, speaks of Zeira's 300 fasts. Cf. Bacher, *Agada der Palästinensischen Amoräer* iii. 6). It is unnecessary to illustrate the prevalence of fasting as a mourning rite (cf. the fast decreed on the death of R. Judah, T.B. *Kethuboth* 104 a); David's action stands out from the normal idea. So, on the opposite side, does Judith's; with certain (rather numerous) exceptions, she fasted all the days of her widowhood (Judith viii. 6. For the medieval Jewish custom of fasting on the anniversary of a parent's death see Shulḥan Aruch, *Yoreh Deah* 402, § 12, gloss).

Fasting as a penitential rite was, in the Rabbinic view, allied to sacrifice. But this idea only came to the front after the destruction of the Temple. The Talmud (T.B. *Berachoth* 17 a) records that R. Shesheth (third century A.D.) on fast days was wont to pray: "Master of the Universe, it is revealed before thee that while the Temple stood, a man sinned and brought a sacrifice, of which only the fat and blood was offered, and this atoned for him; and now I have sat fasting and my fat and blood has been diminished. May it be thy will that it may be accounted unto me as though I had offered it on the altar, and do thou accept it from me with favour." According to some Mishnaic texts, at an earlier period, while the Temple was in existence, the delegation (*ma'amad*) of Israelites who were appointed in association with the priests officiating in Jerusalem, remained in their cities and fasted four times a week during their sacrificial term (Mishnah, *Ta'anith* iv. 3); but this passage is missing in the best texts (including the Cambridge Mishnah, and the Munich codex, on which see Rabbinovicz, *Variae Lectiones*, Ta'anith, p. 160) and cannot therefore be relied upon. One may perceive a trace of the same idea in the preference given to fasting over alms-giving as a means of expiation; alms-giving is a sacrifice of money, fasting of one's body (T.B. *Berachoth* 32 b, top). Yet it must not be forgotten that according to Mar Zuṭra the value of fasting lay in the accompanying alms-giving (*Berachoth* 6 b). Far older and more continuous than the idea of fasting as sacrifice is the association of fasting with initiation and the reception of sacred messages. The Talmud (*Sanhedrin* 65 b) speaks of the one who fasts in order that the spirit of purity may rest upon him (cf. Exodus xxxiv. 28; Deut. ix. 9, 18; Daniel ix. 3). In early Christianity this idea was more fully developed than in the Pharisaic system, for there is no exact Rabbinic parallel to Acts xiii. 2, xiv. 23. But from the Apocalypse of Baruch (v. 7, ix. 2) it is clear that in the latter part of the first century fasting was the "usual preparation for the reception of supernatural communications" (cf. Daniel ix. 3, and several instances in IV. Esdras; see Charles on the Baruch passages). Jesus fasts for 40 days (Matt. iv. 2) as a preparation to his ministry. In later centuries Jewish mystics practised fasting in hope of close communion with God, in the third century already Joshua b. Levi fasted much whereupon Elijah resumed his interrupted visits (see refs. in Bacher, *Agada der Palästinensischen Amoräer* i. 189). On the other hand, though fasting might be regarded as a specific for the preservation of the knowledge of the Torah in a pietist's progeny (see *Baba Mezi'a* 85 a), nevertheless religious joy rather than a mood of sadness was the pre-requisite for the reception of the Shechinah (T.B. *Pesaḥim* 117 a), as also for entering on prayer (*Berachoth* 31 a). This idea must be set against the assumption that Pharisaic fasting was conducted in a dismal manner or with a sad countenance (on the basis of Matt. vi. 17). In the *Testament of Joseph* (iii. 4), the patriarch declares: "I fasted in those seven years, and I appeared unto the Egyptians as one living delicately, for they that fast for God's sake receive beauty of face" (cf. Daniel i. 15). The Day of Atonement was a day of joy (Mishnah, *Ta'anith* iv. 8). How uncharacteristic of

Pharisaic piety, moreover, is the public display of fasting, may be seen from the categorical statement of the Code (Shulḥan Aruch, *O. Ḥ.* 565, 6): "He who fasts and makes a display of himself to others, to boast of his fasting, is punished for this." On occasions of public fasts, naturally the fasting was public, for all the community assembled at devotions in the public ways (Mishnah, *Ta'anith* ii. 1); it was indeed an offence for an individual to dissociate himself from the community on such occasions, perhaps because he was not personally affected by the calamity which had called forth the general fast (T.B. *Ta'anith* 11 a). But on private fasts it was the duty of the pietist to avoid publicity. It is not easy to decide the extent to which private fasts were developed at the beginning of the Christian era. In later times they became very frequent; against bad dreams fasting was declared by Abba Areka as efficacious as fire is against flax (T.B. *Sabbath* 11 a). Excessive private fasting was, however, discountenanced in the second century by Jose ben Ḥalafta, though apparently it was permitted by the general opinion (*Ta'anith* 22 b). From a passage in the Psalms of Solomon iii. 8, 9, it would seem that in the homes of pietists private fasting was common: "The righteous man maketh inquisition continually in his own house to the end to put away iniquity; with his trespass offering he maketh atonement for that wherein he erreth unwittingly, and with fasting he afflicteth his soul." But this may refer to the Day of Atonement. The statement in Luke xviii. 12 has been held to prove that the Pharisees fasted every Monday and Thursday, but it is plausible to explain this as exceptional. "The simplest view seems to be that Luke xviii. 12 (as well as Matthew vi. 1–6, Mark ii. 11, etc.) refers to the exceptional fasts during October—November, when severe pietists fasted on Mondays and Thursdays if the rain failed. At the close of the period every one was required to fast, but the Pharisee of Luke puts himself forward as a specially strict observer of the rite, and such pietists (yeḥidim) fasted several Mondays and Thursdays during the drought (T.B. *Ta'anith* 10 a and b). Didache viii. 1 has the same autumn fasts in mind" (Büchler, *Journal of Theological Studies*, x. 268. Similarly, the trumpet-blowing before giving alms, Matthew vi. 2 etc., refers to the public fasts; the Pharisees were much opposed to public alms-giving and took various measures to prevent the identity of the donor becoming known to the recipient—*Baba Bathra* 10). The Monday and Thursday fasts became more regular later on (*Ta'anith* 12 a), and it is possible that they go back to the age of Luke. After the destruction of the Temple, private fasts became frequent, though the cases of those who fasted constantly must have remained exceptional, as their cases are specifically cited (cf. *Ḥagiga* 22 b; *Nazir* 52 b; *Pesaḥim* 68 b). And opinion was much divided as to the laudability of the habit. Meir held that Adam was a saint in that he fasted for many years and imposed other austerities on himself (*'Erubin* 18 b), while Mar Samuel declared the constant faster a sinner (*Ta'anith* 11 a, foot). A student (talmid ḥacham) was forbidden to fast overmuch as it rendered him physically unfit for "the work of heaven" (*ibid.* 11 b, top). And even in the bitter sorrow which followed immediately on the destruction of the Sanctuary by Titus, Joshua b. Ḥananiah, a disciple of Joḥanan ben Zakkai, opposed excessive asceticism, though actual fasting is not named (Tosefta, *Soṭah*, end; T.B. *Baba Bathra* 60 b). It is also probable that when Paul (II. Cor. xi. 2) refers to frequent fastings, he was referring to that kind of self-denial which is so pathetically described in the Mishnah (Meir—vi. 4 quoted above p. 114).

On the most important aspect of fasting the Pharisaic record is peculiarly clear, though they are habitually assailed on the very subject. If there is one thing evident from the continuous record of Judaism, it is the determined effort made by prophet and scribe to prevent the fast becoming a merely external rite. The fifty-eighth chapter of Isaiah remains, of course, the most spirited homily enforcing the true significance of fasting. But there are several powerful reinforcements of the prophet's protest.

Ecclus. xxxiv. 25, 26.

He that washeth himself after touching
a dead body, and toucheth it again,
What profit hath he in his washing?

Even so a man fasting for his sins,
And going again, and doing the same;
Who will listen to his prayer?
And what profit hath he in his humiliation?

Tosefta, *Ta'anith* i. 8.

If a man keep the object of defilement (shereṣ) in his hand, though he bathe in the waters of Siloam and in all the waters on earth he is not clean.

Mishnah, *Yoma* viii. 9.

He who says I will sin and repent, I will sin and repent, he hath no power of repentance.

The passage quoted from the Tosefta also occurs in the Jerusalem Talmud (*Ta'anith* ii. 65 b) in an interesting context. We have there recorded a series of actual homilies spoken on fast days. Before citing some of these, reference must be made to a more familiar instance. The Mishnah (*Ta'anith* ii. 1) ordains that on a fast after a continued drought, all having assembled with the Ark containing the Pentateuchal Scroll in the public thoroughfare, and having sprinkled themselves (and the Ark) with ashes, the oldest present is to address the assembly in these terms: "Our brethren: it is not said of the men of Nineveh that he saw their sackcloth and their fast, but he saw their acts, that they turned from their evil way (Jonah iii. 10), and in the prophet (Joel ii. 13) it is said: Rend your heart and not your garments." In the Jerusalem Talmud (*loc. cit.*), besides the homily referred to above, we have the address of R. Tanḥum bar Illai, on the text (II. Chron. xii. 6, 7): "Then the princes of Israel and the king humbled themselves, and they said, The Lord is righteous. And when the Lord saw that they humbled themselves, the word of the Lord came to Shemaiah, saying, They have humbled themselves, I will not destroy them." On which the Rabbi comments: "It is not written here *they fasted*, but *they humbled themselves, I will not destroy them.*" Of R. Ḥaggai the same passage tells us that he always cited on every fast day the saying of R. Eliezer: "Three things annul the decree: prayer, alms-giving and repentance, and all three are derived from the same text (II. Chron. vii. 14): 'If my people, which are called by my name, shall humble themselves, and pray, and seek my face, and turn from their wicked ways, then will I hear from heaven, and will forgive their sin, and heal their land'" (*seek my face* is defined to mean alms-giving on the basis of Psalm xvii. 15). It is manifestly unjust to charge with ritualism fasts on which such homilies were a regular feature.

The main point was that neither fasting nor confessing sufficed unless with it went a practical amendment of conduct (T.B. *Ta'anith* 16 a). No doubt alms-giving may degenerate into an external and mechanical rite, but it was sought to so combine it with an inward sense of sin and a conscientious aspiration towards amendment that the danger of degeneration was lessened. It was an old theory, and Tobit (xii. 8) already expresses it: "Good is prayer with fasting and alms and righteousness." A fine turn was given to the idea when the alms-giving was not regarded as a direct agent in turning away the divine disfavour, but as an imitation of the divine nature. R. Tanḥuma (*Genesis Rabbah* xxxiii. 3) addressed his assembled brethren on a fast day in these terms: "My children, fill yourselves with compassion towards one another, and the Holy One blessed be he will be full of compassion towards you." It must moreover be remembered that, after the fall of the Temple, Joḥanan ben

Zakkai comforted his mourning disciples with the saying that the loss of the Sanctuary by removing the sacrifices had not deprived Israel of the means of atonement. Charity remained. And the word used by Joḥanan for charity is not alms-giving but the bestowal of loving-kindness (גמילות חסדים) and the Rabbi cites the text (Hosea vi. 6): I desire loving-kindness and not sacrifice (*Aboth de R. Nathan*, ch. iv., ed. Schechter, p. 11). It was the same Rabbi who before the destruction of the Temple had said: "Just as the sin-offering atones for Israel, so charity (צדקה) atones for the Gentiles" (T.B. *Baba Bathra* 10 b).

## XVII. THE SABBATH.

In no other detail of the differences of the Gospels with the Pharisees do the latter appear to more advantage than in their attitude towards the Sabbath. As against his critics Jesus, indeed, sums up his position in the reasonable epigram: "The Sabbath was made for man, not man for the Sabbath" (Mark ii. 27), but the Pharisees would have done, nay, did do, the same. In the higher sense, it is true, this principle cannot be maintained. The Philonean conception of Sabbath was that of the divine effortless activity (*De Cherub.* xxvi., I. 154), and man was most closely imitating the divine exemplar when he made the approach to such a state the ideal purpose of his being. So the Rabbis also taught. The observance of the Sabbath constitutes a man the partner of God in the creation of the world (T.B. *Sabbath* 119 b); if he keep the Sabbath man *makes* it (Mechilta on Exod. xxxi. 16, ed. Friedmann, p. 104); by hallowing the Sabbath, Israel brings redemption to the world (T.B. *Sabbath* 118); and by fulfilling the Sabbatical precepts, man bears testimony to the divine ordering of the Universe (Mechilta on Exod. xx. 17, ed. Fr., p. 70 b). In this higher sense then, man was made for the Sabbath, the destined purpose of his being was the establishment of harmony with the divine. God kept the Sabbath before man kept it (*Jubilees* ii. 18 seq.), and man was made that he might fulfil on earth the custom of heaven.

But in its practical application to ordinary human life, the Gospel rule is salutary. Life must be fitted to religion, not religion to life; but there can be neither religion nor life when the one is allowed to crush out the other. And this the Rabbis felt. The commandments were given that man might live by them (וחי בהם Levit. xviii. 5), and this text was the basic ground of the Rabbinic permission of many acts which, in themselves, and apart from their necessity for the preservation of human life, were more or less flagrant invasions of the Sabbatical rest (T.B. *Yoma* 85 b). The parallel between the view of

Jesus and that of the Pharisees is, however, still closer. For, as is well known, a principle almost verbally identical with that of Mark ii. 27 is found in the name variously of R. Simon b. Menasya (Mechilta on Exod. xxxi. 13, ed. Fr., p. 103 b) and of R. Jonathan b. Joseph (T.B. *Yoma, loc. cit.*). Both these authorities were Tannaim, the latter belonging to the beginning, the former to the end of the second century. The variation in assigned authorship suggests that the saying originated with neither, but was an older tradition. For the principle that the Sabbath law was in certain emergencies to be disregarded was universally admitted (T.B. *Yoma* 85 a), the only dispute was as to the precise Pentateuchal text by which this laxity might be justified. Such discussions always point to the fact that a law is older than the dispute as to its foundation. One Rabbi bases the principle on the text (Leviticus xviii. 5) already cited; another—in the Talmud, Simon b. Menasya—on the text: "Wherefore the children of Israel shall keep the Sabbath *to observe the Sabbath throughout their generations*" (Exod. xxxi. 16), and the Rabbi argued that one may profane a particular Sabbath to preserve a man for keeping many Sabbaths. Then follows another suggested justification: "The Sabbath; holy *unto you*" (Exod. xxxi. 14): *unto you* is the Sabbath given over, and ye are not given over to the Sabbath" (לכם שבת מסורה ואי אתם מסורים לשבת). As I have previously contended (*Cambridge Biblical Essays*, p. 186), the wording of the Hebrew saying is noteworthy. *Given over* is from *masar* (= *to deliver up*). The maxim seems to go back to Mattathias. War was prohibited on the Sabbath (*Jubilees* ii. 12) but the father of the Maccabee, under the stress of practical necessity, established the principle (1 Macc. ii. 39) that self-defence was lawful on the Sabbath day, for to hold otherwise was to "deliver up" man, life and soul, to the Sabbath. In the age of Josephus, Jewish soldiers would not march, bear arms, or forage on the Sabbath (*Antiquities* XIV. x. 12), just as at an earlier period they would not continue the pursuit of a defeated enemy late on a Friday afternoon (2 Macc. viii. 26). But these acts were not necessary, in a primary sense, and therefore were avoidable; self-defence fell into a different category, and Josephus attests (*Antiquities* XII. vi. 2) that "this rule continues among us to this day, that if there be necessity, we may fight on the Sabbath days." The distinction, however, between offensive and defensive warfare was not without its dangers (see Josephus *Antiquities* XIV. iv. 1; *Wars* I. vii. 1; II. xi. 4), and the Judæans suffered from the distinction when Pompey took advantage of it. Shammai held that though offensive warfare might not be initiated, an offensive already in progress might be continued (*Sabbath* 19 a). Thus though Shammai and his school took a severer view than did Hillel and his followers, the former made concessions to necessity.

The exact limits within which the early halacha permitted the infringement of the Sabbath law are not easily defined, for no subject is more intricate than the history of the principle of the subordination (דחייה) of Sabbatarian rigidity. It has been maintained (*e.g.* by F. Rosenthal in the Breslau *Monatsschrift*, 1894, pp. 97 seq.) that the earlier law was the more lenient, and that custom became continuously more severe. But this is not accurate. It is only necessary to compare the prescriptions of the *Book of Jubilees* with the later halacha to see that there was evolution in lenity as well as in severity. Compare, for instance, the asceticism in the marital life of *Jubilees* (xlix. 8) with the very opposite attitude in T.B. *Kethuboth* 82 b (and commentaries on *Nedarim* viii. 6). The Essenes (Josephus, *War* II. viii. 9) avoided other bodily necessities on the Sabbath, but such rigidity was quite opposed to the Pharisaic view (*Sabbath* 81 a). Or again, the *Book of Jubilees* is firm in its refusal to admit the presence of heathens at the Sabbath meals of Jews: "the Creator of all things blessed it [the Sabbath], but he did not sanctify all peoples and nations to keep Sabbath thereon, but Israel alone: *them alone he permitted to eat and drink* and to keep Sabbath thereon on the earth" (*Jubilees* ii. 31). The later halacha radically modified this attitude, for not only might meals be provided for heathens on the Sabbath (T.B. *Beza* 21 b), but the very compiler of the Mishnah himself gave a banquet in honour of Antoninus on the Sabbath (Genesis, *Rabba* xi. § 4). It is even open to question whether the halacha, as developed by Hillel, did not introduce the important rule which permitted the bringing of the paschal lamb on a Sabbath (פסח דוחה שבת).

It is clear, then, that the later halacha permitted certain relaxations of the Sabbath law. From this, however, it cannot be inferred that in the time of Jesus there was such rigidity as would account for his antagonism to the Pharisees. It may well be that greater severity prevailed in Galilee and the North than in Judæa and the South (see some references by J. Mann in the *Jewish Review*, iv. 526). In that case, and if the dispute really occurred in Galilee, the controversy between Jesus and his opponents was *local*, and has no relevancy to the Sabbath law as established by the school of Hillel. For it is just on the points in which the conflict occurred that the Pharisaic law must already have reached its humane position in the first century at latest. The controversies between the schools of Hillel and Shammai are concerned with some details of Sabbath observance, but in no case do these controversies touch the points raised by Jesus. The established general rule was that the Sabbatical regulations might be, nay must be, waived in order to save life, and this is throughout implied in the Synoptic incidents. The Rabbinic phrase expressing this general rule (*Yoma* 85 a פקוח נפש דוחה שבת) was derived from a special case, that of removing a person from under a fallen mass of débris (פקוח נפש), whence the term came to apply, in general, to all acts necessary for saving an endangered life (see dictionaries *s.v.* פקוח). The Mishnah treats the rule as well established even in case of doubt: "Any case in which there is a *possibility* that life is in danger thrusts aside the Sabbath law" (Mishnah, *Yoma* viii. 6, Tosefta, *Sabbath* xv. 16). A generous inclusiveness marked the limits of this bare possibility. No Sabbatical considerations would have prevented the actual preparation of food for those in danger of actual starvation. Ears of corn might not be plucked and ground on the Sabbath under normal circumstances, but so soon as the element of danger to life entered, such and any other acts requisite for saving that life became freely admissible (cf. the collation of the early Rabbinic laws in Maimonides, Hilchoth *Sabbath* ch. ii.). "And such things" (says the Baraitha, T.B. *Yoma* 84 b and Tosefta, *Sabbath* xvi. 12, of all active infringements of the Sabbath law in cases of emergency) "are not done by heathens but by the great men of Israel" (ע״י גדולי ישראל)—*i.e.* these breaches of the law were to be performed personally by the leading upholders of the law. So, too, in the similar case of the Day of Atonement, the Mishnah (*Yoma* viii. 5) allows a sick man to be fed on the fast at his own desire, in the absence of doctors, or in their presence even if they thought the patient's need not pressing, but in the case of the presence of experts, the patient might be fed if they recognised the necessity. The Talmud (T.B. *Yoma* 83 a) explains this to mean that whereas the patient, who himself desired it, was on his own demand to be fed, whether experts were present or not, he was to be fed, even against his own inclination, if experts declared him in danger. Thus even though the ministrations of the doctors involved *them* in a profanation of the Sabbath (for the Day of Atonement was also a Sabbath) they were required to compel the patient to accept those ministrations, however unwelcome it might be to him.

On the other side the case is different with unnecessary interruption of the Sabbath rest. Normally, food eaten on the Sabbath must be provided on the Friday. On this rule the older and the later halacha agree. *Jubilees* (ii. 29, l. 9) already lays this down with emphasis: "they shall not prepare *thereon* anything to be eaten or drunk." This restriction might easily be derived from an expanded application of the Pentateuchal law concerning the manna (Exod. xvi. 23, 25), and from the direct prohibition against kindling fire on the Sabbath (Exod. xxxv. 3). It is scarcely doubtful but that the prohibition of preparing food on the Sabbath, involving as it must a variety of more or less laborious operations, was essential to any real observance of the day of rest. Even so, certain work, such as the removal of heavy boxes of produce, might be performed on the Sabbath to make room for the reception of wayfarers (Mishnah, *Sabbath* xviii. 1), but whatever could be done on Friday was to be done on that day (*ibid.* xix. 1, specifically of the circumcision rite, according to Aqiba). Friday is therefore called in the Greek sources *the day of preparation* (παρασκευή), a title authenticated by Josephus (*Antiquities* XVI. vi. 2) as well as by the Synoptics (Mk xv. 42; Mt. xxvii. 62; Luke xxiii. 54; cf. John xix. 14 with reference to the Passover). There is no exact Hebrew or Aramaic term corresponding to this, but later on, at all events, the technical word הכנה (T.B. *Beṣa* 2 b) seems to show that παρασκευή must have been the paraphrase of some such older phrase. At all events substantially the Greek word represents the fact. An important element of this preparation was the provision of ample Sabbath meals for needy wayfarers (Mishnah, *Peah* viii. 7). Such entertainment was not to be accepted lightly, and those who refused to avail themselves of this relief were praised (*ibid.* § 9). On the other hand, one who, if absolutely destitute, declined the food provided (not on Sabbath only) was esteemed a self-murderer (כאילו שופך דמים). Fasting, moreover, was forbidden on the Sabbath, this was an old and continuously observed rule (*Jubilees* l. 11, *Judith* viii. 6). It has been ingeniously suggested (E. G. Hirsch in *Jewish Encyclopedia* x. 597) that Jesus practically charges his critics with having neglected charity, in not providing Sabbath meals for the needy. "Thus he answers their charge with another. For the act of his disciples there was some excuse; for their neglect to provide the Sabbath meals there was none." But this view, arrestive as it is, hardly fits the language of the Synoptics. The argument turns on the lawfulness or unlawfulness of certain acts on the Sabbath. It cannot be, on the other hand, that Jesus alleges that even the Galilean Pharisees would admit *no* abrogation of the Sabbath law to meet a pressing necessity, for his whole contention assumes that certain abrogations *were* permitted. The incidental question as to travelling on the Sabbath does not arise, for in the Gospels this aspect is ignored, and we must suppose that the disciples had not engaged on a long journey, for such a proceeding would constitute an entire breach with the spirit of the Sabbath rest. If the disciples were in imminent danger of starvation, then the Pharisees must have admitted the lawfulness of their act under the pressure of circumstances. But it is scarcely asserted in the Gospels that the necessity was so absolute as this. The citation of the precedent of David does not involve this. Though there are variations in detail in the accounts of the Synoptics they all agree in the reference to David (Mark ii. 25, Matt. xii. 3, Luke vi. 3). "When he (David) had need and was an hungered" says Mark, and the other Gospels say much the same thing: in 1 Sam. xxi. it is not specifically said that David's young men were in a condition of starvation, for the context implies haste rather than destitution as the ground for using the holy bread. The Midrash (*Yalqut ad loc.*), however, clearly asserts that it was a case of danger to life. (It may be remarked incidentally that the Midrash supposes the David incident to have occurred on a Sabbath, and this would make the Synoptic citation of the parallel more pointed.)

All things considered, it would seem that Jesus differed fundamentally from the Pharisees in that he asserted a general right to abrogate the Sabbath law for man's ordinary convenience, while the Rabbis limited the licence to cases of danger to life. The difference is shown, too, in the citation of Temple analogies. The Pharisees thought that work permitted in the Temple was to be specially avoided in general life on the Sabbath (T.B. *Sabbath* 74 a), but Jesus cites the Sabbath work of the Temple as a precedent for common use (Matt. xii. 5). But the real difference lay in the limitation assigned by the Pharisees, according to whom all labour, not pressing and postponable, was forbidden on the Sabbath. That this is the true explanation is confirmed by the cases of healing, and is indeed forcibly suggested in Luke xiii. 14: "There are six days in which men ought to work, in them therefore come and be healed, and not on the day of the Sabbath." And this argument of the ruler of the synagogue remains unanswered; it is regrettable that the Synoptics do not in other cases present the Pharisaic case so precisely. Pharisaism speaks with no uncertain voice, and it is the voice of moderation and humanity. Every remedy for saving life or relieving acute pain, such as those of child-birth

(Mishnah, *Sabbath* xviii. 3), the curing of snake-bites (Tosefta, *Sabbath* xv. 14), the relief of various pains (T.B. *Yoma* 84), cooking for the sick (Tosefta, *ibid.* § 15), these and many other matters are detailed in various parts of the old halacha (see the collation of these passages in Maimonides, Hilchoth, *Sabbath* ch. ii.). It is interesting to note that John vii. 22 reports Jesus as defending his general position from the analogy of circumcision. Here we have yet another instance of the Fourth Gospel's close acquaintance with Hebraic traditions, for the most notable relaxation of the Sabbath law was just in cases of circumcision (see Mishnah and Talmud, *Sabbath* ch. xix.). In *Yoma* 85 b the very words of John vii. 23 are paralleled, and the saving of life derived by an *à fortiori* argument from the rite of circumcision. Jesus, however, traverses the Pharisaic position, in that he had no objection to treat long-standing diseases, lingering maladies, and in general cases where the treatment could be postponed without fear of dangerous consequences. Jesus concedes, nay his argument is based on the assertion that the Pharisees would permit the relief of an animal's distress on the Sabbath—indeed the principle was laid down in various places (Tosefta, *Sabbath* xv., T.B. *Sabbath* 128 b צער בעל חיים דאורייתא). But Jesus went further. No act of mercy, whether the need pressed or not, was to be intermitted because of the Sabbath. This is an intelligible position, but the Pharisaic position was as intelligible, and it was consonant with the whole idea of the Sabbath rest. For there are many categories of acts, clearly servile, and yet which might be brought within the definition of the merciful, thus first invading, and finally destroying, the day set aside for repose and communion with God. The Pharisees permitted, nay required, the performance of all necessary works of mercy, but refused to extend the licence too indiscriminately, and never reconciled themselves to the theory that in general the performance of a duty justified the infringement of a prohibition. Whatever may be urged from other points of view against the Rabbinic treatment of the Sabbath, and much may be so urged, it is just on the subjects in dispute in the Gospels (cf. *Orient* ix. 62) that their withers are entirely unwrung.

## XVIII. THE PERSONAL USE OF THE TERM "MESSIAH."

In the Hebrew Bible there is no indubitable instance of the use of the term Messiah (Greek χριστός) as a personal description of the instrument of the future redemption. There are several passages which tend in that direction, but as Dalman remarks no single passage can be made responsible for the use of the title. Dalman's discussion of the whole subject is full, and, in the main, satisfactory (*The Words of Jesus*, Edinburgh, Clark, 1902, pp. 268 ff., 289 ff.). The reader may be referred to Dalman for much careful information on the Rabbinic uses of the term Messiah. That, as applied to the future salvation, the term is pre-Christian is shown by the Psalms of Solomon (between 70 and 40 B.C.), where however it has been doubted whether the reading (xvii. 36) χριστὸς κύριος is right or merely a mistranslation of משיח יהוה. It should be mentioned that earlier Jewish critics have altogether doubted the Jewish provenance of this passage; Geiger held that the Greek translator, Graetz (*Geschichte der Juden*, III. ed. 2, p. 439) that the author, was a Christian, because of this very phrase (Ryle and James, *Psalms of the Pharisees*, Cambridge, 1891, pp. 141—143, notes). A similar remark applies to the use of the phrase in Pss. of Solomon xviii. 6—8. But for this suspicion there seems no sufficient ground, for in the passages cited (especially xvii. 36) the Messiah is a scion of King David in contradistinction to the Hasmonean kings. This falls well in line with the developed Pharisaic tradition in which David becomes almost inseparably associated with the Messiah. Almost, but not absolutely, for Aqiba recognised Bar Cochba as Messiah, though there is no claim in the sources that he was of Davidic descent. It is not possible to regard the non-Davidic origin of the Messiah in any document as, of itself, evidence that the document is Sadducean.

The simplest view seems to be that when a name was sought for the king of salvation, the old phrase used of the royal dignitary משיח יהוה Ar. משיחא דיי "the Anointed of the Lord" was appropriated. The transference would be helped by the Apocalyptic literature, and it may be also by the existence of a military official the "Anointed of War" (משוח מלחמה, Mishnah Soṭa viii. 1). This office was probably filled by Judas Maccabeus. As regards the mere name, the word Messiah, with or without the article, is the common appellation in the Babylonian Talmud for the personal Messiah. Dalman (*op. cit.* p. 293) thinks that "the Babylonian custom of using משיח as a proper name is incapable of being verified in regard to Palestine. It cannot, therefore, be regarded as old, or as having had a determining influence in Christian phraseology." This distinction, however, is one hard to draw. What may be asserted is that the name Messiah does not become common in Rabbinic usage till after the destruction of the Temple. Its application to Jesus occurs at the moment when the name began to be widely used, and the New Testament usage here, as in many other points, is parallel to Rabbinic development and forms a link in the chain. After the Bar Cochba war (135 A.D.) the name was well established.

Assuming then that the older phrase-form was משיח יהוה, it remains to account for the dropping of the word "Lord." In Daniel ix. 25—6 the term is used absolutely, "an anointed one"; and in the *Zadokite Fragment* (ed. Schechter) we find "his anointed," and also "an anointed from Aaron—Israel" (p. 20, l. 1). In another place the text has "anointed of Aaron" (12, l. 1). Dalman (p. 291) urges that "as the Tetragrammaton was not pronounced, and as there was a reluctance to name God [a reluctance which Dalman thinks, p. 196, was shared by Jesus], so here, as in other commonly used titles, the name of God was omitted and only המשיח Aram. משיחא was said." But though this explanation has cogency, it must be supported by another consideration which Dalman omits. It rather seems that it was a Hebrew tendency to omit the qualifying noun in titles, whether the qualifying noun was the name of God or not. We have an instance in Sirach. The Hebrew text of ch. xliv. is headed שבח אבות העולם "Praise of the Fathers of the World," whereas the later Greek translator abbreviates this into πατέρων ὕμνος, "Praise of the Fathers." Then later again the term "Fathers" was used to mean the older Rabbis without any qualifying noun. We see the same process in two famous titles which subsequently were much used. These were Nagid (probably abbreviated from נגיד עם אל, cf. שר עם אל of 1 Macc. xiv. 28) and Gaon (abbreviated from גאון יעקב Psalm xlvii. 5). At a far older period Nasi (נשיא) seems an abbreviation of a longer expression. It may be noted in passing that the term Nasi like Messiah was transferred from a political to a spiritual function, and that at an earlier period than we can definitely trace the same reference in the case of Messiah.

## XIX. GOD'S FORGIVENESS.

Rabbinic Judaism rested its confidence in the divine forgiveness on God's justice—based on his knowledge of human nature, and on his mercy—based on his love. Divine pardon is the logical correlative of human frailty. "He knoweth our frame"—as the Rabbis translated it "our yeṣer, our evil propensities"—"he remembereth that we are dust" (Psalm ciii. 13). Hence, Repentance forestalled sin in the order of creation; the means of grace was premundane; the remedy preceded the disease (*Aboth*, ii. 4). All moral basis for the world was lacking until this pillar of Repentance was set firm in place (*Pesaḥim*, 54 a; *Pirke R. Eliezer*, iii.; *Genesis Rabba*, i. 4. Cf. Schechter, *Rabbinic Theology*, 128, 314). This idea of premundane grace was deftly supported by the citation of two juxtaposed verses of Psalm xc.: "Before the mountains were brought forth, or ever thou gavest birth to the world...thou didst turn man back to dust, saying, Return, ye children of man." Again, God desires man's reverence, and to this end he forgives. "There is forgiveness with thee, that thou mayest be feared." A human tribunal punishes in order to vindicate the majesty of the Law, but God maintains his reverence by mercy, he as it were coaxes man to virtue by generously overlooking vice, and by making the sinner realise that he has not erred beyond the range of pardon. For the father yearns for the return of his erring children: "Like as a father pitieth his children, so the Lord pitieth them that fear him" (Ps. ciii. 13), and as we have just seen, this fear is on its side won by the mercy which is the response to fear. He has no desire for the death of the sinner, but would have him return and live (Ezekiel xxxiii. 11).

"Neither the national and individual experiences recorded in the Old Testament, nor the words and general language used, seem to suggest any fundamental difference in the idea of forgiveness from that which we find in the New Testament....Indeed so far as the relation between the individual and God is concerned, there is nothing to indicate that the forgiveness granted by God in the experience of his people before the coming of Christ, was different in kind from that which Christ proclaimed" (Bethune-Baker, Hastings' *Dictionary*, II. 56). This is clearly true, unless it be the fact that Jesus claimed the function of mediatorship between man and God in the matter of forgiveness. The Old Testament—especially in the Psalter—assumes that man has direct access to the Father, and Pharisaism more than accepted—it confirmed and emphasised—this assumption. The prophet—whether John the Baptist or another—might bring men to forgiveness; he did not bring forgiveness to men; it was not his to bring. The mediatorial idea—suggested by the allegorising interpretation of scripture on the one hand and by the inroad of angelology and the doctrine of ancestral virtue with its mediatorial appeal on the other—was not altogether absent from later Rabbinic theology, but on the whole it is true to assert that the principle was left intact that God and God alone is the object of worship and the sole and immediate source of forgiveness. A human potentate is reached through his ministers; but the presence of God is attainable without any such interpository etiquette. (This, for instance, is the moral drawn in *Jer. Berachoth*, 13 a, from Joel ii. 32: Whosoever shall call on the name of the Lord shall be delivered. Cf. Schechter, *op. cit.* p. 45).

Important as this aspect of the relation between God and erring humanity may be theologically, it is not more important practically than another phase of the problem as to the direct and inalienable accessibility of the divine mercy. Churches and Creeds do tend to raise barriers between man and God. They ought to join; they too often seek to keep asunder. They write their cheerless *Quicunque vult* over the threshold of heaven. Israel, on his side, is the peculiar treasure of God, for whom the rest of the world is of lower concern; not entirely so (for see p. 149 below) but to a considerable extent. On their side, of the rest of the world each group has its own key to the Presence, and the only route thither is marked on its especial and exclusive chart. As a corrective to this natural dogmatism, there recurrently rises an equally natural but a far more gracious humanism. It cannot be that any quality of human nature can disqualify man from the father's love; be that quality inborn or acquired sinfulness or unbelief. Inhumanity itself cannot rob its unhappy possessor of the rights of humanity. "The Lord is gracious and merciful; slow to anger and of great loving-kindness. The Lord is good to all; and his tender mercies are over all his works" (Ps. cxlv. 8, 9). "He dealeth not with us after our sins, nor rewardeth us after our iniquities" (Ps. ciii. 10). But it is superfluous to multiply texts; the real, sufficing, ultimate text is inscribed on the tablets of every humane heart. As Philo says (*De opif. mund.* 61), "God exerts his providence for the benefit of the world. For it follows of necessity that the Creator must always care for that which he has created, just as parents do for their children."

Two reasons, however, produce some inevitable modifications of this amiable conception. In the first place, religion is disciplinary. It must, in the interests of morality, somehow take account of consequences in order to affect antecedents; it must make forgiveness in some measure dependent on desert. And, secondly, human nature, because it is imperfect, tends to find analogues to its own imperfections in the divine nature. In 1779 Erskine, defending Lieutenant Bourne for challenging to a duel his commanding officer Admiral Wallace, said: "There are some injuries which even Christianity does not call upon a man to forgive or to forget, because God, the author of Christianity, has not made our natures capable of forgiving or forgetting them." Men go further, and assimilating God to their own image, assert that there are injuries which God neither forgives nor forgets. To what extent have Judaism and Christianity followed a similar course in this curious limitation of God's mercy? "Out of the depths have I cried unto thee....O Israel, hope in the Lord; for with the Lord there is mercy, and with him is plenteous redemption. And he shall redeem Israel from *all* his iniquities" (Ps. cxxx.). There is no limitation here. Or again: "But thou hast mercy on all men, because thou hast power to do all things, and thou overlookest the sins of men to the end that they may repent. For thou lovest all things that are, and abhorrest none of the things which thou didst make; for never wouldst thou have formed anything if thou didst hate it. And how would anything have endured, except thou hadst willed it? Or that which was not called by thee, how would it have been preserved? But thou sparest all things, because they are thine, O Sovereign Lord, thou Lover of men's souls" (Wisdom xi. 23—26). And similar ideas may be readily enough found also in the Gospels. "Knock, and it shall be opened unto you...and to him that knocketh it shall be opened" (Matthew vii. 7). "He maketh his sun to rise on the evil and the good, and sendeth rain on the just and the unjust" (Matthew v. 45). And though it be difficult for certain men to enter into the Kingdom of God, yet such things "are possible with God" (Luke xviii. 27). "I will arise and go to my father," says the Prodigal Son, but "while he was yet afar off, his father saw him, and was moved with compassion and ran and fell on his neck and kissed him" (Luke xv. 18—20). In such passages there is the fullest possible admission of the divine accessibility to all men. Jesus indeed was animated by a strong, one may even say a unique, sense of his own relation to and unbroken intercourse with God. But this sense of nearness is weakened for all other men when the intercourse with God is broken by the intrusion between them and God of the person of Jesus. In this respect—of the universality of access—the Pharisaic position varied, but it was in the main,—as no doubt the Gospel position was—represented by such thoughts as are enshrined in the following Parable:

A King's son went out into evil courses, and the King sent his guardian (παιδαγωγός) after him. "Return, my son," said he. But the son sent him back, saying to his father: "How can I return, I am ashamed." His father sent again saying: "My son, art thou indeed ashamed to return? *Is it not to thy father that thou returnest?*" (לא אצל אביך אתה חוזר. *Deut. Rabba* ii. § 24, in the name of R. Meir).

The Synoptists, not once or twice but often, dispute the general access to God. The contrast of sheep and goats, of wheat and tares—the gnashing of teeth and weeping of the iniquitous as they are cast into the fire while the righteous bask in the sunshine of God—of narrow and broad ways; the declaration that those who refuse to receive Jesus or his apostles are in a worse case than the men of Sodom and Gomorrah; the invariable intolerance and lack of sympathy when addressing opponents, and the obvious expectation that they will be excluded from the Kingdom—these things make it hard to accept current judgments as to the universality of all the Gospel teaching in reference to the divine forgiveness.

Under the stress partly of dogmatic controversy, partly of psychological experience, certain sinners were generally declared outside the pale of pardon. Philo, whose doctrine on the divine relation to man is, on the whole, so tenderly humane, holds that those who blaspheme against the Divine, and ascribe to God rather than themselves the origin of their evil, can obtain no pardon (*De prof.* 16, Mang. I. 558). This is parallel to, though less emphatic than, Mark iii. 29: "he that blasphemeth against the Holy Spirit hath no forgiveness for ever." Similarly, there are Rabbinic passages in which "the sin of the profanation of the Name of God" is described as exempt from forgiveness (*Aboth de R. Nathan*, 58 b). So, too, the man who causes many to sin *cannot* repent

(*Aboth*, v. 18). But the inability was not absolute—for, as some texts of *Yoma* 87 a read, it is only said to be *well-nigh* (כמעט) not entirely out of the power to repent. And in such cases "death atones" (*Mechilta*, 69 a, *Yoma*, 86 a. Comp. Schechter, *Aspects of Rabbinic Theology*, pp. 328 seq.). Yet it is true that certain sinners are "excluded from a portion in the world to come" (Mishnah, *Sanhedrin*, x. [xi.] 1), having "denied the root-truths of Judaism" and thus "gone out of the general body of Israel." (Comp. Maimonides on the Mishnah cited, and see *Jewish Quarterly Review*, XIX. p. 57).

Such views, however, were theoretical metaphysics rather than practical religious teaching. In its dogmatic precisions religion may think of exclusions; in its humane practice it thinks of inclusions. "God holds no creature for unworthy, but opens the door to all at every hour: he who would enter can enter" (Midrash on Ps. cxx). This is the basic doctrine of all religion, including Pharisaism, and it is repeated again and again in various terms in Rabbinic literature. (For references see Montefiore in *Jewish Quarterly Review*, XVI. 229 seq.)

God owes it, as it were, to his own nature to forgive. "God, the father of the rational intellect, cares for all who have been endowed with reason, and takes thought even for those who live a culpable life, both giving them opportunity for amendment, and at the same time not transgressing his own merciful nature, which has goodness for its attendant, and such kindness towards man as is worthy to pervade the divinely ordered world" (Philo, *de prov.* Mangey, II. 634). But this view is not new to Philo; it underlies the whole Biblical and Rabbinic theory as to Providence (see E. G. Hirsch in *Jewish Encyclopedia*, X. 232—3). In the oldest liturgical prayer the "Eighteen" Benedictions—a prayer in essence pre-Maccabean in date, as all authorities are now practically agreed—God is the sustainer of the whole world in all its natural and human relations, and immediately after the expression of his omnipotence comes the appeal to him as the God who "delights in repentance," who "is gracious and doth abundantly forgive." This last phrase is from Isaiah lv., a chapter which is a most gracious comparison of God's fertilising energy in nature to his ever-ready love to the erring human soul. "Let the wicked forsake his way and the unrighteous man his thoughts; and let him return unto the Lord, and he will have mercy upon him; and to our God, for he will abundantly pardon." And this graciousness is based on the very greatness of God. "As the heavens are higher than the earth, so are my ways higher than your ways," and this power is correlatively shown in the divine interest in the affairs of men. No passages in scripture are more often cited in the Rabbinic literature than this, unless it be Hosea's messages (ch. xiv), Ezekiel's (ch. xviii.), Isaiah's noble utterances in xliii. 25, xliv. 22, and Daniel's (ix. 9). "To the Lord our God belong mercies and forgivenesses." Rabbinic exegesis had no doubt as to the *categorical* sense of Isaiah i. 18, "Though your sins be as scarlet, they shall be as white as snow," though the moderns mostly render this sentence interrogatively.

This last fact is of some importance. To render: "*If* your sins be as scarlet, shall they be white as snow?" may suit the context in Isaiah better, but it is doubtful grammar. However, Rabbinic exegesis does often throw much light on the point we are considering. Forgiveness was an inherent attribute of the divine nature, as Philo says and as the Rabbis also maintain. But the texts on which the Rabbis base their conclusion as to the divine mercy are statements also of the divine retribution. In particular is this the case with the greatest text of all, Exodus xxxiv. 6—7, "The Lord, the Lord, a God full of compassion and gracious, slow to anger and plenteous in mercy and truth; keeping mercy for thousands, forgiving iniquity and transgression and sin: and that will by no means clear (the guilty); visiting the iniquity of the fathers upon the children, and upon the children's children upon the third and the fourth generation." The difficulty might have been met by the application of the principle that Morality and the Law are the expression, not of God's mercy or any other quality, but simply of the divine will. This idea is expressed in the passage (T. J. *Berachoth* v. 3) which denounces the ascription of such laws as that of the bird's nest to the mercy of God. It is the divine will that bids man show kindness to the bird, and not the divine love. This idea of Will did not, however, find much favour in Rabbinic theology, for it was directed against Gnosticism and had but a temporary value and vogue. That, on the contrary, the Law is an expression of Love was deep-rooted and permanent in that theology. Man's mercy to man was a reflection of God's mercy to man (see p. 166 below). God is the "Merciful One," "the Loving One" (רחמנא), and the very same epithet is transferred to the Law itself, which is often cited as "The Merciful" (see dictionaries of Levy and Jastrow s.v.). Hence, the retributive conclusion of the great pronouncement of God's mercy must be explained in terms of mercy.

This mercy is sometimes expressed in terms of *postponement*. This is not to be confounded with *limitation*. God's power and readiness to forgive are absolute. But even in his attribute of judge he is not harsh, and again and again postpones sentence. Philo's words (II. 634) re-appear in the Midrash (*Tanḥuma* Buber, Numbers 12 b): "the Merciful does not become the Tyrant (אין המוחל נעשה אכזרי)." But, on his side, man must not behave as though God's patience is infinite. God holds over thrice, but he strikes the fourth time (*Yoma* 86 a on basis of Amos ii. 6). This is not literal, and the stress must be laid on the *thrice* of the forgiveness, not on the *fourth* of the punishment. Yet though there is no limitation to God's forgiveness, there must be a limit to man's taking advantage of it. (*Aboth de R. Nathan* xxxix). How does Pharisaism reconcile the contradiction?

This was done by calling into play the other note in the harmony between God and man. If it be the nature of God to offer forgiveness, it is the nature of man to need and to crave it. God's *métier* is pardon, man's part is repentance. But though God's grace is in large measure conditioned by man's desire for it, by his repentance, nevertheless God makes repentance easy (*Pesiqta* xxv. 163 b). "He who sins and regrets his act is at once forgiven" (*Ḥagiga* 5 a). God would have men seek him in reverence, therefore he forgives. He is long-suffering, and does not requite offence with penalty. He holds it over, giving the sinner a long respite. He visits the sin of the fathers on the children —if the children carry on the tradition of sin. He is merciful and so he accepts the repentant. This is the meaning attached to the phrase quoted above from Exodus. The Rabbis do not translate ונקה לא ינקה (Exod. xxxiv. 7) "he will by no means clear the guilty," but stop at the emphatic infinite (ונקה) "and he will altogether clear" the repentant, though (לא ינקה) "he will not clear" the unrepentant, unless amendment follows at least in a subsequent generation (*Yoma* 86 a).

But this very idea of *postponement* is practically identical with the idea that no man is ultimately obdurate. Even the worst type of sinner—"he who makes others sin"—is not regarded as in a hopeless case, even he may come to repent (*Yoma* 87 a). This thought underlies the liturgy. It will be noticed, e.g., that the Confession of Sins on the Day of Atonement—a confession older according to Dr Rendel Harris than the Didache—includes offences of the most varied kind, including breaches of the Decalogue and also those sins ("profanation of the name" and so forth) which in the theoretic theology were pronounced unpardonable. Yet after enumerating them the worshipper adds: "For all these, O God of forgiveness, forgive us, pardon us, grant us remission." Now, as Philo put it, God's mercies are uncircumscribed, but not so the faculties of the recipients" (Drummond, *Philo Judaeus*, II. 57). Because God is to man as a father, therefore he does not forgive without discipline. God judges while he pities. "He not only pities after he has judged, but he judges after he has pitied: for with him pity is older than judgment" (*Quod deus immut.* M. I. 284). Yet he also judges, in relation always to man's finitude. God works on human nature, a nature which though imperfect is not impotent for good. In a sense the Jewish doctrine is something like the *synergism* of Erasmus, which as his opponent saw was radically opposed to the Pauline theory of grace. Repentance and confession lead to grace, says Philo (*De excer.* 8, II. 435), and the Rabbis held the same view. Suppose there is no repentance, is there grace? The Rabbis would probably have answered that the supposition is a wild one, but that in any case there is grace. One by one they rescued from the category of the unforgivable the few individuals whom by name they had relegated to the category. For God cannot divest himself of his attribute of mercy. This is the meaning of God's prayer to himself that his grace may overcome his wrath (*Berachoth*, 7 a, *Moed Qaton*, 16 b). This is the meaning of Aqiba's saying (*Aboth*, iii. 20) that "the world is judged by grace (בטוב), yet all is according to the amount of the work." The antinomy is the ultimate doctrine of Pharisaism. Man's part in the divine scheme of mercy must be real. He must turn and live. But the world is nevertheless judged by grace. This does not mean that man can or ought to escape the consequences of sin. Man must pay: but God is a lenient creditor, and he himself provides the coin for the remission of the debt. Man recognizes, too, that God has the right to bring man back to himself by any means that he chooses. The main thing is that man must take his part *seriously*. Sometimes man cries to be turned back to God by mild means. There is a very human note in the prayer of Rabah (*Berachoth*, 17): "O my God, before I was formed I was nothing worth, and now that I have been formed I am but as though I had not been formed. Dust am I in my life: how much more so in my death. Behold I am before thee like a vessel filled with shame and confusion. O may it be thy will, O Lord my God and God of my fathers, that I may sin no more, and as to the sins I have committed, purge them away in thine abounding compassion though not by means of affliction and sore diseases." As Maimon puts it in his Letter of Consolation (*Jewish Quarterly Review*, II. 68): "When a child is rebellious against us, we punish him in a gentle way, giving him instruction, inflicting pain upon him, the effect of which, however, will not be permanent, with a thong which gives pain, but leaves no trace, and not with a whip which leaves a permanent mark, or with a rod, which would make a mark for the time, but cleaves not the flesh, as it is said, "If thou beatest him with a rod, he shall not die" (Prov. xxiii. 13). This idea readily passes over into the idea of "chastisements of love" (*Ber.* 5), which on the one hand are not the stripes for sin but the stigmata of service, a means of repentance. On the other hand, the prevalent idea is that God is the father, who corrects "as a father chastises his son" (Deut. viii. 5), who demands from his son genuine tokens of contrition and amendment, but whose love goes out to those who are weakest and least able to return. Philo on Genesis xxviii. 3 has a striking explanation of Isaac's selection of Esau for the blessing. He determines, in the first instance, to bless Esau not because he prefers him to Jacob, but because Esau is in greater need of the blessing. Jacob can "of himself do things well," but Esau is "impeded by his own character, and has no hope of salvation but in the prayer of the father." Thus, the father forgives just because the son does not deserve it. The Pharisaic position will never be understood by those who fail to realise that it tried to hold the balance between man's duty to *strive* to earn pardon, and his *inability* to attain it without God's gracious gift of it. Perhaps the point may be made clear by contrasting two Rabbinic parables. The first is from Deut. *Rabba* ch. iii.:

A King's bride brings two gems as her dowry, and her husband gives her two other gems. She loses her own gems, and the King takes back his two. When she again finds her two gems, he restores his two. So Israel brought into the covenant with God the gems of *justice and righteousness* (Gen. xviii. 19), inherited from Abraham. God added two other gems, *loving-kindness* (Deut. vii. 12) and *mercy* (xiii. 18). When Israel lost his gems (Amos vi. 12) God took away his (Jer. xvi. 15). When Israel again finds his lost gems (Isaiah i. 27), God restores his gift (Isaiah liv. 10) and the four jewels of *justice*, *righteousness*, *loving-kindness* and *mercy* together form a crown for Israel (Hosea ii. 21).

Here we have the idea that God's mercy is a gem the possession of which is conditioned by Israel's righteousness. It is surely noble teaching, but it is not the whole truth. The other half is told in another type of thought. If, in the famous saying of Antigonos of Socho (*Aboth* i. 3), Israel must serve without hope of reward, then on the other side God's gifts must be bestowable by him without condition. Israel must work without pay; God must pay without work. On the text: *I will be gracious to whom I will be gracious, and I will show mercy on whom I will show mercy* (Exodus xxxiii. 19) the Midrash has a remarkable passage. It occurs on this text in the *Rabba* (ch. xlv. end), *Tanḥuma*, and *Yalquṭ* (§ 395). It proclaims that though righteousness will receive its reward, God's grace extends in full measure to those who have not deserved it. The idea is the same in all versions, except that in the *Yalquṭ* the point is missed that the last treasure was the *largest*. (This point is brought out in the prose rendering of S. Singer in *Lectures and Addresses*, London 1908, p. 74.) The following verse translation was made from the *Yalquṭ* (Alice Lucas, *Talmudic Legends*, London 1908, p. 10):

A legend tells, that when th' Almighty Lord
Proclaimed to Moses his eternal word,
He in a vision showed to him likewise
The treasures that lie stored in Paradise.
And at each one in turn the heavenly voice
Spake: "This the treasure is, that shall rejoice
His soul who freely giveth alms, and here
His portion is who dries the orphan's tear."
Thus one by one were all to him made known,
Until unnamed remained but one alone.
Then Moses said: "I pray thee, what is this?"
And answer made the Lord most High: "It is
The treasure of my mercy, freely given
To those who else were treasureless in heaven."

This idea, that the Father gives undeservedly, is strongly brought out in the Philonean passage oft-alluded to, and now quoted as follows. (For another version see Eusebius, *Prep. Evangel.* viii. 14, Mangey II. 634, Aucher, *de Providentia* II. 53):

*Quaestiones in Genesim*

Δυοῖν ὄντων υἱῶν, τοῦ μὲν ἀγαθοῦ, τοῦ δὲ ὑπαιτίου, τὸν μὲν ὑπαίτιον εὐλογήσειν φησίν· οὐκ ἐπειδὴ τοῦ σπουδαίου προκρίνει τοῦτον, ἀλλ' ὅτι ἐκεῖνον οἶδε δι' αὑτοῦ κατορθοῦν δυνάμενον, τοῦτον δὲ τοῖς ἰδίοις τρόποις ἁλισκόμενον, μηδεμίαν δὲ ἔχοντα σωτηρίας ἐλπίδα, εἰ μὴ τὰς εὐχὰς τοῦ πατρός· ὧν εἰ μὴ τύχοι, πάντων ἂν εἴη κακοδαιμονέστατος.

(J. Rendel Harris, *Fragments of Philo Judaeus*, 1886, p. 43.)

*Genesis xxvii.* 3

§ 198. Quippe quod duo sunt filii: unus bonus, alter sub causa (sc. crimine, culpa). Istum itaque, qui sub causa est, benedicere ait, non quod plusquam bonum praeferat hunc, sed quia scit illum per se solum posse recte rem perficere; istum vero ut a suis moribus detentum impeditumque, spem salutis habere in sola patris oratione: quam si non assequatur, prae omnibus miser erit.

(Aucher's Latin translation from Armenian, p. 400.)

The Rabbis have another form of the same thought when they pronounce the penitent sinner superior to the righteous; the former has overcome a weakness to which the latter is not susceptible. The same thought underlies the Rabbinic discrimination between Jew and Gentile in regard to God. Often there is strong particularism in favour of Israel (*Jewish Quarterly Review*, XVI. 249 seq.), and Judaism did, under the stress of the Roman persecution, regard the obdurately unrepentant heathen as resting under the divine wrath, much as we find it in the Apocalypses, and in the particularist passages of the Synoptics. But the inherent universalism of Rabbinism reveals itself not only in the beautiful hope for the heathen contained in the liturgy (in the *Alenu* prayer), not only in such a saying as that the righteous of all nations have a share in the world to come—a saying which Maimonides raised to the dignity of a Jewish dogma—but the nations are actually represented as finding repentance easier than Israel finds it. (On the salvation of the heathen see M. Joseph, *Judaism as Creed and Life*, ch. x, ed. 2, 1910, p. 116.) And most striking of all is the use made of the story of Nineveh. The Book of Jonah is read on the Day of Atonement, and it was also in earlier times the subject of a discourse on fast days (Mishnah, *Ta'anith*, ii. 1). Thus the accepted repentance of a heathen nation was the model for the repentance of Israel. "The Lord is good unto all; and his tender mercies are over all his works." This is a verse in the 145th Psalm which was introduced thrice daily into the Rabbinic liturgy. Characteristically enough, too, it was the recitation of this particular Psalm which, it was held, opened the doors of paradise to men (*Berachoth* 4 b). And it is an absolutely universalistic Psalm.

Some other aspects of the questions treated in this note will be considered further in Note XX on "Man's forgiveness."

## XX. MAN'S FORGIVENESS.

The Mishnaic tractate *Aboth* (Fathers) contains a collection of maxims by the Tannaim, the teachers of Pharisaism from the century before till the end of the second century after the beginning of the Christian era. Among these maxims occurs one which is of unusual character, for it consists merely of the citation of a passage of Scripture without addition or comment. The maxim referred to is found in ch. iv. (§ 19 or 26) of the tractate: "Samuel ha-Qatan was wont to say: Rejoice not when thine enemy falleth, and let not thine heart be glad when he stumbleth." This citation from Proverbs xxiv. 17 is remarkable. Samuel belonged to the end of the first century, and was associated in esteem with Hillel (T. J. Soṭah ix. § 12) as one "worthy of the Holy Spirit." The ingrained weakness of human nature, the desire for revenge against an enemy, is thus pointedly attacked by a great Pharisee, and in a manner as remarkable for its position as for its form.

In the Old Testament inculcation of kindliness to man Pharisaism found a firm basis for its own treatment of the subject. This doctrine does not consist of a few stray texts; it is of the essence of Old Testament religion. With regard to the special point before us, the repression of rancour and vindictiveness, the Hebrew Bible is permeated with example and admonition. No two nobler instances of forgiveness are to be found in literature than the records of Joseph's conduct to his brethren and of David's to Saul, culminating as the latter does in the Dirge of "magnanimous forgiveness" with which—to use Sir G. A. Smith's phrase—the second book of Samuel opens. And the admonition finds expression in every part of the Bible. It is found in the Law not in one but in many precepts. To the eternal glory of the Old Testament, the great texts "love thy neighbour as thyself," "hate not thy brother in thy heart," "avenge not," "bear no grudge," "love the stranger," are part of the Hebrew law of holiness.

There was little left for religion in subsequent ages except to draw out the full consequences of these and similar injunctions. Nothing that has been added can compare in sheer originality and power to the first formulation of these great principles. Theology, unhappily, has been engaged in belittling the Old Testament contribution to the gracious store, whittling away its words, or at best allowing to them grudgingly the least that the grammatical words compel! For instance, in the note on Leviticus xix. 18, in the *Cambridge Bible for Schools* (Leviticus Volume, 1914, p. 109), the editors are painfully anxious that the young student should not over-rate the text before him. And he is pointedly warned that the "stranger" of verse 34 is only the "stranger who worshipped Israel's God." Did Israel, then, worship Egypt's Gods? Yet the "stranger" is to be loved because the Israelites "were strangers in the land of Egypt." Must, then, the same word *gêr* mean two different things within the compass of the same Hebrew sentence? Whatever *gêr* means in other contexts, and in later ages, it is clear that in Leviticus xix. 34 it has a wide connotation. (On the whole question of the Rabbinic law on the stranger see D. Hoffmann, *Der Schulchan-Aruch und die Rabbinen über das Verhältniss der Juden zu Andersgläubigen*, Berlin, 1885.)

This, however, is a minor point. All honour to the great teachers of later times who set themselves to read as much into the law of brotherly love as they could. But the law is Hebraic. And it is not the Pentateuch alone which contains it. The prophetical teaching is saturated with the love of mercy. There is no need to quote. Zechariah sums up what he regards as the message of the older prophets: "Execute true judgment, and show mercy and compassion every man to his brother: and oppress not the widow, nor the fatherless, the stranger, nor the poor; and let none of you imagine evil against his brother in your heart" (Zech. vii. 9, 10; cf. viii. 16, 17 where there is added "love no false oath," with the glorious conclusion "for all these things are things that I hate, saith the Lord").

Similarly with the Wisdom literature of the Old Testament. Job, Proverbs, Ecclesiasticus, have splendid sayings on the subject of forgiveness. Again, there is no need to quote more than one passage. I select this passage, partly for its intrinsic merit, partly for its position in the Mishnah as already indicated, but mainly because it became a fundamental principle of Pharisaism.

> Rejoice not when thine enemy falleth,
> And let not thine heart be glad when he is overthrown:
> Lest the Lord see it, and it displease him,
> And he turn away his wrath from him. (Prov. xxiv. 17—18.)

What does this mean? Ibn Ezra among the older, and Dr Charles among the newer, commentators interpret the words to mean that malicious joy defeats its own end. This would not be a low standard, for many a bitter opponent has been restrained by the knowledge that to press revenge too relentlessly rouses for the victim a sympathy which would not otherwise be felt. But the great majority of interpreters, ancient and modern, read the sentence differently.

C. H. Toy's explanation in the Proverbs volume of the *International Critical Commentary* (p. 448) runs thus:

> "The *turn his anger from him* (that is from the enemy) is not to be understood as affirming that God will cease punishing a wicked man, because another man is pleased at the punishment; the full force of the expression is 'turn from him to thee,' and the stress is to be laid on the 'to thee.' 'Thou,' says the sage, 'wilt then become the greater sinner, and Yahweh will be more concerned to punish thee than to punish him.'"

The same view is taken in the Kautzsch Bible, where Kamphausen (p. 808) renders the verses Proverbs xxiv. 17–18 thus: "Wenn dein Feind fällt, so freue dich nicht, und wenn er hinsinkt, frohlocke nicht dein Herz, dass nicht Jahwe es sehe und Missfallen empfinde und seinen Zorn von jenem hinweg [auf dich] wende." On this insertion, Wildeboer in Marti's *Kurzer Hand-Commentar* remarks: "Kamphausen rightly inserts the words *to thee*." In the "Century" Bible G. C. Martin takes the same view: "*from him*, i.e. 'lest the Lord turn His anger from the wicked man to you.'" As will be seen later, the Pharisaic theory consistently was that the unforgiving injured party became the *sinner* through his implacability.

That the moderns are, however, supported by older exegetes is clear. Thus, the most popular commentary on the Mishnah, that of Obadiah of Bertinoro, has this remark on the passage already cited (Aboth iv. 19 [26]): "והשיב מעליו אפו: since it is not written וישב but והשיב, the meaning is: He will transfer his anger from thine enemy and will place it upon thee." The commentary on Aboth ascribed to Rashi interprets similarly. So does Gersonides, and so again does the popular Hebrew writer David Altschul in his commentary on Proverbs. Accepting this meaning it is a noble saying, just as in the very same chapter (Prov. xxiv. 29) is found that other noble verse: "Say not, I will do so to him as he hath done to me; I will render to the man according to his work." This is the highest possible expression of forgiveness as opposed to retaliation, unless the saying in Prov. xx. 22 be higher still: "Say not thou, I will recompense evil; wait on the

Lord and he shall save thee." Here, certainly, there is no reference at all to revenge; God does not avenge, he saves.

The doctrine read in, or into, Proverbs xxiv. 18 by most commentators is confirmed by the opening of the great passage on forgiveness to be found in Ecclesiasticus xxvii., xxviii. The passage is quoted below; here we are concerned with two introductory verses:

> Wrath and anger, these also are abominations;
> And a sinful man shall possess them.
> He that taketh vengeance shall find vengeance from the Lord;
> And He will surely make firm his sins. (Ecclus. xxvii. 30, xxviii. 1.)

This seems to mean that God exacts vengeance from the vengeful, just as Prov. xxix. 18 teaches. At all events, the Pharisaic principle was just that. *The unforgiving man is the sinner* (see quotations below). And following on his elaboration of this principle, Maimonides (*Laws of Repentance* ii. 10) adds:

> It is prohibited for a man to be hard-hearted and refuse his forgiveness; but he shall be "hard to provoke and easy to pacify" (Aboth v. 14). When the sinner seeks pardon, he must forgive with a perfect heart and a willing mind. Even though one has oppressed him and sinned against him greatly, he shall not be vengeful nor bear a grudge. For this is the way of the seed of Israel and those whose heart is right. But the heathen, of uncircumcised heart, are not so, for they retain their anger for ever. Therefore does the Scripture say of the Gibeonites (2 Samuel xxi. 2), in that they pardoned not and proved relentless, "They were not of the children of Israel."

No doubt it is a good thing for men to see themselves as others see them, and the Pharisees have enjoyed the privilege without stint! Is it not well, too, for others sometimes to see men as they see themselves? Let the Pharisees enjoy this privilege too!

It is important to observe the reference made by Maimonides to the incident of the Gibeonites' revenge. The claim of Maimonides that forgiveness was a characteristic of Israel is made in the Talmud also in reference to the Gibeonites (Yebamoth 79a). Often it has been urged that the presence of vindictive passages in the Psalter must have weakened the appeal of the finer sentiments in other parts of the Psalms and of the Scriptures generally. But the argument is a fallacy. The New Testament teaching is not all on the same level as the Sermon on the Mount, there are passages which express a vindictive spirit. But Christians rightly treat such passages as negligible in presence of the nobler sayings, which dominate and colour the whole. So with the Jew and the Old Testament. He was impelled invariably to interpret the lower in terms of the higher. The noblest ideas dominated the rest. Never do we find in the Rabbinic literature appeal made as precedents to those incidents at which the moral sense boggled. What was disliked was explained away. "Eye for eye" was never applied in practical Jewish law. Taken over theoretically from the Code of Hammurabi, the lex talionis was not acted on in Israel. *No single instance of its application is on record.* The unfavourable reference to the law in Matthew v. 38 no more than the favourable allusion to it in Philo (II. 329) implies that the law was extant as a legal practice. The Talmud is emphatic that the retaliation was not by mutilation of the offender but by the exactment of compensation by fine. (*Baba Qama* 84 a, where only one authority argues for a literal interpretation.) Perhaps the Dositheans were literalists in this respect, but the phrase "eye for eye," with which so much play is made in non-Jewish literature, was not familiar on Rabbinic lips. Some writers do most erroneously confuse "eye for eye" (a principle of human justice) with "measure for measure" (a theory of divine retribution). The one is a truculent policy, the other a not ungracious philosophy. The Pharisees who like the Synoptists adopted the theory of "measure for measure," like them also rejected the principle of "eye for eye." In fact the very objection to the lex talionis as literally conceived was used to support the need of traditional interpretation; the law as written cannot be understood without the Pharisaic mitigations (see the quotations from Saadiah in Ibn Ezra's elaborate note on Exodus xxi. 24). Similarly with the imprecatory Psalms. These could not mean what they seem to say, and why not? Because they do not consist with the forgiving spirit of other parts of the Scriptures. Thus Psalm xli. 11 reads "Raise me up that I may requite them." This contradicts the humaner spirit of Psalm xxxv. 13, vii. 5, and so David must have meant: "Raise me up that I may requite them *good for evil*" (see the quotation from Saadiah in Qimḥi's note to Psalm xli.). This may be poor exegesis, but it is rich humanism. There is another fact to remember. The imprecatory Psalms never received a personal private interpretation.

Theologically we see the same phenomena. Anthropomorphisms are brought into harmony with the developed spiritual conception of the Godhead, by explaining them away, allegorising them. Economists tell us that base coin drives out the genuine. But in Jewish history we see the reverse process; the genuine drives out the base. This tendency is shown in the Bible itself. Contrast 1 Chron. xxviii. 29

with 1 Kings ii. 1–12, whence it is seen that the author of the Book of Chronicles entirely omits the passage assailed, thus revealing that the feeling of the Chronicler was quite as tender and unvindictive as that of any modern moralist. The example of Joseph so very deeply impressed Jewish thought, that it is set up as an exemplar for God himself! Here is an oft-repeated idea; it occurs in the Pesiqta Rabbathi ed. Friedmann, p. 138 a, also in the Pesiqta d. R. Cahana, in the Canticles Rabba on viii. 1, and elsewhere:

*Comfort ye, comfort ye my people, saith your God* (Isaiah xl. 1). This is what the Scripture hath: *O that Thou wert as my brother* (Cant. viii. 1). What kind of brother?...Such a brother as Joseph to his brethren. After all the evils they wrought unto him Joseph said, *Now therefore fear ye not: I will nourish you, and your little ones. And he comforted them and spake to their heart* (Genesis i. 21)....Israel said unto God: Master of the World, come regard Joseph. After all the evils wrought by his brothers he comforted them and spake to their heart; and we, on our part, are conscious that we caused Thy house to be laid waste through our iniquities, we slew thy prophets, and transgressed all the precepts of the Law, yet, *O that Thou wert as a brother unto me!* Then the Lord answered: Verily, I will be unto you as Joseph. He comforted his people and spake to their heart. So, as for you, *Comfort ye, comfort ye my people. Speak unto the heart of Jerusalem and say unto her that her warfare is accomplished, that her iniquity is pardoned.*

The ideal traits of the Biblical heroes and saints were set up for imitation, their faults never.

Like the Book of Proverbs, the Wisdom of Sirach (Ecclesiasticus) inculcates a lofty ideal on the subject of forgiveness. It is clear that the teaching is on the same line as that of the Synoptics: as is manifest from the passages set out in parallel columns:

| | |
|---|---|
| Forgive thy neighbour the hurt that he hath done unto thee;<br>So shall thy sins also be forgiven when thou prayest. | When ye stand praying, forgive, if ye have aught against any one;<br>That your father also which is in heaven may forgive you your trespasses.<br>MARK xi. 25; MATT. vi. 14; LUKE vi. 37. |
| One man cherisheth hatred against another,<br>And doth he seek healing from the Lord?<br>He sheweth no mercy to a man like himself,<br>And doth he make supplication for his own sins?<br>Being flesh himself he nourisheth wrath:<br>Who shall atone for his sins?<br>ECCLUS. xxviii. 3—5. | Forgive us our debts, as we also have forgiven our debtors.<br>For if ye forgive men their trespasses, your heavenly father will also forgive you.<br>But if ye forgive not men their trespasses, neither will your father forgive your trespasses.<br>MATT. vi. 12, 14, 15. |

Now this teaching of Jesus son of Sirach is absolutely identical with that of Jesus of Nazareth. Dr Charles, who holds that the Testaments of the Twelve Patriarchs belong to the second century B.C., cites from these Testaments a view on forgiveness which he characterises as "no less noble than that of the New Testament." I will repeat the quotation made by Dr Charles from Test. Gad vi. 1.

3. Love ye one another from the heart; and if a man sin against thee, cast forth the poison of hate and speak peaceably to him, and in thy soul hold not guile; and if he confess and repent, forgive him. 4. But if he deny it, do not get into a passion with him, lest catching the poison from thee, he take to swearing, and so thou sin doubly. 6. And though he deny it and yet have a sense of shame when reproved, give over reproving him. For he who denieth may repent so as not again to wrong thee: yea he may also honour and be at peace with thee. 7. But if he be shameless and persist in his wrongdoing, even so forgive him from the heart, and leave to God the avenging.

Thus the line of connected Jewish teaching is complete: Proverbs, Sirach, Twelve Patriachs, Synoptics. Other links in the chain could be indicated. Philo, with much else as elevated, has these sayings (cited by C. G. Montefiore in his *Florilegium Philonis* in *J. Q. R.* VII. 543): "If you ask pardon for your sins, do you also forgive those who have trespassed against you? For remission is granted for remission" (Mang. II. 670). "Pardon is wont to beget repentance" (II. 672 συγγνώμη μετάνοιαν πέφυκε γεννᾶν). "Behave to your servants as you pray that God may behave to you. For as we hear them, so shall we be heard; and as we regard them, so shall we be regarded. Let us show pity for pity, so that we may receive back like for like" (*ibid.*).

The teaching of Judaism on the subject of forgiveness is in fact the brightest and strongest link in its golden chain. The doctrine was adopted by medieval moralists who insist on it with extraordinary frequency. And it was introduced into the authoritative Codes. As Maimonides puts it in his Code (*Laws of Repentance* II. 9, 10): "The man who does not pardon a wrong doing to him is the sinner; it is prohibited for a man to be vindictive (אכזרי, lit. *cruel, hard-hearted*) but he must forgive with a perfect heart and an eager soul." This is the spirit in which the Jew approaches God with his supplication for mercy on the great Day of Atonement. This is the teaching of Pharisaism. To attribute any other doctrine to it is unhistorical. There is no justification for representing as in a moral "backwater" the humanitarian religion of Hillel, Joḥanan ben Zakkai, Neḥunya ben Haqana, Meir, and the rest of a long, continuous line of teachers in

Jewry, who are organically connected with Sirach though they neither begin nor end with him.

That there are "imprecations" in the Psalter, that the Pharisaic literature shows some narrowness of sympathy where sectarians are concerned, and that through its whole course, until the rise of the liberal movement, Judaism has retained a "particularist" taint,—these facts must neither be ignored nor exaggerated. As to the Psalms, an admirable treatment of the question may be found in an anonymous little book (with Introduction by the Rev. Bernard Moultrie) entitled *The Use of the Psalms in the Christian Church with special reference to the Psalms of Imprecation* (St Leonards-on-Sea, 1908). The author shows how Paul, in warning Christians against revenge (Rom. xii. 19, 20), uses words borrowed from the Old Testament (Levit. xix. 18; Deut. xxxii. 35; Prov. xxv. 21, 22). Job in the course of his spirited protest, which contains the most perfect ideal of virtue ever formulated in literature, exclaims (xxxi. 29, 30)

> If I rejoiced at the destruction of him that hated me,
> Or lifted up myself when evil found him;
> (Yea, I suffered not my mouth to sin,
> By asking his life with a curse;)

As the author of the volume cited justly asserts (p. 63): "The opposition to revenge is so little peculiar to the New Testament, that the strongest and most numerous passages against it are to be found in the Old." The author goes on to show that, on the other hand, imprecations are found in the New Testament. (He cites: Rev. vi. 15—17; Matt. xiii. 56, xxiii. 33—36, xxiv. 50, 51, xxv. 41; Heb. x. 31, xii. 29; 2 Thess. i. 6—12.) But these, like the "imprecations" of the Psalter, are all based on the theory: "Do not I loathe them, O Lord, that hate thee: and am I not grieved with those that rise up against thee?" (Psalm cxxxix. 21). If this theory be no longer tenable in modern times, then those few whole Psalms, and single verses in other Psalms, which are based on like theory, should be expunged from public worship without casting a stone from the superior virtue heap at the former generations of Maccabean Zealots or English Puritans who saw in the theory nothing lowering or dangerous. The Synagogue has no need to eliminate Psalms lix. and cix. (the chief of the imprecating Psalms) because they are not used in regular Jewish public worship!

Of these two Psalms only this need be said. Of the imprecations in Ps. cix. (6—19) it is almost certain that the "Psalmist *quotes* the imprecations of his enemies in his complaint to God against them"

(W. Emery Barnes, *Lex in Corde*, 1910, p. 176). This view is disputed, but there is much in its favour. Of Psalm lix. it is equally certain that the imprecations are not directed against a personal enemy. It may well be that the objects of animosity are the Samaritans, and that the Psalm belongs to Nehemiah's age.

Mr Montefiore's lament that Jesus displayed animosity against the Pharisees has been resented by critics of his volumes. His comment, it has been said, is due to psychological misunderstanding. If this be so, ought not the same principle to apply to the Pharisaic animosity —such as it was—against sectarians? If Jesus might with propriety assail the Pharisees with threats of dire retribution, the same measure must be meted out to them, when they are the assailants of those whom they thought wilfully blind to truth and open rebels against righteousness. In no age have the sects loved one another over much, and much as one may sigh at this display, among all creeds, of human nature red in tooth and claw, it is happily true that the consequences have not been entirely bad for the world. The prophet is almost necessarily a denunciator, and the sect must fight if it would maintain the cause. "The emulation of scholars increases wisdom" (B. Bathra, 21 a), and the same principle applies to sectarian differences. The Pharisees of the age of Jesus were no doubt good fighters against internal heresies, just as they were good fighters against the common enemy, Rome. But there was more of this a century before and a century after Jesus than in his actual age. For it is in fact found on examination that the Jewish ill-feeling against the "nations" is correlated to the ill-feeling of the "nations" against Israel. The Maccabean spirit of exclusiveness was roused by the Syrian plot against Judaism, just as the later Pharisaic exclusiveness was roused by the Roman assault on the religious life of Israel. And the same is true even of the apocalypses, with their tale of doom. All of them must be placed in their proper historical background if the picture is to be just. Undoubtedly, with the terrible experience of the Great War before our eyes, with the recollection of much said and written and done burnt into our minds, our world is better able to judge the past. And it is not necessary to appeal to our own immediate experience of the hour. One would not deduce the theory of brotherly love held by Dutch Christendom from the language of Boers regarding English during the South African War; one would not entirely gauge the condition of Elizabethan Anglicanism in relation to the forgiving spirit by its language or actions regarding Spanish Catholics. Nor would one be just to Puritanism if one read a complete theory of its attitude towards the persecutors of the Church into Milton's fiery sonnet on the massacre by the Piedmontese:

> Avenge, O Lord, thy slaughtered saints, whose bones
> Lie scattered on the Alpine mountains cold!

National, sectarian, animosities, even humanitarian indignations against the cruel and the unrighteous, do indeed stand on a different plane to personal vindictiveness, and men sometimes do well to be angry.

It is, however, not the case that the Pharisaic liturgy enshrines any vindictiveness against Christianity. This denial is obviously true of the first century, but it is also absolutely true of later centuries. As a Jewish heresy, early Christianity was the subject of antipathy, as an independent religion it was scarcely assailed at all. Paganism was another matter; against idolatry the Synagogue waged war, and sometimes idolaters came in for their share of the attack, and were, in moments of stress, regarded as outside the pale of the brotherhood of man. But even then, it was internal heresy that was more bitterly resented, and the deliberate sinner, the man of immoral and heretical life within the fold, was far more the object of recrimination than any one who stood outside. Here, again, we have a fact of human nature, not of Pharisaic nature only, and it is a pity that the Pharisees are made to bear the burden which should be put on the shoulders of mankind.

The Rabbinic sayings to the effect that it is permissible to "hate" the wicked within the fold, have no reference to personal wrongs. The offences which make "hatred" justifiable are invariably breaches of morality or of the law of God which should not be condoned until the offender had repented. The personal foe does not come into the category. The same page of the Talmud (*Pesaḥim* 113 b) which records the duty to show detestation of the adulterer records also that beloved of God is he who forgives wrongs personal to himself. "I believe it to be quite one of the crowning wickednesses of this age that we have starved and chilled our faculty of indignation" (Ruskin, *Lectures on Art*, 1870, p. 83; compare Sir J. Stephen, *History of the Criminal Law of England*, 1883, Vol. I. p. 478). In the category of those who were to be the object of this "indignation," were sometimes included the heretic and the disloyal (*Aboth de R. Nathan* xvi.). But almost always the offences were indeed detestable (e.g. *Ta'anith* 7 b). Beruriah, the wife of R. Meir, in an oft-quoted passage explained

Psalm civ. 35 as a prayer that sin not sinners should be made an end of (*Berachoth* 10 a). It is not easy, in this tender fashion, to discriminate between sin and sinners, but one ought never to lose sight of the general Pharisaic repugnance against hatred. "Hatred of mankind" (the term used is the widest possible שנאת הבריות) is one of the three things (the other two are the "evil eye" and the "evil *yeṣer*"—envy and lust) which "put a man out of the world" (Mishnah, *Aboth* ii. 11 [15]). So that we have in a late Midrash the splendid generalisation that: Whoever hates any man is as one who hates Him who spake and the world was (*Pesiq. Zuṭ.* on Numbers viii. seq.). This prohibition applied to all men, even to Rome (see the strong rebuke in Eccles. *Rabba* xi., on the text Deut. xxiii. 8). Even the command to remember Amalek was explained by one Rabbi to mean: Remember your own sins which led up to Amalek's assault:

A King owned a vineyard, round which he built a fence. He placed inside the fence a savage dog. The King said: Should one come and break through the fence, the dog will bite him. The King's own son came, and broke down the fence. The dog bit him. Whenever the King wished to mention how his son had offended in the matter of the vineyard, he said to him: Remember what the dog did to you! So, whenever God wishes to recall Israel's sin at Rephidim (Exod. xvii. 8), he says unto them: Remember what Amalek did to you! (*Pesiqta K.*, iii. 27 a).

In passing, though the fact is of more than passing importance, let note be taken of the quotation from the *Pesiqta Zuṭarta.* To hate man is to hate God. We have the same thought underlying the preference shown by Ben Azzai for Genesis ii. 4 as the "greatest commandment" (cf. p. 20 above). R. Aqiba declared in favour of Leviticus xix. 18 "Love thy neighbour as thyself." But this is open to the objection that if a man is himself in despicable state, he may despise his neighbour (הואיל ונתבזיתי יתבזה חבירי). Hence, says Ben Azzai, greater is the text: "These are the generations of the heaven and the earth when they were created" (Gen. ii. 4). As R. Tanḥuma comments: "If thou showest low regard for any man, remember whom thou art despising: for the text says: In the image of God made he man."

Another aspect of the sectarian question is apt to be overlooked. Sects, while their first inspiration is fresh and their numbers small, have always been distinguished for the strength of brotherly love within their own body. But when the membership transcends local bounds, and the initial impulse is materialised into a systematised organisation, that warmth of complete and unreserved fraternity is necessarily apt to cool. It is superfluous to show how Christianity was compelled by its own success to become less a brotherhood than a Church. Within Judaism we find at every epoch, from the period before the Christian era down to the present time, the continuous formation of new unions, which display intensity of brotherhood while young and small, and which progress in the normal way towards greater aloofness as the body grows older and bigger. Religion is kept fresh by the outbreak of sectarianisms; this is the great good accruing from the creation of new sects. For these recurrent outbreaks of sectarianism are also outbreaks of brotherliness within the new sect, they are the renewals of the religious stream, the openings up of new wells of the humane spirit which comes direct from God. And so we find Hippolytus saying of the Essene: "He will observe righteousness towards men and do injustice to none: he will not hate anyone who has done him injustice, but will pray for his enemies" (*Refutatio Omnium Haeresium*, IX. 18—28. Cf. Kohler, *Jewish Encyclopedia*, V. 239; Josephus, *War*, II. viii. 6—7). So, passing across many centuries, we have Luria (the mystic leader of Safed, 1534—1572) *opening the day* with the invocation: "Lo! I hold myself ready to fulfil the divine behest: Thou shalt love thy neighbour as thyself," and at night *closing the day* with the declaration: "Lo! I pardon everyone who has angered, or provoked me, or sinned against me, and I pray that no man whatsoever shall be punished because of me." (Cf. Steinthal, *Zu Bibel und Religionsphilosophie*, p. 161.)

And the same sensitiveness is observable at normal periods. There is, for instance, a whole series of more ancient personal prayers preserved in the Jerusalem Talmud (*Berachoth* iv. § 2). "May it be thy will, O Lord my God and God of my fathers, that hatred and envy of us enter not into the heart of man, nor hatred and envy of any man enter into our heart." On the same page may be seen the student's prayer. "May it be thy will, that I be not angered against my fellows, nor they against me." Yet another prayer occurs in the same context. "Bring us near to what thou lovest, keep us far from what thou hatest." These beautiful petitions may be paralleled by that of Mar Zuṭra, who every night on retiring to his couch said: "Forgiveness be to all who have troubled me" (שרי ליה לכל מאן דצערן *Megillah* 28 a).

Turning from the necessary distinction suggested above between public, national, humane enmities and private, individual, inhuman vindictiveness, we are arrested by an aspect of the subject which is an important element in the Pharisaic doctrine of forgiveness. The injured party must forgive, but what of the man who has done the wrong? Pharisaism did not reserve all its sympathy for the inflicter of the wrong; it had sympathy, too, with the sufferer of the wrong. It said to the injurer: You, too, pray for God's mercy, but you must not go to God red-handed. Before you ask God's forgiveness, seek the forgiveness of your injured fellow-man. Not even the Day of Atonement atones for wrongs done by man to man (Mishnah Yoma viii. 9). The man who brought a sin-offering and remembered at the very altar that he still held the stolen goods, was ordered to stop his sacrifice, make restitution, and then come back to his sacrifice (Tosefta, Baba Qama x. 18, p. 368. Cf. *Cambridge Biblical Essays*, 1909, p. 189; see also Philo *de opif.* chs. i and iv). And if the sin-offering prescribed in the Pentateuch was thus of no avail unless practical atonement had preceded, it is not surprising that we find the same declaration of the futility of prayer to God unless it had been preceded by an appeal to the injured neighbour. Undo the injury, beg your neighbour's forgiveness, realize the wickedness of wrong-doing, do not throw *all* the burden of reconciliation on the person wronged. *He* must forgive, but you must try to earn his forgiveness. It is not merely a piece of French wit: *Que messieurs les assassins commencent!* The criminal must not expect *all* the consideration, he must show some on his part to the rights of society. The Pharisees softened punishment by their theory that it was part, the main part of atonement: the prisoner came out, not crushed by disgrace, but ennobled if chastened by the sense that he had borne punishment to put himself right with the outraged moral law. It then became the duty of society to forgive on its part: to clean the slate, and forget the record. And so with regard to wrongs which do not fall within the scope of the law at all. Here, too, the perpetrator of the wrong must bear his share in the hard labour of atonement. It is almost pathetic to read in Jewish moral books how the offender must humble himself, must again and yet again present himself before his offended brother, seeking pardon, refusing to accept a rebuff. (Cf. Yoma 87 b.)

The Synoptics, on the whole, imply the same view. The Gospel exhortations to forgive take it for granted that, though the response must be prompt and complete, it is response rather than initiative that is contemplated. There are thus two elements: (*a*) approach by the offender, (*b*) pardon by the offended. Some theologians who, without foundation in fact, contrast the Pharisaic doctrine unfavourably with the Gospel teaching, in their just admiration of (*b*), which the Pharisees fully shared with the Synoptists, ignore (*a*), which the Synoptists fully shared with the Pharisees. The Gospel view is most clearly seen in the effective Parable of Matthew xviii. 23—35. The defaulting debtor is forgiven the debt after admitting it and praying for patience (v. 26—7). The debtor then refuses a similar prayer by *his* debtor (v. 29). In punishing this act—and the Parable of forgiveness a little loses its grace by making over vindictive the lord's resentment of unforgiveness—the lord says: "Thou wicked servant, I forgave thee all that debt, *because thou besoughtest me*" (v. 32). This be it remembered is the illustration of the injunction "until seventy times seven" (v. 22). Clearly the injured is expected to do his part in seeking pardon from the injured (cf. Hermas, *Mandate* IV. 8, 9).

And if the injured party be dead? Then at his grave must pardon be asked: the living appealing to the dead (Maim. Teshuba, ii. 11; Yoma 87 a). This terrible aspect of the case had great weight in completing the practical Pharisaic mechanism of forgiveness. For there are wrongs done by us over which we weep in vain. It is not that our friend *will* not always forgive; sometimes he *cannot*. The injury may have passed beyond him: it may have affected too many: you may fail to catch up with all its ramifying consequences. Or he may have died. It is the most heart-breaking experience, especially in family dissensions. You are hard, you will not bend: then you relent too late: the other side has hardened: or the other side has passed from earth, and heart cannot find the way back to heart this side of the grave.

It was this last consideration that impelled the Rabbis to pour all the vials of their indignation on the man who increases the inherent difficulty of reparation by his obduracy when asked to forgive. Such a one, Maimonides on the basis of the Mishnah (Baba Qama viii. 7 etc., Bam. Rabba § 19, Berachoth 12, Yalqut Samuel i. § 115) pronounces a sinner and a typical representative of the spirit of cruelty and hard nature. Here the theory of measure for measure was applied, the theory which finds so effective an expression in the Lord's prayer ("Forgive us our trespasses as we forgive them that trespass against us"). "If a man offends his neighbour and says: I have sinned, the neighbour is called sinner if he does not forgive" (see refs. just cited). "So long as thou art forgiving to thy fellow there is One to forgive thee; but if thou art not pitiful to thy fellow, there is none to have mercy on thee" (Buber Tanḥuma Genesis, p. 104, cf. Sabbath, 151 b). The Midrash also argues that Job and Abraham received signal instances of God's beneficence *when they had prayed for the pardon of others*, and much more to the same effect. *The injured party must pray for the pardon of his injurer* (Tosefta B. Qama ix. 29 ed. Zuckermandel, p. 366 top), otherwise, he himself will suffer (Midrash Jonah, p. 102).

On the other side, of Neḥunya ben Haqana it was said (Megilla 28 a) that the curse of a comrade never went to bed with him. In response to R. Aqiba he said: "I never stood on my rights" (to exact revenge or even apology): and so Rava said (*loc. cit.*, and Rosh Hashana 17 a, Yoma 23 a): He who forgives (המעביר על מדותיו) received forgiveness, for in the Scripture (Micah vii. 18) the words "pardoneth iniquity" are followed by the words "passeth by transgression, i.e. God pardoneth the man who passes over wrongs." There is no self-righteousness here, no aggravating sense of superior virtue. Those, of whom the Rabbis speak, who humbled their spirit and heard their "reproach in silence," were, the same sentence (Pesiqta Rabbathi, p. 159 a) continues, also those who "attributed no virtues to themselves." To bear reproach and answer no word was an oft-praised virtue (Sabbath 88 b, Sanh. 48 b—49 a). This noblest of all applications of the principle of measure for measure which goes back to Psalm xviii. 25, 26 is found again and again in the Rabbinic writings. It is not "incidental" to them, it is permeative. "R. Judah says in the name of Rabban Gamliel: See, the Scripture saith, And He will show thee mercy and have compassion on thee and multiply thee; this token shall be in thy hand, Whilst thou art merciful, the Merciful will have mercy on thee" (Tosefta Baba Qama ix. 30).

The principle of "measure for measure" (see Matthew vi. 14—15) supplies the most efficient motive for forgiveness, but passing beyond that, the Rabbis make the duty of forgiveness absolute. The unforgiving man was the denier of God (Yalqut on Judges viii. 24); many private Rabbinic prayers breathe the most thorough feeling for a state of mutual good-will between men (e.g. Berachoth in both the Talmuds on iv. 2). In the future world there is to be no enmity (Berachoth 17 a), which is the Rabbinic mode of setting up the same ideal to be striven for on earth. The acme of the saintly disposition is slowness to be enraged and quickness to be reconciled (Aboth v. 11). And although we do not find in the Rabbinic literature a parallel to the striking paradox *Love your enemies*, we do find the fine saying (already quoted by Schöttgen): "Who is mightiest of the mighty? He who makes his enemy his friend" (מי שעושה שונאו אוהבו, Aboth de R. Nathan, xxiii). This ancient saying received more than lip-homage. Samuel ibn Nagrela was made Vizir of Habus, the Berber king of Granada in 1027. Near the palace of Habus, says Graetz (*History of the Jews*, E.T. III. viii.), there lived a Mussulman seller of spices, who no sooner beheld the Jewish minister in the company of the king, than he overwhelmed him with curses and reproaches. Habus, indignant at such conduct, commanded Samuel to punish this fanatic by cutting out his tongue. The Jewish Vizir however knew how to silence him who cursed. He treated him generously, and by his benefactions converted the curses into blessings. When Habus again noticed the seller of spices, he was astonished at the change, and questioned Samuel about it. The minister replied, "I have torn out his angry tongue, and given him instead a kind one." So, to return to the older period, the greatest crown of all was that won by Moses when he entreated God, not on his own behalf, but to forgive sinful Israel (Yalqut on Ps. xc. 1).

*A Prayer of Moses* (Psalm xc. 1). To what is the matter like? To three men, who came to seek the royal amnesty. The first came and made obeisance.—"What seekest thou?"—"Amnesty for my rebellion." His petition was granted. So with the second. Then came the third. "What seekest thou?"—"For myself, nothing. But such and such a Province is laid waste, and it is thine; command that it be rebuilt." Said the King, "That is a great crown—it is thine." So David and Habakkuk pray on their own behalf (Psalm xvii. 1, Habakkuk iii. 1). When Moses came, God asked him: "What seekest thou?"—"Forgive the iniquity of this people" (Numbers xiv. 19). God answered: "This is a great crown—it is thine, in that I change my will because of thee" (*Yalquṭ*, Psalms, § 841).

Very fine too is the following expression given to the desire to convert enemies into friends by the exhibition towards them of love:

> If thine enemy be hungry, give him bread to eat,
> And if he be thirsty, give him water to drink;
> For thou shalt heap coals of fire upon his head,
> And the Lord shall reward thee. (PROV. xxv. 21—22.)

R. Ḥama b. Ḥanina said: Even though he has risen up early to slay thee, and he come hungry and thirsty to thy house, give him food and drink. Why? *Because thou heapest coals of fire on his head and the Lord will make him at peace with thee* (v. 22). Read not *yeshalem*, will repay, but *yashlimenu*, will *make him at peace with thee* (Midrash *ad loc.* Cf. T. B. *Megillah* 15 b. See the passages as quoted in *Yalquṭ ha-Machiri*, Proverbs, p. 58 b).

As another Rabbi could claim, at the close of a long life (*Megillah* 28 a), "I never went to bed with the curse of my fellow" (לא עלתה קללת חברי על מטתי).

By a natural, and assuredly not dishonourable, stretch of moral chauvinism, this very quality of forgiveness, which is so rashly denied to the Pharisees, was by them treated as a special characteristic of Israel (cf. p. 153 above). "He who is merciful towards all men (הבריות) thereby shows himself of the seed of Abraham" (Beṣa 32 b. In all such passages the context shows that רחמן *merciful*, used indeed in the widest sense, is particularly employed in the meaning *forgiving*). Carrying to the extreme the maxim "Be of the persecuted not of the persecutors" (Baba Qama 93 b and elsewhere), the Rabbis even said "He who is not persecuted does not belong to Israel" (Ḥagiga 5 a). "Three gifts the Holy One bestowed on Israel: he made them forgiving, chaste, and charitable" (Bam. Rabba viii., Yebamoth 79 a). Or to sum up: "Ever shall a man bestow loving-kindness, even on one who does evil unto him; he shall not be vengeful nor bear a grudge. This is the way of Israel" (Midrash le'olam, ch. vii.).

And why? Because Israel is the child of God, and must strive to be like his Father. The great foundation of the forgiving spirit is not to be sought in the principle of measure for measure. Its basis is the *Imitatio Dei*, an idea which is very old, very frequent in the Pharisaic literature, and included by Maimonides as one of the precepts of the Pentateuch (Affirmative laws § 8). Portia, in her sublime praise of the quality of mercy, says:

> But mercy is above this sceptred sway,
> It is enthronèd in the hearts of Kings,
> It is an attribute to God himself;
> And earthly power doth then show likest God's,
> When mercy seasons Justice.

Her rebuke, cast at the Jew, almost reads like a quotation from the Jew's own books. "As God is merciful and gracious, so be thou merciful and gracious," is the Pharisaic commentary on "Ye shall be holy, for I the Lord am holy" (Sifra 86 b, and many other passages, Mechilta 37 a, Sabbath 133 b, and often. See Schechter, *Some Aspects of Rabbinic Theology*, ch. xiii.). "The profession of the Holy One, blessed be he, is charity and lovingkindness, and Abraham, who will command his children and his household after him 'that they shall keep the way of the Lord' (Gen. xviii. 19), is told by God: 'Thou hast chosen my profession, wherefore thou shalt also become like unto me, an ancient of days'" (Genesis Rabba, lviii. 9, Schechter, p. 202). Or to cite but one other passage (Soṭa, 14*a*), "Rabbi Ḥama b. R. Ḥanina said: What means the Biblical command: Walk ye after the Lord your God? (Deut. xiii. 4). Is it possible for a man to walk after the Shechinah? Is it not previously said: The Lord thy God is a consuming fire? (Deut. iv. 24). But the meaning is: to walk after the attributes of the Holy One. As he clothed the naked—Adam and Eve in the Garden (Genesis iii.)—so do thou clothe the naked; as the Holy One visited the sick (appearing unto Abraham when he was ailing, Genesis xviii.), so do thou tend the sick; as the Holy One comforted the mourners (consoling Isaac after the demise of his father, Genesis xxv.) so do thou comfort the mourners; as the Holy One buried the dead (interring Moses in the valley, Deut. xxxiv.), so do thou bury the dead. Observe the profundity, the ingenuity of this Rabbinic exegesis: from first to last, from Adam's days in the beginning to Moses' death in the end, from Genesis to Deuteronomy, the law, according to the Rabbi, bids the Israelite *Imitate God*" (cf. *Jewish Addresses*, 1904, pp. 41—51). Most frequently this *Imitatio Dei* interprets itself as an admonition to mercy. God imparts of his attribute of mercy to men that they may be merciful like himself (Gen. R. xxxiii.). That the connection of the law of holiness with the *Imitatio Dei* goes back to the beginning of the Christian era is shown from Philo's saying: "Holiness consists in imitating the deeds of God," just as "earthly virtue is an imitation and representation of the heavenly virtue" (μίμημα is used several times in this context), a "warder-off of the diseases of the soul" (*De alleg. legum*, I. 14, Mangey, I. 52). For God is the supreme archetype (see Drummond, *Philo-Judæus* II. 81), and as all virtue is a reflection of his moral nature, so man becomes moral when he strives to liken his character to the heavenly exemplar. So the "rewards of the virtuous, which fill the soul with a transcendent joy" are, with Philo, the attainment to some share in the nature of God (Drummond, II. 323). This extension of the idea is Pharisaic as well as Philonean (Pesiqta R. xi. end). On earth man is an appanage of God, cleaving to him in the desire to imitate. But hereafter man becomes self-existent in his resemblance to God (הם הווים ודומים).

## XXI. THE LIFE OF THE RESURRECTION.

The question as to the exact physical conditions of life after death has often divided Jewish opinion. Maimonides (Hilch. *Teshubah* viii. 2) unreservedly asserts: "In the world to come there are no bodies, but only the souls of the righteous, without bodies like angels." This view Maimonides based on Talmudic authority; but some of his critics protested against it and quoted such Rabbinic sayings as clearly inculcate the view that at the resurrection the dead arose with the same physical defects as in life (T.B. *Sanhedrin* 91 b), though these were forthwith healed, that the dead arose clothed (*Kethuboth* 114 a). So, in the Apocalypse of Baruch l. 2: "the earth will then assuredly restore the dead, making no change in their form," though (li.) the aspect of the resurrected saints would thereafter be transformed.

On the other hand, Maimonides rested his statement on the saying (*Berachoth* 17 a): "In the world to come there is neither eating nor drinking, no marital relations, no business affairs, no envy, hatred nor quarrelling; but the righteous sit with their garlands on their heads, enjoying the splendid light of the Divine Presence (Shechinah) as it is said: And they beheld God and they ate and drank (Exodus xxiv. 11)."

This saying (parallel to Mark xii. 25) is cited by the Talmud in the name of Abba Arika (Rab), who died in 247 A.D. But the main ideas involved in his sentence are all much older, and are not inconsistent with the belief in the bodily resurrection. In the first century the schools both of Hillel and Shammai believed in the restoration of the material form (*Genesis Rabba* xiv., ed. Theodor, p. 129; *Leviticus R.* xiv.). But it is certain that this bodily resurrection was only regarded as one stage in the process of attaining to immortality, and much ingenuity has been exercised (as by Naḥmanides in *Shaar hagemul*) in reconciling with one another the various Rabbinic statements (including the famous parable of the lame and the blind, on which see p. 98 above).

The main metaphors in Rab's picture of the future life are (1) the banquet, (2) the light, (3) the crown. "The righteous sit with garlands on their heads, enjoying, etc." is a figure obviously derived from the banquet (Löw, *Gesammelte Schriften* iii. 417). It is a familiar figure which the evidence shows goes back in Rabbinic literature to the first century. In a famous passage of the Mishnah, Aqiba (*Aboth* iii. 16, last words) speaks of the future life as a banquet, which is prepared for all, wicked as well as righteous, for the sinner is to enjoy it when he has paid the penalty for his evil life (this universal interpretation is clearly derivable from the context, and the Bertinoro rightly so interprets). Aqiba held that the judgment on the wicked in Gehinnom lasted only twelve months (Mishnah, *Eduyott* ii. 10). The same figure is carried out in the Mishnaic saying of R. Jacob (*Aboth* iv. 16). He compares the earthly life to the πρόθυρον (vestibule or outer door) and the future world to the τρίκλινον (dining hall. The force of R. Jacob's comparison is well brought out by L. Löw, *Gesammelte Schriften* i. 127; cf. also iii. 417). An amplification of the figure, belonging, however, to an earlier date, is seen in the parable of the wise and foolish guests (T.B. *Sabbath* 153 a. This parable is ascribed to Joḥanan b. Zakkai by the Talmud, and to Judah the Patriarch in Eccles. Rabbah on ix. 8. The former ascription is adopted by Bacher, *Agada der Tannaiten*, ed. 2, vol. i. p. 36, and it is the more probable seeing that R. Meir knew it. The figure is frequently found in the Rabbinic literature of later centuries; cf. T.B. *Pesaḥim* 119 b; *Baba Bathra* 74 b, where the Leviathan appears as the main dish at the banquet).

Even older is the idea of the heavenly light which the righteous were to enjoy. In Daniel xii. 2 the resurrected saints are to shine as the brightness of the firmament, and in the Ethiopic Enoch (cviii. 12) they are to be clad in raiments of light. The term light played a great part in Jewish mystical terminology. The angels fed on the shining light of the Shechinah (*Numbers Rabba* xxi. 16) and the mystics made much play with the thought. The figure of the crown is also an old conception. Thus in *Wisdom* (v. 15 seq.) the righteous live for ever, and they shall receive the royal robe (βασίλειον) and the diadem of beauty (διάδημα τοῦ κάλλους) from the Lord's hand. It is not clear from the context whether this crowning of the righteous is regarded as part of the protection on earth or whether it is a feature of the life hereafter, but the two ideas lie near together. The crown may imply the notion of victory, or possibly the exact thought is of freedom. The phrase "with their crowns on their heads" occurs in the Sifra (*Behar* Perek ii., ed. Weiss, p. 106 d) in a context which leads Weiss to make this suggestion (foot of the page cited): the freed slaves "ate and drank and rejoiced *with their crowns on their heads*" between the first and tenth of Tishri in the Jubilee year. In his book, *The Immanence of God in Rabbinical Literature* (p. 88), Dr Abelson has a fine passage in which he summarises the view of Naḥmanides. In Exodus xvi. 25 the text says of the Manna: "to-day ye shall not find it in the field," on which the Mechilta remarks: "Ye shall not find it in this life, but ye shall find it in the life to come." Dr Abelson thus reproduces Naḥmanides' comment: "The worthy Israelite will find his manna, i.e. his source of continued vitality, even after death; he will find it in that blessed union with the Shechinah for which he has qualified himself in ascending stages of spiritual saintliness. He will wear the crown upon his head. Does not the prophet predict that 'in that day the Lord of Hosts shall be a Crown of glory' (Isaiah xxviii. 5)? There will be a complete merging of the human life with the divine life."

# INDEX I

*Of Names and Subjects*

# INDEX II

*Of New Testament Passages*

## MATTHEW



## MARK

LUKE



JOHN



ACTS



ROMANS



1 CORINTHIANS



2 CORINTHIANS



GALATIANS



2 THESSALONIANS



1 TIMOTHY



HEBREWS



REVELATION

# STUDIES IN PHARISAISM AND THE GOSPELS

BY

I. ABRAHAMS, M.A.

READER IN TALMUDIC, UNIVERSITY OF CAMBRIDGE,
FORMERLY SENIOR TUTOR, JEWS' COLLEGE, LONDON

*SECOND SERIES*

Reprinted by permission of Cambridge University Press.
First Published 1924.

# PREFACE

THE generous reception accorded to the First Series of these Studies has encouraged me to prepare a further Series on the same plan and method. The plan is open to objection, no doubt. To take up particular topics, and treat them in short essays written at long intervals of time, involves both superfluity and deficiency, the former owing to repetition, the latter to omission. Such essays overlap, and never can present a complete view. But I have endeavoured to cite different quotations where the same subjects recur, and the plan has the advantage of concentrating, in the various chapters, on main points of interest, without overloading them with details. I have improved, I hope, on the plan of the former volume by the introduction of foot-notes, in which details better find their place than in the main text. In two of the chapters the notes proved so extensive that they are collected at the ends of those chapters, and the opportunity was used for entering into fuller consideration, among other matters, of Philo's views on the Imitation of God, and the recorded particulars of Polycarp's noble martyrdom.

Though this plan is, as has been conceded, open to objection, I cannot concede so much as regards the method. Only one of my readers (Prof. A. T. Robertson) has, so far as I am aware, mistaken what the method is. The statement in my previous preface, that I felt no impulse towards a directly challenging style, was in this one case turned into an admission that I found nothing to challenge, but accepted the very views which my book was designed to oppose. I am still convinced that what is needed by students of the New Testament, be they Christian or Jewish students, is not polemics but exposition, not controversy but balanced discussion. The Gospels should no more be used as a foil to Pharisaism, than the Talmud as a foil to the Gospels. Jesus, in his teaching, was not always thinking of the Pharisees. His value is depreciated by so narrowing the application or motive of his appeal. Some of his finest, his most vital, criticisms of conduct and standards of conduct tend to be cheapened by a recondite search for justification in supposed Pharisaic vices. There is patent enough justification in the ordinary and admitted facts of human nature. Pharisaism will never be understood by those who treat everything that Jesus said as an attack on Pharisaism. I do not think that Dr Charles can long persist in his latest theory that though the Pharisees were not conscious deceivers, yet they were self-deluded. This, it is true, is more genial than treating them as types of hypocrisy and externalism. To treat morality as law, as on the whole the Pharisees did, spells neither self-delusion nor lack of spirituality. On the other hand, to treat morality as an autonomous principle, as Jesus on the whole did, spells neither licence nor vacillation. Ordinary society tends, it is true, to convert legalised morality into mechanism, and autonomous morality into anarchism. For ordinary society, then, a compromise is necessary between the Pharisaic ideal of moralising the organised community and the evangelical ideal of free self-development of the individual. On the cultural side, as Butcher said, Hellenism and Hebraism must be confluent in the stream of civilisation; so on the purely ethical side, legalism and individualism must be somehow made confluent in the stream of religion. The compromise, the confluence should not be difficult, for on neither side is the tendency absolute or isolated. Christianity knows of organised conventions, Judaism of free action of the conscience. Legalism and autonomy thus already have much in common.

The time has passed for "disputations" of the medieval type, and students can throw off the older recrimination and mutual suspicion. Above all we must avoid what I have termed hand-to-mouth exegesis. The Gospels represent varying moods, and nothing is gained by commentators applauding a principle in one context and decrying it in another context, using Pharisaic material as a foil in the one case and forgetting the same material in the other. Surely students are no longer seeking to score points off each other. What we should rather seek is to add to the common total of points scored by truth in its contest against falsehood, by humanism against obscurantism. I have myself learned so much from Christian scholars in my understanding of Jesus, that if these can derive any trifling help from my work in their understanding of the Pharisees, I shall rejoice at having repaid a small instalment of a heavy debt.

Amidst the weeds of Pharisaism are flowers, amidst the evangelic flowers are weeds. I cannot overcome my preference for the flowers. I am no gatherer of weeds. If I had for a moment been tempted to diverge from these, my inmost sentiments, I should have been kept straight by the gracious words of one of the most gracious of men. The reference made to one of my readers induces me to allude to this other. It was a genuine pleasure to win the approval of the late William Sanday, a theologian whose mission to the scholarly world was to inculcate good-will, appreciation, and tolerance tempered by firmness. He contributed an essay on the "Language of Vindictiveness" in liturgy and life to the second of the Tracts on Common Prayer published by the Oxford Press under the title *The Use of the Psalter* (Oxford, 1918). On page 60 he wrote: "I have in my hands a book which I believe will mark a distinct step in advance in the whole treatment of this problem" (of the relation of the Gospels to Rabbinism). The book was the First Series of these *Studies in Pharisaism and the Gospels*. "We see," Dr Sanday continued, "the spirit of true scholarship at work." For, he adds, "It is scholarship to which I should be inclined to attach somewhat pre-eminently the epithet *humane*. The writer is above all things a *humanist*, and that in a field where in the past *humanism* has been too much wanting. Perhaps there is a little more of apology than he thinks in what he writes. But it is at least amiable apology, intent on bringing out really good things, and free from carping disparagement of the other side."

I quote these words, so characteristic of Dr Sanday's generosity, not because I think them deserved by my achievement, but because they completely reveal my intention. Undoubtedly Dr Sanday was just in his detection of unsuspected apologetics in my exposition. But his praise is a stimulus to mitigate the lurking unfairness, which cannot be altogether eradicated. His statement of the humanistic demands of scholarship will, I am sure, be treasured by all of us who are engaged in researches which ought to call for a unanimous and indignant protest against the *odium theologicum* which has been anything but an adornment to the Queen of Sciences.

The actual contents of this volume, which for the present at least concludes the whole work, correspond to a large extent with the promises made in the Preface to the First Series. Certain subjects there indicated are missing, while others not there indicated are introduced. Two chapters (on "Prayer" and on "Pharisaic Delicacies") have been previously printed, but these have been revised. In one case, the chapter on "The Imitation of God," the address form has been retained. I had the privilege of submitting several of the Studies to criticism at the Universities of Oxford, Cambridge, Harvard and Yale, and at the Union Theological Seminary of New York. I greatly profited by this criticism, and at the same time was urged to proceed with the publication of the Studies in question. It was at the suggestion of several friends that I appended the series of Miscellaneous Notes with which the volume ends. The larger portion of the book has been in type for some time, and for this reason I have been unable to use some important books which have recently appeared. This particularly applies to Strack and Billerbeck's *Commentary on Matthew*, Büchler's *Types of Jewish Pietism*, K. Kohler's *Visions of Heaven and Hell*, and C. G. Montefiore's *The Old Testament and After*. I observe that the last-named anticipates me in several important points, while his exposition often adds considerations which I had overlooked. My whole work on the New Testament was suggested by his example, an example emphasised by his urgent pressure. The humanism, which William Sanday so genially detected in me, derives primarily from C. G. Montefiore. His Commentary on the Synoptic Gospels was the work of a pioneer from the Jewish side. Those of us who follow his method are proud to recognise in him a master and a guide.

I. A.

*August*, 1923

# CONTENTS

## I. "THOU HAST SAID."

Various attempts have been made to certify the affirmative significance of this answer (σὺ εἶπας)[1] from Rabbinic usage. But these attempts cannot be regarded as successful. Wellhausen, in the first edition of his Introduction[2], without offering any evidence treated the phrase as an Aramaism afterwards obsolete but current in Jesus' day, with the force of an emphatic "yes" (*ja!*). But in his second edition he silently erased the statement. "Aramaisms" may be now current, now disused; but this change must be attested historically, not assumed to meet exegetical presuppositions.

There is, in fact, no such Rabbinic idiom. The only common use of the phrase "Thou hast said" in Rabbinic has no reference to question and answer. It is an exegetical formula, introducing a deduction from a scriptural text[3].

In his excellent essay on the subject, H. Thayer[4] rightly rejected as irrelevant the only Rabbinic passage previously quoted in support of the existence of a Rabbinic idiom[5]. In about the year 220 A.D. Judah the Patriarch, editor of the Mishnah, was dying in Sepphoris. In their anguish at the imminent catastrophe, the people declared that they would kill the bearer of the dread tidings of Judah's demise. Bar Qappara appeared before them in mourning garb. He addressed them in parable: "Men and Angels took hold of the Tables of the Covenant (= the soul of Judah); the Angels prevailed and seized the Tables." The people cried: "Is Rabbi dead?"; whereupon Bar Qappara

[1] Matt. xxvi. 25 (concerning Judas), 64 (where Mk xiv. 62 has ἐγώ εἰμι), xxvii. 11 (σὺ λέγεις), Mk xv. 2, Lk. xxii. 70 (ὑμεῖς λέγετε ὅτι ἐγώ εἰμι), xxiii. 3. Some authorities (e.g. Preuschen) who regard the answer at the trial as ambiguous ("Thou hast said it, not I") are disposed to regard Matt. xxvi. 64 as decidedly affirmative.

[2] *Einleitung in die drei ersten Evangelien*, Berlin, 1905, p. 41; second ed. 1911.

[3] אמרת. For instances (especially from the Mechilta) see Bacher, *Die aelteste Terminologie der jüdischen Schriftauslegung*, Leipzig, 1899, p. 6. See also the same author's *Die exegetische Terminologie der jüdischen Traditionsliteratur*, Part II, Leipzig, 1905, p. 11.

[4] In *Journal Hist. Biblical Literature*, xiii. (1894), 40—46. Cf. the comments of A. Merx on Mt. xxvi. 25.

[5] T.J. Kilaim, ix. 3. Cf. T.B. Kethuboth, 104 a. It is cited by Schoettgen, *Horae*, p. 225, but *not* used in this inaccurate way by Lightfoot who well knew the passage (see his *Horae*, p. 144, ch. lxxxii. of the Introduction).

answered: "Ye have said." This is the version of the Palestinian Talmud. Even without the variant in the Babylonian Talmud: "*Ye* have said it, *I* have not said it[1]," it is clear that Bar Qappara's remark has no bearing on the meaning of the answer of Jesus.

More recently, however, another Rabbinic testimony of considerably earlier date has been adduced. It is cited by two competent authorities, who both regard it as practically decisive[2], but curiously enough in opposite senses. While Dalman[3] thinks that *Thou hast said* "means exactly *thou art right*," and this would be, though "not strictly speaking a form of affirmation," nevertheless a form "of concession," Chwolson[4] regards it as an "absolute" repudiation. The passage, which would refer to a period some 25 years after the death of Jesus, is this[5]:

One may enter the space between the porch and the altar, without previously washing hands and feet. So holds R. Meir, but the Sages are of the opposite opinion. Said R. Simeon haṣanua', in the presence of R. Eleazar: "I went between the porch and altar unwashed of hands and feet."—Eleazar rejoined: "Who is the more considerable, thou or the high priest?"—Simeon was silent.—Eleazar said to him: "Art ashamed to say that the high priest's dog is more important than thou!"—Simeon said to him: "*Rabbi, thou hast said.*"—Said R. Eleazar to him, "By the Temple service! even a high priest would have had his skull split with clubs. How didst thou contrive to evade the notice of the watchman?"

We have quoted Dalman's interpretation. Supporting himself with a note of Elijah Wilna[6], Chwolson regards Simeon's cryptic utterance as a complete denial. He holds that the phrase, in Jesus' mouth, is

[1] Cf. Luke xxii. 70. In T.B. Pesaḥim, 3b (foot) Joshua son of Idi reports the death of R. Kahana in indirect method. "Is he dead?" they ask. And he answers: "I have not said it." The reason for the periphrastic formula is a dislike of bearing ill tidings, and a desire to give a more pleasant turn to the phraseology employed. Wuensche goes beyond the facts when he talks (*Neue Beiträge*, p. 329) of a Rabbinic habit of answering ambiguously to dangerous questions. On the other hand indelicate or coarse expressions were to be avoided by the use of roundabout phrases.

[2] A. H. McNeile in his *Comm. on Matt.* (p. 381) supports his view—that σὺ εἶπας (Mt. xxvi. 25) is "clearly an affirmative, probably with the force of an admission"—by a reference to this same passage.

[3] *The Words of Jesus*, Edinburgh, 1902, pp. 309 *seq.*

[4] *Beiträge zur Entwicklungsgeschichte des Judentums*, 1910, p. 55.

[5] Tosefta Kelim, I. i. 6.

[6] "*Thou hast said*, i.e. I am indignant (angry) at thy saying this to me!" Clearly the passage can bear this meaning. It may be doubted, too, whether Eleazar himself was serious; it would be exceeding probability, as Chwolson argues, to suppose that both he and Simeon would hold the Sadducean high-priesthood in such high esteem as Simeon's *assent* would imply.

a less full denial; not a denial of the *fact* alleged, but a repudiation of having *asserted* the fact. He strengthens this view by his interpretation of Simeon's phrase. "Thou hast said, but in truth it is not so, though I do not care to answer rudeness by rudeness and give you the lie direct." Eleazar son of Hyrqanos was noted for his rough and domineering manner, and his jibe deserved at least the mild protest which Chwolson reads into Simeon's words. Or he may have simply intended a refusal to take Eleazar's taunt seriously. At the best Simeon's words are ambiguous, and the passage cannot be used as evidence, from the Rabbinic side, that "Thou hast said" is a formula of affirmation or even of consent.

Dalman expresses a fairly general view when he writes: "Since Mark (xiv. 62) has simply ἐγώ εἰμι for σὺ εἶπας, it is obvious that there existed a tradition to the effect that the answer of Jesus was understood to be a real affirmative." But we must then add that since Matthew and Luke avoid the simple ἐγώ εἰμι of Mark, it is equally obvious that there was a tradition that the answer was not a direct affirmative. We can scarcely talk of a *tradition* at all with regard at all events to the incidents of the *trial*. If there be indeed tradition, then we have two traditions, not one. It must always be open to doubt which of the two is older[1]. Nor can we be quite certain that the words used by Mark are intended as an unqualified affirmative[2].

[1] Dalman, *op. cit.*, p. 308. For an enlightening discussion of the problem see Merx, *op. cit.*, p. 384 (cf. his *Comm. on Mk*, p. 161).

[2] It is barely possible that ἐγώ εἰμι was understood as an "evasion," and identical in force with σὺ εἶπας. The Rabbinical commentators were much troubled by Jacob's false answer to his father (Gen. xxvii. 24). "Art thou my very son Esau?", asks Isaac; and Jacob replies: "I am." The LXX renders καὶ εἶπεν Σὺ εἶ ὁ υἱός μου Ἠσαύ; ὁ δὲ εἶπεν Ἐγώ, where some authorities read Ἐγώ εἰμι. Rashi seeks to save Jacob from a charge of direct lying by his comment: "Jacob did not say I am Esau, but I am," i.e. "I am I; Esau is thy firstborn." Though there is no mention of this interpretation in the older literature, yet it is possible that Rashi derived it from an ancient source. It is one of the curiosities of exegesis to find this very Ἐγώ εἰμι treated by a Jewish commentator as an evasion.

## II. THE YOKE.

There is, to use Mr C. G. Montefiore's words, "exquisite grace and tenderness" in the famous passage beginning (Matt. xi. 28—30): *Come unto me, all ye that are heavy laden.* The passage is, indeed, as the same commentator remarks, "largely made up of quotations[1]." Neither for the first, nor for the last, time in literature has a mosaic, pieced together from other designs, attained to artistic originality and independent beauty.

The passage is peculiar to Matthew. Yet it seems so bound up with xi. 25 as to justify its recognition as a genuine part of the whole, even if that whole cannot safely be attributed to Jesus. As, however, Luke (x. 21) does record the same thought as is conveyed by Matt. xi. 25 (which, judging by the parallels, cannot be treated as independent of xi. 28—30), it is not necessary to reject the passage, unless we persist in misunderstanding its meaning.

Are the modern commentaries right in reading into it an attack on the Pharisees? Was Jesus never thinking of anything else but his immediate opponents? *My yoke is easy, and my burden is light* is usually taken as an implied censure of the difficult yoke and heavy burden of the Rabbinical law. But must every saying of the Gospels be treated as controversial? Does a "scientific criticism" really demand such a method of interpretation? Ought we, by introducing the disturbing irritant of polemics, distort the serene pathos of the passage before us? Must the comfort that it has brought to so many afflicted souls be won at the cost of afflicting the souls of so many others?

The sayings of the Gospels, in brief, deal often with human nature at large, and not with Pharisaic nature in little. We moderns have still something to learn from the older commentators, who with less sense of the historical than we possess, had on occasion a fuller understanding of the moral background of the Gospels.

Chrysostom[2], for instance, is quite clear that the contrast of the easy with the hard yoke is not between the new teaching and the old,

[1] Jer. vi. 16; Ecclus. li. 1 and 23 *seq.* (cf. especially the Hebrew text of li. 26 a). The passage in Ecclus., with its allusions to *youth* and *yoke*, is clearly related to Lam. iii. 27. See also Midrash on Psalm lv. 23.

[2] Homily 38 on Matthew.

but between the two never-relaxed pulls of virtue and vice. Some of his words may be quoted, though it is hard to do justice to his splendid homily by selecting a few sentences from what constitutes a finely-sustained, perfectly-balanced argument.

If virtue seem to thee an irksome thing, consider that vice is more irksome. And this very thing he was intimating, in that he said not first, *Take my yoke upon you*, but before that, *Come, ye that labour and are heavy laden*; implying that sin too hath labour and a burden that is heavy and hard to bear. This the Prophet, too, was speaking of, in that description of her nature *As a heavy burden they weighed heavy upon me* (Psalm xxxviii. 4[1]). And Zacharias too, describing her, saith that she is a *talent of lead* (Zech. v. 7, 8). And this moreover experience itself proves. For nothing so weighs upon the soul, and presses it down, as consciousness of sin; nothing so much gives it wings, and raises it on high, as the attainment of righteousness and virtue.

And after describing the enslaving effect of such vices as envy, dishonesty, sensuality and pride, Chrysostom concludes:

Fear not thou, therefore, neither start away from the yoke that lightens thee of all these things, but put thyself under it with forwardness, and then shalt thou know well the pleasure thereof. For it doth not at all bruise thy neck, but is put on thee for good order's sake, to persuade thee to walk seemly and to lead thee into the royal road, to deliver thee from the precipices on either side and to make thee walk with ease in the narrow way.

This is good, sound sense. Virtue and vice are both burdens. In the epigram of Simeon b. Pazzi, man torn between the two appeals exclaims: "Woe to me for my yoṣer, woe to me for my yeṣer[2]." If a man yield to his yeṣer, his lower impulses, he is accountable to his yoṣer (God, the Creator); if he obey his yoṣer, then he suffers from his yeṣer, from the pains of unsatisfied desires. Life is conflict[3]. Whichever of the two win, be it virtue or vice, the victory is won at a heavy cost. For the broad way is the way to destruction, the disciple must bear his cross[4]. The Pharisee felt this, but was also ready to see the other side. For of Virtue, as personified in Wisdom or Torah, he said with Proverbs (iii. 17): *Her ways are ways of pleasantness, and all her paths are peace. She is a tree of life to them that lay hold upon her: and happy is every one that retaineth her.* This "tree of life" was indeed

[1] The Midrash on this verse also points out that virtue leads to a lightening of the burden imposed by vice.

[2] T.B. Ber. 61 a אוי לי מיוצרי ואוי לי מיצרי. Cf. ‘Erub. 18 a.

[3] That life itself is a "heavy yoke" is already expressed in Ecclus. xl. 1: *ζυγὸς βαρύς*: Heb. עסק גדול חלק אל׳ ועול כבד על בני אדם.

[4] Matt. vii. 13—14, x. 37 *seq.*; Luke xiv. 26 *seq.*; Rom. viii. 35 *seq.*

on the broad way, its branches so wide-spread, that a man might journey for half a millennium before encompassing the tree[1]. Yet the life, the happiness, was not of this world, and bliss hereafter must be attained by tribulation here. That such tribulation would not suffice to hold a man from devotion to the ideal, does not imply that the sacrifice is the less real. The sufferer rejoices indeed in such an opportunity, he is victor not victim. Paul the critic of Pharisaism, and Aqiba its champion, were at one in this regard[2]. The toil, the anguish, is the sure road to happiness[3]. Yet one must discriminate. What of the terms of Matt. x. 37? The Rabbinic parallels cited are not real. Philo is no nearer[4], though he perhaps gives the clue to the particular phraseology of Matt. viii. 21, 22 (Luke ix. 59, 60). But what Philo says, in explanation of the law denying the High-Priest the privilege of attending to the burial of a near relative, is that he who has been assigned to God must not be turned from his duty by the sorrows of ordinary life. He must be beyond the contagion of such sorrows. And, with regard to family feuds and social strife, which are the mark of the new age in rare Talmudic sources[5], these refer (like similar apocalyptic phrases) to the upheaval which is to precede the new order, they are the culminating type of evil, not the condition for attaining the good. Much nearer is the Pharisaic thought as regards proselytes to Judaism; the parable which follows only expresses one side of the Rabbinic attitude on the subject[6], but the last phrases of the parable have an interesting similarity to Matt. viii. 22[7].

*The Lord loveth the righteous; the Lord preserveth the (gerim) strangers* (Ps. cxlvi. 8, 9). To what is the matter like? To a king, who owned a flock of sheep, which went forth to the pasture (in the morning) and returned home in the evening. Thus did the flock every day. Once a gazelle joined itself to the flock, placed itself among the goats, and browsed with them. When the sheep returned to their shed, the gazelle returned with them; when they went out to the pasture, it

[1] Baraitha in T.J. Ber. i. § 1. Cf. T.B. Ta'anith 7 a, and Midrash on Psalm i. (§ 19).

[2] Acts v. 41; T.J. Ber. ix. § 5, T.B. Ber. 61 b.

[3] Pereq R. Meir (Aboth vi.) § 4.

[4] Mon. ii. 12 (M. II. 229).

[5] T.B. Sanh. 97 a; end of Mishnah Soṭa; cf. p. 62 below.

[6] Cf. *Jewish Encyclopedia*, x. 222.

[7] On the other hand, unless the prophet's remark is to be interpreted as a rebuke, there is a deep contrast between the Gospel text and 1 Kings xix. 20. Though the Rabbinic parable quoted is of uncertain date, it would seem to be early, and may belong to the first century.

accompanied them. They said to the king: This gazelle has attached itself unto the sheep; feeds with them daily, goes out with them, and with them it returns. The king loved the gazelle, and when it went to the meadow he appointed a good shepherd, bidding all take special care that no man should strike it. And when it returned with the flock, the king said to them: Give it drink. So greatly did he love it. The shepherds said unto him: O master! how many he-goats hast thou, how many ewes, how many kids! Concerning these thou dost not exhort us, but concerning this gazelle thou dost daily give us orders. Then the king answered: As for sheep, willy nilly, 'tis their nature to feed in the meadow every day, and by night to return to sleep in the shed. But as for gazelles, they sleep in the desert, 'tis not their way to enter into the settlements of men. Shall we not then show regard unto this one, which has left all the great wide wilderness, the abode of all the beasts, and has come to stand in (our) courtyard? So must we treat with tender consideration a stranger (ger, proselyte), who has forsaken his family, and his father's house, who has left his people and all the peoples of the world, and has betaken himself to us[1].

That there were true and false yokes must have been a thought familiar enough in the first century, when on the one hand the Roman government, and on the other the Pharisaic Law, were operative as rivals in Jewish life. It is this rivalry that gives point to the well-known first-century saying of Neḥunya b. Haqana[2], a contemporary of Joḥanan b. Zakkai. "He who takes on himself the yoke of the Torah is freed from the yoke of the kingdom and the yoke of worldly affairs; but on him who casts off the yoke of the Torah is set the yoke of the kingdom and the yoke of worldly affairs." The general sense of the passage is clear. It could only incidentally signify that the student was excused from the burden of secular office; only incidental, too, is the idea of reward. The willing acceptance of the yoke of the Torah brings its reward, just as the violent rejection of it brings its punishment, in relation to exile and foreign oppression. Here, however,

[1] Numbers Rabba viii. § 2; Mid. to Psalm cxlvi. (ed. Buber), p. 536.

[2] Aboth Mishnah iii. 5. Cf. also the idea that virtue is freedom (Pereq R. Meir, Aboth vi. 2); and compare p. 213 below. Bacher (*Agada der Tannaiten*, i. 54 [58]) adopts a reading of Aboth iii. 5 which omits the words "the yoke of the kingdom and." In Deut. xxviii. 47—48, the "iron yoke" of foes is imposed because Israel refused to serve God in joy. Eleazar ben Pedath interprets the "iron yoke" as the constant burden of care under tyranny; he uses the word הרעיון which Jastrow renders by "greed." But Eleazar's thought is scarcely that servitude leads to so special a burden, and even in its Biblical usage the word is more general. So, too, the same word (הרעיון) is used in explanation of "every disease" of Deut. vii. 15; here Jastrow renders the word by "ambition." Bacher more aptly translates: "lastende Sorge" (*Agada der Pal. Am.* ii. 41). The Rabbinic interpretations cited may be found in T.J. Sabbath xiv. § 3.

consequence rather than recompense is implied. "From over-anxiety on such matters—oppression and the struggle for existence" comments C. Taylor, "an absorbing devotion to Torah frees a man." Or, to cite the paraphrase of R. T. Herford, "Devotion to Torah frees a man from oppression and care by setting his mind on things above." That the higher casts out the lower, that the good yeṣer is empowered to resist the evil yeṣer by the Torah, which acts as a spiritual prophylactic, is genuine Pharisaism[1] as well as sound psychology. In particular, the interpretation just accepted of Neḥunya's maxim is confirmed by another recorded utterance of the same teacher. "He who sets his heart on things of Torah is delivered from things of foolishness." Similarly, in the first recension of the Aboth de R. Nathan there is a fuller saying of like import[2]. Quoting Psalm xix. 9: *The precepts of the Lord are right, rejoicing the heart; the commandment of the Lord is pure, enlightening the eyes*, Neḥunya expounds that he who sets the Torah on his heart is freed from many disturbing thoughts—famine, folly, fornication and anxiety because of the *yoke of flesh and blood*[3]. The last phrase explains and expands the similar phrase, the *yoke of kingdom*, implying an antithesis between the *yoke of man* and the *yoke of God*. The actual phrase the *yoke of the Holy One*[4] appears in the later Rabbinic books, but mostly we find (as in Lam. iii. 27) either an abbreviation (simply the *yoke*), or paraphrases avoiding anthropomorphic suggestions (the *yoke of heaven*, the *yoke of the kingdom of Heaven*, the *yoke of the Law*, the *yoke of the Commandments*). Another interesting phrase is the *yoke of the Name*. If Israelites paid regard to the Torah,

[1] T.B. Ber. 5 a; Sifrê on Deut. vi. 6 and the references in Porter's *Yeçer Hara*, pp. 127—8. The yeṣer wounds, the Torah heals (T.B. Qiddushin 30 b). Contrariwise, it is when the heart is empty of the yeṣer that the Torah can find a lodging-place there (Mid. Mishle, p. 96).

[2] Aboth de R. Nathan xx (ed. Schechter, p. 70). This fuller saying is attributed to another contemporary Rabbi Ḥanina, but the Midrash Haggadol (as cited by Schechter, p. 71, note 7) rightly assigns it to Neḥunya.

[3] Schoettgen in his *Horae* has a good section on the yoke. But he has no justification for his paraphrase (p. 119) of "jugum carnis et sanguinis" by "h.e. veteris Adami." In T.B. Soṭa 47 b the yoke of flesh and blood is contrasted with the yoke of heaven. Cf. Tosefta Soṭa xiv. 4.

[4] Exod. R. xxx. § 1. Because Israel refused to accept the yoke of the Holy One, they fell into Sennacherib's hand and were carried into exile. More generally, Agur (Prov. xxx. 1), clean of sin, bore the yoke of God, and was divinely inspired. In this rare use of the phrase, the yoke of God is identical with the reception of the holy spirit (Machiri and Yalquṭ on Prov. *loc. cit.*).

they would escape other yokes. And what did the Torah demand? "Receive upon yourselves the Yoke of the Kingship of My Name, and reconcile each other in the fear of God, and conduct yourselves each with each in loving kindness[1]." Curiously enough, the shortest form (simply the *yoke*) grew most familiar on the negative side. To cast off the yoke became synonymous with a denial of the fundamental principles of Judaism[2]. The main types of the phrase, positively applied, were two: the yoke of the kingdom or kingship of Heaven and the yoke of the commandments. That these types, though closely alike, were not identical is clearly shown by the distinction drawn by a disciple of Aqiba. "Joshua son of Qarḥa said: Who do we recite (in the daily liturgy) first Deut. vi. 4—8 and then Deut. xi. 13—21? In order first to accept the yoke of the Kingdom of Heaven, and afterwards the yoke of the commandments[3]." A parallel idea is expressed in relation to the Decalogue, which starts with the declaration *I am the Lord thy God* and with the injunction *Thou shalt have no other God before me*, and subsequently lays down specific laws. At Sinai Israel accepted the Kingship of God with joy and unanimity[4]. The precepts are, in other words, the mandates of the King. It is necessary in the first instance to acknowledge the Kingship of God, in order to realise at once that the precepts have divine sanction, and that the performance of them is the fulfilment of the Divine Will[5]. "Ye have accepted my Kingship, accept my decrees"—so Simeon b. Yoḥai interprets[6]. It was

[1] Sifrê, ed. Friedmann, p. 138 b.

לו חכמו ישכילו זאת · אלו נסתכלו ישראל בדברי תורה שניתנה להם לא שלטה בהם אומה ומלכות · ומה אמרה להם ? קבלו עליכם עול מלכות שמי והכריעו זה את זה ביראת שמים והתנהגו זה את (r. עם) זה בגמילות חסדים :

On the Name in this connection see Annotations to Prayer Book, p. li (on ברוך שם כבוד מלכותו). See also the fine passage in the Sifrâ (ed. Weiss, p. 93 b). Obedient Israel is God's (לשמי) in that through God's choice of him, Israel separates from sin and accepts the Kingship of heaven נמצא פורש מן העבירה ומקבל עליו מלכות שמים.

[2] Apoc. Baruch xli. 3; Aboth iii. 5 use the fuller phrase.

[3] Mishnah Berachoth ii. 2 (T.B. 13 a); Mechilta on Exod. xx. 3 (ed. Friedmann 67 a).

[4] Mech. ed. Friedmann 66 b.

[5] It became also a common Rabbinic phrase that Israel obeyed the Torah to give gratification (נחת רוח) to God. Cf. T.B. Ber. 17 a; and see p. 179 below.

[6] Sifrâ on Levit. xviii. (ed. Weiss 85 b). The Law was the decree (גזירה) of the King, and submission was necessary even to precepts for which no reason was discernible. Cf. passages in E. Ben Yehuda, *Millon* ii. 744.

the acceptance, the joyous and unqualified acceptance, of the Kingship of God that gave moral dignity and spiritual glow to pietism, that made its burden light in life, and ultimately transfigured the martyr's death into a demonstration of devoted love and loyalty to the King[1].

In another passage dealing with the *burden* (Matt. xxiii. 4, Luke xi. 46) the attack is on the Pharisees, or on a section of them. The differences between the three Gospels is here of considerable interest. Mark altogether omits the passage. In Luke (xi. 45) a distinction is drawn between the Pharisees and the lawyers (νομικοί); in Matt. there is no such distinction. All this would strengthen the view that the Gospel attack is directed (here and elsewhere) not against Pharisaism but against certain Pharisees. These are charged with binding heavy burdens on men's shoulders, which burdens they will not move with their finger. We have above expressed appreciation of the older Christian exegesis; but in connection with this passage we find an indication of a newer method. Chrysostom thus moralises[2]:

> He mentions here a two-fold wickedness, their requiring great and extreme strictness of life, without any indulgence, from those over whom they rule, and their allowing to themselves great security; the opposite to which the truly good ruler ought to hold; in what concerns himself, to be an unpardoning and severe judge, but in the matters of those whom he rules, to be gentle and ready to make allowances; the contrary to which was the conduct of these men. For such are all they who practise self-restraint in mere words, unpardoning, and grievous to bear, as having no experience in the difficulty in actions.

The last part of this interpretation is a deft rebuke to the arm-chair moralist who fails to take into account the practical difficulties of life. But as against the Pharisaic system, modern commentators rightly hesitate to concede that the Rabbis were open to the charge of imposing on others burdens they were themselves reluctant to bear. Such a charge is altogether inconsistent with the other charge that the Pharisees were over-punctilious in their pietism. We read, both before and after the destruction of the Temple, of individual Pharisees who adopted a peculiarly severe rule for themselves; we do not read of individuals who permitted themselves a laxity denied to others[3]. Indeed we have

[1] T.B. Ber. 61 b and parallels. [2] Hom. 72 on Matthew, §§ 1—2.

[3] On the contrary, the greater the saint, the more his need of severity against himself; for the righteous are punished for such offences as would be treated as venial in the case of less scrupulous pietists (T. debe E. ii., the whole chapter is interesting on the subject of the *yoke*). The following late utterance (Exod. Rabba xxv. 8) may be cited as illustrating the present discussion: "*His bread shall be*

the rule very clearly indicated to the contrary: "Shammai said: make thy Torah a fixed thing; so that thou art neither easier nor harder to thyself than to others." The ideal principle is to use the same standard in all cases. Ezra's example is quoted (Ezra vii. 10); he "set his heart to seek the law of the Lord and to do it, and to teach in Israel statutes and judgments." He himself did what he ordained on others[1].

It is however becoming usual to interpret the charge as implying that the Pharisees impose many burdens but remove none; they are always adding to the weight, never relieving it. In a broad sense this would be a true criticism of Pharisaism, but before it could be admitted, it would need to be considerably qualified. At every period we find the Rabbis relieving burdens. The process was historically continuous. In a well-known anecdote, Simeon b. Sheṭaḥ (*c.* 100 B.C.) is introduced as straining the law to free 150 Nazirites from the cost of sacrifices[2]. Hillel (in the reign of Herod) practically abrogated the law of Deut. xv. 1 in relief both of creditors and debtors[3]. So, too, after the destruction of the Temple, there was an ascetic wave which sought to enforce the avoidance of meat and wine (because these were used at the sacrifices). Joshua b. Ḥananya prevented this excess. He, indeed, had a just contempt for the "foolish saint," the man whose pietism led him to stupid extremes, he was also a stern critic of pietism which was the veil for hypocrisy[4]. So, Joshua b. Ḥananya warned his colleagues against burdening the age with unrestrained mourning over Zion. The general rule established then, and obeyed with reasonable consistency before and after was: "No decree must be made for the

*given him and his waters shall be sure* (Isa. xxxiii. 16), this refers (in the first clause) to God, who exacts of the sons of the Torah, Say not I have heard [a tradition] when thou hast not heard, be not one who forbids to others and permits to himself (אוסר לאחרים ומתיר לעצמו), but let what cometh from thy lips be faithful, as in the case of Moses, and (as in his case) I will show thee beauty face to face as it is said, *Thine eyes shall behold the king in his beauty* (Isa. xxxiii. 17)."

[1] Aboth de R. Nathan II ch. xxiii.; cf. I ch. xiii.

עשה תורתך קבע· שלא תהא מקיל לעצמך ומחמיר לאחרים· או תהא מקיל לאחרים ומחמיר לעצמך· אלא כשם שאתה מקיל לעצמך כך תהא מקיל לאחרים· וכשם כאתה מחמיר לעצמך כך תהא מחמיר לאחרים· שנאמר כי עזרא הכין לבבו לדרוש את תורת ה׳ ואחר כך וללמד לישראל חוק ומשפט:

Compare also the references given in Jastrow p. 353 at foot (on the phrase לעובדא, as a personal in contrast to a traditional ruling of conduct).

[2] Gen. Rabba ch. xci. [3] See *Jewish Encyclopedia*, x. 219.

[4] Mishnah Soṭa iii. 4. Cf. Mishnah Yadayim iv. 3.

community which the majority of the community could not endure[1]." The tendency of Pharisaism was, in certain very important directions, so emphatically towards alleviation that the Rabbinic law practically abolished capital punishment and introduced a whole system of equity by the side of law. The tendency towards severity in other directions was itself called to account: against those inclined to it was cited the text (Eccles. ii. 14): *the fool walketh in darkness*[2]. It is clear enough that there was an acute struggle, sometimes amounting to physical violence, between the Jewish parties in Palestine in the first century[3]. This fact, however, is itself of two-fold significance. On the one hand it might account for some of the Gospel polemics. But, on the other, if those polemics are justifiable by the possibility well summarised by A. H. McNeile (on Matt. xxiii. 4): "The school of Hillel, indeed, tended to laxity, but in the time of Jesus they were probably in a minority[4]"—if that be so, then we can perceive how ill-conceived is the method of the Schürer school, who convert the Gospel attack on the school of Shammai into a condemnation of Pharisaism, which, as a system, emerges historically with the school of Hillel triumphant!

This consideration, however, must not for a moment be held to dispute the patent fact that the Pharisaic system was a highly developed scheme of duty. When, in the history of Rabbinic tradition, the easier or lighter régime of the Hillelites is contrasted with the harder or heavier requirements of the Shammaites, this is by no means the same as claiming that the Hillelites were establishing anything but a severe rule of obligation. Under the Hillelite régime, which became predominant, the requirements of the Law, both moral and ritual, were far-reaching, intricate, manifold. They did not merely affect the great concerns of life, but fussed over the small; they left few things untouched, and their touch was mostly, though far from invariably, a heavy one.

[1] Tosefta Soṭa (end). T.B. Baba Bathra 60 b. For this and other lightenings of burdens see Bacher in *Die Agada der Tannaiten*, i. 158 (164) and in *Jewish Encyclopedia*, vi. 397.

[2] Baraitha in T.B. 'Erubin 6 b; Rosh Hashana 14 b. While he who adopts all the "light" rules of both the Hillelites and the Shammaites is a rascal, he who adopts all the "heavy" rules of both is a fool.

[3] T.B. Hagiga 3 b, T.J. Sabbath i. 4; cf. Bacher, *Agada der Tannaiten*, 11—22 (14—25).

[4] That in some points Jesus was in agreement with Shammai has been alluded to above (First Series, p. 71). Shammai, too, as against Hillel is in agreement with the spirit of such ideas as Matthew v. 28 (see Mechilta, p. 91 b, foot).

But this is the real problem. Burden, weight, are psychological as well as physical concepts. When Jacob served seven years for Rachel, "they seemed unto him but a few days, for the love he had to her" (Gen. xxix. 10). In the same way, with the Pharisee, the Torah became ever more the object of Israel's affection. On Israel's side, service was the token of love, on God's side the opportunity of service was a precious gift, bestowed as a loving privilege[1]. As in the famous Mishnah of Ḥananya son of Aqashya (Makk. iii. 16), the Holy One was pleased to make Israel worthy by giving them a copious Torah and many commandments. If it seem that this puts the thought too much like a barter, it must be remembered that service for love, arising out of the acceptance of the Kingdom, was the ideal which overrode all such considerations[2]. Matthew (vi. 33, cf. Luke xii. 31) is at much the same standpoint. Nor was the law so given to lose its charm out of familiarity. The Sifrê on Deut. vi. 6 lays stress on the phrase *this day*. "These words which I command thee *this day* shall be upon thy heart." They are not to be regarded as an old set of ordinances, but as new, which men eagerly rush towards[3]. This is moral of a host of parables, which became so luxuriant in Rabbinic literature between the second and fourth centuries, though they go back to an earlier period. Sometimes it is Israel, as the King's son, who receives the Father's gift[4]; sometimes it is Israel, the King's bride, who is loaded with ornaments by her Husband[5]. For it is only to the son or the beloved spouse that all the keys of the treasury are entrusted. Or the figure is the garden, whose fruits and flowers are cultivated by the son because of his love for the father. Or again, the figure is that of a banquet, at which the ordinary guest receives one dish, one cup of wine, while the son has access to the whole larder and to the cask[6]. So Israel has the prerogative of knowing and obeying all the precepts. Much

[1] Deut. Rabba vii. § 9.

[2] Sifrê on Deut. xi. 13, ed. Friedmann, p. 80 (top). It is to be noted that this comment to serve from love

כל מה שאתם עושים לא תעשו אלא מאהבה

is made on a context which was interpreted of the acceptance of the Kingdom, and is usually pointed to as one of the strongest Pentateuchal enunciations of reward for righteousness.

[3] אשר אנכי מצוך היום · שלא יהו בעיניך כדיוטגמא (διάταγμα) ישנה שאין אדם סופרה אלא כחדשה שהכל רצים לקראתה :

On the reading סופרה see Friedmann's note p. 74 a n. 2.

[4] Cant. R. ii. 3; Pes. Rabbathi 100 a.

[5] Yalquṭ Deut. § 238.

[6] T.B. Pesaḥim 53 b; Exod. R. xxx. § 9; Cant. R. i. 2.

less onerous duties are required of the rest of the world than of the son who was admitted to the innermost secrets of the father. In fact, the possession of these secrets is the *evidence* of sonship[1]. Yet another figure is that of the Torah as the King's only daughter, who is given in marriage to Israel. The King is desolated at parting with her, and bids the son-in-law wherever he sojourns to set an apartment for the father to occupy when he visits his daughter[2]. Indeed it is impossible by mere extracts and generalisations to convey the intensity of feeling for the Torah, all the tenderness of human affection, all the glow of mystic union. If to the authors of these parables, to those who shared these emotions, service was a yoke, it was hardly a yoke that galled[3].

It would be interesting to follow out in detail two contrasted lines of thought which eventually, however, converge. On the one hand, there is joy in the very weight of the yoke, in the abundance of the service. So the Midrash[4] turns Ps. lxviii. 20: Blessed be the Lord in that he adds unto us commandments and statutes day by day. On the other hand, in comparison to the might of God, the service demanded by him is small[5]. In this sense, there is frequent insistence on the lightness of the burden. A human king exacts far more homage than does the divine King[6]. No doubt the Torah, a necklet to the obedient, is a chain to the disobedient, who, from another point of view, is just he who casts off the yoke. The Pharisaic view is well brought out in two consecutive verses of the Apocalypse of Baruch, xli. 3, 4:

> For lo! I see many of thy people who have withdrawn from thy covenant, and cast from them the yoke of thy law.
>
> But others again I have seen who have forsaken their vanity, and fled for refuge beneath thy wings.

Galled by the yoke, or feeling it a profitless burden, the one casts it off. But another, willingly assuming it, finds it no yoke, but a refuge under the wings of the Divine Presence[7].

[1] Pes. Rabbathi 14 b. [2] Exod. R. xxxiii. 1.

[3] In the foregoing paragraph, only a small fraction of the evidence is adduced as to the Pharisee's joy in the Law, and his conviction that the very multitude of its obligations was at once a distinction here and a source of happiness hereafter.

[4] Ed. Buber, p. 319. The Targum renders the text in the same manner.

[5] Cant. R. vii. 2. [6] Yalquṭ on Micah vi. 3.

[7] Yalquṭ Gen. § 34; Pes. Rabbathi 138 a; Deut. R. iv. 2. Cf. T.B. Sanhedrin 94 b. The Ten Tribes (sinners) "lightened the yoke," the people of Hezekiah "make it heavy" upon them, that is remained faithful. On the general question of the moral effect of "Nomism" see the excellent remarks of E. Ehrhardt in Hastings' *Encyclopaedia of Religion and Ethics*, ix. 381.

## III. THE LIGHT OF THE WORLD.

Were it not that in Matt. v. 14 the disciples are termed "the light of the world" (τὸ φῶς τοῦ κόσμου) it might be possible to uphold the distinction between the source—"light"—as applied to Jesus (John viii. 12) and the derivative—"lamp" (λύχνος)—as applied to the ministers (John v. 35, Matt. v. 15). To some extent there may be force in the distinction (cf. Alford's note on John v. 35). But the use of the terms as poetical parallels in Prov. vi. 23 militates against the reality of the distinction.

Whether a similar distinction is to be drawn between the Rabbinic uses of two similar terms (אור *light* and נר *làmp*) is not clear. Israel is a light to the nations (Is. xlii. 6). But God is the Light of the World, not Israel: God lights Israel's lamp (Ps. xviii. 29), He is the Light of the world (אורו של עולם) and Light dwells with Him (Daniel ii. 22). Israel's kindling of the lamp in the Temple is in some sense, however, parallel to God's action in the world[1].

This parallel becomes almost identity in a saying of Bar Qappara (end of second century). Quoting the verse from Ps. xviii. already referred to (*For thou wilt light my lamp*), Bar Qappara expounded thus: "The Holy One said to man: thy lamp is in My hand, My lamp in thine. Thy lamp is in My hand—as it is said *The lamp of the Lord is the soul of man* (Prov. xx. 27). My lamp is in thy hand, to kindle the perpetual lamp. The Holy One said: If thou lightest My lamp, I will light thine[2]."

It was Adam who was specifically named by the Rabbis as the "Lamp of the World" (נרו של עולם[3]). Adam enjoyed the sight of the primeval light, by which he could gaze from end to end of the world, but this was "hidden" because of the sins of the generations of Enos, the tower of Babel, and the flood, and becomes the reward of the righteous hereafter. The earthly Sabbath in some sense partakes of this light, but the idea tends to become Messianic[4].

[1] Cf. Num. Rabba xv. § 5. [2] Leviticus Rabba xxxi. § 4; cf. p. 154 below.

[3] T.J. Sabbath ii. 6 (end); and the parallels cited in the Yalquṭ ha-Machiri on Prov. xx. (ed. Grünhut, p. 18 a).

[4] Gen. Rabba xii. § 6; xi. (ed. Theodor, p. 88; cf. also pp. 102—3) and notes *ibid.*; T.B. Ḥagigah 12 a (ed. Streane, p. 59); T.B. Taanith 15 a. Cf. Enoch xlv. 4, *Adam and Eve*, § 26. Cf. Kohler in *Jewish Encyclopedia*, i. 176. The Gospel metaphors are clearly based on Isaiah, else one might be tempted to suggest that the symbol was due to the Pauline conception of Christ as the second Adam.

The epithet "Lamp" was early applied to Rabbis. When Joḥanan b. Zakkai's disciples visited him during his illness, they address him as "Lamp of Israel[1]" according to some readings, and as "Lamp of the World" according to others. The difference, in this context, is not very significant, but the former may be the more original reading[2].

Another application of the phrase Light of the World is made in relation to the holy city. Jerusalem is the Light of the World[3], as it is said (Isaiah lx. 3): and nations shall walk by thy light. And who is the Light of Jerusalem? The Holy One, blessed be He, as it is said (verse 19): the Lord shall be unto thee an everlasting light. This last Hebrew phrase (אור עולם) is of course translatable by "the Light of the World[4]." Arresting, too, is the thought that the olive oil in the Temple lamp was the Light of the World[5], apparently just as Noah's olive-branch proved that there was light and peace to the world after the flood[6].

The two ideas, of the Temple and of the Teachers of the Torah as the Light of the World, are brought together in the lengthy dialogue between Baba b. Buṭa the blind contemporary of Herod and that King. Baba was spared after the siege of Jerusalem in 37 B.C., and he it was who induced the King to expiate his sins by re-constructing the Temple. How, asks Herod, can a man such as I atone his crimes? He, replied Baba, has quenched the Light of the World (the Teachers)—as it is said: for the commandment is a lamp, and the Law is light (Prov. vi. 23); let him occupy himself with the Light of the World (the Temple), of which it is written: all nations shall find light therein. There is, of course, a play on the verb *nahar*, which means both "to shine" and "to flow[7]."

[1] In T.B. Ber. 28 b the reading is "Lamp of Israel"; in some texts of the Aboth de R. Nathan it is "Lamp of the World" (see ed. Schechter, p. 159; on p. 79 he also reads "Lamp of the World"). With Luke (xvi. 8) has been compared Enoch (cviii. 11) "generation of light," "sons of light."

[2] For a fine analysis of the ideas connected with Light in Jewish literature see Kohler in *J.E.* viii. 83. For an elaborate Midrash on the degrees of the illuminating function of the righteous see Mid. on Psalm xi. (ed. Buber, p. 101, with the parallels given there in note 42).

[3] ירושלים אורו של עולם.

[4] Genesis Rabba ch. lix. § 5. Cf. Friedmann, *Seder Eliahu Zuṭa* (Vienna 1904) p. 33.

[5] השמן זית אורה לעולם.

[6] M. Tanḥuma on Exod. xxvii. 20 (ed. Buber, *Exod.* p. 96 and מט).

[7] T.B. Baba Bathra 4 a.

הוא כבה אורו של עולם דכתיב כי נר מצוה ותורה אור׳ ילך ויעסוק באורו של עולם דכתיב ונהרו אליו כל הגוים

W. Bacher details the whole dialogue in *Jewish Encyclopedia*, ii. 392.

## IV. CONFESSION OF FAITH.

It is a familiar fact that the Hebrew for *confess* is, like the English equivalent, employed in the double sense of proclaiming God and acknowledging sin[1]. The two ideas are closely connected. The greatness of God, particularly in the divine aspect of fidelity, contrasts, almost of itself, with the littleness of man, particularly in the human aspect of infidelity. It was in his moments of fidelity that man was most like God. Hence the word for human faith in God is the same as the word for the divine steadfastness to purpose[2]. Man, accordingly, in his prayers would feel impelled to confess God as a preliminary to confessing his own shortcomings. Or rather, the two confessions were part and counterpart of the same experience.

Very closely is this discernible in a text which became potent both in Rabbinic theology and liturgy. "Thou, even Thou, art Lord alone," begins Nehemiah (ix. 6); this leads up to his admission (ix. 33) that Israel's sufferings were the just recompense for Israel's ill-doings: "Thou art just in all that is come upon us, for thou hast dealt truly, but we have done wickedly[3]." Resignation to the will of God is at once an act of allegiance and of self-abasement[4]. In the Prologue to the Exodus, in reply to the question of Moses, God answers: "Thus shalt thou say unto the children of Israel, I am hath sent me unto you" (Exod. iii. 14). Here, and in many other texts, God proclaims, witnesses to, himself. In Peter's "Confession" (Mt. xvi. 16, Mk viii. 29, Luke ix. 20) the position is reversed. Jesus asks and Peter answers: "Thou art the Christ." Yet other, again, is the situation at Carmel, where the demonstration of divine power calls forth the acclamation: "The Lord, he is God; the Lord, he is God" (1 Kings xviii. 39[5]). This acclama-

[1] See *Oxford Gesenius Dict.* s.v. ידה and *N.E.D.* s.v. *confess*.

[2] See *Dict.* s.v. אמן.

[3] This is the motive of many of the Atonement prayers of the Synagogue. Cf. also the use of the idea in the burial service (Annotated ed. of Hebrew Prayer Book, p. 318 and notes).

[4] Sifrâ on Levit. x. 3, ed. Weiss, p. 45 a (of Abraham, Aaron and David); Jer. Soṭa viii. 3 (of Zedekiah); T.B. Aboda Zara 18 a (of those condemned to death); Ber. 19 a, Taanith 11 a (of the man afflicted with sorrows).

[5] This exclamation has great liturgical influence; it is the concluding phrase of the Day of Atonement service. In the present liturgy the phrase is repeated seven times; originally, however, the words were (as in the Scripture) used twice only. This is shown clearly in the liturgical commentary of Judah b. Yaqar.

tion is not, however, entirely spontaneous, for the cry of the people is practically the response to the prophet's challenge (verse 24).

The protestation of faith is, in the Old Testament, often associated with a recital of the divine intervention in the life of Israel. "God in History" was the underlying basis of Rabbinic optimism. The declaration at the bringing of the first-fruits (Deut. xxvi. 5—10) is paralleled by Psalms lxxviii and cvii[1]. The former was included in the domestic service of the first night of the Passover at an early date[2]. On the model of the historical Psalms the liturgy of the Synagogue revels in its laudation of God as revealed in the history of Israel and the world. Even the Decalogue, which was daily recited in the Temple, connects the Law with the miraculous redemption of Israel from Egypt (Exod. xx. 1[3]). There were also declarations of faith which had no such historical framework. Foremost among these was the *Shema*, opening with the enunciation of the unity and uniqueness of God (Deut. vi. 4). Now this passage, like the Decalogue, was part of the daily office of the Temple[4]. The *purpose* of this recital is not stated in the sources, but it can hardly be that it was introduced merely as a scriptural lesson[5]. It was not only an important text in itself, but was the most significant of the "confessional" passages of the Old Testament. For the phraseology is remarkable. Four verses of the Hebrew Bible open with the invocation: "Hear, O Israel." All four occur in Deuteronomy (v. 1, vi. 4, ix. 1, xx. 3). Now, in all but the one before us (vi. 4) the invocation is followed up by the *second* person; only here is the *first* person used ("the Lord *our* God"). The older Midrashim perceived this verbal difference. "The Lord our God the Lord is one,"—the Lord, who in the first instance is our (Israel's) God, is to be the One God also to the nations (quoting Zechariah xiv. 9[6]). This conception enormously added to the importance of the text as a testimony to God, and there seems no reason to doubt that the exegesis was ancient. The whole idea of witnessing to God was, moreover, of this two-fold nature; it was a personal acknowledgment by Israel, it was a universal proclamation

[1] Stephen's address in Acts vii. is thus in the true form. It is in the *sequel* that he differs from Hebrew models.

[2] Mishnah, Pesaḥim x. 4.

[3] On the dogmatic significance of this, cf. S. Schechter, *Studies in Judaism*, first series, pp. 145, 186.

[4] Mishnah, Tamid v. 1. Cf. the First Series of the present work, p. 9.

[5] Yet Friedmann so holds (Sifrê, Deut. 72 b, note 17, citing T.B. Menaḥoth 99 b).

[6] Sifrê on Deut. vi. 4; cf. the commentary of Naḥmanides on the same text.

to the world. Thus it was a true exegetical instinct which led to the combination of Zech. xiv. 9 with Deut. vi. 4.

Nor does the evidence end here. In the Synagogue liturgy the recital of the Shema is followed by the clearest declaration of faith known to the Hebrew prayer book[1]. "Yea, *it is true*—this thy word...*It is true* that the God of the Universe is our King." This passage, based (on the authority of Rab) on Ps. xcii. 3, is the nearest to a Creed that the Synagogue liturgy ever attained before the late Middle Ages. In essence the passage is old, belonging according to the best authorities to the period of the Hasmonean revival. The wording has been expanded and varied in course of the ages, but in substance it retains its original character[2].

Another liturgical example also deserves special consideration. The *Alenu* Prayer, so named from its opening word, is very generally held to be pre-Christian in date[3]. The whole congregation prostrated itself while confessing faith in the one God, and proclaiming the hope of the universal acceptance of the Divine Sovereignty. Probably this passage was originally recited once annually, at the autumn New Year; later, it was introduced into the daily liturgy. Later again it formed the dying confession of martyrs[4].

We have ground, therefore, for holding that the "confession" of God was a regular feature in the Temple ritual. God, as we have already seen, testifies of himself that he is God. Ps. l. 7 is very emphatic on this head, however we interpret the verse[5]. But though

[1] Apart, of course, from the dogmatic implications. The thirteen articles of Maimonides (both in their prose and poetical versions) now appear in most Hebrew prayer books. Naturally, however, these are not earlier than the thirteenth century (see Annotated ed., etc., pp. 3, 89 and notes).

[2] See the Annotated ed., etc., pp. 42, 98 and notes. The passage is referred to in the Mishnah and Talmud (Tamid v., Berachoth fol. 12—13). The Geniza MSS preserve much shorter (and more primitive) versions than are now used. For views affirming the antiquity of the passage see: L. Löw, *Gesammelte Schriften*, i. 49; Zunz, *G.V.* p. 370 (ed. 2, p. 382); E. G. Hirsch in *Jewish Encyclopedia*, ii. 148—9. The saving efficacy of the response "Amen" is also to be noted. Cf. *Jewish Encyclopedia*, i. 492. The response Amen to doxologies was both in Synagogue and Church equivalent to a Confession of faith. See particularly T.B. Sabbath 119b.

[3] Cf. First Series of these Studies, p. 149. As to the pre-Christian date, see Kohler (*Jewish Encyclopedia*, i. 336 *seq.*). Cf. also I. Lévi (*Revue des Études Juives*, lxiv. p. 177).

[4] *Emeq ha-bachah*, ed. Wiener, p. 31.

[5] A.V. "I will testify *against* thee," R.V. "I will testify *unto* thee." The latter is the rendering of the LXX, which has the well-known phrase: ὁ θεὸς, ὁ θεὸς σού εἰμι ἐγώ (with a possible reminiscence of Exod. iii. 14).

God thus testified to himself, it was incumbent on Israel to testify also. The relation was reciprocal. On the one hand: Unless Israel witness to God (Is. xliii. 10, xliv. 8) God will be a quick witness against Israel (Mic. i. 2, Mal. iii. 5[1]). On the other hand: When Israel does witness to God, God witnesses to Israel. A first-century saying brings this out fully on the basis of the text (Deut. xxvi. 17—18): "Thou hast avouched the Lord this day to be thy God...and the Lord hath avouched thee this day to be his peculiar people." Just as Israel proclaims the One God (Deut. vi. 4) so God proclaims the one people (1 Chr. xvii. *passim*. Note in particular the consecution of ideas in verses 20 and 21[2]). The Sovereignty of God over earth was due, as it were, to man's proclamation of it. "Before our father Abraham came into the world, the Holy One (as it were) was King only over the heavens, as it is written (Gen. xxiv. 7): 'the Lord *God of heaven* who took me from my father's house.' When, however, our father Abraham came into the world, he made God King over *heaven and earth*, as it is written (*loc. cit.* verse 3): 'and I will make thee swear by the Lord, the God of heaven and the *God of earth.*'" The Kingdom of God, as S. Schechter well says, is "based upon mankind's knowledge of him, and the realisation of his nearness[3]." Otherwise expressed, the thought is that Israel's virtue is the exaltation of God, obedience to the divine will increases the divine power[4]. He is greater than the praises of him[5], yet his throne was not established until the children sang praises unto him[6].

The reciprocity of the relation is illustrated by Matt. x. 32 (cf. Mk viii. 38, Luke xii. 8): "Whoever shall confess me before men, him will I also confess before my Father which is in heaven." There is something here, no doubt, of the idea of martyrdom. The martyr of Synagogue as of Church has ever been buoyed up by this sure sense that his open

[1] See C. Taylor's note, *Sayings of the Jewish Fathers* (ed. 2), p. 117.

[2] T.B. Hagigah 3 a—b. This same Deuteronomic text was used in the Synagogue Hymn printed in Annotated ed. etc. p. ccl. In this Hymn the reciprocal relations between Israel and God are expressed in much detail.

[3] Sifrê on Deut. xxxii. 10 (ed. Friedmann 134 b). S. Schechter, *Aspects of Rabbinic Theology*, 33, 84. With this thought may be compared the Rabbinic idea that though God was desirous of living in his world from the beginning he only did so when the Tabernacle was built (Pesiqta Rabbathi v. and vii. (27 b) and parallels). The contrasting and complementary reference to the heavenly and earthly jurisdiction of God is illustrated by the phrase of the Lord's Prayer: "thy will be done on earth as in heaven."

[4] Deut. Rabba iv (§ 7); cf. Mechilta, ed. Friedmann 39 a. Cf. p. 173 below.

[5] Mechilta, Shira § 1.

[6] Exod. Rabba xxiii. (§ 1).

and fearless confession of God places him in a special relation to the God whom he confesses[1]. Confessing God or his Name (Ps. vii. 18, liv. 8) in the sense of gratitude for the divine benefits belongs to the same category, yet really stands higher. In 1 Kings viii. (esp. verse 33) the transition between the senses of confession as praise and as admission of guilt is very marked. What so elevates the idea of confession as praise is the Messianic hope that it will survive the confession of sin. The thank-offering will last on eternally, though the sin-offering will be superseded in the age of innocency and bliss. But there will be no end to the "sacrifice of praise" (Heb. xiii. 15[2]).

In the Middle Ages an actual confession of faith was used on the death-bed. This was based, in its terms, on Maimonides' formulation of the Creed. But its introduction was the work of the mystics, who did not feel it at all inconsistent to adopt the phraseology of a rationalist so pronounced as Maimonides[3].

[1] On the connection between martyrdom and the "Sanctification of the name of God," see Hastings' *Encyclopaedia of Religion and Ethics*, vol. ix. p. 178.

[2] Cf. Annotated edition, etc., p. xxxii.

[3] Several instances of this Confession of faith will be found in the author's forthcoming collection of Hebrew Testaments or Wills to be issued by the Jewish Publication Society of America as a volume of the "Jewish Classics."

## V. THE HIGH PRIEST'S CONFESSION.

There is no reason for surprise in the fact that the Synoptics make no allusion to the Day of Atonement. The Gospel allusions to fasting are to special occasions, not to the great annual rite[1]. The silence of the Synoptics is paralleled by that of the Old Testament, a silence which in the latter case is explicable on the ground of a post-exilic date for the Day of Atonement[2]. As to the Synoptics, one must remember that the Day was uniquely a day for the Temple; it did not compare in national significance with the Pilgrim feasts, which drew vast crowds to the capital from the provinces[3]. There would have been no opportunity for Jesus to discourse or discuss in Jerusalem on the Day of Atonement, given over as it was to the ritual of the Temple. The day was so fully occupied with this ritual, that it was impossible for one and the same witness to be present at it all. Thus we are specifically told in the Mishnah (Yoma vii. 2) that he who was present at the reading of the scriptural lesson by the High Priest was unable to see also the complete ritual of the sacrifices. In the synagogues outside Jerusalem, the day must have been spent in prayer. We have Philo's direct testimony that this was the case in the diaspora. The prayers went on from morning to evening, and were directed for pardon, not on the ground of the worshipper's merit, but in reliance on the compassion of a Being who prefers forgiveness to punishment (M. II. 296). Isaiah lviii. may be a homily spoken in Jerusalem on the Day of Atonement, and the habit is illustrated also in the Pesiqtoth. The latter were not, however, so much spoken on the Day itself, as on the previous Sabbath, which continued to be the occasion for such homilies right through the

[1] Compare First Series, ch. xvi.

[2] Is. lviii. possibly, though not certainly, was spoken with reference to the Day of Atonement. The chapter forms the prophetic reading of the Synagogue for the morning of that day.

[3] Jeroboam recognises the national importance of the Pilgrim feasts (1 Kings xii. 32). It was with reference to Tabernacles, not the Day of Atonement, that during the Roman War, "when Cestius had marched from Antipatris to Lydda, he found the city empty of its men, for the whole multitude had gone up to Jerusalem for the feast of Tabernacles" (Josephus, *War*, II. xix. 1). Thus, though the Fourth Gospel alludes to discourses of Jesus on Tabernacles (First Series, p. 11), it does not mention any on the Day of Atonement.

history of the Synagogue. Not even the Fourth Gospel records any such discourse or discussion. There was no popular custom to make a point of being present in Jerusalem for the Fast, as there was e.g. for the Passover, the ritual of which, though largely associated with the Temple, was also essentially domestic and associated with the life outside the Temple precincts. Except that the goat was despatched beyond the city, the Day of Atonement rites were confined to the Temple enclosure.

This is not to deny that the Day of Atonement filled a great place in popular Jewish life. Some aspects of it were quite independent of the Temple; in the first instance the fast itself, in the second the discipline of repentance. In this discipline, a recital of the Temple doings held a high place, and the point of stress was the Confession of the High Priest. Such Confession, beginning perhaps with this recital, became rapidly, as the liturgy of the Synagogue developed, more and more one of the prime elements of atonement.

Hence considerable importance attaches to the precise terms of the Confession as pronounced by the High Priest on the Day of Atonement. This importance is increased by a noteworthy change. Whereas in Leviticus xvi. 30 it is the *priest* who is agent: "he shall make atonement for you"—where *he* is the priest, in the period before 70 A.D., in the Mishnaic formulation of the High Priest's Confession *God* is the subject. *Kappêr nâ*, "O Lord, do *Thou* atone for the iniquity, the sins, and the transgressions." The scapegoat, it must be remembered, was not sacrificed but Confession was made over it. Hence, with regard to prayer and Confession, Hosea xiv. 3 could easily be made to apply in later ages. There is no ground for doubting that the Mishnah reproduces the three-fold formula actually employed in the Temple. Atonement was to be made by the High Priest for himself, and for his house and for the people. The Mishnaic tradition as to the formula is clearly based on the terms of the Biblical prescription (Lev. xvi. 21): he shall confess "all the *iniquity* of the children of Israel, and all their *transgressions*, and all their *sins*" (והתודה עליו את כל עונת בני ישראל ואת כל פשעיהם לכל חטאתם). The order of the words—iniquities, transgressions, sins—is noticeable, for the Synagogue liturgy has re-arranged them in accordance with the Talmudic criticism of the view of R. Meir as contained in the Mishnah. The Mishnaic order is, as the Talmud points out, confirmed by Ex. xxxiv. 7: "forgiving *iniquity* and *transgression* and *sin*" (נשא עון ופשע וחטאה.). But the arrangement, as applied to public worship, is objected to on the ground that there is an anti-climax. For, argues the Talmud, חטא = an inadvertent sin, עון a presumptuous iniquity, and פשע a transgression, a deliberate act of rebellion[1]. If the High Priest first asked pardon for transgressions, it would be superfluous to pray in behalf of lighter offences. Hence the Talmud prescribes that the order of confession should be: sin, iniquity, transgression[2]. Confirmation for the arrangement—חטא עון פשע—is found in Ps. cvi. 6, 1 Kings viii. 48, Dan. ix. 5, in none of which, however, does פשע occur, though otherwise the citations bear out the Talmudic contention which has been accepted in the current Synagogue liturgy for the Day of Atonement[3]. (Shulḥan Aruch, Oraḥ Ḥayim.) The *Abodah*, literally service, was most probably recited outside Jerusalem in the synagogues on the Day of Atonement even in Temple times; and the *Abodah* was in essence a narrative of the High Priest's doings on that day and contained the formula of confession. The present liturgical forms of the *Abodah* go back according to J. Derenbourg[4] to the fifth or sixth century. But some forms of the *Abodah* must have been in synagogal use many centuries earlier than that. One of the most important facts bearing on the history of the liturgy is the spiritual association of the provincial synagogues with the ritual ceremonial of the Temple. Though the rite of the Day of Atonement was specifically associated with the Temple, there was a liturgical analogue in all Jewish congregations throughout the ancient world.

The Confession (the text of which will be discussed immediately) in the Palestinian Version runs thus:

O the NAME, I have done iniquity, I have transgressed, I have sinned before Thee, I and my house. I beseech, O Name [or according to the other reading By the Name], pardon the iniquities, the transgressions and the sins which I have in-

[1] On "Sin as Rebellion" cf. S. Schechter, *Some Aspects of Rabbinic Theology*, ch. xiv. He bases his conception on such passages as Sifrâ 80 d (on Levit. xvi.); cf. also T.B. Yoma 35 b; Tosefta. The exact words are · עונות אילו הזדונות פשעיהם אילו המרדים · חטאתם אילו השגגות.

[2] While there is no doubt that פשע is a stronger term than חטא, it is not so certain that there is any idea of climax in the order of the terms when employed together. Thus Isaiah lviii. opens: "Shew my people their *transgression* (פשעם), and the house of Jacob their *sins* (חטאתם)." Here the words are simply parallel.

[3] The Geniza fragments in many instances differ from the current liturgical usage, for the fragments often preserve the order of the Mishnah (עויתי פשעתי חטאתי).

[4] *Revue des Études Juives*, vi. 70.

iquitously done, sinned, and transgressed against Thee, I and my house: as it is written in the Law of Thy servant Moses, saying, For on this day shall atonement be made for you to cleanse you from all your sins before the Lord ye shall be clean (Levit. xvi. 30). And they answered after him: Blessed be the Name of His Glorious Kingdom for ever and ever.

The Mishnah records that the High Priest used this same formula thrice, with certain variations, on the Day of Atonement[1]. The second recitation only differs from the first by the addition of the words "and the sons of Aaron, Thy holy people" in the confession. The third recitation alters the terms to "Thy people, the house of Israel." But it adds (in the Palestinian Version) in the *third* recitation only a passage which, in some versions, occurs all three times:

And the priests and the people who stood in the Court at the time when they heard the Name, coming forth from the mouth of the High Priest, bent the knee, prostrated themselves and fell on their faces and said: Blessed be the Name of His Glorious Kingdom for ever and ever.

As the formula is, in any case, one of the oldest liturgical confessions extant, it is worth considering the exact text in detail. The text is taken in what follows from the Mishnah of the Palestinian Talmud (ed. W. H. Lowe, pp. 50 a ff.) and the main variants are indicated.

(i)

(Mishnah Yoma iii. 8 [9]; T.B. Yoma 35 b; T.J. Yoma ii. 7, 40 d.)

אנא השם עויתי פשעתי חטאתי לפניך אני וביתי · אנא בשם[a]
כפר נא לעונות לפשעים[b] ולחטאים שעויתי שפשעתי[c] שחטאתי
לפניך אני וביתי · ככתוב בתורת משה עבדך לאמר כי ביום הזה
יכפר עליכם לטהר אתכם מכל חטאתיכם לפני יי תטהרו · והן[d]
עונים אחריו · ברוך שם כבוד מלכותו לעולם ועד :

(*a*) T.J. (ed. Venice) in Mishnah reads השם throughout: but in Talmud T.J. iii. 7 reads בשם in second clause each time. T.B. (ed. Venice) השם (so Maimonides). Tosefta, Yoma ii. 1 reads בשם. (*b*) T.B. ולפשעים, Rabbinovicz על העונות ועל הפשעים ועל החטאים. (*c*) T.J. ed. Venice and T.B. ושפשעתי ושחטאתי (so Maimonides). (*d*) Maimonides (Cambridge MS. Add. 1020) והכהנים והעם עונים וכו'.

[1] Cf. for the modern usage, the *Service of the Synagogue* (ed. Davis and Adler), Day of Atonement, Part II, pages 161 *seq.* On the response "Blessed be the Name" etc. see Annotated edition of the Prayer Book, p. li. On the Shem Hamephorash, the Tetragrammaton, see *J.E.* xi. 262.

(ii)

(Mishnah Yoma iv. 2; T.B. Yoma 41 b.)

אנא[(a)] וכו׳···וביתי ובני אהרן עם קדושיך אנא בשם[(b)] וכו׳···וביתי ובני אהרן עם קדושיך ככתוב וכו׳:

(*a*) T.J. in Mishnah, ed. Venice, reads השם. In this clause T.B. (ed. Venice) reads: אנא השם חטאתי עויתי ופשעתי, and in the second clause: לעונות ולפשעים ולחטאים שעויתי ושפשעתי ושחטאתי. (*b*) T.B. השם.

(iii)

(Mishnah Yoma vi. 3 [2]; T.B. Yoma 66 a.)

אנא השם עוו[(a)] פשעו חטאו לפניך עמך בית ישראל אנא בשם[(b)] כפר נא לעונות[(c)] ולפשעים ולחטאים שעוו ושפשעו ושחטאו לפניך עמך בית ישראל ככתוב וכו׳···לעולם ועד: [(d)]הכהנים והעם העומדים בעזרה בזמן ששומעים את שם המפורש[(e)] שהוא יוצא מפי כהן גדול כורעים משתחוים ונופלים על פניהם ואומרים ברוך שם וכו׳:

(*a*) T.B. later eds. read חטאו עוו פשעו, retaining the same order throughout the paragraph. Rabb. has עוו ופשעו וחטאו. (*b*) T.J. Mishnah, ed. Venice, reads השם; but T.B., ed. Venice, here (and here only) reads בשם. Some eds. T.B. read השם throughout, and Maimonides seems to have done the same. (*c*) T.B., ed. Venice, לחטאים ולעונות ולפשעים. (*d*) T.B., ed. Venice, omits the whole paragraph beginning הכוהנים והעם; other eds. contain it, reading והכוהנים, כשהיו שומעים, משתחוים, היו כורעים (so Maim.). (*e*) Liturgies read: את השם הנכבד והנורא מפורש יוצא מפי כהן גדול בקדשה ובטהרה היו כורעים ומשתחוים ומודים ונופלים וכו׳.

Like the Palestinian Mishnah, the Liturgies for the most part read אנא בשם in the second clause, throughout the three formulæ; but this is not the case in the Roman Machzor (ed. Bologna, 1540) which has השם throughout. The Geniza fragments vary considerably in their phraseology, but do not confirm the current liturgical texts.

There is considerable significance in the variations in reading revealed in the preceding notes. Geiger[1] fixed attention on two facts: (1) there is evidence for the occurrence of the reading אנא בשם once only and that in the second clause of the third formula, and (2) in the Mishnah the prostration of the assembled people is mentioned once only,

[1] *Ozar Nechmad*, iii. 118.

and that at the close of the third formula. From these facts Geiger inferred that the High Priest uttered the Tetragrammaton once only, and not as is commonly supposed nine times during his three-fold confessions. Geiger elsewhere maintained that whereas in Alexandria (and subsequently throughout Jewish circles) אדני (Lord) was substituted for the Tetragrammaton, in Palestine the substitute was השם (The NAME). Thus the High Priest really said אנא השם except on the last occurrence of the phrase, when he actually pronounced the Tetragrammaton, a fact indicated by the Mishnaic formula אנא בשם.

I think that Geiger's view can be supported by another piece of evidence. The description in Ecclesiasticus ch. 50 of the ceremonies of the Day of Atonement most clearly includes only one prostration during the confession[1]. That there was only *one* prostration during the confession is quite conclusively shown by verses 20—21:

20 אז ירד ונשא ידיו על כל קהל ישראל וברכת ײ בשפתיו ובשם ײ התפאר

21 וישנו לנפל שנית (העם כ)ל(ו) מפניו

A *second* prostration occurred during the priestly *benediction* during which, as we know from other sources, the Tetragrammaton was pronounced. The reading of the last clause of *v.* 21 is uncertain; but the first clause is undoubted. The Greek text of Sirach (*καὶ ἐδευτέρωσεν ἐν προσκυνήσει* "And he bowed himself down in worship the second time") obscures the fact revealed by the Hebrew text that it was the assembled people who for the *second* time fell on their faces (וישנו לנפל שנית); hence they had only *once* done so previously. It must be pointed out, moreover, that Derenbourg who offers objections to Geiger's theory gives no acceptable explanation of the phrase אנא בשם; he suggests that השם is

[1] The Tosefta (Yoma ii. 2) declares that the High Priest mentioned the Name ten times on the Day of Atonement, "six times over the bull, thrice over the goat, and once at the casting of the lot (between the two goats)." This takes no account of the Priestly benediction, which according to the Mishnah, occurred four times during the Day of Atonement (Mishnah Taanith iv. 1) in the Synagogues, after the destruction. At all events it must have been uttered once in the Temple. Moreover, the Tosefta says nothing (in its summary) of the number of prostrations. It may be pointed out with reference to the Hebrew of the fiftieth chapter of Ecclesiasticus that the term להזכיר in verse 16 refers to confession. This confirms B. Jacob's view as to the meaning of that word in the headings of Psalms xxxviii. and lxx. (*Zeitschrift für die alttestamentliche Wissenschaft*, xvii. 48).

used in the first clause as a simple invocation, and בשם in the second clause as an adjuration. But there is no evidence that אנא was ever followed by the preposition ב in an adjuration.

Reverting to the terms used, no clear light is thrown by the LXX. It uses ἁμαρτία, ἀδικία, ἀνομία without much discrimination, though it is interesting to observe that in Leviticus xvi. 21 (as in Exod. xxxiv. 7) it gives ἀνομία for עון, ἀδικία for פשע and ἁμαρτία for חטא. In the N.T. (as in the LXX) the favourite word for sin is ἁμαρτία, which is the literal sense of חטא (for the Hebrew like the Greek means a *miss*, a failure to reach the mark)[1]. The LXX is mostly followed in the N.T. but there are interesting variations. Thus Mark xv. 28 (καὶ μετὰ ἀνόμων) is closer to the Hebrew of Isaiah liii. 12 (ואת פושעים) than the LXX (ἐν τοῖς ἀνόμοις)[2]. 1 Pet. ii. 22 has ἁμαρτία for the חמס of Is. liii. 9 (where LXX has the stronger ἀνομίαι); in iv. 8, as also in James v. 20, ἁμαρτία stands for פשע (Prov. x. 12). In Rom. iv. 7—8 (following LXX of Ps. xxxii. 1—2) we have ἀνομία for פשע, and ἁμαρτία for both חטא and עון. In Matt. vii. 23 ἀνομία corresponds to און. The Synoptics use ἀνομία (peculiar to Matthew) and ἀδικία (peculiar to Luke). Rom. xi. 26—27 uses ἁμαρτία for חטא and ἀσέβεια for פשע (Is. xxvii. 9, lix. 20—21). It is interesting to note that in Hebrews (which alone in the N.T. has a clear reference to the Day of Atonement, ix. 6—10, x. 19—22), some texts of viii. 12 (in the quotation from Jeremiah xxxi. 34), while reading ἀδικία (for עון) and ἁμαρτία (for חטא), add the clause καὶ τῶν ἀνομιῶν αὐτῶν (thus adding ולפשעיהם to the Hebrew text)[3].

[1] This fact is a curious comment on the contrast drawn between Greek and Jewish ideas of sin by R. W. Livingstone in his charming book on *The Greek Genius and its meaning for us* (p. 27). "They (the Greeks) regarded their offences as shortcomings and called them ἁμαρτίαι 'bad shots.' But to S. Paul departures from the path of righteousness are not shortcomings or misses or frailties or failures but sins."

[2] Does this fact throw light on the authenticity of the text in Mark, despite its rejection by most editors? Mark's genuine use (i. 2) of Malachi iii. 1 is partly at least independent of the LXX (cf. *Cambridge Biblical Essays*, 1909, p. 179).

[3] For the use of the Aramaic חוב in such contexts see Levy, *Chald. Wörterbuch*, pp. 240 ff. On the inferences to be drawn as to the phraseology of the Lord's Prayer, see commentaries. Allen quotes the Targum of Isaiah liii. 5, where פשע=חובא.

## VI. WHITED SEPULCHRES.

The metaphor is obscured in Matthew (xxiii. 27—28), while Luke (xi. 44) is curiously at variance. Luke actually satirises the *absence* of those marks, the *presence* of which is the basis of the irony of Matthew. "Woe unto you! for ye are as the tombs which appear not[1], and the men that walk over them know it not." If the tombs were "whitened," this figure of Luke would be pointless. On the other hand, Matthew's metaphor is not a natural one. The whitening of the tombs is referred to in the Mishnah[2] as taking place in Adar, before the Passover. "There was no objection to a layman's becoming unclean, except when he wanted to enter the Temple," as C. G. Montefiore accurately observes. As the pilgrims for the Passover *did* so want, it was necessary to whiten the tombs and re-mark them with lime if the "latter rains" obliterated the earlier indications. But as A. H. McNeile comments "White-chalked graves do not afford a good simile of hypocrisy, since they proclaim to all, instead of concealing, their inward pollution[3]." It was this feeling perhaps that led to the insertion of what most critics regard as a gloss: "which outwardly appear beautiful." It is hard to decide whether ornamental graves were at all common in ancient Palestine; we have the historical instance of Simon's mausoleum with its seven pyramids in Modin, and an allusion or two in Josephus[4]. On the whole, however, Jewish graves were simple and not visible above ground; otherwise the "whitening" of the approaches would have been unnecessary[5]. Ob-

[1] Lightfoot suggests that Luke refers, in his phrase τὰ μνημεῖα τὰ ἄδηλα, to the קבר תהום "grave of the depth," the site of which has passed out of the memory of man (כל שאין אדם זוכרו). T.J. Nazir ix. 2; T.B. Pesaḥim 80 ff. The idea of "defilement of the depth" is referred to in the Mishnah (Pesaḥim vii. 7, Nazir ix. 2); the phrase being generalised to denote (particularly in the case of the Nazirite) an unknown cause of defilement.

[2] Sheqalim i. 1, T.J. *ad loc.* On the Jewish tombs cf. S. Krauss, *Talmudische Archaeologie* (1911), ii. 79 ff.

[3] *The Gospel according to St Matthew* (1915) p. 339.

[4] 1 Macc. xiii. 27; Josephus, 16 *Antiq.* vii. 1, 4 *War* ix. 7. Cf. *J. E.* xii. 187. The "whited wall" of Acts xxiii. 3 reminds one of Renan's remark (*Mission de Phénicie*, p. 822) that, in the rock-cut Palestinian tombs of soft limestone, entire *walls* were noticeably preferred to pillars.

[5] On the use of tombstones cf. Krauss and *J. E. loc. cit.* A well-known second century saying (T.J. Sheqalim ii. 5) has it: "They make no monuments for the righteous: their words are their memorial." This was possibly meant as a rebuke

viously the graves themselves must have been quite inconspicuous. The gloss would be much more likely to arise from a knowledge of Roman than of Jewish sepulchral ornaments.

A very strong metaphorical application of the *grave* to *hypocrisy* is to be found in the fifth Psalm. There is a play on the words *qeber* (sepulchre) and *qereb* (inward part). "There is no faithfulness in their mouth; their *inward part* is very wickedness, their throat is an open *sepulchre*." Here the point of the figure is that they seek to deceive by their speech, by outward appearances, both the fact that their hearts are false and their designs fatal. In Jeremiah v. 16, the quiver of the Scythians is so full of deadly missiles that it is called "an open sepulchre[1]"; there may possibly be an undercurrent of contrast to the people's declaration that there is no truth in the prophet's mouth (verse 13): "Because ye speak this word, I will make my words in thy mouth fire and this people wood, and it shall devour them."

The context in which the phrase "whited sepulchres" appears is a sweeping and unrestrained attack on the Pharisees. Much of Matt. xxiii, there is critical reason for assuming, belongs to a period later than Jesus, and reflects an antipathy which grew during the struggle of the new faith to find a home in the abode of the old. The assault on Pharisees almost amounts to an assault on Pharisaism, though not even in this chapter is the identification formally made. "Scribes and Pharisees, hypocrites!" reverberates again and again. Luke prefers simply "Pharisees," omitting the first and third words. The attack is too indiscriminate to be effective. It has been often pointed out how forcibly the Pharisaic leaders themselves satirised and denounced hypocrisy. They appreciated the danger, a danger which is common to all religions but is more intrusive in a system of more than in one of fewer forms[2]. One would have imagined that the Pharisaic exposure of hypocrisy (and no one doubts that it was very thorough)[3] could only have one significance,

to the habit of ostentatious monuments, adopted as a passing fashion at the time (cf. *J. E.* xii. 191). Mishnah Erubin v. 1 also seems to refer to a period much later than Jesus.

[1] The LXX omits the phrase in Jeremiah v. 16; it has, however, the words τάφος ἀνεῳγμένος in Ps. v. 10.

[2] I. Elbogen has some good remarks (in an opposite sense), for he thinks that "es ist ganz gleichgiltig, ob die betreffende Religion, wenig oder viele Formen hat, oder ob sie gar auf ein blosses Bekenntnis des Glaubens sich beschränkt" (*Die Religionsanschauungen der Pharisäer*, Berlin 1904, p. 33).

[3] T.B. Yoma 86 b; T.J. Ber. ix., Soṭa 5, T.B. Soṭa 22 b.

viz. that hypocrisy was abhorrent to the "scribes," the authors of the exposure. It is disappointing to have again and again to argue this point. One *ought* to be met by the Ciceronian protest "utitur in re non dubia testibus non necessariis." But recent theologians persist in turning the Pharisaic indignation against themselves. The fact that the Pharisees denounce hypocrisy proves—that the Pharisees were hypocrites! Otherwise what the need of the denunciation? Out of their own mouths you prove the justice of the Synoptic attack[1].

To the specific charges the Pharisees have their answer, sometimes a meticulously precise rebuttal, sometimes the tenure by the criticised of a point of view opposed to that of the critic. Take only one instance, the tithe: scrupulously given, while "judgment and mercy and faith" are neglected (Matt. xxiii. 23). A typical Pharisee gives the commentary. Gamaliel I, the reputed teacher of Paul (Acts xxii. 3), was not a man to neglect the weightier matters of the law. In the trial of the disciples in Acts v. 34 ff. Gamaliel appears in a gracious light, "open-minded and liberal." Similarly Rabbinic sources agree in eulogising his moral character[2]. But it was this very man who most emphatically urged the duty of scrupulous exactitude in tithing. "Rabban Gamaliel said, Make to thyself a master, and be quit of doubt; and accustom not thyself to give tithe by a conjectural estimate[3]." These things ye ought to do and not leave the other undone, might be fairly inscribed by Pharisaism as the motto on its banner.

This last assertion is no mere controversial paradox. It is the simple truth about *all* the many Pharisaic teachers of whom the Rabbinic literature has any detailed record. It is true of them in all ages. It

[1] "Certainly no one would say that all the Pharisees were hypocrites. Nor did Jesus mean that, but simply that hypocrisy had come to be the distinguishing characteristic of Pharisees as a class or party. *To this fact the Talmud itself bears clear testimony*." The writer in evidence quotes the famous Rabbinic satire on the types of sham Pharisees (A. T. Robertson, *Jesus and the Pharisees*, London, 1920, pp. 23, 26).

[2] Mishnah Soṭah ix. 15; Gamaliel is there also represented as the typical exponent of Pharisaism.

[3] Aboth i. 17. ואל תרבה לעשר אומדות. Taylor comments: "Let (such) duties be defined as far as may be by rule; let doubts be resolved by authority; leave as little scope as possible for personal bias and the temptations of self-interest." D. Hoffmann (*Die erste Mischna*, 1882, pp. 31 ff.) argues that Gamaliel II is the author of this saying. Were this so, the argument of the text would not be affected. But most authorities (Geiger, Weiss, Taylor, Herford) are agreed that Gamaliel I is referred to. W. Bacher specifically rejects Hoffmann's view (*Jewish Encyclopedia*, v. p. 559).

is true of Hillel, it is true of Aqiba, it is true of Rab—Pharisees who cover the first three centuries. It is true of innumerable others. One cannot take up the records of the Pharisees *at any age* without lighting on such men not singly but in battalions. Now as W. Bacher justly says of Hillel: "In the memory of posterity Hillel lived, on the one hand, as the scholar who made the whole of the traditional law his own....On the other hand, he was known as the saint and sage who in his private life and in his dealings with men practised the high virtues of morality and resignation just as he taught them in his maxims with unexcelled brevity and earnestness[1]." A curious type this of the whited sepulchre! Aqiba was another of the same calibre. We read of his devotion to ritual—how in his excitement in private prayer he would begin in one corner of the room and end in another corner; how in prison he used up half his scanty pittance of water to wash his hands ritually[2]. Yet not only did this same Aqiba take a very ideal view of the fundamentals of religion[3], but went to a death of cruel torture, not reluctantly but joyously (as he expressly said), happy to prove by the willing sacrifice of his life his love of God[4]. A curious type this of hypocrisy! And as for the third named out of hundreds, Abba Arika, known as Rab, the founder of the College at Sura, to whom the Babylonian Talmud with all its mazes of law and ceremonial owes its origin—he was not less famed as moralist than as ritualist[5]. It was this same Rab to whom is attributed this short confession for use on the Day of Atonement[6]: "Thou knowest the secrets of eternity and the most hidden mysteries of all living. Thou searchest the innermost recesses, and triest the reins and heart. Nought is concealed from thee, or hidden from thine eyes." A curious type this of externalism!

A recent writer already referred to in this Note (Prof. A. T. Robertson) says of the charge of hypocrisy that it "stirs the modern apologists of Pharisaism to rage." It may well do so, though some of us try to keep our temper. We understand too fully the need and value of the exposure of hypocrisy, to do other than ask those who would judge Pharisaism fairly, to investigate besides the faults to which the system was liable, the virtues which it actually revealed.

[1] *Jewish Encyclopedia*, vi. p. 397.
[2] T.B. Berachoth 31 a; Erubin 21 b.
[3] Cf. First Series, Index s.v. Aqiba.
[4] T.B. Berachoth 81 b, T.J. Ber. ix. 5; and parallel passages.
[5] Cf. Bacher's summary of his moral utterances in *J. E.* i. 30—the summary is of itself an apt commentary on Matthew xxiii.
[6] T.B. Yoma 87 b; cf. Singer ed. of Prayer Book, p. 259.

## VII. THE GOOD SAMARITAN.

Among the special Sources of Luke there may have been a Collection of Parables *based on Scriptural Texts*, a Collection attributing (probably in large measure truly) stories and reflections to Jesus. Whether such a Collection should be termed (with Wright) "Pauline" is doubtful. It would be rather of the nature such as we find in various sections of the Midrash. It has been already suggested[1] that the Prodigal Son is related to the history of Jacob and Esau in Genesis. The Good Samaritan would be a fitting illustration of Leviticus xix. 18, on love of one's neighbour. Several other instances might be cited, as e.g. Luke xiv. 16 ff. On comparing this with Matthew xxii. we seem to find a clue to some of the differences between the reports of Parables in the first and third Gospels.

| Matthew xxii. 5–6. | Luke xiv. 18–20. |
| --- | --- |
| But they made light of it, and went their ways, one to his own farm, another to his merchandise: and the rest laid hold on his servants, and entreated them shamefully, and killed them. | And they all with one consent began to make excuse. The first said unto him, I have bought a field, and I must needs go out and see it: I pray thee have me excused. And another said, I have bought five yoke of oxen, and I go to prove them: I pray thee have me excused. And another said, I have married a wife, and therefore I cannot come. |

Apart from the difference in the moral at the termination of the passages, Luke reminds us of an Old Testament context far more clearly than Matthew does. The latter possibly had an oral, not a written source; while Luke's source was written not oral. Luke may, in brief, have had before him a Collection in which there were Parables illustrating Deuteronomy xx. 5 ff. In this passage, the exclusions from military service are laid down. "What man is there that hath built a new house, and...that hath planted a vineyard...that hath betrothed a wife?" We can in our age fully realise the aptness of Jesus' sarcasm against the unconscientious shirkers of duty by appeal to the law protecting the conscientious. Deuteronomy differs from the modern law, in that the former openly released from military service those who honestly proclaimed themselves faint-hearted (Deut. xx. 8). It will be observed

[1] First Series, p. 11.

that Luke continues to supply reminiscences of this same chapter. In xiv. 28 he refers to "building a tower," in xiv. 31 to conditions of peace and the embassage (cf. Deut. xx. 10 ff.). Thus there is a good deal in this fourteenth chapter of Luke that recalls the twentieth chapter of Deuteronomy. It is possible, too, that the Barren fig-tree (Luke xiii. 6) is a parabolic comment on Deut. xx. 20. Luke xii. 52 was, again, possibly spoken on occasion when Micah vii. 6 had been read in the Synagogue; and Luke xvi. 1 on the Unrighteous Steward might have been a parable suggested as a comment on Deut. vii. 9. God's faithfulness is contrasted in many Midrashic parables with man's unfaithfulness[1]. Luke ix. 5 again may be compared with Midrashic homilies on Psalm x. 1[2].

Whether or not the Good Samaritan was originally a Midrashic illustration of Leviticus xix. 18, its effectiveness for that end is, as the Parable now stands, indisputable. Hence it is hard to follow Mr Montefiore in his more or less partial approval of J. Halévy's criticism, forcible and ingenious though it is[3]. The latter put forward the view that in the original Parable the three persons were not Priest, Levite, Samaritan, but Priest, Levite, Israelite. It is quite true that the latter gives an excellent climax—Israelite of course would mean layman. "Priest and Levite who live by the pilgrims' gifts, and who ought to set an example of charity to the masses, abandon piteously a poor wounded pilgrim on an unfrequented road; a simple Israelite, consulting only his heart, takes care of him and saves him from certain death[4]." But, as we shall see, the sudden appearance of the third term Samaritan where we should

[1] See the series of Parables (several of them *royal*) on Deut. vii. 9 in the Midrash Debarim Rabba iii. § 3.

[2] Midrash Tehillim, ed. Buber, pp. 92–3.

[3] C. G. Montefiore, *The Synoptic Gospels*, p. 936; J. Halévy, "Sens et Origine de la parabole évangelique dite du bon Samaritain" in *Revue des Études Juives*, vol. iv. pp. 249 ff.

[4] Halévy, *op. cit.* p. 255. "Ce sens particulier de la dénomination *israélite* était naturellement incompréhensible par le cercle pagano-chrétien, auquel saint Luc a emprunté la parabole. Pour les chrétiens recrutés parmi les païens, la mention d'un israélite, après celle d'un prêtre et d'un lévite qui sont aussi israélites, n'avait aucun sens et gâtait par sa présence la belle ordonnance de la parabole. Pour remédier à cet inconvénient on se crut autorisé a corriger Ἰσραηλίτης en Σαμαρείτης, et cette correction fut accueillie d'autant plus favorablement qu'elle donnait satisfaction à un besoin réel, celui de rattacher à Jésus l'idée de la supériorité des chrétiens païens sur les Juifs non convertis." But would such a contrast be so strange even to a Gentile Christian in the light of Psalm cxviii. 2–3?

expect Israelite, gives special point to the whole conception, and in Mr Montefiore's admirable words, makes the parable "one of the simplest and noblest among the noble gallery of parables in the Synoptic Gospels. Love, it tells us, must know no limits of race and ask no enquiry. Who needs me is my neighbour. Whom at the given time and place I can help with my active love, he is my neighbour and I am his." Curiously enough, it is the heirs of the Pharisees who most strenuously insist on this. Merx remarks[1]: "Modern Jewish teachers of religion explain *rea* (neighbour) as equivalent to all fellow-men." Certainly they do so, in every Synagogue pulpit, in every Jewish text-book. "This," continues Merx, "does all honour to their morality, but is incorrect historically." Even so, it is undeniable that the Christian advance in the significance of *rea* has its counterpart in a similar Pharisaic advance, if any advance was really necessary on the Old Testament teaching[2].

Leaving this discussion for the moment, attention may be drawn in this context to a remarkable passage in the Sifrâ. Here the collocation "Priest, Levite, Israelite" is referred to in terms which for their universal sympathy are worthy to be placed side by side with the moral of the Parable of the Good Samaritan. The text, Leviticus xviii. 5, runs thus: "Ye shall keep My statutes and My ordinances, which, if a man do, he shall live in (or by) them: I am the Lord." Whereon the Sifrâ has this comment:

*Which, if a man do.* Rabbi Jeremiah[3] was wont to say: Whence does one infer that even a heathen who performs the Law is accounted as a High Priest? The text proves this, when it says, "which, if *a man* do, he shall live by them." Similarly, the Scripture says: "This is the law"—it does not say "This is the law of Priests, Levites, and Israel," but "This is the law of *man*, O Lord God" (2 Sam. vii. 19)[4]. Thus also the text does not say "Open ye the gates that Priests, Levites and Israelites may enter," but "Open ye the gates, that *the righteous heathen*[5] which keepeth truth (or faithfulness) may enter in" (Isaiah xxvi. 2). Similarly the Psalmist (cxviii. 21) does not say: "This is the gate of the Lord; Priests, Levites, and Israelites shall enter into it," but, "This is the gate of the Lord; the *righteous*

[1] *Das Evangelium Matthaeus nach der Syrischen*, etc. (1902), p. 293.

[2] Cf. First Series, ch. ii and p. 151.

[3] In T.B. Sanhedrin 59 the same idea is quoted in the name of R. Meir, who belongs to the second century, while Jeremiah is a fourth century Palestinian (cf. Bacher, *Die Agada der Palaestinensischen Amoräer*, iii. 95 ff.).

[4] R.V. "and this too after the manner of men."

[5] Evidently to be so translated in this passage; cf. the beginning and end of the citation.

shall enter into it." So, too, with Ps. xxxiii. 1, the call is not to Priests, Levites and Israelites, but to *the righteous* to rejoice in the Lord. Nor does the text (Ps. cxxv. 4) say: "Do good, O Lord, unto Priests, Levites and Israelites," but "Do good, O Lord, unto those that be good, and to them that are upright in their hearts." Hence even a heathen who performs the law is accounted as a High Priest.

Nowhere can contrast be more easily discerned between Paulinism and Pharisaism than in the respective uses made of the ground text (Leviticus xviii. 5) on which this remarkable homily is based. Paul quotes the text twice (Romans x. 5 and Galatians iii. 12). To him, the abrogation of the Law makes it possible for all men to be one in Christ (Gal. iii. 23–28). To the Pharisee, all men may become one in and because of the Law[1]. To Paul the collocation Jew, male, freeman was objectionable; to the Pharisee the collocation Priest, Levite, Israelite. Both Paul and the Pharisee would embrace all mankind in the one gracious possibility of divine love.

The appearance of the Samaritan among the personages of the Parable is explicable, not only on such general grounds, but also as a device of moral art. To castigate one's own community, it is sometimes effective to praise those outside it. We have a very early instance of it in the Talmud[2]; the traditions of it are many; it clearly emanates from an age when the Temple still stood. The hero of the story is Dama, son of Netinah. He was a non-Jew, an idolator, dwelling in Askelon; evidently a man of means, and a πατήρ βουλῆς[3]. "To what limits should a son go in honouring his father?" asked the Rabbi. "Go forth and see what a certain idolator of Askelon did" is the answer. On one occasion he was silent and respectful when his mother publicly insulted him, and on another occasion refused to disturb his father who lay asleep with his head on the key of the box containing the gem which the agents of the Sanhedrin wished to purchase for the High Priest's

[1] Not the whole law, for the "Noachide" precepts were alone necessary for the heathen's salvation according to Pharisaism. See *Jewish Encyclopedia*, vii. 648. According to Maimonides the pious of all nations who have a part in the world to come are those who observe these fundamental laws of morality (Hilchoth Melachim viii. 11). Opinions are divided on the point in the Talmud (T.B. Sanhedrin 105). Maimonides adopts the view of R. Joshua, which indeed has been generally accepted by the Synagogue.

[2] T.B. Qiddushin 31 a, Aboda Zara 23; T.J. Peah i. 1; Deut. Rabba i. § 3; Pesiqta Rabbathi xxiii (xxiv) ed. Friedmann, p. 123 b.

[3] S. Krauss (*Biz. Zeitschrift*, ii. 528; *Griechische und Lateinische Lehnworter im Talmud*, etc. (1899), ii. 438) gives the title as παροβούλη, local magistrate. See also *Jewish Encyclopedia*, iv. 415.

vestment. Though a very high price was offered, he refused to disturb his father, and the sale was not effected. In this way, a heathen was put forward as the model of love and reverence towards parents. This is a Pharisaic parallel to the choice of a Samaritan in the Lucan Parable. The parallel is even closer when Luke quotes Jesus as pointing to a Samaritan as a "stranger" (ἀλλογενής) as the only one out of ten cleansed lepers who "returned to give glory to God" (Luke xvii. 16). As J. A. Montgomery aptly remarks[1]: "The gratitude of the Samaritan was made to point a moral to the Jews even as was the faith of a heathen centurion upon another occasion (Matthew viii. 5 ff.)[2]."

All art, even the highest, is necessarily imperfect, and so fine an example of the Parabolic art as the Good Samaritan does not escape the universal condition. In order to include the moral becomes exclusive; to bring the Samaritan into the category of "neighbour," the Priest and Levite are excluded. Jülicher[3] asks these questions with much force, and concludes that verses 30–35 belong to a different context in which the question related not to the definition of "neighbour," but to the qualifications for admission to the Kingdom. The merciful alien better deserves admission than the Jewish Temple-official enslaved to selfishness. (Cf. Romans ii. 14 ff.) By this means, however, the situation is not saved. For we are again, indeed, faced by the real paradox in the Gospel criticism of the Pharisees; it excludes *them* from the gracious message which Jesus brought. This, as Jülicher argues, is not a forward step, but a step backward from Pharisaic doctrine. That by Priest and Levite are meant the Pharisaic leaders cannot be seriously questioned. John (i. 19) preserves a true tradition of this method of classifying the official representatives of Judaism, and it is not without significance that while the Synoptists generally use the dichotomy Pharisees and Scribes,

[1] *The Samaritans* (1907), p. 160.

[2] Simeon b. Gamaliel also praised the Samaritans in that "every law which the Samaritans accepted, they are more punctilious in observing than the Jews" (*op. cit.* pp. 161 and 170).

[3] *Die Gleichnisreden Jesu* (1910), ii. p. 595: "Soll aber Jesus den Begriff des Nächsten auf den engen Kreis derer, denen gegenüber man zum Dank verpflichtet ist, eingeschränkt haben? Wäre das nicht ein ärmlicher Standpunkt und trotz der eventuellen Einbeziehung von Heiden und Ketzern ein Rückschritt gegen die jüdische Schullehre, die *jeden* Volksgenossen als Nächsten zu lieben befahl? Meinte Jesus, jener Ueberfallene hätte den Priester und den Leviten, die ihn im Stich gelassen, nicht mehr unter die Nächsten rechnen sollen? Auch das σὺ ποίει ὁμοίως sichert für Lc das Gefühl, dass im vorigen ein Muster des Thuns, nicht des Wissens und Erachtens gegeben worden ist."

we have in the chapter of Luke under discussion the Johannine division. And there is this difference between the Lucan parable and the Rabbinic use of a non-Jew as model. The Rabbis do not forget that their own class is capable of the same virtue. A very similar story to that of Dama is in fact told of Safra, a very Pharisee of the Pharisees[1].

The question as to Pharisaic teaching on the universality of brotherly love has already been partly discussed in these pages. It is necessary to add that the citations made by Lightfoot on Luke x. 29 (and among more recent writers by Merx on Matthew, p. 293) are irrelevant. Such a quotation as that of Lightfoot from the Aruch[2], is misinterpreted. The exclusion of a heathen's ox from the category of a "neighbour's ox" (Exod. xxi. 35) is purely legal, and refers only to the question of compensation[3]. The principle was one of equity; only those who paid regard to the injuries inflicted on others (obeying the seven Noachide precepts) are to receive compensation. In general, those who incurred the *obligations* of the Law would enjoy the Law's *amenities*. Thus as *legally* defined, "neighbour" would be restricted to those who observed the Noachide precepts. The definition was legal and reciprocal. It has nothing whatever to do with humane and personal relationships. The distinctions drawn between fellow-Israelite and heathen in such matters were, moreover, concerned only with times of war, and did not apply to normal times of peace[4]. And while Maimonides[5] most regrettably includes an obsolete and ephemeral opinion that it was not a duty

[1] Cf. Rashi on T.B. Makkoth 24 a (Sheiltoth 36). Safra, engaged in prayer, took no notice of the offers (gradually increasing in amount) made for an article he had for sale. When he had ended his devotions he sold the article for the lowest price first offered, for he had made up his mind to accept that sum and refused to gain by the delay. To Safra was applied the text Psalm xv. 2 ("He speaketh the truth in his heart").

[2] s.v. בן ברית (Kohut, *Aruch Completum*, ii. 112).

[3] Cf. Mishnah Baba Qama iv. 3 (also T.B. same tractate 9 b); Maimonides Nizqe Mamon viii. 1.

[4] Soferim xv. 10 (note 27 p. 211 in Müller's edition).

[5] Laws of רוצח iv. end. Against this may be set the idea that the helping of the straying ox of an *enemy* was a special means of overcoming man's tendency to vindictiveness (Sifrê on Deut. ed. Friedmann, p. 115 a). Maimonides himself was in his own conduct and thought remarkably tolerant. As a theologian he was in advance of his age in his pragmatic appreciation of other religions. As a physician, he spent his strength in healing the poor Jew and Gentile alike without distinction. (See Yellin and Abrahams, *Maimonides*, chs. vi. and xi.)

to save a heathen from drowning, Eleazar b. Shammua actually did so save.

It is indeed remarkable how many stories are to be found in the Rabbinic sources of conduct very like that of the Good Samaritan. A series of anecdotes at the end of Tractate Peah in the Jerusalem Talmud show how keenly the Pharisees felt it their duty to relieve distress on their way, even when their benevolence was being exploited by impostors. The story of Abba Tahna has already been told above[1]; how at the anticipated sacrifice of all his goods he carried to the city a leper whom he found by the way-side. Nahum of Gimzu acted less promptly, but the sharpness of his remorse and the severity of the retribution that met him are full of significance. Carrying a gift to his father-in-law, he was accosted by a leper who begged alms. "On my way back" answered Nahum. On his return he found the leper dead. He exclaimed: "May my eyes which saw you and gave not be blinded! my hands that stretched not out be cut off, my legs that ran not to thee be broken!" And so it happened to him. To R. Aqiba he declared: "My remorse is great, and my sufferings are the just requital of my wrong towards this poor fellow[2]."

Even more to the point are the stories told in the Midrash[3]. Bar Qappara walking by the shore of the lake at Caesarea comes to the help of a Roman officer who had lost his all in the wreck of his vessel. The Rabbi gives him two selas[4], takes him home, and then gives him three other selas, saying so great a man can use this larger sum. Then there is the incident of Eleazar ben Shammua. He it was who, in reply to the question, How can man escape the travails precedent to the coming of the Messiah? answered, By study of the Law and by the bestowal of loving-kindnesses[5]. Hence it is not surprising that, though he was a pupil of Aqiba who suffered martyrdom at the hands of Rome, Eleazar ben Shammua included Romans in his wide-embracing benevolence. The Rabbi succours a shipwrecked Roman, clothes the sufferer

[1] First Series, p. 110.

[2] Cf. T.B. Taanith 21 a.

[3] On Ecclesiastes xi. 1.

[4] This is curiously like the two pence of Luke x. 35; though otherwise Bar Qappara is even more generous than the Good Samaritan.

[5] T.B. Sanhedrin 98 b. Bacher (*Agada der Tannaiten*, ii. 277) considers the story of Eleazar ben Shammua as legendary, but on insufficient grounds. Even so, the fact that the story was devised is almost as apt an illustration of Luke's Parable as would be the historical fact of the occurrence, which there is no real reason to question.

in his own robe of honour, takes him home, feeds him and presents him with 200 denarii, and on his departure accompanies him part of the way. The Roman subsequently has a full opportunity (which he utilises) to show his gratitude[1].

[1] Very arresting is the claim (and admission) of *brotherhood* between Jew and Roman—bitter enemies though they were in the field. The shipwrecked Roman says to the Jew: "I am of the sons of Esau your brother" (מן בני עשיו אחוכון אנא). The oppressed Jews appeal to the Roman, "Are we not your brothers?" (אנחנו לא אחיכם). Cf. Bacher, *op. cit.* p. 278.

## NOTE ON ROMANS ii. 14.

The quotations in Weber, which commentators copy, need rectification. Thus the quotation, that an idolator's prayer was not heard (Deut. Rabba ii.), misconceives the passage, in which the point made is that an idolator's prayer is *insincere*. With 1 Kings viii. before them, the Rabbis could not have laid it down as a principle that a heathen's prayer is not heard. Compare p. 76 below.

A most interesting feature in the text in Romans is the reference to the "Gentiles who do *by nature* the things of the Law." This accords literally with what Philo writes of the Patriarchs. These fulfilled the law before the law, as laws of their own nature. Paul's *φύσει τὰ τοῦ νόμου* corresponds to Philo's *πρὸς τὸ βούλημα τῆς φύσεως* (*De Opif. Mundi* § 3) and his *διατάγματα τῆς φύσεως* (*De Abrah.* § 5). So the Pharisees held that Abraham kept laws before Sinai (Mishnah Qiddushin, last words). The idea that much of the Law was derivable from natural reason (T.B. Yoma 67 b) is firmly expressed by A. Ibn Ezra in his Yesod Morah ch. v.: all the decalogue except the Sabbath law is so derivable. Yet Abraham observed the Sabbath (Yoma 21 b). In Jubilees ii. 23 Jacob is the first to observe it. So, the Patriarchs observed other festivals, Jubilees vi. 17, xvi. 20, xxxii. 4.

## VIII. THE SECOND DEATH.

It seems directly due to Schoettgen that the phrase the *Second Death* (ὁ θάνατος ὁ δεύτερος) has come to be described as "Rabbinic[1]." This, however, is scarcely the case. The phrase is not to be found in the older Rabbinic literature at all; it nowhere occurs in the Talmud or earlier Midrash, just as it is absent from the Gospels. Certainly, if Schoettgen's quotations were correct, the scholars who have relied upon him (or rather on his imitator Wetstein) would have been justified[2]. Wetstein, it may be remembered, published his Commentary in 1752; Schoettgen's *Horae* saw the light in 1733. The former does not blindly copy the latter, in this as in other matters; it is clear that Wetstein verified most at least of the quotations which he derived from Schoettgen. But he unfortunately allowed himself to be misled. In brief *all* Schoettgen's quotations (for the occurrence of the phrase *Second Death*) from Talmud and Midrash are wrong.

This is the more remarkable seeing that Schoettgen was well aware of the true sense of his quotations; but on consideration he actually preferred the misinterpretation. Finding in the older literature a phrase which means *strange death* (i.e. unnatural, sudden, or violent) he renders it by *second death*, against all sense and authority. We have here an illustration of the truth that second thoughts may be worse than first thoughts[3]. In fact, with the exception of the Targumim and Revelation, the phrase *Second Death* does not occur in the older literature. Nor is

[1] In addition to the commentaries on Revelation (ii. 11, xx. 6, 14, xxi. 8) this description is boldly used in Preuschen, Greek-German Dictionary to the N.T. (1910, p. 501). Grimm in his Lexicon Graeco-Latinum (4th ed. 1903, p. 198) more accurately speaks of the *Second Death* as Targumic (ut apud Targumistas).

[2] See Schoettgen pp. 1136–7, Wetstein ii. p. 756.

[3] Schoettgen's exact words are: "Mortem alteram vocant (Judaei) hebraice מיתה משונה *mortem iteratam*, et chaldaice מיתה תנינא. Prius illud vidi a viris doctis versum esse mortem *repentinam* vel *violentam*: sed tum phrasis, tum res ipsa docet aeternae mortis notionem huc potius quadrare." In T.B. Soṭa 35 a, Baba Bathra 10 a–b, Taanith 11 a the meaning is not *second death* but *unnatural death*. Nor is there any reference to *second death* in T.J. Kilaim (ix. 3) or Genesis Rabba (xcvi.), quoted by Wetstein. In Baba Bathra 10 a–b *charity that delivers from an unnatural death* (Prov. x. 2) is defined as such alms as neither giver nor recipient knows recipient and giver respectively. On *untimely* death, and the influence of Adam's sin, see Apoc. of Baruch liv. 15, lvi. 6 and Charles' notes.

it to be found in Philo, though he is sometimes cited in evidence. Philo indeed speaks of death with its two-fold guise, but he has no thought of a first and a second death. He merely discriminates between the state of death and the state of dying: death may or may not be a good, but dying is always an evil. Cain's condition after his crime against his brother was, as it were, a long-drawn-out living death[1]. Philo elsewhere perhaps comes nearer the idea of two deaths, when he contrasts immortal with ephemeral life. The term "immortal" applies equally to the highest earthly life of spiritual love of God and to life after death. Even so, when Philo discriminates between death, as separation of soul from body, and death as "the ruin of virtue and the reception of vice," a peculiar death of the soul itself, he is not really quite at the standpoint which discriminates between a first and a second death[2]. On the other hand, Plutarch (*On the Face in the Moon*, 942–3) does speak of a first and a second death, as Wetstein notes. Plutarch regards life as composed of three elements: body, soul, mind, of which the third is highest. "Mind is as much better a thing and more divine than the soul, as soul is than body." Hence there are two deaths; the one terrestrial, when the soul and mind are together separated from the body, the other lunar, when the mind is freed from the soul. "The death which we die is of two kinds: the one makes man two out of three, the other makes him one out of two." Thus Plutarch's language is no parallel to the *second death* of the Targumim and of Revelation. To Plutarch the second death is not a penalty but a privilege, it is the select only who enjoy it. Some even who reach the moon are cast back into the abyss without acquiring the boon of the second death[3]. A *third* death would be needed to equate Plutarch's scheme to that of the Apocalypse.

[1] Philo's remark runs: *θανάτου γὰρ διττὸν εἶδος, τὸ μὲν κατὰ τὸ τεθνάναι, ὅπερ ἀγαθὸν ἐστιν ἢ ἀδιάφορον, τὸ δὲ κατὰ τὸ ἀποθνήσκειν, ὃ δὴ κακὸν πάντως καὶ ὅσῳ χρονιώτερον βαρύτερον* (*De Praemiis et Poenis*, M. 419, Cohn v. 351).

[2] Cf. C. G. Montefiore's quotations in his "Florilegium Philonis" in *Jewish Quarterly Review*, first series, vol. vii. pp. 503 ff. The Philonean citations made by him are I. 65 (cf. I. 200); I. 264; I. 554; I. 557.

[3] In a sense this is true also of the particular Rabbinic view that certain types of sinners did not even enjoy the privilege of rising at the resurrection, to endure judgment and, if so decreed, to die again. Their first death was final. This is said, in one opinion, specifically of the generation of the flood, who will not arise even at the judgment, but are absolutely annihilated (Mishnah Sanhedrin xi. 3; cf. Talmud, folio 108). This view is controverted by other Rabbis. The whole of Chapter XXXIV of the *Chapters of R. Eleazar* is interesting on this topic. Cf. p. 44 below.

Seeing, then, that the "Rabbinic" parallel to the *Second Death* is Targumic[1], it is astonishing that the most significant of the Targumic passages is ignored by the commentaries on Revelation. I refer to the appearance of the *Second Death* in the Onkelos Targum. It so appears once, and once only, in the translation of Deut. xxxiii. 6: "Let Reuben live and not die." In what may be termed the normal Rabbinic method, this sentence is interpreted as a Pentateuchal indication of immortality. *Let Reuben live* in this world *and not die* in the world to come[2]. Obviously it is entirely foreign to the usual Rabbinic method to turn the phrase into a *denial* of immortality to any class. Yet, as we shall see, this is what Targum Onkelos does. Elsewhere Onkelos acts otherwise. "Ye shall therefore keep my statutes and my judgements: which if a man do *he shall live by them*" (Levit. xviii. 5)—Onkelos renders the final clause: "And live by them in eternal life[3]." The Deuteronomic passage, however, is so rendered by Onkelos as to include the term *Second Death*, a fact which naturally roused the surprise of N. M. Adler in his commentary on Onkelos, in that the latter departs from Rabbinic usage. Onkelos (Deut. xxxiii. 6) runs: "Let Reuben live in eternal life, and not die the *Second Death*[4]." Obviously, the *Second Death* here does not refer positively to a state of torture but negatively to a state of annihilation[5]. As to the phrase itself, one is inclined to think that it has crept into Onkelos from the other version of the Targum to which it really belongs, and in an inexact form[6].

At all events, it is open to question whether the expression the *Second Death* rightly belongs to the Pentateuchal Targum at all. The "Jerusalem" Targum certainly contains it; not so, however, the so-called Targum Jonathan. But even the "Jerusalem" Targum gives a

[1] The passages cited from Yalquṭ Reubeni add nothing by way of early evidence.

[2] T.B. Sanhedrin 92 a. Cf. Sifrê on Deut. xxxiii. 6 (ed. Friedmann p. 144 a). The latter runs: "But assuredly Reuben died! What then is the meaning of *and not die*? In the world to come?"

[3] לחיי עלמא. Cf. the commentary of Naḥmanides וחי בהם לעולם הבא.

[4] יחי ראובן בחיי עלמא ומותא תנינא לא ימות.

[5] Adler, *loc. cit.*, and Levy, *Chaldäisches Wörterbuch*, p. 546, both correctly interpret in this way.

[6] The current reading in Onkelos is, however, cited by Saadiah in his *Emunoth ve-deoth* ix. 1. This work was finished in 933 (see Bacher in *Jewish Encyclopedia*, x. 581). So, too, it is quoted in the same terms in the Commentary of Baḥya (died 1340) on the passage in Deuteronomy. Baḥya interprets Onkelos to mean that Reuben would enjoy immortal life, and not return thence *into the body* to die a second death.

turn quite other than that of Onkelos, for it renders (Deut. xxxiii. 6): "Let Reuben live *in this world*, and not die the *Second Death*, which the wicked die in *the world to come*[1]." In Onkelos the whole scene is played in the future; in the "Jerusalem" Targum, it is partly in this world, and partly in the future. The meaning, however, seems to be the same. This is complicated by the more frequent occurrence of the phrase in the Targum to the Prophets. On Isaiah xxii. 14 ("Surely this iniquity shall not be expiated from you till you die"), the Targum simply has "*till you die* the second death." Qimḥi's interpretation that the *Second Death* refers to the "death of the soul in the world to come" cannot be accepted without qualification. For in its paraphrase of Isaiah lxv. 6 the Targum uses the expression: "I will deliver unto the *Second Death* גויתהון *their bodies*," implying a resurrection followed by punishment. On the other hand, in Jeremiah li. 39, 57, the phraseology is again less precise: "They will die the *Second Death* and *not live in the world to come*," which simply implies annihilation[2]. The *Second Death* would then mean the deprivation of the second life. Thus these Targumim waver between the two ideas of (*a*) negative annihilation, and (*b*) a positive condition of punishment, as the meaning of the *Second Death*[3]. It is this first sense which predominates in the Targums while it is the second sense which is used in Revelation. Anyhow, the phrase *Second Death* is found only in the Targumim and in Revelation—that is to say neither in Talmud nor Gospels—and this points to the conclusion that the phrase is Apocalyptic rather than Rabbinic.

This conclusion is confirmed by the further fact that the most remarkable use of the phrase (outside Revelation) occurs in the *Chapters of Rabbi Eleazar*, a pseudepigraphic Hebrew work which, in its present shape, belongs to the ninth century, though the contents are to a large extent very much older[4]. Its general character may be described as

[1] T. Jonathan Deut. xxxiii. 6 ייחי ראובן בעלמא הדין ולא יימות במותנא תניינא דמייתון בה רשיעיא לעלמא דאתי:

[2] T.J. Isaiah xxii. 14 עד דמתותון מותא תינייתא (the inference would be that the *Second Death* was an expiation, with the consequence that forgiveness would ensue). T.J. Isaiah lxv. 6 ואימסר למיתא תניינא ית גויתתהון. T.J. Jeremiah li. 39, 57 יימותון מותא תיניינא ולא יחון לעלמא דאתי.

[3] An interesting light on the medieval Jewish thought on this subject may be found in the Hebrew poems of Immanuel of Rome, a contemporary of Dante; see the quotation in B. Halper's *Post-Biblical Hebrew Literature, an Anthology*, Philadelphia, 1921, vol. ii. pp. 188 ff.

[4] Cf. the English edition by G. Friedlander (*Pirḳê de Rabbi Eliezer*, London 1916), Introduction p. liv.

nearer the Apocalyptic than the Midrashic type. The passage that follows is often repeated in later Hebrew books[1]; it was evidently found interesting. "See now that I, even I, am He, and there is no God with me: I kill, and I make alive, I have wounded and I heal, and there is none that can deliver out of My hand" (Deut. xxxii. 39). Why did the Scripture repeat the pronoun: *I, even I*? Because the Holy One, blessed be He, said: I am He in this world, and I am He in the world to come. I am He who redeemed you from Egypt, I am He who in future will redeem them at the end of the fourth kingdom[2]. Therefore is it said, *I, even I, am He.* Every nation[3] which says that there is a second God, I will slay it with a *Second Death* wherein is no resurrection; and every nation which says that there is no second God, I will quicken it for the life of the world to come, slaying those and quickening these, wherefore it is said *I kill and I make alive*[4]. I have wounded Jerusalem and her people in the day of My wrath, but with great mercy I will heal them. Therefore is it said: *I have wounded and I heal.* No angel or seraph can (or will) deliver the wicked from the judgment of Gehinnom, as it is said: *and there is none that can deliver out of My hand.*

The above-cited remark of Qimḥi—distinguishing the bodily death (as first death) from the spiritual death (as *Second Death*) is not confirmed by this passage. In the Rabbinic conception body and soul were judged together[5], and when cast into Gehinnom were cast there together. An early passage speaks of certain sinners as spending a year in Gehinnom[6], and thereafter "their body is consumed and their soul burned,

[1] Yalquṭ Deut. § 946; Midrash Tannaim, ed. Hoffmann, p. 202.

[2] An Apocalyptic term for the beginning of the Messianic age.

[3] Schoettgen wrongly reads *idolator* (כל עכו"ם). Some texts (cf. the Yalquṭ) read "whoever" (כל מי) for "every nation" (כל גוי).

[4] In the first edition (Constantinople 1514) the reading is: I will slay (the former) with a death without resurrection, and will quicken the latter (read שאין for שיש) *at the Second Death, for the life of the world to come.*

[5] Cf. First Series, p. 98.

[6] This is not the purgatorial period of the "intermediate" class between the perfectly righteous and the perfectly wicked. Allen on Matthew x. 28 refers to the passage cited in my next note, and adds: "But, as a rule, both in Apocalyptic and Talmudic literature, the punishment of the wicked is regarded as eternal." On the contrary, the "intermediate" class would be the majority, and a purifying purgatorial period normal. Cf. K. Kohler on *Purgatory* in *Jewish Encyclopedia*, x. 274; S. Singer, *Is Salvation possible after Death?* (in *Lectures and Addresses*, 1908, p. 55).

while a wind scatters them under the feet of the righteous." But here, too, body and soul are annihilated together, just as with certain major sinners, "the great seducers and blasphemers," body and soul undergo endless tortures in Gehinnom[1]. This seems the sense, also, of Matthew x. 28: "Fear not them which kill the body, but are not able to kill the soul, but rather fear him which is able to destroy *both soul and body* in Gehenna." If Matthew really means to distinguish between body as mortal and soul as immortal, his thought (as Weiss justly remarks) would be Greek rather than Hebraic. Luke's version the same commentator regards as the more original. This may be so, but Matthew, in the words italicised, undoubtedly comes back to the Hebraic thought as more clearly expressed in Luke. For Luke xii. 4–5 has a fuller form which (as will be seen) reminds one very forcibly of a famous Rabbinic episode, contemporary with (or a little earlier than) the compilation of the third Gospel. Johanan ben Zakkai, the hero of the episode which took place on his death-bed, died somewhere about 80 A.D. To turn to Luke, the sentences run: "And I say unto you, my friends, Be not afraid of them which kill the body, and after that have no more that they can do. But I will warn you whom ye shall fear: Fear him, which after he hath killed hath power to cast into Gehenna; yea, I say unto you, Fear him." It will be noted that Plummer's emphatic conclusion that by *him* is meant God and not Satan is strongly supported by Johanan ben Zakkai's words. Not that there is wanting in Rabbinic thought a personification of the Evil Impulse (yeṣer hara) as both Satan and the Angel of Death[2].

The final act in Johanan ben Zakkai's life is thus described in the Talmud[3]:

When Rabban Johanan b. Zakkai was ill, his disciples went in to visit him. On beholding them, he began to weep. His disciples said to him, "O Lamp of Israel[4], right-hand pillar (cf. 1 Kings vii. 21), mighty hammer! Wherefore dost thou weep?" He replied to them, "If I was being led into the presence of a human being who to-day is here and to-morrow in the grave, who if he were wrathful against me his anger would not be eternal, who if he imprisoned me the imprisonment would not

[1] Tosefta Sanhedrin xiii. (ed. Zuckermandel, p. 434); T.B. Rosh Hashana 17 a.

[2] T.B. Baba Bathra 16 a; Sukkah 52 a. The Yeṣer, however, though it seeks to kill and testifies against man after death, is not an uncontrolled force, for God finally slays the Yeṣer itself.

[3] T.B. Berachoth 28 b. I quote from the excellent version by A. Cohen (Cambridge 1921) p. 188.

[4] Cf. p. 16 above.

be everlasting, who if he condemned me to death the death would not be for ever[1], and whom I can appease with words and bribe with money—even then I would weep; but now, when I am being led into the presence of the King of kings, the Holy One, blessed be He, Who lives and endures for all eternity, Who if He be wrathful against me His wrath is eternal, Who if He imprisoned me the imprisonment would be everlasting, Who if He condemned me to death the death would be for ever[2], and Whom I cannot appease with words nor bribe with money—nay more, when before me lie two ways, one of the Garden of Eden and the other of *Gēhinnōm*, and I know not in which I am to be led—shall I not weep?" They said unto him, "Our master, bless us!" He said to them, "May it be His will that the fear of Heaven be upon you [as great] as the fear of flesh and blood." His disciples exclaimed, "Only as great!" He replied, "Would that it be [as great]; for know ye, when a man intends to commit a transgression, he says, 'I hope nobody will see me[3].'" At the time of his departure [from the world] he said to them, "Remove all the utensils because of the defilement[4], and prepare a seat for Hezekiah[5], King of Judah, who is coming[6]."

It has often been noted that in Matthew x. 28 and Luke xii. 4 the phraseology (φοβεῖσθαι followed by ἀπό) is Hebraic; it corresponds not merely to Septuagint usage but to the later Hebrew construction. "Dost thou not fear the Roman Government?" asks Papos of Aqiba; and the latter replies by the fable of the fishes, whom the fox advises to leave the troubled waters and come to dry land. Much as he had to fear by disobeying the Government and obeying God, even at the risk of life

[1] In the parallel narrative in Aboth d. R. Nathan xxv. (ed. Schechter p. 79) the reading is "his anger...imprisonment...condemnation is only *in this world*" (בעולם הזה). Cf. the saying of R. Simeon that he who makes a man sin is more criminal than he who slays him. For the latter does not, while the former does, rob his victim of his future bliss, slaying him here and hereafter (המחטיאו הורגו בעולם הזה ולעולם הבא) Mid. Tanḥuma Numbers, ed. Buber p. עו, and Sifrê § 252 ed. Friedmann, p. 120 a. See also the usages in Lev. xix. 32 and Exod. ix. 30.

[2] In A. d. R. N. "his anger is in this world and in the world to come" (בעולם הזה ובעולם הבא).

[3] "If there be a witness he desists. Remember, then, that God is always a witness; so have the same fear of Him that you have of a human being" (Cohen).

[4] Caused by the presence of a dead body.

[5] To accompany him into the next world; Hezekiah's Messianic quality is referred to in T.B. Sanhedrin 94 a.

[6] Lightfoot's oft-quoted comment on this story of Joḥanan b. Zakkai's end may be read in ch. 15 of his *Mattaêo Praemissa* (prefatory to the *Horae*): "Ah miseram et languentem Pharisaei in morte fiduciam." But it is rather self-confidence than confidence that is lacking. Lightfoot curiously stops before the reference to Hezekiah. Joḥanan clearly had no doubts as to his friendly guidance to the future life.

itself, far worse would be his plight were he to seek safety from Rome by apostasy from Heaven. In this story[1] the phrase used is מתירא מפני which exactly corresponds to φοβεῖσθαι ἀπό[2]. A similar idiom occurs much earlier than Aqiba (martyred *c.* 132 A.D.). The dying Alexander Jannaeus in 78 B.C. counselled his wife Salome Alexandra (who succeeded him on the throne) to fear neither Pharisees nor their honest opponents but the hypocrites. He uses the phrase אל תתיראי מן[3]. As regards Johanan b. Zakkai's prayer that men should fear God as much as they do man, an excellent illustration may be cited from the Tosefta[4]. The thief who steals in the owner's absence is more heavily penalised by the law than is the open robber who carries off his booty under the owner's very eye—because the latter at all events does not fear man more than he does God! Splendid use was made of this idea by the later Jewish moralists, who urged their readers and disciples to act in private as in public under the constant sense of the King's presence and the reverence due to royal dignity[5]. There was no question, again, but man must die for the truth. No Pharisee but shared the Aqiba spirit which knew when to die. The marginal references in the English versions of Matthew and Luke rightly point to the Second Maccabees, to the stories of martyrdom under Antiochus IV. As a modern writer beautifully remarks[6]: "There shone out in that intense moment the sterner and sublimer qualities which later Hellenism, and above all the Hellenism of Syria, knew nothing of—uncompromising fidelity to an ideal, endurance raised to the pitch of utter self-devotion, a passionate clinging to purity. They were qualities for the lack of which all the riches of Hellenic culture could not compensate. It was an epoch in history. The agony created new human types and new forms of literature, which became permanent, were inherited by Christendom. The figure of the martyr, as the Church knows it, dates from the persecution of Antiochus;

[1] T.B. Berachoth 61 b.

[2] A just distinction is drawn by Plummer between the μὴ φοβηθῆτε ἀπὸ in Luke xii. 4 and the φοβήθητε τὸν of verse 5 as marking the transition from shunning an oppressor and fearing God. Neo-Hebraic idiom does not seem to use the phrase התירא מפני or התירא מן of the fear of *God*.

[3] T.B. Soṭa 22 b. It will be observed that the idiom is used in the Gospel passages before us in a similar context—a denunciation of hypocrisy.

[4] Baba Qama vii. (beginning), T.B. Baba Qama 79 b; cf. Bacher, *Agada der Tannaiten*, i. 32 (ed. 2, p. 29).

[5] Cf. Maimonides, *Guide of the Perplexed*, vol. iii. ch. 52; Oraḥ Ḥayyim i. 1.

[6] E. R. Bevan, *The House of Seleucus*, ii. 174.

all subsequent martyrologies derive from the Jewish books which recorded the sufferings of those who in that day 'were strong and did exploits' (Daniel xi. 32)." And as the Church knows the glorious figure of the martyr so does the Synagogue. Each was not free from the offence of creating the martyr, needless to discuss whose offence was more heinous. But if the blood of the martyr is the seed of the Church, perhaps the more gracious future may turn the martyrdoms of Church and Synagogue into seeds of mutual respect and admiration[1].

[1] As this is passing through the press, I am reading Mary Johnston's new romance *Admiral of the Ocean-Sea.* At the beginning of the third chapter I found these sentences, the last of which seems to me worth italicising. Not for the first time is a theologian confirmed in his humanism by a romancer! "The Moor was stained and the Spaniard, the Moslem and the Christian and the Jew. Who had stains the least or the most God knew—and it was a poor inquiry. *Seek the virtues and bind them with love, each in each!*" The saying is put into the mouth of Jayme de Marchena about to sail with Columbus to find America in the very year (1492) which saw the expulsion of the Jews from Spain. Soon the Moors were to follow. It is well to pluck out of so disastrous a *dénoûment* a message of brotherhood with Miss Johnston's hero.

## IX. TABERNACLES.

The three "tabernacles[1]" of the Transfiguration would be temporary shelters such as were erected for watchmen in gardens and vineyards, for soldiers in war, for cattle, and even as a temporary protection against the sun for workers in the fields. They were of the same type as the little lodges raised by the modern fellahin in Palestine. Some loose stones, or where procurable some sticks or tree trunks mostly as a tripod but sometimes as a square with an old mat as an awning, constitute at the present day, frail sleeping apartments for guardians against thieves and jackals. The "tabernacle" or *sukkah* of the Israelites (used during the end-of-summer festival) had, and has, a roof of cut branches. Indeed the root from which *sukkah* is derived denotes to intertwine branches[2].

The ephemeral character of the tents referred to is often used, as in Isaiah i. 8, as a symbol of desertion and desolation. Among the figures in which Hezekiah's prayer depicts the hopelessness of life, the first is that of "a nomad's tent, easily pitched and soon removed" (Skinner): "My habitation is removed, and is carried away from me as a shepherd's tent" (Is. xxxviii. 12). It may be that this O.T. text underlies the use of the phrase "tent" as a metaphor for the body in various N.T. passages[3].

[1] *σκηνάς* Mk. ix. 5, Mt. xvii. 4, Lk. ix. 33. The *ποιήσωμεν* of Mark (and Luke) becomes *ποιήσω* in Matthew. The LXX uses *σκηνή* for סכה (Is. i. 8) and for אהל (Is. xxxviii. 12). Similarly the "Tabernacle" of Meeting (אהל and משכן) appears as *σκηνή*.

[2] For an account of the structure of these booths see I. Abrahams, *Festival Studies*, ch. ix. On the root סכך see Oxford Gesenius, p. 697 and the Talmud dictionaries of Levy, Jastrow and Kohut, ii. 523–525, 990, vi. 47 respectively.

[3] 2 Cor. v. 1, 4; 2 Peter i. 13. Bigg's note on the last passage (in the *Inter. Crit. Comm.*) may be cited. "*Σκήνωμα*, a tent; this metaphor for the body suits well with the general conception of life as a pilgrimage 1 Pet. i. 1, ii. 11. St Paul uses *σκῆνος* in the same sense 2 Cor. v. 1. The apostles derived the metaphor from the history of the Patriarchs, but according to Clement of Alexandria, *Strom.* v. 14. 94, Plato also called the body *γήινον σκῆνος*." In Isaiah xxxviii. 12 the figure is not of a pilgrimage, as the next metaphor proves: "I have rolled up my life like a weaver"—who rolls up the completed web. It is the shortness of life, its premature close, that confounds Hezekiah (then in the thirty-ninth year of his age). The LXX (though not following the M.T.) gives the sense of Isaiah admirably: "like one who strikes a tent having but just pitched it."

On the other hand, the ephemeral quality of the tabernacle must not be exaggerated. To do so misses the point of Amos ix. 11: "In that day will I raise up the tabernacle of David that is fallen, and close up the breaches thereof; and I will raise up his ruins, and I will build it as in the days of old." Driver conceives that Amos changes the metaphor. "The term *tabernacle* itself denotes a very humble structure, which here, in addition, is represented as *fallen*. In the following words the figure of the booth is neglected; the *breaches* being those of a wall or fortress (cf. iv. 3, Is. xxx. 13)." But in Amos iv. 3 the meaning (as Driver himself notes) may be "a gap in a fence" through which a herd of cows might go one behind the other. So with Amos ix. 11. The herdsman of Tekoa may have had in mind a kind of structure which well fits the two ideas of easy overthrow and of equally easy re-construction. In the fields and vineyards, besides the temporary hut (*sukkah*) was built the stone tower (*migdal*), which was more substantial[1]. These towers were preserved from season to season, and were used as storehouses. Of this kind must have been the Sukkah of Gennesareth mentioned in the Talmud, intended for the olive-garden. That it was strongly made is clear from the fact that it was turned to permanent domestic uses. But the point of Amos' metaphor is yet to be explained. When I was in the vineyard at Moza, near Jerusalem (and not many miles from Tekoa), I was shown a solid building made of stone. It had a domed roof, was very substantial, yet was put together without mortar or cement of any kind. You see everywhere stone huts of this kind, but the one I examined most closely recalled to me the words of Amos. For this large, solid stone hut, had a stone staircase running up the outside. On mounting this, one came to the roof, on which was placed a genuine Sukkah, an alcove covered with Arabian vines, poor as to fruit, but excellent as a shade. It was wonderful to note how cool this was, how wide the prospect, how admirable a look-out for a watchman by day. At night the lower edifice is curiously warm, and is a fine protection against the heavy dew and frequent cold. I think that Amos had just such a structure in mind when he foretold that God would raise up the fallen tabernacle, and

[1] In illustration of ἀγραυλοῦντες in Lk. ii. 8 it may be noted that לון is used alike of shepherds, fruit-watchers, and turret-keepers "dwelling" or rather "passing the night" in city and field in the Tosefta, Erubin iii. (ii.) 9, ed. Zuckermandel, p. 142, l. 19, הרועים והקייצים והבורגנין ושומרי פירות שדרכן ללון בעיר׃׳׳ובזמן שדרכן ללון בשדה

close up the breaches thereof. The same kind of structure throws new light on Isaiah iv. 6, as the reader will easily see by turning up the passage. So, too, with the 31st Psalm. God's shining face, like brooding wings, shelters the faithful from the storm of human passions, as in a Sukkah from the heat, and from the wind and rain as in the more solid stone covert in which it was set.

Oh how great is Thy goodness, which Thou hast laid up for them that fear Thee,
Which Thou hast wrought for them that put their trust in Thee, before the sons of men!
In the covert of Thy presence shalt Thou hide them from the plottings of man:
Thou shalt keep them secretly in a pavilion (*sukkah*) from the strife of tongues[1].

It may even be that in Isaiah lviii. 12, "the old ruins" (used in the context of a "watered garden"), which are to be rebuilt, refer to the structures which needed but a little labour for their resuscitation. Similarly in lxi. 4, where the same phrases are used, the context is "trees of righteousness," "the planting of the Lord." Thus we have another point of contact between the "tabernacle" and eschatological or Messianic hopes. Very significant indeed is the citation of the passage from Amos ix. in Acts xv. 16–18, where the rebuilt tabernacle of David corresponds, in the exposition of James, to the "restored or Messianic theocracy" (J. V. Bartlet).

The Rabbinic parallels, often quoted in illustration of the "tabernacles" of the Transfiguration scene, are also eschatological and Messianic. The tents (sukkah or ḥuppah, both words being used) were to be made for the righteous from the Leviathan's skin—an eschatological reference[2]. Or the "seven canopies" of the Messiah are to be made by God of precious stones and pearls, while from each canopy flow four streams of wine, honey, milk, and pure perfume[3]. The "cloud" of the Transfiguration may be paralleled by the fancy that (in connection with the Sukkah) "God protected Israel under clouds of glory[4]." Even closer, however, is the thought in the Midrash Tanḥuma (on Pinḥas), that in the future God will make for every righteous man a canopy out of the clouds of glory, quoting Isaiah iv. 5[5].

[1] Part of the preceding is quoted from *Festival Studies*, p. 60.

[2] T.B. Baba Bathra 75 a; Pesiqta (Buber) 186 a–b. Cf. the *shade* (צל) which God will make hereafter, for various categories of the righteous (T.J. Soṭa vii. § 4, on the basis of Eccles. vii. 10).

[3] Pesiqta R., ed. Friedmann, p. 163 a.

[4] Pesiqta 186 b.

[5] עתיד הקדוש ברוך הוא לעשות לכל צדיק וצדיק חופה מענני הכבוד שנאמר וברא ה׳ על כל מכון הר ציון וגו׳

A large element in the last discourses in the Pesiqta with reference to Tabernacles is Messianic. Very significant, too, is the association of the Prayer for Rain (introduced at Tabernacles) with the Resurrection of the Dead. "We make mention of the Rain in the benediction of the Revival of the Dead," says the Mishnah[1]. This idea is not fully explained by the fact that the rain revives nature, for in Hebrew poetry that function would rather be assigned to the Dew. The War of Gog and Magog (which had so much influence in the Apocalypses) described in Ezekiel xxxviii. 18—xxxix. 16 is read in the Synagogues as a prophetic lesson during Tabernacles[2]. The very remarkable prominence given to Tabernacles in Jubilees xvi. points in the same direction[3]. Again if Isaiah xxix. was, as most commentators (including Skinner, Marti and Duhm) think, spoken on Tabernacles, then it is a further evidence for the point now being made that as it proceeds the chapter becomes eschatological[4].

Before turning to another matter, it may be remarked that the collocation of Moses and Elijah in the Transfiguration narratives needs no recondite explanation. Allen's note on Matthew xvii. 3 says all that is necessary; especially important being the remark of Joḥanan b. Zakkai. Though this occurs in a late source, it is obviously of early origin, there being no reason for doubting its ascription to Joḥanan (first century). Moses and Elijah are to rise together[5]. The association

[1] Berachoth v. 2; cf. T.B. Berachoth 33 a.

[2] On the date of the introduction of this reading, see A. Büchler, *Jewish Quarterly Review* (first series) vi. 29. In the early part of the second century there were rival views as to the month of the future redemption, opinion being divided between Nisan (Passover) and Tishri (Tabernacles). See T.B. Rosh Hashana 10 b. In the third year of the Triennial Cycle, the prophetic lesson for the feast of Tabernacles was Isaiah iv. 6—a Messianic passage. Cf. T.B. Baba Bathra 75 a. For Messianic associations see also Levit. R. xxx.

[3] Abraham keeps the feast at the *Well of the Oath* (Beersheba); and there is reference to going round the altar with branches seven times (Jubilees xvi. 20, 31). These phrases seem to refer to the Joy of the Waterdrawing, a Temple celebration. On this see J. Hochman, *Jerusalem Temple Festivities*, pp. 54 *seq.*, where much useful material is collected.

[4] See Skinner's note on Isaiah xxix. 15.

[5] Debarim Rabba iii.; Moses and Elijah are associated in Megillah 19 b. Cf. on Elijah Volz, *Jüdische Eschatologie*, pp. 191–3. Volz thinks that the coming of Elijah as an eschatological theory is older than the reappearance of Moses. Certainly Joḥanan's phraseology points in this direction: "In the world to come when I bring unto them Elijah the prophet, the two of you (Moses and Elijah) shall come together." In the same Midrash, however, ii. § 9, Moses, we read, was buried before

of Moses and Elijah goes back, it may be suggested, to the same O.T. passage at the end of Malachi, on which the Messianic reappearance of Elijah depends. "Remember ye the law of Moses my servant...Behold I will send you Elijah the Prophet." Possibly this may be the reason why in so many illuminated MSS of the Transfiguration Moses appears with the Tables of the Law on his arm.

We may now turn to the clearest and most influential of the O.T. associations of Tabernacles with the range of eschatological ideas. This is the fourteenth chapter of Zechariah. The chapter is read on Tabernacles in the Synagogue, because the reference to the feast is so unequivocal. The whole world is to come up from year to year, to worship the King, the Lord of Hosts, and to keep the feast of Tabernacles, with dire penalties in case of failure (Zech. xiv. 16 *seq.*). It was this that gave point to the saying: "The Messiah cometh not except to give to the nations two commandments, such as the Sukkah and the Palm[1]."

If we examine Revelations vii. there are striking indications that the apocalyptist has the Feast of Tabernacles in mind. The palms of verse 9 are not perhaps conclusive. But when combined with phrases of the Hallel there is little doubt left[2]. The Hallel (Psalms cxiii.–cxviii.) was associated with all three Pilgrim Feasts (and with other occasions), but in a special degree with Tabernacles (Mishnah Sukkah iv. 1). Moreover the Hallel was regarded as in part Messianic. In the Jerusalem Talmud (Megillah ii. § 1), R. Abin expounds that Ps. cxiv. refers to the past, Ps. cxv. to the present, Ps. cxvi. to the days of the Messiah, Ps. cxviii. 27 to the days of Gog and Magog, and Ps. cxviii. 28 to the future time (which would succeed the temporary era of the Messiah). A similar thought, with variations in details, occurs also

reaching Canaan so that at the Resurrection of the Israelites who died in the wilderness, Moses should rise at their head. So, too, in the Targum Yerushalmi to Exod. xii. 42, Moses and the Messiah appear during the Gog and Magog war.

[1] Yalquṭ Psalms § 682. For variant readings see Buber's note on the Midrash to Ps. xxi. (p. 177). The Yalquṭ seems to have retained the true reading *two*, but even if this be not the case, the Messianic connection between Tabernacles and the Gentile world is none the less clear.

[2] John xii. 13 was perhaps the direct source of Revelation vii. 9. But in John there is a transference of Tabernacles rites to the Passover, and the Jewish author of Rev. vii. would be thinking not of the fourth Gospel but of Zechariah. The Synoptics know nothing of the palms in Jesus' triumphal entry into Jerusalem. In Matthew's account, some spread garments, others branches on the road (Matt. xxi. 8). This is derived from Mk. xi. 7. In Luke xix. 36 only the garments are mentioned, not the branches at all.

in the Babylonian Talmud (T.B. Pesaḥim 118 a). The presence of these variations argues that the Messianic ascription of part of the Hallel was very old. Again it may well be that the Psalmic cry "Salvation" in Rev. vii. 10 comes less from Psalm iii. 8, than from the Hallel, with its oft-repeated watchword of salvation. The O.T. citations throughout the latter part of the chapter are indeed so very remarkably mosaic, that it is difficult to disentangle the references. At all events the association of palms with psalms points almost unmistakably to the Feast of Tabernacles, with its eschatological implications. It may be objected that the association occurred also at Ḥanukkah. In 1 Macc. xiii. 51 "the praise and the palm-branches" are associated at the re-dedication of the Temple. This association, however, does not recur in future observances of Ḥanukkah, the Maccabean anniversary, and 2 Macc. x. 6, 7 explicitly states that "they kept eight days with gladness in the manner of Tabernacles, remembering that not long before, during the Feast of Tabernacles, they were wandering in the mountains and in the caves after the manner of wild beasts. Wherefore, bearing wands wreathed with leaves, and fair boughs, and palms also, they offered up hymns of thanksgiving." Seeing how frequent is the use of Zechariah in other parts of Revelation, it is most reasonable to suppose in chapter vii. also the same use was made. "Owing to the apparently Jewish or Jewish-Christian character of vii. 1–8 and the universalistic character of vii. 9–17, critics have for the most part decided against the unity of the chapter" (Charles on Revelation, i. 189). But Zechariah xiv., as we have seen, is as markedly universalistic as it is Jewish. Hence, with this model before us, and with Zechariah's symbolism of the Feast of Tabernacles in mind, we may assume, without overmuch improbability, that the whole chapter emanated from one hand. All that the Christian redactor needed to do was to insert the references to the Lamb, as he has done in other passages of Jewish provenance[1].

[1] See Kohler in *J.E.* x. 390 *seq.* The figure of the lamb was earlier, of course, applied to Israel (Isaiah liii. 7, Jeremiah xi. 19). Later on, Israel was the troubled lamb among seventy wolves (nations). See Esther Rabba on ix. 2. The lamb also is a figure of Israel in a late (medieval) apocalypse which contains some ancient elements (*The Words of Gad the Seer*, a MS in the Cambridge University Library, Oo 1, 20).

## X. THE PERSECUTIONS.

It is generally recognised that the persecutions of the Christians described in the Synoptics must be referred to a period posterior to the death of Jesus. The anticipations of trials and maltreatment are either associated with the mission of the twelve, or are interpolated into the short but pregnant Jewish Apocalypse which has been incorporated into Mark and the other Synoptics[1].

In a large degree these descriptions accord with the statements of Acts. But in what sense are they historical? This is a question which cannot now be precisely answered. One need not go the length of Gibbon in minimising the extent to which the early Christians were persecuted, and yet one may be fairly convinced that the numbers of the victims and the extent of the tortures were exaggerated by Christian authors, just as no doubt the numbers and extent of the sufferings of Jews at the hands of the Romans were over-estimated in Jewish sources. Fortunately we are not required here to examine this question at all. The problem before us is not the treatment of Christianity by the Romans, but by the Jews.

Now the accounts which we have of Jewish persecution of the new religion all of them emanate from a period when the mission to the Jews themselves had failed. It is far-fetched to suppose that the Synagogue became vicious because jealous of the transference of Paul's propaganda to the Gentiles. The Jewish sources have a good deal to say about Christians, but almost invariably it is *Jewish* Christians that are the object of castigation. Even supposing that in the course of time some passages were censored or suppressed, yet it is assuredly an extraordinary fact that it is scarcely possible to cite a single clear attack against Gentile Christianity in the early Rabbinic literature. The Synagogue was concerned with its own internal affairs; it had to keep itself free from *minuth* (a phrase which, though not always identical with, in the passages now under review refers to Judeo-Christianity); and its endeavours were directed primarily to self-defence. The key-note is struck in the short Rabbinic Apocalypse referred to in Note 1 below. The saddest feature is the prospect of internal dissension, when, in the words of Micah (vii. 6), which it cites, a man's enemies are those of his

[1] See Note 1 at end of chapter.

own household. The Synagogue had far less quarrel with Gentile Christianity, and until the organised Church had become imperial and was in a position and displayed the will to persecute the Synagogue, Christianity as such was not the object of much attention, still less of attack. (The foregoing conclusions are similar to those arrived at by Graetz and Joel, and more recently by R. T. Herford in his *Christianity in Talmud and Midrash*, e.g. p. 393.) The very development of Christianity from a dependent Jewish sect (*minuth*) to an independent world-religion made the new faith less obnoxious to the Synagogue. As Inge well writes: "Paul, he [Tyrrell] says, 'did not feel that he had broken with Judaism.' But the Synagogue did feel that he had done so, and history proved that the Synagogue was right" (*Outspoken Essays*, p. 163)[1]. It may be of interest to add that some observers of the present day conditions (owing to the changes in Palestine), are of opinion that a revival of the Judeo-Christian phenomenon is not impossible.

The protagonists of a new movement, and their heirs and historians in later ages, are always inclined to mistake opposition for persecution. A Jewish reader of Acts, making allowance for Paul's temperament, refusing to accept as literal his account of the persecutions he inflicted as Saul or suffered as Paul, sees some of the facts in a different perspective. Paul, to take the incidents which lead up to the change in his attitude, visited the Synagogue at Antioch of Pisidia on the Sabbath day. After the lessons had been read, he received a courteous invitation to speak a word of exhortation to the people. He used the opportunity to discourse of the divinity of Jesus (Acts xiii. 15). The Jews "contradicted the things which were spoken by Paul" (verse 45). This is the essential fact. In self-defence, the Jews put before their own brethren their objections to Paul's teachings. There is no hint of impeding Paul until he persistently preached Christianity in the Synagogues. Had Paul from the first directed his aims to the conversion of Gentiles the case might have been quite otherwise. One wonders what would be the fate of a zealous Imâm who should on a Sunday appear at St Paul's Cathedral and, after the lesson from the Gospel, urge the assembled Anglicans to prefer the claims of Mohammed to those of Jesus, on the ground that the coming of Mohammed had been prophesied by Christ.

[1] See Note 2 at end of chapter.

It is this inability to place himself at the Jewish point of view that sets even Harnack among those who give a wrong colour to the facts, and persist in alleging that in the first and second centuries there was a steady and insidious campaign by the Synagogue against Gentile Christianity. In his *Expansion of Christianity* (English Translation, i. p. 65) Harnack has a very strong passage on the subject, which is quoted and relied upon again and again as though it were history instead of conjecture. He says: "The hostility of the Jews appears on every page of Acts, from chapter xiii. onwards. They tried to hamper every step of the Apostle's work among the Gentiles; they stirred up the masses and the authorities in every country against him; systematically and officially they scattered broadcast horrible charges against the Christians, which played an important part in the persecutions as early as the reign of Trajan; they started calumnies against Jesus; they provided heathen opponents of Christianity with literary ammunition; unless the evidence is misleading, they instigated the Neronic outburst against the Christians; and as a rule whenever bloody persecutions are afoot in later days, the Jews are either in the background or the foreground."

To begin with, this generalisation altogether overlooks the evidence of Acts xvii. At Athens, Paul reasons with the Jews in the Synagogue, but also with any whom he met in the Agora. "And certain also of the Epicurean and Stoic philosophers encountered him. And some said, What would this babbler (σπερμολόγος) say? other some, He seemeth to be a setter forth of strange gods (ξένων δαιμονίων)." Where is the Jewish instigation here? Stoics and Epicureans had their own case. When a Rabbi came into conversation with Greek philosophers, his purpose was to uphold the "wise men of the Jews" against "the ancients of Athens" (cf. Bacher in *J. E.* vii. 291). E. Hatch has some admirable remarks in his Hibbert Lectures (pp. 9 ff.) on heathen opponents of Christianity. But Harnack does more than accuse the Jews of literary animosity. They were the open or secret prompters of persecutions, particularly those of which Nero was guilty.

For such strong accusations one has the right to demand equally strong evidence. But Harnack fails to provide it. It has been left to P. Corssen in recent times to find in Josephus the instigator of Nero's savagery. Harnack was not able to suggest so simple a solution. "*Unless the evidence is misleading*, they instigated the Neronic outburst against the Christians," says Harnack. When pressed as to his meaning, he admits that he is relying solely on conjecture. In a later passage (vol. ii. p. 116) he returns to the same charge, but in the text modifies his assertion to the less emphatic statement that "the Neronic persecution" was "*probably* instigated by the Jews," and on the word *probably* he has this foot-note: "Without this hypothesis it is scarcely possible, in my opinion, to understand the persecution." The Jews are charged in the most violent terms with instigating the Neronic persecution, and the only evidence adduced by the author of the charge is that he needs the hypothesis to explain the event! Others have been quite able to explain the event without this hypothesis, and without the equally unfounded guess that Nero was induced to his cruelty against the Christians by female Jewish influence at court[1]. Neither Tacitus, nor Suetonius, nor any of the original sources for the history of Rome has a hint of Jewish complicity. And if there is nothing but conjecture for the specific cases alleged by Harnack, still less can his general indictment ("as a rule whenever bloody persecutions are afoot in later days, the Jews are either in the background or the foreground") be held justified by anything like historical evidence. There is only one single period at which it would appear likely that some active persecution occurred. That was the age of Bar Cochba, when national feeling ran high, and the leader of the revolt against Hadrian may as Justin states (*Apology*, i. 31) have directed his animosity (Justin says nothing of "bloody" persecution, his language only points to the ordinary judicial flagellation though he has over-coloured the picture) against those Jews who had accepted Christianity and refused to join Aqiba in recognising Bar Cochba as the Messiah. There is no question here of Gentile Christians; the objects of the rebel leader's wrath were those of his own countrymen who refused to join the rebellion. The animosity is comparable to that felt by many Englishmen against Conscientious Objectors during the recent War. Tarphon and Meir, who were among the Rabbis who helped to repress the Christian movement, were also concerned simply and solely with the heresy within their own body; the danger was that this *minuth* was present secretly in some of the synagogues. It is a very plausible theory that the paragraph introduced at the end of the first century into the Liturgy (in the Eighteen Benedictions) against the *minim* was designed to separate the sheep from the goats and compel the

[1] See Note 3 at end of chapter.

*minim* to declare themselves (see Graetz as cited below and R. T. Herford, *op. cit.* pp. 381 *seq.*). The reader should note in particular the quotation (p. 378) from Jerome—*Ep.* 89 *ad Augustin.*—who speaks of a heresy of the Jews "quæ dicitur Minæarum...qui credunt in Christum...sed dum volunt et Judæi esse et Christiani nec Judæi sunt nec Christiani." Cf. also the extracts made by Mr Herford (on pp. 264, 272, 322, and 339) from the Epistle to the Hebrews, in illustration of the relations between the Jews and the Jewish Christians. The reader may also refer to Prof. W. Bacher's articles in the *Jewish Quarterly Review*, 1905, pp. 171 *seq.*, and in the *Revue des Études Juives*, xxxviii. p. 45, and to Graetz, *Geschichte der Juden*, iv². p. 433.

The same conclusion must be drawn from the citations which are often quoted from the Church Fathers in evidence of the animosity displayed by the Jews against the early Christians[1]. In very few of these citations can be found any such evidence. For the most part they merely show that the Jewish authorities took energetic steps to warn *their fellow-Jews* against the new faith. The language of Justin is too exaggerated to be taken literally. He goes so far as to protest that the Jews aided "evil demons and the host of the devil" against the lives of the saints (*Dialogue*, cxxxi). Such phraseology is obviously that of an advocate rather than of a historian. In reality, what the Jewish authorities did was, more or less, *defensive*. That this is so may be seen most clearly from the very passage on which Harnack chiefly relies for the opposite view, viz. that the Jews were occupied in an anti-Christian campaign throughout the Gentile world. "By far the most important notice," says Harnack, "is that preserved by Eusebius (on Isaiah xviii. 1 f.) although its source is unfortunately unknown." (It may be suggested that the source is Justin, *Dialogue*, cxvii.) The passage, "by far the most important" authority for the oft-repeated charge as to the all-pervading efforts of the Jews at home to assail the Christians of the Gentile world, runs as follows: Εὕρομεν ἐν τοῖς παλαιῶν συγγράμμασιν, ὡς οἱ τὴν Ἱερουσαλὴμ οἰκοῦντες τοῦ τῶν Ἰουδαίων ἔθνους ἱερεῖς καὶ πρεσβύτεροι γράμματα διαχαράξαντες εἰς πάντα διεπέμψατο τὰ ἔθνη τοῖς ἁπανταχοῦ Ἰουδαίοις διαβάλλοντες τὴν χριστοῦ διδασκαλίαν, ὡς αἵρεσιν καινὴν καὶ ἀλλοτρίαν τοῦ θεοῦ, παρήγγελλόν τε δι᾽ ἐπιστολῶν μὴ παραδέξασθαι αὐτήν (Migne, *Patr. Graec.* xxiv. col. 213). That is: "We have found in the writings of the ancients that Jerusalem priests

[1] See Note 4 at end of chapter.

and elders of the Jewish people sent letters to all the Jews everywhere traducing the doctrine of Christ, as a new heresy alien to God, and admonishing them in letters not to accept it." If such encyclicals were actually sent so extensively as this, Eusebius' ancient authority merely states that the central authorities at Jerusalem sent warnings *to their own brethren* in the diaspora exhorting them to turn a deaf ear to the efforts of Christian missionaries, in that the new religion was not compatible with Judaism. So far from this being evidence of Jewish aggression, it is on the contrary a statement of efforts needed for self-defence. The same is the true inference to be drawn from the majority of the complaints of the fathers. The Jewish defence of Judaism sometimes assumed the form of an attack on Christianity, and this attack would not invariably be fair or in good taste. But only in the rarest cases is it directly alleged (e.g. Origen, *Against Celsus*, vi. 27) that the Jews initiated specific charges, and it is noteworthy that Origen does not assert this of his own experience. Mostly the complaint is that the Jews actually defended themselves by placing before their brethren the fundamental objections to Christianity from the Jewish side, and these arguments were also, no doubt, sometimes adopted by heathen opponents of Christianity (Justin, *Dialogue*, xvii., cviii., cxvii. It is only in this sense that Tertullian's remark, *Ad Nat.* i. 14, is credible). Besides the other Jewish criticisms of Justin, cf. M. Freimann's essay "Die Wortführer des Judentums in den ältesten Kontroversen zwischen Juden und Christen" in the Breslau *Monatsschrift*, lv, 1911, pp. 555 *seq.* For the majority of their arguments the heathens had no need of Jewish aid, they are derived directly from a study of the Christian writings. In fact Celsus was as bitter an assailant of Judaism as he was of Christianity. Nay the latter was the object of his scorn just *because* it grew out of the former (i. 2). As Origen himself says (i. 22): Celsus "thinks that he will be able the more easily to establish the falsity of Christianity, if, by assailing its origin in Judaism, he can show that the latter also is untrue." Jews could hardly have been behind Celsus! And the same is true of other Gentile assailants. Judaism was as unsparingly denounced and ridiculed as was Christianity. The Jews were the object of constant attack by heathen satirists and were not very gently treated by the Christian controversialists; their own attitude towards Gentile heathendom was one of a favourable and attractive presentation of the Jewish case, while their general policy towards Gentile Christianity was a propaganda of self-defence in which both heathendom and Christianity were criticised. That such self-defensive propaganda was not unnecessary is shown by the opening lines of the passage from Jerome, the latter part of which has already been cited. Jerome speaks of the presence of Judeo-Christians within the Synagogues of the whole of the Orient even in his time: "Usque hodie per totas Orientis synagogas inter Judæos hæresis est, quæ dicitur Minæarum...qui credunt in Christum." The Jews were far more concerned with purging the Synagogue of those who were in Jerome's phrase *nec Judæi nec Christiani* than with assailing the openly avowed Christianity of the Gentile Church[1].

## NOTE I.

The most important Synoptic texts are Mark xiii. 9; Matt. x. 16—23, xxiv. 9—14; Luke xii. 11—12, xxi. 12—19. It is a critical mistake to take too literally apocalyptic references to persecution. All apocalypses, whether Jewish or Christian, have this feature in common. It is a recurrent element in the world-drama as unrolled in the visions of the end; the heroic saints suffer, and the poet is not over-anxious to discriminate as to the personality of those who cause the suffering. With the "Short Apocalypse" of the Synoptics, may be compared (apart from the formal apocalyptic books) the passage with which Mishnah Soṭa ends. The passage, however, scarcely belongs to the Mishnah, but to the Talmud (T.B. Soṭa 49 a). On the other hand, practically the same "Apocalypse" is found elsewhere (T.B. Sanhedrin 97 a) as a *baraitha*, and is of the same age and character as the Mishnah. For our present subject, the most important point is, that among the signs which are the foot-prints of the Messiah in advance (a curious phrase based on Psalm lxxxix. 51) is the item: "The Kingdom shall be turned to *minuth*." This phrase does not occur in Sanhedrin, but appears in Soṭa. Is it an elision in the former or an interpolation in the latter? The view of M. Friedländer (*Die religiösen Bewegungen innerhalb des Judentums im Zeitalter Jesu*, Berlin, 1905, p. 175) that the passage is an ancient and pre-Christian Jewish apocalypse has little probability. On the other hand, the clause "the face of the generation will resemble the face of a dog," i.e. for impudence, may be pre-Christian, for it was the heathen gods that were termed dog-faced as a term of contempt (T.J. Aboda Zara iii. 43 a). What is quite certain

[1] See Note 5 at end of chapter.

is that *minuth* is, in Jewish sources, a purely *Jewish* heresy (cf. T.B. Ḥullin 13 b), and sometimes at least refers to Judeo-Christianity (never to Gentile Christianity). It is not possible therefore to regard the phrase as an interpolation made when Christianity had become a world-wide power. Now, in Sanhedrin the author of the Short Apocalypse is Judah son of Ilai (Bacher, *Agada der Tannaiten*, ii. 222); he was a younger contemporary of Bar Cochba. The refusal of the Jewish Christians to join in the latter's revolt against Rome and the triumph of Rome over the Jewish nationalists, may well have appeared to Judah b. Ilai (supposing the phrase to be really his) an indication that the "Kingdom shall be turned to *minuth*," and that another than Bar Cochba must be looked for as the Messiah. Against this suggestion, that the phrase was Judah b. Ilai's and the reference to Rome, is the fact that this Rabbi was an admirer of certain aspects of Roman civilisation—their roads and bridges and baths (T.B. Sabbath 33 b). For some notes on the Soṭa Apocalypse see A. Büchler in *J. Q. R.* xvi. 151 and E. Ben Yehuda in *Millon* i. 297 b foot. With regard to the phrase "heels" of the Messiah (עקבי המשיח), Professor Burkitt has suggested to me that in Genesis xxv. 26 Esau's heel is the *fore-runner* of Jacob's birth.

## NOTE 2.

The accounts of the relations between Jews and Christians are much obscured by the many more or less opposed groups roughly designated by these two names. Harnack's essay quoted a few lines later brings out very clearly the many shades and grades between pure Judaism and pure Christianity. There were, we may roughly put it, first the Jews: then the heathen proselytes to Judaism: then the Jewish Christians, the heathen-Jewish proselytes to Christianity, and the Gentile Christians generally. There was possibly another overlooked class: heathens who accepted Judaism viâ Christianity. The existence of one such is alleged by Epiphanius (*De Ponderibus et Mensuris*, xiii.—xvi.), who records that Aquila (the translator of the Bible and the disciple of Aqiba) was first a Christian, who after excommunication by the Church became a Jew (an allegation which L. Ginzberg finds reflected in the Talmud, *Jewish Encyclopedia*, ii. 37). There is this interest in Epiphanius' legend, that he describes Aquila, after his second change of faith, as vindictively anti-Christian. That the notorious zeal of proselytes might well make these more royalist than the king is a point that deserves more attention than it has received. This would apply also to heathen proselytes to Judaism and Jewish proselytes to Christianity. Thus Justin (*Dial.* cxxii.) says "The proselytes not only do not believe, but blaspheme Christ's name two-fold more than you, and endeavour to put to death and torture us who believe in him." Ignatius speaks with unmeasured scorn of the "circumcised teaching Christianity and of the uncircumcised teaching Judaism" (*Philadelphians*, vi.). Harnack cites the passage as testifying to the bitterness of the heathen-Jews in the diaspora towards Christians (*Judentum und Judenchristentum in Justins Dialog mit Trypho* in Texte und Untersuchungen, xxxix. Leipzig, 1913, p. 81). It may be from such a source that was derived a current argument (Eusebius, *Prep. Ev.* i. 2). Let heathens either remain good polytheists, worshipping the gods, or accept Judaism; Christianity is neither sound paganism nor customary Judaism. Jews, however, were in the main too much concerned with Grecian antisemitism and Roman persecutions against themselves to be the instigators of similar sufferings. Pagan philosophers, from Seneca onwards, and pagan rulers needed no such prompting. And, as against Justin, the evidence of Tatian is a strong support to the conclusion that the attacks on Christianity arose mainly, if not entirely, from the non-Christian, non-Jewish heathen side. "Be not, O Greeks, so very inimically disposed towards the Barbarians," is the opening appeal of Tatian's Address to the Greeks. "For what reason," he asks, "men of Greece, do you wish to bring the civil powers, as in a pugilistic encounter, into collision with us?" (ch. iv.; cf. also xxv.). This utter silence of Tatian, pupil though he was of Justin, as to any complicity of Jews is remarkable. His whole protest, moreover, is directed against *Greek* attacks on Christianity. His argument as to the priority of Moses to Homer (ch. xxxvi. *seq.*) is hardly the kind of weapon that Tatian would have directed against Greeks behind whom Jews were arrayed. It is a natural idea to suggest that the Jews resented the passage of their heathen proselytes over to Christianity, which in Dr Parry's words (*Corinthians*, p. xi) "would reap the harvest of their (the Jews') own endeavours." But against this may be set the fact that, in certain epochs at all events, the converts made by Synagogue and Church did not consist of the same classes. There was no direct competition. The former belonged to the aristocratic circles, the latter to the masses (Graetz, *Die jüdischen Proselyten im Römerreiche unter den Kaisern Domitian, Nerva, Trajan und Hadrian*, Breslau, 1884, p. 33).

M. Joel, in his essay *Der Kampf des Heidenthums gegen die Juden und Christen in den ersten Jahrhunderten der römischen Cäsaren*, long ago expressed the conviction, that when the Gentile Christianity grew independent of Jewish connection and was clearly differentiated from *minuth* (Jewish-Christianity), there was no lack of friendship and intercourse between Jews and the former (*Blicke in die Religionsgeschichte zu Anfang des zweiten christlichen Jahrhunderts*, Breslau, 1880–1883, i. p. 30—ii. p. 80 and *passim*). Joel's work deserves to be better known. Charges brought against each other by Jews and Jewish Christians of acting as *delatores* are perfectly natural. In the Talmud (e.g. T.B. Rosh Hashanah 17) the *minim* are associated with the *denouncers*, just as Christian apologists return the compliment. Attention may here be drawn to a new and thorough investigation of "The Attitude of the Jew towards the non-Jew" by Prof. J. Z. Lauterbach (of the Hebrew Union College) in the *Year-Book* of the Central Conference of American Rabbis, vol. xxxi. 1921, pp. 186—233. This essay does not touch closely our present problem, but it is of value for the general question with which it is occupied.

## NOTE 3.

Especial attention may be drawn to J. B. Lightfoot's view expressed in his *Philippians*. He rejects Merivale's view (adopted by Harnack) that Jews of Rome informed against the Christians. "I do not feel justified" writes Bishop Lightfoot (*op. cit.*, ed. 1879, p. 24) "in setting aside the authority of both Tacitus and Suetonius in a case like this, where the incident recorded must have happened in their own lifetime; an incident moreover not transacted within the recesses of the palace or by a few accomplices sworn to secrecy, but open and notorious, affecting the lives of many and gratifying the fanatical fury of a whole populace." Later on (p. 41) Lightfoot equally disputes the suggestion that Poppaea, instigated by Jews, prejudiced the emperor against Paul. "Doubtless she *might* have done so. But, if she had interfered at all, why should she have been satisfied with delaying his trial or increasing his restraints, when she might have procured his condemnation and death? The hand reeking with the noblest blood of Rome would hardly refuse at her bidding to strike down a poor foreigner, who was almost unknown and would certainly be unavenged. From whatever cause whether from ignorance or caprice or indifference or disdain, her influence, we may safely conclude, was not exerted to the injury of the Apostle." For an equally firm protest see Max Radin's *Jews among the Greeks and Romans* (Philadelphia, 1915) pp. 319 and 408. He has also some good remarks on the Roman disposition to regard religious propagandists as leaders of sedition (p. 292).

How conscious Harnack himself was of the tenuity of the evidence on which he relied is naïvely proved by his seizing on the late *Carmen apologeticum* of Commodianus. "Who in Rome in 64 could have indicated the Christians and discriminated them from the Jews? *but so far a literary testimony was lacking.*" He finds the missing testimony in an oblique passage in Commodianus' poem, which is full of historical confusions, and at earliest dates from the third century (Harnack in *Analecta zur ältesten Geschichte des Christentums in Rom*, vol. xxviii. Texte und Untersuchungen, pp. 7—9). Probably its true date is the beginning of the fifth century. That Harnack, after his earlier confidence, should admit that he had no "literary evidence" (but only his subjective conjecture) for a very fierce charge most extravagantly formulated, and then rely on the "evidence" of Commodianus is a curiosity of historical criticism, to which happily parallels are scarce. Certainly the rather earlier Pseudo-Senecan Epistles to Paul have at least as much weight as Commodianus. These Epistles were the work of one who, well-knowing Poppaea's Jewish sympathies, nevertheless speaks (Epistle xii.) of *Jewish* as well as Christian victims of the false charge of incendiarism. Lightfoot (*Philippians*, pp. 329—331) strongly holds that the Epistles are the same as those referred to by Jerome. Yet, despite the indisputable fact that there is no evidence whatever for the charge of Jewish implication in the Neronian persecution of Christians, modern writers continue to cite Harnack's baseless conjecture as though it were founded on historical sources. Thus (without any reference whatever to evidence) we are told of the Jews' "calumnious delation" of the Christians to Nero in Ferrero and Barbagallo's *Short History of Rome* (1919, ii. 214). It may be added that O. Hirschfeld (Mommsen's successor in the Berlin chair of Roman History) absolutely rejects Harnack's bizarre inference from Commodianus (*Kleine Schriften*, pp. 409 ff.).

## NOTE 4.

The *Martyrdom of Polycarp* is the "earliest known history of a Christian martyrdom, the genuineness of which is unquestionable" writes Prof. Kirsopp Lake in his edition of the Apostolic Fathers (Loeb Classics, vol. ii. p. 329). This narrative also leads the way in the charge that the Jews were implicated in such cruel catastrophes. But while the martyrdom itself is fully attested, and the nobility of Polycarp's end stands out in imperishable glory, the narrative itself is not to be relied on as a historical account of the incidents which occurred at Smyrna on Feb. 23 of an uncertain year (the dates suggested vary between 155 and 166 A.D.). The many miraculous elements, and the reminiscences of the martyrdom described in the second Maccabees, are, of themselves, a warning not to treat the account as sober fact.

Nor is this all. That the "writer desires to bring out the points of resemblance to the Passion of Christ" is perfectly obvious. But Prof. Lake adds: "The coincidences are remarkable, but none are in themselves at all improbable." Cumulatively, however, the improbability is so great, that no other conclusion is reasonable than that the story is imitative of the Gospel accounts of the Passion. Polycarp "waited to be betrayed as also the Lord had done" (i. 1), and we should accordingly *expect* to find the Jews implicated by the narrator, seeing that this author has been clearly *influenced by the fourth Gospel.* This accordingly is the case. But here the narrative is patently unhistorical. There is absolutely nothing in the charge for which Polycarp suffered that points to Jewish testimony. Yet the Jews supply the faggots and after the martyr's death demand the body (xviii. 1), apparently lest it be treated with supernatural honours. All this is embellishment, not history. And assuredly the case against the Jews is unintentionally but effectively disproved by xii. 1, 2: "And with these and many other words he (Polycarp) was filled with courage and joy, and his face was full of grace so that it not only did not fall with trouble at the things said to him, but that the Pro-Consul, on the other hand, was astounded and sent his herald into the midst of the arena, to announce three times: 'Polycarp has confessed that he is a Christian.' When this had been said by the herald, all the multitude of heathen and Jews living at Smyrna cried out with uncontrollable wrath and a loud shout: 'This is the teacher of Asia, the father of the Christians, the destroyer of our gods, who teaches many neither to offer sacrifice nor to worship.'" That Jews should have participated in such a shout is so absolutely incredible, that the gravest doubt is thrown on the other references to the Jews. The dramatic writer probably had in mind John xix. 15: "We have no king but Caesar." Jewish participators were a necessary stage-property.

The clear design of the writer to identify the details of Polycarp's martyrdom with the Gospel Passion perhaps explains the difficulty of the date. It is clear that the martyrdom occurred Feb. 23 (the year being uncertain). The actual day seems also to have been a Saturday. But the narrative particularises, and we are told that the day was a "great Sabbath." In viii. 1 we read: "And they set him (Polycarp) on an ass, and led him into the city, on a great Sabbath day (*ὄνῳ καθίσαντες αὐτὸν ἤγαγον εἰς τὴν πόλιν, ὄντος σαββάτου μεγάλου*)." The attempt to identify this with the Sabbath before Purim is not plausible. Lake's suggestion that the "great Sabbath" was actually Purim itself is out of the question. C. H. Turner's view is that the Sabbath *before* Purim was so termed, but despite the authority of A. Neubauer whom he cites, there is no evidence whatsoever that Jews ever so described the Sabbath preceding Purim (*Studia Biblica et Ecclesiastica*, Oxford, 1890, vol. ii. p. 115). Nor is there much plausibility in the view of E. Schwartz that locally, in Smyrna, the Jews kept the Passover as early as February 22 in the year 156. Yet the "great Sabbath" can mean nothing else than the Sabbath before Easter. In other words, the narrator gives the right date Feb. 23, and then, in order to equate his story with John xix. 31, identifies it wrongly with "the great Sabbath." This is exactly what was done a century later in the narrative of the martyrdom of Pionius, which likewise fell on Feb. 23 "on a great Sabbath." As Schwartz points out, in this case the "great Sabbath" is unhistorical: "der *grosse Sabbat* ist aber Erfindung" (*Die Christliche und Jüdische Ostertafeln* in the Göttingen Abhandlungen, viii. 1905–6, p. 137).

It is extremely doubtful whether the Jews described any Sabbath as "the great Sabbath" until later. The only argument in favour of an early date is its occurrence in John xix. 31. The entire absence of the term from the early Rabbinic sources led Zunz to the view that the Synagogue adopted it from the Church (*Die Ritus des synagogalen Gottesdienstes geschichtlich entwickelt*, Berlin, 1859, p. 9). A. Jellinek had previously disputed this, but his only early source is the fourth Gospel

(Fürst's *Orient*, 1851, p. 287). Zunz's view is accepted by Elbogen (*Die jüdische Gottesdienst*, Leipzig, 1913, p. 551). Much later the Jews applied the title to the Sabbath before Passover, Pentecost, New Year, and Tabernacles, never of course to the Sabbath before Purim.

If, however, we accept (as all critics do) the statement that Polycarp's martyrdom occurred on a *Saturday*, this adds another very strong argument against the participation of the Jews. They would hardly have joined on such a day in "preparing wood and faggots from the workshops and baths" (xiii. 1). Nor could any Jews on any day have been associated with the appeal to Philip the Asiarch to "let loose a lion on Polycarp" (xii. 2). Jews agreed with Christians in their detestation of such practices (Mishnah Aboda Zara i. 8; T.J. Aboda Zara *ad loc.*). For a view, similar to the above, of the incredibility of the Jewish participation in the martyrdom of Polycarp and like inhumanities, cf. M. Joel, *Blicke*, ii. 151 *seq.* One general conclusion may be formulated without room for dispute. If any so-called "Jews" acted in the manner described in the *Martyrdom of Polycarp*, they were altogether alien in mind and conduct from any actually known class to whom the name "Jews" might be accurately applied. Another suggestion has been made by Salomon Reinach, on the basis of a passage in Pionius' fourth century *Vita Sancti Polycarpi* (ed. L. Duchesne, Paris, 1881). Reinach suggests that the Jews' part was not to kindle, but to extinguish flames. He compares this function to the modern Oriental *touloumbadjis*, and concludes that "les Juifs de la Smyrne romaine étaient les prédécesseurs des touloumbadjis" (*Revue des Études Juives*, xi. 238).

## NOTE 5.

That Jewish apostoli were really despatched for specifically Jewish objects is clear from several sources. Up to the very end of the fourth century (Cod. Theod. xvi. 8, 14) such messengers (sheluḥim) collected money in the diaspora for the maintenance of teachers in the Holy Land, and supervised the affairs of the local communities during their visits. They also conveyed information as to the fixation of the Calendar (T.B. Sanhedrin, 26 a; Mishnah Yebamoth, end). This system of apostolê, it has been plausibly conjectured, grew out of the Temple tax, and may thus go back to 70 A.D., the date when the

Sanctuary was destroyed. Such envoys may also, at times, have concerned themselves with the question of *minuth* in the synagogues of the diaspora; but there is no Jewish evidence that such concerns were made the primary object of the apostolê. That notice was given to the diaspora of the objection to association with the *minim* in worship is, however, quite likely (cf. Graetz, *Geschichte der Juden*, iv. 115). But for the type of anti-Christian embassies alluded to by Justin there is no confirmation in any Jewish source nor in any independent Christian or pagan authority.

The Jewish embassies to Rome of which we have the clearest evidence were unmistakably self-defensive. This is true of Philo's day, and it is also true of the later embassy to Trajan, on which fresh light is thrown in vol. x. of Grenfell and Hunt's *Oxyrhynchus Papyri*, p. 112. The Jews defending themselves against Alexandrian antisemitism find some favour with the Empress Plotina and Trajan. The latter is indignant at the Alexandrian taunt that the Imperial council is dominated by Jews. What comes out of the story most clearly is that when the Jews received anything like a favourable audience the opposite side (in this case the persecutors and oppressors) would at once protest against packing the court with "godless Jews" (*op. cit.* p. 118). Trajan, the account continues, is turned from any such favour by the "sweat which suddenly broke out on the bust of Sarapis which the envoys carried." Incidentally there is the statement that "each party took their own gods" (ἕκαστοι βαστάζοντες τοὺς ἰδίους θεούς); but there is an unfortunate gap in the text. The editors remark: "It would have been very interesting to know what divine symbols accompanied the Jewish envoys." Possibly a Scroll of the Law, mistaken by the Greek narrator for a "god." On the Jewish account of the famous embassy to Rome between those to Caius and Trajan (in 95 A.D.) when Gamaliel II was accompanied by three colleagues, including Aqiba, see Bacher (*Agada der Tannaiten*, i. 79). The points discussed include a defence against heathen attacks on the Hebrew Scriptures (cf. Mishnah Aboda Zara iv. 7 and Elmslie's note p. 67). Only in one legendary controversy in Rome is there any hint of Christian controversy, and there the Rabbi Joshua b. Ḥananya—one of the actors in a curious pantomimic display (T.B. Ḥagigah 5a)—is, in the Talmudic account at all events, by no means the aggressor (cf. on this Bacher, *op. cit.* pp. 165 *seq.*). Justin actually makes it a matter of complaint against the Jews that the "Rabbis charge the Jews never at all to give ear to us who explain them (i.e. Christological interpretations of the Scriptures), nor to hold any communication with us" (*Dialogue*, ch. cxii). Through this avoidance of controversy the Jews "are unable to derive any benefit whatever from the prophetic writings" (*ibid.*), for they go on explaining them in a non-Christian sense. This points the way to the age-long reluctance of Jews to enter into polemical disputes with Christians regarding their faith. Practically all the polemical literature of the Middle Ages, from the Jewish side, is defensive, though of course sometimes the defence takes the form of counter-attack.

It will be observed that Justin here specifically represents the efforts of the Jewish authorities as irritatingly defensive. The same is true of the mission to Rome, in the second part of the second century, when the object of Simeon b. Yoḥai and Eleazar b. José was purely defensive (T.B. Meilah 17 b). On a survey of the whole evidence it may be firmly asserted that no charge of an active persecution of Gentile Christianity can be proved against the Jews, except possibly against some proselytes to Judaism, themselves of Gentile birth. How readily, however, such charges would be formulated is shown by St Ambrose's attribution of the burning of the churches in Gaza (at the end of the fourth century) to the Jews. But as G. F. Hill remarks: "The ordinary Gazaean population scarcely needed their [the Jews'] assistance in such an affair" (*The Life of Porphyry*, Oxford, 1913, p. xxx). Mark the Deacon's persistent references to the "idol-mania" (*εἰδωλομανία*) of the pagan foes of Gazaean Christianity certainly confirm Dr Hill's scepticism.

## XI. SOME RABBINIC IDEAS ON PRAYER.

If it be true that the ordinary Hebrew word for praying (*hithpallel*) comes from a root meaning "to rend," then it may follow that with the primitive Hebrews prayer implied "cuttings of the flesh," by which men sought to influence the Deity[1]. Thus the origin of the most profoundly spiritual conception which the world owes to Hebraism must, on this theory, be sought in Sympathetic Magic, with which Sir J. G. Frazer has so familiarised us[2]. Some religious students are rather depressed by such theories; they seem to think that religion is being degraded by the connections suggested between their own most cherished ideas and the crude, unlovely rites of savages. But surely this feeling of repugnance is unjustifiable. One has reason for pride, not shame, that human nature has shown itself capable of transforming, under the impulse of the Divine Spirit, the ugly into the beautiful, magic into religion. From this point of view there is nothing disturbing in the theory that Hebraic prayer originated in savage rites[3]. If, again, we stride from the beginning to the end, from the primitive Hebraic origin to the developed doctrine of Pharisaism, we are told by Schürer that "even prayer itself, that centre of religious life, was bound in the fetters of a rigid mechanism[4]." Starting as magic, Hebraic prayer thus culminated in routine. Is this credible? Between the two extremes lie the prophetic religion, the Psalter, and the earliest liturgy of the Synagogue. That all this faded away into an "external function" is either one of the most painful failures of human nature, or one of the

[1] For this view of W. Robertson Smith (*Religion of the Semites*, 321, 337), based on Wellhausen (*Reste arabischen Heidenthums*, 126), see Prof. T. K. Cheyne's excellent article on "Prayer" in the *Encyclopaedia Biblica*. Prof. Cheyne's treatment of the whole subject is as just as it is original.

[2] Cf. Dr Frazer's *Lectures on the Early History of the Kingship*, 1905, pp. 38, 52, etc.

[3] Cf. pp. 138, 159 below. In his *Permanent Values in Judaism*, New York, 1923, the writer develops the thesis that such lower origins may even leave a trace for good in the developed principle or institution.

[4] E. T. II. ii. p. 115. This was repeated in the fourth (latest) German edition, Leipzig, 1907, ed. ii. p. 569.

least reasonable of delusions to which German theologians have fallen victims[1].

But the purpose of this Note is not controversial, unless it be controversial to attempt to present what seems to the writer a little more of the truth over against less of the truth. At all events, little if any negative criticism will be indulged in; rather it will be sought to present positively the developed conception of prayer as it is to be found in the Rabbinic literature. That conception is, on the whole, the conception formed before the first century and still predominant in Judaism; and it has seemed more useful to explain this developed conception than to trace the steps by which it was evolved. To the historian path is as important as goal; not so, however, to those who would fain derive from all religious systems the best that they have to offer.

It is, one must admit, not easy to speak of a Rabbinic conception of prayer at all. This is true equally of the New Testament, wherein (as with Pharisaism) prayer covers the whole range of thought from the complete acceptance of the Divine Will (Luke xxii. 42) to the belief in the objective validity of special supplications (James v. 15), from the most rigid brevity (as in the Lord's Prayer) to the acclamation of prayers continual and incessant (Acts vi. 4, Eph. vi. 18, 1 Thess. v. 17). Theology, in fact, is never systematic while religion is in the formative stages. Pharisaism from the beginning of the first to the end of the fifteenth century remained in this formative condition. Rabbinic theology is a syncretism, not a system. To the earliest Pharisees the Bible as a whole, to the later Rabbis the Bible and the traditional literature as a whole, were the sources of inspiration. Hence they adopted and adapted ideas of many ages and many types of mind, and in consequence one may find in Rabbinic Judaism traces of primitive thought side by side with the most developed thought. Especially is this true of prayer. A conspectus of Rabbinic passages on prayer would cover the whole range of evolution, from the spells of a rain-producing magician to the soul-communion of an inspired mystic. A slip in uttering the formulae of prayer was an evil sign[2]; on the

[1] Bousset's *Religion des Judentums im neutestamentlichen Zeitalter* is in many respects thoroughly unacceptable: but the author's remarks on prayer (p. 157, ed. 2, p. 202) are not lacking in truth and insight. They form in essence a severe criticism of Schürer, for Bousset perceives that the Pharisaic organisation of prayer did deepen the spiritual life of the masses.

[2] Mishnah, Berachoth, v end (B. Berachoth, 34 b). The passage concerning Ḥanina b. Dosa cited later on occurs at this same reference.

other extreme, the finest prayer may be made without any formula or word at all[1]. The Rabbis, again, believed on the one hand in the efficacy of the prolonged prayers of the righteous in general[2], and on the other hand they, like a certain school of modern Evangelicals, sometimes confided in the possession by gifted individuals of a special faculty for influencing the powers above. Such individuals were mighty men of prayer, able to force their will on a reluctant providence; they would argue, importune, persuade. It has always remained an element in the Jewish theory of prayer that man can affect God; what man does, what he thinks, what he prays, influence the divine action. It is not merely that God cares for man, is concerned with and for man. God's purpose is affected, his intention changed by prayer. These phases of belief are, however, never altogether absent from prayer, even in its most spiritualised varieties. They are noticeable in the Psalms, and, when one remembers the influence of the Psalter, one need not wonder to find these phases of belief in the extant liturgies of all creeds. Perhaps we may put it that in the Pharisaic theology there was a fuller belief in special providences than is now thought tenable; but after reading some of the papers in a recent volume entitled *In Answer to Prayer*[3] one must hesitate before assuming that this view was peculiar to Pharisaism[4]. The Rabbis somewhat mitigated the crudity of the belief in special providences by holding that all miracles were pre-ordained, and were inherent in the act of creation. But the order of nature is a modern theory: one would look for it in vain whether in Rabbinic or early Christian books. Now so soon as one believes in special providences, he is liable to seek them by special petitions, and

[1] Cf. Midrash on opening phrases of Psalm lxv. Moreover, silent prayer, even though for the most part the prayer itself was in prescribed terms, was a regular feature of the Pharisaic services. But within the prescribed forms the individual (again silently) meditated his own personal supplications (T.J. Berachoth v. 2. יחיד שואל צרכיו בשומע תפלה). Such private interpolations were at most only semi-audible.

[2] המרבה בתפלה נענה T.J. Berachoth iv. § 1.

[3] London, Isbister, 1904.

[4] Allied to the power of prayer is the power of faith. There is a great passage in the Mechilta (ed. Friedmann, p. 33 b) on Exod. xiv. 31 ("and they believed in the Lord"). It was through Israel's faith that the Holy Spirit rested on the people and inspired the Song of Exod. xv.; it was faith through which Abraham (Gen. xv. 6) inherited this world and the next. It is Israel's faith that in the end will bring redemption. R. Neḥemya says: "Whoever receives upon himself a single precept in faith is worthy of the reception of the Holy Spirit." The whole passage is very fine.

prayer may degenerate into importunity. Onias the circle-drawer would not leave his circumscribed standing-place until the rain fell, and he told people in advance to place under cover all perishable things, so sure was he that God must send the rain for which he prayed[1]. Ḥanina ben Dosa could always tell from his fluency or hesitancy when he prayed for sick men whether the patients would live or die. And though such cited cases are rare in the Talmud, and are perhaps Essenic rather than Pharisaic, still it was generally believed that specific prayer for a specific end might hit the mark[2].

It *might* hit the mark, but it was not certain to do so. Therein lies the whole saving difference. If Rabbinism is firm in its assertion that prayer *may* be answered, it is firmer still in its denial that prayer *must* be answered. The presumptuous anticipations of Onias the circle-drawer were rebuked by some Rabbis. Haughty prayer, under all circumstances, was obnoxious to the humble spirit of a Hillel. Seeing some of his brethren puffed up by their prayer, as though they were doing God a favour by their praise of him, Hillel reminded them of the uncountable myriads of angelic hosts (Job xxv. 3) who minister to God, and in comparison with whose majestic adorations man's worship is a puny affair. But when Hillel perceived that his brethren's heart was broken, he changed his note of rebuke against arrogant Israel, to one of encouragement for contrite Israel. Yea, he said, there are these myriads of myriads of angels, but God prefers Israel's praises to theirs; for it is written of David (2 Sam. xxiii. 1) that he was "the man raised on high, the anointed of the God of Jacob, and the sweet Psalmist of Israel," and further (Psalm xxii. 4): "But Thou art holy, O Thou that art enthroned upon the praises of Israel[3]." Prayer was efficacious, but its whole efficacy was lost if reliance was placed upon its efficacy. As the Prayer Book version of Psalm xxvii. 16 runs: "O tarry thou the Lord's leisure: be strong, and he shall comfort thine heart; and put

[1] Mishnah, Taanith, iii. 8. Cf. note p. 81 below. Onias and Ḥanina are both held to have been Essenes. Prayer for rain must only be uttered near the rain-season (*ibid.* 1, 2). Does this imply a belief in the order of nature? Such prayer had to be sincere; on Tabernacles men did not pray for rain till the end of the festival, when the duty of dwelling in the tabernacle was over, so that "men might pray for rain with a perfect heart." On Onias cf. First Series, p. 110.

[2] Compare further the quaintly interesting discussion as to the relative efficacy of Repentance and Prayer in annulling the evil decree (גזירה) caused by sin (Levit. Rabba x. § 5; Pesiqta R. ed. Friedmann 188 b; T.B. Sanhedrin 37—38).

[3] Aboth d. R. Nathan ii. 27; T.J. Sukkah v. § 4.

thou thy trust in the Lord." But the wicked man is in a hurry. Like Tom Tulliver in *The Mill on the Floss*, his faith cannot survive the failure of divine answer to a petition that he may know his Latin verbs in school next morning. The recovered Hebrew original of Sirach gives us the fine text: "Be not impatient in prayer[1]." The answer, though sure to come in the end, need not be immediate. The possible postponement of answer takes the sting out of the impropriety of expecting an answer at all. The Rabbis put it that the wicked denies God if he happen to pray in vain; the righteous man receives affliction as the mead of virtue yet never questions the justice of God. Solomon's Prayer on dedicating the Temple is thus summarised in the Midrash: When, O Lord, a Hebrew prays to thee, grant what seems *good to thee*; when a heathen prays, grant what seems *good to him*[2]. The meaning of this is: the heathen entirely rests his belief in God on an immediate, specific answer to his prayers, and Solomon entreats God to give the heathen such specific answer in order to retain his allegiance. The true believer is, on the contrary, free from such reliance on the objective validity of his supplication; to him *that* is good which God pleases to ordain[3]. And if it be held right that the petition of one mighty in prayer should be answered, this was for two reasons. In the first place, the ignorant hearing such a man pray in vain, would be liable to infer the impotence of God from the inefficacy of the man who appealed to him[4]. Secondly, the same conclusion is

[1] Sirach (Hebrew) vii. 10. אל תתקצר בתפלה In the Oxford Apocrypha (ed. Charles), vol. i. p. 339, Box and Oesterley have this valuable note: "As Smend points out, תתקצר is an abbreviated form of קצרה רוח; for this phrase see Job xxi. 4; Prov. xiv. 29. G. μὴ ὀλιγοψυχήσῃς, cp. iv. 9, Jas. i. 6, and the Midrash Debarim Rabba iii. 24: 'Pray and pray, again and again; a time will come when thou wilt be answered.' See also Matt. xxi. 21, 22; Mark xi. 24."

[2] Buber's Tanḥuma, Genesis, p. 134 (Toledoth, § 14).

[3] This is the force also of the final phrase *for good* in Rab's famous prayer (T.B. Berachoth 16 b, A. Cohen's E. T. p. 108): "May it be thy will, O Lord our God, to grant us long life, a life of peace, a life of good, a life of blessing, a life of sustenance, a life of bodily vigour, a life marked by the fear of sin, a life free from shame and reproach, a life of prosperity and honour, a life in which the love of Torah and the fear of Heaven shall cleave to us, a life wherein thou fulfillest all the desires of our heart for good." The implication is that God, and not man, knows whether the things prayed for are a real boon: it is God who fulfils for good, though man may ignorantly desire what is not good. Cf. First Series, p. 117.

[4] T.B. Taanith 23 b. The ignorant could not discriminate between the Father who gives rain and the "father" who has no such power by his prayers:

עשה בשביל אילו שאין מכירין בין אבא דיהיב מיטרא לאבא דלא יהיב מיטרא

drawn from a higher line of thought. David begs for an answer because the community *relies* on him. Hear my prayer, David entreats, in that I pray for all Israel. The people's eyes are fixed on mine, as my eyes are fixed on Thee. When I am answered, they are answered. Similarly with the leader in prayer for the congregation. His eyes are on God, the congregation's eyes on him, as the Psalmist (xxv.) exclaims: "Unto Thee, O Lord, do I lift up my soul. O my God, I trust in Thee, let me not be ashamed;...yea, let *none that wait on Thee be ashamed*[1]."

At this place a word must be interposed on a category of what the Rabbis call vain or fruitless prayer (*tephillath shav*). "Though a sharpened sword is held at a man's throat, he shall not withhold himself from mercy[2]," that is: Prayer and penitence may avail even at the eleventh hour. But not at the twelfth. I do not assert that the Rabbis disbelieved in the possibility of salvation after death[3]. But it was during a man's life-time that prayer had its value, not from man's

[1] Midrash on Ps. xxv. 3 (ed. Buber, p. 211).

אמר ר׳ פנחס · כך אמר דוד לפני הקב״ה · רבונו של עולם! בשעה שאני עומד לפניך בתפלה אל תהי תפלתי מאוסה לפניך · מפני שעיני ישראל תלויות בי · ועיני תלויות בך · ואם תשמע תפלתי כאילו תשמע תפלתם: וכן אתה מוצא בתענית צבור · שבשעה שהצבור מתענין שליח צבור יורד לפני התיבה · לפי שעיניהם של צבור תלויות בו · ועיניו תלויות בהקב״ה שהוא שומע תפלתם: לכך אמר דוד גם כל קויך לא יבושו · יבושו הבוגדים ריקם · אלו בני אדם המתענים בלא תשובה:

"Said R. Phineas, Thus did David speak before the Holy One, blessed be he: Master of the World! In the hour when I stand before thee in prayer let not my prayer be rejected, for their eyes hang on me, and my eyes hang on thee, and if thou hearest my prayer, it is as though thou hearest their prayer. So one finds it with regard to the communal fast, that in the hour when the congregation fasts, the delegated leader descends before the Ark, because the eyes of the congregation hang on him, and his eyes hang on the Holy One that he hears their prayer. Therefore David said, none that wait on Thee shall be ashamed, but they shall be ashamed that deal treacherously in vain—these are the men who fast without repentance."

In another version (Yalquṭ § 702) the saying is cited as emanating from R. Phineas in the name of R. Alexander. This should be added to Bacher's list, *Agada der Pal. Amoräer*, i. 199. R. Phineas was possibly also relying on R. Alexander in his view that the efficacy of prayer depends on a knowledge of the Divine *Name* (cf. Midrash to Ps. xci. 15 with the Midrash to Ps. iv. 2).

[2] T.B. Berachoth 10 a (foot).

[3] See S. Singer's fine essay on the subject in *Lectures and Addresses* (1908), pp. 55 *seq*.

side only, but from God's. In explanation of David's phrase "the dead praise not God" (Ps. cxv. 17), the Talmud remarks that it is from a man's devotion in his life-time that God enjoys praise[1]. Particularly the Rabbis held that it was in this life futile to pray *ex post facto*. Thus: "He who supplicates God concerning what has already come to pass utters a vain prayer[2]." If you are going to look at an honours list, you waste your time in praying that your name may be found there or found in a particular position. As the Rabbis otherwise put it, You must not *rely* on miracles. Thus certain prayers are ruled out by the Rabbis from the very possibility of answer. To this category belong also such prayers as one which Raba overheard and blamed. He once heard a man praying that he might win the love of a certain maiden. Raba bade him cease his prayer, urging: "If she be destined for thee, nothing can part you; if thou art not destined to get her, thou deniest providence in praying for her[3]." For marriages are made in heaven, and are beyond praying for.

Against *conditional* prayers, there was strong objection raised. The Rabbis in the Mishnah (Erubin iii. 9) refused, for instance, to accept the view of Dosa b. Harkinas, that the leader in prayer might say on the New Moon of Tishri, "Give us strength, O Lord our God, on this New Moon to-day or to-morrow," in reference to the doubt as to the exact date of the festival. Even more to the point is the Rabbinic denunciation of what they term *Iyyun Tephillah*. The word *Iyyun* means thought, calculation. Sometimes it is used with regard to prayer in a good sense, to connote careful devotion as opposed to mechanical utterance of prescribed formulæ. But there is another word for that, viz. *kavvanah*, which may be rendered devotion, than which no more necessary quality can be conceived of in the Rabbinic theory of prayer. But *Iyyun Tephillah* is very often used in a bad sense. Calculation in prayer is the expectation of an answer to prayer as a due claim, and the Rabbis protest with much vehemence against such *expectation* of a divine response to prayer of any kind whatsoever. "He who prays long and relies on an answer ends in disappointment." Again: "To three sins man is daily liable—

[1] T.B. Sabbath, 30 a. Cf. p. 179 below.

[2] Mishnah, Berachoth, ix; T.B. Berachoth, 60 a, has many sayings on תפלת שוא.

[3] T.B. Moed Katon, 18 b. On the idea that "Marriages are made in Heaven" see my *Book of Delight*, pp. 172 *seq*.

thoughts of evil, reliance on prayer, and slander[1]." Thus the expectation of an answer to prayer is an insidious intruder, difficult to avoid, and branded as sin. Perhaps the point can be best illustrated from another side. Not only do the righteous expect no answer to prayer, but they are reluctant to supplicate God for personal benefits. "The Holy One," we are told, "yearns for the prayers of the righteous." God's throne was not established until his children sang songs to him; for there can be no king without subjects. And as God wishes for man's praise, so he longs for man's petitions. But the righteous cannot easily be brought to make petitions. This is the Talmudic explanation of the barrenness of the Patriarchs' wives; God withheld children to compel the reluctant saints to proffer petitions for them. And so also, from a somewhat different point of view, with the whole people of Israel. Why did God bring Israel into the extremity of danger at the Red Sea before effecting a deliverance? Because God longed to hear Israel's prayer, and rather than have Israel silent he made Israel suffer[2].

There is a hint here of another note, but we can hear it elsewhere more unmistakably. "Honour the physician before thou hast need of him," says Ecclesiasticus. This passage is used in the Talmud to criticise the common practice of praying only under the pressure of necessity. "The Holy One said: Just as it is my office to cause the rain and the dew to fall, and make the plants to grow to sustain man, so art thou bounden to pray before me, and to praise me in accordance with my works; thou shalt not say, I am in prosperity, wherefore shall I pray; but when misfortune befalls me then will I come and supplicate. Before misfortune comes, anticipate and pray[3]." It will be seen that such passages as this carry us far beyond the conception of prayer as

[1] See on עיון תפלה, T.B. Berachoth, 32 b, 55 a; Baba Bathra, 164 b. He who prays thinking he deserves answer receives none. Rosh Hashanah, 18 a. On the other hand: "Whoever performs the will of heaven and directs his heart devoutly to his prayer receives an answer." Exod. Rabba, § 21; cf. Berachoth, 6 b (foot). The distinction may be said to be in this. Devout prayer is answered, *but* the expectation of an answer is not to enter into the thought of the utterer of the prayer. And the failure of an answer must not disconcert the worshipper. As he does not start relying on an answer, he is not overwhelmed by receiving none. "What is good in thine own sight do" (see p. 91 below). This was the final attitude. Of course God does what he thinks good; prayer makes man perceive that what God thinks good is good. Cf. note 3, p. 76, above.

[2] Cf. First Series, p. 103, and the parable from Exodus Rabba there quoted.

[3] Exod. R., ch. xxiii. Tanḥuma, § מקץ (near end).

petition. It is an attitude of mind, a constant element of the religious life, independent of the exigencies of specific needs or desires. And that, one may say, on a review of the whole evidence, is a predominant thought in the Rabbinic theory of prayer.

From one side this is illustrated by the importance attached to public worship. This importance partly arose from the regularity of that worship. It was not a casual impulse, but a recurrent feature of the daily round. But there lay much more than this in the Rabbinic glorification of public prayer. The prayer of a community may be selfish as against the welfare of other communities, but the selfishness is less demoralising than when an individual prays for what may entail injury to another individual. Even selfishness of the first kind, that is, communal selfishness in prayer, is castigated in some famous Rabbinic passages. "The Angels," it is said, "wished to sing praises to God while the Egyptians were drowning in the sea, and God rebuked them, saying, Shall I listen to your hymns when my children are perishing before my eyes?[1]" This was no mere pious expression, for the Passover liturgy of the synagogue has been permanently affected by this Rabbinic idea. On the Jewish festivals the noble series of Psalms of Praise (Hallel)—Psalms cxiii to cxviii—are a regular feature of the synagogue service. But on the seventh day of Passover—the traditional anniversary of the drowning of the Egyptians in the Red Sea—these psalms are curtailed, on the basis of the Talmudic utterance just cited. The Pharisees, and the religion derived from them, thus honour the text: "When thy enemy falls do not rejoice."

There are, no doubt, imprecatory passages in the Psalter, and some (by no means all) of these have found their way into the service of synagogue and church. But, except in times of bitter persecution (as in the Puritan struggle against tyranny in England, or in occasional synagogue hymns written during the Crusades), these imprecatory petitions have not been interpreted personally. Still, Jew and Christian could do without them. There is enough in the Psalter without these[2].

An interesting incident bearing on the same point is related by Josephus. Aretas, the Nabatean king, was besieging Jerusalem about 67 B.C. with a combined force of Arabians and Jews. "Now there

[1] T.B. Yebamoth, 64 a. On public worship see Berachoth, 8 a. Prayer for the wicked (that they may repent and be saved) is enjoined. T.B. Berachoth, 10 a. For the passage about the Egyptians see T.B. Megillah, 10 b; Soṭa, 36 a.

[2] Cf. First Series, p. 157.

was a man whose name was Onias, a righteous man, and beloved of God, who, in a certain drought, had prayed to God to put an end to the intense heat, and whose prayer God had heard and had sent rain. This man had hid himself, because he saw that this civil war would last a long while. However, they brought him to the Jewish camp, and desired that as by his prayers he had once put an end to the drought, so he would in like manner utter imprecations on Aristobulus and those of his faction. And when, on his refusing and making excuses, he was still compelled to speak by the multitude, he stood up in the midst of them, and said: 'O God, King of the whole world, since those that stand now with me are thy people, and those that are besieged are also thy priests, I beseech thee that thou wilt hearken neither to the prayers of those against these, nor bring to effect what these pray against those.'" Such impartiality was not pleasing to the lower minds and violent partisans who claimed God as exclusively on their side, as is the wont of the mean and the partisan in all ages. When the "wicked among the Jews who stood around him" found that he, whom they had brought to curse, refused the amiable rôle assigned to him, they speedily made an end of Onias[1]. But the underlying idea of Onias's prayer meets us elsewhere. A human judge, we are reminded, hears only one side at a time; God hears the whole world at once. The Shechinah, or Divine Presence, rests on ten when praying together—ten forming a quorum for public worship. It is possible that some irresistible power was attributed to the prayers of a congregation, and one catches suspicious echoes in Rabbinic literature of this unworthy belief, but it is nowhere explicitly enunciated. The idea rather seems to be that the individual petition counts less in such

[1] Josephus, 14 *Antiquities*, ii. § 1. Schürer's treatment of the episode (i. 293, 294) is worth noting. He includes it as one of the "Episodes highly characteristic of the contemporary Jewish pietism (*Frömmigkeit*)." His final comment is: "But the people was so little in sympathy with this brotherly spirit of Onias that they at once stoned him." But Josephus says that the stoning was done by *οἱ πονηροὶ τῶν Ἰουδαίων*, "the wicked of the Jews," and has pointedly stated previously that the noblest of the Jews had left the country for Egypt (*οἱ δοκιμώτατοι τῶν Ἰουδαίων ἐκλιπόντες τὴν χώραν εἰς Αἴγυπτον ἔφυγον*). This Onias becomes a popular hero in the later Jewish tradition, and it was "highly characteristic" of the Jewish *Frömmigkeit* that it held precisely the brotherly view of Onias in the positive as his was held in the negative form. "A human being cannot hear two people appealing to him at once; but the Holy One, even though *all creatures on earth* come and cry before him, hears their cries, as it is written, O thou that hearest prayer, unto thee shall all flesh come" (Mechilta, Shira, § 8; ed. Friedmann, 41 b).

prayers, and the individual's own peculiar claims are merged in and reinforced by the mass. "All are equal when they pray before God, women and slaves, sage and simpleton, poor and rich." "When one prays with the congregation it is like a number of rich men who are making a crown for the king, and a poor man comes and inserts his mite. Shall the king think less of the crown because of this poor man's contribution? So when a wicked man joins in prayer with the righteous, shall God reject this joint prayer because of him?" Congregational prayer thus levels up, and makes irrelevant any distinction between righteous and unrighteous. It is heresy (*minuth*) to say, Let the good praise Thee, for just as the malodorous galbanum was mixed with aromatic herbs in compounding the incense, so the pious at prayer must associate the impious with their orisons. Or the same idea may be derived from a text in Amos (ix. 6). God buildeth his upper chambers in heaven, and founds his vault upon the earth. Perhaps Abaye would have us render *agudah* not by "vault" but by bundle or band[1]. This same consideration constituted an element in the superiority of prayer over sacrifice. For while God rejected the sacrifices of the wicked, he was ready to accept their prayers. The "iron wall" which the destruction of the Temple erected between God and Israel was permeable by prayer[2]. Or take this saying, "When various congregations pray, the angel appointed over prayer gathers their supplications together and sets them as a garland on the brow of the Most High[3]." That, at all events, part of the Rabbinic predilection for public prayer was due to this greater unselfishness, is seen by the frequency with which men are urged to pray for one another. "A prayer uttered in behalf of another is answered first"; "He who loses a chance of praying for another is termed sinner"; "Elimelech and his sons were punished for their failure to pray for their generation[4]." They left Judea, it will be remembered, for Moab, and thus subtracted their

[1] Mishnah Megillah iii. (iv.) 9 האומר יברכוך טובים הרי זו דרך המינות. This may have a polemical intention. Not so, however, the passage in T.B. Kerithoth 6 b, which in reference particularly to fasting demands the union of the righteous and the sinner to make the ascetic act completely deserving of the name.

א״ר שמעון חסידא כל תענית שאין בה מפושעי ישראל אינה תענית ׳ שהרי חלבנה ריחה רע ומנאה הכתוב עם סממני קטרת ׳ אביי אמר מהכא ׳ ואגודתו על ארץ יסדה :

[2] Sifrê 71 b; T.B. Berachoth 32 b.

[3] Exodus Rabba, xxi; Echa Rabba, s.v. נדר בעדי.

[4] Baba Qama, 92 a; Baba Bathra, 90 a–91 b; Berachoth, 10 b.

prayers from those that ascended on behalf of the famine-stricken congregation. Perhaps this point best comes out in a Rabbinic prayer which at first sight may seem queer enough. "Let not the prayer of wayfarers find entrance, O Lord, before thee[1]." For wayfarers would selfishly ask for fine weather when the general good of the land needed rain. Selfishness can no further go, nor can one conceive a subtler rebuke of selfishness than this.

Unselfishness in prayer is clearly a rare virtue. An instance or two are as much as we can expect to find in any literature. Such an instance is Ḥanina b. Dosa. This first-century Rabbi was renowned for his successful prayers, and many stories are told of his efficaciousness. But the most noteworthy feature of his devotion was his unselfishness. He was once caught in the rain, and successfully prayed for its cessation. But realising that the world needed the rain, he changed his note. "Master of the world, shall all the world be distressed while Ḥanina enjoys his comfort?" Whereupon copious showers fell. But though by his prayers he thus fertilised the fields of others, he himself was extremely poor. So that "Every day a Daughter of the Voice issues and proclaims: The whole world is nourished for the sake of my son Ḥanina, but my son Ḥanina is satisfied with a measure of carob fruit from one sabbath to the next." Ḥanina does not stand quite alone. For we read of a Mar Zuṭra who is cited as a man who always prayed and fasted for others, never for himself. He is not so well-known a personality as Ḥanina, but he was sufficiently admired to have his name recorded as an ideal of altruistic supplication. It is consoling for human nature that in the Talmud Mar Zuṭra is regarded as an illustration of a class rather than as a unique exception[2].

Now, all the Pharisaic ritual laws which so trouble the spirit of German theologians refer to this public prayer. That this ritualism had its serious dangers is clear enough. The inevitable result of a

[1] T. Jer. Yoma, v. hal. 2. (Cf. Buber, Tanḥuma, Lev. p. ל for parallels.)

[2] T.J. Maaser Sheni, v. § 5. On Isaiah xlvi. 6 (ye stout-hearted that are far from [the rewards of] righteousness) one interpretation describes the people (illustrated by Mar Zuṭra) who themselves profit nothing from their prayers.

כל טובות ונחמות הבאות לעולם בזכותם והם אינן נהנין מהן כלום · כגון מר זוטרא דמצלי על חורנין ומתעני ועל נפשיה לא מתעני :

On Ḥanina see T.B. Berachoth 17 b. In the former passage occurs the parallel to Mt. xi. 12, Lk. xvi. 16. Cf. Bacher, *Agada der Pal. Am.* i. 359 note 2, and *Agada der Bab. Am.* p. 11 note 58.

fixed liturgy is rigidity. The fixation of times and seasons and formulae for prayer does tend to reduce the prayer to a mere habit. But what can be done at any time and in any manner is apt to be done at no time and in no manner. The Rabbis thus attached great importance to habits. "Fix a period for thy study of Scripture[1]" is the well-known maxim of Shammai. The study of Scripture was, of course, an act of worship, it was higher than prayer. Raba declaimed against men who "put aside everlasting life [the Scriptures] and concern themselves with temporal life" [prayers for maintenance]. To know the will of God was more important than to seek to turn God's will in man's favour. Therefore, "Fix a period for thy study of Scripture." Dangerous fixity of a good custom, we exclaim. But is it not curious how inclined we are to detect this danger only in our more ideal habits? We read our morning newspapers as a matter of habit, yet we do not fear to become thereby only mechanically interested in the news of the world. But in the case of prayer the difficulty is supremely urgent. If prayer is to mean anything it must retain its spontaneity. And therefore the Rabbis did their utmost to counteract the inherent weakness of a settled liturgy. Hebrew was the preferable but not the necessary language of prayer; men might pray in any tongue. And though the study of the Law was to be a fixed thing, prayer was not to be a fixed thing. Rabbi Eleazar formulated this in a general principle: "Make not thy prayer a fixed thing but a supplication for mercy[2]." Fix the study of God's word by which his will was made

[1] Mishnah, Aboth i. 15. In the *Jewish Encyclopedia*, x. p. 166 b, Dr J. D. Eisenstein writes: "The higher class, that is the scholars, would not be disturbed in their studies, which they considered of superior importance to prayers. R. Judah recited his prayers only once in thirty days (Rosh Hashanah, 35 a). R. Jeremiah, studying under R. Ze'era, was anxious to leave his study when the time for prayer arrived: and Ze'era quoted: He that turneth away his ear from hearing the Law, even his prayer shall be an abomination (Prov. xxviii. 9; T.B. Sabbath, 10 a)." The reference here is to the set times and forms of prayer. Individuals prayed spontaneously at all times. R. Aqiba, we are expressly told, prayed briefly in public, but lengthily in private.

[2] Aboth, ii. 13; Berachoth, iv. 4 (cf. T.B. Berachoth, 28 b). Cf. First Series, p. 9. "At first," writes Prof. L. Blau, "there were no written prayers; a scribe of the end of the first century says: The writers of benedictions are as those that burn the Torah. A man who was caught copying some at Sidon threw a bundle of his copies into a wash-tub (Sabbath, 115 b). In no case was written matter used during public worship. Prayer-books appear about the seventh century" (*Jewish Encyclopedia*, art. Liturgy, vol. viii. p. 138 b).

manifest, but do not make a fixed thing of prayer, for prayer is at once the human attempt to realise God's will and the human confession of inability to realise that will,—prayer is at highest a cry for mercy. What is the objectionable fixed thing in prayer? One Rabbi answers: "If a man's prayer is a burden"; another answers: "If the man does not pray as one seeking mercy"; a third answers: "If the man fails to introduce personal variations into the fixed forms." Ostentation was particularly discouraged. Again and again worshippers are cautioned not to pray too loudly. "He who shouts in prayer belongs to those who are of little faith." Even in such a context, allowance is made for individual temperament. For as Rab Huna observes, while there are men who can direct their heart Godwards while whispering their devotions, others need the sound of the spoken prayer to enable them to win the desired concentration. But while this relaxation of the ideal rule was permitted to one praying alone, it was forbidden in congregational worship to pray so audibly as to disturb others[1]. Silent prayer, moreover, was laudable because it avoided publicly putting sinners to shame[2]. A devotional heart, a humble attitude, are prescribed. The Pharisee, boasting in his prayer that he is not as other men, is not typical, for Pharisaism conceives all men equally destitute of saving virtue. Confession of sin, not profession of superior sinlessness, was the Pharisaic accompaniment of prayer. Eyes to earth, heart to heaven—is a Rabbi's suggestion for a prayerful posture[3].

These prescriptions could not completely succeed. But at this early period one must remember that public worship was of short duration. The length to which Jewish services have now grown was a slow evolution, and until the first decades of the fourteenth century the actual ritual of public worship was to a large extent in a very fluid condition. When we talk, then, of a fixed liturgy in the time of Jesus, we must not think of anything like the current Synagogue Liturgies or the Anglican Book of Common Prayer. Nothing is more remarkable than the extraordinary number of original individual prayers in the Talmud[4], and the faculty and process of ready impro-

[1] T.B. Berachoth, 24b, 29a.

[2] Mishnah, Soṭa x. 5 תפלה בלחש שלא לבייש עוברי עבירה.

[3] T.B. Yebamoth, 105b עיניו למטה ולבו למעלה.

[4] Some excellent examples are given by C. G. Montefiore in his *The Old Testament and After* (1923) pp. 351 ff. The whole of this part of his book is an apt and valuable interpretation of Pharisaic views on Prayer.

visation for public as well as private worship has continued with copious flow to our own times in the synagogue, though the stream of such inspiration was more generous in the spacious times which preceded the age of printing. The latter invention did more than Pharisaism to give rigidity to Judaism. It is not possible to give by quotations any true impression of the vast mass of new prayers which entered the publicity of the synagogue liturgy or the privacy of the Jewish home during the first fourteen centuries of the Christian era.

Then again, the Rabbis, though they sometimes emphasise the value of lengthy prayer, often declaim against it. The subject was not always approached from the same point of view, and it was admitted that there is a time to prolong and a time to shorten prayer[1]. The Emperor Antoninus asked R. Judah the Prince: "May one pray at all times?" "No!" said the Rabbi, "it is treating God with levity." The Emperor was not convinced. So the Rabbi got up early next morning, went to the Emperor, and greeted him with the salutation, "My Lord!" An hour later he returned, and exclaimed, "O Imperator!" After another hour the Rabbi accosted him for the third time, with "Peace be to thee, O King!" Antoninus could no longer endure it. He angrily retorted on the Rabbi: "You are making mock of my royalty." "So!" said the Rabbi, "Thou, a king of flesh and blood, find these repeated greetings disrespectful; shall then man trouble the King of Kings at all times?[2]" On this Rabbinic parable Miss Martha Wolfenstein—gone from us all too soon—based a pathetic little story. "Genendel the Pious" was an old Ghetto Jewess who was noted for the regularity with which, during her days of poverty, she attended synagogue. Then her son, who had emigrated to America, sends her a monthly allowance, and Genendel leaves off going to synagogue. This is the cause of much scandal, and the Rabbi taunts her with her ingratitude to God. He quotes the text: "Jeshurun waxed fat and kicked...then forsook the God who made him," and adds: "Now that the Lord has provided for thee, thou no longer hast need of him—what?" But Genendel, pious soul, puts another face on the matter. This is her explanation:—

[1] Mechilta on Exod. xv. 25 (ed. Friedmann, p. 45 b). שהיה אומר יש שעה לקצר ויש שעה להאריך

[2] Tanḥuma, מקץ. The passage, taken from Miss Wolfenstein's story, is quoted from *A Renegade and other Tales* (Philadelphia: the Jewish Publication Society of America, 1905; p. 200). R. Joḥanan thought that men might pray all day, but others limited the lawful times of prayer to three (Berachoth, 21 a, 31 a).

It is because I fear the Lord that I do not go to Schul [synagogue]. Many a day I feel that I would like to go—even though I no longer have need of it—for it has become a strong habit with me, this Schul-going. But I do not go. I bethink me of a story which my father—peace be to him—used to tell about their Count in Poland, where he lived. This Count was a very charitable man. Every day, when he came out of his house to go to the hunt, his doorstep would be full of beggars, and to all he gave. There was one beggar—his name was Mattis—who was there every day. No sooner did the Count come out of his door than there was Mattis crying, "O, your Grace, I *am* so poor and wretched." And the Count would give him bread or wood or money, as was his need. But in a day or two he would be there again, crying, "O, your Grace, I *am* so poor and wretched." Well, one day when there were not so many beggars the Count looked at Mattis, and his heart ached for the beggar. "It is sad," he said, "that an old, feeble man should have to beg here in the cold," and he gave orders to his servants that Mattis be given a gulden every week so long as he lived, that he need no longer beg. And Mattis was happy. He bought bread and herring, and a new coat—in short, he was a made man. But Mattis had gotten so used to standing every day on the Count's doorstep that he didn't know what else to do, and a few days thereafter, when the Count came out of his house to go to the hunt as usual, there was Mattis standing again on his doorstep. "For heaven's sake, Mattis," the Count cried, "what dost want now? Have I not provided for thee?" Then Mattis began to cry, "Yes, your Grace, I thank your Grace, but O, your Grace, I *was* so poor and wretched; O, I *was* so poor and wretched." The Count got terribly angry. He took Mattis by the collar and threw him down the steps, so that he fell and broke both his legs, sprained his hand, and bumped his head, and moreover he injured his inwards. Nobody blamed the Count. He had done what he could for the beggar, and he wanted Menuchah (rest). "So it is," concluded Genendel, "with the Lord and me, Rebbe Leben (dear Rabbi). For years I cried to him every day, and he has had mercy on me; he has not let me starve, though, God knows, there was often not enough from one day to the next. But now he has helped for good. He has done what he could for me, and now he wants to be rid of me, for, God knows, there are enough beggars to bother him. Nay, Rebbe Leben, whenever I feel I want to go to Schul I bethink me of Mattis, and stay at home."

But the parable of Rabbi and Emperor is dangerous teaching if it mean more than this: Man must not importune God. Against this may be set another Rabbinic parable[1]. A man visits his friend and the friend greets him cordially, placing him on the couch beside him. He comes again, and is given a chair; again and receives a stool. He comes a fourth time and the friend says, "The stool is too far off, I cannot fetch it for you." But God is not so; for whenever Israel knocks at the door of God's house the Holy One rejoices, as it is written: For what great nation is there that hath a God so nigh unto them as the Lord our God is, *whenever* we call? The Rabbis, like

[1] Midrash on Ps. iv.; T.B. Yoma 76 a. Cf. Bacher, *Agada der Tannaiten*, ii. 137.

ourselves, would have been shocked at the supposition that God is at any time inaccessible to the broken-hearted and contrite. "The gate of tears is never shut," said a Rabbi[1].

Much of what precedes touches only the surface of the subject; we must now try to penetrate a little deeper. The essential relevancy of prayer depends on the nature of God and his relation to man. If God is the absolute, if he is the unchangeable, then prayer must be identical with submission and praise. The worshipper registers his sense of the divine power and as a correlative his own weakness; he adds the corollary that the all-powerful is likewise the all-good. Praise has therefore always formed a large item in the liturgies of the religions which had their source in Judaism. In the Psalter, in the Prayers of Nehemiah and Daniel, on which so many subsequent prayers were modelled, praise is introductory to petition. The oldest of old Psalmic refrains is the *Hōdū*: O give thanks unto the Lord, for he is good; for his loving-kindness endureth for ever.

Rabbinic Judaism took a very strong line on this subject[2]. It attributed to Adam the authorship of Ps. xcii: It is a good thing to give thanks to the Lord and to sing praises to thy name, O Most High; and it declared that when all sacrifices cease in the Messianic age, for as men will no longer sin they will offer no more sin-offerings; when all propitiatory and penitential prayers are discontinued, for men will in that period of grace have nothing to repent of or ask pardon for,—when all other sacrifices and prayers cease, the thank-offering and the service of praise will remain eternally. Thus from Adam to the Messiah, in the Rabbinic conception, man's duty and delight is to utter the praises of God. First praise, then supplicate, is the recurrent Rabbinic maxim for writers of prayers. Praise God for sorrow as well as for happiness. What is an affliction of Love, asks the Talmud? It answers, among other things, Such affliction as does not deprive the sufferer of the power to pray[3]. So long as prayer is possible, God's hand, though heavy on the unhappy, rests on the unhappy not in anger but in love. The countless benedictions prescribed in the Talmud for every conceivable and inconceivable act of life are all praises. There may have been in this some notion of gratitude for favours to come; but this notion, however degrading as between man and his fellow, is

[1] T.B. Berachoth, 32 b.

[2] Leviticus Rabba, § 9: T.B. Berachoth, 6 and 31 b, and 32 a.

[3] T.B. Berachoth, 5 a. Cf. First Series, p. 147.

not a low conception as between man and his God—even if, while testifying thanks, the worshipper implies a hope. Or again, there may be in this rubric of praise an element of propitiation—you mollify an irresponsible autocrat by the incense of flattery. But such an idea cannot be said to have consciously invaded the mind of Pharisaism. In many "Royal" parables the relation of God to man is contrasted with, not equated to, the relation of earthly autocrat and his abject slave. The *mind* of Judaism came largely into the domain of prayer, for the study of the Law was not only in itself an act of worship, but the school was often the place of prayer. And the intellect, whether directed to universal history or to personal experience, perceived recurrent ground for praise and thanksgiving[1]. But prayer is not only or chiefly a matter of the mind; it is a matter of the heart.

Now, while the mind appreciates that the only prayer should be praise, the heart is not satisfied by eulogising God. Every term of praise may bring the Divine Presence nearer to Israel[2], but when that Presence is nearest man seeks to supplicate it as well as adore it. Through the whole history of human life runs the cry for mercy. As men suffer irrespective of creed, so do they all appeal to God's mercy; to quote the late S. Singer, "pain is undenominational and so is pity." And here we come face to face with a peculiar Rabinnic dualism—the Mercy and the Justice of God. A few citations will be better than a long exposition of this dualism. The righteous are they that strengthen God; they help him to be merciful. Why are the prayers of the righteous symbolised as a spade? Just as the spade turns the grain from place to place, so the prayers of the righteous turn the divine attributes from the attribute of wrath to the attribute of mercy[3]. And God himself prays to himself in the same strain. At the Creation God made himself a tent in Jerusalem, and therein he prayed. And he said: May it be my will that my children do my will, so that I destroy not my house of prayer. But when Israel's sins made the Holy One destroy the house, then God prayed: May it be my will that my children repent, so that I may rebuild my house. R. Ishmael relates how he once (as a priest) entered the innermost sanctuary to offer incense, and saw there God who asked a blessing, and Rabbi Ishmael said: May it be thy will that thy mercy subdue thy wrath, and God nodded in

[1] Cf. I. Abrahams, *Poetry and Religion*, pp. 52 *seq.*

[2] Genesis Rabba xlviii. § 7 (end).

[3] Tanḥuma, מקץ (end); T.B. Sukkah, 14 a.

assent[1]. Weber sees in such passages merely the notion of a supreme despot who may or may not permit mercy to temper justice. But though some of these passages are crude, and even childishly naïve, they represent a phase of the attempt to bring God into relation with man, an attempt which is at once the supreme aim and the despair of every religion. And the climax is reached when the Rabbis tell us that God teaches man the very formulae of prayer; he bids Moses to pray to him, and tells him to say: O God, turn the bitter into sweet[2]. "From thee I fly to thee," wrote Solomon Ibn Gabirol in his *Royal Crown*, the most inspired Hebrew hymn after the Psalter.

The just God judges, but his tender mercies are over all his works. It is this belief in the all-pervading mercy of God that makes Jesus' words, "Thy will, not mine," the supreme utterance of the Jewish consciousness on the subject of prayer. These words express more than resignation: they express also a confidence that God's will is man's ultimate good. Uttered in agony, they are rich in spiritual joy, for Gethsemane is a gate to Heaven. Prayer thus becomes something more than petition, something beyond praise; it becomes a harmony between the human and the divine. It is the divine in man going out to meet the divine in God; it is the upward rise of the soul to its heavenly fount. A praying man, as the Pharisees said, is in the Divine Presence[3]. Prayer, in the language of a Jewish mystic, is as flame to coal: it unites the upper and the lower worlds[4]. Prayer, said a Rabbi, is heart-service[5]; it lays the heart of man on the altar of God. No man prays acceptably unless he makes his heart flesh[6]. Thou shalt love the Lord thy God with all thy heart: thus is Israel warned that in the hour of prayer he must not have a divided heart, part for God, and part for worldly aspirations[7]. It is the fear of God that gives virtue to prayer. One self-inflicted heart-pang is more saving than many stripes[8]. Prayer turns aside doom, but it is prayer associated

[1] Midrash, Yalquṭ, on Ps. lxxvi. 3; T.B. Berachoth, 7 a. Cf. First Series, p. 146.

[2] Exodus Rabba, § 43.

[3] T.B. Sanhedrin, 22 a; Yoma, 53 b.

[4] Zohar ויקהל, 213 b. See *Jewish Encyclopedia* (J. W. Eisenstein), vol. x. p. 169, for further citations.

[5] Sifrê, ed. Friedmann, p. פ (on Deut. xi. 13); T.B. Taanith, 2 a.

[6] T.B. Soṭa, 5 a.

[7] Tanḥuma, on Deut. vi. 5.

[8] T.B. Berachoth, 7 a.

with charity and penitence[1]. Note, in passing, how the old magical force of prayer has been transfigured in such a saying—one of the most popular in the Jewish liturgy. God wants the heart, is another famous utterance. Prayer purifies[2]. God is the Fountain of Israel. As the water cleanses the unclean, so the Holy One cleanses Israel. Which goeth to which? The fountain to the defiled or the defiled to the fountain? The defiled goeth to the fountain, descends, and bathes. Thus is it with prayer. But the fountain is near. If thou canst not go to the house of prayer, pray on thy couch: if thou art unable to frame words, let thy heart meditate in silence[3]. And finally, Rabbi Eleazar said: Thus shall a man pray: "Do thy will, O God, in heaven above, and bestow tranquillity of spirit on those who fear thee below, and what is good in thine own sight do. Blessed art thou, O Lord, thou that hearest prayer[4]."

But there is neither space nor need to add more quotations. In his fine book on *The Psalms in Human Life*, Mr R. E. Prothero (Lord Ernle) says: "The Psalms, then, are a mirror in which each man sees the motions of his own soul. They express in exquisite words the kinship which every thoughtful human heart craves to find with a supreme, unchanging, loving God, who will be to him a protector, guardian, and friend. They utter the ordinary experiences, the familiar thoughts of men; but they give to these a width of range, an intensity, a depth, and an elevation which transcend the capacity of the most gifted. They translate into speech the spiritual passion of the loftiest genius; they also utter, with the beauty born of truth and simplicity, and with exact agreement between the feeling and the expression, the inarticulate and humble longings of the unlettered peasant. So is it that, in every country, the language of the Psalms has become part of the daily life of nations, passing into their proverbs, mingling with their conversation, and used at every critical stage of existence."

[1] Jer. Sanhedrin, x. 28 c; Numbers Rabba, § 12; Pesiqta (Buber), 191 a. It is in this sense that we must interpret the saying of Eleazar b. Jacob that "one hour of prayer is better than good deeds" יפה שעה אחת בתפלה יותר ממעשים טובים.

[2] San. 106 b; Exod. R. xxii; Mechilta (בשלח), § 6. [3] Yalquṭ, on Ps. iv.

[4] T.B. Berachoth, 29 b (towards end). On the other fine remarks of this early Rabbi (Eleazar b. Hyrqanos) on prayer, cf. Bacher, *Agada der Tannaiten*, i. 108–110 (ed. 2, 103–4). These sayings are, in essence, more closely parallel to Mark xiv. 36, Matth. xxvi, 39, Luke xxii. 42, than is Aboth ii. 4, though that passage is also rightly quoted in the commentaries on the Gospels, and is an apt illustration of John vii. 17, just as Eleazar's saying is of Matth. vi. 10, etc.

Mr Prothero traces out, by well-chosen and eloquently described historical instances, how these Psalms, with their deep consciousness of sin, their fine note of humility in the hour of victory, "Not unto us, O Lord, not unto us," their contrite yet assured aspirations after a renewed communion with God,—how these Psalms have become the breviary and viaticum of humanity. In estimating the Jewish conception of prayer, some are apt to forget that the Psalms were not only Jewish in origin, but the most constantly prized, the most dearly beloved of all the sacred literature of Judaism[1]. Priests and Levites sang psalms at the daily sacrifices, and when the Temple fell, psalms took the place of sacrifices. The Psalms have been to the Jews a well-spring of consolation, a support in tribulation, a reassurance under sin. And the Jewish theory of prayer is—the Psalter. Rabbinism re-interpreted and re-enforced the Psalter, but abated nothing and surrendered nothing of it. Rabbinism saw in the Psalter, in Heine's words, "sunrise and sunset, birth and death, promise and fulfilment—the whole drama of humanity." And the synagogue absorbed the Psalter into its inmost soul. In the eleventh century, Ibn Gabirol wrote the following Invocation to Prayer, which appears in many modern Jewish liturgies, and is uttered by many Jewish worshippers daily in the early morning:

[1] An inspiring and pathetic chapter could be written on the use of the Psalms in Jewish life. *The Authorised Daily Prayer Book*, ed. S. Singer, contains about half the Psalter. But besides liturgical use, there are many historical records of the application of the Psalms in times of stress under danger and martyrdom, of gratitude under salvation, of acceptance of God's will and inspiration to courageous endeavour—which prove the fertile influence of the Psalter on Jewish life in all ages. Here is one famous instance. In the tenth century, the captain of a corsair vessel had captured Moses b. Ḥanoch and his fair wife. The pirate became enamoured of his beautiful captive. One day she asked her husband in Hebrew if those drowned in the sea rose again at the Resurrection. He answered her with the Psalmic text: "The Lord said, I will bring again from Bashan, I will bring again from the depths of the sea" (Ps. lxviii. 22). Fortified with this hope, and resolved to save her honour, she threw herself in the sea. So, too, Nathan b. Yeḥiel (c. 1035—1106), the author of the *Aruch*, when all his sons died in infancy, solaced his broken heart by combining two consecutive texts of Ps. cxvi.: "Trouble found I and sorrow, and I called on the name of the Lord." This was not merely an act of resignation (as in T.B. Berachoth 60 b) but a sturdy determination to devote to the service of heaven a life with little earthly joy left in it. Cf. Nathan's poem in Kohut's edition viii. 299 and *Jewish Encyclopedia*, ix. 180.

i

At the dawn I seek thee,
Refuge, Rock sublime;
Set my prayer before thee
in the morning,
And my prayer at eventime.

ii

I before thy greatness
Stand and am afraid:
All my secret thoughts thine
eye beholdeth
Deep within my bosom laid.

iii

And withal what is it
Heart and tongue can do?
What is this my strength, and
what is even
This the spirit in me too?

iv

But indeed man's singing
May seem good to thee;
So I praise thee, singing, while
there dwelleth
Yet the breath of God in me.

This rendering is by Mrs Salaman[1], and it beautifully and exactly reproduces the Hebrew. "Mechanism," "pharisaism," and all such phrases are intolerably inappropriate when applied to a Rabbinic theory of prayer which, despite all the vagaries and intricacies of its later liturgical rules and rubrics, found and continues to find its frequent expression in such meditations as this.

[1] In *Songs of Exile* (Macmillan) and *Service of the Synagogue* (Routledge). In Hebrew the prayer is included in Baer's classical edition of the daily Liturgy, and in many other versions, including the Annotated edition of the Singer Prayer-book, and the Prayer-book of the Liberal Jewish Synagogue, London. The poem, in Hebrew and English, also appears in *Solomon Ibn Gabirol* (the Jewish Classics Series, Philadelphia, 1923), p. 2.

## XII. THE LORD'S PRAYER.

Impressed by citations, made by previous writers of parallels to the Lord's Prayer, and possibly moved also by a desire to express disapproval of contemporary liturgical innovations, Hugo Grotius offers the generalisation that the "very Lord of the Church kept aloof from every affectation of unnecessary novelty[1]." Similarly, in modern times, several Christian theologians have recognised in the Lord's Prayer a strong Jewish influence. "True prayer," says Wellhausen, "is the creation of the Jews, and the Paternoster also follows Jewish models." But as he justly adds this is not identical with the assumption that the Paternoster is a mere "cento" from any existing prayers of the Synagogue[2]. It is not unnatural that the failure to discriminate between slavish imitation of Jewish formulae and a general resemblance to Jewish liturgical ideas, has led to an even more extreme claim of absolute independence. Thus E. Bischoff categorically asserts that from its first phrase "Our Father," to the final "Amen," the Lord's Prayer is altogether original[3].

1 The passage (in comment on Matt. vi. 9) runs thus: "Docent autem nos ea quae ex Hebraeorum libris ab aliis sunt citata, non tam formulam hanc à Christo suis verbis conceptam quam in eam congestum quicquid Hebraeorum precibus erat laudabile: sicut et in admonitionibus passim utitur notis eo seculo proverbiis. Tam longe abfuit ipse Dominus Ecclesiae ab omni affectatione non necessariae novitatis" (*Annotationes in Libros Evangeliorum*, Amsterdam 1641, p. 142). Lightfoot, a little later (1648), speaks in much the same terms.

2 Wellhausen on Matt. vi. 9: "Das wahre Gebet ist die Schöpfung der Juden, und auch das Vaterunser folgt jüdischen Vorbildern, wenngleich es nicht bloss ex formulis Hebraeorum zusammengesetzt ist." Wellhausen finds a closer parallel to the Lord's Prayer in the Qaddish than in the Amidah. Both these Jewish prayers went through a long liturgical history. See p. 102 below. J. Jacobs uses the term "cento." He says: "The Lord's Prayer is a cento from the Jewish Amidah, being a shortened form of five of the original six of the Eighteen Blessings" (*Jewish Contributions to Civilization*, Philadelphia, 1919, p. 99).

3 "Auch im AT. kommt 'unser Vater in Himmel' nicht vor; Jesus ist vielmehr, soviel wie ich sehe, der *erste*, der diesen Ausdruck als Anrede für Gott anwendet" (Dalman, as Bischoff regretfully concedes, is of quite the opposite opinion). Again: "*Amen* als Schluss eines eigenen Gebetes ist *erst* von Jesus eingeführt" (*Jesus und die Rabbinen*, Leipzig, 1905, pp. 75 and 82). The chief weakness of Bischoff's argument is that while he sets Jewish liturgical parallels at far too late a date, he assumes that *every word* in Matthew vi. 9—13 was actually spoken by Jesus himself.

There is in particular one petition of the Lord's Prayer which gives us the key to a truer estimate. It is a petition common to Matthew (vi. 12) and Luke (xi. 4). The wording, it is true, differs, and that not merely or chiefly in Luke's use of ἁμαρτίας (sins) for Matthew's ὀφειλήματα (debts). This difference is not very significant, and more seems to have been made of it than is justifiable. Matthew no doubt points to a more accurate reproduction of an Aramaic original. But as Luke, in the second clause, actually introduces the verb (παντὶ ὀφείλοντι ἡμῖν), his use of ἁμαρτίας may be no more than an elegance of style. The significant difference lies rather in the introductory phrase; for while Matthew has ὡς καὶ ἡμεῖς ἀφήκαμεν, Luke's reading is καὶ γὰρ αὐτοὶ ἀφίομεν. Chase (*op. cit.*, p. 56) thinks Luke here more original, and that in its primitive form the clause ran "remit to us and we will also remit." So regarded, "the whole petition becomes thus a prayer and a promise, a prayer for forgiveness, and a promise that the suppliant *will* forgive." This, however, seems less in keeping with the general Gospel teaching (cf. Mk xi. 25), which would rather require human forgiveness to *precede* the hope of divine remission. Dr Chase ingeniously confirms his view by a citation of Matt. xviii. 23 ff. "This interpretation [that the future "we also will remit" is original] has very strong support in the parable of the unmerciful servant. Here the divine forgiveness precedes, and is represented as the model of, human forgiveness (comp. Col. iii. 13, Eph. iv. 32). The servant is forgiven, but lacks the grace to forgive. The remission of the debt which he owed becomes invalid, when he refuses remission to another." Matthew's text of the Lord's Prayer reverses the order, and places man's forgiveness first. As he forgives so shall he be forgiven. And of course Matt. xviii. 23 ff. can be explained as illustrating the principle that "the divine forgiveness is represented as conditional upon the forgiveness by men of their fellows" (W. C. Allen). And certainly this accords with what follows the Lord's Prayer in Matthew (vi. 14, 15): "For if ye forgive men their trespasses, your heavenly Father will also forgive you. But if ye forgive not men their trespasses, neither will

Yet Wellhausen, like many others, denies the latter opinion (seeing that the Lord's Prayer is not found in Mark). Harnack strongly protests, but he reduces Matthew's *seven* petitions to *three*. Bischoff's argument is therefore unsound at both ends. An apt comment on his idea as to "Amen" is to be read in F. H. Chase's *The Lord's Prayer in the Early Church* ("Texts and Studies," Cambridge, vol. i. no. 3, 1891): "That the true text of St Matthew's Gospel had no doxology at the close of the Lord's Prayer cannot be considered doubtful" (p. 168).

your Father forgive your trespasses." And this agrees with the teaching of Sirach, where man's pardon of his neighbour seems a precedent to God's pardon of the forgiving man[1].

It is clear that, whichever form we regard as more primitive, some sort of conditional connection is established between man's forgiveness and God's. If this be so, we have in this clause of the Lord's Prayer a petition which is altogether without Jewish parallel. The idea is Jewish, but not its *liturgical* adaptation. It may be interesting to record that it is only quite the other day that anything of the kind was ever included in a Synagogue Service. The following hymn, based on Sirach, was written by the present writer in order to fill up what seemed to him a liturgical gap.

In suppliance before the Lord
  We stand, and pardon crave
For cruel deed and wrathful word;
  O Father, deign to save!
For mercy unto Thee we pray,
  O teach us also mercy's way!

Healing from Thee we freely seek,
  Shall we not strive to heal?
Do we, on others, anger wreak,
  And dare for grace appeal?
O, in our heart may pardon live,
  Ere we entreat Thee to forgive!

To fellow-men, whom rancour lured,
  Let us forbearance show;
Forgive the hurt we have endured,
  Then to our Father go.
Let flesh 'gainst flesh from anger cease,
  And find at one Atonement's peace[2]!

It will be noted that in this hymn there is no condition asserted from the point of view of God's forgiveness. Man ought not to expect to receive what he is not ready to give—it is good discipline to lay this truth to heart. But, none the less, God's forgiveness is absolute. It was found hard by some Rabbis to admit that even the future Messianic redemption was conditional on man's previous repentance. The point was an early topic of discussion (T.B. Sanhedrin 97 b, foot of page). In the Jewish liturgies, man admits his sin and prays for pardon—he

[1] Ecclus. xxviii. 3. Cf. above First Series, p. 155.

[2] Printed (with some verbal variations) in the hymn-book of the Jewish Liberal Synagogue, London.

throws himself unreservedly on the divine mercy and knows no limits to it. Never does a Synagogue prayer assign any limits to it. Hence the Jew prays for forgiveness *sans phrase.* Hence the normal Synagogue form is: "Forgive us, O our Father, for we have sinned: pardon us, O our King, for we have transgressed. Blessed art thou, O Lord, who art gracious and dost abundantly forgive[1]." Precedent to this is the prayer of Repentance: "Cause us to return, O our Father, unto thy Law; draw us near, O our King, unto thy service, and bring us back in perfect repentance unto thy presence. Blessed art thou, O Lord, who delightest in repentance." But there is no conditional connection in this collocation of ideas, the prayer for power to repent and the prayer for pardon, though it was probably suggested by Isaiah lv. 7: "Let the wicked forsake his way, and the unrighteous man his thoughts: and let him return unto the Lord, and he will have mercy upon him; and to our God, for he will abundantly pardon." Liturgically, however, the Synagogue did not make man's repentance a precise *condition* of God's pardon. Still less did it make man's forgiveness a condition. The unforgiving man does not deserve pardon, but who does? The unforgiving, we can hear the older Jew saying, is most in need of forgiveness, precisely of his own hard-heartedness. Mr G. W. Gwilliam acutely sees this distinction when he writes with reference to the Lord's Prayer: "It cannot be, as is sometimes stated in devotional exegesis, that we are to pray God to measure His boundless pity by our imperfect attempts to forgive; but we plead that we have endeavoured to remove what would be a bar to His grant of pardon: and this is expressed clearly in Luke[2]." But not in Matthew, surely, especially when we read the verses that, in the first Gospel, follow the Lord's Prayer. "A condition is laid down," as J. C. Lambert observes[3]. Hence, Eb. Nestle (expounding Zahn) goes too far when he writes: "A Jew knowing nothing of Christ, and having no wish to have anything to do with Him, was able and is still able to-day to pray it. The saying of Matthew v. 17 that He came to fulfil, is true also of the Lord's Prayer[4]." On the whole no Jew feels himself out of sympathy with the Prayer, except with regard to the condition regarding forgiveness apparently imposed in Matthew's form,

[1] This is the sixth of the "Eighteen Benedictions" (*Authorised Daily Prayer Book*, p. 46).

[2] Hastings' (one volume) *Dictionary of the Bible* (1909), p. 553.

[3] Hastings, *A Dictionary of Christ and the Gospels*, vol. ii (1908), p. 62.

[4] *Op. cit.*, p. 60.

which has no Jewish liturgical parallel whatever. It is not here suggested that, on a valuation of significance, Matthew is higher or lower than the Jewish sentiment. But he is not at the same standpoint.

The point strikes very deeply. Jesus could be very exacting in the light of his teaching on forgiveness of man by man. Moreover, if the son of man has power to forgive[1], then in a sense God himself forgives through man (cf. Ephesians iv. 32), not through man's intermediation but through man's exemplification of the divine mercy. This would involve a *nuance* unfamiliar if not unknown to Jewish theology. All these considerations suggest the conclusion that this particular petition in the Lord's Prayer emanates, not from Jewish models, but from the peculiar thought of Jesus himself.

Hence, while seeing as every student must see the close parallels that exist between the Lord's Prayer and Jewish thought and liturgy, Wellhausen is right in regarding it as an exaggeration to describe the former as compiled "ex formulis Hebraeorum[2]." Regarded more generally it cannot be appropriately described as a "cento." Such a compilation would present more of a patch-work appearance. "As to the beauty of the prayer," to use Mr C. G. Montefiore's words, "there can be small question. It is not original in its ideas[3], but it is original in the choice of ideas, and in their grouping. Whoever put it together chose with fine religious feeling and insight." It is interesting to compare with the Lord's Prayer a real "cento," consciously put together and with considerable skill in a publication issued in Berlin a few years back[4].

Our Father, who art in Heaven[a]. Hallowed be Thine exalted Name in the world which Thou didst create according to Thy will. May Thy Kingdom and Thy lordship come speedily, and be acknowledged by all the world, that Thy Name may be praised in all eternity[b]. May Thy will be done in Heaven, and also on earth give

[a] A common invocation in the Jewish prayer book (Dalman, *Die Worte Jesu*, 152 ff.).

[b] In the Qaddish, in the Qedushah, and in the Eighteen Benedictions of the daily liturgy, after Ezekiel xxxviii. 23.

[1] ἐπὶ τῆς γῆς Mt. ix. 6; Mk ii. 10; Lk. v. 4.

[2] This is Wetstein's phrase: "Tota haec oratio ex formulis Hebraeorum concinnata."

[3] This must be qualified by what is said in the text above.

[4] *Christentum und Judentum, Parallelen.* I believe that Dr I. Elbogen was the editor of this interesting little work. There are two Appendices, I. "Die Bergpredigt nach jüdischen Quellen," and II. "Das Vaternoster in jüdischer Fassung." It is this second Appendix that is translated above, with the references of the original.

tranquillity of spirit to those that fear Thee, yet in all things do what seemeth good to Thee[c]. Let us enjoy the bread daily apportioned to us[d]. Forgive us, our Father, for we have sinned[e]; forgive also all who have done us injury[f]; even as we also forgive all[g]. And lead us not into temptation, but keep us far from all evil[h]. For thine is the greatness and the power and the dominion, the victory and the majesty, yea all in Heaven and on earth. Thine is the Kingdom, and Thou art Lord of all beings[i] for ever! Amen.

[c] Tosefta Berachoth iii. 7; T.B. Berachoth 29 b; cf. I Samuel iii. 18, I Macc. iii. 60.

[d] Proverbs xxx. 8; Mechilta to Exod. xvi. 4; T.B. Bezah 16 a.

[e] Daily prayer in the Eighteen Benedictions.

[f] T.B. Megillah 28 a.

[g] Mishnah Yoma (end). Cf. Tosefta Taanith i. 8; T.B. Taanith 16 a[1].

[h] Daily morning prayer. Cf. T.B. Berachoth 16 b; Sanhedrin 107 a; Qiddushin 81 b; Sukkah 52 b.

[i] I Chronicles xxix. 11—13.

This is a good "cento"; with some refinement of style, it could be made even better. A very beautiful ancient example of a Jewish "cento" is to be found in what is known as the shortened form of the 12 or 13 central paragraphs of the Eighteen Benedictions. There are various forms of this abbreviation, to which apparently reference is already made in the Mishnah. In place of the longer prayer, says R. Joshua, a prayer containing the "substance of the Eighteen" was all that was necessary for daily use[2]. Joshua ben Ḥananya was a disciple of Joḥanan b. Zakkai, and his view therefore belongs to the first century. The Mishnah, however, does not give us the text of the shortened form. This is displayed in the Talmud, being cited in the name of the third-century Rabbi, Samuel, though there is no reason to assume that he was the author of it[3]. A fine English translation may be read in S. Singer's edition of the Hebrew and English Prayer Book[4].

[1] As argued above, these quotations do not bear out the precise phraseology of the text.

[2] Mishnah, Berachoth iv. 3, when R. Eleazar pronounced against *all* fixed forms. The shortened form is usually known as *Habinenu* from the first word (הביננו). The original form of the Eighteen Benedictions was shorter than those in the modern synagogue rituals. A shorter (and clearly more primitive) form "Palestinian" was published by S. Schechter (*J.Q.R.* x. 654), and is reprinted by G. Dalman in *Die Worte Jesu*, 1898, p. 299. This is not included in the English translation of Dalman's work. The German edition also contains the Palestinian and Babylonian versions of *Habinenu* (p. 304). It also includes the Qaddish. For the present liturgical texts see the Authorised Hebrew Prayer Book (ed. S. Singer) with the present writer's Annotations (pp. 37, 42 ff., 55).

[3] T.B. Berachoth 29 a.

[4] P. 55.

The Lord's Prayer, however, is clearly not altogether of this type. Composed under the inspiration of Hebraic ideas, modelled to a large extent on Jewish forms, it was not in its primitive form a mosaic but a whole and fresh design. Originality in prayers is almost always relative. It is remarkable, for instance, that just when a Psalmist spoke of a "new song" he was liable to be least original. In the mouth of Isaiah (xlii. 10) the phrase was an original note, for the "new song" of which he speaks was not inspired by simple gratitude for new mercies, but corresponds to that wider sweep of the creative imagination which led the Prophet of the Return to "announce new things," affecting not Israel only but "the end of the earth, the countries and the inhabitants thereof." The Psalmists, however, take up Isaiah's phrase, and with it reproduce Isaiah's message[1]. *Their* newness consisted in applying the new prophetic message liturgically. In other words, besides originality of idea, there may be a liturgical originality of application—and though the second type is not of the same rank as the first, it is none the less real. The relation is not unlike the relation of applied to pure science.

As it stands in Matthew (and even in Luke) the Lord's Prayer is a mosaic. It is very generally felt that it has suffered accretion. But this impression of a mosaic is weaker if we suppose (with Harnack and others)[2] that originally the Paternoster consisted only of *three* petitions: "(*a*) Give us to-day our bread for the morrow, (*b*) forgive us our debts as we forgive our debtors, (*c*) lead us not into temptation[3]." The second of these three petitions was, as has been argued above, certainly not derived from any other extant Jewish prayer. On the other hand the petition "Thy will be done *as in heaven so on earth*" (peculiar to Matthew, for its presence in Luke is not authentic) has distinctly a derived appearance[4]. The phrase "Thy will be done" by itself

[1] This is especially true of Pss. xcvi. and xcviii. 1, these "evidently involve reminiscences of Isaiah" (Cheyne); a "lyrical counterpart of Isaiah xl—lvi" (Kirkpatrick).

[2] J. Weiss and Loisy contest this opinion.

[3] Cf. C. G. Montefiore, *op. cit.*, p. 534. On the other hand Luke (though he is shorter) agrees with Matthew in the opening petitions "Hallowed be Thy name: Thy kingdom come." It is these petitions, when combined with the remainder, that give the mosaic appearance of the prayer, especially when rounded off by Matthew's doxology.

[4] It is closely allied to the prayer of Eleazar b. Hyrqanos (T.B. Berachoth 29 b), which may be as early as 65 A.D. In the parallel in the Tosefta (Zuckermandel, p. 7) for בתחת is read בארץ which makes the similarity even closer. Of course the ultimate source is Biblical (Ps. cxxxv. 6).

might be original (cf. Matt. xxvi. 42, Luke xxii. 42) but hardly in this context. Then, too, it is difficult to resist the suggestion that the final petition (ἀλλὰ ῥῦσαι ἡμᾶς ἀπὸ τοῦ πονηροῦ) has a reference to the Jewish doctrine of the evil yeṣer[1]. Luke's omission of it (in certain MSS) confirms the suggestion that the phrase is redactionary in Matthew.

Such mosaic appearance, as the Lord's Prayer really presents, is explicable on the theory that it is the work not of Jesus himself but of disciples who knew his career and interpreted his mind. It is possible to find for each of the clauses basis either in the experiences or doctrines attributed to Jesus. The doctrines are expressed more dynamically, but the Lord's Prayer would weld them into a static whole. This theory would account both for the close parallel to Jewish prayer and for a certain intrinsic difference. The compilers (on this view) would be men familiar alike with the mind of Jesus and with the simple prayers of the early Synagogue.

The variations between Matthew and Luke belong to an interesting general problem. Do variants in ancient documents strengthen or weaken their credibility? Does the existence of two accounts, which agree in some respects and differ in others, prove both false? Certainly it would seem so on any theory of verbal inspiration. The verbal inspiration failing, the whole must be untrue, unless we assume that the variants refer to two different occasions, both of which are recorded with meticulous accuracy. One's inability to accept this does tend to scepticism regarding both accounts. But there is another way of looking at the matter. Two accounts may both be true *because* they are not identical. The very fact of their differences may point to a genuine tradition rather than to mere copying one by the other. A copyist would be more likely to reproduce the exact terms of his model.

Though there are phrases in Matthew which make one inclined to prefer his version of the Lord's Prayer, it is generally felt Luke places it in a more natural setting. The contexts are not only different, they are somewhat inconsistent. The "hypocrites" love to stand[2] and pray in

[1] Cf. particularly Taylor, *Sayings of the Jewish Fathers*, ed. 1, p. 142 (ed. 2, p. 128).

[2] On standing in Synagogue, cf. above First Series, p. 8. On posture in prayer, cf. the excellent remarks of L. Ginzberg, in *Jewish Encyclopedia*, i. 290: "About the time of Jesus there was a dispute between the Hillelites and the Shammaites concerning the proper attitude in which to recite the Shema. The latter in opposition to the former, who were indifferent as to posture, insisted that this prayer must be said standing in the morning; but that, in the evening, the posture of solemn

the Synagogues, "that they might be seen of men." But the disciples are (like Daniel vi. 10) to retire to an inner chamber and pray in private. So far Matthew (vi. 5, 6). But in Luke, Jesus is himself seen of his disciples, one of whom, having seen him in prayer, said unto him: "Lord, teach us to pray" (Luke xi. 1). There is no wisdom, however, in taking every phrase of Matthew as implying an attack on Pharisaic methods of prayer. Lightfoot's quotations here are peculiarly inept, he actually cites admirable Pharisaic prescriptions as defects when they are truly merits. In certain commentaries on Matthew vi. 5 *seq.* we have a suggestive instance of the manner in which the Gospel criticisms of the Pharisees have been exaggerated by modern German theologians. Matthew distinctly complains that "vain repetitions" and wordy prayers were the fault of heathens[1]. But Lightfoot, J. Weiss, Bousset, and Bischoff persist in applying the complaint to the Pharisees[2]. So little was it a Pharisaic institution to pray at excessive length in the age of Jesus[3] that the same Eleazar b. Hyrqanos already cited lays it down that there was no rule on the subject, except that there should be no rule. A disciple of this Rabbi prayed briefly and his comrades jeeringly called him the "Shortener." This was reported to Eleazar,

inclination was the appropriate one. This dispute lasted until nearly the end of the first Christian century (Mishnah Ber. i. 3). The chief prayer, the Eighteen Benedictions, was, however, always said standing. Hence the name *Amidah* (Standing) for the Eighteen Benedictions." The whole subject of forms of Adoration is well treated by Dr Ginzberg in the article quoted.

[1] Weiss suggests that the reference is to magical formulae. "A man shall not stand in the midst of a plain and pray *like the heathens*" says a late Jewish source (Yalquṭ Deut. § 934), nor in the public way, but shall stand by a tree or a wall. So Hezekiah acted (II Kings xx. 2).

[2] J. Weiss, *Die Schriften des Neuen Testaments* (1906), vol. i. p. 263; Bousset, *Die Religion des Judentums* (ed. 2, 1906, p. 205); Bischoff, *op. cit.*, p. 70. See I. Elbogen's criticism of Bousset in *Die Religionsanschauungen der Pharisäer*, Berlin, 1904, p. 80.

[3] Bischoff (p. 71) quotes T.B. Berachoth 36 b (read 32 b) in which it is said that the former pietists spent an hour before prayer, an hour at prayer, and an hour after prayer thrice daily. But this was a merely fanciful exaggeration. The real passage is in the Mishnah (Ber. v. 1): "Man must not stand to pray except in a reverential frame of mind. The earlier pietists used to wait an hour before praying in order to attain to a devotional spirit." Neither here nor in the Talmud is there any question of prolonging the prayers beyond the set forms. Kohler (*J.E.* i. 28) quotes a similar admonition from the *Apostolic Constitutions*, vii. 24, "Pray thrice a day, *preparing yourselves beforehand*, so as to be worthy of being called the children of the Father, lest when ye call him 'Father' unworthily you be reproached by Him."

who rejoined: "He was no briefer than Moses, whose prayer for Miriam's recovery consisted only of five words" (Numbers xii. 13). On another occasion, a disciple prayed at length, and they dubbed him "Prolonger." Whereupon Eleazar said: "He was no longer than Moses, who fell down before the Lord forty days and forty nights" (Deut. ix. 18)[1]. In course of time the Synagogue liturgy tended to become very long and to include many repetitions. But all liturgies are inclined to prolixity with age. Not that there is an intrinsic evil in length or repetition. These qualities sometimes arise from the historical circumstances of liturgical development. The two-fold recitation of the Lord's Prayer itself in the Church, like the manifolding of the Qaddish in the Synagogue, was due to the combination of various offices once distinct into a single office. The real point of the Gospel reprobation is not against Pharisaic prayer, but against ostentatious prayer, and ostentation is neither a vice from which Pharisees were free, nor a vice of which they had a monopoly. As Dr Oman truly says[2]: "Most of what he (Jesus) says to the Scribes and Pharisees applies to the dangers of outward organised religion at all times." Or to quote that older Christian writer, Chrysostom[3], to whom one rarely turns without profit, "Here it is well to sigh aloud and to wail bitterly: for not only do we imitate the hypocrites, but we have even surpassed them." Pharisaism, because of its theory of Law, was more liable to the fault than less legalistic systems. But in the ultimate diagnosis the fault is not Pharisaic, it is a fault of human nature[4], which needs stern rebuke by the homilists of every age. Unfortunately insincerity is a hydra which to-day's denunciation cannot scotch for to-morrow.

The initial likelihood that Jesus did himself formulate a short prayer is often supported by the example of many of the Pharisees. It certainly was a frequent custom with the Rabbinic teachers to use or

1 Mechilta on Exod. xv. 25 (ed. Friedmann, p. 45 b). Eleazar sums up in the maxim: "There is an hour to be brief and an hour to be long" (יש שעה לקצר ויש שעה להאריך). He went so far as to deny that prayer by rule was true prayer at all (Mishnah Berachoth ii. 4). For other remarkable sayings of Eleazar on the subject of prayer (it was he who said: "Know before whom thou standest") see Bacher, *Agada der Tannaiten*, ii. 108 (ed. 2, p. 103). Cf. p. 84 above.

2 *Grace and Personality*, ed. 2, 1919, p. 171.

3 Hom. xx. on Matt. Oxford, 1843, i. p. 306.

4 Cf. above First Series, p. 159. It should be added that some things which, observed by an outside critic, seem ostentatious, take on another aspect when experienced by a devotee from within.

compose a favourite form. Do the terms of the Lord's Prayer fit in with such a parallel? Dr Plummer[1] asks us to "notice how entirely free from Jewish elements the Prayer is. It is not addressed to the 'Lord God of Israel,' nor does it ask for blessings upon Israel." But this is precisely a feature of the short Rabbinic prayers associated with the names of individual Rabbis. They are remarkable for the rarity of their references to Israel[2]. In this respect, the analogy with the Rabbinic prayers is close.

Interesting is the problem of the *number*. The Lord's Prayer uses the *plural*; the Rabbinic prayers for the most part the *singular*. Does the opening in Luke (Πάτερ)[3] as contrasted with the opening in Matthew (Πάτερ ἡμῶν) point to a primitive form from which *our* and *us* were absent? The detail is not of great moment, for it is the fact that various texts of the Rabbinic prayers differ in this respect, some texts using the singular (as "My God" and "Our God" in Berachoth 16 b)[4]. Yet it must be confessed that the change from singular to plural is at times clearly due to liturgical pressure. Thus the Talmudic early morning prayer: "May it be Thy will, O Lord *my* God, and God of *my* fathers" (Ber. 60 b) becomes in the liturgy "O Lord *our* God and God of *our* fathers[5]." Even more obvious is this change in regard to Jeremiah xvii. 14: "Heal *me*, O Lord, and *I* shall be healed; save *me*, and *I* shall be saved; for Thou art *my* praise." In the liturgy (p. 47) this becomes: "Heal *us*, O Lord, and *we* shall be healed; save *us*, and *we* shall be saved; for Thou art *our* praise." It was not, however, till

[1] Intern. Comm. on Luke xi. 2 (p. 295), where Latham, *Pastor Pastorum*, p. 416, is quoted.

[2] Cf. the prayers in T.B. Berachoth 16 b ff.; R. Eleazar's prayer Ber. 29 b; Ber. 60 a—b; Yoma 87 b. As Rabbi Eleazar's prayer has been often cited, the text is here quoted in the original:

עשה רצונך בשמים ממעל׳ ותן נחת רוח ליראיך מתחת׳ והטוב בעיניך עשה׳ ברוך אתה יי שומע תפלה:

On the reading cf. p. 91 above; Taylor, *op. cit.*, p. 125.

[3] On *Abba* (Father) as an invocation in prayer see K. Kohler's valuable article in *Jewish Encyclopedia*, i. 28. "Abba," says Dr Kohler, "was the formula for addressing God most familiar to Jewish saints of the New Testament times." Cf. the early (pre-Christian) reference in T.B. Taanith 23 a, where the invocation Abba is cited as used by Simeon b. Sheṭaḥ (second to first cents. B.C. Cf. Schürer, 1, i. 298).

[4] See Rabbinovicz, *Dikduke Soferim* (Variae Lectiones in Mischnam et in Talmud Babylonium), vol. i. pp. 76 ff.; Annotated edition of the Singer Prayer-Book, pp. xix, lxiii.

[5] There is, however, MS authority for the plural in the Munich Codex.

the beginning of the fourth century that any Rabbi sought to make it a rule that prayers must be in the plural. It was in regard to this very point that Abaye (died 339) declared: "A man must always associate himself (even in private prayer) with the community[1]."

Another attractive question is this: Are the final petitions in Matthew's version *connected* as effect and cause? Is "bring us not into temptation," to be interpreted by "but deliver us from the evil one"? It would be natural to assume so, were it not for the omission of the second clause in those MSS of Luke on which, e.g., the R.V. so far relies as to delete it. The two ideas are indeed associated in Talmudic prayers, which are ancient, but whose antiquity is not demonstrably older than the second century[2]. If "the evil one" is the Rabbinic yeṣer ha-ra ("Evil Inclination"), the association with temptation is explicable enough. Of the Evil yeṣer, Dr Schechter says that its "main activity consists in seducing and tempting[3]." Yet it may be doubted whether "temptation" (Hebrew *nissayon*, Greek πειρασμός) bore this meaning in the first century. The Greek verb (πειράζειν) is the ordinary LXX translation of the Hebrew *nissâh*, which as Driver points out "is a neutral word, and means to *test* or *prove* a person[4]." Man's prayer, to be spared the ordeal of such trial, is natural enough. The ordeal is universal[5], yet God only subjects to it those who are capable of bearing it, as the potter tests by striking only sound vessels, not those with flaw; the flax-worker only beats out his good threads; the husbandman only puts the yoke on a strong animal. In another Midrash the figure is that God tests men according to their power of endurance, just as the refiner puts silver in the fire, but gold in the crucible[6]. Such trial is an exaltation of the righteous, such as Abraham, to whom the trial (*nissâh*) becomes as a ship's pennant (*nês*), adorning it and proclaiming its worth[7]. In the early part of the second century

[1] T.B. Berachoth 29b. Cf. p. 81 above.

[2] T.B. Berachoth 16b, 17b, 60b (especially the last). These passages are quoted in full and translated by Taylor, *op. cit.*, Excursus V. ("The Lord's Prayer").

[3] S. Schechter, *Some Aspects of Rabbinic Theology*, p. 248.

[4] Driver's note on Exod. xvii. 2 (in the Cambridge Bible for Schools) is very instructive. On the other hand, the use of "temptation" in the first chapter of the Epistle of James may illustrate the double use of the term. But could the author of the chapter have known the Lord's Prayer?

[5] Cf. First Series, p. 115. Cf. p. 206 below.

[6] Genesis Rabba, ch. xxxii (ed. Theodor, p. 290). Cf. I Cor. x. 13.

[7] Gen. R. lv., quoting Psalm lx. 6, with a play on נסה and נס; Yalquṭ Samuel, § 89.

we find an opinion that it was right to place oneself into temptation *in order* to overcome it[1]. But David who first challenged God to *try* him ("*Examine me, O Lord, and prove me*") was glad to cry off ("*Enter not into judgment with thy servant, for in thy sight shall no man living be justified*[2]"). But the outstanding instance is Solomon, an awful example of the fall of the self-confident. This was why, we are told, the Law so rarely assigns reasons for its injunctions. "In two cases the Torah gave reasons and the greatest of men stumbled over them." For the Law said: the King shall not multiply horses, lest he cause Israel to return to Egypt; nor shall he multiply wives, that his heart turn not away[3]. But Solomon said, I will multiply wives and I will not turn, I will multiply horses and not take the people back to Egypt. And with fatal results[4].

Bishop Lightfoot was justly astonished at the persistence with which Matt. vi. 34 (μὴ οὖν μεριμνήσητε εἰς τὴν αὔριον) is quoted against the interpretation of τὸν ἄρτον ἡμῶν τὸν ἐπιούσιον as meaning "our bread for the coming day." One might just as well say that a Pharisee like Eleazar was inconsistent in praying for a good harvest (as he did in the ninth of the Eighteen Benedictions) while holding that "whoever has a morsel in his basket and says What shall I eat to-morrow? is among those of little faith[5]." As Lightfoot well expresses it: "The fact is that as μέριμνα means *anxiety*, *undue thought* or *care*, prayer to God is not only consistent with the absence of μέριμνα, but is a means of driving it away[6]." Lightfoot seems to think that the Hebrew equivalent would be *da-ag* (as in I Samuel ix. 5), to be solicitous, anxious. It rather seems that we ought to compare another verb (*qapad*) of frequent occurrence in Rabbinic Hebrew. Abraham was promised blessing and greatness, yet immediately on the promise (Gen. xii. 2), he was plunged into famine (Gen. xii. 10). Yet he neither complained nor

[1] T.B. Aboda Zara 17 a—b.

[2] Ps. xxvi. 2, cxliii. 2, cf. the Midrash on the former passage (ed. Buber, p. 216 and notes).

[3] Deut. xvii. 16, 17.

[4] I Kings x. 26, xi. 3. T.B. Sanhedrin 21 b; Yalquṭ on Deut., § 913. C. Taylor brings the petition against temptation into relation with the petition for daily bread, which he connects with the Manna (*op. cit.*, p. 127, quoting Exodus xvi. 4, which uses of the manna the phrase למען אנסנו).

[5] T.B. Soṭa 48 b. Cf. p. 192 below.

[6] J. B. Lightfoot, *On a Fresh Revision of the English New Testament*, 1872 (ed. 2), p. 204. Cf. pp. 170 *seq.*

expressed anxiety as to God's action[1]. The Hebrew verb (used in the hiphil *hiqpîd*) has the double significance of "to feel resentment and anxiety," which gives a peculiar *nuance* to the religious use of the Greek *μέριμνα*. So too the Hebrew noun *qapdan* is the impetuous, as contrasted to the *invetan* or patient, which was the true spiritual attitude for prayer. The connection of the verb *qapad* with prayer may be illustrated by the Targum and the Hebrew Sirach. In Exodus vi. 9 we are told how the people hearkened not unto Moses' message of hope "for shortness of spirit[2]," anguish or impatience (as the R.V. text and margin have it). The Targum renders shortness by *qephiduth*. In the Hebrew text of Sirach vii. 10 we have the word *shortness* used of prayer. "Be not impatient in prayer[3]." The point here no doubt rather is directed against despondency at the apparent failure of divine response. But all these ideas are closely connected.

Much has already been written in the commentaries as to the *general* parallels between the Lord's Prayer and Rabbinic sentiments and liturgy. It is unnecessary to add to these illustrations. To the older literature may be added some more recent contributions. Eb. Nestle (in the article already referred to) gives a careful analysis of the various retranslations that have been proposed. The oldest of these translations is that of Shemtob b. Shaprut, made in the latter half of the fourteenth century[4]. C. Taylor has been several times cited in the course of this note. There are some good suggestions in G. Klein's *Die Aelteste Christliche Katechismus* (Berlin, 1909), pp. 256 ff. He in particular works out the parallel between Matthew and the Jewish prescriptions that a prayer must consist of three parts: Praise, Petition, Thanks[5], and suggests that Ezekiel xxxvi. 23—31 was the model. Dalman's *The Words of Jesus* has valuable material. So has F. Perles' article on "Jewish Prayer" in vol. x (pp. 191 *seq.*) of Hastings' *Encyclopaedia of Religion and Ethics*. One of the best contributions from Jewish scholars is Dr K. Kohler's article in the *Jewish Encyclopedia*, vol. viii. p. 183[6]. On the liturgical use of "Amen," L. Ginzberg's article in the

[1] Genesis Rabba, ch. xl. (ed. Theodor, p. 382): ולא קרא תגר ולא הקפיד.

[2] מקצר רוח.   [3] See p. 76 above.

[4] See A. Herbst, *Des Schemtob ben Schephrut hebraeische Uebersetzung des Evangelium Matthaei*, Göttingen, 1879.

[5] שבח׳ תפלה׳ הודיה (Debarim Rabba, ch. ii).

[6] E. Bischoff (*op. cit.*) on the one extreme, and on the other G. Friedlander (*The Jewish Sources of the Sermon on the Mount*, London, 1909) contain useful material; both are controversial. F. H. Chase (*op. cit.*) gives a careful discussion

first volume of the same work, may be consulted with advantage. The forthcoming commentary on Matthew by H. Strack will undoubtedly be found to possess much valuable material on this, as on many another, subject of importance for students of the Gospels[1].

As to the general influence of Synagogue liturgies on the Church services compare R. M. Woolley in Hastings (*op. cit.*) viii. 177.

of all important points, and may always be consulted with advantage. On pp. 147 *seq.* he displays the parallels between the "Songs" in Luke and ancient Jewish prayers.

[1] Vol. i. of this work has appeared after the present volume was printed, and before the writer was able to utilise its contents.

## XIII. PHARISAIC DELICACIES.

In the course of his account of Gezer, Prof. R. A. S. Macalister has some trenchant comments on the conventional use of the term "Philistinism." He asserts that "the most artistic objects found in all the excavation come from them" (i.e. the Philistine tombs). The popular misconceptions, which have given "Philistinism" its contemptuous connotation, "have been derived from a misunderstanding of the records of their implacable enemies the Hebrews[1]." If this judgment be confirmed, it is perhaps a not unjust revenge that a section of the Hebrews themselves should have become, in their turn, victims of a similar misuse of terms. "Pharisaism" will no doubt enjoy lasting vogue to express what the N.E.D. summarises as "formalism," "hypocrisy," "self-righteousness," while "Philistinism" is too useful to surrender, as a designation of persons who, to quote again the N.E.D. definition, are "deficient in liberal culture and enlightenment[2]." Yet, according to Prof. Macalister, the Philistines were really distinguished by their "superior culture," just as it appears certain to some investigators of the Pharisees, that they were marked by often quaint and sometimes charming delicacies of feeling and thought, by a pervading attraction to the sincere, the simple, the non-ostentatious.

Hence, it may be useful to include in these Studies a short, desultory, uncontroversial and good-tempered account of this aspect of Pharisaism, an aspect which ought not to be ignored in any balanced estimate of a system, the faults of which are better known than are its virtues. And as modern instances may illustrate ancient habits and conditions, I start with two curious and even amusing experiences which fell my way in Jerusalem a few years ago. Pharisaism, one might premise, will never be understood without a sense of humour.

During the whole forenoon of a day near the Passover, I went the round of the poorest quarter with a resident Jewish doctor. The latter

[1] *The Excavation of Gezer* (P.E.F.), 1912, i. 297, 298. Again it was to the Philistines that was due the introduction of wrought iron into Palestine (ii. 269). The "superior culture" of the Philistines, superior i.e. to that of the Hebrews, is another general phrase of Mr Macalister's (ii. 351).

[2] The N.E.D. unfortunately uses language which accepts the conventional use of "Pharisaism" as justified by the history of the Pharisees; in the case of "Philistinism" it correctly avoids propounding any such judgment.

was a severe pietist of the olden Pharisaic order, but a fine fellow, some will say despite, others may prefer to say because of, that. The round was heavy, and the doctor and his companion were unable to take lunch until a very late hour. The doctor was obviously more than hungry, he was famished. I remonstrated with him for allowing himself to fall into so faint a condition, reminding him with a smile of the Talmudic injunction that a man must not so weaken himself by fasting as to disable himself from his work[1]. "But," protested the doctor, "I never break my fast till my round of these wretched folk is over. Were I full, how could I sympathise with the empty?" Indeed the doctor had for the most part written not prescriptions for medicines but orders for food. "What these poor souls needed," added he, "was nourishment, not drugs. And well I knew it from my own condition."

This delicate sincerity was in fact a piece of antique Pharisaism. Aforetime, in Jerusalem, when public fasts were proclaimed under stress of scarcity, no man was allowed to lead in prayer unless he, too, had an empty larder at home[2].

The second experience occurred two days later. I then paid a visit of ceremony to the Haham Bashi, the head of the Sephardic Jews in the Holy City. It was the first day of Passover, and the Rabbi's salon was crowded. He received his English guest with Oriental courtesy, but offered no refreshments. The Haham apologised. "On Passover," he exclaimed, "it is my rule never to partake of food away from home. I cannot therefore invite you to eat in my house." In other words, since his scrupulosity as to the Passover diet made him decline to eat abroad, he refused to presume (as he might well have done) that I would recognise in him so superior a pietist as to consent to do with him what he would not do with me.

It was a whispered confidence. The Haham Bashi would have been appalled at the suggestion of making a display of higher virtue. And his nicety, like the doctor's sensitiveness, had its roots in the past. Whatever else he was, the olden Pharisee was a gentleman. For one boorish Pharisee who thanked God for not making him a rustic[3], there was a whole group of more mannerly Pharisees who refused to boast that they were not as other men. At the time of the fall of

[1] T.B. Taanith 22 b.

[2] Mishnah, Taanith ii. 2: עמדו בתפלה מורידין לפני התיבה זקן ורגיל וביתו ריקם ׳ כדי שיהא לבו שלם בתפלה :

[3] Tosefta Berachoth vi. 23.

Jerusalem the Sanhedrin moved to Jabne. "There was," records the Talmud, "a familiar saying in the mouths of the Rabbis of Jabne running thus: I am God's creature, so is my fellow-man; my work is in the city, his in the field; I rise early for my work, he rises early for his; as he cannot excel in my work, so cannot I excel in his work. Dost thou indeed say: I do much, he does little [in the service of God]? Nay, we have been taught: It matters not whether one offers much or little, so long as the offerer directs his heart to Heaven![1]"

There is an apt practical illustration of this spirit, in the story of that noted student and mystic, Simeon son of Yoḥai, who fell under the displeasure of the Emperor Hadrian. To evade the imperial attentions, Simeon and his son took refuge in a cave. A wonder happened. Hard by there sprang up a stream of water and a carob tree. Naked they sat up to the neck in sand, engaged in study the livelong day. They reserved their clothing for the hour of prayer; having prayed, they undressed again, to save their garments from attrition. In this manner they spent twelve years, when Elijah appeared to announce the death of Hadrian. Father and son thereupon emerged, and came across some men ploughing and sowing. "See," cried Simeon, "how these fellows forsake the things of eternity, and busy themselves with the things of earth." Wherever their angry glances fell, flames burst forth. Then was heard a Daughter of the Voice saying: "Have ye come out to devastate My world? *Back to your cave!*" They returned, and remained in seclusion for another twelve months, the period appointed for the probation of the wicked in Gehenna. At the close of the year the Daughter of the Voice again spoke: "Ye may now come forth![2]" So emphatic a lesson in manners must have proved a capital corrective to overmuch contempt for the *am ha-areṣ*.

In one sense the examples quoted may all be said to belong to a code of manners. It was certainly a striking feature of Rabbinic etiquette to avoid hurting other people's feelings. It went far beyond mere etiquette, however. To bring pallor to a man's face—the Rabbinic equivalent of our putting a man to the blush—was more than bad manners. It was to shed blood; you see the red go and the white

[1] T.B. Berachoth 17 a. The final phrase (אחד המרבה ואחד הממעיט ובלבד שיכון לבו לשמים) is found very frequently elsewhere: e.g. Ber. 5 b (with regard to study of the Law). It is also used with regard to sacrifices in a Mishnah in Menaḥoth (end of tractate). Cf. First Series, p. 57.

[2] T.B. Sabbath 33 b; Bacher, *Agada der Tannaiten*, ii. 73.

come[1]. Pathetic is the self-humiliation of the Rabbi who jeered at another's ugliness. Joshua b. Ḥananya was rather of opinion that ugliness went with wisdom. "Are there no handsome men who are wise?" "Perchance," he rejoined, "were they ugly they would be wiser still[2]." On the other hand, the martyred R. Ishmael was "one of the seven most beautiful men in the world." Acts of inconsiderateness for others' feelings render their perpetrators not, as we should say, unfit for polite society, but as the Pharisees said, unfit for the life to come. The same Hebrew phrase which means good manners also means good morals. Thus the original and derived connotations of the Latin *mores* are combined in the Hebrew *derech ereṣ*. To render food noisome was blasphemy as well as waste. For a man of parts to use foul language was comparable to a palace with an open sewer running through it[3]. If you trod out a path in another's field, you were not only an intruder on his privacy, you were a despoiler of his property. Joshua son of Ḥananya used such a path. "Is this a public way?" asked the little daughter of the owner. The Rabbi replied that it was a clearly marked track. "Yes," said the girl, "thieves like yourself have made it so." Discourtesy merges into dishonesty[4].

But it is not the purpose of this note to cite examples of Pharisaic manners as elements in morality. It is a tempting theme. Hillel bathed as a religious duty; he was keeping pure the body, created in the Image[5]. The material delicacies which loaded the table of the olden régime were not more toothsome than the delicacies of table manners[6]. Comparable with these are the unique Pharisaic rules regarding the physical life of man, especially the conjugal intercourse of the sexes, rules of a wonderful refinement, in which the bodily and the spiritual are syncretised. Delicacies of this type were more than guides to decent life, they were part of the great law of holiness. All this, however, is rather off our present point.

[1] T.B. Baba Meṣia 38 b. It should be noted that in this passage Simeon b. Yoḥai plays a much more amiable rôle.

[2] T.B. Taanith 7.

[3] Derech ereṣ iii. On the meaning of the phrase דרך ארץ see Jastrow's Dictionary, p. 323, col. 2.

[4] T.B. Erubin 53 b.

[5] See First Series, p. 96. Cf. the saying concerning washing face, hands, and feet daily for the honour of God (T.B. Sabbath 50 b).

[6] On this subject cf. my essay on Table Customs in the first volume of the *Jewish Year Book* (London, 1895).

For our present point is simply this. Pharisaism, whatever else it was, and it was much else, was a system of morality expressed as law[1]. We are all familiar with the uglier side of this system, with its defects and dangers. They are attacked by the Prophets, assailed by the Evangelists, and denounced by the Pharisees. But a more engaging side of legalism is far less known. Many think of the Pharisee as a legalist, but omit to remember that he carried his principle into the delicacies of sentiment as well as into the niceties of ritual. He derived the one as well as the other from the Law itself. To insure fulfilment of the law he erected fences, but he also broke down barriers. To avoid transgression he went *beyond* the law. But with the same object he also stepped *within* it. He established equity as part of law. "Within the line of law[2]" is the Rabbinic description of the righteousness which tempers rights. The Pharisee carried this principle of action "within the line of law" to remarkable lengths. Beloved of God is he who does not exact his full rights; beloved of man he who does not stand on his dignity[3]. Abba the Priest always kept away from crowds, to avoid troubling the people to salute him. Very interesting is the comment of a colleague, who thought Abba wrong, as it is not a bad thing for people to receive an opportunity to show respect where it is due. Yet it was not thought right to allow a workman to fatigue himself by rising before the wise[4]. Another Rabbi paid an unjust demand, rather than tempt his neighbour to swear falsely to his claim. Jerusalem, said a Rabbi, was laid waste because the judges in that dire age decided by the letter of the law instead of passing "within the line." Thus, in the Pharisaic philosophy of history, it was a fatal, unforgivable offence to fail in that delicacy of touch which rarely goes with law, but did go with Rabbinic law[5].

The aged Rabbi Ishmael was on the road, and met one laden with wood. The latter put his burden down to rest, and then asked the

[1] Cf. the fine paper on the subject in J. Jacobs, *Jewish Ideals* (1896).

[2] This is the famous conception known as לפנים משורת הדין, on which cf. Jastrow's Dictionary, pp. 301, 1542, and see the quotations in Bialik's *Sefer ha-Aggada*, Part v, 213–4 (Odessa, 1910). This series of volumes is an admirable collection of Pharisaic sayings, and might profitably be used in conjunction with W. Bacher's works on the Agada. A. Büchler (whose book on "Types of Pietism" was published too late for me to use) has some excellent remarks on this topic (pp. 36 ff.). Cf. also C. G. Montefiore, *The Old Testament and After*, pp. 431 ff.

[3] T.B. Pesaḥ in 113 b; cf. First Series, p. 164.

[4] T.B. Ḥullin 54 b.

[5] T.B. Baba Meṣia 30 b; Giṭṭin Mishnah iv. 4.

Rabbi to help him to reshoulder it. Now, being old, Ishmael was not bound by law to help the wayfarer. Nevertheless, as he could not render help, he purchased the wood, for, says the Talmud, Ishmael acted within the line of the law. We are told of the judge who would decide in favour of the richer litigant who was in the right, and then refund the money to the poorer out of his own pocket. Thus did he fulfil the text (II Samuel viii. 15) which describes David as executing "justice and charity," for so the Rabbis translate the phrase. Justice to the rich, by delivering a true verdict, charity to the poor, by making his loss good[1].

Principles of this type, enforced by many anecdotes, led to a wide expansion of the concept of bribery. No Rabbi might sit as judge when either litigant had rendered the Rabbi the slightest service. Abba Areka refused to try a case which involved the keeper of the Inn at which the Rabbi sometimes lodged. Mar Samuel followed the same course when one of the litigants was a man who had helped him to alight from a ferry. When Ishmael's gardener, for the latter's own convenience, carried to town for the Rabbi's use a basket of the Rabbi's own fruit on a Thursday instead of on the usual Friday, the Rabbi refused to try a case in which the gardener was a party. A man gave Rabbi Elisha the first shearings as his priestly due. He then brought his case. Elisha declined both the shearings and the case[2]. The present writer was refused a hearing on a small ritual matter by the Cairo Rabbi because he had been introduced by a common friend. "I cannot," said he, "but be affected in your favour by my regard for him who sent you." In face of certain recent complaints by English judges of loquacious jurymen, may be cited the rule that no member of the Court might say after the verdict, "I was for you but I was outvoted[3]." It might be well perhaps if Judges, on presenting a majority decision, adopted the same reticence.

All this delicacy, as Prof. Amram well indicates, the Pharisees justified on *legal* grounds[4]. For the text does not prohibit the acceptance of money; it forbids the taking of bribes. One may be bribed by other things than money. There is prejudice; there is friendship. The poorer litigant must not be required to stand, while the richer was honoured with a seat[5], for such difference might affect the mind of the Court.

[1] T.B. Sanhedrin 6 b. [2] T.B. Kethuboth 105 b. [3] Sanh. Tosefta vi.
[4] *J.E.* iii. 380. The whole of Prof. Amram's article on Bribery is excellent.
[5] Tanḥuma Shofeṭim (ed. Buber, p. 30).

A. was not permitted to attend court in fine clothes, while his opponent B. was poorly clad. They said to A., "Dress like B. or provide him with a suit as good as yours[1]." Regard the poor as the rich who have lost their former wealth, for they are all descendants of the Patriarchs[2]. Appearances influence. "I never judge a student," said one Rabbi, "for I love a student as my own soul, and no man is a competent judge of his own soul[3]." "Judge not friend or foe," said another; "for in a friend one sees no evil, in a foe no good[4]." There is besides usury a "dust of usury," subtle, often impalpable advantages of a usurious nature. In Pharisaic language, one must keep aloof from what is foul and from what seems foul[5]. Yet there are numerous instances of fine refusals to put an evil interpretation on the suspicious conduct of others[6].

This refinement of feeling, and herein is its peculiarity, is a direct product of legalism. "Sanctify thyself in what is permitted to thee"—do not exceed even in lawful pleasures[7]. The case is stronger than has been so far indicated. For it is a refinement consciously derived from the Law itself. Amid his counsels to Moses, Jethro advises: "Thou shalt teach them the statutes and the laws, and shalt show them the way wherein they must walk, and the work that they must do" (Exod. xviii. 20)[8]. One would expect, if the conventional view of Pharisaism were adequate, to find this last phrase developed into a system of practical ritual. But the Pharisaic exegesis was quite other. The "work that they must do" refers not only to law, but also to that which is "within its line," a phrase, as we have seen, of the most delicate significance. When, too, Wisdom is eulogised, in that he who subjects himself to her guidance, "may walk in the way of the good" (Prov. ii. 20), Pharisaic exegesis tells us that the way of the good is the way that leads within the line of law[9].

Nearly akin to this conception is another, equally derived by Pharisaic lawyers from the law. They made great moral play with the

[1] T.B. Shebuoth 30 a. [2] Baba Qama 90.

[3] T.B. Sabbath 119 a. [4] T.B. Kethuboth 105 b.

[5] Aboth de R. Nathan, I. ii. (ed. Schechter, p. 9): הרחק מן הכיעור ומן הדומה לכיעור:

[6] Aboth i. 7 (cf. Taylor's note); and see the anecdotes in Aboth de R. Nathan, I. viii.

[7] T.B. Yebamoth 20 a.

[8] See Targ. J. on the verse; Mechilta (ed. Friedmann), p. 59 b.

[9] B. Meṣia 83 a.

term *oppression*[1]. The Pharisaic Code of Law (the Mishnah) lays down this principle: "Just as there is oppression (imposition) in cases of buying and selling, so there is oppression in words. One shall not say to another: What is the price of this article? when he has no intention to purchase it. One shall not say to another who has repented: Remember thy former deeds. One must not say to descendants of proselytes: Recollect the deeds of your forefathers. For it is said (Exod. xxii. 21): And thou shalt not vex, neither shalt thou oppress him[2]." To these illustrations of the earlier Code, the later Talmud adds others. If a proselyte would learn the Bible, say not to him: Shall the mouth that ate carrion recite the words spoken from the mouth of Power? One who has no money must not cast his eyes on wares, thus raising in the vendor an unfounded hope. Where there has been a hanging in a family, do not speak of hanging fish in presence of a relative[3]. How persistently quaintness rubs shoulders with human insight in the Pharisaic utterances!

Very subtle is another closely allied idea. Supposing Ziggud knows of Tobiah's crime, but also knows that he is the only witness. If he bring the charge, Ziggud is punished. For he is well aware that a single witness is insufficient for a legal hearing, and under the circumstances if he tender a charge, he merely brings Tobiah into disrepute without opportunity of condemnation or acquittal by process of law. "Tobiah has sinned and Ziggud is flogged[4]," ran the resultant and well-founded proverb. Using a beautiful phrase, which, were certain critics of Pharisaism right, ought never to have been on Pharisaic lips, the Rabbi characterised all these things as "matters *entrusted to the heart*[5]." Runs the text: "Ye shall not oppress one another, but thou shalt fear the Lord" (Lev. xxv. 17). Oppression, wrong which is not penalised by the letter of the law, is a matter of conscience, it is part of that inner sin which the fear of God should cast out. "Stealing the mind" is another term for this type of offence. The worst thief is he who leaves

[1] On this subject cf. Lazarus, *Ethics of Judaism* (E.T.), Part II. pp. 151 *seq.*

[2] Mishnah, Baba Meṣia iv. 10. As H. E. Goldin points out on p. 94 of his useful edition of this Tractate (New York, 1913): "Maimonides in his Commentary on the Mishnah says that a violation of any of the rules of law enumerated in this Mishnah (paragraph) is much graver a crime, and is considered a much greater violation of the principles of morality, than overreaching in cases of bargain and sale."

[3] T.B. Baba Meṣia 58, 59.

[4] T.B. Pesaḥim 113 b.

[5] Sifrâ Qedoshim (ed. Weiss, p. 88 b), and often.

another under a misapprehension[1]. You must not pretend to open a new cask of wine for a friend's delectation, when you would have had to open it in any case. You must not advise a man (even though the advice is good) to sell his field, when you want to buy it. You ought not to invite a man to dine with you on a day on which, as you have good reason for knowing, he is already engaged. If you encounter a friend by chance do not let him imagine that you had designed to meet him[2].

These refinements, odd as some of them are, easily pass into magnanimity. The Pharisees are high in their praise of the heathen upon whom a delegacy of the Sanhedrin waited for the purchase of a gem for the High Priest's vestment. They offered their price, but the heathen refused to sell until his father, under whose pillow the jewel rested, woke from his sleep. The delegacy raised their price in vain. On the father's awakening, the bargain was completed. But the vendor refused to accept more than the price first offered. "I had made up my mind already to take what you tendered," he explained. Simeon son of Sheṭaḥ, to quote another well-known incident, bought an ass, and a jewel was found round its neck. He restored the jewel, saying, "I bought an ass not a jewel[3]." Ḥanina b. Dosa would not make use of the eggs laid by a hen which he found; when the eggs were hatched, he sold the chicks and bought goats which he gave to the original owner of the hen[4]. All such things, where one party is cognizant of facts hidden from the other, or who even profits by his expert knowledge over the inexpert, are among the matters "entrusted to the heart," for which man is directly accountable to God. And he who comes well out of the test "sanctifies the Name[5]."

Such delicacies, some few illustrations of which have been cited out of hundreds, penetrate to the depths. Equally notable is their range. No aspect of life is left untouched. Do not seek to console another while his dead lies before him, yet delay not too long, lest you remind him of a forgotten sorrow. It is like a man, who broke his leg and it was cured. Comes a surgeon and says, I will break it again to show you how skilfully I can cure it[6]. On the other hand, Mar Uqba and his wife took refuge in the oven lest a beneficiary of theirs should see

[1] Tosefta Baba Qama vii. 8 (ed. Zuckermandel, p. 358).
[2] T.B. Ḥullin 94 b.
[3] Deut. Rabba iii. Cf. p. 36 above.
[4] T.B. Taanith 24 a: cf. First Series, p. 102.
[5] Sifrâ as cited on p. 116.
[6] Aboth iv.; T.B. Moed Qaton 21.

them[1]. A man must not walk in his field on the Sabbath to observe what work needs doing on the morrow[2]. The broken tablets, as well as the second perfect pair, were placed in the Ark; so a decrepit scholar who has forgotten his learning must not be without honour[3]. Tell the truth and nothing but the truth, but 'tis no perjury to call a homely bride beautiful. And, in general, never decry your neighbour's bargain. No man must retain in his pocket a spurious coin, nor keep in his house an inaccurate measure[4]. Let the student sanctify God by paying his bills promptly[5]; as a later sage put it, Go to bed without supper and rise up without debt. Over stolen bread beware that you utter no blessing to the Lord[6]. If a man owes you money, avoid him; he will think you are thinking of the loan[7]. Never fail of a promise to a child, lest he learn to lie[8]; never strike an adult son, lest you tempt him to reprisals[9]. Never use the crown of the Law for self-aggrandisement. Tarphon escaped from a dangerous predicament by declaring his identity, and regretted his act throughout his life[10]. He had made a personal use of the crown of the Law. Remove thine own blemish first. Rabbi Jannai's tree overhung the street. So did the tree of X. The people brought an action against X. for trespass. The case came before Jannai, who deferred the hearing for twenty-four hours. Overnight he cut his own offending branches; next day he ordered X. to do likewise. It is significant that the Talmud, after recording the incident, thinks it necessary to inquire why Jannai had not sooner lopped off his branches. The answer is that he thought the public enjoyed the shade, but when they entered action against X. he realised that they considered it a nuisance[11].

Once Rabbi Judah said to his class: He who has eaten garlic, let him depart. R. Ḥanina rose and went out, not that he had so eaten, but not to shame him who had[12]. Eleazar of Bartutha was so excessively charitable that collectors hid themselves when they saw him coming their way[13]. Of Tarphon many stories are told which reveal his refined nature. He outdid Raleigh in courtliness. His mother once had to cross the courtyard barefoot. Under her feet Tarphon placed his hands.

[1] T.B. Kethuboth 47 b.
[2] Levit. Rabba xxxiv. § 16.
[3] T.B. Baba Bathra 14 b.
[4] T.B. Baba Bathra 89.
[5] T.B. Yoma 86 a.
[6] T.B. Baba Qama 94 a.
[7] T.B. Baba Meṣia 75 b.
[8] T.B. Sukkah 46 b.
[9] Midrash on Levit. xix. 14.
[10] T.B. Nedarim 62 b.
[11] T.B. Baba Bathra 60 a.
[12] T.B. Sanhedrin 11 a.
[13] T.B. Taanith 24.

On another occasion, Tarphon was reading with his students, when a poorly-clad bride passed by on her way to her wedding. The Rabbi had her fetched into the house, where the ladies attended to her toilet, decked her out becomingly, and escorted her in dancing procession to her destination[1]. Why should the Rabbi not do this, seeing that God himself decked out Eve as Adam's bride[2]? It is the spirit of the gift that counts. There were two sons. One fed his father on dainties and inherited Gehinnom. The other made his father grind the mill and won Paradise. For the former flung the dainties at his sire as to a dog. The latter sent his father to the mill, for millers were free from the royal draft (how modern it sounds!). The son remained at home and was taken[3].

Such a miscellany of familiar anecdotes and maxims could be indefinitely enlarged. We have encountered Simeon b. Yoḥai in a self-assertive mood. But the same Rabbi reveals himself also in a far from arrogant aspect. He could express his gratitude that he was not called upon to pronounce on a capital charge. "Blessed be the All-Merciful," he exclaimed, "in that I am not qualified to judge[4]." Or, again, what could be finer than this? Hast thou wronged thy neighbour a little? Esteem it much. Hast thou rendered him a great service? Esteem it little. Has he done thee a small good? Esteem it great. Has he wrought against thee a great injury? Esteem it small[5]. On a hot day, Simeon b. Ḥalafta asked his daughter to fan him, offering her a rose. A cool wind blew from the sky. How many roses, quoth he, do I owe to the Giver of this breeze[6]? But enough has been quoted. Much of it has been quaint. In a sense, a chapter has been written in the history of the curiosities of manners. But it is obvious that there is more in it than that. An aroma of the beauty of holiness hovers o'er it all. We have been enjoying the scent of blossoms which flourished on the stem of pietism. Pharisaism grew weeds; it also grew flowers.

[1] T.B. Qiddushin 31 b; Aboth de R. Nathan, I. ch. 41 (ed. Schechter, p. 133).

[2] Aboth de R. Nathan, I. 4 (ed. Schechter, p. 19). T.B. Erubin 18.

[3] T.J. Qiddushin i. § 7. Cf. Aboth de R. Nathan, I. xiii. (ed. Schechter, p. 57).

[4] T.J. Sanhedrin i. § 1. א״ר שמעון בן יוחי · בריך רחמנא דלינא חכים מידון:

[5] Aboth d. Rabbi Nathan, I. xi.

[6] T.B. Baba Meṣia 86 a.

## XIV. THE CESSATION OF PROPHECY.

In a sense it is true that the growing devotion to the Law was one of the causes of the cessation of Prophecy. Dr Charles is very emphatic on this point. "The absolute supremacy of the Law" he says[1] "carried with it the suppression of Prophecy—at all events the open exercise of the prophetic gifts." This, however, was not a peculiarity of the Law, it applied to the Gospels equally. After a conspicuous revival in the Apostolic Age, Prophecy, in the technical sense, again died out as completely in the new Church as in the older Synagogue. This occurred largely for the same reasons. There was a conviction, not always consciously realised, that Prophecy was a phenomenon of the past, of certain defined periods. False prophets, especially those who, like the apocalyptics, interpreted the "signs of the times," had to be suppressed. This suppression may be compared with the Pharisaic antipathy to those who "calculated ends," and caused scepticism of the End when the specific predictions failed to materialise[2]. Even more important was the sense that the authoritatively admitted Scriptures contained all that men needed for perfection here and salvation hereafter. As E. K. Mitchell puts it: "The Law and the Prophets had sufficed for Israel, and the Old Covenant needed only to be supplemented by the New with its apostolic guarantees. Prophecy was thus placed under the restraint of written records, and it was considered more important to interpret the old prophecies than to utter new ones[3]." "Despise not prophesyings" (1 Thess. v. 20) could not stand against the misusers of the charisma. The Montanist movement was able neither to uphold the thesis that

[1] *Apocrypha and Pseudepigrapha of the Old Testament* (Oxford 1913), vol. ii. Introduction vii.–ix.; and page 1.

[2] T.B. Sanhedrin 97b. In his *Iggereth Teman* Maimonides fully expounds the import of this view, based as it is on Habakkuk ii. 3, "though it tarry wait for it." This, in the last resort, was the real Jewish objection to Apocalypses, and must have influenced the comparative absence of them in certain periods. This absence is always comparative, never absolute. Even Maimonides, objecting to calculations, has his own calculation. The hope of salvation itself was never to be abandoned. "Hast thou hoped for salvation?" (צפית לישועה) is a question put to each at the judgment after death (T.B. Sabbath 31a foot).

[3] On the cessation of Christian Prophecy see J. C. Lambert in Hastings' one-volume *Dictionary of the Bible* (1909), p. 765, and E. K. Mitchell in the *Encyclopaedia of Religion and Ethics*, x. (1918), p. 383.

the line of prophets was continuous, nor that ceasing with John the Baptist it revived in those inspired by the Paraclete[1]. With the necessary qualifications, this is as true of Jewish as of Christian Prophecy. We must thus allow for four factors, to account for the cessation of Pro phecy: (1) the intrusion of false prophets, an old abuse, which must throw discredit even on genuine inspirations; (2) the natural quality of Prophecy that makes it necessarily intermittent; (3) the degradation of Prophecy into mere prediction; and (4) the fixation of the Scriptural Canon. The first of these factors was very ancient; it finds frequent expression in the Hebrew prophets (particularly in Zechariah xiii. 1–5), and in early Christian literature. We see signs of the third factor throughout the Maccabean age. The references to the cessation of Prophecy point to the popular degradation of its significance. When, in the (Maccabean?) Psalm lxxiv. 9, the tortured saint moans: "We see not our signs, there is no longer a prophet, neither is there any among us that knoweth how long"—the prophet is clearly identified with the seer. The allusion in 1 Macc. iv. 46 stands in a separate category, for it points forward to a time (afterwards if not then conceived Messianically) when difficulties—here as to the disposal of the defiled altar stones—would be resolved[2]. But in 1 Macc. ix. 25–27 we have a different point of view. After the death of Judas, Bacchides exacted full toll of vengeance on the surviving adherents of the fallen hero; "there was great tribulation in Israel, such as was not since the time that no prophet appeared unto them." This can hardly refer to Malachi. Josephus feels the difficulty and paraphrases "they had had no similar experience since the return from Babylon[3]." The writer of 1 Macc. probably alluded to the "prophetic" deliverances. There was no Elijah or the like to effect a miraculous salvation. The prophet whom he missed was not a Malachi. Similarly with another interesting allusion, in the same book (1 Macc. xiv. 41). All classes, sacerdotal and lay, were well pleased with the election of Simon as prince and high-priest for ever, "until there should arise a faithful prophet." In other words, the popular choice would hold until a direct oracle con-

[1] On Montanism see H. J. Lawlor in Hastings' *Encyclopaedia*, viii. 828 ff.

[2] On this point see the excellent remarks of L. Ginzberg in *J.E.* v. 126. Elijah was to remove all difficulties (T.B. Menaḥoth 45 a; Num. Rabba iii. § 13; Aboth de R. Nathan I. xxxiv. ed. Schechter, p. 101). Cf. also the same scholar's remarks in *J.E.* i. 637 (col. 1), where he adds a reference to Mechilta on Exod. xvi. 33 (ed. Friedmann 51 b).

[3] 13 *Antiq.* 1 § 1.

firmed or annulled it[1]. The thought in the historian's mind was, it may be suggested, something like the confirmation of Saul's election by means of Samuel. The prophet, in short, is conceived in his oracular aspect.

If such were the degradation of the prophetic ideal, the cessation of Prophecy was gain not loss. Its work was done. The intermittence, or rather the sporadic occurrence, of genuine prophecy is one of its outstanding qualities. In the Synagogue it had served its day, just as it was soon found to have served its day in the early Church[2]. The written teachings of prophet and evangelist sufficed to form texts on which the religious genius of Rabbi and Priest could work, adding to the ancient messages while they expounded them, giving new life to them as they drew life from them. In what sense had Prophecy served its day? We have an effective illustration in a small composition which emanated from the dark days of the Maccabean tribulations. This is the Prayer of Azariah, on the theology of which commentators might have said finer things than, for the most part, they have done[3]. The author again laments the absence of prophet, in language reminiscent of Hosea iii. 4, except that, be it noted, he uses "prophet" where Hosea uses "ephod and teraphim." But was the prophet, in the old true sense, really absent? For note how the Prayer proceeds:

> Neither is there at this time prince, or prophet, or leader, or burnt offering, or sacrifice, or oblation, or incense, or place to offer before thee and find mercy. But in a contrite heart and a humble spirit let us be accepted, like as in the burnt offerings of rams and bullocks, and like as in ten thousands of fat lambs; so let our sacrifice be in thy sight this day, and grant that we may wholly go after thee, for they shall not be ashamed that put their trust in thee. And now we follow thee with all our heart, we fear thee and seek thy face. Put us not to shame, but deal with us according to thy forbearance[4], and according to the multitude of thy mercy (verses 15–20).

[1] Cf. Schürer, vol. i. (ed. 1901), p. 249. It is clear at all events that the prophet in this passage is not thought of as the announcer of a new moral message, but as one competent to work the oracle. Compare Ezra ii. 63, Neh. vii. 65, where the "priest with Urim and Thummim" fulfils the same function as is ascribed in 1 Macc. to the prophet. Later Jewish theology was strongly opposed to the view that the Prophet was a mere soothsayer: his work was to bring Israel and mankind to human perfection (Maimonides, *Guide* II. xxix.; Albo, *Ikkarim* iii. 12).

[2] Besides the references given in the articles referred to p. 120 n. 3, see Charles on Revelation i. 6 (vol. i. 16–17).

[3] This is even true of W. H. Bennett's admirable edition in Charles, vol. i. pp. 625 *seq*.

[4] See Bennett's note on this word (ἐπιείκεια), *op. cit.* p. 634.

This is in the true prophetic spirit. If, as Bennett says, and truly says, the Prayer of Azariah illustrates "some of the features of Jewish theology about the beginning of the Christian era[1]," it is clear that the devotees of the Law had absorbed some features of Prophecy at its best. Similarly with the early Church. The popularity of the Canonical Gospels would render the prophet superfluous. Preacher and teacher, unfolding, nay enlarging, Law or Gospel took the prophet's place. This the visionary could not possibly do. You must look for the "Higher Theology" of Synagogue and Church elsewhere than in the Apocalypses, though you may find in the latter a considerable aid to a somewhat disputable philosophy of history. It was the Fathers of the Synagogue and the Church Fathers, Rabbis and Ecclesiastics, Members of Synhedrins and of Councils, Preachers before Ark or Altar, who could appropriate Elijah's mantle and wear it not without distinction. But only in metaphor can we speak of the continued wearing of the same mantle. For the forms in which new messages express themselves cannot remain constant. The prophetic form is no exception to this invariable rule. "Thus saith the Lord," and "I say unto you," are not formulae for all times and teachers[2]. Is there no originality, no fire and passion, in the Rabbinic cry: "Be bold as a leopard, swift as an eagle, fleet as a hart and strong as a lion, to do the will of thy Father which is in Heaven"? Is there nothing which even a prophet could have envied in the Rabbinic elevation of the fear of God even above the study of the Law? Woe to the man who has no house, yet maketh the doors thereto—cries Jannai[3]. There is a driving force, too, in such a sermon as the 4 Maccabees, a driving force drawn from Moses rather than from Stoicism. It does not follow that there are lacking inspired teachers of power and originality in all times except those to which

[1] How difficult it is to generalise on theology is shown by contrasting the Prayer of Azariah (verses 5, 6, 14) with the Maccabean Psalm xliv. As Bennett points out, in the former Israel's misfortunes are explained by Israel's sins, while in the latter, Israel protests as an innocent martyr. The difference is hardly accounted for by the suggestion that "the sins confessed here (in Azariah) are probably those of the nation in the past." The confession is very present in its tone. The true explanation is that the two writers, though contemporary, were not quite at one in their moods. Theology is, after all, largely a matter of moods.

[2] Maimonides quotes (*Guide* ii. ch. 39) a Midrash, otherwise unknown, which points out how the Prophetic formula "God said unto me" was unknown before Moses, though there were prophets before him.

[3] Mishnah Aboth, ch. v (end). T.B. Sabbath 31 a.

the cited formulae were appropriate. Moreover, a vulgarised style, whether in literature or religion, spells convention of thought as well as of manner. The prophet, as Dr Inge has wisely said, suffers more from his disciples and imitators than from his critics and opponents. Not everyone who opens "Thus saith the Lord" is a prophet, just as not everyone lacks prophetic gift because he opens "It is written." The prophet, it is true, claimed to speak the indisputable word. Sometimes he reasoned with his hearers; more often he pronounced his message as an authoritative word needing no confirmation[1]. By the nature of the case, Prophecy could not flourish unless the Synagogue and the Church were prepared to reconsider their attitude towards the immutability of the older revelations. Two sentences from Dr Charles may be noted: "Prophecy was driven forth from the bosom of Judaism, and has never since been suffered to return"; "In modern times Judaism is striving to recover the liberty of prophesying." The former sentence, as we have seen, is too sweeping; the latter does not put the truth quite correctly. A liberal movement in Judaism is, in a sense, a return to the prophetic spirit, not at all because Pharisaism was ever a departure from that spirit; not mainly because such a movement attaches itself more naturally and more fruitfully to an Isaiah than to a Joshua; but because liberalism in religion places, on the whole, its chief stress and reliance on the direct power of great ideas, because in its re-statement of those ideas it is in a creative frame of mind. Religions, all round, tend to lose their creative faculty. This was true even of the Greek religion, though, as Mr Livingstone reminds us, the Greeks had no Bible. Prophecy returns with the return of the creative impulse which, curiously enough, finally emerges from what begins as a destructive criticism of documents. Of course vital religion is always partially creative. The Jew who believed in the perfection and immutability of the Law, the Christian who upheld the perfection and immutability of the Gospel, may seem to us, with our modern knowledge of the growth of texts and the clash of readings, in a static condition. Yet Synagogue and Church have been all along developing despite their loyalty to Canonical Scriptures, so much so that Moses would be to-day as strange in a Synagogue based on the Law, as Paul would be in a Church founded on the Gospel.

[1] This distinction was realised in the Talmud: "They made their words like words of prophecy" (עשו דבריהם כדברי נביאות). So R. Johanan describes a Tannaitic rule which was handed down without any reason assigned.

To return to our immediate concern, the belief in the perfection and immutability of the Law was or is a belief which does not deserve the condemnation with which some critics assail it. It was and is an inspiring belief, and (be it remembered) the prophetic books and the Hagiographa as well as the Law were included in the Canon. Law and Prophecy and Psalter were not antagonistic; they were parts of one whole. The Rabbis delighted to point out how each of the three divisions confirms the other two. When Ḥananya ben Teradyon wished to prove his thesis that when two sit together studying the Torah the Shechinah abides between them—not an ignoble effect of the Torah assuredly—he used texts from Malachi (iii. 16); just as R. Simeon, when maintaining that those who speak words of Torah at meal-times are as though they had eaten at the table of the Omnipresent, cited Ezekiel (xli. 22)[1]. So, too, the Pharisees delighted to find confirmation for the same ideas in all the three sections of the Hebrew Canon concurrently. "'Tis written in the Law, repeated in the Prophets, and a third time stated in the Writings"—so the phrase of reinforcement went[2]. The Pentateuch occupied, undoubtedly, a higher place than the rest of the Scriptures. It pre-existed Creation and will survive the End[3]. But though the Law proper was thus elevated, it was partly because the Law in fact contained within itself the teachings of the Prophets and Hagiographa. There has been much misunderstanding as to the Rabbinic statements regarding the eternity of the Law as against the rest of the Scriptures. There would be no innovations of practical law, the older prescriptions were immutable and in no need of supplement, but the prophetic exhortations would be unnecessary in an age when as Jeremiah prophesied (xxxi. 34) all men would know God, from the least of them to the greatest. Every man, woman and child would be a natural prophet[4]. Nor was the opinion of the eternity of the Law unqualified. With regard to the Pentateuchal sacrifices, for instance, some held that

[1] Mishnah Aboth iii. 3–5, ed. Taylor (1897), p. 43.

[2] See e.g. the use of the sentence by Joḥanan bar Nappaḥa (died 279) in T.B. Megilla 31 a. Joshua b. Levi employs the same phraseology in T.B. Aboda Zara 19 b. These are two examples out of many. Cf. T.B. Sukkah 52. See also Genesis R. ch. xlviii. § 11. In the latter reference there is also the notable saying that the evil Yeṣer does not rule in the time to come, : אין יצר הרע שולט לעתיד לבא

[3] Cf. L. Blau in *J.E.* xii. p. 197. This article needs cautious use.

[4] Cf. Num. xi. 29. The text from Jeremiah is rightly quoted in the commentaries to the Jerusalem Talmud as explaining Megilla i. § 5

ר' יוחנן אמר הנביאים והכתובים עתידין ליבטל וחמשת ספרי תורה אינן עתידין ליבטל

they would all be abolished in futurity with the exception of the Thank-offerings, which would endure eternally[1]. Jeremiah xxxiii. 11 is quoted as the authority for this remarkable idea[2].

In the sense of Jeremiah xxxi. Prophecy, so far from ceasing, must endure eternally. The coincident appearance of Moses with Elijah at the Transfiguration is taken to imply that Law and Prophecy (of the Hebrew Bible) were regarded by the Evangelists as both abrogated. But in the Jewish view this was not the case. According to Philo, as Drummond (i. 14, cf. ii. 282–3) puts it, "Communion between God and man is among the permanent possibilities of our race; and Philo goes so far as to say that every good and wise man has the gift of Prophecy." Maimonides says much the same, and holds, with other Pharisaic authorities, that the restoration of Prophecy will be one of the boons of the Messianic age[3]. The Pharisees were certainly regarded as the successors of the prophets: "R. Abdimi of Haifa said, From the day whereon the Temple was laid waste, Prophecy was taken from the prophets and given to the Sages[4]." This saying is no mere eulogisation of the Sages

[1] Levit. Rabba ix. § 7; Midrash on Psalms lvi. and c. (ed. Buber, pp. 295 and 426). This was no isolated opinion, as may be seen from the group of Rabbis cited as authority for it. The passage occurs in several other places besides those quoted above, as may be seen from Buber's notes.

[2] On the possibility of the Law itself being abrogated in futurity, in favour of a new Torah, see the important remarks of Kohler in *J.E.* v. 216. Very arresting is the saying of Yalquṭ on Isaiah § 296: God will in futurity sit in Paradise surrounded by the righteous and the angels, with sun at his right and moon at his left, and He will expound a new Torah which he will give by hands of the Messiah (והקב"ה יושב ודורש תורה חדשה שעתיד ליתן על יד משיח), and at the end of the Lesson Zerubbabel son of Shealtiel will rise and say the Qaddish, and all the universe including the wicked in Gehinnom will cry Amen, whereupon the wicked will be admitted to Paradise. In another version of the same passage God does not expound a new Torah but the reasons for the old (see Seder R. Amram, p. 13).

[3] Cf. Maimonides, *Guide* ii. ch. 37 (end). For an exposition of Maimonides on Prophecy cf. I. Abrahams in *Mind*, xi. (1886), pp. 102–3. The Midrash on Psalm iii. 6 (ed. Buber, p. 39) runs:

אני שכבתי ואישנה׳ אמרה כנסת ישראל אני שכבתי מן הנבואה ואישנה מרוח הקדש׳ הקיצותי על ידי אליהו שנאמר הנה אנכי שולח לכם את אליהו הנביא׳ כי ה׳ יסמכני׳ על ידי מלך משיח:

"*I laid me down and slept; I awakened, for the Lord sustaineth me.* I laid me down from Prophecy, I slept from the Holy Spirit; I awakened through Elijah, as it is said, Lo I send unto you Elijah the prophet; for the Lord will sustain me, by the hands of King Messiah."

[4] T.B. Baba Bathra 12 a.

as a caste. Every man could become a Rabbi. But beyond this the idea is in line with the thought of Jeremiah and of Joel (ii. 28 [Heb. iii. 1]).

In a foot-note to his *Religion des Judentums*[1], W. Bousset asserts that it is surprising how little influence Joel had on subsequent thought. But in the first place we have, of course, the famous and fertile use of the passage, with its characteristic modification, in Acts ii. 16 *seq.* Nor is a similar use lacking in the Midrash. In connection with Numbers xi. 17 the Midrash remarks: "The Holy One, blessed be He, said: In this world individuals were given prophetic power, but in the world to come all Israel will be made prophets, as it is said (Joel ii. 28): And it shall come to pass afterward, that I will pour out my spirit upon all flesh; and your sons and your daughters shall prophesy, your young men shall see visions: and also upon the servants and the handmaids in those days will I pour my spirit. Thus did R. Tanḥuma son of R. Abba expound[2]." We can understand from this how it came about that Prophecy and the incidence of the Holy Spirit were identified in several Rabbinic passages. In the Targum to Isaiah xi. 2, the phrase "And the spirit of the Lord shall rest on him" is rendered "The spirit of Prophecy shall rest on him." This is in full accord with other Rabbinic views. In this sense there can be no thought at all of the cessation of Prophecy[3]. The Holy Spirit has never ceased, can never cease, to operate in the lives of men. God himself covenanted that the Spirit which was upon man and the words put in his mouth should never depart out of his mouth, nor out of the mouth of his seed, nor out of the mouth of his seed's seed, from thenceforth and for ever (Isaiah lix. 21)[4]. The endowment with the divine Spirit and Word was not to be for

[1] Ed. 1 (1903), p. 229. Bousset's mistake was pointed out the same year in *J.E.* v. 213 b foot, but is verbally repeated in Bousset's second edition, 1906, p. 276. On the other hand, Bousset has some valuable comments on Prophecy in the Apocalypses (*loc. cit.*).

[2] Numbers Rabba, end of ch. xv.; Tanḥuma, end of בהעלותך (Buber iii. p. 61). The significant words run:

אמר הקב"ה בעולם הזה יחידים נתנבאו אבל לעולם הבא כל ישראל נעשין נביאים:

[3] Perhaps the clearest evidence for the identification of Prophecy with the Holy Spirit is the fact that the ten terms cited in Genesis Rabba xliv. § 6 (ed. Theodor, p. 429) as describing Prophecy, are in another text (Aboth de R. Nathan i. ch. 34, ed. Schechter, p. 102) cited, with a single variant, as describing the Holy Spirit.

[4] This passage is recited daily in the Synagogue (see *Authorised Hebrew and English Prayer-Book*, p. 73). For date see Annotated Edition of the same Prayer-Book, p. lxxxii. The Holy Spirit, according to Phineas b. Yair, was attainable by

a day but for all time. At all events, though prophets came and ceased, God remains to fulfil. Said R. Phineas the Priest, son of Ḥama: "Though they who conveyed the promise—the prophets—are dead, yet God—the Author of the promise—lives and endures[1]." And in all ages he imparts of his grace to man, but not in all ages by the same means.

the fear of God (Mishnah Soṭa ix. end): יראת חטא מביאה לידי רוח הקדש: This is the reading in the Cambridge Mishnah (ed. Lowe, p. 106 a). The usual reading substitutes חסידות for יראת חטא.

[1] Pesiqta R. ed. Friedmann, p. 1 a:

אמר ר׳ פנחס הכהן בן חמא׳ אע״ פי שמתו המבטיחים אלו הנביאים׳ אבל האלהים שהבטיח חי וקיים:

This thought represents a main element in the Rabbinic philosophy of history. For though God's steadfastness is (as in the Yalquṭ on Mal. iii. 6) often contrasted with Israel's vacillation (cf. p. 178 below), yet Israel's continuity is assured by God's eternity. Malachi is thus interpreted in the Pereq ha-Shalom, cf. Tanḥuma ed. Buber, Exodus, p. 27 and note 105 there. Prophecy in one sense was the result of Israel's infidelity, since the prophetic exhortations would have been otherwise unnecessary and only the Hexateuch would have been required (T.B. Nedarim 22 b). And yet, in another sense, prophecy—Israel's communion with God—was a feature of Israel's whole career. Browning puts the thought more generally into his Rabbi Ben Ezra's mouth: "Earth changes, but the soul and God stand sure." God cannot endure Joseph's tears, so he restores the Holy Spirit to Jacob (Pesiqta R. iii. p. 12 a).

## XV. THE TANNAITE TRADITION AND THE TRIAL NARRATIVES.

So much has been written, and for the most part so well written, on the relation of the Trial Narratives in the Gospels[1] to the Rabbinic account of legal procedure[2], that it is not proposed in this Note to deal again with the subject. Only one point will be considered, and that a point recently raised anew by the Rev. H. Danby in a brilliant essay which has attracted well-deserved attention[3]. And even this one point can only be treated superficially.

The point is: Can the Mishnaic Code be used at all in commenting on the Gospel Trial Narratives? Most critics of the Mishnah are agreed in holding that the Code, as we have it, is in some respects idealised; theoretical of the later schools, not representative of the historical procedure of earlier times. Mr Danby, however, equipped with exceptional learning both on the Roman and Pharisaic sides, goes much further. The Sanhedrin of the Mishnah is the academic Sanhedrin known to it, not a Council which operated before the loss of national life. The Mishnah when it deals with legal procedure is "of such a nature that it is of little or no value as a picture of native law as practised during the period in question." The code is not merely idealised in parts (as more or less all agree), but is through and through an academic throw-back from the Sanhedrin as it existed after the destruction of the Temple to the Council as it was conceived to have been in the life-time of Jesus.

I find it difficult to assent to this view. Not only is the Mishnaic Code confirmed in several particulars[4], but its basis must have been authentic tradition. The authority for some of the main assignments of constitution and function is not to be lightly esteemed. José ben Ḥalafta, who records some most important particulars regarding the

[1] Mk xiv. 53—65, xv. 1; Mt. xxvi. 57—68, xxvii. 1; Luke xxii. 54, 63—71, xxiii. 1; [John xviii. 12—14, 19—24, 28].

[2] Chiefly Mishnah and Tosefta Tractate Sanhedrin, now translated into English by H. Danby and published by the S.P.C.K. There are other important passages, e.g. Tosefta Ḥagigah ii. 9.

[3] See "The Bearing of the Rabbinical Criminal Code on the Jewish Trial Narratives in the Gospels," in the *Journal of Theological Studies* (Oxford), vol. xxi (October, 1919), pp. 51—76.

[4] Mr Danby cites some instances, and these could be added to considerably. Cf. e.g. Mt. xxvi. 65 with Mishnah Sanh. vii. 5; Mt. xxvii. 34, 48 with T.B. Sanh. 43 a.

older Sanhedrin, belongs to the second century A.D., but his reputation as a chronologist was of the highest. No Rabbi enjoyed fuller esteem for his historical accuracy and caution. There is, therefore, no ground whatever for questioning his statements. They are historical, not academic[1]. And it must be remembered that the Patriarch Judah, who compiled the Mishnah, was a disciple of José, and eulogistically said of him after José's death: "Just as was the difference between the Holy of Holies and the profanest of the profane, so is the difference between our generation and the generation of Rabbi José[2]." As gold to dust was another characterisation. When, then, he was codifying the traditions relating to the Sanhedrin, the compiler of the Mishnah had a trustworthy guide, on whom we may fairly assume he relied.

This unquestionable fact suggests the allowance of less weight than might at first sight seem proper to certain "academic" derivations of rule from Biblical texts. For instance, "Strangulation," though not a Pentateuchal form of execution, is one of the four methods described in the Rabbinic Code. The Mishnah itself gives no explanation, but the Talmud[3] has what is really an "academic" discussion of the origin of this penalty. That, however, strangulation was, historically, a method of execution is proved by Josephus. Incidentally, he proves something more. The Mishnah, for instance, asserts in what looks eminently like an "academic" regulation[4]: "The King may neither judge nor be judged." Now Herod, in one form of the story of Hyrcanus' death given by Josephus[5], wishing to put his veteran predecessor to death, charges him with treasonous correspondence with Malchus, governor of Arabia. He does not try Hyrcanus himself, but refers the case to the Sanhedrin. It is in the following paragraph in Josephus that we come across "strangulation" as a mode of inflicting the death penalty. In this rival version it is apparently Herod himself who orders the

[1] This high opinion of José's historical capacity is strongly expressed by I. H. Weiss in his History of Jewish Tradition (*Dor Dor Ve-doreshov*, ii. 163) and W. Bacher in his *Agada der Tannaiten*, ii. 151 *seq.*, and in his admirable article on the Sanhedrin in Hastings' *Dictionary of the Bible*, iv. 399. José, in the latter passage, is described as "well known as a chronologist and a source of historical information." His reputation in this respect was so high that, in the Talmud (T.B. Yebamoth 82 b), Joḥanan (the Palestinian Amora) ascribed to him the *Seder Olam*—the main source of Rabbinic chronology. On this ascription see Bacher, *Agada der Tannaiten*, ii. 155, 156 (note 1).

[2] T.J. Giṭṭin, end of ch. vi.

[3] Mishnah Sanh. vii. 1, T.B. Sanhedrin, 52 b.

[4] Sanh. ii. 2.

[5] 15 *Antiq*. vi. 2, 3.

execution. "He gave order that he should be strangled[1]." This Roman method of inflicting the death penalty does not arouse Josephus' surprise; it had evidently become acclimatised among the Jews. Thus it is not the Mishnaic statement as to the use of this method that is unhistoric; it is the later discussion as to its origin that is "academic." It is not an unfair inference that the same is true of other features of the Rabbinic Code.

Another case of a similar nature is the assertion in the Rabbinic sources of a Court consisting of twenty-three members. Mr Danby concedes some basis for this in actual practice, "considering the Mishnah's heroic effort to find scriptural sanction for it[2]." But it is hardly the case that "nowhere outside the Mishnah do we find the mention of any court consisting of twenty-three members, the number required for the Lesser Sanhedrin." Twice in the Tosefta[3] is such a Court named, and what is most important the author of the statement is José b. Ḥalafta. Thus the anonymous assertion of the Mishnah is fully justified by the authenticated assertion of the Tosefta. The attempt to derive this Court of twenty-three is indeed "heroic," it is palpably academic and theoretic[4]. We again see, therefore, that the Court of twenty-three was historical, but its origin quite unknown to the later Rabbis. There are quite enough references, moreover, to local courts in extra-Mishnaic sources to confirm our conclusion[5]. I cannot see that the Mishnah (i. 4) assumes that the small local courts had the right to try capital cases. Such cases would only be tried in Jerusalem, and in Jerusalem a quorum of twenty-three was sufficient. The full body of seventy-one would not be necessary, though no doubt a plenary session would be held in important cases[6].

[1] ἀπάγχειν προστάξαι τὸν ἄνδρα.

[2] Mishnah Sanh. i. 6.

[3] Ḥagigah ii. 9, Sanh. vii. 1.

[4] Underlying the attempt to explain the number 23 may be a historical fact—that (in a civil litigation) each side would nominate 10, each 10 would coopt one, while another was coopted to the 22 so as to constitute an odd-number, 23, lest there should be an equality of votes on the two sides. From the civil custom the number 23 might have passed over into criminal proceedings.

[5] Mr Danby quotes Mk xiii. 9, Mt. x. 17, Josephus 2 *War* xiv. 1.

[6] This is confirmed by Josephus in 2 *War* xx. 5, but this confirmation is not of great value. The tendency, however, to quote Josephus as historical evidence *against* the Mishnaic theorisation also needs caution. Thus Josephus' Court of *seven* is cited against the Mishnaic Court of three, but the historian is here patently in error. "Let there be seven men to judge in every city" (4 *Antiq.* viii. 14) is, for Josephus, a *Mosaic* law. It was on this error that he based his own course in Galilee (2 *War* xx. 5). The Mishnah more credibly regards the number seven as occasional only (Mish. Sanh. i. 2).

One side issue of some importance is raised by Mr Danby with regard to the commonly accepted view that no attempt was allowed, in Rabbinic law, to seek to make an accused person incriminate himself. Here the argument is that this rule is not even Mishnaic, but the device of Maimonides in the twelfth century. "This same assertion [that no self-incrimination was to be sought]," writes Mr Danby, "is made in every study of the subject, and seems to be copied each time without verification. There is no trace of such a prohibition in the Mishna or Tosefta. It is first put forward as a principle of rabbinical jurisprudence in the commentary of Maimonides, followed by Bartenora and Cocceius (all of whom were made accessible to Christian students for the first time in Surenhusius' Latin translation of the Mishna, Amsterdam, 1698) on *Mish. San.* 6, 2: 'Lex nostra neminem condemnat mortis propria ipsius confessione.' Salvador quotes this as a final authority—'Le principe des docteurs sur ce point est précis'—and since his time every writer on the Trial has brought this 'rule' forward, and made great play with it as a standing indictment against the conduct of the High-priest in demanding what might be a confession of guilt from the Accused." But though no such formal rule is given in the Mishnah, it is throughout implied. There is no examination of the accused at all, only of the witnesses. It is they who are examined and cross-examined, and it is on their testimony that the verdict is founded. The inference is fully confirmed by two facts. First, the only allusion in the Mishnah to evidence by the accused is that, after the verdict and even at the moment of execution, the carrying out of the sentence is postponed, and the verdict reconsidered again and yet again if the condemned man asserts that he has some overlooked consideration to urge in his own favour. Secondly, it is only when the fatal decision is decided and the condemned man is on the way to the place of execution, that he is exhorted to confess[1]. The purpose of this exhortation was that his death, if acquiesced in as just, was an "atonement for all his iniquities." The confession was made only when the condemned was within ten cubits of the "stoning house," and the execution was irrevocable. Thus, to the end, no self-incrimination was lawful. The Court did not even ask him to confess after it had passed sentence, for the sentence might be cancelled. Only at the final moment, when there was no longer room or opportunity for cancellation, was the appeal for confession made. Thus, though the Mishnah and Tosefta enunciate no

[1] Mishnah Sanh. vi. 1, 2.

such rule in set terms, it is so clearly implied in what these sources do enunciate, that Maimonides represents the Rabbinic and not his personal view[1].

But it is of interest to look a little closer into the statement of Maimonides. Let us read it in full. The Mishnah appeals to the precedent of Achan, to whom Joshua appealed in these terms[2]: "My son, give, I pray thee, glory to the Lord, the God of Israel, and make confession unto him; and tell me now what thou hast done; hide it not from me." Then Achan confesses, and though the lot had fallen on him, there was no evidence whatever against him but his own admission. It is he who reveals the details of his offence, it is he who betrays the hiding-place of the stolen Babylonish mantle, the two hundred shekels of silver and the wedge of gold. When the Mishnah cites the precedent of Achan, it does so for one feature only, the confession; it does not mean that the method of trial was a precedent, without eye-witnesses of the crime, without any evidence but the offender's own extorted admission. Therefore Maimonides has a note, to understand which it must be read in full: "Know thou that Joshua's execution of Achan was an emergency decision[3], because our true Torah does not inflict the penalty of death on a sinner either by his own confession or by the declaration of a prophet that the accused had done the deed." Maimonides was obviously justified in asserting that the execution of Achan was not in accordance with Pentateuchal prescript, while the Rabbinic Code did accord with it. To some extent, the disregard of precedent in some other instances may be explained on other grounds than lack of historicity. Thus in two cases in the Mishnah Sanhedrin precedents are rejected. The one is hard to explain in this way. A precedent as to the method of execution by burning is rejected as being ordered by an "inexpert Court[4]," according to the Talmud the Court was Sadducean[5]. The other case is more simple. The Mishnah holds that no woman might be hanged[6]. To which it is objected that Simeon b. Sheṭaḥ in fact did hang women in Askelon. To this the

[1] See T.B. Sanh. 9 b.

[2] Joshua vii. 19.

[3] הוראת שעה "a decision of the hour," a special act not to be treated as a precedent. Many of the difficulties which modern critics find in the Old Testament are explained by this device in the Rabbinic books. This is especially the case when the Historical Books seem irreconcilable with the Pentateuchal Code, as in Achan's case.

[4] Mishnah Sanh. vii. 2.

[5] T.B. Sanh. 52 b.

[6] Mishnah Sanh. vi. 4 [8].

reply is made that Simeon executed many women in one day, while the Rabbinic Code forbade two condemnations on one and the same day. Hence Simeon's act was no precedent in any particular[1]. Whatever be the historicity of the rule itself, clearly the precedent really was quite exceptional. To this extent, the rejection of precedent is not a clear indication that the Mishnah's own rule was purely academic. Moreover, there is a legendary ring about all these stories concerning Simeon, so that the Codifiers were justified in regarding the cited precedent with scant respect. On the other hand, the Mishnaic account of death by burning certainly reads like an effort of the imagination.

This method is defended on the principle that death was to be inflicted as painlessly as possible: "Love thy fellow-man as thyself—Choose for him an easy (or pleasant) death[2]." Does this type of humanitarianism so colour the Mishnaic Code as to rob it of its historicity? On this point Mr Danby judiciously writes: "Though not constituting a fair argument against the historicity of the Mishna's contents, there is another feature which must, to say the least, have coloured the whole presentation of its subject. One of the rabbinic canons of truth seems to have been that their code must 'shew mercy in judgement' to the highest degree. This *middath r'hamim* 'quality of mercy' is carried to lengths which it is difficult to believe can ever have been possible in practice. We certainly find no example of its working in what we know of Jewish criminology from non-rabbinic sources[3]. But according to the Mishna the judicial body was imagined as best fulfilling its functions when it sought to act as 'counsel for the defence.' If there were no extenuating circumstances in the prisoner's favour, the judges were to do their utmost to find some. The whole scheme of judicial procedure is characterised by the same attitude.

[1] It would be another case of הוראת שעה, a special course necessitated by special circumstances.

[2] T.B. Sanh. 52 a, ברור לו מיתה יפה.

[3] Two actual incidents might be cited. Not long before the siege of Jerusalem by Titus, the Idumeans wished to have Zacharias, son of Baruch, done to death. They appointed a tribunal of seventy. "Now the seventy judges brought in their verdict that the accused was not guilty, choosing rather to die themselves, rather than to have his death laid at their door" (Josephus, 4 *War* v. 4). Another case is the trial of the apostles before the Sanhedrin. Gamaliel's intervention easily inclines the Sanhedrin to revise its thought of putting the accused to death (Acts v. 34—40). When we add the case of Hyrcanus cited above from Josephus, it may be said that that historian conveys the clear impression that Jewish tribunals were reluctant to pass sentences of death.

The verdict of acquittal can be reached quickly, but that of conviction only as a result of most leisurely deliberation. The prisoner must be robbed of no chance which might in any way tell to his advantage. The excessive mercifulness of the rabbinic ideal finds its strongest expression in *Makkoth* i. 10: The Sanhedrin which condemns to death one man in seven years is accounted murderous. According to R. Eleazar ben Azariah it would be a murderous court if it condemned one man in seventy years. R. Tarphon and R. Aqiba assert that if they had been in the Sanhedrin, no man would have been condemned by it. Rabban Shimeon ben Gamaliel may well have replied: 'Then they would simply have multiplied bloodshed in Israel.'"

Yet we have the express testimony of Josephus that, historically, such mildness was the case. "*And indeed the Pharisees generally are by nature indulgent in the application of punishments*[1]." This assuredly is emphatically conclusive; and the interesting point is that it is a comment suggested by an incident that occurred more than a century B.C. Nor is the Mishnaic characterisation as blood-thirsty of a Sanhedrin which decreed frequent executions a late invention. It is clearly older than Eleazar son of Azariah, who was a disciple of Joḥanan b. Zakkai. The statement in Makkoth thus may date from the early part of the first century, and belong to the epoch when the Sanhedrin functioned. The addition of Aqiba and Tarphon actually implies that the earlier part of the passage refers to the pre-destruction period. And though the Mishnah does carry humanitarian considerations to an extreme, it is actually hard to see how capital punishments could have been frequent, seeing that two eye-witnesses of the crime were absolutely required by Pentateuchal law for the establishment of the charge and the conviction of the criminal. The testimony of Eleazar b. Azariah amounts to this—that the strict enforcement of the Pentateuchal law did virtually abolish capital punishment. And with all due respect to Rabban Simeon son of Gamaliel, the world would be better and not less safe if the Rabbinic reluctance to shed even guilty blood were universally adopted. As against a well-known witticism, the Rabbis (had they spoken French) might have retorted "Que messieurs les Juges commencent."

While, therefore, it is certain that the later Rabbis discussed many legal points without regard to actuality, but as possible to arise in the

[1] 13 *Antiq.* x. 6 οὐ γὰρ ἐδόκει λοιδορίας ἕνεκα θανάτῳ ζημιοῦν, ἄλλως τε καὶ φύσει πρὸς τὰς κολάσεις ἐπιεικῶς ἔχουσιν οἱ Φαρισαῖοι.

Messianic age (הלכתא למשיחא) or in order to perform the duty of studying the Torah (דרוש וקבל שכר Sanh. 51 b), it is not to be assumed that they were not arguing on the basis of known facts. For it should not be overlooked that the Pharisaic humanitarianism is in one important case demonstrably historical and not theoretical or the effect of later ratiocination. The Biblical text mentions only one form of corporal punishment, viz. flagellation. The culprit had to be beaten in presence of the judge, and the maximum number of stripes was *forty* (Deut. xxv. 2, 3). But the Rabbis limited the number to 39 (Mishnah Makkoth iii. 10). This limitation, and the arguments by which the Rabbis supported it, are of the very type which raises suspicion of humanitarian idealisation. Yet it is a fully attested fact that 39 and not 40 was indeed the legal number practically administered by the courts. We must not rely on the circumstance that Josephus (4 *Antiq.* viii. 23) actually states the forty stripes less one as the Pentateuchal law. But there is the direct evidence of II Cor. xi. 24, "Five times received I forty (stripes) less one." These facts are no doubt well known, but it seemed appropriate to recall them in this argument. The Pharisaic humanitarianism, in this case at least, corresponded to actual fact.

Of course the main ground for suspicion of the historicity of the Mishnaic account of procedure before the Sanhedrin is the constitution of the Court and the personality of its President. Even, however, if on these constitutional matters the Mishnah reflects later rather than earlier conditions, does it follow that the same is true of the regulations recorded? For myself, I am inclined to accept Dr A. Büchler's theory that there were *two* Courts in ancient times—the one political, the other religious[1]. This theory does largely reconcile the conflicting statements in the Greek and Hebrew sources, in Josephus and the New Testament on the one hand and the Rabbinic books on the other. But for our present discussion a main point is this. Bacher, who however wrote before the publication of Büchler's work on the Sanhedrin (1902), impartially sums the matter up in these terms: "As the Jewish people itself, immediately after the destruction of Jerusalem, began a new life...so also the Sanhedrin of Jerusalem experienced a kind of resurrection....This notion of the persistence of the Sanhedrin

[1] G. A. Smith rejects the theory (*Jerusalem*, i. 422); J. Z. Lauterbach accepts it (*Jewish Encyclopedia*, xi. 42). Cf. my remarks s.v. *Sanhedrin*, in Hastings' *Encyclopaedia of Religion and Ethics*, vol. xi.

even after the destruction of Jerusalem...has largely influenced the traditions about the Sanhedrin. What was true of the new institution was transferred to the ancient one, and the historical picture of the latter was thus essentially changed. Yet it may be assumed, on the other hand, that faithful adherence to tradition about the ancient Sanhedrin secured the retention in the new body of many peculiarities of the institution as it had existed in its last decades. In this way even the statements about the Sanhedrin preserved in Tannaite tradition and in halachic theory may be treated as historical evidence[1]."

Particularly would it be the case with those aspects of criminal procedure which had become practically obsolete. On the one hand, continuity of experience failed, and this must be allowed for as a cause of imaginative representation. On the other hand, because of the gap between present and past, there would be less tendency to read the past in the light of the present. On the whole, when every allowance is made for the theoretical and academic tendencies in the Mishnaic account of legal procedure, there seems no adequate reason why that account should not be utilised, cautiously and critically, in discussing and illustrating the Trial Narratives of the Gospels. The latter were not nearer in time to the facts than are many records of the former. So great, indeed, is the discrepancy between the Rabbinic and the Gospel trials, that the Mishnah (Sanh. iv. 13 end) almost looks like a polemic of the former against the latter. This suggestion would naturally strengthen Mr Danby's thesis. The Gospel narratives would, however hardly have been familiar to Jews before the date of this Mishnah.

[1] Hastings' *Dictionary of the Bible*, iv. 398.

## XVI. THE IMITATION OF GOD.

My primary duty is to thank the Society* for the honour which it has conferred on me. If I pass on without further preface, it is not because my gratitude is perfunctory, but because many words would only obscure, without adequately expressing, my appreciation.

I take it that I am in this position of undeserved dignity because we, of this Society, believe that different theologies are not necessarily antagonistic. The representatives of those different theologies may agree, not merely in a general devotion to truth, but even in certain particular truths at which, by various routes, they arrive.

Hence I have been led to a choice of subject—the Imitation of God—by two considerations. First, there is the greatness of the idea itself; second, its ubiquity. And by this I do not merely mean that the idea was as Pharisaic as it ever was Pauline. (Cf. First Series, p. 166.) I doubt whether it is commonly realised, certainly I did not formerly realise myself, how wide-spread in time and place this stupendous idea is. All religions have accepted it; most have added something to it. The highest formula of moral or ascetic perfection, the theme of some of the greatest of the world's books, it finds its place also in totemistic cults, which side by side with the idea of tabu, or separation between gods and men, place what may in the present context be taken as the idea of mana or identity. This is a profound fact. "Keep off—Come near"—the double cry of the divine to the human, is the antinomy of all religions, including yours and mine. Well then, the ideal of the Imitation of God forms the crown of Judaism and of Christianity, but it graced also the brow of Pythagoras[1]. A tradition that Stobaeus cites ascribes to Pythagoras the precept ἕπου θεῷ—"Follow God." Plato took it from the Pythagoreans, and though no doubt Philo was strongly influenced also by the story of man's creation in Genesis, and by his glorious conception of the Vision of God as man's highest good—Philo certainly owed some of the eloquence with which he expounds the idea to Plato[2]. In Buddhism, too, according to

* This chapter formed the Presidential Address before the Oxford Society of Historical Theology on November 3, 1921. It is here printed as delivered, but the extra notes at the end are additions to the spoken lecture.

[1] See Note 1 at end of chapter. [2] See Note 2 at end of chapter.

Dr Estlin Carpenter's latest and greatest book, the *Imitatio Buddhae* prevails[3]. So, too, with the older religions of Egypt and Assyria. Of course I cannot cover all this ground, nor do more than make this passing allusion to the acts of imitation, of dressing up and mimicry, in rite and drama, to represent deity,—or recall an Alexander assuming the god, affecting to nod, or a self-deified Antiochus wearing Jove's costume and coiffure. Suffice it to generalise that, though this idea of the Imitation of God is the crown of the highest religions, yet gems of itself, however rough and ill-cut, may be discerned on the masks of painted savages.

Nay, it may even be argued that but for the legacy left by the primitive cults we should have lost many a fine element of religion. Could we readily abandon, for instance, all that is involved in the metaphor of Potter and Clay, as effective in Omar Khayyam and in Browning as it was in Jeremiah and the poets of the medieval Synagogue? But such a metaphor must have originated in a crudely anthropomorphic environment. Keeping, however, strictly to the subject now before us, but for this legacy from primitive thought, it is hard to see how the idea of the Imitation of God could have survived in advanced religions. Herein lies a fine moral for the humanist. The Victorian poets, not least Tennyson, were much worried by the apparent waste of life in red-toothed Nature; but there has been no waste of life in the domain of the spirit. Superstition, as the author of *Psyche's Task* has proved, by the very agency of its tabus, strengthened, if it did not create, some of the fundamental institutions on which modern civil order rests: the protection of human life and property, the support of authority, the sacredness of marriage[4]. Similarly, we may add, superstition has worked in the spiritual concerns of mankind. There has been no waste. This noble ideal of the Imitation of God derives from primitive notions as to the nature of God. Had not these primitive notions once operated, or had they failed to leave their indelible mark on the authors of Leviticus and of the Gospels, it is difficult to see how the Imitation of God could ever have arisen, or how, having arisen, it could have survived. The idea obviously needs as its basis an anthropomorphic conception of God. Man's intimate realisation of himself as made in the Image of God is the correlative of his persistent tendency to make God in his own image. The cynical jests

[3] See Note 3 at end of chapter.

[4] See Note 4 at end of chapter.

against this tendency are ill-conceived[5]. They go back very far, to Xenophanes.

> The Ethiop gods have Ethiop lips,
> Bronze cheeks, and woolly hair;
> The Grecian gods are like the Greeks,
> As keen-eyed, cold, and fair.

It was indeed Israel's task, on revising his experiences, to conceive God at Horeb with no manner of form. But with Israel, too, not only was this a slow process, for in the earlier account of the theophany in Exodus there was a perceptible anthropomorphic element, but the traces of the old stages and strata are visible even in the final product in Deuteronomy. How could it be otherwise? Religion is continuous, and as, in Toy's words, "the god's character is shaped by all the influences that go to form the tribal life, and the god thus embodies from generation to generation the tribe's ideals of virtue"—as this is the case, and as, though we do not like to admit it, tribalism is still the badge of all our faiths, it follows that God, to the end as far as we know the end, must in a certain sense stand for ourselves idealised, in the ideal to which we desire to reach. For, passing beyond crude anthropomorphism, what can we do but speak of God in terms of our own nature, while we aim at elevating that nature to something above itself? What else can we mean by God in such a context? We cannot be thinking of the Absolute, for as Philo said, the Absolute is inimitable. Is that why à Kempis speaks not of the Imitation of God but of the Imitation of Christ? Albertus Magnus, on the other hand, entitles a delightful little treatise of his *De adhaerendo Deo*. Be that as it may, many readers will, I think, have found Mr A. I. Tillyard "quietly persuasive" in his recent defence of the anthropomorphic frame of mind. On page 260 of his *Manuscripts of God*, Mr Tillyard writes:

> We take our ideas of Beauty, Truth, and Goodness, and as it were produce them to infinity; then we assign them as attributes to the All-maker and the All-powerful.... We found our ideas of God on ourselves; but we raise them as high as we can above ourselves....Man has an instinct for perfection, and the idea of God is the satisfaction of it.

This is, naturally, not intended to be a final analysis, for we still have to explain the source of our ideas of Beauty, Truth, and Goodness, which we produce to infinity; we have to explain how we came by

[5] See Note 5 at end of chapter.

"the instinct for perfection." If I may borrow the term and re-apply it, this "instinct for perfection," I suggest, is not at all a bad summary of the underlying motive for Imitating God. For though, as I have said, Mr Tillyard's analysis of God Himself is not final, it does help to explain the variety of phases in which the Imitation of God appears among the higher religions. Man's conception of himself and of God act and interact in the conception of the model to be imitated, as well as in the making of the copy. Sometimes, nay often, man seeks for his model a concrete example, not God Himself, but an ideal representative of God,—a personality, not the Absolute, but regarded by the imitator as the nearest to the Absolute that has come within his experience or vision. Abu Said, the tenth century Moslem mystic, says: "I did everything that I had heard of as having been done by the Prophet. Having read that when he was wounded in the foot in the Battle of Uḥud, he stood on his toes to perform his devotions, for he could not set the sole of his foot upon the ground—I resolved to imitate him, and standing tip-toe, I performed a prayer of 400 genuflexions." This, be it noted, was not an exercise of mere pietism, but a discipline enabling the disciple to grow into the likeness of the "perfect man" as the Arab mystics styled Mohammed. In the same spirit the Buddhist saint takes up the Master's begging bowl. When Paul said "Imitate me as I Christ,"—compare 1 Cor. xi. 1 (*μιμηταί μου γίνεσθε, καθὼς κἀγὼ Χριστοῦ*) with 1 Thess. i. 6 (*καὶ ὑμεῖς μιμηταὶ ἡμῶν ἐγενήθητε καὶ τοῦ Κυρίου*)—when Paul used such terms, he not only showed profound knowledge of human nature, but was making allowance for the fact that to imitate a concrete imitator was easier than to follow in the track of an idea. There is a Philonean echo in this, for to Philo, who coined the phrase "heavenly man," and places him between the Absolute God and the earthly man—to Philo, as to Paul ordinary humanity stands third off from God; there is first God, then the Archetype, in whose image (according to Philo) Adam was made. It is this Archetype, not the Absolute, that man must hope to imitate. But we must restrict ourselves for the moment to this one thought—that the content of the ideal to be imitated largely depends concretely on the imitator's construction of the model. The law-loving, transcendental Pharisee thinks chiefly of moral perfection as the goal of imitation; the ascetic and mystic lover of Christ, like the author of the *Imitatio*, thinks of the passion and the sacrifice[6]. Polycarp "waited to be betrayed as also the

[6] See Note 6 at end of chapter.

Lord had done," and we see the same spirit charmingly shown in the Old French ballads of chivalry. In the Chançun de Willame, written about the date of the first Crusade, Vivien first entreats God to save his life from the Saracens, but forthwith retracts his prayer, exclaiming: "Christ was not saved, why should not I suffer too?" All this substitution of a concrete model in place of an Absolute ideal means that men are making the model, or at all events selecting their favourite qualities of the model, as well as copying it. In Judaism, too, we find recurrent phases of the imitation of concrete personalities—Abraham, Aaron, Hillel, and in the sixteenth century onwards Isaac Lurya. None of these personalities, not even I think Christ, is conceived of as Absolute Deity, but the qualities of Deity are conceived of as represented (in the act of imitation) by these personalities. This remark applies less to the Jewish than to the other examples; the mediate stage between God, the model, and Israel the imitator, consisted mainly of the *attributes* of God rather than of any concrete exemplifier of those attributes. In the desire to counter the Islamic claim that Mohammed was "perfect man," Maimon might be almost tempted to assign that rôle to Moses. But the Pharisaic thought does not, in the main, set up individuals as perfect models. It turns to God's example in his attitude to man as the model for man's attitude to his fellow. In certain phases of Jewish scholasticism the divine attributes, as just defined, may almost be termed the bridge by which man might, very imperfectly, cross the gap between human and divine nature. The attributes are not God, but the means by which he may be known and approached.

All these forms of mediation between God the Absolute and the model for imitation, are steps in the progress away from that anthropomorphism out of which the Imitation of God arose, and from which it still derives a good deal of its driving power. After transferring to God certain qualities found in man, it idealises these as God's, and suggests their re-appearance by way of imitation in man. This process is apparent in the Book of Genesis itself. God creates man in his Image (ṣelem)—an anthropomorphic statement if ever there was one. Melito of Sardes contended, with a good deal of justice, that the original text must have meant the resemblance to be physical. Origen whimsically replies: If so, why has man only two eyes and not the seven eyes of the Lord in Zechariah's vision; or, why is man wingless, while the Psalmist's God has wings under which man may take refuge? It was an early device to cut the knot by assuming that the image in which Adam was made was not God's but Adam's ordained type. "In his (man's) image, in an upright form, God made man," is the rendering of Symmachus. This "upright form" idea of the image has an interesting history[7]; in the Aboth de R. Nathan the serpent envies Adam's erect stature; it recurs in Ovid and in Milton, being a favourite with the poets. The notion of an archetype of the human form, on the other hand, has had theological rather than poetical following. We have seen that it is Philo's view, and it has left its trace in the marriage service of the modern synagogue. There is a remarkable passage in Baba Bathra (58 a) regarding Bannaah, the Old Mortality of the Talmud. He enters the patriarchal burial caves, sees Jacob, but when about to inspect Adam, is warned off by a Daughter of the Voice: "Thou hast looked on the likeness of my Image, at my actual Image thou mayest not look." Bannaah, we are told, had already caught a glimpse of the soles of Adam's feet, and noted that they were like two suns[8]. Philo, of course, denies all physical likeness between man and God. Like Marcus Aurelius, he thinks of mind as the "fragment of God" in man. "The resemblance," says Philo, "refers to the mind: for the mind of man has been made after the likeness of that One Mind which is in the Universe as its primitive model." In Daniel certainly the human-angelic form is spiritual. Now there would seem to be in the editor's treatment of the Genesis story something of the same tendency[9]. I am much attracted by Jastrow's suggestion. He regards the anthropomorphic phrase "in God's Image" as a survival from Babylonia which has been intentionally mitigated by the addition of the clause "according to our likeness," which the LXX wrongly introduces with καὶ as an independent clause, while it is really a limiting gloss.

> This term, 'according to our likeness,' (says Jastrow) is added without a conjunction as an explanatory term with the evident intention of weakening the anthropomorphism of the phrase 'in the Image of God.' The old phrase no longer satisfied an advanced age, and a new turn was accordingly given to it by the supplementary expression. The writer warns us, as it were, not to interpret the word literally. He seems to say to us: Be careful. The verse does not mean that God has a human form, but that man is like unto God—has divine attributes.

Here then we are at the heart of the problem. What *are* the divine attributes which man possesses, and by virtue of which he is able, in some sense, to make God a model for imitation? It will, I fancy, be

[7] See Note 7 at end of chapter.
[8] See Note 8 at end of chapter.
[9] See Note 9 at end of chapter.

most profitable if I turn for my answer chiefly to Jewish theology, some such restriction being compulsory in a short address. Nor can I examine those Old Testament passages, into which some critics (I think wrongly) read the Greek idea of the Envy of the Gods—the idea that the Gods do not desire too close an imitation, but seek to keep certain privileges and possessions for themselves. The Lord's jealousy is directed not against man, but against arrogance, be it of men or of rival gods[10]. Still less will I spend myself on Philo—delightful though the task would be. Philo, on Imitation, is admirably expounded by Drummond, though he occasionally misinterprets. A new, revised, enlarged edition of Drummond's *Philo-Judaeus* is a real desideratum. In the older Midrash, which in such contexts is much influenced by the Alexandrian Judaism, man is described as compounded of elements from the upper and lower worlds[11]. He is part beast, part angel. With the beast he feeds, excretes, reproduces his kind, is physically mortal. With the angel, he stands erect, he speaks, he has intellect, and though he dies he lives again. He has the freedom of will to rise on the stepping-stones of his angelic traits to higher things, or to sink down to the level of his bestial traits. Plato has a similar idea. Later Jewish writers are more generous in their allowance to man of angelic or divine qualities. Sabbethai Donnolo, the Hebrew physician of Oria (913–982), carries out the idea of the upper and lower in an analogy of the microcosm and macrocosm which seems in part original to himself. He does not only compare man to the Universe, but also man to God. Donnolo does this in a commentary on the Image of God texts in Genesis. God governs, so does man; God knows past and future, so does man, by memory and dream; God sustains the universe, man his family; God knows good and evil, so does man; God creates, so does man, by his agriculture. Man resembles God in every quality except the possession of the yeṣer and mortality. The yeṣer, it is, that gives man the capacity to rise or fall. This, I repeat, is not at all what we usually understand by the microcosm-macrocosm analogy; with Donnolo the terms of the analogy are God-Man, as well as Nature-Man. If we go a little onwards in time, we note the gathering strength of the thought that all the divine attributes, possessed by man latently, may be brought into action by man's conscious imitation[12]. This advance in comprehensiveness was made under the influence of the Zoharist mysticism, though we must pass over the

[10] See Note 10 at end of chapter.
[11] See Note 11 at end of chapter.
[12] See Note 12 at end of chapter.

Zohar itself, that unique jumble of conventional Cabbalism and daring spiritual originality. Let us stop at Moses Cordovero, a member of the famous Safed group of Jewish mystics, founded by Isaac Lurya in the early part of the sixteenth century. Cordovero is a philosopher of some historical importance, for his thought is claimed to have influenced Spinoza, his younger contemporary. Cordovero distinguished God from man metaphysically, but mystically he says: "From God we all proceed, in him we are all contained; our life is interwoven with his...Nor is vegetable and animal life outside him...all is one and nothing is separate from him." (Cf. *J. E.* x. 370–1.) But we are not concerned with Cordovero's main works; what is of special import for our discussion is a little book of his, as popular as it is wonderful. The British Museum alone possesses a dozen editions; I bought mine for a few pence in Whitechapel. What do anti-Semites, with their talk of international financiers and Bolsheviks, really know of the Jews, seeing that such books are among their favourite literature? Cordovero's book is called *Tomer Deborah*, "Deborah's Palm-Tree"—like many a mystic Cordovero was fond of fanciful titles, his greatest treatise is the *Pardes Rimmonim*—"the Garden of Pomegranates." He opens "Deborah's Palm-Tree" with the sentence: "Man must liken himself to his Master" (*kono*, a word hard to translate—purchaser, owner, and even maker). He then quotes Micah vii. 18–20:

> Who is a God like unto thee, that pardoneth iniquity, and passeth by the transgression of the remnant of his heritage? He retaineth not his anger for ever, because he delighteth in mercy. He will turn again and have compassion upon us; he will tread our iniquities under foot: and thou wilt cast all their sins into the depths of the sea. Thou wilt perform the truth to Jacob, and the mercy to Abraham, which Thou hast sworn unto our fathers from the days of old.

Cordovero sees in these verses the thirteen divine attributes, every one of which man must copy. He takes the clauses one by one, explains God's method, and then calls on his reader to go and do likewise. Thus, man must bear insult; must be limitless in love, finding in all men the objects of his deep and inalienable affection; he must overlook wrongs done to him, and never forget a kindness. Cordovero insists again and again on this divine patience and forbearance, on God's passing over man's many sins and on his recognition of man's occasional virtues. So must man act. And he must temper his justice with mercy, must be peculiarly tender to the unworthy. His whole being must be attuned to God's being. His earthly eye must be open to the good in all men, as is the Heavenly eye; his earthly ear must be deaf to the slanderers and the foul, just as the Heavenly ear is receptive only of the good[13]. For God loves all men, whom he made in his very Image, and how shall man hate where God loves?

I have quoted from Cordovero because I so love the book, and also because I wished to enforce the fact that this type of literature has a vast Jewish public. But the question arises, to what extent had Cordovero a precedent in the older Jewish literature? Now the text Deut. xi. 22 ends thus: "To love the Lord your God, to walk in all His ways, and to cleave unto Him"—a frequent combination this, in Deuteronomy—to love God, to walk in His ways, to cleave to Him. Whereupon the Sifrê remarks: "*In all His ways:* these are the ways of the Holy One, blessed be He: the Lord, the Lord, merciful and gracious, longsuffering and abundant in goodness and truth, keeping mercy for thousands, forgiving iniquity and transgression and sin" (Exod. xxxiv. 6, 7). So says this text, while another text tells us (Joel iii. 5): Whoever shall be called (reading yikkare?) by the Name of the Lord shall be saved. But how is it possible for a man to be called by the Name of the Lord? Only thus: As the Lord is called merciful and gracious, so do thou be merciful and gracious, offering gifts to all without price; as the Lord is called righteous: "The righteous in all His ways," so be thou righteous; as the Lord is called "loving in all His doings" (Psalm cxlv.), "so be thou also loving." This is by no means an isolated passage; there are very many others, some of which are quoted in chapter 20 of the First Series of these Studies. Thus on Deut. xiii. 4, the Talmud (Soṭa 14 a) calls on man to imitate God, who clothed the naked (Adam and Eve), visited the sick (Abraham), and buried the dead (Moses). The whole Torah from Genesis to Deuteronomy thus bids Israel imitate God. On this idea a whole Code of moral perfection is built up; on no other idea (except perhaps that of holiness which, as we shall see, enters essentially into the ideal of imitation) is the Rabbinic scheme of the God-like life so thoroughly and consistently worked out[14].

These ideas connect themselves with three Hebrew words: to love, to walk, to cleave, words often collocated in Deuteronomy. Following after God, cleaving to Him, are in fact declared in Deut. xiii. 3, 4 to be the tests of Israel's love. Love the motive, obedience and attachment the results. Deuteronomy thinks primarily of devotion

[13] See Note 13 at end of chapter. [14] See Note 14 at end of chapter.

to the Lord as contrasted with other Gods, of performance of his commandments as an act of obedience to himself. But these limitations do not exhaust the meaning of the Pentateuch. Hence, quite properly, these verbs became the especial darlings of Christian as of Jewish exponents of the Imitation of God. Moreover they were fully appreciated by the Jewish legalists. Maimonides opens his enumeration of the affirmative precepts of the Law with the precepts to love, to cleave, to imitate. To love, to follow, to cleave—ahab, halach, dabak—to love even unto death, to follow through fire and water, to cleave in face of tempting calls to detachment—these words, and the thoughts they convey, recur in the literature of saintliness, martyrdom, and self-abnegation, above all in the literature of Imitation, Jewish and Christian alike.

Take two famous Christian books already referred to, to which, had I time, I would refer at greater length. "He that followeth me shall not walk in darkness," proclaims the "Light of the World" in the Fourth Gospel. It is with this text that Thomas à Kempis opens the "world's own book." The oldest English version (1519) accordingly entitles the *Imitatio* "Ye folowynge Jesu cryst." But though this is confirmed by other editions, the English title somewhat obscures the intention of à Kempis. The German *Nachfolgung* is nearer, better even is *Nachahmung*. À Kempis could so easily have taken the specific incidents of the life of Jesus as specific models; it would have been so natural to trace the Master's footsteps, and at every stage point the moral of imitation. À Kempis does not, however, make what seems to an outsider the mistake of some modern Christians who treat Jesus as a law-giver—witness some of the recent discussions on divorce. The author of the *Imitatio* does something far bigger; he makes surprisingly few allusions to the concrete facts of the life of Jesus. It is not a copy of Christ's acts or precepts, but conformity with, surrender to, his mind that à Kempis pleads for. For this reason it is the renunciation and passion of Jesus that à Kempis alone cites; for it is these that he sets up as his ideal[15].

Much the same is true of the other fine Christian book to which I refer, the *De Adhaerendo Deo* of Albertus Magnus. *Adhaerere* is the regular Vulgate translation of *dabak*, cleave; in fact I do not think that any other Latin word is ever used by Jerome, when he is rendering *dabak*. Yet, strangely enough, Albertus was not thinking of *dabak*

[15] See Note 15 at end of chapter.

when he wrote of adhering to God. He does not quote Deuteronomy; he does not quote the 63rd Psalm—that Psalm of passionate desire: "My soul thirsteth for Thee, my flesh longeth, my soul cleaveth after Thee." Bearing such texts in mind it is intelligible that the verb *dabak*, and the derived noun *debekuth*, became the specific late Hebrew not merely for the most absorbed devotion in prayer, but for the closest, most immovable and most immediate attachment to God, and for the eager, sometimes overstrung emotion of seeking union with Him. In Jeremiah the figure is strongly used. "For as the girdle cleaveth to the loins of a man, so have I caused to cleave unto me the whole house of Israel" (xiii. 11). This, however, was not strong enough for the later Hebrews. In Numbers (xxv.) we read of Israel joining itself to Baal Peor, the verb being *ṣamad*, which also appears in *ṣamid* bracelet. Yes, says the Talmud, to Baal Peor, sinful Israel was lightly set as a bracelet on a woman's arm, but faithful Israel is clasped to me in actual (and inseparable) contact (Sanh. 64 a). But Albertus Magnus cites none of these passages. The text of his *De Adhaerendo Deo* is certainly a passionate enough outpouring: it is Psalm lxxiii. 28 : *kirbath elohim li tob*: Mihi autem adhaerere Deo bonum est. This is not the true Vulgate rendering (which rightly has *propinquare*, not *adhaerere*); it is taken from the earlier Latin Psalter which (like the Anglican P.B. version) survived and ousted the Authorised Vulgate in public worship of the Roman Church. This earlier Latin Psalter was translated not from the Hebrew but from the Greek, which in this sentence has προσκολλᾶσθαι to be stuck to, to be glued to, hence to cleave to. Now προσκολλᾶσθαι is the ordinary LXX rendering of *dabak*. The LXX probably read *dibkath* for the *kirbath* of the M.T., a genuine variant which, like so many others, is ignored in the Kittel edition. Though, however, Albertus Magnus does not quote Deuteronomy textually, his thought is in line with it, for, as we have seen, the idea of cleaving is frequently associated in Deuteronomy with the idea of loving, just as, in English, attachment comes to mean affection. So, says Albertus in a passage from which I would that I could quote more: "It is love only that turneth us towards God, that transformeth us into God, that we cleave to God by, and that maketh us become one spirit with him." Yet, after all, cleaving is hardly the last word which the idea of Imitation has to speak. Absorption and union, as we find them in Thomas and Albertus, are not the same as sharing independently. Unless the copy become as the model, the Imitation is imperfect. If Imitation is likeness, the likeness must eventually be of equals. So we find in an old Midrash this bold parable: "A king entered his park to go the rounds with his gardener, but the latter hid from his master. Why hidest thou, asked the king; lo I am like thyself. So in futurity will the Holy One, blessed be He, take pleasure strolls with the righteous. But the righteous, seeing Him, will tremble before Him. The Lord will answer: Am I not like you[16]?" Or in another passage (Pesiqta Rabbathi 46 b): "In this world Israel cleaves to the Holy One; hereafter they will be, and be like Him." The goal is reached, not in absorption but in equality, the copy and the original are of one order, though the idea of reverence remains. Naturally such an idea is delicately treated in the Rabbinic literature, but that it was not infrequent is curiously evidenced by a manipulation of text to avoid it. On Exodus: this is my God *veanvehu*—Abba Saul said: "I will be equal to Him, merciful and compassionate as He." Obviously he explained *veanvehu* as *ani vahu* "I and He,"—an expression of equality which the editors of the Rabbinic text have quite obliterated, though it clearly underlies what has been left, and makes its reappearance in a very ancient Mishnaic phrase which has survived from Temple times into the Synagogue liturgy for the Feast of Tabernacles[17].

By throwing this consummation to the life hereafter, a formal breach with the divine supremacy and transcendentalism was avoided. But this is not all. In the Hebrew Bible God is far removed from man, though he is brought near by prayer. God's nature is, however, discriminated from human nature by Power, Wisdom, Eternity, Constancy, Uniqueness, Holiness. Judaism never has abandoned, never can abandon, this transcendental idea of God. But just because of the anthropomorphic background of the Scriptures, the separation was never complete in language, and the mystics had no difficulty in reconciling their immanent theories with the Hebrew transcendentalism. Israel's uniqueness on earth, corresponds to God's Uniqueness in heaven. Power—this was not altogether denied to man; by virtue of being made in the Image of God, Adam is to have dominion over nature, a thought that recurs in the eighth Psalm wherein man, little lower than God, is crowned with glory and honour and dominion. These very words are the same as are used elsewhere in doxologies of the Almighty. Nor would it seem that eternity was originally denied to man. There

[16] See Note 16 at end of chapter. [17] See Note 17 at end of chapter.

is much to commend Frazer's theory that the two trees in Eden were, in the oldest form of the myth, a Tree of Life and a Tree of Death, the one allowed the other forbidden. With a belief in Immortality, the "Tree of Life," aided by the poetical use of the figure in Proverbs, becomes quite a conventional symbol. So the Wisdom of Solomon, permeated by the belief in Immortality, not only denies that God created death but asserts that "God made man for incorruption and made him the image of His own everlastingness," which seems the true reading in ii. 23. The murderer, as a familiar Rabbinic epigram runs, diminishes the Image of God, tampers with the divine eikon. Similarly with Wisdom. To Job (xxviii.) Wisdom is a unique possession of Deity, but wisdom is also frequently ascribed to man, for, in Rabbinic phrase, God shares his Wisdom with those who fear Him (T.B. Berachoth 58 a). "The mind of the wise," says Philo, "is the palace of God." Transcendental in fine, as the Rabbinic God ever remains, the Biblical references to God's paternal love for his creatures made it easy for the Talmud to formulate as a simple matter of common belief a most thoroughgoing expression of Immanence—"Three are partners in every human birth—God, father, mother" (Qiddushin 30 b)[18].

But what of the Divine Holiness? Does it not stand for the supreme and unique hall-mark of Deity, the fence to his unapproachable Self? Here, surely, imitation is impossible; and if so, what becomes of the Imitation ideal? But, as with the divine Uniqueness so with the divine holiness—there is the constant correlative, the derived holiness of Israel. Holiness means separateness, but it is a separateness in which man may have his reflected part. How the old idea of separateness clung to the term is seen from the comment of the Sifrâ on Leviticus xix. 2. "Be ye holy—be ye perushim" (separated), "even as God is parush" (separated). And then, since separateness means aloofness from the foul, the unchaste, the cruel, the term "holiness" came to concentrate in itself the whole of the perfect life as Israel understood it; life perfect ritually, morally, spiritually. The word *kadosh* grows ever richer in significance with the ages. Ritual cleanliness, dietary abstinences, communal separateness, detestation of the grosser indulgences and vices and moral licentiousness, the inspiration to purity of thought, action and belief,—in brief the hallowing of life, and of the martyr's sacrifice of life for the hallowing of God—all these ideas, and more, accumulated round the Jewish conception of *kedushah*

[18] See Note 18 at end of chapter.

(holiness). "It is," as Dr Kohler well says, "holiness which permeates the thoughts and motives of life, and hence it is the highest possible principle of ethics." And since the Pentateuch has chosen to put the Imitation formula in terms of holiness, it is therefore quite natural that the Jewish commentators should connect Leviticus xix. 2 with Genesis i. 26. The formula of Imitation is "Be ye holy, for I am holy"; and, "created in the Image of God" man imitates God by stretching upwards towards the Holiness which resides in Him.

Now, with this idea of holiness went the other idea expressed by the term *tamim*, perfect, without blemish, whole-hearted God-wards. It is at first sight tempting to hold that this is why Matthew (v. 48) expresses the Imitation formula in the terms "Be ye perfect, even as your heavenly Father is perfect." Such a formula would be a not unnatural derivative from "Be ye holy, for I the Lord am holy[19]." Yet there is no verbal parallel in Rabbinic literature to Matthew's form, it is original to him, and unique in the Synoptics. Luke's version (vi. 36) "Be ye merciful as your Father is merciful" has, on the other hand, many Pharisaic parallels as we have seen. We find in Midrashim side by side with the text "Be thou perfect" texts like "as for God his way is perfect," but the Midrash has no thought there of Imitation, it only expounds that man may become perfect by obedience to the perfect Law. Matthew's phrase remains unparalleled. Though, however, he differs in wording from Luke, he intends much the same, except that the first Gospel's "perfection in love" as the aim of imitation is a fuller concept than the third Gospel's "perfection in mercy." Chrysostom's comment on Matthew is admirable. Certainly, he urges, we must love our enemies, for they are our best friends—giving us the opportunity of imitating the divine love extended as it is to the evil and good alike. Very fine, too, is a Rabbinic note on such passages as "Vengeance is mine." It is the *Lord* alone, who in Nahum's phrase is *baal ḥemah*—rendered "Master of Wrath." Man's anger masters him, God masters His anger[20]. The implication clearly is that He only can exercise the retributory function. He alone is not swayed from lasting right by momentary sense of wrong. It would seem that the association of such an idea with God's holiness is as old as Hosea. God, says Hosea almost in so many words, is not diverted from his eternal purpose by the emotion of anger which often moves men away from their ideals. "I will not execute the fierceness of mine anger, I will

[19] See Note 19 at end of chapter. [20] See Note 20 at end of chapter.

not return to destroy Ephraim: for I am God and not man; the Holy One in the midst of thee." (Hosea xi. 9.) There would then be, besides such qualities of Deity which man, however humbly, can and may imitate on earth—certain other qualities which he must not *attempt* to imitate at all. Thrice was Moses angry, say the Rabbis, and thrice he failed to reproduce the mind of God. (T.B. Pesaḥim 66 b; Levit. R. xii. § 1.) The whole Rabbinic literature might, I believe and at all events hope, be searched in vain for a single instance of the sterner of the Old Testament attributes of God being set up as a model for man to copy[21].

This is not the case with the Greeks. We appreciate Plato's attack on the Poets when we remember the appeal made, in the *Eumenides*, to the example of Zeus' ill-treatment of his father Cronos, as a precedent for current imitation. Mahaffy thinks that the case was even worse; that there was positive demoralisation, and that the Homeric poets transferred to the gods the immoral ideas of a later age, the rhapsodists reading their own vicious tastes into the purer character of the older Gods—inventing for the immortals a degradation to match the prevalent corruption of mortals. Plato's own conception was far higher. To become like God, he says, in the *Theaetetus* (176), is to become holy, just, and wise. This is a "Pythagorean" passage, but it would have troubled neither Christian nor Jew to find a most cherished ideal anticipated by the Greeks. As Josephus said, and as Church and Synagogue went on believing throughout the Middle Ages, "Pythagoras transferred a great many of the ideas of the Jews into his own philosophy[22]."

On the positive side Plato fails to reach Paul's exquisite figure that the followers of Christ are "transformed into Christ's image." But on the negative side Plato has a thought to which one of my earlier Midrashic quotations is a parallel. Plato sees so clearly that the slave of evil gradually transforms himself into the Image of Evil. "There are two patterns," says Socrates, "eternally set before [the unrighteous], the one blessed and divine, the other godless and wretched, but they do not see them, or perceive that in their utter folly and infatuation they are growing like the one and unlike the other, by reason of their evil deeds; and the penalty is they lead a life answering to the pattern they are growing like." This is a profound warning against setting up any lower model than the highest. But Plato was not ready to make

[21] See Note 21 at end of chapter. [22] See Note 22 at end of chapter.

the one step further which, at all events, Jewish theology did occasionally make, if only by implication. In another Dialogue, discussing the nature of Holiness, Socrates raises the question which is after all the fundamental: Is the holy what is loved by God, or is it holy because God loves it? We should put it: Is the Model before the Imitator, or does the Model grow out of the Imitation? Socrates accepts neither alternative and gives no solution, but asserts the proposition that it is absurd to talk of making the gods better by attention to them, or profiting them by service. Holiness, says Socrates, is not a barter between gods and men, taking what we need, giving what they need.

This is the absolute standpoint—just as the Hebrew prophets ridiculed the notion that God was in any way advantaged by the sacrifices brought by his worshippers. But, to come to my last point, though God is not affected by man, man's idea of God is so affected, and it is man's idea of God that man imitates. I think that Jewish theology goes even further, and by a bold step crosses the bounds of the relative into the confines of the Absolute. When men pray, the Angel appointed over prayer catches each act of homage and sets it in the Crown of the Most High. The Crown itself is thus beautified by man's devotion. So acts of human generosity are models for God Himself to imitate; Abraham's readiness to suppress his feelings in offering Isaac is to be matched by God's readiness to suppress his wrath. God consents, in another Midrash (see First Series, p. 155), to copy Joseph's forgiveness of his brethren: "I will be unto Israel a brother like unto Joseph." Then again the distressed Lord (alub) gains satisfaction, tranquillity of soul (naḥath ruaḥ) from Israel's service[23]. Further, there is the whole range of ideas connected with the "Sanctification of the Name." On the one side, God because of Israel's love and holiness sanctifies His name in Israel, becoming for Israel's sake a "*man* of war" (Mechilta ed. Friedmann, p. 38 a). On the other side, God's divine nature is manifested and sanctified by human excellence. From the virtue of the creature you infer the virtue of the Creator—this is the moral drawn from a fine act of delicate honesty by Simeon b. Sheṭaḥ. The esteem in which God is held depends on man. Can we go yet farther? "Seeing," writes Naḥmanides, "that we imitate God, every foul act of ours profanes the model." Does man's virtue sanctify the model? Simeon b. Yoḥai seems to say that it makes the model. The

[23] See Note 23 at end of chapter.

act of sanctification of God does more than glorify God—it, as it were, makes him God. On Isaiah xliii. 12: "Ye are My witnesses and I am God," Simeon b. Yoḥai comments: "If ye are My witnesses, then I am God; but if ye are not My witnesses, then I am not God." The Midrash (Pesiq. d. R. Kahana 102 b) adds the warning formula—*ki-beyachol*—if man may use such language without blasphemy. For Simeon b. Yoḥai's thought is not one to be rested in incautiously or too long, and the Midrash very emphatically asserts elsewhere that God's holiness is quite independent of man's conduct or opinion. "I am holy whether ye sanctify Me or not," says God in the Sifrâ (86 b). But there is something infinitely moving in this hankering of Israel and of all the children of God after the conviction, or perhaps I had better say the self-persuasion, that God and man are correlated ideas, like king and subject, father and child; and that neither side of the relationship is significant without the other. God needs nothing, except our praise, says Clement of Rome (Ep. i. ad Cor. c. 52). But that is a great exception, surely. It is man's reverence that constitutes the whole worth of the world to its divine Creator (T.B. Sabbath 31 b). God is Israel's light, and God yearns for the light which Israel kindles in the sanctuary (Levit. R. xxxi. 1).

The same analogy may be drawn between Model and copy. Plato saw and said that, by persistent surrender to the lower impulses, man grows to the pattern of his vices. Pattern and copy are thus interdependent. We may even assert that a bad copy makes a bad model. For, if artists go on long enough painting ugliness, they may destroy the very ideal of beauty. And, on the positive side, each beautiful work of art helps to enrich and refine the beautiful type[24]. If God must, to man, always somehow correspond to man's concept of Him, it follows that the nobler the imitator the nobler the Imitated. The more a man puts into his ideal of the Model, the more he gets into his copy. Nor need we distress ourselves with the suspicion that this is to move in a circle. For the God-made Idea of Himself comes at last to meet the man-made idea of Him across the void; and man, having made the best copy he could on earth, comes face to face with the Model in heaven.

[24] See Note 24 at end of chapter.

## NOTE I.

Perhaps the most convenient quotation, illustrative of the Pythagorean doctrine of *Imitation*, and the Platonic adoption of the idea, is a passage from Prof. Burnet's informing article on "Pythagoras and Pythagoreanism" in Hastings' *Encyclopaedia of Religion and Ethics*, x. 526:

> If we may also regard the famous description of the true philosopher in the *Theaetetus* (176 B—D) as inspired by Pythagorean teaching, we may go a step further and attribute to Pythagoras the doctrine that the end of man is to become like God (ὁμοίωσις τῷ θεῷ). We are not able to prove this indeed, but it is so far confirmed by the fact that Aristoxenus makes 'the following of God' (τὸ ἀκολουθεῖν τῷ θεῷ) the keynote of the Pythagorean system as expounded by him; and an unknown writer excerpted by Stobaeus (*Ecl.* ii. 249, 8 Wachsmuth; cf. Aristoxenus ap. Iambl. *Vita Pyth.* 137) gives 'Follow God' (ἕπου θεῷ) as a Pythagorean precept, and calls attention to the agreement of Plato with it.

Plato, like the New Testament writers, often uses *μίμησις* or *μιμητής* in such contexts. It may be observed, too, that the Hebrew Bible uses two terms which more or less correspond to the two Pythagorean expressions. The one is the term דמות (which would equal ὁμοίωσις) and the other various constructions with the verb הלך. A familiar Hebraism in Matt. x. 38, Mark viii. 34 (but not Lk. ix. 13) is the construction of ἀκολουθεῖν with ὀπίσω τινος.

The prevalent Hebrew idiom is to *walk after* (הלך אחרי יי, e.g. Deut. xiii. 15), to *walk with* (התהלך עם, e.g. Gen. vi. 9) or to *walk before, in presence of* (התהלך לפני, e.g. Gen. xvii. 1). It is remarkable how often the idea of *walking* is associated with *perfection*. Thus the last quoted text runs: "The Lord appeared to Abraham and said unto him, I am God Almighty; *walk* before me and be thou *perfect* (תמים)." So, of Noah (Gen. vi. 9): "Noah was a righteous man *perfect* in his generations, and Noah *walked* with God." Compare הולך תמים, Prov. xxi. 10, Ps. lxxxiv. 12. It may be that such texts really underlie the choice of phrase in Matt. v. 48.

An interesting LXX use of ἀκολουθεῖν is in Ruth i. 14—Ῥοὺθ δὲ ἠκολούθησεν αὐτῇ, where the Hebrew has the verb דבק (Ruth clave unto her). The LXX is rather shaky in rendering this Hebrew verb in more than one place. On the other hand, the LXX seems never to use any form of μιμέομαι.

The Deuteronomic use of דבק may profitably be illustrated by textual quotations. In Deut. xi. 22, parallel to a diligent fulfilment of the commandment in the previous passage is the phrase: *to love the Lord your God, to walk in all his ways, and to cleave unto him* (ולדבקה־בו). In Deut. xxx. 19, 20: "I call heaven and earth to witness against you this day, that I have set before you life and death, the blessing and the curse: therefore choose life, that thou mayest live, thou and thy seed, to love *the Lord thy God, to obey his voice, and to cleave unto him*, for he is thy life and the length of thy days." To this Joshua xxii. 5 is partly parallel. Then, again, in Deut. x. 20 "*Thou shalt fear the Lord thy God, him shalt thou serve, and to him shalt thou cleave*, and by his name shalt thou swear." Cf. Deut. xiii. 5 (and Joshua xxiii. 8), and finally Deut. iv. 4: "But ye *that cleave unto* the Lord your God, are alive every one of you this day." There is assuredly more in these passages than loyal devotion, however close. There is intensity of feeling which easily rises into the passionate sense of nearness and attachment expressed in the Psalms:— "My soul cleaveth (A.V. followeth hard) after thee, thy right hand upholdeth me," Ps. lxiii. 8; and "I cleave unto thy testimonies," Ps. cxix. 31. The same verb is used of cleaving to idolatry. More to the point is its employment of a man's cleaving in love to a woman (Gen. ii. 24, xxxiv. 3, 1 Kings xi. 2). Of man's friendship to man or woman's to woman the relationship is also expressed by the same verb (Prov. xviii. 24, Ruth i. 14). It is this passion of affection that led, even more than the Deuteronomic passages, to the fondness of the later Jewish mystics for the term דביקות (close cleaving) to represent their sense of devotion, rapt attachment, man's absorption in relation to God, especially during prayer. There is no commoner word than this in the vocabulary of moralists with a mystical turn of mind. The word, however, rarely loses its practical connotation. Cleave to God's laws as well as to his attributes (דבק במצותיו ובמדותיו, Sheloh fol. 2 b). For an earlier expression of the same thought see Numbers Rabba xiv.

## NOTE 2.

Nowhere is Philo's syncretism of Hebraism and Hellenism clearer than in his development of the idea of the Imitation of God. One conclusive piece of evidence will suffice. Philo *quotes* both Deuteronomy and Plato. In *De Migr. Abrahami* 23 (M. I. 456, Cohn-Wendland, ii. 293), the *end* is to follow God: "τέλος οὖν ἐστι κατὰ τὸν ἱερώτατον Μωυσῆν τὸ ἕπεσθαι θεῷ, ὡς καὶ ἐν ἑτέροις φησίν Ὀπίσω κυρίου τοῦ θεοῦ σου πορεύσῃ"—where Deut. xiii. 5 [4] is directly cited. (Note that Philo does not quote exactly the LXX version of אחרי יי אלהיכם תלכו, for the LXX correctly has the plural while Philo uses the singular.)

On the other hand, in *De Fuga* 15 (M. I. 557, C.-W. iii. 126) Philo directly quotes Plato's *Theaetetus* 176—the finest Platonic context for the Pythagorean doctrine of imitation. Indirectly too Philo's metaphor of *fleeing* to God in this chapter is derived from the same passage in Plato. Philo's constant refrain that man must strive to imitate God *as far as he can* is distinctly Platonic. "As far as man can" is indeed a common formula in this context; Marcus Aurelius, for instance, uses it.

A summary of Philo's view on Imitation is to be found in J. Drummond, *Philo-Judaeus*, ii. 286. For the "Vision of God" (ὅρασις θεοῦ), see e.g. *De ebrietate* 20 (M. I. 369, C.-W. ii. 185). Cf. also H. A. A. Kennedy, *Philo's Contribution to Religion* (1919), pp. 192, 234. Maimonides was at one with Philo in interpreting the approach to God as being equivalent to Knowledge of Him (*Guide* I. xviii. and lx.; II. xxxvi.). Elsewhere (*Guide* I. liv.) Maimonides thinks more of the *moral* side of the relationship.

It may be pointed out that, unlike Irenaeus, Origen and Tertullian, Philo draws no distinction (any more than Plato does) between ὁμοίωσις (similitudo) and μίμησις (imitatio). Thus: man must *imitate* God as far as he can, omitting nothing which may lead to the attainable *similarity* (*De Humanitate* 23, M. II. 404, C.-W. v. 319 μιμεῖσθαι θεὸν καθ' ὅσον οἷόν τε, μηδὲν παραλιπόντα τῶν εἰς τὴν ἐνδεχομένην ἐξομοίωσιν). Here Philo was possibly influenced by Hebraic thought. How can man *resemble* God? Only by *imitating* his attributes. In this view, Imitation = the only Resemblance attainable by man.

On the parallel to another Philonean idea in Pharisaic thought (ἀρεσκεία) see Note 23 below.

Philo's description (quoted in the course of the text) of mind as a "fragment" or "shred" of God occurs in *De Somniis*, i. 6 (M. I. 625, C.-W. iii. 212, ἐν ἀνθρώπῳ δὲ νοῦς, ἀπόσπασμα θεῖον ὤν). Philo quotes Gen. ii. 7. This idea persisted in later Jewish thought. Thus Aaron of Rawicz, at the beginning of his Ethical Will (סדר הדרכה, Breslau, 1830), writes that the Israelite's soul is a portion of the divine substance (נשמת האדם מישראל היא חלק מעצמותו ית' סוד האדם העליון). See also the informing article by L. Ginzberg on Adam Ḳadmon ("the original man") in *Jewish Encyclopedia*, i. 181 *seq.*

For Philo's enunciation of the doctrine that the Model which man imitates is *mediate*, the following passage will suffice (Eusebius, *Evan. Prep.* vii. 1, ed. Gifford III. (1) p. 349):

Why, as if speaking of another God, does he say, In the image of God I made man, and not in the image of himself? With consummate beauty and wisdom is this oracle expressed. For nothing mortal could be made in the likeness of the Most High God and Father of the universe, but in the likeness of the second god, who is the Word of the former. For it was right that the rational character in the soul of man should be impressed on it by the divine Word; since the God who is prior to the Word is superior to every rational nature; and it was not lawful for any created thing to be made like to him who is set above the Word in the most excellent and unique nature.

Elsewhere Philo expresses himself without reference to the Logos, when he describes man's mind, on the basis of Genesis i. 26, as the element of resemblance. Nothing earth-born is more like God than is man, but the likeness is not bodily (ἡ δὲ εἰκὼν λέλεκται κατὰ τὸν τῆς ψυχῆς ἡγεμόνα νοῦν), "the mind which exists in each individual has been created after the likeness of that One Mind which is in the universe as its primitive model, being in some sort the God of that body which carries it about and bears its image within it (τρόπον τινὰ θεὸς ὢν τοῦ φέροντος καὶ ἀγαλματοφοροῦντος αὐτόν). In the same rank that the great Governor occupies in the universal world, that same as it seems does the mind of man occupy in man" (*De Opif. Mund.* xxiii., M. I. 16, C.-W. i. 23). There is a fine comparison of the soul of man to the Holy One in T.B. Berachoth 10 a (ed. Cohen, p. 60).

On the Hellenistic contrast between the supreme and unknowable God and the secondary, creative, knowable God, see J. Burnet, *Greek Philosophy*, vol. i. p. 169. For some valuable comments on the relation of Philo's doctrine to the Rabbinic thought, cf. N. I. Weinstein, *Zur Genesis der Agada*, Frankfort a. M. 1901, pp. 46 seq.

In further illustration of Philo's syncretism of "Midrash and philosophy, Plato and the Rabbis," reference may again be made to L. Ginzberg's article on Adam Ḳadmon in the *Jewish Encyclopedia*, vol. i. p. 181. The whole article is of great importance.

Philo's phrase "heavenly man" (οὐράνιος ἄνθρωπος) occurs in *Leg. Alleg.* i. 12 (M. I. 49, C.-W. i. 69)—this "heavenly man, as the perfect image of the Logos, is neither man nor woman" (*De Opif. Mund.* xlvi. M. I. 32, C.-W. i. 46–7) just as in the other passage just cited, the original or heavenly man "as being born in the image of God has no participation in any corruptible or earthlike essence; whereas the earthly man is made of loose material, called a lump of clay." For the close Rabbinic parallels see L. Ginzberg (*loc. cit.*).

The *mediate* character of the Model in the Philonean phraseology is paralleled in the Synagogue Marriage Service (T.B. Kethuboth, 8a) where in the benediction God is eulogised thus: "He made man in his image, in the image of a form created by him" (בצלמו | בצלם דמות תבניתו), i.e. as Ginzberg notes, "Adam was created after the image of a God-created type." (Cf. Aqiba's saying in Mishnah *Aboth*, iii. 14.) Primordial Adam was the "idea" and created man the "image." On the Marriage Service comp. my note in the Annotated ed. of the *Hebrew Prayer Book*, p. ccvi. See also Note 8 below.

## NOTE 3.

The reference to J. Estlin Carpenter is to his *Theism in Medieval India*, 1921, p. 62. Cf. "His (Buddha's) person is the pivot on which all Buddhist thought turns, and the ideal at which every believer should aim" (M. Anesaki in Hastings' *Encycl. R. and E.* v. 448).

On Buddha cf. also C. Eliot, *Hinduism and Buddhism* (ii. 9), where he compares the Bodhicaryâvatâra of Sântiveda (seventh century) to à Kempis' *De Imitatione Christi*. Cf. also E. M. Bowden, *Imitation of Buddha*, p. 8; this writer notes the element of kindness to animals. Cf. Midrash Tanḥuma (ed. Buber) p. 17, and notes 63, 64 with the parallels.

The quotation from Abu Said (the tenth century Moslem mystic) is summarised from R. A. Nicholson's *Studies in Islamic Mysticism* (1921) pp. 15 seq.; on the "perfect man" see *op. cit.* 86, 88, 206. On Maimon's eulogy of Moses see L. Simmons in the *Jewish Quarterly Review*, 1890, ii. 65.

## NOTE 4.

Sir J. G. Frazer's *Psyche's Task*, a "Discourse concerning the Influence of Superstition on the Growth of Institutions," first appeared in 1909; a second edition was published in 1913. In the Introduction, the author sums up his thesis in four propositions:

I. Among certain races and at certain times Superstition has strengthened the respect for government, especially monarchical government, and has thereby contributed to the establishment and maintenance of civil order.

II. Among certain races and at certain times Superstition has strengthened the respect for private property and has thereby contributed to the security of its enjoyment.

III. Among certain races and at certain times Superstition has strengthened the respect for marriage and has thereby contributed to a stricter observance of the rules of sexual morality both among the married and unmarried.

IV. Among certain races and at certain times Superstition has strengthened the respect for human life and has thereby contributed to the security of its enjoyment.

An optimistic moral has never been more brilliantly drawn from the history of human institutions. Is it possible to extract a parallel solace from human nature itself? Some Pharisaic teachers thought it possible. "And God saw every thing that he had made, and behold, it was good exceedingly" (Genesis i. 31). "Every thing?" asks the Rabbi. "He hath made every thing beautiful in its time" (Eccles. iii. 11). Again the Rabbinic query: "Every thing?" The answer is affirmative, for it is the evil yeṣer which is intended in Genesis by the adverb *exceedingly* good. (In other versions, for which see Theodor's notes in his edition of Genesis Rabba, pp. 71–2, the deduction is made from other verbal elements of the text, such as the conjunction *and* behold.) Is, then, the evil yeṣer a good? Yes, for but for it a man would not build a house, nor marry a wife, nor bear children, [nor pursue business, nor plant a vineyard, so that the world order would not be maintained]. The words in brackets occur in some versions. In the Midrash in Psalm xxxvii. (ed. Buber, p. 252) the same useful social ends are ascribed, from another text, to men's envy of one another. In Theodor's edition of Gen. Rabba, ch. ix. § 7 the words are simply:

נחמן בשם ר׳ שמואל. הנה טוב מאד זה יצר טוב. והנה טוב מאד זה יצר הרע. וכי יצר הרע טוב מאד הוא אתמהא. אלא שאלולי יצר הרע לא בנה אדם בית ולא נשא אשה ולא הוליד בנים. וכן שלמה אומר (קהלת ד׳ד) כי היא קנאת איש וגו׳:

This passage is referred to in First Series p. 69 and the whole subject is further treated in the present writer's *Permanent Values in Judaism* (New York 1923), Lecture I on "The Permanent Value of Primitive Ideas."

The same profound idea, that the evil in man may be made to subserve a good purpose, is expressed in several other early Rabbinic passages. In the text Deut. vi. 5 the word for "heart" is לבב (with *two beths*). On which the Sifrê (ed. Friedmann, 73a): "And thou shalt love the Lord thy God with *all thy heart*, with thy two yeṣers, the good and the evil yeṣer. Or, alternatively, *with all thy heart*, that thy heart be not divided towards the Omnipresent." The same thought is found in the Mishnah Berachoth ix. 5 and in the Talmud on the passage; cf. Tosefta vi. 7 ed. Zuckermandel, p. 15, and Targum J. on the Deuteronomic text. Maimonides explains that the idea is that even in moments of transgression or anger man must not omit his consciousness of loving duty towards God. But the thought is far deeper than that. It points to the organic unity of human nature, compounded though it is of two elements, one good and one evil, and both elements must be used to do God's work in the world. (Cf. Abrahams and Montefiore, *Aspects of Judaism*, 1895, p. 95.)

So, too, in another side of the Rabbinic conception of the evil yeṣer. This yeṣer must be captured for good ends by the good yeṣer. Not only must "a man excite his good yeṣer (impulse) against his evil yeṣer, for it is said Be ye angry and sin not" (Ps. iv. 10, T.B. Berachoth, 5a), but the evil yeṣer must be forcibly deported to the house of learning and compelled to join in the discipline of study. "If that ugly one (the evil yeṣer) meets thee, drag him to the house of learning" (T.B. Qiddushin, 30 b). Or, finally, the good yeṣer may unite the evil yeṣer with itself, so that the two may cooperate in good. Thus is explained Psalm lxxxvi. 11 (where again the form לבב with two *beths* is found). "Unite my heart to fear thy name"—the unwilling cattle must be forced to bear the yoke so that the two may plough together (Midrash, *ad loc.*). "I will praise thee, O Lord my God, with all my heart (בכל לבבי)" exclaims the Psalmist. "With the good yeṣer and with the evil yeṣer," comments the Midrash (ed. Buber, p. 374) "so that I may pray with full sincerity" (this seems the meaning of the last clause). The recognition of the lower instincts leads to man's self-knowledge, and this to a frank effort to make the best of his composite nature, and to direct his very passions to a divine end.

## NOTE 5.

Kipling, in *Buddha at Kamakura*, satirises the tendency in the last stanza of that wonderful poem:

> But when the morning prayer is prayed,
> Think, ere ye pass to strife and trade,
> Is God in human image made
> No nearer than Kamakura?

As a warning against Western "superiority," the satire is just. Mr Tillyard, however, better realises the full significance and validity of this anthropomorphic tendency. Jehuda Halevi much earlier also said that "we shall find nothing resembling God more finely than the rational soul"—in other words, the perfect faculty as found imperfectly in man (*Cusari* iv. 3, ed. Hirschfeld, p. 209).

On the complaint of Xenophanes (fr. 16) that the Ethiopian gods are black and snub-nosed, while those of the Thracians are blue-eyed and red-haired, compare J. Burnet, *Greek Philosophy*, vol. i. p. 35. See also Frazer, *Golden Bough*, "Taboo" p. 387; the "Dying God" pp. 3, 194.

Xenophanes' proviso that for man to make a god in his own image required belief and artistic power, really gives away his argument. Whence came the belief and the power? This is the real question. One answer, and not the least plausible, is that the source is Kinship of human and divine, for which Xenophanes makes no allowance. Nor is it clear why P. Shorey, in the last volume of Hastings' *Encyc. Rel. and Ethics* (xii. 48), says of the other side of the relationship—"the assimilation of the human to the divine"—that "it is not a practicable final philosophy of the supreme human good for any race of men in whom the will to live persists." True, the Imitation tends towards "other-worldliness." But there can be no absolute divorce between this and "worldliness." Xenophanes thought it ridiculous for God to be depicted as like man. Are the moderns to think it equally ridiculous for man to aim at godlikeness? Toy well argues that the Imitation of God is one of the most advanced triumphs of religion (*Introduction to History of Religions*, 1913, pp. 3, 266–7).

## NOTE 6.

Sacrifice also had its part in the Pharisaic ideal. It has often been pointed out that the *aqeda* (binding) of Isaac fills an important place in Jewish thought, parallel to that of the Crucifixion in Christian martyrdom. Israel Lévi has devoted an important essay to the subject ("Le Sacrifice d'Isaac et la Mort de Jésus" in *Revue des Études Juives*, vol. lxiv. 1912, pp. 161 seq.). Appeal is made to the Sacrifice of Isaac in two ways, (1) in its redeeming function, as a ground for the divine mercy to Isaac's descendants, and (2) as a model for martyred Israel to imitate in all ages. Very significant is the phrase "perfect burnt-offering" (עולה תמימה) applied to the aqeda (Genesis Rabba, ch. lxiv).

Equally arresting is the sentence that because of Isaac offering himself on the altar, God will in futurity quicken the dead (Pesiqta de R. Kahana, ed. Buber, 200 b). All this, and the use of the aqeda in the Synagogue liturgy, is fully discussed by Lévi.

As to the date at which the aqeda attained this position in Judaism, opinions differ. A. Geiger (*Jüdische Zeitschrift*, 1871, vol. x. p. 171) places it in the third Christian century, and thinks that the Synagogue was indebted to the Church. I. Lévi contests this view. "The Synagogue Ritual for the New Year was already in existence in the first century, and as the passage relating to the aqeda is an integral part thereof, we may be certain that the doctrine was already popular at that time" (*op. cit.* p. 178). Lévi discusses the relation of the Pauline treatment of the Crucifixion to the Pharisaic use of the aqeda, in the same essay.

Obviously, the Rabbinic use of the Sacrifice of Isaac is essentially an element in the doctrine of the "Merits of the Fathers" (זכות אבות). On this doctrine much has been written. A. Marmorstein has recently devoted a special monograph to the subject, and has usefully collected and discussed a large number of passages.

As an incentive to martyrdom for Judaism, the aqeda is often cited in the Middle Ages. This application of Isaac's Sacrifice is pathetic in the extreme. It reaches through the ages; thus it is very strongly enforced by Isaiah Horowitz, a famous mystic and rabbi who, born in Prague in 1555, died in Safed *c.* 1630. The equation of the martyr to Isaac may be found in his master-work *The Two Tables of the Covenant* (Shene Luḥoth ha-Berith), fol. 61 a (foot). To quote a very much earlier passage (dating from a period between 63 B.C. and 38 A.D.), the author of the (so-called) Fourth Book of the Maccabees has this appeal (ch. xvi. 16—25):

My sons, noble is the fight; and do ye, being called thereto to bear witness of our people, fight therein zealously on behalf of the Law of our fathers. For it would be shameful if, while this aged man (Eleazar) endured the agony for religion's sake, you that are young men shrank before the pain. Remember that for the sake of God ye have come into the world, and have enjoyed life, and that therefore ye owe it to God to endure all pain for his sake; for whom also our father Abraham made haste to sacrifice his son Isaac, the ancestor of our people; and Isaac, seeing his father's hand lifting the knife against him, did not shrink....With these words the mother of the seven encouraged every single one of her sons to die rather than transgress the ordinance of God; they themselves also knowing well that men dying for God live unto God as live Abraham, and Isaac, and Jacob, and all the patriarchs.

And so, in his peroration, the preacher (xviii. 20) can exclaim: "Ah, cruel was the day, and yet not cruel, when the cruel tyrant of the Greeks set the fire blazing for his barbarous braziers," and so forth. (On the date of IV. Maccs. see L. B. Townshend in Charles' *Apocrypha and Pseudepigrapha*, vol. ii. p. 654.) For a similar Talmudic application of the martyrdom of the seven sons, see T.B. Giṭṭin 57b, and compare Midrash Echa Rabba (on Lamentations i. 16).

## NOTE 7.

The "upright form" as man's peculiar quality is part of Ovid's picture in *Metamorph.* i. 76—88; cf. Milton, *Paradise Lost*, iv. 288—299. This recalls the ὄρθιον of Symmachus.

Z. Frankel (*Vorstudien zu der Septuaginta*, Leipzig, 1841, p. 188) called attention to the same idea in the LXX of I Samuel xxviii. 14. The Witch of Endor sees "gods coming up out of the earth," and in answer to Saul's further question, she replies, I saw "an erect man (ἄνδρα ὄρθιον) coming out of the earth." E. Nestle, who inaccurately claims to be the first to compare this with Symmachus' rendering of Gen. i. 27, rightly contends that we have here the conception that the upright human stature was an element in the god-like image (*Marginalien und Materialien*, Tübingen, 1893, p. 3). Wellhausen thinks that the LXX read זקף for the זקן of M.T. He refuses to accept Frankel's suggestion that the LXX refers to the myth that usually, in necromantic recalls, persons appear upside-down (T.B. Sanhedrin, 65 a), Samuel appears in his upright (usual) shape (*Der Text der Bücher Samuel*, 1871, p. 13).

It may be suggested that the confusion in the LXX rendering of Eccles. vii. 29 is due to an underlying reference to the same idea. The Midrash, applying all this context to Adam, may also have thought of the idea in relation to the text ("God made man upright" ישר).

According to the Aboth de R. Nathan, ch. i. (ed. Schechter, p. ג) the serpent was envious of man's upright form. Because of this desire, the serpent was doomed to crawl on the ground; previously the serpent had feet (Genesis Rabba, xx. § 5, ed. Theodor, p. 186. Cf. p. 177). This idea is referred to by Josephus: "Depriving him (the serpent) of his feet, God made him trail and crawl on the ground" (I. *Antiq.* i. end).

In Daniel, as in Pharisaic Judaism generally, the "human form" is contrasted to the bestial to imply spirituality. (Cf. A. Bevan, *Daniel*,

p. 119; C. Toy, *Polychrome Ezekiel*, p. 96.) There is a pretty poetical combination of the physical and spiritual, the upright form and quality of soul, in the description of Adam (Pirque R. Eleazar, ch. xi). He "stood upright adorned with the Image of God" (מתואר בדמות אלהים עמד על רגליו).

## NOTE 8.

An excellent account of the facts and legends associated with Bannaah (or Bannayah) is given by L. Ginzberg in the *Jewish Encyclopedia*, ii. 494. Add, for the sun-like heels of Adam, a reference to Midrash Rabba on Eccles. viii. (beginning), and parallels. Compare further the "coats of light" in which (according to R. Meir) Adam and Eve were clothed in Paradise after their disobedience (Gen. Rabba xx. § 12). See also Odes of Solomon xxv. (and elsewhere). Adam obviously recovered his pristine garb of light after his bodily death.

According to Rashi it is Jacob who is intended by the phrase

נסתכלת בדמות דיוקני · בדיוקני עצמה אל תסתכל

This is derived from Gen. Rabba lxviii. § 12, on the basis of Isaiah xlix. 3: "Israel in whom I am glorified (or I glorify myself), thou art he whose eikon is engraved on high." C. F. Burney refers to this passage in discussing John i. 51 (*Aramaic Original of the Fourth Gospel*, p. 115). In Luke's Genealogy (iii. 38) the direct propinquity of *Adam* to deity seems expressed in τοῦ 'Αδάμ, τοῦ θεοῦ, unless the last words go back to the beginning of the genealogy ("—a gigantic parenthesis" as Plummer well objects).

On דיוקן (possibly δείκανον, but more probably a variant of איקונין εἰκόνιον, εἰκών), see S. Krauss, *Griechische und Lateinische Lehnwörter im Talmud, Midrasch und Targum*, vol. ii. 1899, p. 202. Cf. also *op. cit.* p. 40, where many references are made to the use of the word in Rabbinic literature.

Here only one or two remarks need be made. The murderer tampers with the eikon of God (Exod. Rabba xxx. § 16). A very strong use of the simile occurs in T.B. Sanhedrin, 46 b. The hanged criminal must be speedily cut down (Deut. xxi. 23), because of man's likeness to God. "R. Meir said: It may be likened to twin brothers who resemble each other; one of whom is king over the whole world, and the other became a robber. The latter was caught and crucified (צלוב). Every passer-by said: It seems as though the king is hanging here. The king commanded: Take him down." From the other side, the man who fails to bring to life, by abstaining from begetting children, "diminishes the likeness" (ממעט בדמות, T.B. Yebamoth, 63 b). Human life is defined as דמות דיוקני (T.B. Moed Qaton, 15 b top).

Another characteristic figure is the *mould* from which coins are struck. The divine Image is God's sela (סלע שלי, T.B. Aboda Zara, 54 b). Yet there is a difference. Man casts many coins from the same mould (חותם), and all are alike. But God made all men from the mould of Adam, and not one resembles his fellow-man (T.B. Sanhedrin, 37 a).

## NOTE 9.

There is no need to summarise the discussions of the Genesis texts, which are so fully and ably elaborated in the commentaries, particularly in S. R. Driver's edition in the "Westminster," and J. Skinner's in the "International Critical" series. It may be well to make a reference to Saadiah's Commentary, and to David Qimḥi's Commentary on Genesis, edited by A. Ginzburg (Pressburg, 1842), where there are very lengthy notes on the Adam story and the creation of man. With these may be compared Qimḥi's terser remarks *s.v.* צלם in his Dictionary (Sefer ha-Shorashim). See also Maimonides, *Guide of the Perplexed*, Part I, chs. 1—3 (English ed. by M. Friedländer, vol. i. pp. 28 seq.). The reader will also find it profitable to consult M. Friedländer's *Essays on the Writings of Abraham Ibn Ezra* (1877), pp. 24 seq., especially with regard to the prevalence of the theory of the microcosm (עולם הקטן), which became "a favourite among the Jewish writers of the Middle Ages." On the same subject there is an article in the *Jewish Encyclopedia*, viii. pp. 544 seq.; the articles in the same work on Sabbethai Donnolo (iv. p. 639) and Moses Cordovero (x. p. 370) may also be named. Donnolo's views on the creation of man in the image of God are contained in his פירוש נעשה אדם בצלמנו, ed. Jellinek (Leipzig, 1854). A valuable discussion of Gen. i. 26 etc. may be read in A. Geiger's article in *Jüdische Zeitschrift für Wissenschaft und Leben* (Breslau, 1862), vol. i. pp. 40 seq. (Cf. the same author's *Urschrift*, p. 329.) Again, the first chapter of V. Zapletal's *Alttestamentliches* (Freiburg, 1903) deals fully with "Das Ebenbild Gottes im Menschen."

## NOTE 10.

The force of the divine "envy" in the O.T., as Rabbinically interpreted, is well brought out by the Rabbinic contrast between Ps. c. 3 and Ezekiel xxix. 3. The Psalmist says of God "he made us"; Pharaoh boasts that *he* is the author of his own existence (Genesis Rabba, ch. c. § 1). Incidentally the next remark in the Midrash deserves attention. "R. Aḥa said: He made us and we must perfect (or complete) our soul unto him" (ולו אנו משלימים את נפשותינו). Throughout life and at its close, man is God's. Of Noah's son Shem we are told (Mid. Tanḥuma on Gen. ix. 18, ed. Buber, p. 46) that "he was stainless and perfect unto his Creator (כשר ומושלם לבוראו)." Shem was a great favourite with the Rabbis; his and Eber's "academy" was the prototype of the Pharisaic houses of study (*Jewish Encyclopedia*, xi. 261).

It was not to be expected that the Rabbis would discuss Genesis iii. 22 in relation to the Greek doctrine of the "envy of the gods." Philo, naturally, was in a different case. He has the Greek theory clearly in mind, for he uses the very word (*φθόνος*) common in Herodotus and other writers in such contexts. He emphatically disputes the suggestion that Genesis implies the Greek doctrine. "There is no uncertainty or envy in God" (*οὔτε ἐνδυασμὸς οὔτε φθόνος περὶ θεόν*). Sometimes, continues Philo, God acts quite differently to man, sometimes he disciplines man as a father his son. It is not God but man who hesitates, "lest perchance he put forth his hand." As for God: "It is altogether impossible that God should envy either immortality or any good whatsoever to any other. Here is an indisputable proof." God made the world without pressure from anyone; he ordered it with a vast harmony of blessings. God's very denial of earthly immortality to man after his depravity was a boon; for the longer the life of the depraved the greater his misery, a grave misfortune to himself and to others. See Aucher, *Philonis Judaei Paralipômena Armena* (1826), pp. 57 seq.; J. Rendel Harris, *Fragments of Philo Judaeus* (1886), p. 15; C. D. Yonge, *The Works of Philo Judaeus* (1855), vol. iv. pp. 312 seq.

Philo does not discuss this question in relation to the Hebrew phrase ("a jealous God," Exod. xx. 5, etc.) which verbally comes so close to the *φθονερὸν ἐὸν τὸ θεῖον* of Herodotus (i. 32). But God's jealousy in the Hebrew idea is simply his claim to uniqueness, there must be no rival near the throne.

The Midrash on Exod. vii. 1 ranges together for obloquy the "four men who claimed divine quality" (שעשו את עצמן אלהות). See Tanḥuma ed. Buber, Exodus, p. 23, and compare Exod. Rabba on the text quoted. Besides Pharaoh (already referred to), there are Hiram (Ezek. xxviii. 2), Nebuchadnezzar (Isaiah xiv. 14) and Joash (2 Chr. xxiv. 17). "Because Pharaoh made himself a god, go thou and become a god over him, drive him down to contempt even as he raised himself high." The view of the Midrash here is identical with the proverbial maxim: "Pride comes before a fall." (There is closer parallel between Hebrew and Greek thought concerning ὕβρις than φθόνος). Cf. for a similar range of ideas Proverbs xxix. 23 and Matthew xxiii. 12, with T.B. Erubin ("Whoever exalts himself God brings low," כל המגביה עצמו הקב"ה משפילו), and the other parallels cited in the Commentaries. Particularly good is A. Wuensche who, in his *Neue Beiträge zur Erläuterung der Evangelien* (1878), pp. 281—2, has a fine collection of Pharisaic praises of humility. For a famous medieval eulogy of the same virtue, attention may be directed to the oft-printed Letter of Naḥmanides addressed from Palestine to his son in Spain. The Letter appears in several editions of the Synagogue Prayer-Book, and both the text and an English translation are included in B. Halper's *Anthology of Post-Biblical Hebrew Literature*, Philadelphia, 1921, vol. i. p. 130 and vol. ii. p. 171. Philo's treatment of the Stoic οἴησις (self-conceit) is admirably analysed by C. G. Montefiore in his *Florilegium Philonis* (*Jewish Quarterly Review*, 1894, vol. vii. pp. 504 seq.). The whole of Mr Montefiore's *Florilegium*, as original as it is penetrating, should be carefully studied by those who wish to understand Philo's religion. It is a necessary supplement to Drummond's work.

In fine, Genesis iii. 22 connects itself less with Gen. i. 26 than with the episode described in Gen. xi. The divine anxiety as to man's assumption of the divine rôle is, as it were, justified by man's arrogant attempt to storm the heavens. (Cf. A. Ehrenzweig in Marti's *Z. A. W.*, vol. 39, 1921, p. 83.) Cf. also Isaiah's satire on Lucifer's arrogance in ch. xiv.

## NOTE 11.

See particularly, for the part-angelic part-bestial nature of man, Genesis Rabba, ch. viii. § 11 (ed. Theodor, pp. 64 seq.), and the parallels quoted in Theodor's notes. With this compare Hitopadesa Prastavana 25: "Food, sleep, fear, and sexual intercourse—this (set is) the common property of men with brutes." But the Indian parallel does not continue to the other half, for it trails off into the generality: "Virtue is the great distinction of men." How influential this view, of the part-angelic part-bestial nature of man, has been through the ages may be seen in Pico della Mirandola's Oration (published after the author's death in 1493), and in the recent revival of the thesis by Dean Inge.

## NOTE 12.

The tendency to extend the older Rabbinic illustrations of the Imitation of God was the natural outcome of the tradition. Mercy and loving-kindness were specially cited by the earlier Pharisaic imitationists. Later writers built upon this structure. See further Note 17 below.

The following passage is a characteristic exposition of the method:

It is a positive duty derived from the Law for man to resemble God (להדמות אליו ית׳), as it is written: And thou shalt walk in his ways (Deut. xxviii. 9). Our Sages, of blessed memory, traditionally explained this to mean: As he is merciful, be thou also merciful. This is what God said concerning Abraham, that he would command his children after him, to keep the way of the Lord (Gen. xviii. 19). *And so with all the qualities of God, man must see to it that he, too, shall possess every such attribute* (וכן כל הכינוים בו להקב״ה יראה האדם שגם הוא יהיה בו מדה זו).

This passage occurs (ch. i. § 11) in the Shorter Form of Eleazar Azkari's ספר חרדים (Book of the Godfearers), printed at the end of Abraham Danzig's ס׳ זכרו תורת משה (Wilna, 1828). Abraham Danzig, be it noted, was a spiritual heir of the Pharisees. His popular Guide (the *Life of Man*, חיי אדם) combines, in genuine Pharisaic style, obedience to ritual rules with the response to the individual appeal of inward religion. Indeed among the favourite Hebrew moral books are just those which combine legalism with mysticism. Particularly to be noted is the opening of Danzig's *Life of Man*, which like Maimonides' Code places the Imitation of God in the forefront of the religious life.

Eleazar Azkari's work, written at Safed in 1588, bases itself on the text: All my bones shall say, Lord, who is like unto thee? (Psalm xxxv. 10). Hence he groups all religious discipline, thought and emotion round the "eight organs"—heart, eye, mouth, nose, ear, hand, foot, head (cf. Pesiqta R. ix. p. 32 a). Incidentally, it may be observed that to Azkari the Imitation of God is mediate, not absolute—the model is present in God's attributes, not in God himself (ch. v. p. 12 a). On the question of Attributes in Jewish scholasticism, see I. Husik, *A History of Mediaeval Jewish Philosophy* (1906), Index *s.v.* Attributes.

These later ideas attach themselves to the older. In the Song of Songs i. 15, "Lo thou art fair, my love," God is taken as addressing Israel—"My loved one, in that thou walkest in my ways." (Midrash Zuṭa ed. Buber, p. 16.)

That Jewish theology, in the main rationalistic in the Aristotelian sense, sets up not the Absolute God but God's moral attributes as the subject of man's emulation is well expressed by K. Kohler (*Jewish Theology*, 1918, p. 102) as follows:

Scripture says of God that he "walketh in holiness" (Ps. lxxvii. 14), and accordingly morality in man is spoken of as "walking in the ways of God" (Deut. x. 12, xi. 22, etc.). "Walk before me and be perfect!" says God to Abraham (Gen. xviii. 19). Moses approached God with two petitions,—the one, "Show me thy ways that I may know thee!" the other, "Show me, I pray thee, thy glory!" In response to the latter God said, "No man can see me and live," but the former petition was granted in that the Lord revealed himself in his moral attributes (Exod. xxxiii. 13—23). These alone can be understood and emulated by man; in regard to the so-called metaphysical attributes, God will ever remain beyond human comprehension and emulation.

Mystical Judaism would not accept this limitation, but it is a limitation deep-set in rationalistic Judaism. The scholastic discussion, beginning with Saadiah, as to the lawfulness of ascribing positive attributes to God, does not concern our present subject. (On the attribute question see *Jewish Encyclopedia*, ii. 294 seq.) A hymn like Jehuda Halevi's *God, whom shall I compare to thee?* expresses both man's inability to penetrate to the divine mystery and the power to know God through his moral manifestation, while the fuller knowledge comes hereafter.

Deep, deep beyond all fathoming,
Far, far beyond all measuring,
We can but seek thy deeds alone;
When bow thy saints before thy throne
Then is thy faithfulness made known.

Pure souls behold thee, and no need
Have they of light: they hear and heed
Thee with the soul's keen eye, although
The ear of flesh be dull and slow.
Their voices answer to and fro.

The whole poem may be read in *The Jewish Year* by Alice Lucas (1898, p. 5). Such thoughts are common in the Synagogue hymnology. Compare and contrast the extracts from Ibn Gabirol's *Royal Crown* in the same volume, pp. 140 seq.

## NOTE 13.

Cordovero's analysis has its analogue in Pharisaic phraseology. The heavenly ear and eye (אזן של מעלה עין של מעלה) are terms used already by Johanan b. Zakkai. (Tosefta Baba Qama vii. 2.) Cf. Bacher, *Agada der Tannaiten*, i. 32 [ed. 2, p. 29]. Here, too, reference may be made to Johanan b. Zakkai's remarkable eulogy of the Agada (homiletic and spiritual interpretation of Scripture) as leading to Imitation. "If it be thy desire to recognise him who spake and the world was, learn the Agada, for by that means thou understandest the Holy One, and cleavest to his ways" (Ṡifrê to Deut. xi. 22). In this exposition we have represented the ideal side of the Pharisaic "Schriftgelehrten" upon whom so much scorn is sometimes thrown. For the meeting-house of the Rabbis is the place where God's wondrous greatness is taught (ששם היו מתנים גדולותיו של הקב"ה). Cf. Bacher, *op. cit.* 31 [27].

Again Cordovero's reference to God as the Model for man's imitation in regard to suffering abuse in silence, is paralleled in the Midrash to Psalm lxxxvi (ed. Buber, p. 372). "Preserve my soul, for I am godly (חסיד): whoever hears himself cursed and is silent, though he has the power to destroy (his assailant) becomes a partner with God, who hears the blasphemies of heathens and ignores them. David heard himself reviled (by Shimei), but was silent. Therefore he says: Preserve my soul, for I am godly."

## NOTE 14.

In order to be the Perfect Model for Israel's imitation, God himself sets an example of obeying his own law. In the Introduction to his translation of T.B. Berachoth, thinking of such passages as fol. 6 a, 7 a, A. Cohen writes:

> God is perfection, and man can only strive after perfection by imitating his way. He is the Pattern upon which human life should be modelled.
>
> Starting from this principle, it is a natural step to regard God as the *complete* exemplar of conduct, and the ideal life demanded by Judaism but a reflection of his. Not only are the divine attributes of holiness, justice, charity and mercy to become human attributes, but if God has commanded the Israelite to obey the precepts of the Torah, he himself shows the way by submitting to them. He has enjoined the sacred act of prayer; therefore he too must pray, so that his creatures should do as he does. He has ordained the wearing of the phylacteries; he obeys his ordinances, and his people must follow in his ways.

This explanation throws new light on the Talmudic statements that God studies his own Torah daily (T.B. Aboda Zara 3 b), and, besides phylacteries, wears the fringed garment or tallith (T.B. Rosh Hashana 17 b). Weber ascribes such ideas to the "Judaizing" (Judaisirung) of the God-idea, as a coarsening process (*Jüdische Theologie*, § 32). The anthropomorphic tendency of such passages, however, is best explained, with Mr Cohen, as an element in the idea of Imitation. Looked at from another side of the same idea, such conceptions are explicable as an attempt towards what S. Schechter described as "humanising the Deity." As the same writer remarks: "A great number of scriptural passages, when considered in the light of Rabbinical interpretation, represent nothing else but a record of a sort of *Imitatio hominis* on the part of God" (*Some Aspects of Rabbinic Theology*, p. 38). That God, in the exhibition of his might, nay *in order* to exhibit his might, is merciful to sinners, is expressed in the very strongly human phrase (T.B. Yoma 69 b) that God "conquers his yeṣer" (כובש את יצרו) which some modern editors would weaken to "his wrath" (כובש את כעסו). As has been argued elsewhere, the *Imitatio hominis* is a logical correlative of the *Imitatio Dei.*

In this connection there is an interesting parallel between Talmud and New Testament. God not only prays himself but he teaches Israel how to pray (T.B. Berachoth 7 a, Rosh Hashana 17 b as cited above). With this compare both the fact of the Lord's Prayer itself, and the preliminary to it in Luke xi. 1: "One of the disciples said unto him, Lord, teach us to pray." In Rosh Hashana 17 b we read: "The Holy One, blessed be he, enwrapped himself and showed to Moses the order of prayer (והראה לו למשה סדר תפלה)."

## NOTE 15.

In August 1649, Sir Kenelm Digby was banished, and hastily crossed the Channel. While at *Calis* (Calais) in October, he translated Albertus Magnus' *De Adhaerendo Deo*. The version was published in London in 1654. The opening passage of the Dedication to his mother is so attractive, that the temptation is irresistible to find space for it:

When lately I was commanded out of England, I was so streightened in time, that I was not able to carry anything with me, besides what I had about me. And the difficulties that my servants met in bringing my carriages after me, made me remain here sometimes in want of my ordinary attendants, and of such necessaries as I had dayly need of. I was not so sensible of any, as of the deprivation of my bookes: which in all fortunes I have ever found my best companions; and in whose conversation I as well profited, as pleased my self. And therefore in all my journies (even the longest and most cumbersome) I have ever used to have a convenient store of them with mee. I was now reduced to have none other by me, but a short discourse of Albert the great, concerning the perfection of a spiritual life; which at my setting forth from London, I had put into my pocket; invited thereto, by the dignity of the subject, the excellency of the author, and the smallnesse of the bulk of it. I read it over with much delight; And judged it so profitable a work, that I desired to impress the contents of it as deep as I could in my memory: and indeed to convert the whole treatise into the very substance of my soul, as hoping, it may one day serve mee for a rule to govern my poor devotions by; as far as my feeble eyes may be able to see by the light of so dazzling a sunne. This occasioned me to employ my self in rendring in my own tongue the expressions which this author had made in Latin. For I believe, scarce any study do'th so vigorously digest an other mans notions into the nourishment of ones own minde, as doth the translating or the paraphrasing of them.

It is of interest to note what Albertus Magnus writes elsewhere on Ps. 73 [72] 28, the text (Mihi adhærere Deo, bonum est) from which he took the title of his little treatise.

Et] etiam *bonum est mihi adhærere Deo*, tanquam sponso dulcissimo. *Genes.* 2 Propter hoc relinquet homo patrem et matrem, et adhærebit uxori suæ. [He adds:] Et simili lege sponsa patrem relinquet et matrem, et adhærebit sponso suo, tanquam amico fidelissimo. *Psal.* Adhæsit anima mea post te: ut tota conglutinetur tibi per charitatem. 1 *Reg.* 18 Anima Jonathæ conglutinata est cum anima David. *Deuteron.* 10 Patribus nostris conglutinatus est, et adamavit eos. Tanquam Regi potentissimo. *Psal.* Innocentes et recti adhæserunt mihi, quia sustinui te.

Et hoc valde bonum: quia sibi adhærentes illuminet: quippe in *Psal.* dicitur: Accedite ad eum, et illuminamini. Multo ergo fortius adhærentes et illuminatos ad se magis trahit. *Cant.* i. Trahe me post te, et curremus in odorem etc. *Glossa.* Non trahitur nisi adhæret. Tractos unit sibi. 1 *ad Cor.* 6 Qui adhæret Deo, unus spiritus est. (*Operum* Tom. VII. ed. 1651, p. 41.)

## NOTE 16.

The passage in the Sifrâ (ed. Weiss, p. 111a) on Leviticus xxvi. 12 ("And I will walk among you") runs thus, with the necessary emendations from the Yalquṭ Levit. § 672:

והתהלכתי בתוככם. משלו משל למה הדבר דומה? למלך שיצא לטייל עם אריסו בפרדס והיה אותו אריס מיטמר מלפניו. אמר לו המלך לאותו אריס מה לך מיטמר מלפני? הריני כיוצא בך! כך עתיד הקב"ה לטייל עם [בין .Y] הצדיקים בגן עדן. וצדיקים רואים אותו ומזדעזעים מלפניו. והקב"ה אמר להם לצדיקים מה לכם שאתם מזדעזעים מלפני? הריני כיוצא בכם!

But the equality must not imply the obliteration of the distinction between Creator and creature, between God and man. Even in the boldest flight of the Imitation idea, such a thought was so foreign to the conventional Pharisaism, that the necessary gloss was inserted. Thus the Sifrâ and Yalquṭ (cf. Rashi's Commentary on the Pentateuch) guard against the thought which the quotation just made might suggest by continuing:

יכול לא יהיה מוראי עליכם. תלמוד לומר והייתי לכם לאלהים ואתם תהיו לי לעם וגו':

The whole text runs (Levit. xxvi. 12–13): "And I will walk among you, and will be your God, and ye shall be my people. I am the Lord your God, which brought you forth out of the land of Egypt, that ye should not be their bondmen; and I have broken the bands [or bars] of your yoke, and made you go upright." It is notable that the Midrash and Talmud bring the last phrase into relation with Adam (cf. Note 7, p. 164 above), for R. Simeon interprets that men were to be 100 cubits tall like Adam, or in another view 200 cubits, double Adam's stature. (Cf. T.B. Sanhedrin 100 a with the Sifrâ.) Similarly tall were to be the women. "Our daughters are fashioned after the pattern of the (nave of the) temple" (Ps. cxliv. 12) which was 100 cubits high. It is clear that the original homilists had in mind throughout their interpretation of Leviticus xxvi. 12 the connection of the Imitation idea with the Creation story, and its final exaltation into a spiritual relationship between God and man in the future life.

Another arresting passage is Deut. Rabba ch. i. § 12. The Midrash interprets the text (Deut. i. 10) והנכם היום ככוכבי השמים לרב: Lo ye are to-day like the stars of the heaven, [but in future you will resemble] the Master.

(היום אתם ככוכבים אבל לעתיד לבא לרב אתם עתידין להיות דומין לרבכם).

For God is a fire (Deut. iv. 24) and Israel's light will become a fire and His holy One a flame (Isaiah x. 17). And, says R. Levi b. Ḥama, as idolators resemble their idol (Ps. cxv. 8), how much more must the servants of the Lord resemble Him.

## NOTE 17.

It is scarcely possible to explain the remarks of Abba Saul and R. Ishmael on any other theory than Friedmann's, that the latter was disturbed by the former's comment, and emphatically denies its accuracy.

Comparing the Mechilta with the Yalquṭ (§ 244) on Exodus xv. 2, and following the hint of Rashi on T.B. Sabbath 133 b the true text would seem to be:

זה אלי ואנוהו. אבא שאול אמר ואנוהו (אני והוא). תדמה לו מה הוא רחום וחנון אף אתה רחום וחנון. רבי ישמעאל אומר וכי אפשר לו לבשר ודם להשוות [Mechilta reads להנוות] לקונו? אלא אתנאה לפניו במצות וכו׳:

Rashi's note on Sanh. 133 b is very important as to the significance of Abba Saul's thought.

הוי דומה לו. ולשון אנוהו אני והוא אעשה עצמי (כצ״ל) כמותו לדבק בדרכיו:

In the text I have connected this idea with the curious invocation during the procession round the altar on Tabernacles (Mishnah, Sukkah iv. 5). The phrase אני והו is usually interpreted as an equivalent to אנא יהוה (Psalm cxviii. 25). See the Dictionaries of Levy (i. p. 110) and Jastrow (p. 84). For the suggestion that Plutarch (*Symp.* IV. vi. 2) confused the phrase with the Bacchic cry Evoe, see A. Büchler, *Revue des Études Juives*, xxxvii. 181 ff. Cf. also J. Hochman, *Jerusalem Temple Festivities*, p. 78 onwards, with the Notes at end of the volume.

It seems to me that the Mishnah, amid the confusions which have led to the present readings, points to Exodus xv. 2 as the original source. The invocations would thus have arisen from varying interpretations of ואנוהו. "Beauty is thine, O altar!" would emerge from the interpretation "and I will beautify him." The אני והו[א] would attach to the interpretation given in the text. It was naturally imagined by later authorities that the Hallel (Ps. cxviii. 25) was alluded to, especially as the invocation is followed by the prayer "Save us." But Exodus xv. 2 distinctly connects the idea of *salvation* with ואנוהו. The verse runs:

עזי וזמרת יה ויהי לי לישועה. זה אלי ואנוהו אלהי אבי וארוממנהו:

The appeal for salvation might well be based on Israel's consciousness of his duty to model his nature and life on the divine attributes. The same verse may also underlie the other phrase of the Mishnah ליה ולך מזבח and also the formula אנו ליה וליה עינינו (Sukkah v. 4).

That this appellation of God "Ani ve-hu"—"I and He"—points to a sort of identification of God with Israel, is forcibly maintained by G. Klein (*Der aelteste Christliche Katechismus und die Juedische Propaganda-Literatur*, Berlin, 1909, pp. 44–49). Klein (p. 48) explains Abba Saul's saying quoted above as based on the explanation equating ואנוהו with אני והוא. He compares Abba Saul's further simile, Sifrâ on Levit. xix. 2: "Thou shalt be holy, for I the Lord your God am holy:

the retinue of a King imitates the royal example": פמליא של מלך מה עליה ? להיות מחקה למלך. Klein concludes: "This is the secret of the Shem ha-mephorash (Tetragrammaton). It conceals within it the deepest secret of Religion, the *unio mystica*—the demand to be one with God."

Another text which must not be ignored in this discussion is Numbers xi. 16: And the Lord said unto Moses, Gather unto me seventy men of the elders of Israel. On this the Midrash Tanḥuma comments (ed. Buber, p. 60, § 26): Gather unto Me: this is what the Scripture says (Prov. xxii. 11), He that loveth pureness of heart, and hath grace in his lips, the King shall be his friend. Why did he not say seventy *anashim* (plural), but seventy *ish* (singular)? Because these were seventy uniquely qualified men, *like Me and thee*: for the Lord is a Man (*ish*) of War (Exod. xv. 3), and of Moses it is said And the man (*ish*) Moses (Numbers xii. 3):

אספה לי· זה שאמר הכתוב אוהב טהר לב חן שפתיו רעהו מלך· למה לא אמר לו שבעים אנשים אלא שבעים איש? אלא אמר לו שבעים איש מיוחדים שהם דומים לי ולך· ה׳ איש מלחמה והאיש משה:

Again, on the text Exod. xv. 2 we have the thought that man *recognises* God by His acts and attributes (Mechilta ed. Friedmann, p. 37, n. 13). Cf. also Sifrê on Deut. vi. 6: Set these words on thine heart, and by that means thou wilt *recognise* the Holy One and wilt cleave to his ways:

תן הדברים האלה על לבבך שמתוך כך אתה מכיר את הקב"ה ומדבק בדרכיו:

## NOTE 18.

For a fuller form of the same saying שלשה שותפים באדם הקב"ה ואביו ואמו, where various parts of the body are assigned to each human parent, and the life, soul, senses, intelligence and so forth are attributed to God's part in the birth, see T.B. Niddah 31 a.

This baraitha was not an isolated statement. With it may be compared the saying of R. Simlai (Genesis Rabba, ch. viii. § 9, ed. Theodor, p. 63, where the notes are important). "And God said, We will make man in our image, after our likeness. In the past man was created from the earth, and Eve was created from Adam. From now onwards in our image after our likeness—not man without woman, nor woman without man, nor both of them without the Divine Presence (Shechinah)"—(לא איש בלא אשה. ולא אשה בלא איש. ולא שניהם בלא שכינה).

## NOTE 19.

The Midrash Tanḥuma on Gen. xvii. 1, with reference to Abraham, combines with this text Psalm xviii. 31: התהלך לפני והיה תמים זה שאמר הכתוב האל תמים דרכו. The contrast between the texts relating to Noah and Abraham is often developed (cf. Midrash Rabba on Gen. vi. 9 and xvii. 1 and Numbers R. on xvi. 3). Noah walked *with* God, needing his help; Abraham walked *before* God, in his own strength. Moreover, Abraham was the herald of the Lord, the King being preceded by his court (*familia*, Aboth de R. Nathan xxvii.). Cf. the saying of R. Nehemiah (second century) cited in Genesis R. ch. xxx. § 10. Abraham, in another figure, goes in front, God being either as the Shepherd who looks on while his sheep (Abraham and the other patriarchs) pass before him, or as the Prince who follows his retinue. In the first view (R. Joḥanan's) God is watching over Abraham, in the second (Resh Laqish's) God is receiving honour. Nay God *needs* man's honour; thus the Midrash (*loc. cit.*) ends off the chapter with the words:

על דעתיה דרבי יוחנן אנו צריכים לכבודו · ועל דעתיה דרשב"ל הוא צריך לכבודנו:

"In the view of R. Joḥanan we need his honour; and in the view of R. Simeon b. Laqish he needs our honour." These two Rabbis were brothers-in-law. Cf. Note 23 below.

C. J. Ball (*The Book of Job*, 1922, p. 96) remarks that "*Correct* or *irreproachable* would be a better rendering of תם than *perfect*." If, however, the poet of chs. xxix. and xxxi. may be regarded as expounding the idea of the prose Prologue, the conception passes so far beyond "correctitude" into the domain of tenderness and sensibility, that any other word than "perfect" would be too weak.

## NOTE 20.

"I am master of envy and envy is not master of me" is God's expansion of the text for "I the Lord thy God am a jealous God." See the Mechilta on Exod. (ed. Friedmann, p. 68 a). More fully the thought is expressed in the Midrash on Psalm lxxxiv. (ed. Buber, p. 417) and in Genesis Rabba xlix. § 8 (ed. Theodor, p. 508): "Man's anger controls him, but God controls his anger, as it is said (Nahum ii. 2): The Lord avengeth and is master of wrath (ה' נוקם ובעל חמה); man's jealousy overpowers him, but God overpowers jealousy, as it is said: The Lord is God over jealousy and avengeth (ה' אל קנא)."

"God is not man that he should lie (fail)"—Numbers xxiii. 19, and "My thoughts are not your thoughts, nor my ways your ways"—Isaiah lv. 8 mean, at all events among other things, that God (unlike man) is moved by eternal, not temporary, purposes. God's constancy differentiates him from man. Yet even so, it is by virtue of this very fact that man's life has a continuity which is a reflection of the divine self-consistency. This may be the sense of Malachi iii. 6 "I, the Lord, change not, and ye sons of Jacob are not consumed." God's permanence gives continuity to ephemeral man.

So while in a large number of Rabbinic parables God is likened to an earthly king, in others he is differentiated from any human ruler. For the most part, however, these differentiations are on the ground of God's greater condescension, ampler love, easier accessibility, milder justice, which he tempers with mercy and readiness to forgive. Such parables are numerous. There are many instances in Ziegler's *Königsgleichnisse des Midrasch* (Breslau, 1903).

## NOTE 21.

When the moral is drawn, for instance, from Samuel's greater severity than Saul's towards Agag, the verdict is not that Samuel's severity is to be imitated, but that Saul's clemency is open to suspicion. "He who is kind to the cruel is apt to be cruel to the kind," says the Midrash in contrasting Saul's treatment of Agag and the priests of Nob (see Yalquṭ Samuel, § 149). The Synagogue liturgy cites Saul's kindness to Agag, and, as an item of Haman's evil disposition, blames him that "he remembered not the mercy of Saul, through whose compassion for Agag the enemy was born" (*Authorised Hebrew and English Prayer Book*, ed. Singer, p. 277). It was during the respite granted by Saul that Agag became father of Haman's ancestor (T.B. Megilla 13 a; Second Targum to Esther iv. 13). Hence the severe injunction to Saul had proved justified. Perhaps an exception to the generalisation in the text is to be found in the idea that just as God hates the presumptuous sinner, who is enemy to God, so man may hate God's enemies, his own persecutors. But even with regard to that idea there is much on the other side.

## NOTE 22.

Josephus, *Apion* I.22. (Cf. *Apion* II.17.) On the long life of this quaint fancy, that the Greek philosophers were indebted to Moses and other Jewish teachers, see the article of N. Samter "Der *Jude* Aristoteles" in the *Monatsschrift für Geschichte und Wissenschaft des Judenthums*, Breslau, 1901, vol. xlv. pp. 453 seq. Cf. I. Abrahams in *Mind*, 1888, vol. xiii. pp. 468 seq. See also the article of L. Ginzberg in the *Jewish Encyclopedia*, ii. 98 seq. M. Steinschneider gives a complete list of the pseudo-Aristotelian writings (including those in which the Greek admits his indebtedness), in his *Hebraeischen Uebersetzungen des Mittelalters*, Berlin, 1893, vol. i. pp. 229–273.

## NOTE 23.

The idea, that God receives not merely honour but also satisfaction, pleasure, gratification, from man's service, is common to Philo and Pharisaism. Obedience is in Philo's phrase *θεοῦ τιμῆς καὶ ἀρεσκείας ἕνεκα*. By *ἀρεσκεία* Philo must mean much the same thing as the Pharisees meant by נחת רוח, usually rendered "tranquillity of spirit," in translating such passages as T.B. Berachoth 17a. It is, however, a less pallid emotion that is implied. R. Joḥanan said: R. Meir, on concluding the reading of the Book of Job, used to say: It is the fate of man to die and of cattle to be slaughtered, and death is the common destiny. Happy is he who has grown in Torah and whose labour has been in Torah: who has caused gratification to his Creator—נחת רוח ליוצרו—advanced in good repute, and departed from the world with a good name. Of such a one said Solomon, "A good name is better than precious oil, and the day of death than the day of one's birth (Eccles. vii. 1)." God, having made man for his glory, derives a kind of contentment and gratification when his design attains success.

Cf. also קורת רוח in Tana debe Eliahu, a text permeated with the Imitation ideal. A reference to this text should be added on p. 169 above.

On the "Sanctification of the Name" see F. Perles, *Juedische Skizzen* (ed. 2, Leipzig, 1920), pp. 100 seq.; I. Abrahams in Hastings' *Encyclopaedia of Religion and Ethics*, vol. ix. p. 177.

On the significance of the caution expressed, in the passage quoted in the text on p. 154 by the phrase כִּבְיָכֹל (or כִּבְיָכוֹל) much has been written. The sense is clear: it guards against the application to God of phrases which approach the objectionable. Jastrow (Dict. p. 577a) renders: "*as though it were possible, as it were* (ref. to an allegorical or anthropomorphous expression with reference to the Lord)." In illustration Jastrow cites the well-known thought that the Divine Majesty always, *as it were,* shares in Israel's enslavement (as in Egypt). Israel said to God "thou hast, *as it were,* redeemed thyself" (Mechilta on Exod. xii. 41, ed. Friedmann, p. 16a). Levy, vol. ii. p. 240 of his *Neuhebräisches und Chaldäisches Wörterbuch* takes the same view. W. Bacher explains the phrase differently. Following the view of N. Brüll (in Kobak's *Jeschurun* vii. Hebrew section 1–5), Bacher regards כביכול as an ellipsis of

כ[אלו] [נאמר] ב[מי ש]יכול [אתה לומר זה]

"as though it were said concerning one of whom thou canst say this." Bacher compares *sit venia verbo.* The phrase belongs to the oldest Tannaitic terminology, being used by Joḥanan b. Zakkai (Bacher, *Die älteste Terminologie der Jüdischen Schriftauslegung*, Leipzig, 1899, p. 72). Another cautionary phrase is אלמלא מקרא כתוב אי אפשר לאומרו— "were it not written in the text of Scripture, it would be impossible to say it." Further illustrations of the use of both phrases may be consulted on p. 78 of the second volume of Bacher's work, dealing with the Amoraim (vol. i. is concerned with the Tannaim). The second volume appeared in 1905.

A very strong instance of the phrase illustrating the general subject of this Note, with which compare Note 19, occurs in the Midrash on Lamentations i. 6 (Mid. ch. i. § 33). When Israel does God's will, the celestial power is strengthened; while that power is—"if the expression be permitted"—weakened by man's neglect to do God's will. God's very capacity to help is reduced by Israel's lapse from obedience to his Law.

ר׳ יהודה בר׳ סימין בשם ר׳ לוי בר׳ פרטא [אמר]· בזמן שישראל עושים רצונו של הקב״ה מוסיפים כח בגבורה של מעלה כמד״א (במדבר י״ד י״ז) ועתה יגדל נא כח ה׳· ובזמן שאין עושים רצונו של הקב״ה כביכול מתישין כח של מעלה· והולכים גם הם בלא כח לפני רודף:

(Cf. Pesiq. K. xxvi. For a weaker form see Yalquṭ Psalms § 779.)

Thus far, on the basis of Numbers xiv. 17 ("And now, I pray thee, let the power of my Lord be great." In other versions Ps. lx. 14 is cited). Cf. the homilies in the Yalquṭ on Deut. xxxii. 18 which the Midrash paraphrases "There is weakness in the Sculptor that made thee": צור ילדך תשי התשתם כחו של יוצר. God is likened to a sculptor (or potter), whose art is nullified by the vacillation of the model.

Again God is exalted when his children observe justice (Deut. Rabba v. § 7:
אמר הקב"ה לישראל בני חייכם בזכות שאתם משמרים את הדין אני מתגבה).

Further, the pure service of God, rendered without self-seeking, is service for God's need (לצורך אלהים Midrash on Ps. xxxi. ed. Buber, p. 240), or possibly we should translate "on God's prescription," or "at God's requirements."

It is needless to add that these, and other Rabbinic passages in a similar sense, are paralleled and completed by many in which God's independence of man is firmly posited. Malachi i. 11 scathingly warns recalcitrant Israel that he has other worshippers. And, more generally, God reigned before the world, during man's existence in the world, and in the final end. Cf. I. Abrahams, *Festival Studies* (1906), p. 180; Annotated edition of the Prayer Book (1914), p. viii. The significant passage quoted from the Sifrâ (86 b) runs: "Be ye holy, for I am holy. If ye sanctify yourselves I will esteem it as though ye sanctify me, and if ye do not sanctify yourselves, I shall esteem it as though ye did not sanctify me. Or does it mean, unless ye sanctify me I am not sanctified? No, I remain in my holiness whether ye sanctify me or not" (בקדושתי אני בין מקדישים אותי ובין אין מקדישים אותי:).

Philo has a fine passage at the end of his comments on the first two commandments. God calls men to honour the one truly living God, not that he needs this honour (ἑαυτοῦ τιμῆς οὐ προσδεόμενος—οὐ γὰρ ἑτέρου χρεῖος ἦν ὁ αὐταρκέστατος ἑαυτῷ), but that he desires to direct men into the right road, the knowledge of the real God, the first and most perfect Good (ὅς ἐστι τὸ πρῶτον ἀγαθὸν καὶ τελεώτατον), from whom, as from a fountain, blessings flow down to the world and its inhabitants (*De Decalog.* xvi., M. II. 194, C.-W. iv. 287). It is man that needs God, not God man. For the same thought in other literature cf. J. Rendel Harris on Ode iv. 9 of the Odes of Solomon (ed. 1909, pp. 91–92). This passage in the Odes runs: "Thou hast given us of thy fellowship: it is not that Thou wast in need of us, but we that are in need of Thee."

The two ideas, that while God stands in no need of man, yet he acquires gratification from man's service, are well brought out in relation to sacrifices. These are for *man's* good, God has neither need of them nor gain from them. And yet he derives pleasure from man's obedience to the command to bring the sacrifices. "It is a gratification to me in that I ordered and my will is done" (נחת רוח לפני שאמרתי ונעשה רצוני). See Sifrê §§ 107 and 143 on Numbers xv. 7 and on xxviii. 2 (ed. Friedmann, pp. 30 a and 54 a). In later Jewish ethical literature the conferment of this gratification on God becomes a frequent motive to obedience. It is difficult to convey an adequate idea of the tender and affectionate if familiar attitude implied between the Father and his children.

Somewhat akin to the same conception is the Rabbinic explanation of Psalm cxv. 17: "the dead praise not the Lord." (T.B. Sanhedrin 30a.) Man must occupy himself in his life-time with the study of the Torah and the performance of the precepts, for at his death he is no longer in a position to so occupy himself. The Holy One, blessed be he, then has no praise through him (ואין להקדוש ברוך הוא שבח בו). David, in effect, prays for life in order that he may continue to render homage to God. The phrase cited indicates that God as it were loses something precious to Himself by a man's death.

## NOTE 24.

S. Alexander, in his 1920 Gifford Lectures (*Space, Time and Deity*), reaches a similar goal by a very different route. "If we apply to the new quality of deity what we learn from the succession of lower empirical qualities, we conclude by analogy that the process by which good overcomes evil in the region of mind is one of the conditions of the emergence of deity; so far, that is, as human endeavour contributes to the generation of this quality. Thus goodness or good will is material on which deity is built, and deity is in the line of goodness not of evil." So, too, "the victory of the lower type which is good makes possible the rise of its successor to the higher level" (vol. ii. p. 413).

The passages quoted on p. 154 are (Sabb. 31 b):

אין לו להקב״ה בעולמו אלא יראת שמים בלבד

and (Levit. R. xxxi. 1)

אתה מאיר לכל באי עולם· ואתה מתאוה לאורן של ישראל:

Cf. p. 15 above.

## XVII. MISCELLANEOUS NOTES.

### (a) *Let the dead bury their dead* (Mt. viii. 22; Lk. ix. 60)

"The apparent harshness and obscurity of the saying is a guarantee for its authenticity" (A. Plummer). It becomes less harsh and less obscure if we adopt a clever suggestion of F. Perles (in Preuschen's *Zeitschrift f. d. neutest. Wissenschaft*, xix. 96). He points out that turned into Aramaic, the Greek ἄφες τοὺς νεκροὺς θάψαι τοὺς ἑαυτῶν νεκρούς would run: שבוק למיתיא למקבר מיתיא דילהון. This, says Perles, was beyond doubt the original text. The "Greek translator" simply misread the third word, understanding it as the infinitive pe'al (לְמִקְבַּר) i.e. "to bury," while it is in reality the pa'el participle (לִמְקַבַּר) "to the burier." Hence the saying would mean: "Leave the dead to their burier of the dead."

Perles points out that the pa'el קַבַּר is used both in Targum (Onqelos Num. xxxiii. 4, Ezekiel xxxix. 15) and Peshitto (1 Kings xi. 15). The description of the burier as מקבר מיתיא corresponds precisely to the new Hebrew קובר מתים (T.B. Niddah 24 b).

It may be added that Perles' suggestion by no means prejudices the decision as to the original language of the Gospels. It has been felt that Jesus may have been quoting a proverbial saying (cf. W. C. Allen on Mt. viii. 22). Such a proverb would be in Aramaic, whatever the language of the Gospel. All that Perles' suggestion requires is that the first translator of the proverb into Greek mispunctuated a word in the proverb.

It is possible that other instances of Aramaic proverbs may be detected. "If the salt have lost its savour, wherewith shall it be salted?" (Mt. v. 13 ἐὰν δὲ τὸ ἅλας μωρανθῇ, ἐν τίνι ἁλισθήσεται;). In Mk. ix. 50 the reading is: ἐὰν δὲ τὸ ἅλας ἄναλον γένηται, ἐν τίνι αὐτὸ ἀρτύσετε; Lk. xiv. 35 has ἀρτυθήσεται for ἁλισθήσεται, otherwise agreeing with Matthew. It would seem that the first Gospel has here preserved the true reading. In T.B. Bechoroth 8 b occurs the saying: מילחא כי סריא במאי מלחי ליה "Salt if it has lost its savour, wherewith shall it be salted?" This corresponds exactly with the reading in Mt. It should be added that the Talmudic saying again has all the look of a proverbial phrase. It may be that another slightly mistranslated Aramaic proverb lurks in Luke's words *οὔτε εἰς γῆν οὔτε εἰς κοπρίαν εὔθετόν ἐστιν.* Perles turns this into Aramaic: לא לְתַבָּלָא ולא לְזַבָּלָא כשר "fit neither for seasoning nor for manure." The word תַּבָּלָא (spice) was, on this theory, confused with תֵּבֵל which the LXX repeatedly renders by *γῆ*.

## (*b*) *Shed for the remission of sins* (Mt. xxvi. 28)

The words (*εἰς ἄφεσιν ἁμαρτιῶν*) occur, in this context, only in Mt. xxvi. 28 (they are absent in Mk. xiv. 24, Lk. xxii. 20, 1 Cor. xi. 25). "Mt., by adding these words, shows that he understood the covenant to be a covenant between God and the many, by which remission of sins was secured to them, the sign of this covenanted forgiveness being the shed blood" (Allen). As a general principle, however, it is only in Hebrews ix. 22 that we find the rule: "apart from the shedding of blood there is no remission" (*χωρὶς αἱματεκχυσίας οὐ γίνεται ἄφεσις*). Apart from O.T. texts (particularly Levit. xvii. 11) there is the practically identical Rabbinic generalisation אין כפרה אלא בדם "There is no atonement except with blood" (Baraitha in T.B. Yoma 5 a, Zebaḥim 6 a; to which oft-cited passages add the note of the Sifrâ on Lev. i. 4, ed. Weiss p. 5 d § 9: אי זהו המכפר? זה הדם · שנא' כי הדם הוא בנפש יכפר). All that this meant was that the sacrificial rite was invalid without the pouring and sprinkling of the blood. The Biblical prescriptions required the blood, hence there was no atoning power in the sacrifice without it.

The force of these ideas is well brought out by K. Kohler in *J.E.* ii. 276 (first column). Interesting is his remark (*op. cit.* 278 col. 1) based on the text in Mt. (as also on Heb. x. 12, Col. i. 20) that it was owing to the destruction of the Temple, and the cessation of the sacrifices, that "a large number of Jews accepted the Christian faith in the Atonement by the blood shed for many for the remission of sins." Joḥanan b. Zakkai (see note (*l*) below) thought otherwise.

But what was the Rabbinic *theory*? The Talmud never formulates a theory on the subject at all. Rashi (1040–1105) on Levit. xvii. 11 is the first who is quite clear on the point. His note runs: "For the life (nefesh) of the flesh, of every created thing, is dependent on the blood, and therefore I have given it to atone for the life of man, *let life come and atone for life.*" (Comp. R.V.; while A.V. ends: "for it is the blood that maketh atonement for the soul," R.V. has "for it is the blood that maketh atonement by reason of the life.") Rashi's note: תבוא נפש ותכפר על הנפש has all the appearance of being based on an old authority, possibly a no longer extant reading in the Sifrâ, but there is no passage known to me in the early Rabbinic books, as we have them, which can be cited as Rashi's source. Yet, seeing that according to Ezekiel xviii. 13, and also according to some Rabbinic statements (e.g. R. Ḥanina b. Gamaliel in Mishnah Makkoth iii. 15 העובר עבירה אחת נוטל נפשו עליה He who transgresses a single transgression gives up his life therefor)—every sin entails death, the sacrifice through its blood would be a substitute for death. But this does not satisfactorily explain Rashi's unequivocal statement of theory. For Ḥanina b. Gamaliel seems merely to put his view about sin and death the more emphatically, so that he may continue—as he does in the Mishnah *loc. cit.*—"If he who transgresses a single transgression gives up his life therefor, he who performs a single commandment, how much more is his life given unto him." In order to emphasise the life-giving power of virtue, he emphasises the deadliness of vice.

Apparently Rashi has, thus, no ancient authority. In the most conspicuous Scriptural example of transference—the scapegoat—the animal was not offered, nor was its blood sprinkled. The Talmud even much later than the cessation of sacrifices seems only to hold that the sacrificial blood atonement had to be personal and individual, and that the blood poured out must be such as actually caused the animal's death (T.B. Pesaḥim 65): דם שהנפש יוצאה בו מכפר דם שאין הנפש יוצאה בו אינו מכפר. It bases this on texts, not at all on a theory. It may be well, however, to quote the view of J. Z. Lauterbach (*J.E.* x. 625 col. 1): "The sacrifice cleanses only through the blood that is sprinkled, the blood symbolising the life of the one sacrificing, which, but for the substitution of the victim, would have to be surrendered in expiation of the sin (T.B. Zebaḥim 6 a)." It must be observed, however, that the Talmud itself, in the passage last cited, offers nothing in the nature of such a *theory* of substitution. It merely asserts in the same phraseology as cited from Yoma 5 a above, the necessity of the blood in the sacrificial atonement rite, as of course it was bound to do in face of Levit. xvii. 11. On all these points the Rabbis, on the whole, had no *theory*, the prescriptions of the Law must be accepted and they sufficed without explanation. As Joḥanan ben Zakkai said of the Red Heifer, it was not the corpse that defiled nor the water that purified—it was simply the decree of God that asserted both the source of defilement and the means of purification (Pesiqta Parah ed. Buber, p. 40 b; Pesiqta Rabbathi xiv, ed. Friedmann, p. 65 a).

### (c) *Why callest thou me good?* (Mk. x. 18; Lk. xviii. 19)

It would seem that the reading of Mk. and Lk. is preferable to that in Mt. (xix. 17). Unless the epithet "good" had been applied to Jesus in the question, it is difficult to explain the answer of Jesus in Mt. εἷς ἐστὶν ὁ ἀγαθός. In fact the "editing" of Matthew is betrayed by the use of ἀγαθός and ἀγαθόν. The epithet "good" applied to a teacher is unusual but not entirely unknown. "There is no instance in the whole Talmud," says Plummer (p. 422), "of a Rabbi being addressed as *good master*, the title was absolutely unknown among the Jews." There is, however, a quite clear instance (quoted by Dalman in the *Words of Jesus*, Edinburgh, 1902, p. 337). There was a drought at Hagronia (Agranum?) when Raba (in M. the reading is incorrectly Rab) visited the place. He ordained a fast, but no rain fell. Next day he inquired whether anyone had had a dream. R. Eleazar of Hagronia replied that he had heard in his vision the address: "Good greeting to the good teacher from the good Lord, who of his goodness doeth good to his people" (שלם טב לרב טב מרבון טב דמיטוביה מטיב לעמיה:). Raba regarded this as a propitious hour; he ordained a further prayer, and the rain descended. It is not quite clear from the context whether the term "good master" was applied to Eleazar or to Raba.

There are many instances of God being called "the good" (Mishnah Ber. ix. 2 etc.). There is also the liturgical usage referred to in *Cambridge Biblical Essays* (1909, p. 191). For the liturgical text see particularly S. Schechter in *Jewish Quarterly Review*, x. (1898) 654–9; and the same texts reprinted in Dalman's German edition (*Die Worte Jesu*, Leipzig 1898, p. 299). Moreover, Moses is described as "good." Seeing that his mother saw that "he was good" (Exod. ii. 2), the Talmud (Soṭa 12 a) assigns Tob or Ṭobiah as a name to Moses. Very remarkable is the passage in T.B. Menaḥoth 53 b, regarding the reception of the Law by Moses. "Let the good (Moses) come and receive the good (the Law) from the Good (God) unto the good (Israel)": יבא טוב ויקבל טוב מטוב לטובים. The texts referred to are Exod. ii. 2; Prov. iv. 2; Ps. cxlv. 9; Ps. cxxv. 4.

The idiom in Mk. οὐδεὶς ἀγαθὸς εἰ μὴ εἷς ὁ θεός is thoroughly Hebraic. Cf. for instance אין טוב אלא תורה (T.B. Berachoth 5 a): "There is nothing good except the Torah." Matthew's alteration is obviously designed (as the commentators agree) to avoid words which would be derogatory to Jesus. They, however, read into the passage more than is needed. "Here as always," as Dalman aptly remarks, "the honour due to the Father was the first consideration with Jesus." He desired no flattery, still less would he tolerate irony. In the Midrash Adam refuses the homage of the ministering angels (Genesis Rabba viii. § 10 and parallels).

### (d) *Sons of the Kingdom* (Mt. viii. 12)

Luke in the parallel passage (xiii. 28) does not use this phrase: and though Mt. repeats it (xiii. 38), it is unknown to Mark. It is equally unknown in Rabbinic usage. Matthew here innovates. In Parables, we often have "sons of kings"—to represent the sons of the royal family (Ziegler, *Die Königsgleichnisse des Midrasch*, 1903, ch. xi.). But we never find the phrase "son of the kingdom." The nearest to Mt.'s phrase would be "a son of the covenant" and "a son of the world to come." The former occurs in the well-known prayer of R. Judah, the compiler of the Mishnah, and has found its way from T.B. Berachoth 16 b to the daily prayer book of the Synagogue (ed. Singer, p. 7). Still, there is this to be urged in favour of Matthew's phrase. He also uses (xxiii. 15) the converse, viz. "son of Gehenna" (υἱὸν γεέννης). This, while it does occur in the Talmud (T.B. Rosh Hashana 17 a), is extremely rare. Hence Mt.'s other phrase ("son of the kingdom"), though peculiar to him, may have been a genuine usage, though very occasional, and with no extant parallel.

"The sons of the theocracy are those who belong to it in virtue of their birth, who thereby have a natural right to the possession of it" (Dalman, *Words of Jesus*, p. 115). Similarly "sons of the Kingdom is in Semitic idiom equivalent to those who should inherit it, its rightful heirs" (Allen, *Matthew*, p. 78). No doubt this underlies Matthew viii. 12, especially in the light of the illustration quoted from Philo (*De execrationibus* vi. M. ii. 433, C.-W. v. 371). Nevertheless, though "son" and "heir" are naturally associated, this is by no means regularly the case with the Rabbinic "son of the world to come." In a very large number of passages a "son of the world to come" does something to deserve it and does not acquire it by privilege of birth. So numerous are these passages that it may even be generalised into a rule, that the "son of the world to come" had earned his right of entry (T.B. Ber. 4 a;

Sabb. 153 a; Meg. 28 b; Taanith 22 a, and often). Even when the term "inherit" is used (T.B. Soṭa 7 b; Qiddushin 39 b, and often) the idea of deserving the heritage comes in. Another common phrase is that a man is ready, quickly qualified (מזומן), for the world to come (Taanith 29 a; B. Bathra 75 b, and often); or he has become worthy (זכה) of the future world (Giṭṭin 68 b, and often), or he is announced to be (מבושר) of the future world (T.J. Sheqalim iii. end). The obvious question arises: If *every* Israelite has a portion in the world to come (Mishnah Sanhedrin ch. ḥeleq), how comes it that of individuals only it is said that they are so destined? The true answer would be that at different periods different views were taken as to the universality of Israel's right to future bliss. Or it may be that the difference was that while eventually all are saved, to some salvation comes quicker. This is the explanation given in the tosafot (gloss) on Kethuboth 103 b (top). But the Mishnah itself in the same tractate is inconsistent, as we should justly expect it to be in face of a problem of this kind. Thus while in Mishnah Sanh. x. (xi.) 1, every Israelite is contemplated as possessing a portion in the world to come, in the same tractate vi. 2, the criminal is only so blessed if he makes open confession of offence. Great is the saving power of repentance (Sanh. 90 b). In general, the conception of a "son of the world to come" was moralised. Among such sons of salvation were the gaoler who maintains decency among the prisoners of opposite sexes, and the jester who cheers men and pacifies the quarrelsome (T.B. Taanith 22 a), the kindly Roman executioner (B. Bathra 75 b), or more generally: "Who is a son of the olam haba (the coming world)? He who is modest and lowly; who bends the knee as he goes in and out; who continually occupies himself with Torah, and seeks no advantage for himself" (T.B. Sanhedrin 88 b). Thus so far from inheriting the future world, something had to be done to acquire it. Hence the common phrase that a man "acquires his world" (קונה עולמו), sometimes in a single hour, by a short act of virtue, sometimes in many years, by a lifetime of devotion (T.B. Aboda Zara 10 b, and elsewhere). The realisation of such inequalities was a fine safeguard against the mechanical claims of pietism as well as against the presumption that a seat in Eden was a birth-right.

### (e) *The kingdom of God is within you* (Luke xvii. 21)

R.V. retains the old A.V. rendering: it would be almost a sacrilege to lose so fine a phrase, even though as a translation it is clearly inadmissible. The R.V. relegates the true alternative *in the midst of you* to the margin; the A.V. did the same with the alternative *among you.* To the moderns whom Plummer cites as upholding "*within you,*" must be added Dalman (*Words of Jesus*, pp. 143 seq.). His grammatical argument is not persuasive, while he fails to meet the exegetical objection. "Against *within you* (בגוכון) it appears an objection that it is the Pharisees who are addressed; but this cannot be considered a final criterion, for the historical situation, where the saying of the Lord is introduced, cannot lay claim to the same degree of certitude as the saying itself." But the genuineness of the saying is no more authenticated than the context. It is true, as Dalman argues, that Luke uses ἐν μέσῳ several times for "among."

The same uncertainty is shown, however, in the Greek renderings of the parallel Hebrew equivalent of Luke's phrase. Thus in Exod. xxxiv. 9 ילך יי בקרבנו (A.V. "Let my Lord, I pray thee, go among us," R.V. "Let the Lord, I pray thee, go in the midst of us"), the LXX has μεθ' ἡμων, Sym. and Th. ἐν μέσῳ ἡμῶν and A. ἐντὸς ἡμῶν.

More interesting is another O.T. text, not usually quoted among the many illustrations of Luke. Though it assuredly had no influence on the third Evangelist, it was of some importance in Jewish mysticism. I refer to Hosea xi. 9. Here the Hebrew text is בקרבך קדוש (LXX ἐν σοὶ ἅγιος): "the Holy One in the midst of thee." (Cf. Isaiah xii. 6, though there the word גדול interferes with the use of the text mystically. The LXX has ἐν μέσῳ αὐτῆς.) But this text of Hosea was the basis of a sentence in the Introduction to the Roqeaḥ (*Perfumer*) of Eleazar of Worms (early part of the 13th century). The sentence runs: "Know that the Holy One is within thee, therefore let thy life be one of holiness, self-denial, and purity." (A good study of this book, by M. Joseph, may be read in the *Jews' College Jubilee Volume*, London 1906, pp. 171–190. See also *J.E.* v. p. 100.)

The comment on this text from Hosea, in the Talmud (T.B. Taanith 5a), by R. Joḥanan illustrates (as is well-known) the heavenly Jerusalem of Revelation. Said R. Joḥanan: "(God says) I will not enter Jerusalem on high (ירושלים של מעלה) until I enter the Jerusalem below"—i.e. on earth (ירושלים של מטה); until, that is, the earthly seat is fit for God's holy presence, the heavenly revelation is withheld. The idea of a *second* Jerusalem on high is here derived from Psalm cxxii. 3, where the word שחברה is interpreted in the sense of a "companion city." There are other Rabbinic sources of the idea.

## (*f*) *Lend, never despairing* (Luke vi. 35)

The R.V., after a long life to the Vulgate *nihil inde sperantes* (A.V. "hoping for nothing again"), for the first time put what seems the true rendering into an authoritative English translation. Plummer's excellent note fully deals with the textual questions, and with the influence (he calls it "mischief") wrought by the old interpretation. His foot-note to p. 188 puts the truth in a nutshell.

The only point on which a remark is here offered is that to Luke a loan to the necessitous was an act of benevolence. The whole context proves this. Whether he had the refinement in mind that in certain circumstances it may be truer charity to lend than to give is not clear. What he emphasises is that loans should be made to all classes in need, without overmuch anxiety as to the character of the borrower or the security for the debt. The question of repayment was not to enter into the lender's consideration.

The Hebrew attitude towards lending was the same. It was regarded altogether as an act of benevolence (cf. W. H. Bennett in Hastings' *Encyclopaedia of Religion and Ethics*, xii. 555–6). "The wicked borrows and does not repay" (Ps. xxxvii. 21). Yet this was not to stop the flow of kindness. For the verse proceeds "but the righteous dealeth graciously and giveth," a clause explained by verse 26: "All day long he dealeth graciously and lendeth," though, the Psalmist seems to say, he knows that his loan is a gift. As Ibn Ezra remarks on verse 21, the righteous makes no difference between friend and foe, and he cites in confirmation Proverbs xxv. 21. This well illustrates the context in Luke.

As regards loans and gifts, the Talmud (T.B. Sabbath 63 a) cites the dictum of Simon b. Laqish to the effect: גדול המלוה יותר מן העושה צדקה ומטיל בכים יותר מכולן: "greater is the lender than the almsgiver, and more than either is he who provides means for making a living." A similar thought (with special reference to the maintenance of students) is attributed to R. Joḥanan in T.B. Pesaḥim 53 b. In another passage we have the delicate idea of R. Meir that to the needy who is reluctant to accept alms, the benefaction may be camouflaged as a loan to save his feelings (Maimonides, *Gifts to the Poor*, vii. 9 on the basis of T.B. Kethuboth 67 b). Other Rabbis (in the same Talmudic reference) add that, contrariwise, a gift may subsequently be converted into a loan. The granting of loans, bearing no interest, has long been a regular feature of Jewish (as no doubt of other) systems of poor relief.

### (*g*) *O ye of little faith* (Mt. vi. 30, Luke xii. 28)

The adjective ὀλιγόπιστοι (Mt. vi. 30, xvi. 8, Luke xii. 28, Mt. viii. 26, xiv. 31) is recognised as the equivalent of the Rabbinic קטני אמנה literally "little ones of faith," i.e. men of little faith. The Hebrew occurs in another form: "lacking in faith" (מחוסר אמנה) as in Genesis Rabba, ch. xxxii. § 6. In the Rabba passage just quoted the sense is not the same as in Mt. and Lk. Noah's lack of faith was not his disbelief in God's power to save, but his scepticism as to God's intention to destroy. Noah (says the Midrash) did not enter the ark until the flood had already made considerable headway. Noah did not enter because God commanded him to do so (vii. 1), but only "because of the waters of the flood" (vii. 7).

But the other Rabbinic phrase, "men of little faith," is used in a sense exactly parallel to the ὀλιγόπιστοι of the first and third Gospels. (Mk. does not use the word, which is also unknown to Classical Greek.) "R. Eleazar the Great (first century) said: Whoever has bread in his basket and asks, What shall I eat to-morrow, is none other than of those of little faith" (T.B. Soṭa 48 b). The occurrence of the Rabbinic phrase so early, and in this particular context, strengthens the authenticity of the ascription of it also to Jesus. Comparable with this use of the phrase is the Rabbinic application of it to the over-anxious by the sea. The men of the Exodus were "of little faith" not only in the wilderness (Exodus xiv.) but also at the Red Sea (Ps. cvi.). See T.B. Arachin 15 a. This reminds us of the use in some of the Gospel texts cited above. It may be added that in T.B. Soṭa 48 b the noun קטנות אמנה occurs, this corresponds exactly to the ὀλιγοπιστία of Mt. xvii. 20. The other reading ἀπίστια has equally a Rabbinic parallel in Num. Rabba xix. § 10, where אין אמנה looks like a noun built on the model of the Greek ἀπιστία, a classical form which occurs several times in N.T. Another interesting use of the phrase is in connection with prayer.

"He who makes his voice heard in his prayer is of those of little faith" (T.B. Berachoth 24 b). Importunity is evidence of distrust (cf. above p. 76). The ideal was to utter the words, but in soft not stentorian voice. "How many weighty rules may be derived from the incident of Hannah! *Now Hannah spake in her heart* (1 Sam. i. 13)—hence it is inferred that one who prays must be devout of heart (lit. must *direct* his heart). *Only her lips moved*, hence, one who prays must pronounce the words with his lips. *But her voice was not heard*—hence it is forbidden to raise the voice when praying" (Ber. 31 a, end).

The converse, "men of faith" (אנשי אמנה) occurs in the Mishnah (Soṭa ix. 12), where the pessimistic exaggeration is uttered that the "men of faith" ceased with the destruction of the Temple. The sad phrase "the men of faith have perished" appears in the medieval Synagogue hymns (cf. Zunz, *Literaturgeschichte der synagogalen Poesie*, pp. 23, 228).

The Rabbinic parallels cited in Lightfoot's *Horae* (on Mt. xxi. 21) and in Wuensche's *Neue Beiträge* (p. 204) for the phrase "to remove mountains," are linguistically very close, but they do not ascribe this hyperbolical influence to faith, but to the power of the government to gain its ends however extreme, or to the faculty exercised by intellectual agility in removing difficulty. Yet the power of faith described in Hebrews xi. 32–39 aptly summarises, in a completely Jewish spirit, the power of faith from the time of Gideon to that of Judas Maccabeus. 4 Macc. insists (xv. 24, xvii. 2) on the same power. The most frequent Rabbinic thought is that man's faith moves God to perform the most miraculous feats on behalf of the faithful. This is the substance of long passages in the Mechilta in its comments on the passage of the Red Sea. Cf. also p. 74 above.

### (*h*) *In presence of the Angels* (Luke xii. 8–9)

For Luke's *before the angels of God* (cf. also xv. 10) Matthew (x. 32–3, xviii. 14) has *before my Father which is in heaven*. Bousset suggests that this is evidence for Luke's Jewish special source, his remark applying particularly to the use of the phrase in Luke xv. (*Die Religion des Judentums*, 1903, p. 308). It is not clear how this paraphrase of the *angels* for *God* can be called a late Jewish usage. The Targum never makes the substitution. In the few instances in which *Elohim* is rendered *angels*, the ground is exegetical not theological (so in Ps. viii.

6), and the Targum is followed by many authorities. Certainly God was called Holy and the Holy Ones are often angels; but this does not justify Bousset.

It is rather unkind of commentators, when dealing with the joy in heaven over the repentant sinner, to quote a Rabbinic sentence: "There is joy before God when those who provoke him perish from the world" (Edersheim, Plummer). For there is much on the other side. In T.B. Berachoth 34 b, Abbahu has the saying that the penitent occupy a place inaccessible to the righteous. Abbahu is, indeed, a late authority, but the Mishnah (Sanhedrin vi. 5) has a touching passage which ought to be quoted as well. It runs thus: "When a man suffers (for his sin), what language does the Shechinah use? Woe to my head, woe to my arm! If the Omnipresent thus suffers when the blood of the wicked is shed, how much more when it is the blood of the righteous." In fact on such questions there were various points of view among Pharisaic teachers, and particular utterances ought not to be used as foils to beautiful Gospel passages which assuredly do not require the darkening of Pharisaism in order to display their light. Moreover, the drawing of such contrasts is apt to produce very bad exegesis. Thus Edersheim in an earlier place deprecates the Pharisaic preference (not a unanimous preference) for the repentant sinner over the perfectly righteous. But he forgets to quote it when dealing with the beautiful saying of Jesus in which more or less the same idea is expressed. This line of argument was forcibly criticised by S. Schechter in his article "On the Study of the Talmud" in the *Westminster Review*, to be reprinted in the third series of his *Studies in Judaism*. The effect on the criticism of the Gospels is as regrettable as the effect on the criticism of Pharisaism. There is a lack of consistency in the standards applied to different parts of the same system. The self-same point of view is blamed or praised according to momentary exigencies or caprice. There thus arises what may be termed a hand-to-mouth exegesis, a danger which the present writer does not flatter himself that he has avoided.

### (*i*) *Spoken through Jeremiah* (Mt. xxvii. 10)

The chief authorities refer this to Jeremiah; the few MSS that omit the prophet's name probably do so to save the ascription to Jeremiah of a quotation made (with minor variations) from Zechariah xi. 13. In Zech. the reading *potter* (יוצר) is supposed by many to be a mistake for *treasury* (אוצר). Wellhausen acutely pointed out that Matthew shows indications of both readings (cf. verse 5 with verse 10). The whole story of Mt. xxvii. 3–10 is missing from Mark and Luke.

How came the author or authors of the legend concerning Judas' death to quote Jeremiah instead of Zechariah? Wuensche thinks of Midrash, and it is true that Midrash would have seen nothing unnatural in welding together various texts containing a reference to the potter. But this is not the case in the present context. Lightfoot ingeniously cites T.B. Baba Bathra 14 b where Jeremiah comes first in the order of the prophets (cf. N. Schmidt in *Encyclopaedia Biblica*, col. 2372; C. D. Ginsburg, *Introduction to the Massoretico-Critical Edition of the Hebrew Bible*, pp. 1–8). Quoting from this section of the Bible, Matthew might cite the passage as from "Jeremiah." There is no parallel to such a method of citation as Lightfoot's theory requires, but his suggestion perhaps deserves more consideration than it has received.

The most likely explanation is that given by C. G. Montefiore, who conceives that "Jeremiah xxxii. 6–15 and xviii. 2 were vaguely in the mind of those who made up the legend." It may be interesting to note that Jeremiah seems to be the originator of the literary use of the potter and clay metaphor. There is no such literary use precedent to him, and J. Skinner is right in asserting that "this classical illustration of the divine sovereignty—the image of the potter and clay—seems to have originated with Jeremiah" (*Prophecy and Religion*, 1922, p. 162). Isaiah's references (xxix. 16, xlv. 9, lxiv. 7) are later, and the older reference (xxx. 14) merely alludes to the fragile nature of the potter's products. The point is even more interesting when we remember that pottery makes a comparatively late appearance among the Jews. The Jewish pottery is nearly all wheel-turned, and dates from the later Jewish monarchy (650–500 B.C.). If Jeremiah spoke the first verses of ch. xviii. between 620 and 610 (Cornill), the potter's house was a novelty in Jeremiah's day. Hence his use of the art in parable had all the interest of a topical allusion, and would have been all the more effective on that account. The notion of the creation of man from clay is old, and we have an Egyptian picture of the XVIIIth dynasty showing Khnûmû moulding Amenhotep III and his double on the potter's table (*KAT* ed. 3, 429; Jeremias, *The Old Testament in the Light of the Ancient East*, 1911, i. 182; Maspero, *Dawn of Civilization*, ed. 5, p. 157). But there is no use of the metaphor in the Babylonian hymns; indeed none seems to have been adduced in any literature prior to Jeremiah.

### (*j*) *Give not that which is holy unto the dogs* (Mt. vii. 6)

Most of the references to "dogs," as an epithet for wicked opponents, are not to be interpreted primarily as contemptuous; they point to the relentlessness and shamelessness of persecutors, for which Psalm xxii. 16 is the model. Bulls and lions typify much the same in this Psalm. The Rabbinic usage agrees with the N.T. usage (Phil. iii. 2, Rev. xxii. 15). The facts are well marshalled by K. Kohler in *J.E.* iv. 632. Neither Talmud nor Mt. is pleasant reading in this connection.

When, however, the commentaries on Mt. persistently assert that the Jews habitually called the heathens "dogs," it is necessary to dispute the assertion, though C. G. Montefiore lends countenance to it. There was no such habitual designation, it is casual at the most, and the wicked and idolatrous are the object of the obloquy. Naturally few moderns give credence to Eisenmenger's absurdity that the Jews described the Christians as "dogs" (*Entdecktes Judenthum*, i. 714–716). Eisenmenger's quotations are, without exception, irrelevant and misconstrued. Nor are Wuensche's quotations (*Neue Beiträge*, p. 189) more fortunate. His statement that the Talmud describes the heathen as "a people like the ass" is not justified by his quotations. The first Nidda 77a is altogether erroneous; while in his other references nothing is said in the Talmud about heathens. The point invariably is as to the legal status of slaves, who are compared (from this point of view only) to such chattels as their master's ass. T. K. Cheyne in *Encyclopaedia Biblica* (col. 1125) repeats Wuensche's inaccuracy.

There is, indeed, a Rabbinic parallel or rather contrast to Mt. xv. 27, "the dogs eat of the crumbs which fall from their masters' table." The passage referred to is in the Midrash to Ps. iv. 8 (ed. Buber, p. 48; Buber, however, has an incorrect reading, for ורשעי ישראל of his text, the Venice ed. 1546 as well as all important MSS read ואומות העולם). "The nations of the world who obey the seven Noachide laws receive their reward in this world; how much more shall Israel, obedient to the 613 precepts, enjoy happiness in the world to come. Hence Israel should rejoice when they behold the table of the heathens, as it is said: Thou hast put joy in my heart, from the time when their corn and their wine increased (Ps. iv. 8 [7]). R. Joshua b. Levi said, It is a parable: like a king who made a feast, and brought in the guests, and placed them at the door of his palace. They saw the dogs come out, with pheasants, and heads of fatted (birds) and calves in their mouths. Then the guests began to say, If it be thus with the dogs, the meal itself how much more so (will it be luxurious). And the nations of the world are compared to dogs, as it is said (Isaiah lvi. 11) Yea the dogs are greedy." It is obvious even from this passage that the description of heathens (in a context where no allusion is made to their wickedness) as dogs was unfamiliar, else there would have been no need to explain it exegetically. The "crumbs" in Joshua b. Levi's parable are rather choice dainties, unless we suppose that it was pheasants' heads rather than pheasants that the dogs carried off. The whole passage has a derived look, it is too sophisticated to be old. The opening part of the passage in the Midrash is anonymous; but Joshua b. Levi (to whom the actual parable is ascribed) was a Palestinian Amora of the first half of the third century.

## (*k*) *As a thief in the night* (1 Thess. v. 2, cf. Mt. xxiv. 43, Lk. xvii. 24)

The phrase in 1 Thess. v. 2 has the appearance of a proverbial phrase, but elsewhere, whether in the Gospels or in Rev. iii. 10, xvi. 15, this does not seem to be the case. The fact that the figure is not found elsewhere, whether in Biblical, apocalyptic, Rabbinic, or classical literatures, justifies McNeile's suggestion that "it may have originated with Jesus." In *J.E.* iv. 51 col. 1 a misprint of quotation marks leaves the impression that, in T.B. Sanhedrin 97 a, the phrase "like a thief in the night" occurs. This is not the case. It is there said that "the Messiah, treasure trove, and the scorpion come unexpectedly" (בהיסח הדעת, i.e. with removal of the mind, absence of expectation).

It is going too far to assert, with Jerome, that the Jews had a "tradition" that the Messiah would come at midnight, at a time corresponding to the Exodus. Such an idea is found, indeed. Cf. T.J. Pesaḥim x. § 1; Exod. R. ch. xviii. § 12. The "open door," still part of the home rite of the Passover eve, is commonly explained as symbolical of the entry of Elijah (L. Landshuth, מגיד מראשית, p. xvi). There are several other explanations, but this seems the most probable.

The unexpectedness of the Messiah's coming is the main point of the figure, and this main point is found in Mk. xiii. 35. Apart from the quotation, made above from Sanh., it has been shown above (p. 120) that it was regarded by certain Rabbis as blameworthy to calculate the date of the Messianic age. So strongly was this objection felt, that in several places condemnation is uttered against a similar impatience with regard to an earlier redemption. Thus, in particular, it is said that the Ephraimites suffered severe casualties in an attempt to enter Canaan at a date which they calculated for the Redemption from Egyptian bondage. (Cf. Mechilta, ed. Friedmann, 24 a top; Pirque de Rabbi Eleazar, ch. xlviii.; cf. *J.E.* v. 189.)

A favourite Rabbinic use of the idea of the secretness with which the thief operates is of another kind. The thief is penalised by the law more severely than the open robber. R. Joḥanan b. Zakkai explained that the thief who steals in the owner's absence stands more in awe of man than of God, coming unobserved lest men should see or hear him, but treating the Heavenly Eye and Ear as though neither hearing nor seeing. The robber in the owner's presence regards neither man nor God: he is the less culpable. R. Meir cites a parable in the name of R. Gamaliel. Two men gave feasts, one invited the people but not the king, the other invited neither. The one who invited neither deserved less punishment (Tosefta Baba Qama vii. 2; T.B. Baba Qama 79 b). The point is that the thief stole in the presence of witnesses but in the absence of the owner. This is an apt instance of the difficulty of entering into the exact sense of a parable, unless the key is provided in the context. Cf. p. 47 above.

### (*l*) *More than all sacrifices* (Mk. xii. 33)

Mark's prophetic attitude towards sacrifice is emphasised in Mt. ix. 13, xii. 7, by the direct citation of Hosea vi. 6. Hosea uses the word "ḥesed," rendered ἔλεος in LXX and Mt. In the plural, and in connection with the noun derived from "gamal," the term is a great favourite of the Rabbinic literature, in which "gemiluth ḥasadim" denotes "the rendering of loving services," services of money and yet more of person (T.B. Sukkah 49 b, on basis of another famous O.T. text in which "ḥesed" appears, the ἀγαπᾶν ἔλεον of Micah vi. 8; cf. also Deut. Rabba v. § 3).

There is a well-known saying to the same effect by Joḥanan b. Zakkai, who, as F. C. Burkitt points out, "was probably only a few years junior to St Paul." Replying to a despondent disciple—Joshua b. Ḥananya—who bewailed the loss of the atoning sacrifices when the Temple fell, Joḥanan said that there was no room for grief, for there remained a means of propitiation equal to the sacrifices, namely "gemiluth ḥasadim," the rendering of loving-kindnesses, even as it is written, I desire loving-kindness and not sacrifice (Aboth d. R. Nathan I. iv., ed. Schechter, p. 21; cf. Bacher, *Agada der Tannaiten*, p. 35; Burkitt, *Schweich Lectures*, p. 8). Joḥanan's opinion was not improvised after 70 A.D. While the altar still stood, Joḥanan had said "Just as the sin-offering atones for Israel, so also alms-giving (צדקה) atones for the nations" (T.B. Baba Bathra 10 b). Thus Joḥanan merely enlarged the idea from alms-giving to loving-kindness, and then extended to Israel after the destruction of Jerusalem, the same principle which he had applied to the rest of the world before that calamity.

If we add to this coincidence the two facts (*a*) that long before 70 Joḥanan foresaw and prophesied the loss of the altar (T.B. Yoma 39 b), and (*b*) that after 70 he anticipated its speedy restoration (T.B. Kerithoth 8 a, Rosh Hash. 31 b, and particularly Sukkah 41 a; cf. H. Graetz, *Die jüdische Proselyten im Römerreiche*, pp. 11–12)—we can understand how it came about that the cessation of sacrifices dealt so much milder a blow at the Jewish system than might have been anticipated. The minds of men like Joḥanan were prepared for the catastrophe, and as time went on and the Temple remained desolate, the religion thoroughly recovered its balance, and gemiluth ḥasadim, first a substitute, becomes *superior* to sacrifices (Deut. R. v. 3). The Apocalypse of Baruch shows us how, after 70, the view became forthwith propounded that the Law was of more permanent efficiency than the sacrifices, that the Law remained though the altar had gone. This idea meets us again and again in the Rabbinic homilies. Then, again, sacrificial language was applied to prayer (Taanith 27 b, Ber. 23 b), to fasting (Num. R. xviii.), to acts of benevolence (Levit. R. xxxiv. § 13), to the table as altar (T.B. Ber. 55 a), to the conquest of lust as a sacrifice of the yeṣer (T.B. Sanh. 43 a), to the giving of alms as payment of the shekel for the tamid (T.B. Baba Bathra 9 a), and already in Justin Martyr's time the theory was propounded by Jews (represented by Trypho) that the sacrifices as such all along had been merely temporary or educational (Dialogue xxii., lxviii.), a theory which finds expression in the Midrash (Levit. Rabba xxii. 8, Yalquṭ on Ps. cxxxii., Gen. R. lxxxvi. § 5, Mechilta p. 60 b), and was afterwards fully developed by Maimonides (*Guide*, iii. 32; see, however, D. Hoffmann, *Leviticus*, Berlin 1905, i. pp. 81 seq.). What has been said of gemiluth ḥasadim applies generally also to the Torah as a permanent means of salvation.

The evidence of Philo is to the same effect. For the diaspora, Justin's evidence shows (Dialogue xxii., lxviii.) that Jews applied Malachi i. 11 to the efficiency of prayer as apart from sacrifice (cf. for an instructive use of this text Pesiqta Rabbathi, p. 192 a. As in Justin so in the Midrash the text is used in a controversy between Jew and non-Jew). But Philo's evidence is the more important as it is so much earlier. Like the Rabbis and the Gospels, Philo has no antipathy to sacrifices as such. They all accept the prophetic standpoint, but point forward to the time when, by the force of circumstances, sacrifices must give way to other methods of appealing for God's mercy. In the process and progress Philo says some fine things. "They who bring themselves (αὑτοὺς φέροντες) are offering the most excellent of sacrifices" (*De Sacrifant.* iii., M. II. 253, C.-W. v. 65). With this may be compared the identical phrase in a Midrash. The word nefesh (soul, life) is mentioned with reference to the meal-offering (Levit. ii. 1). Why? Because it is the poor man who brings such an offering, and God accounts it as though "he offered his soul, himself" כאילו הקריב נפשו לפני (Yalquṭ § 447). The context in Philo also refers to the poor, and thus the parallel is very close. And again: "God delights in fireless altars round which virtues form the choral dance" (βωμοῖς γὰρ ἀπύροις, περὶ οὓς ἀρεταὶ χορεύουσι, γέγηθεν ὁ θεός, *De Plant.* xxv., M. I. 345, C.-W. ii. 154). Philo would not have objected, any more than Maimonides did, to praying for the restoration of the sacrifices. It was not till the modern liberal movement that Jews began to omit such prayers (cf. D. Philipson, *The Reform Movement in Judaism*, 1907, p. 118 etc.).

### (*m*) *The tradition of the elders* (Mk. vii. 3)

The word παράδοσις, often used in Classical Greek, only occurs in this place in the Gospels, and in the parallel passage Mt. xv. 2. A. Merx, on this last-cited text, argues that the word can hardly mean "tradition," for the strict rules of hand-washing and so forth were certainly not old enough in the time of Jesus to deserve such a description. He suggests (with support from the Syriac) that we ought to render παράδοσις by *commandment* (מצוה), or to regard παράδοσις as a late change of the text. Büchler (*Der galiläische Am-ha Areṣ*, 1906, ch. iv.) maintains that hand-washing as a firmly fixed obligation was not introduced till the second century. His book is full of most valuable material, and though his contention regarding hand-washing is disputable, he certainly succeeds in proving, what had been previously urged by Jewish scholars, especially by C. G. Montefiore, that the majority of the purity laws applied only to priests, or to laymen who had occasion to enter the Temple (C. G. Montefiore, *Hibbert Lectures*, 1892, p. 476 and note 4). On this point Dr Büchler's evidence leaves no room for doubt. It certainly does not seem that there was ever a large class of laymen who voluntarily elected to live under sacerdotal restrictions. W. Brandt (*Jüdische Reinheitslehre*, 1910, p. 4) concedes that the passage in Mk. has the appearance of an interpolation. His examination of the Rabbinic evidence is distinguished by its sincerity and objectivity.

Josephus (13 *Antiq.* x. 6) uses the term "tradition of the fathers" (*παράδοσις τῶν πατέρων*) in contradistinction to the written law (*νόμιμα τὰ γεγραμμένα*), and expounds this as the point of contention between Pharisees and Sadducees; on this account Leszynsky (*Die Sadducäer*, 1912, p. 297) conceives that Jesus had Sadducean leanings. Hellenists like Philo were certainly not on the Sadducean side, as is proved by his often-quoted and favourable reference (M. II. 629) to "the ten thousand other precepts which relate to the unwritten customs and ordinances of the nation." It may be doubted whether in Ecclus. viii. 9 there is any specific allusion to such traditions. But in the Prologue to that book it may be that when the writer alludes to "readers and lovers of learning" he is referring not to one and the same class but to two classes. The readers may be those who study the *mikra*, the written law as read from the scroll; while the lovers of learning might be those who study the traditions, which were learned orally, *mishnah*. (Cf. J. H. A. Hart in *J.Q.R.* xix. 284 seq. and my note p. 289.) The earliest clear reference to "two laws"—written and oral—is in connection with a proselyte story told of Hillel and Shammai (T.B. Sabbath 31 a).

### (*n*) *I say unto you, Fear him* (Luke xii. 5)

The context of this saying has already been discussed (p. 46 above). So, too, in First Series (p. 139) reference is made to the Rabbinic turn given to Ps. cxxx. 4: "But there is forgiveness with thee, that thou mayest be feared." God's readiness to pardon leads to the fear of God. A similar idea may underlie Rom. ii. 4 "the goodness of God leadeth thee to repentance."

How old is this use of the idea in, or read into, Ps. cxxx.? It is at least as old as the Letter of Aristeas (on the date of which see *J.Q.R.* Jan. 1902; H. St J. Thackeray in his ed., S.P.C.K. 1918, p. xii.). No reasonable critic places the Letter later than 100 B.C. (cf. H. T. Andrews in Charles' *Apocrypha and Pseudepigrapha*, ii. p. 87).

Now in the course of the discussions at the Banquet, the king inquires (§ 194) how he might inspire terror into his enemies? The sage answers: "If while maintaining an abundant supply of arms and forces he recognised that these things were powerless to secure any lasting and conclusive result. For God *instils fear into the minds of men by granting reprieves* and making merely a display of his sovereignty."

It seems to me that the difficulty found by Wendland in interpreting this passage is removed by a reference to Ps. cxxx. As we should expect, there is no suggestion in the text of Aristeas of any acquaintance with the LXX version of Psalms.

## (*o*) *Barabbas* (Mt. xxvii. 16 seq.)

The name occurs in all four Gospels (cf. Mk. xv. 7 seq., Lk. xxiii. 18, Jn. xviii. 40). The question as to the authenticity of the reading "Jesus" in front of Barabbas has been answered in the affirmative by F. C. Burkitt in his valuable note (*Evangelion da Mepharreshe*, ii. 277) and many authorities are of the same opinion. The purpose of the present note is to call attention to an onomastic suggestion of W. Bacher.

Barabbas naturally means "Son of Abbas" (Abba). "But evidence is wanting that Abba was a proper name" (Plummer on Luke xxiii. 18). It is certainly true that in no instance, except Barabbas, can the personal name Abba be cited quite so early. Yet it is not necessary to suppose that Abba means "father" in this case, seeing that Abba is a well-established proper name and that early enough. A possible contemporary of Joḥanan ben Zakkai was so named (Mishnah Peah ii. 6), and he does not stand alone. (See *J.E.* i. 29, where both those able scholars—W. Bacher and L. Ginzberg—unhesitatingly accept Abba as a personal name.) There was among the Yabne Rabbis a Judah bar Abba (Mishnah Eduyoth vi. 1), if we follow the reading of the Cambridge Mishnah (ed. Lowe, p. 139 a), supported by the Yuḥasin (cf. Bacher, *Revue des Études Juives*, xxxvi. p. 104). The Amora Samuel's father was Abba bar Abba (T.B. Berachoth 18 b). The evidence for the use of Abba as a personal name is quite conclusive.

As to the origin of the name, it may have been originally a title of honour (father = master, Rabbi, cf. Abba Saul) and thence become used as a proper name. But as Bacher points out (*op. cit.* p. 105) it may well be an abbreviation of Abraham. Bacher shows that the full name Abraham is never used in the Talmud. Similarly Moses, Aaron, David, Solomon, are never used in the Talmud of Palestinians, and most of the names cited were equally unused in Babylonia, except that in the latter country we once find a single Moses in the fourth century (T.B. Arachin 23 a, Baba Bathra 174 a) and a single Aaron in the fifth (T.B. Baba Qama 109 b, Menaḥoth 74 b). These names (to which may be added Isaiah and Israel) were not used because of the veneration in which they were held. The names avoided seem to have been the *first* in their respective aspects: Abraham the first Patriarch, Aaron the first high-priest, and so forth. Later on, continues Bacher, these venerated names were given in the hope that those so denominated would imitate the virtues of the original bearers of the names. Yet, as Bacher adds, in the third century a Palestinian Rabbi, Samuel b. Naḥman, expressly asserts that the name Abraham was used (Genesis Rabba, ch. xlix. beginning, cf. Bacher, *Agada der palaestin. Amoraer*, i. 489).

Bacher (p. 105) concludes from these facts that the name Abraham was used at the earlier periods, but in the disguised form Abba. "On ne réussit pas seulement à préserver ainsi de la profanation le nom d'Abraham, mais on a également un des principaux éléments étymologiques de ce nom (אב cf. Genesis xvii. 5) et on rappelle en même temps le titre d'Abraham comme 'père' κατ' ἐξοχήν (אברהם אבינו cf. Isaiah lxiii. 16)." On this view Jesus Barabbas was really Jesus the son of Abraham.

## (*p*) *Abraham's bosom* (Luke xvi. 22)

Some commentators seem to think that this phrase occurs in 4 Macc. xiii. 16–17. This is due to C. L. W. Grimm's note on the passage in *Kurzgefasstes exegetisches Handbuch zu den Apokryphen des Alten Testamentes* (Leipzig 1857): "Vs. 16 werden uns Abrah., Isaak und Jacob *in ihren Schoss* aufnehmen." There is, however, no authority for the words "in their bosom" in the Greek text. Hence this supposed parallel to Luke, so far as the phraseology is concerned, is non-existent.

In a general sense, moreover, the parallel is scarcely good, for according to the text cited the martyrs would resemble Isaac who at the "fatherly hand" yielded himself to be a sacrifice (4 Macc. xiii. 12). Hence they would be worthy of their great progenitors and "after this our passion, Abraham, Isaac, and Jacob shall receive us, and all our forefathers shall praise us." This is less close to the parable of Lazarus and Dives than to Matt. viii. 11: "Many shall come from the east and the west, and shall sit down with Abraham, and Isaac, and Jacob in the kingdom of heaven." The phrase "sitting in Abraham's bosom" (יושב בחיקו של אברהם) occurs once in the Talmud (T.B. Qiddushin 72 b) with reference to a third-century Babylonian Rabbi, Adda bar Ahaba. It is doubtful whether the statement is that Adda "sat in the bosom of Abraham" in his infancy (at his entry into the covenant of Abraham on his circumcision) or at his death (on his entry into Paradise). The latter seems the more probable, though Rashi adopts the former interpretation.

Attention may be called to A. Geiger's suggestion (*Jüdische Zeitschrift*, 1868, vi. pp. 196 seq.) that Lazarus (i.e. Eleazar) is identifiable with Abraham's servant. His citations are interesting. He concludes that at the time of Jesus, or rather at the time when Luke's parable was assigned to Jesus, Eleazar-Lazarus was among the Jewish folk a type of a humble but zealous and God-fearing man of the lower people, fit to be borne on angels' wings to Abraham's bosom, to serve him as it were in Paradise as he had served him on earth (*op. cit.* p. 201).

## (*q*) *They make broad their phylacteries* (Mt. xxiii. 5)

There is no support elsewhere for this particular form of ostentation. The tephillin (nowhere described in Jewish sources as phylacteries) were, however, a proudly borne mark of Judaism, and the display of them (especially the tephillah worn round the head) was only ostentatious in a good sense (as understood by the Pharisees). This is clear from T.B. Menaḥoth 35 b, where the rite is brought into connection with Deut. xxviii. 10 "And all the peoples of the earth shall see that thou art called by the name of the Lord."

Similarly it would seem that it was held needful to specify this rite because of heretical variations, the precise nature of which, however, is not clear. The commentators find it very difficult to explain the "danger" of wearing a *round* phylactery on the head—the context implies that any but a cubical shape was heretical (Mishnah Megillah iv. 8). Is the "danger" some obscure superstition, against which it was desirable to protest? Perhaps this throws light on the use of the word "phylactery" (amulet).

In his *Aramaic Origin of the Fourth Gospel*, C. F. Burney (p. 10) suggests that to Matthew's *πλατύνουσιν γὰρ τὰ φυλακτήρια αὐτῶν* correspond the *μακρὰ προσευχόμενοι* of Mk. xii. 40 and Luke xx. 46. The charge of verbosity in prayer is indeed hard to justify, for early Jewish liturgies were very brief (compare p. 85 above). Dr Burney thinks that the "Aramaic original" was דִּמַפְּתִּין תפיליהון which Matthew rightly rendered "who make broad their phylacteries," while the other Synoptics mistranslated by "who make verbose their prayers." As a comment on a not ignoble *motive* for pietistic display may be cited the Mechilta on Exod. xv. 2 (ed. Friedmann, p. 37 a), where ואנוהו is rendered "and I will beautify him"—and the comment is made, man can "beautify" God by wearing a beautiful fringe and a beautiful tephillah or phylactery (ציצית נאה תפלה נאה). Or again, the Yelamdenu to Genesis xxv. 23 (with a play on גוים and גאים). "Read not two nations (Esau and Jacob), but two proud ones, both of whom glorify themselves: Esau (Rome) prides itself in its *κυκλάς* (state-robes) while Jacob wears the fringe; Esau wears the *χλαμύς* (toga), Israel the ṭallith" (the four-cornered mantle, still used by the orthodox in prayer). This may be compared with the quotation with which this Note opens. Perhaps in the contrast to the Roman *κυκλάς* (literally *round* garment) we have a clue to the Mishnaic objection to a *round* phylactery. The round robe was a feminine attire originally at least, and there would be an objection to use phylacteries which suggested feminine fashions. (On the quotation from the Yelamdenu see Kohut, *Aruch* s.v. ככלא.)

It may be that the objection in Mt. is to wearing of the phylacteries at all. It may have displeased, in particular, Gentile observers. Jerome, on Galatians iv. 22, says that Jews feared to appear in the cities, because they attracted attention; "probably," comments Blau, they were recognised by the tephillah (phylactery, on the head). For a similar reason, the phylactery was not worn openly in times of danger (Mishnah Erubin x. 1). As regards the Jews themselves, however, the practice was not universal, and in some Jewish circles may have been disliked (cf. L. Blau in *J.E.* x. p. 27). Some pietists of recent centuries have adopted large phylacteries; this has not been from motives of ostentation but to enable the texts, inscribed on parchment inside the leathern boxes, to be written clearly. In most cases the boxes are small, and the writing diminutive. It must be remembered that each box contains four texts: Exod. xiii. 1–10, 11–16, Deut. vi. 4–9, xi. 13–21, i.e. 31 verses.

The verb used in Mt. πλατύνουσιν may merely be used as an equivalent to the μεγαλύνουσιν of the latter part of the verse (used in relation to the κράσπεδα, the LXX word for "fringes"). But if the first verb be taken precisely (to widen), it can hardly refer to the boxes, which were cubical. One hardly widens a cube. The difficulty is removed if we think of the straps by which the boxes were attached, rather than of the boxes themselves. The tephillah of the arm (box and strap alike) was invisible. But the head tephillah was displayed, hence its greater importance in Rabbinic eyes. The head tephillah is bound over the brow, the box overhanging the centre of the forehead, and a knob at the middle of the neck, the two ends of the strap hanging over the shoulders in front. There was, however, another method of dealing with the ends of the strap, viz. to tie them round twice or thrice not to leave the ends loose. This method (referred to in Menahoth *loc. cit.*) would explain Mt.'s verb πλατύνουσιν.

## (r) *In his heart* (Mt. v. 28)

The Rabbinic parallels usually quoted in illustration of this great thought are less to the point than are some of the ideas to be read under הרהור עבירה ("unchaste imagination") in the Dictionaries (Levy, p. 493; Jastrow, p. 366; Kohut, III. p. 243). Levy quotes especially (T.J. Yoma 29 a) הרהור עבירה קשה מעבירה "The thought of sin is more serious than sin itself." Kohut cites (T.B. Berachoth 12 b): "*After your eyes* (Numbers xv. 39) means lustful imagination," cf. the Targum *ad loc.*

On the other hand, this ideal doctrine was not pressed to the exclusion of a differentiation between temptation and fall, between intention and act. The Gospel would assuredly not so have pressed it. Transgression for God's sake may be better than piety without such motive (T.B. Horayoth 10 b), but the real differentiation is well brought out in Tosefta Peah i. § 4. A good intention is, as it were, added to, accounted with, the good deed which ensues; not so a bad thought which does not eventuate in an evil effect (cf. T.B. Qiddushin 40 a). The test of true reformation on the part of the unchaste offender was the presence of the same opportunity with the absence of the same yielding to it (*ibid.*). Resistance to temptation was possible; it was a very high virtue (T.B. Yoma 38–39). Who is mighty? He who subdues his yeṣer, his impulse to sin (Mishnah Aboth iv. 2); the stronger the man, the stronger his yeṣer, and therefore the greater his triumph if his good yeṣer prevail (T.B. Berachoth 34 b, Sukkah 52 a; cf. C. Taylor on Aboth ch. IV. note 2 and Additional Note 33). Cf. p. 105 above.

It is in accord with this that unrectifiable crookedness (Eccles. i. 15) is defined as the adultery which produces bastard offspring (Mishnah Ḥagigah i. 7). The Talmud (T.B. Ḥagigah 9 a) records the opinion that the act is just as reprehensible if no such consequence occur. But it is the act, not the mere lust, that is castigated in this connection.

### (*s*) *Love thy neighbour* (Mt. v. 43)

The question whether in Rabbinic exegesis this text was restricted in its application is discussed in the First Series of these Studies.

On the whole that exegesis has a fine record on this text. The only exception specified is that of the heretic and the betrayer. A famous passage of the Aboth de R. Nathan (i. ch. 16, ed. Schechter, p. 64) against "hatred of one's fellow-men" (שנאת הבריות) refers to this case. With this may be compared the Church canons threatening perpetual excommunication against Christian *delatores* (Synod of Elvira, *c.* 306 A.D., can. lxxiii.; cf. Council of Arles, can. xiii.). Even so, however, R. Simeon b. Eleazar (in the same passage) protests that "it is said with a great oath: Thou shalt love thy neighbour as thyself, I am the Lord—I have created him; if thou love him I am faithful to requite fully, if not I am a Judge to exact punishment (from thee)." So, too, on Exod. xxii. 27 the Mechilta ends off with the most general exposition of reverence, not merely for prince and judge, but for all men (שאר כל אדם). Note in the former passage, as in the one cited below, the phrase *with a great oath*; this implies the most emphatic and impressive form of command.

Again, a first-century passage (Aboth de R. Nathan ii. 26, ed. Schechter, p. כז) is of great significance. R. Ḥanina, the deputy high-priest, said of neighbourly love that "it is a thing on which the whole world depends. This command was given with an oath on Mt. Sinai. If thou hate thy neighbour who is as bad as thyself, I will exact payment from thee! If thou love thy neighbour who is as good as thyself, I will have mercy on thee!"

רבי חנינא סגן הכהנים אומר דבר שכל העולם תלוי בו נאמר עליו שבועה מהר סיני
אם שונא חבירך שמעשיו רעים כמעשיך אני ה׳ דיין להפרע מאותו האיש ׳ואם
אוהב את חבירך שמעשיו כשרים כמעשיך אני ה׳ נאמן ומרחם עליך:

(In Rabbinic idiom אותו האיש most probably means *thee.*)

Thus a man must not be hated for the evil in him—the hater being also a sinner; but he must be loved for the good in him, corresponding to the good in the lover. The passage is a little obscure, but this would appear to be its meaning.

Commenting on the variation of text in Exod. xxiii. 4–5 and Deut. xxii. 4 (in the former it is an *enemy's* ox that must be restored, in the latter a *brother's*) the Sifrê, on the latter text, remarks that the inherent readiness of men to exclude others from the fraternal relations induced the Law to specify "enemy," thereby bringing the latter within the category of brother שלא דברה תורה אלא כנגד היצר. (Ed. Friedmann p. 115 a: cf. also note 6.) Cf. T.B. Baba Bathra 32 b: מצוה בשונא כדי לכוף את יצרו. The purpose of the Law concerning an enemy is to restrain, subdue, a man's evil inclination which might prompt him to narrowness of sympathy.

While on this topic, reference may be made to A. Seeberg's book *Die beiden Wege und das Aposteldekret* (Leipzig 1906). He holds that the ἀρχαίοι (Mt. v. 27, 33) are not Moses and the other Biblical authorities but the contemporary exponents of a doctrine of The Two Ways which Jesus was criticising. His argument, though unconvincing, has many points of interest (see particularly pp. 18–22). On the other hand his deduction from the allusions in the Rabbinic literature to "causeless enmity" that a well-founded enmity was lawful, is quite unjustified. "Causeless hatred" was and is a common human fault against which moralists pronounce without implying that any form of hatred was condoned. Baseless animosity and ill-feeling are evils against which no denunciation is too strong. In the Sephardic ritual (ed. Gaster, p. 113) this is well brought out, for the same prayer which is directed negatively against unfounded hatred (שנאת חנם) appeals positively for fellowship in brotherly love and friendliness.

### (t) *A camel through a needle's eye* (Mt. xix. 24; Mk. x. 25; Lk. xviii. 25)

The commentaries rightly quote (from Lightfoot, Wuensche, and others) the Talmudic phrase "an elephant passing through a needle's eye" (T.B. Berachoth 55 b, Baba Meṣia 38 b) to describe something extraordinary. It was obviously a proverbial expression. It is applied in the Talmud to an impossible dream and to over-subtle dialectics (cf. on the proverb L. Dukes, *Rabbinische Blumenlese*, 1844, pp. 119, 212; A. Cohen, *Ancient Jewish Proverbs*, 1911, pp. 113–4).

On the other hand, a similar metaphor is employed in the Midrash in a sense opposite to the meaning of the Gospels. The entrance into God's grace is easy. "The Holy One said: Open for me a door as big as a needle's eye and I will open for you a door through which may enter tents and (?)" (Pesiqta R. xv. ed. Friedmann, p. 70 a). The final word occurs in a great variety of readings. The Midrash on Canticles v. 2 has cut the knot by reading "wagons and coaches." This, as Friedmann argues, is a late emendation. But what was the original text? It varies between כצוצריות, בחצצריות, בצרצריות, כצצרות, and several other forms. Friedmann holds that underlying these variants is the Latin *castra*. It may, however, be suggested that the real reading is the hapax legomenon כרכרות (Isaiah lxvi. 20) where the meaning is probably dromedaries. If this be so the parallel, or rather contrast, is striking. The repentant sinner opens a needle's eye to God, and God opens a gate in which tents and camels might camp. The figure almost seems employed as a foil to the Gospel passages quoted.

### (u) *Sufficient unto the day* (Mt. vi. 34)

The citation from T.B. Sanhedrin 100 b, Wuensche's *Neue Beiträge*, p. 98 (cf. W. C. Allen's *Commentary on Matthew*, p. 65) illustrates James iv. 13, 14 better than it does Mt. vi. 34.

| James iv. 13, 14 | T.B. Sanhedrin 100 b |
|---|---|
| Go to now, ye that say, To-day or to-morrow we will go into this city, and spend a year there, and trade, and get gain: whereas ye know not what shall be on the morrow. What is your life? For ye are a vapour, that appeareth for a little time and then vanisheth away. | Trouble not thyself about the trouble of the morrow, for thou knowest not what a day brings forth. Perhaps on the morrow a man (alive to-day) will not exist, and he will be found having troubled himself concerning a world which is not his (for he may have departed from this world over-night). |

In both these parallels Prov. xxvii. 1 is in the speaker's mind, though the LXX phraseology is unlike that of James. The latter has *οἵτινες οὐκ ἐπίστασθε τῆς αὔριον*, while the former runs: *οὐ γὰρ γινώσκεις τί τέξεται ἡ ἐπιοῦσα.* On the other hand, the repeated use of *καυχάομαι* in the context in James points to a reminiscence of the LXX rendering of the first clause in Prov. xxvii. 1 (*μὴ καυχῶ τὰ εἰς αὔριον*), just as the personification of the "morrow" is common to Matthew and Proverbs. The true parallel to Mt. vi. 34 (as Lightfoot already recognised, and as Wuensche also indicates), is to be found in T.B. Berachoth 9 b (דיה לצרה בשעתיה). The Talmudic phrase is not easily translated. Its meaning is quite clear, however. There is no need to anticipate trouble; it is enough to grieve when the cause arrives, not beforehand. "Time enough for the trouble when it comes" is Jastrow's rendering (*Dict.* p. 1300), which brings out the force well, as does McNeile's "There is enough trouble in its hour." A variant might be suggested: "Trouble has its sufficiency in its hour." In the Talmud the idea occurs in a homiletic exposition of Exodus iii. 14. God is first described as "I am that I am," but at the end of the verse it is "I am" only. The double *I am* is taken to refer to present and future tribulations, to the slavery in Egypt and the captivity in Babylon. In A. Cohen's translation (*Berakot*, p. 54), the passage runs: "*I am that I am.* R. Ammi said: The Holy One, blessed be He, spake to Moses, 'Go, say to the Israelites, I was with you in servitude and I will be with you in the servitude of the kingdoms.' He (Moses) said before Him, 'Lord of the Universe, sufficient is the evil in its time.' The Holy One, blessed be He, said to him, 'Go, say to them, *I am* hath sent me unto you.'" The reference to the Babylonian captivity is thus omitted. The epigram, Sufficient etc., is clearly a proverbial phrase, although collectors of Rabbinic proverbs do not always recognise this fact.

Another parallel quoted by Schoettgen (*Horae*, p. 75) from the Mishnah Soṭa ix. 12 (cf. Wuensche *loc. cit.*) is irrelevant. In the despondent thought of the destruction of the Temple, R. Simeon b. Gamaliel (in the name of R. Joshua), nature itself reflected the catastrophe. Each day brings its curse (אין יום שאין בו קללה), and the dew no longer falls for a blessing, while the very fruits have lost their flavour. In the Talmudic comment (T.B. Soṭa 49 a) Raba piles on the agony: "Raba said, Every day's curse is greater than yesterday's," quoting Deut. xxviii. 67. The saying in Mt., like the parallel in Berachoth, is not so pessimistic as this. Nor is it characteristic of the Rabbinic outlook, which, in its more normal aspect, is reflected in the liturgical passage: "We will give thanks unto Thee and declare Thy praise for our lives which are committed unto Thy hand, and for our souls which are in Thy charge, and for Thy miracles which are daily with us, and for Thy wonders and Thy benefits, which are wrought at all times, evening, morn and noon" (*Authorised Hebrew and English Prayer Book*, p. 51). This benediction is referred to by name in the Mishnah (Tamid v. 1), though the full text of the passage is not recorded so early. Perhaps the most influential Pharisaic utterance on the subject is the optimistic maxim cited in the name of Meir and Aqiba: "Whatever the Merciful does he does for good (or for the best)" (כל דעביד רחמנא לטב עביד). With this saying (T.B. Berachoth 60 b) cf. Romans viii. 28. Dr Pangloss has not entirely laughed this principle out of court. And if joy is evanescent, so is sorrow. Happiness waits for no man, neither does misery. For while to-day's joy may not endure till to-morrow, he who suffers to-day may not be a sufferer to-morrow לא מי שמיצר היום מיצר למחר (Tanḥuma ed. Buber, Leviticus, p. 22).

### (v) *Symposia, symposia: Prasia, prasia* (Mk. vi. 39, 40)

As the commentaries note, this charming pictorial touch is not merely artistic but also chronological. It points to a period near the Passover, when, the rainy season being over, the fields (under the first heat of the sun) are for a while covered with fresh green—not a usual feature of Palestinian scenery. This greenery would be less grass than low-lying shrubs. Mk.'s χόρτος is used in 1 Cor. in such a context. It may be anticipated that the new irrigation of the Jordan valley will considerably change this, as it has done in Egypt. (To the usual authorities on the scenery of Palestine add S. Krauss, *Talmudische Archaeologie* (1911) i. 4, ii. 200.) Mk.'s πρασιά perhaps corresponds to תלם, furrow rather than bed.

Some points of verbal interest may be noted. First, Mk.'s συμπόσιον corresponds (as Schoettgen observes) to the Talmudic ḥabura (חבורה). Naturally the idea is not that of the Greek *drinking* party; it is the *party* that is emphatic. For the use of ḥabura see Jastrow, *Dict.* p. 416. It occurs specifically with regard to the companies united for partaking of the paschal lamb. Again πρασιά may possibly correspond (as Wuensche holds) with the Talmudic shura (שורה) *row*. "The disciples were arranged in rows like (the vines in) the vineyard"

(T.J. Berachoth iv. § 1 end). The grouping in Mark is clearly for the convenience of feeding the five thousand. But the arrangement was also suitable for the audience at a discourse. The rows need not be as Menzies says "rectangular," but straight. For the use of shura see Jastrow, *Dict.* p. 1542. It may be suggested that the symposia were *groups* which were brought into *line* by the directing hand of the Master.

Further, the repetition of the words—an obvious Hebraism—is found in the Talmud precisely in the same context as in Mk., and with regard to the very same word. The passage from Berachoth cited above runs (on the use of the description of the College at Jabneh as the Vineyard): "Was there indeed a Vineyard there? The reference is to the disciples who formed rows, rows, like a vineyard" (אלו תלמידי חכמים שהיו עשוים שורות שורות ככרם). It by no means excluded that the meetings at Jabneh (Jamnia) were actually in a vineyard. At the present day the whole neighbourhood is famous for its successful viticulture. S. Krauss may be right in his contention that the Rabbinical assemblies occurred in the open air (*Levy-Festschrift*, 1912, p. 22). On praying in the open air see First Series, p. 2. Krauss also suggests the Hebrew ערוגות ערוגות and J. Moffatt (*Expositor*, Jan. 1914, p. 90) reminds us of his third suggestion from the Midrash on Cant. viii. 13, where the students sit גנוניות גנוניות which may mean "in the arrangement of small gardens." On the other hand the tendency to compare students to growing plants is an obvious poetical fancy, for which both Biblical and Rabbinic analogies are abundant. Reference may be made to Targum and Midrash on Ecclesiastes xii. 11; cf. T.B. Ḥagiga 3 a—b: "As planting is a thing which is fruitful and multiplies, so too the words of the Law are fruitful and multiply" (ed. Streane, p. 9; the same context gives one of the many parallels to the "binding and loosing" of Mt. xviii. 18). Similarly "as the forest produces blooms מלבלב so does the Temple" (T.B. Yoma 39 b)—a fair legend of golden trees producing golden fruits, fragrant to the passing breezes. To pass from further attractive citations, very pretty is the Rabbinic use of "flower," "blossom" (פרח) to denote the young. The "flowers of the priesthood" are the young priests (cf. Mishnah Yoma i. 7, and Buxtorff, *Lexicon*, col. 1810), to whom practical jokes were not strange. These usages recall and illustrate the picture so fascinatingly drawn in Mark. Such scenes as he depicts belong to the undying charm of the story of Jesus.

## (*w*) *The Blessed* (Mk. xiv. 61)

Mk.'s τοῦ εὐλογητοῦ is possibly more original than Mt.'s τοῦ θεοῦ (Mt. xxvi. 63), but though Mk.'s phrase would be more likely on the lips of a High Priest, to speak of the Messiah as "the son of the Blessed" has no Rabbinic parallel. Dalman (*Words of Jesus*, p. 200) rightly remarks that: *the Blessed* is, as a rule, in Jewish literature only added as an appended epithet (cf. Rom. i. 25, ix. 5, 2 Cor. xi. 31) to *the Holy One* (הקדוש ברוך הוא, "*the Holy One, blessed is* (*or be*) *He*"). In the Aramaic equivalent the *noun* is used, *the Holiness, blessed be He* (קדשא בריך הוא, cf. Dalman, *op. cit.* p. 202).

Yet something must be added to Dalman's further remark (p. 200) that: 'the simple המבורך *the Blessed One*, Mishnah Ber. vii. 3 forms an exception." This may be an exception, but it became the rule in this particular context, for it was taken over by the Synagogue liturgy (cf. the *benedictus* of the Latin Graces). In the Mishnah cited the question is raised as to the form of doxology in the Grace, and various suggestions are made as to the formula to be used in assemblies of varying sizes. Whereupon: "R. Aqiba said: What do we find in the Synagogue? Whether many or few, one says *Bless ye the Lord.* R. Ishmael says: *Bless ye the Lord who is blessed* (ברכו את ה' המבורך)." R. Ishmael thus testifies to a liturgical use, unknown to Aqiba, but Ishmael's view prevailed. For the Talmud (T.B. Berachoth 50 a) on the quoted Mishnah runs: "Rafram b. Pappa visited the Synagogue of Abi Gibar (identified by Wiesner with Edessa). He stood up, read in the Scroll, and proclaimed *Bless ye the Lord*; he then stopped and did not say *who is blessed.* They all shouted *Bless ye the Lord who is blessed.* Raba said: Thou black pot! What hast thou to do with this controversy? Moreover, everybody acts in accordance with the opinion of R. Ishmael." The addition was designed in order to associate the leader with the praise of God to which he summons his fellow-worshippers (cf. annotated edition of the Singer Prayer-Book, Notes p. xli). Many modern translations of the Synagogue liturgy prefer the rendering *who is praised* to *who is blessed.* Moreover, there is uncertainty as to whether we should render המבורך by "who is blessed" or "who is to be blessed." The difference is not very significant, for mostly the invocation is followed by a further benediction.

### (*x*) *The friend of the bridegroom* (John iii. 29)

This is recognised as the bridegroom's best man *shoshbin* (שושבין). The phrase of John *friend* has its exact parallel in the Mishnah, Sanhedrin iii. 5. Neither a man's friend nor his enemy may testify for or against him. The Mishnah defines friend and enemy thus: "A friend is his *shoshbin*, his enemy one who has not spoken to him for thirty days." This last definition throws considerable and favourable light on what the Rabbis mean by enemy. As to the first, the Hebrew is אוהב זה שושבינו.

The word often occurs in the Targum and there is a good article on it in J. Levy's *Chaldäisches Wörterbuch über die Targumim*, p. 464; cf. his Talmudic Dictionary, p. 526. He derives the word from שבב = חבר, to be united in friendship. Sachs (as cited by Levy) explains it as "myrtle-bearer." There is no doubt as to the meaning; the *shoshbin* is, as Dalman puts it, the "Hochzeitskamerad." There was anciently a *shoshbin* for the bridegroom and another for the bride (T.J. Kethuboth i. § 1); but, adds the Talmud, this was not the custom in Galilee.

It may be worth observing in this connection that the Greek word for bride νύμφη passed over into the Targum and Rabbinic literature, though the normal כלתא was ready to hand. It appears in the form נינפי (Targum to Song of Songs iv. 8; Gen. Rabba, ch. lxxi. § 8). In T.B. Rosh Hashana 26 a the word is recognised as foreign: "they call the bride *ninphe*." On this form of the Greek word see S. Krauss, *Griechische und Lateinische Lehnwörter* (1899), ii. p. 361. He rightly recalls that the use of νύμφη for daughter-in-law in Mt. x. 35 is a Hebraism.

### (*y*) *Truth shall make you free* (John viii. 32)

Cf. for some parallels p. 7 above. The Rabbis read "Law" for "truth." It was the Law that produced freedom, cf. Mishnah Aboth, the so-called Sixth Chapter, § 2. Taylor (p. 100) draws the parallel between the Rabbinic saying "thou wilt find no freeman but him who is occupied in learning the Torah" and John viii. 32, James i. 25, ii. 12. He also cites in illustration other Rabbinic sayings on the same subject.

The same thought is to be found in Philo, whose treatise *Quod omnis probus liber est* has a Stoic ring. It was a much admired idea in later Jewish literature. Thus there is the famous epigram by Jehuda Halevi, cited by me in *Poetry and Religion* (1920) p. 46. As a variant to my translation may be cited that of Mrs R. N. Salaman. It is curious to note how widely two translations, both exactly literal, may differ. Mrs Salaman's runs thus:

> Servants of time, lo! these be slaves of slaves;
> But the Lord's servant hath his freedom whole.
> Therefore, when every man his portion craves,
> "The Lord God is my portion," saith my soul.

This is taken from *Songs of Exile* (1901) p. 50. The Hebrew original may be read in A. Harkavy's edition of Jehuda Halevi (Warsaw 1895) ii. p. 90.

### (*z*) *The strong man armed* (Luke xi. 21)

For this phrase (ἰσχυρὸς καθωπλισμένος) there is an interesting parallel in the Aboth de R. Nathan (I. xxix. ed. Schechter, p. מה). "R. Isaac b. Pinḥas said: He who has in his hand Midrash but no halachoth, is an unarmed strong man; he who has in his hand halachoth but no Midrash is an armed weakling; if he possess both he is *a strong man armed* (גבור ומזויין)." In other texts (see Schechter's note *ad loc.*) the first two clauses are reversed. Probably the reversed order is correct (it has good support). The man who studies the Scripture is a strong man, but unless he knows how to apply it to life (in halachoth) he is without weapons.

On the author of this saying compare W. Bacher, *Die Agada der Palaestinensischen Amoraer* (Strassburg 1896, vol. ii. p. 206).

The use of the verb in *Hermas*, Mandate xii. 2, §4 "armed with the fear of God" is perhaps closer to the Rabbinic than the evangelical example. "But put on your desire of righteousness, and resist them (lustful desires), being armed with the fear of God (καθοπλισάμενος τὸν φόβον τοῦ κυρίου). For the fear of God dwells in the desire which is good. If the evil desire see you armed with the fear of God, and resisting it, it will flee far from you and will no longer be seen by you, for fear of your weapons." This is in full accord with Rabbinic phraseology on the two yeṣers. In this particular saying of R. Isaac the context, however, makes no specific reference to the yeṣer. In the previous sentence R. Isaac contrasts the wise and the unwise; the sin-fearer and him who has never tasted the fear of sin: "He who has in his hand Midrash but no halachoth has not tasted the taste of wisdom; he who has in his hand halachoth but no Midrash has not tasted the taste of sin." R. Joḥanan b. Zakkai (Aboth de R. Nathan I. xxii. ed. Schechter, p. 74) has a similar saying: "The disciples asked R. Joḥanan, Who is a Sage who is a Sin-fearer? He said unto them: He is an artisan with his tool of his craft in his hand (אומן וכלי אומנותו בידו). [They asked], Who is a Sage who is no Sin-fearer? and Joḥanan answered, He is an artisan without the tool of his craft in his hand. [They asked]: Who is a Sin-fearer who is no Sage? He answered, He is a man who is no artisan but holds in his hand the tool of his craft."

This passage is further illustrative of the frequent cases in the Gospels and the Rabbinic literature in which disciples address questions to their teacher. It must have been a common form of instruction. The Rabbinic instances are too numerous to quote; there is an interesting series in T.B. Megillah 27 b–28 a.

# INDEX I

## *Of Names and Subjects*

# INDEX II

*Of New Testament Passages*

## MATTHEW



## MARK

## LUKE



## JOHN



## ACTS



## ROMANS



## 1 CORINTHIANS



## 2 CORINTHIANS



## GALATIANS



## EPHESIANS



## PHILIPPIANS

### COLOSSIANS



### 1 THESSALONIANS



### HEBREWS



### JAMES



### 1 PETER



### 2 PETER



### REVELATION